The Asian Yearbook of Human Rights and Humanitarian Law

The Asian Yearbook of Human Rights and Humanitarian Law

The titles published in this series are listed at *brill.com/ayhr*

The Asian Yearbook of Human Rights and Humanitarian Law

VOLUME 7

Edited by

Matthias Vanhullebusch, Steve Foster and Ben Stanford

BRILL | NIJHOFF

LEIDEN | BOSTON

Typeface for the Latin, Greek, and Cyrillic scripts: "Brill". See and download: brill.com/brill-typeface.

ISSN 2452-0578
ISBN 978-90-04-53861-0 (hardback)
ISBN 978-90-04-53862-7 (e-book)

Printed by Printforce, United Kingdom

Contents

PART 3
Human Rights Protection of Vulnerable Persons

PART 4
Human Rights and Democratic Values under Threat

List of Illustrations

Figures

Tables

Editorial

As the world was crawling out of the global pandemic it was faced yet again with another crisis with global proportions. The war in Ukraine violated basic principles of international humanitarian law and triggered a global food and energy crisis in 2022. The spiralling inflation in many parts of the world, including in the Asian region, has caused tremendous suffering upon peoples already in precarious socio-economic situations. The ongoing climate change crisis also hits peoples in the Global South particularly hard. The (in)ability to handle each of those consecutive crises has undermined the belief in humanity's resilience and solidarity. The agenda on the universal protection of human rights too is facing an uphill battle against a human rights fatigue and backlash, and engagement on human rights has increasingly been curtailed by strategic considerations. Conversely, non-interference is the convenient response to limit a dialogue on human rights compliance and accountability.

In spite of such human rights predicaments, striving for fundamental equality and dignity continues to take place in the hearts and minds as well as actions of different share- and stakeholders. In particular, the engagement with human rights by the contributors – Asian and Western scholars alike – to this Volume 7 of the Asian Yearbook of Human Rights and Humanitarian Law shows proof of and pays tribute to such humanitarian spirit across their different jurisdictions, ranging from the Middle East and Central Asia up to South(east) and East Asia. Not only have they criticised the lack of compliance and accountability with human rights, they also propose practical legal solutions to improve the human rights situations of different individuals and groups in society. Such creative legal reasoning is a testimony to the wealth and diversity of academic scholarship in and on the Asian region, and which the Asian Yearbook of Human Rights and Humanitarian Law is thrilled to host and promote. In this regard, Volume 7 of the Asian Yearbook of Human Rights and Humanitarian Law covers a wide range of topics, which have been organized along four central themes.

Part 1 on Human Rights Protection and Erosion during the (Post-) COVID-19 Pandemic addresses human rights challenges which were presented nationally and internationally alike together with their respective responses. Qian Liu and Yucong Zhang carried out an empirical study on the human rights infringements which Chinese people suffered during the COVID-19 pandemic and its long-term consequences upon their civil and political rights – even now, when the zero-covid policy has been abandoned. Nauman Reayat paid particular attention to the role of the Pakistani Supreme Court when it reviewed the national and provincial governments' responses to the pandemic in various fields, including health and economy, demonstrating that juristocracy is there to stay. Mohammad Towhidul Islam and Md Jahid Al-Mamun examined the precarious socio-economic conditions of Bangladeshi home renters, which was aggravated by the governmental lockdown policies and religious injunctions; yet, offering avenues for remediation for the future. Nafees Ahmad examined the consequences of the perennial inter-religious strife between Hindus and Muslims in handling the COVID-19 pandemic and its adverse consequences on the right to religion and the right to health. Zeynab Malakouti Khah and Clive Walker, on the other hand, shed light on an international dimension of the COVID-19 pandemic in Iran examining the perverse consequences of the U.S. sanction regime on international humanitarian relief efforts in Iran.

Part 2 on Economic, Social and Environmental Rights Contestation and Evolution examines various areas where those rights have been undermined and where redress is possible. Muttukrishna Sarvananthan and Navaratnam Sivakaran examined the post-civil war context in Sri Lanka, where discrimination against economic, social and cultural rights continues to be a reality for members of minorities groups, but which can be solved if those rights become justiciable under the proposed new Constitution; thus, also contributing to long-lasting peace on the divided island state. Jayvy R. Gamboa engaged with a new theoretical perspective – Legal Adaptive Capacity – in the discussion of the just transition from an industrial to a post-industrial area in the face of climate change in the Philippines. Through the prism of labour and administrative law, he offered avenues to equitably distribute the costs on the labour force as the economy is required to shift to a low-carbon one. Mohamad Nasir carried out a case study on the mining activities in one of Indonesia's coal-rich provinces, where licencing policies and corruption are contributing to the degradation of the natural environment, and are putting the health of nearby local communities at risks – which additionally have entered into land conflicts with mining companies.

Part 3 on Human Rights Protection of Vulnerable Persons pays attention to different vulnerable groups in society. Saumya Uma performed a comparative study on marital rape in five South Asian jurisdictions: Bangladesh, India, Nepal, Pakistan and Sri Lanka. She traced back their respective marital rape exemption provisions into their colonial past and deconstructed the judicial and legislative reforms that have failed to put an end to this. Furthermore, she engaged with feminist legal theories from the region to change the socio-legal discourses on marital rape. Nadhratul Wardah Salman, Saroja Dhanapal and Shad Saleem Faruqi examined the vulnerable legal status of Malaysian children born outside of wedlock under the dual legal system that prevails in Malaysia, namely under the Common and Syariah Law. They proposed policy changes that could remedy the disparity in both legal systems so that those children enjoy better legal protection. Mohammad Abu Taher, Olivia Tan Swee Leng and Siti Zaharah Jamaluddin examined the deficient legal protection of older persons in Malaysia in the face of financial abuse and exploitation, either by persons in their close circles or by cybercriminals. They explored possibilities to amend the legislation and to further empower the elderly to prevent such abuses in the first place. Adity Rahman Shah comprehensively analysed the status of the indigenous peoples of the Chittagong Hill Tracts in Bangladesh under international (human rights) law and their denial of recognition by the government. She offered different avenues within Bangladesh's domestic legal order to eventually honour their right to self-determination.

Part 4 on Human Rights and Democratic Values under Threat gives the floor to a different perspective that undermine human rights and democracy in various jurisdictions. Pavel Doubek examined the challenges which accompany the narrow definition of torture advanced by Taiwan as it takes steps to criminalize it against the background of rampant torture practices in Taiwan's past. Sergey Marochkin hinted at a return to Russia's authoritarian past in the face of the erosion of fundamental human rights and democratic guarantees under Russia's constitutional regime on behalf of the current leadership, thus portraying a grim future ahead for the protection of those fundamental rights. In the final chapter of this Volume 7 of the Asian Yearbook of Human Rights and Humanitarian Law, Steve Foster unpacked two recent judicial decision of the UK Supreme Court and the European Court of Human Rights which favoured the right of privacy over press freedom and free speech, criticising the potentially adverse consequences of those decisions on those freedoms as well as editorial judgement.

Apart from the brief exploration of the themes of, and contributions to, this exciting Volume 7 of the Asian Yearbook of Human Rights and Humanitarian Law, the editors-in-chief wish to express their gratitude to the entire editorial and production team at Brill, in particular Lindy Melman and Theo Joppe, for the smooth transition of the editor-in-chiefship and the production of this Volume 7. Special thanks goes to the outgoing editors-in-chief Javaid Rehman and Ayesha Shahid for their warm support as they continue to serve on the editorial board, as well as to Alexey Ilin for his impeccable work as assistant-editor.

Matthias Vanhullebusch (Shanghai Jiao Tong University)
Steve Foster (Coventry University)
Ben Stanford (Liverpool John Moores University)
May 2023

PART 1

Human Rights Protection and Erosion during the (Post-)COVID-19 Pandemic

∴

"We Got Nothing to Lose": Covid-19, Excessive Surveillance, and the Right to Privacy in China

Qian Liu and Yucong Zhang

Abstract

This article discusses the roles and long-term consequences of China's deployment of high-tech surveillance and neighbourhood community governance during the Covid-19 pandemic, as well as people's attitudes and responses to excessive surveillance in the authoritarian regime. Drawing upon in-depth open-ended interviews with ordinary Chinese people, we find that over the years China's excessive surveillance through big data and neighbourhood communities has diluted its citizens' interest in fighting for the right to privacy. This is achieved through "slowly boiling the frog alive," meaning constantly testing and pushing the boundary to re-define the new normal. Unfortunately, Covid-19 has provided an opportunity for the authoritarian regime to "justify" its expansion of and investment in high-tech surveillance and community governance, both of which will sustain its repressive governance. Ordinary Chinese people's responses to the authoritarian state's intrusive surveillance mechanisms have gradually changed from "having concerns, thinking critically, and considering resistance" to "giving up resistance and instead making the best out of the hopeless situation."

Keywords

Authoritarianism – high-tech surveillance – community governance – right to privacy – qualitative research

1 Introduction

China's attitude towards human rights during the Covid-19 pandemic is clearly demonstrated in a news article published at the early stage of the outbreak in the Global Times, a daily tabloid newspaper under the auspices of the People's Daily. It says,

> Essentially, public health issues are not an issue of human rights. There must be efficient prevention and control...When facing the challenge of survival, the rights of individuals must be subordinated to the needs of [the] majority. This is the same in both Eastern and Western ethics. When it comes to life and death, we must first solve the problem of survival before considering how to live more comfortably.[1]

The emphasis on the interests of the majority and the postponement of demands for human rights is evident in China's legal responses to past and current pandemics and emergencies.

During the outbreak of Covid-19, the Law on the Prevention and Treatment of Infectious Diseases (1989/2004), the Regulations on Dealing with the Outbreak of Public Health Emergencies (2005), and the Emergency Response Law (2007) are crucial legal documents the Chinese government relies on to respond swiftly as the situation evolves.[2] These legal documents define the duty and obligations of individuals and work units; specify how health care institutes deal with Covid-19 patients and close contacts; stipulate that the police have the right to handle people who refuse treatment or quarantine; and prescribe that local authorities can shut down markets, theatres, schools, and other places where people may gather. These legal documents, however, pay little attention to the right to privacy during the pandemics. The only piece of law that mentions the protection of the right to privacy is the previously adopted Law on the Prevention and Treatment of Infectious Diseases of 2004 and amended in 2013, with Article 12 stipulating that "disease prevention and control institutions and medical agencies shall not divulge any information or materials relating to personal privacy."[3]

The lack of privacy concerns under China's current legal system not only creates room for excessive surveillance in the name of curbing the spread of

---

1 'US Seeks Selfish Gains as China Goes All out to Curtail Coronavirus Spread' *Global Times*, 4 February 2022, https://www.globaltimes.cn/page/202002/1178494.shtml (accessed 1 August 2022).

2 Standing Committee of the National People's Congress, 'Law of the People's Republic of China on Prevention and Treatment of Infectious Diseases,' 17 Order of the President of the People's Republic of China § (2004); General Office of the State Council, 'Regulations on Dealing with the Outbreak of Public Health Emergencies' 376 Decree of the State Council § (2003); Standing Committee of the National People's Congress, 'Emergency Response Law of the People's Republic of China' Pub. L. No. CLI.1.96791, 69 Order of the President of the People's Republic of China (2007).

3 Standing Committee of the National People's Congress, 'Law of the People's Republic of China on Prevention and Treatment of Infectious Diseases (2013 Amendment)' Order No. 5 of the President of the People's Republic of China § (2013), chap. 1, article 12.

the virus but also leaves the abuse of Covid-19 control mechanisms by both central and local governments unchecked. Given that the pandemic provides an opportunity for the authoritarian regime to collect health data and travel histories of its citizens, its long-term consequences are concerning. In this article, we aim to discuss how the lack of legal certainty and transparency, as well as the usage of criminal law to impose harsh punishment, makes everyday resistance to ubiquitous surveillance fruitless and leaves its citizens under pervasive fear during the Covid-19 pandemic in the authoritarian regime.

After the first known Covid-19 outbreak in Wuhan, China benefited greatly from its reliance on excessive surveillance to control. The bottom-up community governance and the top-down high-tech surveillance were the two primary factors that contributed to China's success in combatting Covid-19 in the first two years of the pandemic before the country was hit by the omicron variant in late March 2022. Until December 2022, China strictly enforced the zero-tolerance Covid-19 policy, with the aim to not only curb the spread of the virus but also to ensure the legitimacy of the Chinese Communist Party (CCP) and Xi's preparation for his presidency to a third term.[4]

The CCP considered neighbourhood communities as "a crucial firewall" in the people's war against Covid-19 and the "urban community grid management" the key to virus containment.[5] China's community governance during the Covid-19 pandemic primarily relied on its grid management (网格化管理) system of grass-roots governance, which was an extension of the existing governance structure.[6] This system divides cities, towns, and villages into sections that are then assigned to grid members (网格员) to organize and control.[7] It is estimated that China had mobilized 4.5 million grid members as of January 2022.[8] With the help of grid members who were employed to be the primary

---

4   D Macklin, 'How Long Can Xi Prioritize 'Zero COVID' over the Economy?' *The Diplomat*, 14 May 2022, https://thediplomat.com/2022/05/how-long-can-xi-prioritize-zero-covid-over-the-economy/ (accessed 1 August 2022).

5   F Xu and Q Liu, 'China: Community Policing, High-Tech Surveillance, and Authoritarian Durability' in VV Ramraj (ed.) *Covid-19 in Asia: Law and Policy Contexts* (Oxford University Press 2021) 27, 31.

6   JC Mittelstaedt, 'The Grid Management System in Contemporary China: Grass-Roots Governance in Social Surveillance and Service Provision' (2021) 36 *China Information* 3.

7   Y Wei et al., 'COVID-19 Prevention and Control in China: Grid Governance' (2021) 43 *Journal of Public Health* 76.

8   B Chu et al., 'Living by the Code: In China, Covid-Era Controls May Outlast the Virus' *The New York Times*, 4 February 2022, https://cn.nytimes.com/china/20220130/covid-restrictions-china-lockdown/ (accessed 1 August 2022).

contact for citizens and to collect data and information about residents, the party-state was able to both control and serve its citizens at the same time.[9]

At the outset of the Covid-19 outbreak in China, President Xi Jinping mobilized people to participate in what he called the "people's war against Covid-19," emphasizing that bottom-up initiatives were of great importance in combatting Covid-19.[10] This large-scale mass mobilization was part of Xi's agenda to expand the Maoist "Mass Line" ideological mobilization methodology for social management.[11] Similar to the Cultural Revolution when neighbourhood watch and report was encouraged, people were not only "mobilized into getting tested, undergoing quarantine, and handing over their geolocative data,"[12] but they were also called on to report those who did not comply with Covid-19 restrictions, as the latter were considered enemies in the people's war against Covid-19. [13]

Meanwhile, big data played a significant role in ensuring the government employees' work efficiency and ordinary citizens' compliance with excessive Covid-19 restrictions. All ordinary citizens were required to use color-coded Quick Response (QR) health codes and the Information Big Data Travel Cards, both of which were associated with smartphones. Failure to report one's travel histories and follow Covid-19 restrictions could lead to serious legal consequences such as fines and imprisonment. The efficiency and high compliance rates, however, were achieved at the cost of ordinary citizens' right to privacy and their sense of certainty and security in their everyday lives.

This article discusses the impact of China's reliance on community governance from the bottom up and high-tech surveillance from the top down to contain the virus and the long-term consequences of these control mechanisms. This socio-legal study emphasizes the need to understand the impact from the perspectives of ordinary people who were affected by the state's deployment of excessive surveillance mechanisms.

Drawing upon ethnographic observation, in-depth open-ended interviews, and detailed analysis of media coverage and online discussion, we find that ordinary Chinese citizens were reluctant to resist excessive surveillance and

---

9   Mittelstaedt, *supra* note 6, 7.
10   S Yuan, 'Zero COVID in China: What Next?' (2022) 399, no. 10338 *The Lancet*, 1856; J Jiang, 'A Question of Human Rights or Human Left? – The 'People's War against COVID-19' under the 'Gridded Management' System in China' (2022) 31 *Journal of Contemporary China* 491, 494.
11   *Ibid.*, 497.
12   D Macklin, 'China's Risky Revival of Mao-Era Grassroots Mobilization Methods' *The Diplomat*, 7 June 2022, https://thediplomat.com/2022/06/chinas-risky-revival-of-mao-era -grassroots-mobilization-methods/ (accessed 1 August 2022).
13   Jiang, *supra* note 10, 500.

fight for their right to privacy during the pandemic. Several factors contributed to this reluctance: first, sacrificing one's interest for the interest of the
larger community was considered to be one's obligation as a responsible citizen during the nation-state's combat against the Covid-19 pandemic, which
was reinforced by the CCP's mass mobilization. Second, those who resisted or
considered resisting learned that resistance led nowhere but could have severe
legal consequences imposed on them. Thus, they faced the reality and kept
their heads down. Third, given that all the intrusive high-tech surveillance and
neighbourhood community governance had been in place before the Covid-
19 pandemic and that there was a lack of legal protection of the right to privacy in China, many people held the view that they had better make the best
out of hopelessness when there was nothing to lose. Unfortunately, Covid-19
provided an opportunity for the authoritarian regime, and democratic states
alike, to "justify" its expansion of and investment in high-tech surveillance and
community governance, both of which sustained repressive governance. We
argue that the authoritarian regime's gradual increase of high-tech surveillance
and intrusive community governance diluted ordinary citizens' interests in
fighting for the right to privacy through the process of "slowly boiling the frog
alive."

2   Data and Methods

This article primarily draws on three sources of data collected from December
2019 to March 2022 through ethnographic observations, in-depth open-ended
interviews, and a detailed analysis of news coverage and online discussions.
The ethnographic observation was conducted by the second author from
December 2019 to February 2022, who experienced the first two years of the
Covid-19 pandemic in China. It enabled her to collect firsthand data on lockdowns, high-tech surveillance, and lived experiences in urban neighbourhood
communities. The experience of living in the field was crucial in facilitating an
understanding of how the system worked on the ground in urban communities, as well as how citizens responded to the law in their everyday lives. The
role of the second author was a complete observer, who did not interact with
the members of the setting for the purpose of this research and did not tell
anyone that she was doing a study during her stay in the field.[14]

---

14   For more information about complete observer, see DK Hoonaard and L Scott, *Qualitative*
        Research in Action: A Canadian Primer, 4th edition (Oxford University Press, 2022) 86.

Between January and March 2022, we conducted in-depth open-ended interviews with ordinary citizens across China using Zoom, Voov Meeting, and Wechat.[15] Most of the interviews were conducted by the first author, with the second author attending several sessions and leading four interviews. In total, we interviewed 36 ordinary citizens from across urban China, covering Xiamen, Fuzhou, Quanzhou, Putian, Shenzhen, Guangzhou, Ningbo, Nanning, Xi'an, Shenyang, Hangzhou, Shanghai, Yancheng, and Wuhan. Conducting online interviews enabled flexibility with time and locations when it comes to recruiting participants and scheduling interviews. Sometimes, we were able to speak to multiple participants from different parts of China within one day.

During the interviews, we asked our participants about their attitudes towards high-tech surveillance and neighbourhood communities, their concerns about privacy, their interactions with staff members and volunteers of the neighbourhood communities, their experience using the health QR codes and big data travel cards, the impact of excessive surveillance on their everyday lives, and their overall experience during the Covid-19 pandemic.

Each interview lasted for approximately 90 minutes, with a few extending to more than two hours when our participants were eager to share their insights and experiences. We audio-recorded the interviews and took detailed notes in most sessions. Transcription and data analysis started concurrently with online interviews. The analysis of interview data was conducted on NVivo, a software program designed for qualitative research.

The data presented in this article were primarily collected before the country was hit by the omicron variant and the lockdown in Shanghai since late March 2022. We acknowledge that some ordinary people's attitudes toward the right to privacy and resistance to authoritarian surveillance may not remain the same after the Shanghai lockdown. This is because the crisis during the Shanghai lockdown has led to widespread public dissent about the legitimacy of the CCP both in person and online in China's social media sphere.[16] However, the research team decided not to follow up with our participants nor to reach out to new participants during this sensitive time out of ethical considerations when online discussions about Covid-19 control mechanisms and policies were being censored and closely monitored.[17]

---

15   Voov meeting is a popular meeting platform in China, which is similar to Zoom. Wechat is China's most popular messaging and networking app, which also supports audio and video conferencing.

16   K Thibaut et al., 'Shanghai's Lockdown' *China File*, 29 April 2022, https://www.chinafile .com/conversation/shanghais-lockdown (accessed 1 August 2022).

17   G McGregory, 'China Has Always Banned Dissent. One Man's Story Shows How the Shanghai Lockdown Has Kicked Government Censors into Overdrive' *Fortune*, 26 April

While the lack of voices since the start of the Shanghai lockdown may be a limitation of this study, we believe that data collected before this turning point are valuable because it is extremely difficult, if not impossible, to obtain data that captured ordinary citizens' sentiments during a time when many believed that they should sacrifice freedom and privacy in exchange for an orderly, safe, and economically strong nation state.

3 Social Control from the Bottom Up: Governing through Neighbourhood Communities in the Authoritarian Regime

It has been a long tradition in China for the state to govern through communities and households and hold them responsible for the behaviour of their members. The practice of community governance can be traced back to the practice of *baojia* 保甲, which was created in the eleventh century and peaked in the Ming and Qing dynasties. *Baojia* organized people into a hierarchy—ten households formed a *jia*, and ten *jia* formed a *bao*. At times, *baojia* "became a catchall for local government functions such as mutual surveillance, collective responsibility, policing, bandit suppression, tax collection, census taking, militia organization, and even democratic local self-government."[18] The *baojia* system highlighted mutual responsibility in terms of overseeing and reporting fellow members' wrongdoings, and those who failed to do so would face punishment.[19]

During the 2003 SARS pandemic, "the neighbourhood policing system was rapidly converted to SARS detection."[20] The 2004 Law on Prevention and Treatment of Infectious Diseases explicitly stresses the important role of neighbourhood communities in containing infectious diseases—according to Article 9, "residential committees and village committees should organize residents and villagers to participate in the prevention and control of infectious

2022, https://fortune.com/2022/04/26/china-covid-lockdown-shanghai-internet-censors/ (accessed 1 August 2022).

P Verma, 'Shanghai's Covid Lockdown Posts Skirt China's Censorship Regime' *The Washington Post*, 22 April 2022, https://www.washingtonpost.com/world/2022/04/22 /shanghai-lockdown-social-media-posts/ (accessed 1 August 2022).

18   For more information, see L Harris, 'Baojia' in *Berkshire Encyclopedia of China: Modern and Historic Views of the World's Newest and Oldest Global Power* (Berkshire Publishing 2009) 158.

19   Jiang, *supra* note 10, 498.

20   J Lawson and F Xu, 'SARS in Canada and China: Two Approaches to Emergency Health Policy' (2007) 20 *Governance* 209, 217.

diseases."[21] In other words, lessons learned from the 2003 SARS pandemic led the Chinese state to further emphasize using neighbourhood communities during emergencies.

In the so-called people's war against Covid-19, urban neighbourhood communities (*shequ*, 社区) were at the "frontline," which most urban residents we interviewed considered crucial to China's success before the omicron variant hit.[22] Unlike neighbourhood community associations here in Canada and in many other parts of the world where neighbourhood organizations generally indicate a form of self-governing voluntary association, neighbourhood communities in China are extensions of the authoritarian regime.[23] The leaders of these neighbourhood communities are selected, employed, and installed by the Chinese government. Thomas Heberer classifies the concept of neighbourhood communities as a model of "authoritarian communitarianism" that helps to impose top-down control through local authorities and organizational structures.[24]

Neighbourhood communities perform a political surveillance function in people's everyday lives by acting as a bridge connecting people and the authorities.[25] They have multiple functions in addition to reporting to higher levels about the activities of its residents, including but are not limited to conveying information from the top, helping with public health and emergency measures, organizing social services and volunteers, and assisting residents who had been placed under quarantine or subject to other restrictions.[26]

During the Covid-19 pandemic, grid members heavily relied on Wechat, China's most popular messaging and networking app, to deliver information and disseminate relevant laws and policies through local residents' chatting

---

21   Standing Committee of the National People's Congress, 'Law of the People's Republic of China on Prevention and Treatment of Infectious Diseases' Order No. 17 of the President of the People's Republic of China § (2004).

22   F Xu and Q Liu, 'China: Community Policing, High-Tech Surveillance, and Authoritarian Durability' in VV Ramraj (ed.) *Covid-19 in Asia: Law and Policy Contexts* (Oxford University Press 2021) 27.

23   B Read, *Roots of the State: Neighborhood Organization and Social Networks in Beijing and Taipei*, 1st edition (Stanford University Press 2012) 3, 10, 11; C Göbel, 'The Government Next Door: Neighborhood Politics in Urban China' (2015) 222 *The China Quarterly* 560, 560.

24   T Heberer, 'Evolvement of Citizenship in Urban China or Authoritarian Communitarianism? Neighborhood Development, Community Participation, and Autonomy' (2009) 18 *Journal of Contemporary China* 491, 512.

25   Read, *supra* note 23, 7–8.

26   B Read, 'The Multiple Uses of Local Networks: State Cultivation of Neighborhood Social Capital in China and Taiwan' in B Read and R Pekkenan (ed.) *Local Organizations and Urban Governance in East and Southeast Asia* (Routledge 2009) 121, 132.

groups. Like most urban residents in China, the second author joined the chatting group organized by the grid member in her neighborhood in order to get the most updated information regarding Covid-19 restrictions in her area. Usually, the management team of the property, local police, grid members, and other staff members from the local government were included in these groups. In general, at least one person per household was included in the chatting group of their neighborhoods, which made these groups the primary domain of governance.[27] These groups were the arenas where people get notifications regarding mandatory Covid-19 testing and lockdowns.

Many interviewees spoke highly of the role of the grid management system in containing the spread of Covid-19. Mrs. Sun, a woman in her sixties, said, "The grids are very effective, as they cover every corner of the city. Each individual is always located in a particular grid. With this accurate information, epidemiological investigations can start immediately whenever something happens."[28]

Local authorities, especially neighbourhood community workers, were most aware of the local situation but at the same time had the least power and the most pressure in the combat against the Covid-19 pandemic. They were the ones who knocked on the doors, called their residents to gather information about health status and travel histories, delivered supplies and disseminated information to local residents. However, they were burdened to prioritize policies imposed from above and had limited freedom to adjust the policy implementation on the ground.

For local officials, failures in achieving the goals set by the central government could lead to serious consequences. In the past two years, a large number of local officials across the country were held accountable for outbreaks in their regions.[29] The risk of losing their positions and being held responsible for outbreaks at the local level forced local officials to stick to the policy imposed from the top. This uncertainty led neighbourhood community staff to stick to policies and regulations and refuse to be flexible in accommodating the residents' needs, even though they understood that it was unfair to stick to the letter of the law under certain circumstances.

---

27   Interviews, Mr. Zheng, Miss. Chan, Miss. Wang, January to March 2022.

28   Interview, Mrs. Sun, March 2022.

29   Z Huang, 'China's 'Fragmented Authoritarianism' During the COVID-19 Pandemic' *The Diplomat*, 25 June 2022, https://thediplomat.com/2022/06/chinas-fragmented-authoritarianism-during-the-covid-19-pandemic/ (accessed 1 August 2022).

4   Excessive Surveillance from the Top Down: Governance through
       Big Data and Repressive Laws

Before the Covid-19 pandemic, smartphone apps and mobile phone data have
already been widely used across the world for contact tracing and human
mobility patterns as a way to contain the spread of epidemic diseases. Soon
after the first outbreak of Covid-19 in Wuhan, China adopted these technologies to collect data using Wechat and Alipay, which are two popular apps with
more than one billion users. The data were analysed by an artificial intelligence algorithm which then generated QR codes to indicate each person's
degree of risk and determine where the individual could go.[30] To be allowed
into subways, malls, restaurants, office buildings, and other public spaces, one
would need to have a green QR code. A yellow code limited one's access to
public spaces, while a red code indicated that one has to be in home isolation
or subject to confinement in isolation centres. The QR codes health system had
been combined with the Information Big Data Travel Card, which recorded the
travel history of every individual.[31]

Contact tracing during the Covid-19 pandemic was not the first time that
big data technologies were used by the party-state to control its citizens. In
the past few years, China has been using big data technologies to achieve its
stability maintenance, which has been a top priority since the early 1990s.[32]
Long before the Covid-19 pandemic, China had been promoting and developing its mass surveillance systems, including programs such as the big-data
police video monitoring system, the Sharp Eyes system, the first regionwide iris
database in Xinjiang, and social credit systems.[33] High-tech surveillance ena-
bles the party-state to collect enormous data about people's movement, online
activities, among other things, for law enforcement and social security control.

The Covid-19 pandemic provided China with an opportunity to legitima-
tize its investment and development of mass surveillance capacities across the

---

30   Xu and Liu, *supra* note 22, 32.
31   *Ibid.*
32   Y Wang and C Minzner, 'The Rise of the Chinese Security State' (2015) 222 *The China Quarterly* 339.
33   SkyNet, a big-data police video monitoring system collects images at intersections, gath-
      ering places, and checkpoints, is promoted by the Chinese state as a smart city initiative
      and crime-control mechanism. The Sharp Eyes system links cameras with smartphones,
      vehicles, televisions and appliances with public surveillance cameras. China's social credit
      systems collect data on the behaviour of citizens, who may gain or lose points because of
      their behaviour. For more information, see L Khalil, *Digital Authoritarianism, China and
      COVID* (Lowy Institute for International Policy 2020) 11–12.

country, which include but were not limited to human surveillance networks via grid management systems in neighbourhood communities, facial recognition, security cameras, drones, telecommunications tracing, GPS tracking, and other digital technologies. Some foreign media and Chinese scholars point out that Covid-19 could be a "catalyst" for China to boost and fine-tune its mass surveillance tools,[34] with many of them suggesting that these infrastructures may remain after the pandemic.[35]

While China was by no means the only country that deployed contact tracing apps and other tracing technology to curb the spread of the virus, its operation was unconstrained because of the lack of privacy laws and obligations and transparency.[36] As a result, China left citizens in the dark—there was no information on how authorities handled their data and whether the data would be stored for future use.[37] Furthermore, at a time when the color of one's health QR code meant freedom to move and citizens without a green code were prohibited from entering public spaces, "the authorities have never explained in

---

34   A Kharpal, 'Coronavirus Could Be a 'Catalyst' for China to Boost Its Mass Surveillance Machine, Experts Say' *CNBC*, 24 February 2020, https://www.cnbc.com/2020/02/25 /coronavirus-china-to-boost-mass-surveillance-machine-experts-say.html (accessed 1 August 2022); Khalil, *supra* note 33; *D*; Liang Jingjun 梁昌均, 'qinghua faxue jiaoshou Lao Dongyan tan renlian shibie bie lanyong: dada digu le fengxian, ying jinshen tuiguang 清华法学教授劳东燕谈人脸识别滥用：大大低估了风险，应谨慎推广 [Tsinghua University Law School professor Lao Dongyan talks about facial recognition misuses: the risks are highly underestimated, use with caution]' https://www.sohu .com/a/491743158_115565 (accessed 5 April 2022).

35   R Zhong, 'China's Coronavirus Tracking Apps Stir Privacy Fears as They Linger' *The New York Times*, 26 May 2020, https://www.nytimes.com/2020/05/26/technology/china-coronavirus -surveillance.html?_ga=2.4102960.1612801765.1653516107-1822504096.1650695621 (accessed 1 August 2022); A Ng, 'COVID-19 Could Set a New Norm for Surveillance and Privacy' *CNET*, 11 May 2020, https://www.cnet.com/health/covid-19-could-set-a-new -norm-for-surveillance-and-privacy/ (accessed 1 August 2022).
      K Lily, "'The New Normal': China's Excessive Coronavirus Public Monitoring Could Be Here to Stay' *CNET*, 9 March 2020, https://www.theguardian.com/world/2020/mar/09 /the-new-normal-chinas-excessive-coronavirus-public-monitoring-could -be-here-to-stay (accessed 1 August 2022).

36   Khalil, *supra* note 33, 18.
      I Qian et al., 'China's Expanding Surveillance State: Takeaways from a NYT Investigation' *The New York Times*, 21 June 2022, https://www.nytimes.com/2022/06/21/world/asia/china -surveillance-investigation.html (accessed 1 August 2022).

37   A Dukakis, 'China Rolls out Software Surveillance for the COVID-19 Pandemic, Alarming Human Rights Advocates', *ABC News*, 14 April 2020, https://abcnews.go.com/International/ china-rolls-software-surveillance-covid-19-pandemic-alarming/story?id=70131355 (accessed 1 August 2022); P Mozur et al., 'In Coronavirus Fight, China Gives Citizens a Color Code, With Red Flags' *The New York Times*, 1 March 2020, https://www.nytimes .com/2020/03/01/business/china-coronavirus-surveillance.html (accessed 1 August 2022).

detail how the system decides the color of someone's code, which has caused bewilderment among people who have received yellow or red ones without understanding why."[38] The lack of transparency left government employees on the ground unsure about how to deal with certain circumstances when the situation evolved.

At the same time, high-tech surveillance not only improved the efficiency of community governance but also created opportunities for the implementation of repressive law to punish those who violated Covid-19 restrictions. First, big data provided records of people's whereabouts and health status. These data could be directly used by the neighbourhood communities to govern its residents. Grid management staff members had access to all sorts of data from the household registration system, public transportation system, as well as contact tracing data. Mr. Zheng, a resident in Xiamen, emphasized that, "QR code scanning plays an important role in containing Covid-19, as it records the exact time an individual enters and exits the place. These details are all extremely helpful for epidemiological investigations."[39]

Ms. Kang shared her experience of being contacted by grid management staff members after visiting a local grocery store,

> I received a phone call from a grid member a week after doing my grocery shopping. She requested me to do Covid-19 testing and self-quarantine at home for 14 days. She told me that someone who tested positive visited the store on the same day I did my shopping. I did not scan the QR code at the entrance that day, so I was quite surprised that they still got me. Perhaps they found out from my payment history or something. The most ridiculous part was that she requested me to self-quarantine for seven more days after learning from our conversation that I just returned from Shanghai the day before. So, poor me had to stay home for 21 days.[40]

From Ms. Kang's story, we see that big data enabled neighborhood communities to trace down close contacts and request them to self-quarantine, even if the individual had not scanned their QR codes. The possibility that one's payment history could have been secretly used to identify close contacts is a concerning issue. At the same time, the very fact that the grid management worker requested Ms. Kang to extend the period of self-quarantine based on information gathered from the phone call reflected that law enforcement was uncertain,

38   Zhong, *supra* note 35.
39   Interview, Mr. Zheng, March 2022.
40   Interview, Ms. Kang, March 2022.

non-transparent, and arbitrary at the local level. Power was unconstrained because of the lack of legal regulations to streamline the implementation of the Covid-19 control measures.

Second, the existence of big data surveillance ensured the possibilities to punish whoever pushed their luck in front of a set of harsh laws and regulations. China has been using repressive law and heavy penalties to curb the spread of the virus. Soon after the first known Coivd-19 outbreak in Wuhan, China quickly turned to its existing laws and regulations to emphasize harsh punishment. In particular, China's main takeaway from its battle against SARS was the reliance on its criminal law as a weapon to handle the Covid-19 pandemic. During the SARS outbreak, Wen Jiabao, the then premier of China, emphasized that "we must stress heavily the importance of using legal methods and bring fully into play legal weapons to win the war in preventing SARS."[41] The government imposed severe criminal liability and even went as far as to threaten execution to deter the irresponsible and malicious spread of SARS.[42]

A variety of legal documents were issued to tackle those who transmit the disease since the Covid-19 outbreak. On 10 February 2020, the Supreme Court of China, the Supreme Procuratorate, the Ministry of Justice, and the Ministry of Public Security jointly issued a notice entitled "The Opinions on Punishing Criminal and Illegal Activities that Hinder the Prevention and Control of Covid-19." This notice followed the criminal law tradition of "heavy penaltyism," with the aim to threaten long jail sentences and even execution for anyone who avoids quarantine regulations or spreads the virus. The Amendment (XI) to the Criminal Law of the People's Republic of China (2020), which was put forward in December 2020, stipulates that those who refuse to comply with containment measures and consequently cause the spread of the virus or a grave danger of spread shall be sentenced to a fixed term of no more than three years or criminal detention for the crime of "impairing the prevention and treatment of infectious disease."

To summarize, the combination of community governance from the bottom up and big data surveillance from the top down created a repressive environment that was lacking legal certainty and transparency. To understand the impact of the lack of privacy concerns and the imposition of punishment through repressive laws on ordinary citizens' everyday lives, it is crucial to investigate how people responded to and engage the laws and regulations that were in place to curb the spread of the virus.

---

41   R Keith and Z Lin, 'SARS in Chinese Politics and Law' (2007) 21 *China Information* 403.

42   K. Zou, 'SARS and the Rule of Law in China' in J Wong and Y Zheng (eds.) *The SARS Epidemic: Challenges to China's Crisis Management* (World Scientific Publishing 2004) 99.

5   "We Got Nothing to Lose": Making Sense of Legal Compliance and
         the Lack of Resistance in the Authoritarian Regime

Despite the inconveniences caused by ambiguous Covid-19 restrictions and
the unpredictable process of enforcement, the majority of our interviewees
like Ms. Kang generally supported the usage of big data surveillance and community governance to curb the transmission of the virus during the pandemic,
given that China had such a large and diverse population. They claimed that
the efficiency in tracking down positive cases and close contacts made them
feel safe to move around and live a normal life.

    When asked about the concerns about the violation of rights to privacy
during the Covid-19 pandemic, most of our participants expressed critique of
values embedded in individualism and categorized these questions as westernized. Some participants half-jokingly accused the research team of being
westernized or eroded by the so-called "overseas hostile forces," which the CCP
deployed to refer to "international non-governmental organizations (NGOs),
foreign journalists, agencies of foreign governments, and other foreign actors
actively operating in various domains of Chinese law and governance."[43] We
identify three key themes from the narratives of our participants: willingness
to sacrifice privacy for the interest of the whole community and the nation
state; reluctance to resist in an authoritarian regime; and making the best out
of high-tech surveillance and community governance when privacy did not
exist in China.

5.1   *Sacrificing Rights to Privacy for the Interests of the Community and
         the Nation State*
With few exceptions, our participants emphasized the idea of sacrificing the
right to privacy for the interests of the larger community and the nation state.
There were uncomfortable moments during the interviews when our participants accused the research team of misunderstanding the nature of privacy
and thinking about Chinese issues from a westernized perspective. In an
interview with a 34-year-old civil servant in Quanzhou, the first author asked
whether she was concerned about her right to privacy during the pandemic.
Upon hearing the question, the civil servant shrugged off the privacy concerns
by suggesting that the researcher's understanding of rights to privacy did not
apply to the Chinese context. She said, "privacy only exists among individuals,
and there is no such thing as privacy between individual citizens and the nation

---

43   S Liu, 'The Decline of Two Forces in Chinese Law and Governance' (2022) *Chinese Journal
      of Comparative Law* 1, 1.

state. The state is not interested in your privacy. Only individuals will gossip about you."[44] Seeing the nation state as an abstract concept, the civil servant trusted the state with the ability to use her privacy in an appropriate way.

When reminded of the fact that neighbourhood community staff members collected and had access to much confidential information of all the residents in the community, she said, "local officials at the neighbourhood communities are well-disciplined. The information collected for Covid-19 will be in safe hands because of party loyalty (党性), meaning that all staff members know they cannot make trouble and have to obey the order from the top. You have to understand that neighbourhood communities are the extension of the party state."[45]

One may argue that civil servants would think about rights to privacy differently from other people who are less likely to be exposed to party propaganda. However, our interviews with ordinary citizens who had extensive living experience overseas also pointed in the same direction. Ms. Huang, a local resident in Xiamen, obtained her postgraduate degree in Australia and spent several years in New Zealand as a permanent resident there. In our discussion about rights to privacy, Ms. Huang mentioned a family story from the early days of the Covid-19 outbreak in China to remind the researcher of the danger of emphasizing the right to privacy:

> My cousin came back to Xiamen from Hong Kong for a visit during the spring festival in early 2020. At that time, there was a close contact in our neighbourhood. The neighbourhood community sent out a message to all residents, notifying us the name, age, home address, family members, and ID number of the close contact. I had to say that was not the best practice, but at that time, local officials did not know what to do. My westernized cousin was very upset about the violation of the right to privacy. He said that it was unthinkable in Hong Kong. Looking at the situation in Hong Kong now, our family members laugh at him and his naïve attitude toward the right to privacy. After all, releasing the travel histories and some information of Covid-19 patients and close contacts is crucial in the battle against the virus—at least the authority has to release enough information for ordinary citizens to be cautious and make their own evaluation of the risk.[46]

44   Interview, Ms. Liang, February 2022.
45   *Ibid.*
46   Interview, Ms. Huang, February 2022.

Ms. Huang's emphasis on her family's reaction to her cousin's concern about rights to privacy was an indication of the agreement among family members regarding the need to sacrifice individual privacy in exchange for public health. In addition, Ms. Huang stressed that China could not have been so successful in containing the virus in the first two years of the pandemic without effective coordination and services provided by the neighbourhood communities. For this reason, she considered neighbourhood communities as the most important advantage of China's battle against Covid-19.

The majority of our participants supported the practice of sacrificing the privacy of some individuals for the interests of the larger community and the nation state during crises such as the Covid-19 pandemic. As a resident in Hangzhou suggested, "These are special strategies during an emergency, so I understand it if the authority releases my travel histories to save lives."[47] Similarly, a resident in Shenzhen was willing to sacrifice his privacy when needed: "if exposing my privacy is going to save thousands of lives, then go ahead and expose it. I will find a way to cope with it."[48]

Overall, the majority supported the harsh control measures during the pandemic and spoke highly of using the QR code and travel cards to monitor the compliance of the laws and regulations. As a resident who went through 28 days' mandatory lockdown suggested, "it may affect individual citizens' schedules, but overall it is beneficial for the whole community and the country. Imposing harsher control is much better than putting public health at risk."[49]

Ordinary people's willingness to support and sacrifice one's own privacy for the interests of the larger community and the nation state, however, does not translate into a lack of awareness of the importance of privacy and the risk involved. There were, of course, concerns about submitting health information and travel histories. The reasons why ordinary citizens willingly accepted excessive surveillance control through big data and neighbourhood communities were much more complicated than being exposed to mass mobilization and party propaganda.

Many people subscribed to the moral duty to "sacrifice the 'small self' for the 'great self' [牺牲小我完成大我]," an ideal emerged during the New Culture Movement from 1915 to 1919. The small self is embedded in individual interests and the great self can only be realized by serving society or the nation-state.[50]

---

47   Interview, Ms. Yan, January 2022.
48   Interview, Mr. Zhong, January 2022.
49   Interview, Ms. Hong, January 2022.
50   Y Yan, 'The Statist Model of Family Policy Making' in Y Yan (ed.) *Chinese Families Upside Down: Intergenerational Dynamics and Neo-Familism in the Early 21st Century* (Brill, 2021) 223.

During the Covid-19 pandemic, it was common for ordinary people to hold the view that sacrificing the interest of the self had a long way to go to contribute to the battle against Covid-19. Our participants also pointed to the lack of a better approach than relying on excessive surveillance, given that China is a massive country with a diverse population and limited medical resources.[51] In addition, little room for resistance and the lack of privacy even before the Covid-19 pandemic frequently appeared in the discussions about their acceptance of using big data and neighbourhood communities to contain the virus.

5.2   *Resistance Leads Nowhere*

Although recent studies have identified a high level of satisfaction among ordinary people for the Chinese government's performance during Covid-19,[52] this attitude did not equate with having no concerns with the country's repressive laws and regulations. Our data revealed that those who were critical of the excessive control mechanisms gave up resistance and chose to follow the law to "save trouble." In other words, people obeyed the authoritarian laws and regulations that they considered "illegitimate" in order to protect themselves from inviting unnecessary trouble at a time when resisting the law would likely make no difference.

Those who felt uncomfortable submitting private information and being under excessive surveillance were pushed toward compliance after realizing that there was little room for resistance. Despite her initial concern about privacy, Ms. Ling was among those who gradually got used to showing her health QR code and travel histories in her everyday life in order to access public spaces. At the outset, Ms. Ling, a manager of a state-owned medical supply company, was afraid that once her travel histories were released to the public, their business competitors could take advantage of the information and ruin the reputation of her employer. After a while, however, she became not sure how to resist when citizens in the country were all following the order. Her strategy, therefore, was to avoid travelling and meeting people as much as possible.[53]

Some participants gave up after finding out that resistance usually resulted in endless trouble rather than justice. Ms. Jiao, an instructor in Nanning, was five days into her quarantine when we conducted the Zoom interview. She was

---

51   Interview, Ouyang, March 2022; interview, Wu, March 2022; interview, Hua, March 2022; interview, Weng, January 2022; interview, Mei, February 2022.

52   C Wu et al., 'Chinese Citizen Satisfaction with Government Performance during COVID-19' (2021) 30 *Journal of Contemporary China* 930; Xu and Liu, *supra* note 22; D Chen, 'China's Coronavirus Response Could Build Public Support for Its Government' *The Washington Post*, 27 March 2020, https://www.washingtonpost.com/politics/2020/03/27/chinas-coro navirus-response-could-build-public-support-its-government/ (accessed 1 August 2022).

53   Interview, Ms. Ling, February 2022.

wronged by the big data—her health QR code turned red directly from green one day when she woke up in the morning, which meant that she was subject to 14 days of mandatory at-home quarantine. Ms. Jiao did not understand why her QR code turned red since she did not travel to affected areas. The only possibility she could recall was that she took a train that went through an affected area about 10 days ago,but she did not get off the train. Knowing that it must have been a system error, she complained to the neighbourhood community but was told that she had to stay home and waited for further notice. Four days had passed, and no one from the neighbourhood community solved the problem for her after several rounds of complaining and explaining. She asked the neighbourhood community staff for legal documents that explained the reasons for her quarantine, but there was no such legal document issued to the neighbourhood community to guide their everyday operations when it comes to Ms. Jiao's situation. She decided to resist by calling the municipal government and writing to the central government to report the neighbourhood community. Nothing happened after all her efforts. Disappointed with the process, Ms. Jiao realized that resistance led nowhere and thus made the decision to leave the city after her quarantine.[54]

5.3   *Making the Best out of Hopelessness*
Ordinary people's submission of privacy during the pandemic did not necessarily result from respect and satisfaction with the law and control mechanisms in place. Upon realizing that resistance was pointless and would not lead to any improvement, many of them chose to accept the reality by suggesting that we should make the best of it when there was nothing to lose. The existence of excessive mass surveillance and disrespect for individual privacy long before the Covid-19 pandemic in China greatly contributed to ordinary citizens' acceptance of the state's employment of big data and community governance to curb the spread of the virus. In other words, ordinary citizens in China had experienced the Chinese state's gradual process of having more and more surveillance mechanisms in place to govern its citizens in the years leading up to the Covid-19 pandemic. It is not that they never had concerns about high-tech surveillance. Rather, they found it pointless to resist the state's usage of big data to curb the spread of the virus at a time when they felt that they had no privacy in front of the Chinese state.

Asked about privacy concerns when using QR codes and the Information Big Data Travel Card, some interviewees pointed out that there was no such

---

54   Interview, Ms. Jiao, March 2022.

thing as privacy in today's China. The rationale behind the acceptance of and even approval of mass surveillance using QR codes and Travel Card was the idea of making the best of it when there is nothing to lose. This idea was further reinforced by the belief of sacrificing the small self for the great self.

Ms. Yu, an administrative staff member at an entertainment company in Xiamen, explained "nothing to lose" by saying that "Chinese citizens are very used to having no privacy after years of cell phone verification, facial recognition, and various Apps collecting your data in the background. QR codes and Travel Cards are just one of those Apps."[55] Ms. Yu's narrative was echoed in the first author's conversations with Dr. Ke, a social scientist in Fuzhou who found criticizing QR codes and Travel Cards pointless because facial recognition and online censorship were almost everywhere in China—"When everything you do is monitored by China's Sharp Eyes surveillance system and all you say online are censored, what is the point of fighting against QR codes and Travel Cards?"[56]

Their emphasis on making the best of it when there is nothing to lose resulted from the process of realization, disappointment, and eventually acceptance of one's powerlessness in the highly-controlled social and political environment that left little room for them to fight back and change the rules. The acceptance, according to Ms. Wei, a resident in Xiamen, "comes from the realization of the fact that it is pointless for an individual to fight against the whole system. It is not that I had never thought about resisting but that I knew from the outset that resisting could do nothing. So why not just save the trouble and follow the law?"[57]

The realization and acceptance of one's powerlessness had convinced many of our interviewees to make the best of it. Mr. Qiang, a resident in Fuzhou who received medical training in the U.S., said, "There is no better approach than this in containing Covid-19. Most people in China have smartphones, which have laid a solid foundation for governing through big data. When privacy means nothing in China, it makes sense to use it for the public good."[58] Similarly, a Hong Kong resident who worked in Beijing said, "Violation of the right to privacy in China is nothing new. However, the government does make the best use of big data to safeguard the public health of such a massive country in the past two years."[59] Along the same line, Dr. Ke went one step further and suggested

---

55   Interview, Ms. Yu, February 2022.
56   Interview, Dr. Ke, January 2022.
57   Interview, Ms. Wei, January 2022.
58   Interview, Mr. Qiang, January 2022.
59   Interview, Ms. Chan, March 2022.

that "we should not criticize authoritarianism when it has proved to be more effective in containing Covid-19. Compared with the situations in western countries, we have to acknowledge that authoritarianism has its advantages. There is no problem with making use of these advantages to benefit citizens."[60] Making the best of it when there is nothing to lose, therefore, reflected ordinary people's critical thinking about the law and the consequences of resisting or complying with it. It was a product of ordinary people's constant evaluation of the controlled environment within which they made decisions.

6   Excessive Surveillance and Long-term Consequences

Activists and scholars across the world have raised concerns about the long-term consequences of the impact of China's emergency management response and its development of surveillance technologies and control mechanisms during the Covid-19 pandemic.[61] Covid-19 provided legitimacy and opportunities for the authoritarian regime to develop its surveillance system. From the perspectives of ordinary people who were affected by these control mechanisms, we identify two long-term consequences that will outlast the outbreak.

6.1   *The Boiling Frog: Normalising Excessive Surveillance and Extinguishing Expectations of Privacy*

Among all the consequences, using public health management as an excuse to develop and test out mass surveillance control mechanisms during the Covid-19 has normalized the government's intrusive surveillance via big data and the neighbourhood community's grid management systems. Infrastructures developed during the pandemic will likely stay and become the new normal, as well as the strengthened grid management systems. Things become more complicated when big data and neighbourhood communities often fulfill multiple functions at the same time, combining surveillance with services and convenience.

When asked about expectations toward the role of neighbourhood communities after the pandemic, several participants expressed a demand for a more engaged role of the neighbourhood community to serve ordinary people in

---

60   Interview, Dr. Ke, January 2022.

61   J Liu and H Zhao, 'Privacy Lost: Appropriating Surveillance Technology in China's Fight against COVID-19' (2021) 64 *Business Horizons* 743; J Batke and M Ohlberg, 'State of Surveillance' *China File*, 30 October 2020, https://www.chinafile.com/state-surveillance-china (accessed 1 August 2022); Lily, *supra* note 35.

everyday life. For example, a resident in Yancheng who went through a 28-day mandatory quarantine after her arrival from overseas, spoke highly of the role of her neighbourhood community in providing service during her quarantine and conveying the message from the top to ensure every citizen understood their legal obligations. She said,

> Before the pandemic, we didn't get to see the local officials from our neighbourhood community much. We didn't feel that we had a group of people working for us. During the pandemic, we started to get to know each other—they organized and monitored vaccination and lockdown etc. We got the notice regarding when and where to get vaccinations and Covid-19 testing from them. Ordinary citizens do not have much communication with the government, so we may not know everything about the new laws and regulations. The neighbourhood community is the only channel for us to get to know and confirm the laws that apply to us in the area. That's why I hope they could be more involved in our lives in the future.[62]

Similarly, a resident in Hangzhou suggested that the Covid-19 pandemic reminded the local community officials of their responsibility to serve the residents, which she hoped would continue after the pandemic. When asked whether she was concerned about extensive private information regarding health status, family relations, among other things collected by the neighbourhood communities during the pandemic, she said, "They had much private information long before the pandemic. They are civil servants after all, so I believe they will not take advantage of private information to do anything illegal."[63] Demanding more service and involvement from the neighbourhood communities, therefore, is a result of the acceptance of the long-existing government intrusion via neighbourhood communities as its extension. It offers support to the viewpoint that when resistance leads nowhere, we need to make the best of the hopeless situation.

Ordinary people's gradual indifference to high-tech surveillance is in a similar situation. A law professor in Fuzhou found ordinary people's reluctance to resist high-tech deeply concerning. He stressed several times during the interview that high-tech surveillance in the name of public health management in the past two years had a long-lasting impact on the right to privacy because of the normalization of excessive surveillance in everyday life, as well as the

---

62   Interview, Ms. Hong, January 2022.
63   Interview, Ms. Yan, January 2022.

intolerance of different voices concerning the control mechanisms during the pandemic. While he understood the reasons why many people gave up resistance in a repressive environment, he was concerned about the danger of the silence of the majority.[64]

People's reluctance is also a result of the accumulation of excessive surveillance and gradual submission of privacy to the state for social stability over the years. It is part of people's coping mechanisms during the rise of the Chinese security state and its turn against the rule of law.[65] Sida Liu depicts ordinary people's strategies of refraining from engaging in political affairs and focusing more on personal well-being in today's China as "the art of playing ostrich."[66] In a sense, after years of excessive surveillance and rising authoritarianism in China, citizens are like frogs that are being slowly boiled alive—they have got used to the submission of privacy in their everyday lives and consider it to be the new normal. Avoiding resistance is also a survival tactic in a regime that is increasingly more repressive, especially at a time when resistance and criticizing the regime's Covid-19 control mechanisms would lead to severe punishment both in society and under the criminal law.[67]

6.2   *Further Marginalizing the Marginalized and Oppressing the Oppressed*

The combination of community governance from the bottom up and big data surveillance from the top down affected citizens disproportionately during the pandemic. Excessive surveillance infrastructures developed during the pandemic also have future consequences for those who have already been marginalized or closely monitored. There are two categories of citizens whose interests will be significantly compromised by excessive surveillance put in place in the name of containing the spread of the virus—those who are socially marginalized based on their identities and those who are closely monitored and oppressed by the authoritarian regime due to their involvement in activism or their dissent. This section uses LGBTQ Chinese and dissidents as examples to discuss the impact of the combination of community governance and big data surveillance on those who are marginalized and monitored in the authoritarian regime.

---

64   Interview, Dr. Mai, March 2022.
65   Wang and Minzner, *supra* note 32; CF Minzner, 'China's Turn Against Law' (2011) 59 *American Journal of Comparative Law* 935.
66   S Liu, 'Cage for the Birds: On the Social Transformation of Chinese Law, 1999–2019' (2021) 5 *China Law and Society Review* 66, 79.
67   Liu, *supra* note 43.

6.2.1   Further Marginalizing the Marginalized

The overemphasis of the discourse of for the interests of the majority during the pandemic to justify excessive surveillance and government intrusion has inevitably hit the marginalized heavily, reinforcing existing inequality in Chinese society across gender, class, sexualities, disabilities, ethnicity, places of origin and other factors. China's public health management gives little to no consideration to people with special needs based on their diverse backgrounds. Sacrificing the right to privacy for the interests of the majority also translates into further marginalization of those who have already been marginalized in Chinese society.

The Chinese state is by no means alone when it emphasizes hierarchies of rights. Law and society scholars and human rights activists in South Korea, for example, have criticized the politics of postponement and the state's emphasis on hierarchies of rights in recent scholarship.[68] As Judy Han argues, a postponement of human rights means a deadly deferment of livable lives.[69] While hierarchies of rights exist in all societies across the world, what made it problematic during the pandemic in China was that the Chinese state got to determine whose rights matter most.

Clearly, in a social and political environment that emphasized the interests of the majority, the rights and interests of the already marginalized population were secondary in the people's war against Covid-19. As indicated in the official documents and party propaganda, when a nation is hit by a pandemic, everybody should focus on the big picture [顾全大局] and prioritize the interest of the public; and one should always be ready to sacrifice the small self for the greater self. Against this backdrop, ordinary citizens also consciously or unconsciously embrace hierarchies of rights when evaluating whose rights and which kind of rights are more salient.

At a time when the Chinese state holds the view that "the rights of individuals must be subordinated to the needs of the majority" during public health emergencies, the right to privacy of the individuals has to give way to other rights, such as the right to health of the public. Guiding by this principle of prioritizing the interest of the so-called majority, the rights and needs of those

---

68   E Kim, "'Equal' Second-Class Citizens: Postcolonial Democracy and Women's Rights in Post Liberation South Korea' in CL Arrington and P Goedde (eds.) *Rights Claiming in South Korea* (Cambridge University Press, 2021) 63; JHJ Han, 'The Politics of Postponement and Sexual Minority Rights in South Korea' in CL Arrington and P Goedde (eds.) *Rights Claiming in South Korea* (Cambridge University Press, 2021) 236.

69   Han, *ibid.*, 251.

who have already been marginalized are further marginalized, ignored, and sacrificed in the name of emergency management.

As a Shanghai resident and an international student affiliated with a Canadian university suggested, "it is risky to be different from the so-called majority in China, but 'the majority' is a fluid and unclear concept at the same time. During crises in China, we tend to forget or ignore the suffering of the most marginalized people in the name of the interests of the majority."[70] Marginalized people in China have to fit in and make efforts to be or pretend to be "normal," a strategy the first author refers to as "identity-hopping."[71]

Take gay and lesbians in China, for example—their rights are sacrificed in ways that are usually invisible to the so-called majority before and during the pandemic. As Matthias Vanhullebusch powerfully notes in his work published in the 2019 *Asian Yearbook of Human Rights and Humanitarian Law*, China's recent adaptation of regulations that prohibit reporting on homosexuality online and other forms of mass communication further contributes to the invisibility of the needs of sexual minorities in China.[72] The right to privacy is extremely important to gay and lesbians who have to pretend to be heterosexual in a conservative political and social environment such as China for survival where coming out to the society and family members is usually not an option.[73] According to Erich Hou, "most sexual minorities refrain from publicly discussing their sexual orientation or gender identity in China."[74] While homosexuality is not illegal in China, heteronormative expectations of marriage and children force gay and lesbians to "hide their feelings and prioritize social obligations over individual desires."[75] Social expectations for

---

70   Interview, Ms. Chen, March 2022.

71   Q Liu, 'Qualified to Be Deviant: Stigma-Management Strategies among Chinese Leftover Women' (2021) 17 *International Journal of Law in Context* 284.

72   M Vanhullebusch, 'Crime, Discrimination and Freedom in Asia' (2019) 3 *Asian Yearbook of Human Rights and Humanitarian Law* 473, 488.

73   L Rofel, *Desiring China: Experiments in Neoliberalism, Sexuality, and Public Culture*, (Duke University Press, 2007); Q Liu, 'Unmarried Mothers in China and Their Feminist Resistance: Demanding Rights or Social Understanding?' in G Wu, Y Feng, and H Lansdowne (eds.) *Gender Dynamics, Feminist Activism and Social Transformation in China* (Routledge, 2019); EL Engebretsen, 'Under Pressure: Lesbian-Gay Contract Marriages and Their Patriarchal Bargains' in G Santos and S Harrell (eds.) *Transforming Patriarchy: Chinese Families in the 21st Century* (University of Washington Press, 2016) 163; SYP Choi and M Luo, 'Performative Family: Homosexuality, Marriage and Intergenerational Dynamics in China' (2016) 67 *British Journal of Sociology* 260.

74   E Hou, 'Universalism or Cultural Relativism? Case Study of Same-Sex Marriage in Taiwan' (2019) 3 *Asian Yearbook of Human Rights and Humanitarian Law* 75.

75   GB Radics, 'Human Rights in Asia' in *The Global Encyclopedia of Lesbian, Gay, Bisexual and Transgender LGBTQ History*, 1st edition (Charles Scribner & Sons, 2019) 787; LJ Chua

the younger generation to provide elder care to their parents negatively and disproportionately affect gay and lesbians, especially those who refuse heterosexual marriage.[76]

During the pandemic, quarantine and lockdown posed unique issues for young lesbian, gay, bisexual, transgender, and queer (LGBTQ) Chinese to hide their sexualities, as many of them were constrained within the household with their parents; stigmatization of homosexuality made it difficult for those who live with HIV to receive basic medical care;[77] and according to our interview with a gay man in Fujian, contact tracing using big data significantly discouraged gay men from attending social activities within gay communities and visiting same-sex partners out of town.[78]

The further marginalization of the marginalized and the emphasis on sacrificing the interests of the minority for the majority during the pandemic ran the risk of justifying discrimination against the minority in everyday life. Seeing the rights of the minority as less important and can thus be sacrificed encourages competition among ordinary citizens for "normalcy" at the cost of stigmatization of the marginalized during and after the Covid-19 pandemic.

6.2.2   Further Oppressing the Oppressed

While one cannot deny that the combination of community governance and big data surveillance played a significant role in curbing the spread of the virus at least during the first two years of the pandemic, we should not ignore the fact that the information collected and the infrastructure put in place could also be abused by both central and local governments to oppress citizens who did not share the same political views with the authoritarian regime or even those who simply fought for their own rights by taking their grievance to the street.

After the outbreak of the Covid-19 pandemic, human rights lawyers across the country reported that their travel plans were interrupted by the health code system—sometimes their health codes turned directly from green to red

---

and T Hildebrandt, 'From Health Crisis to Rights Advocacy? HIV/AIDS and Gay Activism in China and Singapore' (2014) 25 *VOLUNTAS: International Journal of Voluntary and Nonprofit Organizations* 1583, 1592.

76   T Hildebrandt, 'The One-Child Policy, Elder Care, and LGB Chinese: A Social Policy Explanation for Family Pressure' (2019) 66 *Journal of Homosexuality* 590.

77   L Iyengar and S Yu, 'COVID-19 Is Further Disenfranchising China's Queer Youth' *The Diplomat*, 23 September 2020, https://thediplomat.com/2020/09/covid-19-is-further -disenfranchising-chinas-queer-youth/ (accessed 1 August 2022).

78   Interview, Mr. Wang, March 2022.

without reasons, preventing them from travelling.[79] Human rights lawyers in China are well-known for their courage in taking on sensitive cases to challenge the party-state—some high-profile human rights lawyers do not shy away from political sensitivity and often intentionally choose cases for their sensitivity in order to attract attention and battle against the system.[80] The success of their activism led to the 709 government crackdown in 2015, with over two hundred activist lawyers across the nation being the targets.[81] Since the crackdown, hundreds of human rights defenders had been forced to chat with the police or be put in detentions of varying lengths.[82]

Community governance and big data surveillance inevitably make it easier to monitor the behaviour and movements of the human rights lawyers. Wang Yu, a well-known human rights lawyer who was among the first lawyers being detained in the 709 crackdown, believes that the authorities have weaponized the health code to try to stop her from working—in the past, security officers had to follow her physically; now with the help of big data surveillance developed during the Covid-19 pandemic, they could restrict her movements from afar. Xie Yang, a human rights lawyer in Changsha, also said on Twitter that his health code turned red before he was about to board a fight to visit a relative of a citizen journalist who was imprisoned.[83] As the New York Times points out, "Chinese officials are turning their sharpened surveillance against other risks, including crime, pollution, and 'hostile' political forces."[84]

Ordinary citizens who did not necessarily disagree with the regime could also become victims of the abuse of the Covid-19 control mechanisms. Local government authorities in Henan, for example, abused the health code system to crack down protests for the goal of ensuring social stability. In 2022, hundreds of people in Henan were unable to access their savings in the banks. When some of them were planning to meet in Zhengzhou to protest the freeze, the local government issued red codes to more than a thousand potential

---

79   Chu et al., *supra* note 8.

80   H Fu, 'The July 9th (709) Crackdown on Human Rights Lawyers: Legal Advocacy in an Authoritarian State' (2018) 27 *Journal of Contemporary China* 554.

81   The 709 crackdown refers to the detention of several public interest lawyers on and shortly after 9 July 2015 on suspicion of a number of national security and public order offences. See, *ibid.*; D Wang and S Liu, 'Performing Artivism: Feminists, Lawyers, and Online Legal Mobilization in China' (2020) 45 *Law & Social Inquiry* 678.

82   E Pils, 'The Party's Turn to Public Repression: An Analysis of the '709' Crackdown on Human Rights Lawyers in China' (2018) 3 *China Law and Society Review* 1.

83   N Gan, 'China's Bank Run Victims Planned to Protest. Then Their Covid Health Codes Turned Red' *CNN*, 15 June 2022, https://www.cnn.com/2022/06/15/china/china-zhengzhou -bank-fraud-health-code-protest-intl-hnk/index.html (accessed 1 August 2022).

84   Chu et al., *supra* note 8.

protesters whose bank deposits were frozen, labelling them as potential or confirmed Covid-19 patients.[85] This strategy was also used on those who were angry about an unfinished construction real estate project and complained to local authorities in Zhengzhou.[86] Those whose health codes turned red must be quarantined for 14 days and would have health officials visiting them and asking them to stay home. Some of the depositors were taken to hotels for mandatory quarantine once their health codes turned red, guarded by police and local officials.[87] The danger of using big data surveillance to contain the pandemic has been powerfully summarized by one of the depositors interviewed by CNN—"The health code should have been used to prevent the spread of the pandemic, but now it has deviated from its original role and become something like a good citizen certificate."[88]

All these stories of authorities' abuse of the health code system to control the movement of citizens have highlighted the fact that China's health code system, like many other algorithmic-based systems across the world, lacks transparency, creating opportunities for the authorities to abuse the system to achieve the goals of control.

7   Conclusion: Ubiquitous Surveillance and Pervasive Fear

China in recent years has increased its reliance on the fear of sanction among ordinary people to govern, a strategy Eva Pils refers to as "rule by fear."[89] Ubiquitous surveillance during the pandemic further normalized this control mechanism, which inevitably led to pervasive fear and anxiety among ordinary Chinese citizens in everyday life. It may be true that governance through excessive surveillance was effective in its initial management of the Covid-19 pandemic in China. However, it came at a price for ordinary citizens and the

---

85   C Jung, 'China's Political Surveillance System Keeps Growing' *The Diplomat*, 23 June 2022, https://thediplomat.com/2022/06/chinas-political-surveillance-system-keeps-growing/ (accessed 1 August 2022).

86   *Ibid.*; 'Strict Use of Health Code Urged as Homebuyers Suspectedly given Red Codes after Complaints against Unfinished Residential Project' *Global Times*, 11 January 2022, https://www.globaltimes.cn/page/202206/1268243.shtml (accessed 1 August 2022).

87   T Wong and BBC Chinese, 'Henan: China Covid App Restricts Residents after Banking Protests' *BBC*, 14 June 2022, https://www.bbc.com/news/world-asia-china-61793149 (accessed 1 August 2022); Gan, *supra* note 83.

88   *Ibid.*

89   E Pils, 'Rule-of-Law Reform and the Rise of Rule by Fear in China' in W Chen and H Fu (eds.) *Authoritarian Legality in Asia* (Cambridge University Press, 2020) 90.

authoritarian state alike—the Shanghai lockdown since late March 2022 is a typical example.

In this article, we have documented the primary strategies adopted by the Chinese party-state to contain the Covid-19 pandemic, as well as people's attitudes towards these repressive control mechanisms. The combination of big data technologies and community governance ensured that the party-state had accurate information regarding its citizens' whereabouts and health status. From people who emphasized the importance of sacrificing the interest of the self for the whole nation, people who gave up resistance, to citizens who were trying to make the best of the current situation, we see that many people were getting used to living under excessive surveillance. The gradual increase of surveillance also resulted from limited room of effective resistance from citizens on the ground.

Nevertheless, it is misleading to blame citizens for not working hard to resist excessive surveillance, nor is it appropriate to assume that each citizen has the obligation to resist under such a repressive environment. After all, if resistance is highly risky and often leads to nothing, making the best of what they have is a reasonable choice. This is a long-existing practice in China—we are familiar with the political apathy and low degree of social trust among citizens in Chinese society, especially after the tragic ending of the Tiananmen student movement.[90] Over the years, Chinese citizens have learned to "refrain from engaging in politics and focus more of their attention on economic prosperity and personal well-being."[91] We have to keep our heads down most of the time because of fear and disappointment. The rise of authoritarianism in recent years makes ordinary Chinese people extremely cautious about what we do and what we say.

What concerns us most is the process of slowly boiling frogs alive by instilling fear and disappointment in those who have thought about fighting for their rights and interests; and by silencing the majority of the population to deter individuals who are thinking about speaking out. The Covid-19 pandemic further provided a chance for the authoritarian state to justify its expansion of surveillance control and make use of the majority's silence and fear for the virus to oppress those who had not given up hope.

In this article, we have discussed how the Chinese state used community governance from the bottom up and big data surveillance from the top down to curb the spread of the virus during the Covid-19 pandemic. We have documented and analysed the perspectives of ordinary people who were affected

---

90   Liu, *supra* note 66, 79; Yan, *supra* note 50, 225.
91   Liu, *supra* note 66, 79.

by the state's deployment of excessive surveillance mechanisms before and during the Covid-19 pandemic, with an aim to attract attention to the authoritarian regime's gradual process of diluting ordinary citizens' interests in fighting for the right to privacy. It is clear that the authoritarian regime prioritized the containment of the pandemic over its economic development and sought the opportunity to crackdown the so-called "overseas hostile forces" amid the pandemic. The self-imposed intellectual isolation would eventually undermine national dynamism and development, especially when China's export industries remain highly dependent on Western demand.[92] As Carl Minzner points out, China's authoritarian revival is undermining its rise.[93] In the long run, governance through ubiquitous surveillance and pervasive fear would lead to severe consequences both for the state and its citizens.

Note on the Contributors

Qian Liu
Assistant Professor of Law and Society, Department of Sociology at the University of Calgary, Canada. Correspondence to Qian Liu, ss 948 2500 University Drive NW, Calgary, Alberta, T2N 1N4, Canada. Email address: qian .liu2@ucalgary.ca

Yucong Zhang
PhD Candidate, Department of Pacific and Asian Studies, University of Victoria, Canada.

---

92   'Fortified but Not Enriched; The Chinese Economy' *The Economist*, 28 May 2022, https://go-gale-com.ezproxy.library.uvic.ca/ps/i.do?p=ITBC&u=uvictoria&id=GALE%-7CA705005219&v=2.1&it=r (accessed 1 August 2022).

93   C Minzner, *End of an Era: How China's Authoritarian Revival Is Undermining Its Rise* (Oxford University Press, 2018).

CHAPTER 2

Juristocracy before, during, and after COVID-19 in Hybrid Regimes: Evidence from Pakistan

Nauman Reayat

Abstract

Juristocracy – a government of judges – undermines the separation of powers and promotes the involvement of judges in political issues in some states. This may undermine judicial independence, the public trust in the judiciary, and democracy. However, juristocracy may lead to democratisation and judicial empowerment in hybrid regimes (a mix of autocratic and democratic features). For example, the process of the emergence of juristocracy brought about a transition to democracy in Pakistan in 2008. The Supreme Court of Pakistan (SCP) was unable to take decisions consistently against the political interests of the Parliament and the executive before March 2009. However, after March 2009, the SCP was able to shape the functions of Parliament and the executive, respectively, influencing policy-making and the enforcement of laws. This emergence of the government of judges during hybrid regimes in Pakistan was further strengthened during the COVID-19 crisis as the SCP ran the government through its orders in *suo motu* proceedings on COVID-19. Such a strengthening of juristocracy has been an understudied phenomenon, a gap which this chapter seeks to fill. Accordingly, it advances the field of comparative constitutional law and politics by arguing that juristocracy in Pakistan refers to the government of judges of the SCP in which judges carry out certain duties of the executive and Parliament on certain issues through its main duty of interpretation of laws. The COVID-19 crisis shows proof that the SCP – in the absence of pandemic legislation – extended its powers not only to govern the COVID-19 crisis but also to mark its political involvement in matters of federalism, accountability, protection of minority rights, and the enforcement of labour laws. The SCP's increasing involvement in shaping policy-making and policy-execution must be seen in light of the absence of policy and the government's reluctance to adopt pandemic policies.

Keywords

Juristocracy – pandemic – COVID-19 – Supreme Court of Pakistan – judicial empowerment – rule of law

1   Introduction

Be it developed democracies like the United States, Australia, or the United Kingdom or developing democracies like India, Kenya, or Pakistan; politically important issues[1] ultimately reach the courts. These matters threaten the authority of the government or involve the fate of important leaders, such as the Prime Minister of Pakistan Nawaz Sharif, international affairs such as the exit of Britain from the European Union, or the powers of the heads of governments such as the UK Prime Minister Boris Johnson.[2] The decisions of courts on these matters indicated a certain degree of judicial power. This made scholars of constitutional comparative law use the term juristocracy interchangeably with judicialisation of politics or judicial empowerment. This use does not adequately explain the concept of juristocracy. For example, Moreno used the decisions of the US Supreme Court against the executive and legislature to explain the origins of American juristocracy.[3] Ran Hirschl used constitutionalisation of rights in New Zealand, Israel, Canada, and South Africa to illustrate the emergence of juristocracy in these countries.[4] According to him, constitutionalisation of rights in these countries provided the judges of higher judiciaries with more powers which indicated that the political system is moving

---

1   D Kapiszewski, *Challenging Decisions: High Courts and Economic Governance in Argentina and Brazil* (University of California Press, 2007); D Kapiszewski, *High Courts and Economic Governance in Argentina and Brazil* (Cambridge University Press 2012); P Vondoepp, 'Politics and Judicial Assertiveness in Emerging Democracies: High Court Behavior in Malawi and Zambia' (2006) 59 *Political Research Quarterly* 389; P Vondoepp, *Judicial Politics in New Democracies: Cases from Southern Africa* (Lynne Rienner, 2009); MS Mate, *The Variable Power of Courts: The Expansion of the Power of the Supreme Court of India in Fundamental Rights and Governance Decisions* (University of California Press, 2010) https://escholarship.org/uc/item/3f164owm (accessed 21 January 2023). These issues usually involve the fate of political leadership, matters of public importance, or issues making headlines in national media. However, the criteria used in this chapter to evaluate the political importance of cases was borrowed from the work of Kapiszewski (2007; 2012) on the high courts of Brazil and Argentina, the work of Mate ibid. on the Supreme Court of India and VonDoepp (2006; 2009).'s work on African countries. They laid down the criterion of politically important cases; cases were politically important if they directly challenged the authority of the government. Mate included extra checks by confirming the political importance of cases with experts. Using their approach, this chapter focuses only on issues involving the fate of political leadership, the authority of the government in power, matters of public importance, and/or issues making headlines in national media.

2   *R (Miller) v Prime Minister/Cherry v Advocate General* [2019] UKSC 41.

3   P D Moreno, *How the Court Became Supreme: The Origins of American Juristocracy* (LSU Press 2023)

4   R Hirschl, *Towards Jursitocracy: The Origins and Consequences of the New Constitutionalism* (Harvard University Press, 2007).

towards juristocracy. This neither captures the complete understanding of the concept of juristocracy nor provides an adequate understanding of the nature and scope of judicial empowerment. This chapter argues that juristocracy is a combination of two words, "juristo" and "cracy". Juristo means judges and cracy means government. Juristocracy means the government of judges. Just like every other form of government, juristocracy carries out three functions: legislation, enforcement of laws, and interpretation of laws. In juristocracy, judges carry out all these functions through decision-making.

Developing an adequate understanding of and explanation for juristocracy became more difficult during the COVID-19 crisis because COVID-19 increased the space for the involvement of courts in political issues and matters of public health policy. The COVID-19 crisis was new for different governments and it limited fundamental rights. Governments across the world took some time to make policy decisions. As a result, different policy-related issues regarding the COVID-19 crisis ultimately reached the courts. Courts across the globe were more obviously involved in matters of public policy and politics during the COVID-19 crisis. Much has been written about the role of courts during the COVID-19 crisis,[5] but the wider literature on comparative constitutional law and politics[6] or the role of courts during the COVID-19 crisis did not discuss

---

5   M Rossner, D Tait, and M McCurdy Justice, 'Justice Reimagined: Challenges and Opportunities with Implementing Virtual Courts' (2021) 33 *Current Issues in Criminal Justice* 94; C Győry and N Weinberg, 'Emergency Powers in a Hybrid Regime: The Case of Hungary' (2020) 8 *The Theory an and Practice of Legislation* 329; S Dhital and T Walton, 'Legal Empowerment Approaches in the Context of COVID-19' (2020) 19 *Journal of Human Rights* 582; J Grogan, 'COVID-19, The Rule of Law and Democracy. Analysis of Legal Responses to a Global Health Crisis' (2022) 14 *Hague Journal on the Rule of Law* 349; E Peluso Neder Meyer, U Levy Silvério dos Reis, and B Braga de Castro, 'Courts and COVID-19: An Assessment of Countries Dealing with Democratic Erosion' (2023) *Jus Cogens.*

6   N Maveety and A Grosskopf, '"Constrained" Constitutional Courts as Conduits for Democratic Consolidation' (2004) 38 *Law and Society Review* 463; S Gloppen et al., *Courts and Power in Latin America and Africa* (Palgrave Macmillan, 2010); JKM Ohnesorge, 'The Rule of Law-Democratization in Indonesia An Assessment' (2007) 3 *Annual Review of Law and Social Science* 99; T Ginsburg and T Moustafa (eds.), *Rule by Law: The Politics of Courts in Authoritarian Regimes* (Cambridge University Press, 2008); L Hilbink, *Judges beyond Politics in Democracy and Dictatorship: Lessons from Chile* (Cambridge University Press, 2011); A Trochev, *Judging Russia: The Role of the Constitutional Court in Russian Politics 1990–2006* (Cambridge University Press, 2008); T Ginsburg, 'Courts and New Democracies: Recent Works' (2012) 37 *Law and Social Inquiry* 720; M Popova, *Politicized Justice in Emerging Democracies: Case Study of Courts in Russia and Ukraine* (Cambridge University Press, 2012); L Hilbink and MaC Ingram, 'Courts and Rule of Law in Developing Countries' https://oxfordre.com/politics /view/10.1093/acrefore/9780190228637.001.0001/acrefore-9780190228637-e-110 (accessed 16 January 2023); PH Solomon, 'Courts and Judges in Authoritarian Regimes' (2007) 60 *World Politics* 122; G Vanberg, 'Constitutional Courts in Comparative Perspective: A Theoretical

the strengthening of juristocracy due to COVID-19. Furthermore, most of the studies on juristocracy discuss the concept of juristocracy in the context of developed democracies[7] but hesitate to discuss in the context of developing democracies where state institutions and democracy are unstable and there is a weak culture of voluntary compliance with courts' decisions.

This chapter addresses the above issue by providing an adequate understanding of juristocracy and explaining how the COVID-19 crisis strengthened juristocracy in Pakistan in 2020 and 2021 ever since the phenomenon became more visible between 2009 to 2013. In doing so, the chapter uses the order sheets issued by the SCP during *suo motu* proceedings[8] on COVID-19 under Article 184(3) of the Constitution of Pakistan 1973, which empowers the SCP to make any decision on enforcement of fundamental rights and on matters of public interest.

The chapter further argues that while courts in other countries of the world received issues limited to a specific area of public policy, the SCP did not only influence the process of policy-making on issues related to the COVID-19 crisis but also ran different organs of the government by issuing directions to them and following up on those directions through reports. In this regard, the SCP carried out the functions of the legislature and executive powers – the other two branches of a government. This indicated the strengthening of juristocracy during the COVID-19 crisis in the context of hybrid regimes, especially the one in Pakistan in 2019 where policy domains such as economic and foreign policy are controlled by the military from behind the scenes. The hybrid regimes are studied by some scholars as a separate regime type and are categorised by them along multiple dimensions. For example, Gilbert and Mohseni examined hybrid regimes by considering civil liberties, competitiveness, and tutelary

---

Assessment' (2015) 18 *Annual Review of Political Science* 167; RE Kapindu, 'Courts and the Enforcement of Socio-Economic Rights in Malawi: Jurisprudential Trends, Challenges and Opportunities' (2013) 13 *African Human Rights Law Journal* 1; J Barnes, 'Bringing the Courts Back In: Interbranch Perspectives on the Role of Courts in American Politics and Policy Making' (2007) 10 *Annual Review of Political Science* 25; EU Petersmann, *Multilevel Constitutionalism for Multilevel Governance of Public Goods: Methodology Problems in International Law* (Hart, 2017).

7 J Smillie, 'Who Wants Juristocracy?' (2006) 11 *Otago Law Review* 183–195; S Ruparelia, 'A Progressive Juristocracy? The Unexpected Social Activism of India's Supreme Court' https://kellogg.nd.edu/documents/1709 (accessed 16 January 2023).

8 *Suo motu* proceedings are the proceedings that court initiate on their own without the submission of any formal petitions. There is no mention of the word "*suo motu*" in the Constitution of Pakistan 1973 but the SCP stretched the scope of Article 184(3) of the Constitution to introduce this term. This article empowers the SCP to make any decisions for the enforcement of fundamental rights and on matters of public interest.

interference.[9] They used dichotomous categories (e.g. competitive versus non-competitive regimes) for their three criteria. Adeney found that regimes in Pakistan since 2008 are hybrid regimes. She examined regimes in Pakistan since 2008 across the three dimensions of competitiveness, civil liberties, and reserved domains.[10] However, she used multiple categories[11] to measure these dimensions. The aim here is not to conceptualise hybrid regimes which has been done by the above studies.

This chapter makes an important contribution to the wider literature on juristocracy in general. The existing literature mostly discusses a certain degree of judicial empowerment to illustrate juristocracy, whereas this chapter discusses how the judges of a higher judiciary shape legislation and enforcement of current policies in addition to their traditional role to interpret legislation. This is a more adequate understanding of juristocracy. Moreover, this chapter develops the existing studies on juristocracy by explaining that the constitutionalisation of fundamental rights or political competition are not the only determinants of juristocracy. In addition, the COVID-19 crisis can also affect a juristocracy. By doing so, this case study advances the field of juristocracy in general and juristocracy during the COVID-19 crisis in the context of hybrid regimes in particular.[12] Furthermore, the strengthening of juristocracy in Pakistan during

9   L Gilbert and P Mohseni, 'Beyond Authoritarianism: The Conceptualization of Hybrid Regimes' (2011) 46 *Studies in Comparative International Development* 270.

10   K Adeney, 'How to Understand Pakistan's Hybrid Regime: The Importance of a Multidimensional Continuum' (2017) 24 *Democratization* 119.

11   For example, Adeney used three dimensions for competitiveness: elected officials, universal suffrage, right to candidacy, and correctly organised free and fair elections. She scoreded these dimensions on the scale of low, medium and high. See Adeney, *supra* note 9.

12   Indeed, little has been written on how juristocracy emerges and flourishes in hybrid regimes. A Trochev and R Ellett, 'Judges and Their Allies: Rethinking Judicial Autonomy through the Prism of Off-Bench Resistance' (2014) 2 *Journal of Law and Courts* 67; Ohnesorge (n 6); Hilbink and Ingram (n 6); MC Ingram, *Crafting Courts in New Democracies: The Politics of Subnational Judicial Reform in Brazil and Mexico* (Cambridge University Press 2016); RASz Urribarri, 'Courts between Democracy and Hybrid Authoritarianism: Evidence from the Venezuelan Supreme Court' (2011) 36 *Law and Social Inquiry* 854; M Popova, 'The Postcommunist Judiciary: One Step Forward, Two Steps Back' in K Engelbrekt and P Kostadinova (eds.), *Bulgaria's Democratic Institutions at Thirty a Balance Sheet* (Lexington Book, 2020); M Popova, 'Politicized Justice in Emerging Democracies: A Study of Courts in Russia and Ukraine' (2012) 9781107014 *Politicized Justice in Emerging Democracies: A Study of Courts in Russia and Ukraine* 1; Ginsburg, *supra* note 6; Trochev, *supra* note 6.

the COVID-19 crisis went unnoticed in scholarship on courts in Pakistan which this chapter seeks to finally address.[13]

The second part of this chapter discusses the emergence of juristocracy in Pakistan before the COVID-19 crisis. The third part discusses the emergence of juristocracy in Pakistan during the COVID-19 crisis focusing on the order sheets issued by the SCP during the *suo motu* proceedings on COVID-19 under Article 184(3) of the Constitution. The fourth part provides a brief overview of juristocracy after the COVID-19. The last part makes conclusions and predicts the future development of juristocracy in Pakistan.

2   Juristocracy in Pakistan before the COVID-19 Crisis

Before 2005, different constitutions were enacted in Pakistan all of which provided adequate constitutional guarantees to the higher judiciary regarding

---

13   D Munir, 'From Judicial Autonomy to Regime Transformation' in L Karpik, MM Feeley, and TC Halliday (eds.), *Fates of Political Liberalism in the British Post-Colony: The Politics of the Legal Complex* (Cambridge University Press, 2012); O Siddique, *Pakistan's Experience with Formal Law: An Alien Justice* (Cambridge University Press, 2013); O Siddique, 'The Jurisprudence of Dissolutions: Presidential Power to Dissolve Assemblies Under the Pakistani Constitution and Its Discontents' (2006) 23 *Arizona Journal of International and Comparative Law* 622; M Khan, 'Genesis and Evolution of Public Interest Litigation in the Supreme Court of Pakistan: Toward a Dynamic Theory of Judicialization' (2015) 28 *Temple International and Comparative Law Journal* 285; MS Khan, 'The Politics of Public Interest Litigation in Pakistan in the 1990s' (2011) 2 *Social Science & Policy Bulletin*; H Khan, *Constitutional and Political History of Pakistan* (3rd edn, Oxford University Press, 2017); S Shafqat, 'Civil Society and the Lawyers' Movement of Pakistan' (2018) 43 *Law and Social Inquiry* 889; D Munir, 'The Pakistani Lawyers' Movement and the Popular Currency of Judicial Power' (2009) 123 *Harvard Law Review* 1705; H Khan, *A History of the Judiciary in Pakistan* (Oxford University Press, 2016); ZS Ahmed and MJ Stephan, 'Fighting for the Rule of Law: Civil Resistance and the Lawyers' Movement in Pakistan' (2010) 17 *Democratization* 492; ZS Ahmed, 'The Role of the Pakistani Mass Media in the Lawyers' Resistance against the Musharraf Dictatorship' (2012) 4 *Pakistaniaat: A Journal of Pakistan Studies* 61; MH Cheema and IS Gilani (eds.), *The Politics and Jurisprudence of the Chaudhry Court 2005–2013* (Oxford University Press, 2015); AA Qazi, *A Government of Judges: A Story of The Pakistani Supreme Court's Strategic Expansion* (The University of Chicago Press, 2018); PR Newberg, *Judging the State* (Cambridge University Press, 1995); I Ahmad et al., *Pakistan's Democratic Transition: Change and Persistence* (Taylor & Francis, 2017); O Siddique, 'The Judicialization of Politics in Pakistan: The Supreme Court after the Lawyers' Movement' in M Tushnet and M Khosla (eds.), *Unstable Constitutionalism: Law and Politics in South Asia* (Cambridge University Press, 2015) 159–191; SA Ghias, 'Miscarriage of Chief Justice: Judicial Power and the Legal Complex in Pakistan under Musharraf' (2010) 35 *Law and Social Inquiry* 985.

judicial appointments, salaries, the age of retirement, and the process for the removal of judges.[14] Judges of the Supreme Court and provincial high courts were given many powers including the power to protect fundamental rights by reviewing the executive's actions or legislation if they undermine fundamental rights. Before 2005, one could not speak of juristocracy in Pakistan since the judiciary could not protect itself against any court-packing and court-curbing actions by the different regimes; let alone compel Parliament to adopt laws or compel the executive to implement laws. In this respect, the military in Pakistan abrogated the Constitution of Pakistan in 1958 and the 1962 Constitution. The higher judiciary could not strike down these constitutional abrogations. Instead, the higher judiciary endorsed this abrogation.[15] The military suspended the 1973 Constitution and populated the judiciary with loyal judges in 1977.[16] The matter ultimately reached the SCP. Unsurprisingly, the SCP upheld the suspension of the constitution. Given that the higher judiciary was packed with judges loyal to the regime, the ability and willingness of judges to make decisions in politically important cases and the implementation of those decisions against the political interests of regimes in power during this period was limited. It could hardly influence policy-making and run different organs of the state through its decisions.

With the transition from the military regime to democracy, which started through the general election of 1985, this would gradually change. From 1985 to 1999, five civilian governments came to power through elections.[17] These five regimes were hybrid regimes because they came to power through elections but the military continued to control foreign policy and economic policy and influence national politics from behind the political scenes. In this period, one regime was led by Muhammad Khan Junejo (1985-1988), two regimes were led by the Pakistan People Party (PPP) from 1988 to 1990 and from 1993 to 1996, and the other two were led by the Pakistan Muslim League-Nawaz group (PML-N) from 1990 to 1993 and from 1997 to 1999. Most of these regimes appointed judges to the SCP and provincial high courts who were loyal to the regime. The President dismissed these governments due to malpractices pursuant to Article 58-2(b) of the Constitution of Pakistan 1973. The issue of these dismissals ultimately reached the SCP. The SCP upheld the two dismissals of PPP-led governments in

---

14   For details, see Khan (2017), *ibid.*
15   *The State v Dosso* (1958) PLD SC 533; *Asma Jilani v the Government of Pakistan.*
16   *Begum Nusrat Bhutto v Chief of Army Staff.*
17   Siddique, *supra* note 13.

1990[18] and 1996.[19] However, the SCP struck down the dismissal of Muhammad Khan Junejo's government in 1988 but did not order the restoration of assemblies.[20] Similarly, the SCP struck down the dismissal of PML-N led government in 1992[21] but upheld the overthrow of PML-N led government by General Pervez Musharraf in October 1999.[22] Autobiographies of judges[23] suggest that PML-N and PPP had been influencing the judiciary by appointing judges who they thought would remain loyal to their regime. The details of the above decisions and political developments of that time have been discussed elsewhere.[24]

However, juristocracy reared its head during the 2000s when the socio-economic and socio-political situation of Pakistan had changed massively. Public access to information increased and the state's control over public opinion decreased. The military regime of General Musharraf (1999-2008) privatised different state enterprises, including, but not limited to, banks, the Pakistan Telecommunication Corporation and the electronic media. As a result, the number of media channels increased from a couple to dozens followed by the establishment of a countrywide cable network in urban city centres during the 2000s.[25] Also, the number of internet service providers and users increased significantly.[26] This suggests that public access to information increased significantly, and it became increasingly difficult to control public opinion.

Furthermore, the size of the middle class in Pakistan multiplied during the 2000s. Pakistan was ranked among the top ten countries in the world in terms of the population of its middle class.[27] The middle class in Pakistan[28] consisted

---

18   *Ahmad Tariq Rahim v. Pakistan*, 44 PLD 646 (1992).

19   *Benazir Bhutto v. President of Pakistan*, 50 PLD 388, 434 (1998).

20   *Pakistan v. Muhammad Saifullah Khan (Haji Saifullah)*, 41 PLD 166.

21   *Muhammad Nawaz Sharif v. President of Pakistan*, 45 PLD 473 (1993)

22   *Zafar Ali Shah v. General Pervez Musharraf*, 52 PLD 869 (2000).

23   Chief Justice (Retd) Ajmal Mian, *A Judge Speaks Out* (Oxford University Press, 2004); SA Shah, *Law Courts in a Glass House* (Oxford University Press, 2001).

24   Siddiqu (2006), *supra* note 13.

25   'PEMRA Annual Report 2009–10' (2010) https://www.pta.gov.pk/en/annual-reports (accessed 1 February 2023); 'PEMRA Annual Report 2010–14' (2014) http://www.pemra .gov.pk/ (accessed 1 February 2023).

26   'PTCL Annual Report' (2014) https://ptcl.com.pk/uploads/Annual Report 2014.pdf (accessed 1 February 2023).

27   N Chun, 'Middle Class Size in the Past, Present, and Future: A Description of Trends in Asia' (2010) 217 *ADB Economics Working Paper Series*, https://www.econstor.eu/bitstream /10419/128515/1/ewp-217.pdf (accessed 1 February 2023).

28   The Pakistani scholarship explained the concept of the middle class in different ways. For example, see Durr-e-Nayab, 'Estimating the Middle Class in Pakistan' (2011) 50 *The Pakistan Development Review* 1; A Adil, 'Our Middle Class' *The News* (15 July 2017) https://www .thenews.com.pk/print/210660-Our-middle-class (accessed 9 April 2020); AS Akhtar,

of professionals such as lawyers, students, representatives of civil society organisations (CSOs), and teachers, most of them living in urban city centres with access to information on the entire world through newly privatised media and internet. They were exposed to information regarding better governance, good qualities of life, low rates of unemployment and inflation, and maximum accountability. As a result, they began to expect good governance, transparency, and decreasing corruption in their own country too. This expectation was visible in public opinion surveys conducted by Gallup Pakistan across different urban and rural areas of Pakistan.[29] According to these survey reports, unemployment was the most important issue in Pakistan. According to another survey Pakistani people were concerned about increasing corruption.[30] The general public viewed these issues to be connected to each other.[31]

It is against this background of social and political changes that the juristocracy emerged in Pakistan whereby the higher judiciary became more able to protect itself against the executive's court-packing and court-curbing actions,

---

'Dreams of a Secular Republic: Elite Alienation in Post-Zia Pakistan' (2016) 46 *Journal of Contemporary Asia* 641; Dr. JA Ghani, 'The Emerging Middle Class in Pakistan: How It Consumes, Earns, and Saves' *International Conference on Marketing* (Institute of Business Administration, 2014) http://iba.edu.pk/testibaicm2014/parallel_sessions/ConsumerBehaviorCulture/TheEmergingMiddleClassPakistan.pdf (accessed 1 February 2023). The middle-class consists of different groups including but not limited to professionals such as teachers, doctors, engineers, small business/enterprises entrepreneurs, lawyers, and journalists. Since this study is not about the composition and behaviour of the middle class in Pakistan, it focuses on lawyers, students, and representative of CSOs only because their involvement the restoration of the judges was reported widely in national media.

29   '61% Pakistanis Believe Unemployment Is the Biggest Problem Today' *Gallup Pakistan* (2014) https://gallup.com.pk/61-pakistanis-believe-unemployment-is-the-biggest-prob lem-today-29-say-the-same-about-the-economy/ (accessed 9 April 2020); 'Pakistanis Perceive Nepotism to Be One of the Top Most Causes for Unemployment -- Gallup Pakistan' http://gallup.com.pk/wp/wp-content/uploads/2016/06/18-5-091.pdf (accessed 1 February 2023); 'Pakistan Unemployment Rate (1980 - 2020) (Data & Charts)' *CEIC*, https://www.ceicdata.com/en/indicator/pakistan/unemployment-rate (accessed 28 March 2020); 'Inflation (49%) Unemployment (21%) and Terrorism(21%) Continue to Be Seen as Most Important Problems in Pakistan. For an Average Citizen External Dangers Take a Back Seat (8%). GILANI POLL/GALLUP PAKISTAN', 25 November 2011, http://gallup.com.pk/wp/wp-content/uploads/2016/02/251111.pdf (accessed 1 February 2023); 'Inflation Is Seen As Top Most Problem In Popular Opinion (55%): GILANI POLL/GALLUP PAKISTAN', 27 January 2011, http://gallup.com.pk/wp/wp-content/uploads/2016/06/27-01-111.pdf (accessed 1 February 2023).

30   '43% of the Urbanites Believe That Corruption Will Increase in the Next 3 Years' (2007) https://gallup.com.pk/43-of-the-urbanites-believe-that-corruption-will-increase-in-the -next-3-years/ (accessed 10 March 2020).

31   Nauman, *supra* note 23.

to make decisions against the executive and parliament and to compel the executive to implement those decisions in different phases from June 2005 onwards. The emergence of juristocracy in Pakistan was marked by six phases.

The first phase began on the day of the appointment of Iftikhar Muhammad Chaudhry as the Chief Justice of Pakistan (CJP) by General Pervez Musharraf on 30 June 2005.[32] Prior to his appointment as the CJP, he was a judge loyal to the military regime. He had participated in those proceedings before the SCP that endorsed the suspension of the Constitution and the direct military intervention of General Musharraf.[33] However, after his appointment as the CJP, his attitude changed. From the first day of his appointment, he was aware of the new context in which the judiciary was operating and, accordingly, indicated his liberal approach towards the SCP and its relationship with other organisations in Pakistani society. In this regard, he referred to the role of CSOs and the media in the process of the dispensation of justice and expressed his concerns about the inaccessibility to justice for the common man.[34] Shortly after his appointment as the CJP, Chaudhry reactivated the Human Rights Cell of the SCP[35] which led to a massive increase in applications from individuals and groups alike. CJP Chaudhry also increased *suo motu* notices. These steps engaged the public at large directly with the SCP.[36] In most of the human rights petitions and for *suo motu* notices, the SCP issued directions which were in favour of citizens and against the interests of the military regime of General Musharraf. These directions and notices already started to show proof of a certain degree of governance by the judges of the SCP. Unsurprisingly, this did not bode well with the military regime of General Musharraf. In reaction, the military regime of General Musharraf suspended the CJP Iftikhar Muhammad Chaudhry on 9 March 2007 to regain control over the autonomy of the higher judiciary.[37]

The second phase began after the suspension of the CJP Iftikhar Muhammad Chaudhry when CSOs, journalists, lawyers, and students held countrywide protests.[38] In addition, these groups along with the CJP challenged the

---

32 A Kalhan, '" Gray Zone" Constitutionalism and the Dilemma of Judicial Independence in Pakistan' (2013) 46 *Vanderbilt Journal of Transnational Law* 1.

33 *Zafar Ali Shah v. General Pervez Musharraf*, 52 PLD 869 (2000)6.

34 Nauman, *supra* note 23.

35 Gilani, *supra* note 12.

36 Nauman, *supra* note 23.

37 A Anthony, 'Supporters Hold Rally for Suspended Pakistani Judge - Reuters' https://uk.reuters.com/article/uk-pakistan-judge/supporters-hold-rally-for-suspended-pakistani-judge-idUKISL19665420070526 (accessed 29 March 2020).

38 *Ibid.*

suspension directly before the SCP under Article 184(3) of the Constitution.[39] The SCP demonstrated its control over the executive's powers by restoring the CJP. The restoration was against the regime's interests and showed how the SCP protected itself against the court-packing measures of the military regime. The suspension and subsequent restoration of the CJP paved the way to the emergence of a genuine juristocracy. The restoration of the CJP Chaudhry marked the end of the second phase of the process of the emergence of the juristocracy.

The third phase began after the restoration of the CJP Chaudhry when the SCP allowed the petition by leaders of PML-N to return to Pakistan from exile.[40] They were previously sent into exile in Saudi Arabia under a deal between the military regime of General Musharraf and Saudi Arabia. The decision to allow these leaders was a policy issue as it involved Pakistan's relationships with Saudi Arabia. The SCP's decision indicated that the SCP was involved in policy-making which falls in the domain of Parliament and the executive. This policy-making by the SCP further contributed to the process of the emergence of the government of judges. Also, the SCP's decision to allow the opposition leaders gained the support of a major opposition political party for the SCP and damaged the political interests of the military regime of General Musharraf.

Facing growing unpopularity, General Musharraf struck a deal with opposition leader, Benazir Bhutto, Chairperson of the PPP. Under the deal brokered by the US government, the former could remain president should the latter's party secure a majority in Parliament.[41] Musharraf had previously initiated criminal proceedings against Bhutto and her husband when Bhutto was in self-exile. Bhutto was in self-exile ever since Musharraf came into power in October 1999. Both husband and wife could not return and participate in politics as they had to face legal proceedings before doing so. In order to avoid these proceedings, they preferred to be in self-exile. Musharraf enacted the National Reconciliation Ordinance (NRO) to quash criminal proceedings against several politicians including members of the PPP as well as bureaucrats. This was aimed at materialising the deal. However, opposition political parties challenged the NRO before the SCP. The SCP stopped the potential beneficiaries from taking any benefit from the NRO until the final decision of the SCP.[42] Again, the NRO was a product of the law-making process but the SCP took on this power under Article 184(3) of the Constitution by connecting it to the matter of the enforcement of fundamental rights and public interest.

---

39   *The Chief Justice Iftikhar Muhammad Chaudhary v the President of Pakistan* (2007).

40   Khan (2017), *supra* note 13.

41   C Rice, *No Higher Honor: A Memoir of My Years in Washington* (Crown 2011).

42   *Dr Mobashir Hassan & others v Federation of Pakistan & others* (2010) PLD 2010 2.

The SCP decisions on the NRO and the issue of the return of PML-N gave the impression that the higher judiciary could continue to take decisions against the interests of the military regime of General Musharraf. Meanwhile, presidential elections were scheduled for October 2007. General Musharraf submitted his nomination papers for the elections to the Election Commission of Pakistan. However, noticing that there is a conflict between the judiciary and executive, opposition political parties challenged Musharraf's eligibility to contest presidential elections. The SCP issued an interim decision that the Chief Election Commission may continue to hold elections but was stopped from issuing the final notification.[43] As a result, the presidential elections were held in October 2007. However, given that the SCP made two important decisions against the interests of General Musharraf, the government could not take its chances to wait for the final decision. Therefore, General Musharraf promulgated an emergency on 3 November 2007, suspended the constitution, introduced a provisional constitution, arrested many lawyers and politicians and shutdown the transmission of several private TV channels.[44] The third phase of the emergence of juristocracy ended on 3 November 2007.

The fourth phase of the emergence of juristocracy began after the promulgation of an emergency on 3 November 2007. However, the emergency catalysed the ousting of General Musharraf. His popularity nosedived and international pressure from the US government increased. The US government advised Musharraf to step down from the office of the Chief of Army Staff (COAS) and move towards a democratic process through the election.[45] In the wake of this pressure, Musharraf lifted the emergency,[46] resigned from the office of COAS, handed over command to the then Director General, Lieutenant General Ashfaq Pervez Kiyani,[47] and announced general elections.[48]

General elections were held in February 2008. Following their result, a coalition government of the PPP and the PML-N led by PPP came into power.[49]

---

43   *Wajihuddin Ahmmad v Chief Election Commission, PLD 2008 SC 13.*

44   TA Qureshi, 'State of Emergency: General Pervez Musharraf's Executive Assault on Judicial Independence in Pakistan' (2010) 35 *North Carolina Journal of International Law and Commercial Regulation* 485.

45   Rice, *supra* note 41.

46   G Witte, 'Musharraf Ends 6-Week Emergency Rule' *The Washington Post*, 16 December 2007.

47   C Gall, 'Musharraf Quits Pakistani Army Post' *The New York Times*, 28 November 2007, https:// www.nytimes.com/2007/11/28/world/asia/28cnd-pakistan.html (accessed 1 February 2023).

48   Quresh, *supra* note 33.

49   T Mehdi, 'An Overview of 2008 General Elections' *Dawn*, 16 April 2013, https://www.dawn .com/news/802815 (accessed 30 March 2020).

The government announced its intention to restore the judges removed on 3 November 2007 and entered into a series of talks with the PML-N regarding the restoration of those judges. Although the latter promised its voters during the election campaign that it would restore the judges, the PPP reneged on its promises because the restoration of judges could bring independent judges into the Court which could limit the government's powers and thus its own powers. As a result, CSOs, lawyers affiliated with opposition political parties, journalists, students, and professionals held the first long march for the restoration of the judges. This mounted the pressure on the government and it reappointed many of those judges except for a few, including the deposed CJP Iftikhar Muhammad Chaudhry.[50]

Meanwhile, the PML-N withdrew from the coalition and joined the opposition. This increased mistrust between the PPP and the PML-N. The SCP packed with judges loyal to the regime disqualified the leaders from holding the membership of the National Assembly in an old case.[51] Following this decision the federal government imposed the Governor's rule in the province of Punjab where PML-N was leading the government.[52] The timing of the case suggested that the PPP used a non-independent judiciary to control the opposition. The PML-N leader openly accused the then PPP leadership of involvement in manipulating the court's decision.[53] As a reaction to the above disqualification, the PML-N announced it would join a second march of CSOs, lawyers, journalists and opposition political parties from different parts of Pakistan.[54]

The second march for the restoration of the remaining judges removed on 3 November 2007 began in the second week of March 2009 and was covered live by most of the TV channels.[55] In the wake of countrywide demonstrations,

50   'Four LHC Judges Take Fresh Oath' *Dawn*, 30 August 2008, https://www.dawn.com/news/319098/four-lhc-judges-take-fresh-oath (accessed 1 February 2023); WA Shah, 'Three PHC Judges to Take Fresh Oath' *Dawn*, 5 September 2008,https://www.dawn.com/news/319861/three-phc-judges-to-take-fresh-oath (accessed 1 February 2023).

51   'Sharifs Disqualified, Punjab under Governor Rule' *Dawn*, 26 February 2009, https://www.dawn.com/news/955822 (accessed 29 March 2020).

52   *Ibid.*

53   'Belligerent Nawaz Lashes out at Zardari' *Dawn*,26 February 2009,https://www.dawn.com/news/346187/belligerent-nawaz-lashes-out-at-zardari (accessed 30 March 2020).

54   S Mullaly, 'A Long March to Justice: A Report on Judicial Independence and Integrity in Pakistan' (2009) *International Bar Association, Human Rights Institute*, https://papers.ssrn.com/sol3/papers.cfm?abstract_id=1615685.

55   'Long March Kicks off amid Use of State Force' *The News International*, 13 March 2009, https://www.thenews.com.pk/archive/print/663211-long-march-kicks-off-amid-use-of-state-force (accessed 1 February 2023); 'Imran Urges People to Join Long March' *Dawn*, 26 January 2009, https://www.dawn.com/news/340424/imran-urges-people-to-join-long

representatives of the European Union, ambassadors of the United States and the United Kingdom, and COAS Ashfaq Pervez Kiyani held discussions with the Prime Minister and President Asif Ali Zardari to resolve the issue. As a result, the government announced the restoration of the remaining judges. The judges were finally restored on 16 March 2009[56] which meant the end of the fourth phase of the emergence of juristocracy in Pakistan.

The fifth phase of the emergence of juristocracy began after the restoration of the remaining judges. Previous phases did not indicate the influence of judges over policy-making and the enforcement of laws as such. Those phases just gave evidence of the struggle of different societal and political groups to successfully protect the judiciary against any court-packing measures of the executive. The successful outcome was building up the momentum which gave rise to the obvious emergence of juristocracy in the fifth phase. This phase showed proof that juristocracy had become operational in Pakistan. The SCP reversed all actions taken by the previous two regimes since 3 November 2007; it removed judges appointed by the previous regimes[57] and made the executive appoint judges approved by the SCP, it struck down the NRO,[58] Contempt of Court Act 2012 and the appointment of the Chairman of the National Accountability Bureau,[59] it reviewed certain parts of the Eighteenth Constitutional Amendment,[60] it disqualified parliamentarians for their bogus academic degrees, it held all those involved in the embezzlement of money at Bank of Punjab[61] accountable and it fixed the prices of petroleum products.[62] The list of these decisions that shaped legislation and enforced laws are indeed long. This was the peak of juristocracy. The judges of the SCP influenced legislation and the enforcement of laws through their interpretation of the constitution and statutory laws in general and Article 184(3) of the Constitution in particular. This phase ended with the retirement of CJP Chaudhry in December 2013.

-march (accessed 1 February 2023); 'Islamabad Sit-in till Restoration of Judges' *Dawn*, 26 January 2009, https://www.dawn.com/news/340433/islamabad-sit-in-till-restoration-of-judges (accessed 1 February 2023).

56   'Nation Celebrates Judges' Restoration' *The News International*, 17 March 2009, https://www.thenews.com.pk/archive/print/663287-nation-celebrates-judges'-restoration (accessed 1 February 2023).

57   'Sindh High Court Bar Association v. Federation of Pakistan' (2009) PLD SC 879.

58   *Dr. Mobashir Hassan & others v. Federation of Pakistan & others.*

59   N Iqbal, 'SC Removes NAB Chief Fasih Bokhari' *Dawn*, 29 May 2013, https://www.dawn.com/news/1014659/sc-removes-nab-chief-fasih-bokhari (accessed 1 February 2023).

60   *Nadeem Ahmed and others v the Federation of Pakistan.*

61   *Bank of Punjab v Haris Steel Industries (Pvt) Ltd* (2010) PLD SC 11.

62   *Iqbal Zafar Jhagra & another v the Federation of Pakistan.*

The sixth phase began after the retirement of CJP Chaudhry and lasted until the outbreak of COVID-19 in 2019. The activism of the SCP slowed down during this phase which was visible in the decrease in number of human rights petitions registered by the Human Rights Cell of the SCP under Article 184(3) of the Constitution. According to the annual report of the SCP 2019–20, the number of human rights petition decreased from 21025 in 2014 to 3109 in 2020. Also, the SCP did not consistently make decisions in politically important cases during this phase. The cases decided by the SCP were mostly targeted at politicians. All this showed that juristocracy faced limitations during this phase. For example, the SCP disqualified the Prime Minister Nawaz Sharif for the latter's concealment of assets[63] but the SCP did not strike down the extension of COAS General Qamar Javed Bajwa. A litigant challenged the appointment of the COAS, General Bajwa, in November 2019. The SCP initiated the proceedings. However, the petitioner withdrew the petition but the SCP changed the proceedings into *suo motu* proceedings and continued looking into the matter. The main issue before the SCP was the law under which the hybrid regime of Pakistan Tehreek-i-Insaaf (PTI) extended the tenure of the COAS Bajwa. It turned out that there was no law under which the SCP could extend the tenure of the COAS Bajwa. The SCP was supposed to strike down the appointment as it was without a legal basis but it eventually did not. Instead, the SCP provisionally approved the extension of the tenure of the COAS Bajwa and deferred the matter to the government to make the law on this issue within six months.[64]

However, the sixth phase of juristocracy was not as obvious as the fifth phase, as during the latter remarks and orders of the SCP made headlines on a daily basis. A major reason for this up and down was the personal choice of chief justices who then led the SCP. The CJP has administrative powers to approve the initiation of *suo motu* proceedings, constitute benches of the SCP, and chair the meetings for judicial appointments in provincial high courts and the SCP. Some chief justices practiced judicial restraint and discouraged the use of *suo motu* actions and the initiation of proceedings in politically sensitive cases. For example, the CJP Tassaduq Hussain Jillani (2013–2014) and CJP Nasir-ul-Mulk (2014–2015) kept a low profile and showed restraint. However, other chief justices such as CJP Mian Saqib Nisar (2016–2019) and CJP Asif Saeed Kosa (January 2019-December 2019) actively looked into politically

---

63   Constitution Petition 29 of 2016, *Imran Ahmad Khan Niazi v Mian Muhammad Nawaz Sharif P.M. Pakistan*, 2017 SCP 87.

64   *Ibid.*

important cases, issued public statements covered by the media and encouraged *suo motu* proceedings.

However, juristocracy took a new turn when COVID-19 reared its head in 2019 and increased space for the influences of the judges of the SCP over legislation and enforcement of laws, as will be discussed next.

3   Juristocracy in Pakistan during the COVID-19 Crisis

3.1   *Judicial Law-making*

COVID-19 emerged in December 2019. Its existence was initially reported in China and ever since spread across the world. However, it took some time to have a noticeable effect in Pakistan. The number of COVID-19 positive cases reached its peak around the summer of 2020. The Parliament in Pakistan did not respond to the new situation adequately. It could not make any new law to tackle the new situation and institutionalise the government's response to it. There were several reasons for the government's inability to respond through legislation. First, like the rest of the world, the situation in Pakistan was getting worse. The government had a limited capacity to first understand the new situation and then to address it. Second, the government wanted to avoid passing any law that could complicate issues regarding COVID-19 rather than address it. The economy of Pakistan was already struggling at that time. Any law on COVID 19 could have restricted people's movement and economic activities.

As a result, the SCP was operating in a legal vacuum. There was a need for policy-making and enhanced governance that could deal with the COVID-19 crisis. However, Parliament did not make any policy and the government did not make any huge efforts to bring about changes to its governance. Nor was any kind of intention on the part of the government that could indicate the Parliament planning to make such laws expressed. Therefore, the SCP responded to this context by initiating *Suo Motu* Case No. 1 of 2020 under article 184(3) of the Constitution which empowers the SCP to decide on issues related to the enforcement of fundamental rights and public importance. Although the Constitution did not specify the exact scope of fundamental rights and public interest, the Court justified its intervention by connecting the COVID-19 crisis to the enforcement of fundamental rights and public interest. Despite the fact that the COVID-19 crisis was more related to policy-making and enforcement of policies, the government did not seriously oppose the SCP stepping into the realm of policy-making and enforcement of laws.

To that end, the SCP initially issued notices regarding steps taken to address the COVID-19 crisis to the different federal and provincial authorities of Pakistan including, but not limited to, the Attorney-General of Pakistan (AGP), advocate generals of the province of Khyber Pakhtunkhwa, Punjab, Baluchistan, and Gilgit Baltistan (GB) and health authorities in these provinces. These notices directed these authorities to inform the SCP about the steps taken by them to deal with the COVID-19 situation. These authorities responded to the SCP's notices by turning up on 7 April 2020. The Court made an observation that there is no law in the country that can provide legal force to the government's response to the COVID-19 crisis. The Court directed the AGP to submit a response to its observation on emergency legislation, and other authorities to submit a report on actions taken by them to deal with the COVID-19 crisis.

The issue of emergency legislation was related to law-making which should have been initiated in Parliament instead. However, in this case, the SCP triggered the legislation process by its directions and observations. By doing so, the judges of the SCP were leading legislative functions and actions of Parliament and of the executive as well as subjecting elected representatives to the Court's directives and observations.

The AGP submitted the Government's response on the next hearing of the above case on 13 April 2020 "that as a matter of policy, the session of Parliament is not being called but the Government is considering such aspect of the matter". Responding to the SCP's previous directions, the AGP further declared that the Prime Minister was holding a high-level meeting with the Chief Ministers of all the Provinces including GB and the Chief Commissioner of Islamabad Capital Territory on the day of the hearing. The meeting would thoroughly deliberate issues relating to the COVID-19 crisis. The federal government would draw up a uniform policy applicable throughout Pakistan without distinction.

In the hearing of 13 April 2020 a lawyer of the SCP informed that the government of Punjab had issued an executive order to stop any inter-provincial movement of people to curb COVID-19. The Advocate-General of Punjab confirmed the issuance of the order. The SCP observed that such an order is a violation of Article 15 of the Constitution and hence cannot be passed by the executive authority. However, the legislature could do so by adopting a new law. The learned Advocate-General assured the SCP that he would advise the government accordingly. However, the SCP struck down and set aside the executive order of the government until such a measure was taken by the Parliament of Punjab first.

In the hearing of 4 May 2020 the government informed the SCP that the Prime Minister and other relevant officials conducted a meeting with stakeholders of all the federating Provinces on 14 April 2020 in which a policy decision regarding the COVID-19 crisis was made and was being implemented by the provincial governments. However, the AGP admitted before the Court that the above policy decision was not broad enough, therefore, another meeting would have to take place to address the issues regarding the COVID-19 crisis more adequately.

In the same hearing of 4 May 2020, the SCP learned that the federal and provincial governments imposed a lockdown all over the country and closure of all business activities all over the country except for a few. The Court found that the said policy decision of 14 April 2020 submitted to it by the government in the previous hearing was not much of a policy and lacked transparency because it only made reference to standard operating procedures (SOPs) on the COVID-19 crisis and identified which industries had been allowed to remain open.

During the above hearing, the government of Sindh informed the SCP that they processed and accepted applications by some businesses and shops to operate. The SCP found this action of the government against the fundamental rights guaranteed in the Constitution and the principle of transparency. The SCP made an observation that the government needed to revisit and re-examine its decision regarding the COVID-19 crisis. The Court held that it expected the government to come up with a comprehensive – non-discriminatory – policy rather than keep accepting exceptions to the lockdown measures. Also, the Court expressed its desire that the federal government should make a policy decision after consulting with the provinces at the national level and apply such a decision uniformly across the whole country. The Court directed all the government stakeholders, federal government and provincial governments to report their coordination efforts to frame a uniform national policy to the court and to ensure that such a uniform policy was enforced all over Pakistan.

It is argued that the SCP was not assigned the role to make the policy by directing the government to make a uniform national policy. Instead, policy-making was the function of Parliament that the SCP was carrying out during the COVID-19 crisis. However, the SCP did not stop at merely issuing directions to the federal and provincial governments to come up with a uniform policy. The SCP also delved into the specifics of the (to be adopted) COVID-19-related policy. For example, in the hearing of 18 May 2020, the National Health Services and Research Centre (NHSRC) submitted a report and the minutes of a meeting of the National Coordination Committee on COVID-19 headed by the Prime Minister of Pakistan through CMA No. 3096 of 2020. The minutes showed the steps taken by the committee to deal with issues including, but not limited to, shopping malls, small community markets in urban and rural areas, and the closure of such shops and businesses on Saturday and Sunday. This was where the SCP stepped in and struck down the decision regarding the closure of shops, markets and businesses on Saturday and Sunday because the decision violated Articles 4, 18 and 25 of the Constitution[65] which allowed businessmen to do their business on all days, which is permissible under the law, subject to the enforcement of SOPs. In this regard, the Court did not find any justifiable rational or reasonable grounds for requiring businesses to close down on these two days. The Court held:

> all days of the week are the same. It is for the convenience of the human beings that the days have been given names, otherwise there is no distinction between others days of the week from Saturday and Sunday..... We may caution the Government of Pakistan so also the Governments of all the four Provinces, ICT and G.B. that looking at the past history of Pakistan, where business activities of private entrepreneurs was interfered with by the Government, such entrepreneurs lost faith in the system and packed up and moved to some other destinations in the world, where they consider their investment to be more safe and profitable. If the businesses and industries remain closed for a long time, their revival becomes doubtful, more and more, and in case they are not revived, millions of workers will be on streets and the Government may be faced with a human disaster and calamity of such a magnitude that to overcome it, may become next to impossible.[66]

The decision to declare public holidays or which days of the week will be working days, however, is the sole discretion of Parliament. It requires proper legislation. Yet, the judges of the SCP legislated on this issue during the COVID-19 pandemic. This suggested that the judges of the SCP were not only carrying out the basic function assigned to the judiciary by interpreting different provisions of the constitution on the fundamental rights and related to the powers of the SCP, but also carrying out the function of Parliament itself.

---

65   Article 4 of the Constitution of Pakistan 1973 provides: "1) To enjoy the protection of law and to be treated in accordance with law is the inalienable right of every citizen. Wherever he may be, and of every other person for the time being within Pakistan. (2) In particular— (a) no action detrimental to the life, liberty, body, reputation or property of any person shall be taken except in accordance with law; (b)no person shall be prevented from or be hindered in doing that which is not prohibited by law; and (c)no person shall be compelled to do that which the law does not required him to do". Article 18 of the Constitution gives the right to every citizen to enter upon any lawful profession or occupation, and to conduct any lawful trade or business. Article 25 of the Constitution provides that "citizens are equal before law and are entitled to equal protection of law".

66   Suo Moto Case No.1 of 2020, the Supreme Court of Pakistan, 2020 SCP 97, supremecourt. gov.pk/downloads-judgements/s.m.c._01_2020_18052020.pdf (accessed 12 January 2023).

Nonetheless, subsequently, when the AGP and Chairman National Disaster Management Authority (NDMA) informed the Court about the drastic increase in the number of COVID-19 positive cases during the hearing of 19 May 2020 and 8 June 2020 respectively, the Court reversed its previous decision by allowing the government to close down shops on Saturday and Sunday and to "make a policy for the opening and closing of shops as per their strategy to meet the dangers of COVID-19".

The reversal of the decision showed that the judges of the SCP were running a government which was stronger and more powerful than the one run by elected representatives of people in an elected democracy. The elected representatives are required to hold debates in the Parliament before enacting a legislation and repeat the same process to change a law. The executive executes the law after enactment and stops to implement it when it is changed. However, the judges of the SCP carried out both functions: legislation and execution. They initially made the above decision in a hearing on the COVID-19 crisis and later reversed it. The court ensured the enforcement of both decisions through follow-up hearing and directing the executive to submit progress reports on implementation of their decisions.

The SCP kept on reiterating its directions to the government to adopt a uniform policy but the government did not do so throughout the COVID-19 crisis. This further justified the involvement of the SCP in governing the matters specifically related to the COVID-19 crisis nationwide. The SCP could not be blamed for taking over the policy-making function of Parliament since the latter failed to assume its prerogatives. In the hearing of 8 June 2020, the learned AGP informed the SCP that the National Coordination Committee made a unanimous policy for dealing with COVID-19. Some provincial governments have adopted laws to deal with COVID-19 but the federal government failed to do so at the national level despite numerous calls from the SCP.

Later in the hearing of 25 June 2020, the learned AGP informed that the federal government had started consultations with provincial governments to prepare a uniform policy that could be applied across the country to deal with the COVID-19 crisis. The policy also included incentives, protective equipment and other facilities for the doctors and other healthcare staff. The SCP directed the AGP to submit a comprehensive report on the implementation of the future policy.

The government's inability to come up with a law increased the space for the judges of the SCP to govern the country instead. Given the global pandemic no one seriously questioned the involvement of the SCP in policy-matters, instead, it received implicit approval as it was addressing the problem. For example, the government or the public at large did not react to the SCP's decision on the closure of businesses during the weekend (discussed above) and the reversal of this decision.

Nonetheless, policy-making was not the only part of the government that the SCP was influencing during the COVID-19 crisis in 2020 and 2021. The SCP also influenced the enforcement of laws by chasing the executive and compelling it through its directions to submit reports and replies, not only on the COVID-19 crisis, but also on issues related to different areas of politics and public policy. These issues included, but were not limited to, resource management for the COVID-19 crisis, accountability, shaping Islamic opinions, the protection of minority rights and the enforcement of labour laws. This is explained in the next section.

3.2   *Policy Execution*

Some of the areas of policy in which the SCP performed the policy execution function were directly related to COVID-19 whereas others were indirectly related to COVID-19. For example, issues such as the government actions regarding lockdown and the safety of legal community were directly related to COVID-19. However, issues such as malpractices of the different government authorities limiting the capacity of the government to deal with COVID-19 were indirectly related to COVID. Therefore, the SCP had to hold them accountable. All these areas of policy-execution are discussed below.

3.2.1   COVID-19 Related Issues

In the hearing of 13 April 2020, the federal government through the learned AGP assured the Court that it was taking all the necessary steps to deal with the COVID-19 crisis and was trying to reduce its effect on the people by taking various measures on the social welfare side and also on humanitarian grounds. Furthermore, the federal government provided medical supplies to the provincial government, including test kits to laboratories, personal protective equipment (PPE) and ventilators to the hospitals. The government initially imported most of these items but later the provincial governments of Punjab and Sindh began to make efforts to manufacture a large number of these items. They put locally manufactured ventilators to the test and planned to produce and distribute these all over the country.

While representing the government of Punjab, the Advocate-General of Punjab submitted a report to the SCP. The report explained the steps taken by the government of Punjab to deal with the COVID-19 crisis there. In response, the SCP expressed its desire that the government of Punjab would continue to make all sorts of other protection against COVID-19 available to all.

While representing the government of Sindh, the Advocate-General of Sindh submitted a separate report on steps taken by the provincial government regarding the COVID-19 crisis there. The report explained the steps taken by the government to control the spread of COVID-19 in the province of Sindh. In one of the hearings, the SCP expressed its concerns over one of the orders of the government of Sindh under which 11 Union Councils (UCs) in Karachi had been sealed. The Advocate-General informed the Court that the government had allowed grocery shops in these 11 UCs to remain open but did not introduce any other programme for these 11 UCs. Also, the government of Sindh distributed free *Rashan*[67] worth Rs. 8.0 billion in Sindh.

The provincial governments of Khyber Pakhtunkhwa and Baluchistan separately submitted their reports during the same hearing. The SCP took those reports into the account and made an observation that the effects of COVID-19 are not too alarming in these two provinces and the overall situation at that time was found to be under control. The SCP directed the federal and provincial governments to provide sanitary staff with proper and secure uniforms. This would help sanitary staff to work without fear of being affected by disease themselves.

During the above hearing, the Chairman of the Pakistan Medical Association informed the SCP that 40,000 applications for registration of doctors were pending before the Pakistan Medical and Dental Council (PMDC). There were numerous cases regarding the PMDC that were pending in the different courts of the country, including the SCP. This pendency had limited the capacity of the health sector to deal with the COVID-19 crisis. The SCP stated that it would address these cases soon in accordance with the law. One of the above pending cases was related to the appointment of Registrar, PMDC. Registrar PMDC was removed because the PMDC Ordinance under which he was appointed was repealed in 2019 through an ordinance by the President.[68] He had challenged his removal before the Islamabad High Court (IHC). The latter allowed the former to work. However, the National Health Services of Pakistan appealed against IHC's decision to the SCP.[69] The position of registrar was important for processing of the above application especially during the COVID crisis when the demand for doctors increased significantly to deal with the COVID crisis. The SCP decided this pending case on 17 April 2020, struck down the IHC's decision and ordered the reconstitution of PMDC for better and efficient

---

67 *Rashan* is an Urdu word for Groceries.

68 N Iqbal, 'SC Reconstitutes PMDC, Sets aside IHC Order' *Dawn*, 18 April 2020, https://www .dawn.com/news/1550118 (accessed 31 January 2023).

69 *Ibid.*

working of the council.[70] This later facilitated the processing of the aforesaid applications.

In the hearing of 20 April 2020, all federal and provincial governments again submitted their reports. These reports explained that these governments had made PPE available to doctors and paramedic staff. This equipped hospitals to deal with all situations arising from this COVID-19 pandemic more effectively. The report also provided that the steps taken by the government ensured that doctors, nurses, paramedics and janitorial staff were present to perform their duties.

The SCP observed that COVID-19 has not reached its peak but COVID positive cases were increasing day by day. The SCP expressed its desire for cooperation among functionaries of all the federal and provincial governments. It stated that it expected them to make a consolidated effort and take decisions by consensus for the betterment of the country. The SCP continued to direct these governments to submit reports on their progress regarding COVID.

In the hearing dated 4 May 2020 the Advocate-General of Baluchistan submitted a report to the SCP. The report explained steps taken by the government of Baluchistan to deal with the COVID-19 crisis. According to the report, COVID-19 was also present in the Province of Baluchistan but did not grow to an alarming level. The report confirmed that the provincial government received all the required facilities for the treatment of the COVID-19 patients. Doctors and paramedics received PPE and the hospitals had no complaints in this regard.

In the hearing of 18 May 2020, the federal and provincial governments submitted new reports to the SCP and informed them about the restrictions imposed over the opening and closure of shopping malls, shops and markets. However, SOPs regarding the COVID-19 crisis were maintained.

In the hearing of 19 May 2020, the AGP requested the SCP to constitute a team of doctors to seek their opinion on the COVID-19 crisis. The Court rejected the request because it did not consider it essential to undertake this exercise. It observed that the government was already consulting doctors and it could obtain the opinion from the doctors.

During the above hearing different departments of the government of Khyber Pakhtunkhwa including, but not limited to, the Health Department, the Home Department and the Relief and Rehabilitation Department submitted a report on the measures they have adopted to address the COVID-19 crisis in their province. According to the report, the government made maximum effort

---

70   *Ibid.*

to provide beds, medicines, and medical devices and there was no shortage of these items for the treatment of COVID-19 patients. The learned Advocate-General informed that 40% of total COVID-19 tests carried out were positive but the situation was under control. However, the SCP directed the government to submit another report on efforts made to deal with the issue of the COVID-19 crisis.

In the hearing of 5 May 2021, the Deputy Military Estates Officers, Headquarter Military Lands and Cantonment (ML & C) and the Ministry of Defence submitted a report stating that the disinfection in the Cantonment areas was being conducted on a regular basis, fines were being imposed for violations of COVID-19 SOP s, i.e., masks, gloves, hand sanitizer and antibacterial soaps, and payment of salaries and other benefits to the sanitary staff, the medical and paramedical staff were regularly being made. As per the report, all essential PPE was provided to the doctors and paramedic staff of the hospitals and dispensaries under the ML & C Department.

The above analysis showed that the SCP was shaping policy-execution by directing the different government authorities of Pakistan to submit their progress reports on actions taken by them to deal with COVID-19. These authorities were executing under the pressure created by the directions of the SCP during the above hearings. However, the actions of the government during the above hearings were general. The SCP went beyond this and shaped specific actions of the executive to deal with specific aspects of COVID-19 related issues. This is discussed in the next section.

3.2.2   Establishment of Quarantine Centres

In the hearing of 20 April 2020, the Court observed that a quarantine centre was established in the Haji Camp in Islamabad. Different newspapers reported inhumane conditions in the said camp. The Islamabad High Court observed the same during a case pending before the Court. The SCP inquired from the Secretary of Health who was present in the Court at that time to confirm the existence of such a quarantine centre. To this the secretary assured the court that he would visit the centre and would submit a detailed report on the conditions there.

Acting upon his assurance, the Federal Secretary, Department of Health submitted the report in the next hearing of 4 May 2020. According to the report, the NDMA had previously established the quarantine centre at Haji Camp. However, Haji Camp was not a proper location as it lacked all facilities which were required for a quarantine centre. Therefore, Haji Camp Quarantine Centre was closed down and the quarantine centre was moved to a hostel which was made available free of cost. There were 48 rooms in the hostel to accommodate the passengers who were found to be COVID-19 positive and where they had to be kept in quarantine. The SCP directed the NDMA to explain the reasons for which the Haji Camp was declared a quarantine centre without confirming if the same could be used as a quarantine centre or not and to disclose any amount spent on making it a quarantine centre.

3.2.3   Resource Management for the COVID-19 Crisis

In the hearing of 13 April 2020, the SCP observed that COVID-19 did not seriously affect Pakistan. According to the Court, there were other serious ailments prevailing in the country due to which people were dying daily and those diseases require more money too. The Ministry of Health informed the SCP that there are other serious diseases such as brain haemorrhage, dengue fever, kidney failure, cardiac failure, hepatitis, and liver failure causing the deaths of hundreds of thousands of people on a yearly basis. The SCP remarked that it expected that the government should not put all its resources into the COVID-19 crisis and make the country all together dysfunctional. The federal government and all provincial governments should address this point.

In the hearing of 19 May 2020, the Chairman of the NDMA explained how the NDMA used funds at its disposal. COVID-19 was a new virus. Therefore, it required special gear, tools and equipment for protection, treatment and control of the same. The gear, tools and equipment were sufficiently available though they were not manufactured in Pakistan. The government allocated funds to immediately purchase the same. They were imported from abroad. The government distributed the gear, tools and equipment harmoniously among all regions of Pakistan. However, now local production facilities had started manufacturing the gear, tools and equipment themselves, thus putting an end to imports.

Similar to the above tools and equipment, the NDMA placed orders for importing 1,187 ventilators from abroad. Of these, 300 had been received and distributed among all the four provinces, ICT and GB. They would receive the remainder soon which would be distributed accordingly. According to the report submitted by the NDMA, they had started manufacturing ventilators to international standards which were also capable of being exported abroad. Therefore, Pakistan would be self-sufficient in all manners to deal with the COVID-19 crisis. Initially, a company of the Pakistan Army, DESTO invested in the manufacturing of PPE and testing kits but later the private sector was also able to manufacture PPE, testing kits and ventilators. The SCP directed the NDMA to submit a report with further details on this matter to the next hearing.

On the next hearing of 8 June 2020, complying with the SCP's directions, the NDMA submitted a report in which it confirmed that Pakistan Ordnance

Factories (POFs), i.e. Wah Cantt and DESTO, manufactured PPE. The Ministry of Defence owned these two companies. According to the report, DESTO recently imported the machinery for manufacture of PPE. The SCP directed the NDMA to submit documents of importation for this machinery along with the next report by the next hearing. The documents that the SCP directed the NDMA to submit included, but were not limited to, the contract of purchase, the letter of credit, the airway bill, the packing list, the invoice, the custom documents, etc., Also, the SCP directed the NDMA to submit a report regarding laboratories operating all over Pakistan which were providing a testing facility for COVID-19. The NDMA complied with the directions of the SCP by submitting the report on the next hearing of 25 June 2020.

In the hearing of 5 May 2021, the SCP noted that COVID-19 patients suffered from breathlessness and they required oxygen. With the rise of COVID-19 positive cases the demand for the availability of oxygen also increased. The Additional Attorney-General of Pakistan (AAGP) informed the SCP that Pakistan Steel Mills Karachi was capable of producing oxygen for COVID-19 patients. However, the government needed to arrange approximately an amount of Rs.1 billion to make the oxygen plant of the Pakistan Steel Mills operational. He further informed the Court that the government would shortly take steps to make it operational for the smooth supply of oxygen to hospitals. This would ensure that no shortage, obstruction or impediment to the supply of oxygen occurred. According to the AAGP, the government constituted a committee of experts who were considering steps required to operationalise the plant.

The Advocate-General of Khyber Pakhtunkhwa informed the SCP that oxygen cylinders were being sold for exorbitant prices and these prices were not being regulated. The Chief Executive Officer, Drug Regulatory Authority of Pakistan submitted to the SCP that the Ministry of Industries & Production handled the very production of oxygen and it was required to regulate the prices of oxygen. The SCP directed the Secretary of the Ministry of Industries & Production to notify a proper price mechanism for the sale of oxygen gas and to submit a report every two weeks in this regard.

3.2.4   Safety of the Legal Community

During the hearing of 20 April 2020, the President of the Islamabad High Court Bar Association and the President of the District Bar Islamabad complained to the SCP that lawyers in Islamabad were not being provided with testing facilities and other medical assistance by the Islamabad Capital Territory (ICT). On this, the SCP issued a notice to the Advocate-General of the ICT to explain what steps were taken by the administration in Islamabad to redress lawyers' grievances for the provision of necessary medical facilities. In the next hearing of 5 May 2021, the Islamabad High Court Bar Association and the District Court Bar Association submitted to the SCP that the ICT administration had taken steps to address their concerns but that they would like to see the Law Minister for redressing further concerns. The SCP directed the Attorney-General of Pakistan to facilitate the meeting of the Presidents of the Bars with the Law Minister as early as possible.

3.2.5   The Protection of Minority Rights

The Constitution of Pakistan provides protection to religious minorities through the list of fundamental rights. Also, as discussed above, the government submitted reports regarding the enforcement of SOPs and health & safety regulations for different groups but these SOPs and regulations were not enforced for religious minorities – a large majority of whom were sanitation staff. The SCP received a complaint that PPE was not provided to sanitary staff. The Court inquired with the Advocate Generals and the learned Attorney Generals of the federal and provincial governments about this matter. They confirmed that the required PPE had been provided to all federal and provincial governments for the sanitary staff. They further assured the Court that more would be provided to them if any such need arose.

Nonetheless, in the hearing of 19 May 2020, Samuel Payara, Chairman of the Implementation of Minority Rights Forum complained that the government did not provide protective gear and salaries for nine months to sanitary staff and pensions to those who are retired in the province of Sindh. He also informed the SCP that some of the sanitary staff were employed by contractors and their living conditions were worse. Samuel was a Christian and most of the sanitary staff are Christians in Pakistan. Christians are a religious minority in Pakistan. The Court noticed that similar situations existed in other provinces. The judges of Court observed that the "sanitary, being a core work of the Government, we fail to understand as to how this work is being done by awarding contracts. Apparently, such contracts are mere sham contracts." Therefore, it protected the rights of minorities by directing the federal and provincial governments, particularly the government of Sindh, to submit reports on the provision of PPE against COVID-19 and the payment of salaries to religious minorities working as sanitary staff. It took an assurance from Advocate Generals of all federal and provincial governments to provide all sort of protective gear within a week and to pay them their salaries and pensions if a sanitary staff member is retired. It also directed the government to pay salaries to those sanitary staff who were employed by contractors.

In the hearing of 25 June 2020, the provincial government of Sindh submitted its report to the SCP. The report showed that there were no funds for the payment of salaries to the Sanitary Staff of WASA/Hyderabad Development Authority (HDA). Yet, the Chief Minister approved a summary of an amount of Rs.140 million for payment of salaries to the sanitary staff for the months of March and April 2020. The Chief Minister approved another summary on 10 June 2020 for the payment of the salaries for seven months. Also, the Board of Directors of HDA increased water charges by 20% from all consumers for payment of salaries to the sanitary staff of HDA. However, the same government allocated Rs 100 billion for the importing of luxury vehicles to be used by the government's employees. The SCP found this allocation unjustifiable and restrained the government from using these funds till the next date of hearing.

3.2.6 Federalism

The issue of the use of powers regarding the movement of people between the federal and provincial governments was a matter related to federalism and to be dealt with by the federal and provincial governments. However, the SCP influenced the issue of interprovincial movement through its directives during the proceedings on the COVID-19 crisis. In the hearing dated 13 of April 2020, the government of Punjab stopped the interprovincial movement of people through an executive order. The SCP initially confronted the Advocate-General of Punjab with Article 15 of the Constitution that provides people with the right of movement. The latter responded that only the legislature could restrict this right of movement through a legislation and that he would advise the government to refrain from stopping the interprovincial movement of people. The SCP struck down the executive order of the Government of Punjab to restrict interprovincial movement of the people until the legislature made a law on this matter.

In the hearing of 19 May 2020, the SCP strengthened the federation by extending the federal government's powers in the provinces in the context of the COVID-19 crisis under Article 149 of the Constitution which provides:

> 149. Directions to Provinces in certain cases. (1) The executive authority of every Province shall be so exercised as not to impede or prejudice the exercise of the executive authority of the Federation, and the executive authority of the Federation shall extend to the giving of such directions to a Province as may appear to the Federal Government to be necessary for that purpose...(4) The executive authority of the Federation shall also extend to the giving of directions to a Province as to the manner in which the executive authority thereof is to be exercised for the purpose of preventing any grave menace to the peace or tranquillity or economic life of Pakistan or any part thereof.

According to the SCP, the provincial governments are mandatorily required to exercise their authorities without impeding or prejudicing the exercise of authority by the federal government. In light of the above provision, the SCP viewed the COVID-19 crisis as a grave menace to the peace or tranquillity or economic life of Pakistan or any part thereof. Therefore, the SCP extended the executive authority of the federation to issue directions to provinces in the manner in which the provincial government had to exercise its executive authority to prevent COVID-19.

3.2.7   Islamic Law and Accountability

In the hearing of 20 April 2020, the SCP looked into religious matters during the *suo motu* proceedings on the COVID-19 crisis. Muslims are bound by their religious belief to give 2.5% of their wealth to the poor if they have assets equal to more than 87.48 grams (7.5 tola) of gold or 612.36 grams (52.5 tola) of silver.[71] The provincial governments in Pakistan run the department of Zakat and Bait-ul-Mal to ensure the collection of Zakat from the rich and its distribution among needy and poor people. The SCP wanted to know about the criteria adopted by the government for making payments to the beneficiaries of the Zakat and Bait-ul-Mal funds. Furthermore, how the collected money is distributed among needy people, how the expenditures on the administration of these two departments are managed, and whether funds collected through the above two departments can be utilized for payment of salaries to their employees and officers. In this regard, the court directed the government to obtain the opinion of the Chairman of the Council of Islamic Ideology and former Judge of Shariat Appellate Bench of this Court Mufti Muhammad Taqi Usmani by the next hearing. Mufti Muhammad Taqi Usmani submitted his opinion at the next hearing of 4 May 2020. The Director General (of Research) of the Council of Islamic Ideology also submitted his opinion on the questions. The Court thanked both for submitting their opinions and acknowledged that the opinion provided guidance to the SCP. However, the SCP did not delve into the theological debate to make a decision on this issue.

In the hearing of 20 April 2020, when the issue of the collection and distribution of funds collected by these governments for poor and needy people was discussed, the SCP also delved into the question of the accountability of federal and provincial governments. Bait-ul-Mal is a department of the federal government that collects Zakat from people who are eligible to pay Zakat.[72]

---

71   'Zakat Calculator 2022 - The Citizens Foundation (TCF)' https://www.tcf.org.pk/zakat /zakat-calculator/ (accessed 29 January 2023).

72   'Pakistan Bait-Ul-Mal' https://www.pbm.gov.pk/ (accessed 29 January 2023).

Bait-ul-Mal distributes the received money among needy and economically under-privileged people. The SCP held provincial governments accountable on the issue of distribution of funds of Bait-ul-Mal by directing these governments to submit a detailed report on the distribution of those funds. The provincial governments submitted their reports but the SCP was not at all satisfied with those reports. Therefore, the SCP directed all federal and provincial governments to submit more detailed information on the distribution of funds which could show more transparency in the distribution of Zakat and Bait-ul-Mal funds.

Following the above directions, these governments submitted detailed reports in the hearing of 4 May 2020. After going through the detailed reports, the SCP observed that Zakat funds and funds of Bait-ul-Mal were not being properly utilized. The Auditor General submitted a separate report to the Court in which he found a lot of irregularities in the use of funds from Zakat and Bait-ul-Mal. The SCP supplied the copies of the Auditor General's report to all the Advocate Generals of the provinces and ICT and directed them to seek instruction from their respective governments and submit a reply to it. The SCP also indicated that it would consider referring the matter to Federal Investigation Agency or National Accountability Bureau which could take further action in the event of irregularities in the spending of those funds.

The SCP did not only hold the federal and provincial governments accountable for the distribution of Zakat and Bait-ul-Mal funds. During the above hearing, it also held the departments of health and police of the province of Khyber Pakhtunkhwa accountable for the mistreatment of doctors in Peshawar. It came to the knowledge of the Court that the government stopped clinics in that area from doing any functions and that police officials mistreated the doctors and consultants and forcefully tried to shut down their clinics. The SCP directed the provincial secretary of the department of health to look into the matter and submit a report to the Court and take necessary action against all those responsible for the maltreatment of doctors. The Court allowed those health clinics to remain open as per the SOPs and directed the provincial government to refrain from any longer obstructing those clinics.

The matter of accountability of the federal and provincial governments was not limited to the health sector and police. The COVID 19 crises provided the SCP with an opportunity to hold different departments of the government accountable. Malpractices within these departments came to surface during the proceedings on the COVID 19 crisis. These malpractices weakened the government's response to COVID-19. Therefore, the SCP held the government accountable on matters not directly related to COVID-19. For example, during the hearing of 19 May 2020, as per previous directions of the

SCP, NDMA was explaining to the SCP the use of funds allocated to it during COVID-19. NDMA informed the Court that it had to spend money on dealing with Locust attack on agricultural fields of Pakistan. During the hearing of 8 June 2020, NDMA stated that it has four Beaver aircrafts out of which one is operational and the other three are non-operational due to lack of availability of pilots. This provided the SCP with an opportunity to look into the matter of the lack of availability of pilots and also scrutinized the Civil Aviation Authority (CAA).

Therefore, during the hearing of 25 June 2020, the SCP asked the AGP about the availability of pilots. The SCP drew the attention of the AGP to the statement of the Minister of Aviation issued on the floor of Parliament and reported widely in national and international media. According to the statement, many pilots flying planes in Pakistan had fake flying licenses. In response to this statement, the SCP, during the same hearing, expressed its concerns on the lives and safety of airline passengers to the AGP and directed the Director-General of the Civil Aviation Authority (DGCAA) to submit a comprehensive report regarding the followings: i. total number of licenses issued; ii. total number of pilots in employment of PIAC; iii. verification of degrees and licenses; iv. how many pilots with fake degrees and/or licenses had been found; and v. what action had been taken against them.

In the hearing of 5 May 2021, DGCAA complied with the SCP's directions by submitting the above comprehensive report to SCP in which the information regarding the initiation of criminal proceedings in trial courts against all those involved in misconduct and crimes was provided. In addition to proceedings in trial courts, disciplinary action within the department was also initiated against them.

During the above hearing, the government informed the SCP that the Pakistan International Airline Corporation (PIAC) was suffering losses. Its losses increased massively during the COVID-19 crisis due to travel restrictions. The issue of the viability of PIAC came to surface during these proceedings. The SCP held the PIAC accountable on the issue of viability of PIAC and fake degrees of pilots. The Chairman of PIAC submitted a report to the court according to which PIAC has surplus staff which were appointed due to their political affiliations with previous regimes and actions had been taken against those officials of the PIAC who violated the laws. This included the list of pilots who were dismissed on account of holding fake academic documents. According to the reports, all those against whom disciplinary actions were taken had obtained stay orders from different courts. The Chairman of PIAC approached the office of the AGP to assist PIAC in vacating injunctive orders.

The Court directed the Chairman of PIAC to take necessary steps for removing surplus and non-required staff to stabilise the airline in order to save it from further financial losses.

Furthermore, the SCP directed the CEOs of the Pakistan international airlines, i.e. AirBlue and Serene Air, to submit a report regarding the verification of the educational degrees and licenses of their pilots for the Civil Aviation Authority and to submit a list of pilots employed along with copies of educational testimonials and licenses of their pilots.

Beyond the accountability within the aviation sector, the SCP also challenged the accountability of provincial governments who had to prioritise their budgets in the face of the COVID-19 crisis. In this regard, it held the government of Sindh accountable on the allocation of Rs. 4 billion for the purchase of luxury vehicles. The SCP noticed that an amount of Rs. 4 billions has been allocated in its annual budget of 2020–2021 to the import of luxury vehicles. The Court observed that the government needed to spend more money on health, water-supplies, infrastructure developments and safety of the people. Thus, the SCP restrained the government of Sindh and directed the government to submit the report on its new budgetary priorities. The government of Sindh submitted the report to the next hearing of 5 May 2021. The SCP found it unsatisfactory because according to the report huge funds were allocated for water supply and sanitation, education, health, and infrastructure development but they were not actually used in these sectors.

3.2.8   Enforcement of Labour Laws

In the hearing of 20 April 2020, the issue of the health and safety of workers in factories of the province of Sindh was discussed before the SCP. The government of Sindh informed the SCP that industrial units were allowed to operate in Karachi, but in accordance with a SOP enforced by the government for the operation of these units in the context of the COVID-19 crisis. The government asked the industrial units to submit all necessary certificates to the government. The SCP highlighted that the 1934 Factories Act required factories owners to provide proper facilities to factory workers and that compliance with this Act would result in a revolutionary change in the factories. In addition, the above steps taken by the Sindh government had to make factories safer places for their workers. The Court observed that factories should ensure the provision of drinking water, proper canteens, where food prepared by the employers was given to the workers at a nominal price as well as proper residential accommodation, clean toilets and proper medical facilities were to be provided to their respective workers. The SCP directed the relevant departments of the government, dealing with the factories, to submit a detailed report on the enforcement of labour laws. The SCP here went one step further by noting that it made the above observation in respect of factories situated in Karachi but that the labour law should be uniformly applied and enforced across Pakistan without any distinction.

4   Juristocracy after the COVID-19 Crisis

The COVID-19 crisis strengthened the culture of the judiciary's involvement in deciding politically important cases including those issues that normally required legislation and the enforcement of laws. This culture became entirely visible in political developments and the decisions of the SCP after COVID-19.

The hybrid regime of the PTI came to power through the general election in 2018. However, opposition political parties made an alliance against the hybrid regime of the PTI under the umbrella of the Pakistan Democratic Movement (PDM). The PDM had been trying to bring about a regime change by bringing a vote of no-confidence against the Prime Minister Imran Khan but was not successful to do so until 2022. According to them, the PTI-led regime was run by the military from behind the scenes and hence was not legitimate. The PDM could not manage to move a motion of no-confidence against the Prime Minister as they did not have the required votes in the National Assembly. In order to gain a majority in the National Assembly, they initially wooed disgruntled members of the ruling party and later held meeting with allies of the government including the Balochistan Awami Party, the Mutahidda Qaumi Movement and the Pakistan Muslim League Quaid-i-Azam group (PML-Q) between January 2022 and April 2022. The PTI-led government attempted to maintain its majority by sending a reference to the SCP to advise on the legality of those party members who collude against its policies.[73] Also, it attempted to retain the support of its allies. In this regard, the PTI leadership held meetings with the leadership of its allies including the MQM and the PML-Q.[74] The leadership offered the

---

73   AQ Siddiqui and M Nawaz, 'Article 63-A: Votes of Dissident Members Cannot Be Counted, SC Announces Verdict' *The News International*, 17 May 2022, https://www.thenews .com.pk/latest/958491-presidential-reference-on-article-63-a-supreme-court-to -announce-verdict-today (accessed 13 December 2022).

74   'No-Trust Motion: PTI, MQM-P Make Contradictory Statements after PM Imran Khan's Meeting' *The News International*, 3 September 2022, https://www.thenews.com.pk/latest /939984-no-trust-move-pm-imran-arrives-at-mqm-p-headquarters-in-karachi (accessed 13 December 2022).

position of Chief Minister of the province of Punjab to Chaudhry Pervez Elahi from the PML-Q and made its incumbent Chief Minister Usman Buzdar resign from his position. In return, the PML-Q supported the PTI while the MQM and the BAP supported the PDM.

Therefore, the PDM successfully submitted the motion to move the vote of no-confidence in the National Assembly in March 2022. The motion was put to debate and voting in April 2022 but just before the voting could start the speaker gave the floor to the then Minister of Information Fawad Chaudhry to address the assembly. The minister drew the attention of the speaker to Article 5 of the Constitution according to which, "loyalty to the state is the basic duty of every citizen". He viewed the motion of no-confidence as part of a conspiracy hatched by opposition political parties and the American government to bring about a regime change and hence demanded the speaker to reject the motion of no-confidence under Article 5. The speaker was also a member of the PTI. He approved the demand of Chaudhry and rejected the motion of no-confidence. Next, the opposition political parties challenged the speaker's ruling directly before the SCP. The SCP struck down the speaker's ruling and restored the proceedings of the motion of no-confidence in the National Assembly in April 2022. The PDM saw its motion passed in the National Assembly and a PDM-led government came into power.

In May 2022, the SCP announced its decision on the reference sent by the previous PTI-led regime according to which votes of party members against the party policy could not be counted and these members would be disqualified.

Meanwhile, after the resignation of the Chief Minister of Punjab, elections for the new Chief Minister had to take place. The speaker of the Punjab Assembly, i.e. Chaudhry Pervez Elahi, was the nominee of both the PTI and the PML-Q whereas Hamza Shahbaz was the nominee of the PML-N. The PML-Q and the PTI did not have a majority of seats. Chaudhry Pervez Elahi – the then speaker of the Punjab Assembly – was reluctant to hold the session. The PML-N approached the Lahore High Court to order the government to conduct elections. The Lahore High Court ordered a session of the assembly be conducted.[75] The session of the assembly was held but a ruckus took place during the session which sabotaged the proceedings of the assembly.[76] Twenty-five members

---

75   R Bilal, 'LHC Orders Punjab Assembly Deputy Speaker's Office Be Reopened' *Dawn*, 11 April 2022, https://www.dawn.com/news/1684496 (accessed 13 December 2022).

76   'Police Arrest Five PTI MPAs in Crackdown inside Punjab Assembly' *Pakistan Today*, 16 April 2022, https://www.pakistantoday.com.pk/2022/04/16/police-arrest-five-pti-mpas -in-crackdown-inside-punjab-assembly/ (accessed 12 December 2022).

of the PTI voted in favour of the PML-N. The deputy speaker, Dost Mazari, continued the voting process in the provincial assembly of Punjab. The majority of the members of Punjab assembly including twenty-five members of the PTI voted for Hamza Shahbaz and against Chaudhry Pervez Elahi. Hamza Shahbaz became the new Chief Minister.

Yet, based on the decision of the SCP on the reference sent by the PTI, Chaudhry Pervez Elahi challenged the election of the Chief Minister separately before the Lahore High Court. The Lahore High Court directed the deputy speaker of the Punjab Assembly to recount votes for the election of the Chief Minister without counting 25 votes of the PTI members.[77] However, the PTI appealed against this decision before the SCP and requested to modify the decision of Lahore High Court to the extent that 25 votes should not be counted and that elections should not take place immediately. The SCP accepted the appeal. As a result, the votes of those 25 members of the PTI who previously voted in favour of Hamza Shahbaz for the position of Chief Minister were not counted. Meanwhile, by-elections were held for 20 seats which were vacated as a result of the SCP's decision on the reference. Most of those were won by the PTI.

In light of changes in the composition of the Punjab Assembly, the provincial assembly was called into the session for the election of the Chief Minister. Chaudhry Pervez Elahi was the nominee of the PTI and Hamza Shahbaz was the nominee of the PML-N. Members of the PTI and the PML-Q voted for Chaudhry Pervez Elahi whereas the PML-N members voted for Hamza Shahbaz. The former secured a majority after the composition of the assembly had changed. However, the speaker talked to the head of the PML-Q, Chaudhry Shujat Hussain, before the voting took place.[78] The latter clarified that the party did not instruct its members in the assembly to vote for Pervez Elahi. Based on the earlier decision of the SCP wherein the Court decided that votes of the party defectors would not be counted, the speaker did not count the voting of the PML-Q members.[79] As a result, votes in favour of Hamza Shahbaz

---

77   R Bilal, 'LHC Orders Re-Counting of Votes for Punjab CM Election Excluding PTI Dissi-
      dents' *Dawn*, 30 June 2022, https://www.dawn.com/news/1697495 (accessed 13 December
      2022).

78   Z Burki, 'Dost Mazari's Ruling Sparks Constitutional Debate' *The News International*, 23
      July 2022, https://www.thenews.com.pk/print/976054-mazari-s-ruling-sparks-constitutional
      -debate (accessed 13 December 2022).

79   *Ibid.*

became more than those in favour of Chaudhry Pervez Elahi. Thus, Hamza Shahbaz became the new Chief Minister.

However, the new opposition challenged the matter directly before the SCP.[80] The former relied on the SCP's observation on the same issue in a previous case in which the SCP observed that votes of those members will not be counted if they vote against the instructions of the party. However, the SCP decided that parts of the decisions in the previous case were observations and they were not the operative part of the decision and if any observation was inadvertently incorrect the same could be corrected in a later case. The SCP distinguished the head of the party from the parliamentary head of the party. The Court held that the former leads the party in general whereas the latter leads the party in the parliament. The members of Punjab assembly did not defect by following the parliamentary head's instruction to support Chaudhry Pervez Elahi. Therefore, the SCP struck down the speaker of Punjab's action that had not counted the votes of those members of PML-Q. As a result, Pervez Elahi supported by the PTI became the Chief Minister.

The above analysis showed that juristocracy after COVID-19 was a continuity of the nature and scope of juristocracy during and before COVID-19. However, it further strengthened itself after COVID-19. The SCP shaped legislation and the election of the head of provincial governments by frequently making decisions on proceedings within the national and provincial assemblies and the powers of the speaker of these assemblies under Article 184(3) of the Constitution.

5   Conclusion

The higher judiciary of Pakistan has been involved in political affairs since 1947. These affairs included, but were not limited to, the legality of regime change. However, until June 2005, there was no juristocracy in Pakistan as such. It only emerged in Pakistan from June 2005 onwards. The population of the middle-class in Pakistan grew enormously during the 2000s. The military regime of General Pervez Musharraf appointed Iftikhar Muhammad Chaudhry as the CJP on 30 June 2005. The SCP under Chaudhry as CJP activated HRC of the SCP and increased *suo motu* notices and decisions against the interests of the military regime of General Musharraf. As a response, the regime suspended the CJP Chaudhry lawyers. CSOs, opposition political elites and journalists held

---

80   *Chaudhary Parvez Elahi v The Deputy Speaker Provincial Assembly of Punjab Lahore, etc*
       2022 SCP 237.

country-wide protests and challenged the suspension before the SCP. The SCP restored the CJP Chaudhry. However, the regime again removed the CJP Chaudhry along with other judges on 3 November 2007. The above groups held two long marches for the restoration of the judges removed on 3 November 2007 as a result of which all those judges were ultimately restored in March 2009. The obvious form of juristocracy emerged after March 2009 when the restored judges made decisions in every area of politics and public policy. It shaped the process of the appointment of judges in the higher judiciary, reviewed the Eighteenth Constitutional Amendment, struck down the NRO 2009, Contempt of Court Act 2012, and Election Act 2017, and disqualified numerous parliamentarians including two Prime Ministers in 2012 and 2017.

However, the COVID-19 crisis increased the space for policy-making and policy-execution by the judges of the SCP. The judges of the SCP were not influencing the process of policy-making but also compelling the executive to enforce laws. The judges carried out their function by initiating *suo motu* proceedings during the COVID-19 crisis under Article 184(3) of the Constitution and by asking the federal government and provincial governments and their departments to submit reports on actions taken to address the COVID-19 crisis during these proceedings. The judges compelled the federal and provincial governments to make SOPs and enforce those SOPs and to adopt a uniform national policy on COVID-19. It influenced the establishment of quarantine centres for COVID-19 patients and the management of available resources to address the COVID-19 crisis. It held different departments of the government and provincial governments accountable on different issues, shaped issues of Islamic legal nature and protected minority and labour rights.

When the peak of the COVID-19 crisis was passed in late 2021, the higher judiciary of Pakistan continued to influence policy-making and legislation. The SCP made decisions on rulings of the speaker of the National Assembly and that of the Punjab Assembly. These were the two main examples that show that the SCP was able to influence the internal mechanisms of those institutions whose main task was to make laws.

The juristocracy in Pakistan will likely expand and strengthen itself in the future. The judges of the SCP will continue shaping the functions of the Parliament and the executive by using their powers of judicial review. They will shape policy-making process by reviewing the legislation and the powers of parliamentarians. The Parliament will not be able to control the expanding juristocracy if political parties do not establish a culture of resolving all political and policy disputes within the Parliament. The Parliament's ability to control juristocracy will weaken if it fails to carry out its basic role of legislation during a crisis such as COVID-19. In addition, the judges will shape the functions of the executive by ensuring the enforcement of their decisions, holding the executive accountable, directing the executive to submit compliance reports, and by holding follow-up proceedings on their decisions. The executive will comply with the decisions of the SCP as long as public support is available to the SCP. This general public support will remain available to the SCP if the latter addresses the issues of the former (e.g. health and safety of the public at large during COVID-19) and the executive fails to carry out its basic role of governance and does not cater to the public needs.

Note on the Contributor

Dr Nauman Reayat
Lecturer in Law, School of Law, University of Leicester.

CHAPTER 3

Home Renters' Protection in Bangladesh during the COVID-19 Pandemic under the Rights' Fabric of the Constitution: Options and Challenges

Mohammad Towhidul Islam and Md Jahid Al-Mamun

Abstract

The lockdown and shutdown policies of the Bangladesh government during the COVID-19 pandemic have created unprecedented job losses, cut-off salaries, etc. As a result, home renters who usually spend almost 40%-60% of their monthly income as the house rent fail to pay the rent during the COVID-19 pandemic and face the eviction from their houses despite the lockdown call to 'stay home and stay safe'. The existing regulatory framework dealing with the landlord-tenant relation is silent about their protection during the emergency pandemic. Against this backdrop, this paper shall analyze the constitutional and other legislative and administrative measures in order to safeguard the interests of pandemic-ridden renters in line with the human rights framework. Accordingly, it shall prescribe a way forward within the constitutional and legislative framework considering global best practices.

Keywords

COVID-19 – right to shelter-renter's protection – enforceability of negative ESC rights – Bangladesh

1 Introduction

The sufferings from the COVID-19 pandemic are alarming worldwide in all spheres of life, including housing, which poses threats to human rights, especially the right to housing; Bangladesh is not an exception surviving all through the emergency. To protect her population from the pandemic following the World Health Organization (WHO) guidelines, like other countries Bangladesh declared nationwide 'lockdown' or 'shutdown' on several occasions ordering the closure of all government, semi-government, autonomous, private offices;

suspension of all modes of public transports; and movement of people outside their homes except on some exceptional grounds like groceries and emergencies needs.[1] The Deputy Commissioners (the most senior public officials in a district), executive magistrates, and the police were empowered to enforce the lockdown orders to prevent the COVID-19 pandemic, and the government deployed the Army to aid the civil administration.[2] The executive magistrates were empowered to try offenses under sections 269, 270, 271 of the Penal Code 1860[3] along with sections 24, 25, and 26 of the Communicable Diseases (Prevent, Control, and Elimination) Act 2018[4], which describe acts likely to spread any infectious disease and break the quarantine rule.[5] To try the offenses, the executive magistrate can hold a summary trial as per the Mobile Court Act 2009[6]. The maximum punishment for those offenses is six months imprisonment or/and a fine of up to 1 lac taka.

Such lockdown measures appear to curtail the right to life, right to shelter, right to health, right to work, right against inhuman or degrading treatment as laid down in the Universal Declaration of Human Rights 1948 (UDHR)[7] and the International Covenant on Economic, Social and Cultural Rights 1966 (ICESCR)[8]. This is because these measures restrict the earning sources of around 50 million people in the informal sector in Bangladesh and thus

---

1 ABP News Bureau, 'Bangladesh Announces Nationwide Weeklong Strict Lockdown from April 14-21; List of Guidelines to Be Followed' *news.abplive.com*, 12 April 2021, https://news .abplive.com/news/world/bangladesh-week-long-lockdown-directions-and-guidelines-to -be-followed-for-fighting-coronavirus-1452767 (accessed 9 July 2021).

2 'Fresh Lockdown in Bangladesh: Experts Sceptical about Having Any Great Result' *Dhaka Tribune*, 13 April 2021, https://www.dhakatribune.com/bangladesh/2021/04/13/fresh-lockdown -in-bangladesh-experts-sceptical-about-having-any-great-result (accessed 9 July 2021); Ridwanul Hoque, 'Bangladesh's Unofficial Emergency: Managing the COVID-19 Crisis by Notifications' *Verfassungsblog*, 6 May 2020, https://verfassungsblog.de/bangladeshs-unofficial -emergency-managing-the-covid-19-crisis-by-notifications/ (accessed 9 July 2021); PTI, 'COVID-19: Bangladesh Army Says Troops Will Be on Streets until Govt Recalls' *The Hindu*, (29 March 2020, https://www.thehindu.com/news/international/covid-19-bangladesh-army -says-troops-will-be-on-streets-until-govt-recalls/article31197469.ece (accessed 9 July 2021).

3 Act No. 45 of 1860, http://bdlaws.minlaw.gov.bd/act-11.html (accessed 17 July 2021).

4 Act No. 61 of 2018, http://bdlaws.minlaw.gov.bd/act-1274.html (accessed 17 July 2021).

5 See *supra* note 2.

6 Act No. 59 of 2009, http://bdlaws.minlaw.gov.bd/act-1025.html (accessed 17 July 2021).

7 Universal Declaration of Human Rights (adopted 10 December 1948) UNGA Res 217 A(III) (UDHR) arts 2-22.

8 International Covenant on Economic, Social and Cultural Rights (adopted 16 December 1966, enforced 3 January 1996) 993 UNTS 3 [hereinafter ICESCR] art 11. Bangladesh ratified ICESCR on 5 October 5 1998. See, 'UN Human Rights Treaty Bodies' (OCHCR.org), https://tbinternet. ohchr.org/_layouts/15/TreatyBodyExternal/Treaty.aspx?CountryID=14&Lang=EN (accessed 22 July 2022).

affects the attainment of other rights including the right to housing.[9] Even approximately 2.5 million people working in the private sector are victims of dismissals, lay-offs, cut-off salaries, etc.[10] This makes them vulnerable since they cannot be able to pay for the costs of food and, most importantly, accommodation. About 50,000 to 60,000 people of Dhaka city are reportedly evicted during the pandemic, and many others are in a threat of being evicted from homes since they would not be able to pay the house rent.[11] So, despite the government's announced lockdown aims to save their lives or the WHO guidelines advise that staying home is a strong weapon to fight against the pandemic, all such measures indirectly make people's lives vulnerable since they cannot earn for their livelihoods and shelters.

To this end in view, in the absence of statutory safeguards or notable policies to protect the interest of home renters in this pandemic the Constitution of Bangladesh can be taken as a legal means to find some redresses as it contains the right to shelter as an economic, social and cultural (ESC) right of ESC rights contained in Part II of the Constitution. However, their judicial unenforceability causes concerns. Against this backdrop, this paper shall analyze the vulnerability of pandemic-surviving home renters, the government response, and the constitutional and legislative vacuum to safeguard their interests in line with the right to life, right to shelter, right to health, right to work, right against inhuman or degrading treatment, and accordingly, it shall prescribe a way forward within the constitutional and legislative framework in light of global best practices.

To be noted that since effective decentralization has not been taken in the unitary country of Bangladesh[12], most headquarters of government, autonomous and non-government organizations, garments, and other industries, private universities, other educational institutions, etc., are situated in its capital city of Dhaka. As a result, people from different stages of life come and settle in Dhaka for different goals, i.e., to work, study, for a better lifestyle, etc. It makes Dhaka seventh among the most populated cities in the world and

---

9   S Akter, 'Covid-19 and Bangladesh: Threat of Unemployment in the Economy' (2020) 3 *North American Academic Research* 79, https://www.researchgate.net/publication /343820206_Covid-19_and_Bangladesh_Threat_of_unemployment_in_the_economy (accessed 15 July 2021).

10   'More than 26 Lakh People Have Become Unemployed during the COVID-19 (translated from Bengali)' *Banikbarta* (4 July 2021).

11   'Low-Income People Leaving Dhaka' *The Business Standard*, 23 June 2020, https://www .tbsnews.net/coronavirus-chronicle/covid-19-bangladesh/low-income-people-leaving -dhaka-96850 (accessed 15 July 2021).

12   The Constitution of the People's Republic of Bangladesh 1972, arts 1, 5.

the number one densely populated city globally with 20,283,552 inhabitants.[13] Further, almost 90% of the dwellers in this city are renters.[14] For this reason, this paper shall limit its scope to the protection of the home renters of Dhaka city.

2   Legislative Protection and the Government's Response towards Protecting Home Renter's Rights during the COVID-19 Pandemic

About 50,000 home renters who usually pay 30% to 60% of their total monthly income as rent,[15] to live in Dhaka, the capital city of Bangladesh, have been forced to permanently leave the city to their birthplaces or an unknown destination during the COVID-19 pandemic.[16] Many of them are students having no job, many have lost their jobs due to lay off, termination, and forced resignation, or are not given a full salary or given a partial salary, and many are forced to stop their businesses – small, medium and even some heavy ones during the pandemic.[17] Being already in a poor condition, struggling with income and expenditure, temporary shutdown of businesses as per the government order, job losses and salary cuts, etc., are the factors responsible for further increasing the urban poverty.[18] Thus, the pandemic causes unprecedented job losses, unemployment, and catastrophic economic hardships upon households and leads to concerns in enjoying the right to life, right to shelter, right to health, right to work, right against inhuman or degrading treatment.[19]

---

13   World Population Review, 'World City Populations 2020' (worldpopulationreview. com2020), https://worldpopulationreview.com/world-cities (accessed 6 March 2022); D Murphy, 'Where Is the World's Densest City?' *The Guardian*, 11 May 2017, https:// www.theguardian.com/cities/2017/may/11/where-world-most-densely-populated-city (accessed 6 March 2022).

14   Abu Shofiun Mohammad Taj Uddin, 'House Owner-Tenant Amicable Relationship through Proper Implementation of Laws in Urban Residential Area' (2016) 10(1) *World Vision*, http://bv-f.org/WV-10/03.%20WV%20Final.pdf (accessed 6 March 2022).

15   *Ibid.*

16   '50 Thousand Tenants Leave Dhaka during Coronavirus Pandemic (Translated from Bengali)' *dw.com* (22 June 2020).

17   MI Hossain, 'COVID-19 Impacts on Employment and Livelihood of Marginal People in Bangladesh: Lessons Learned and Way Forward' (2021) 28 *South Asian Survey* https://journals .sagepub.com/doi/full/10.1177/0971523121995072 (accessed 16 March 2021).

18   S Mollah and M Saad, 'The Caravan of Broken Dreams' *The Daily Star*, 12 June 2020, https:// www.thedailystar.net/frontpage/news/the-caravan-broken-dreams-1928865 (accessed 17 July 2021).

19   EA Benfer et al., 'Eviction, Health Inequity, and the Spread of COVID-19: Housing Policy as a Primary Pandemic Mitigation Strategy' (2021) 98 *Journal of Urban Health* 1, https://link .springer.com/article/10.1007/s11524-020-00502-1 (accessed 17 July 2021).

A recent study shows that about 68% of people in the cities of Dhaka and Chittagong have lost their jobs due to the pandemic, among which the job loss in Dhaka city is 76%.[20] This study further shows that poverty has increased from 23% to 35% during the pandemic.[21] As a result, many home renters, especially middle to low-income people, are now experiencing unprecedented levels of anxiety since they are at risk of being evicted. To them, the much-used catchwords 'Stay Home, Stay Safe,' 'make physical distance,' and 'wash your hands with soap' appear to be paradoxes during the last few months in anxieties of losing works and shelters. However, as per the government lockdown measures and the WHO guidelines, houses are described as forts to fight against the COVID-19 pandemic. Leilani Farha, a United Nations (UN) Special Rapporteur on Right to Adequate Housing, labels housing as the frontline defence against the coronavirus pandemic.[22] However, the precautionary pandemic buzzwords have carried a sarcastic meaning to thousands of Bangladeshi people, who are in constant menace to be evicted from their homes.

Furthermore, neither the Premises Rent Control Act 1991[23] nor the Communicable Diseases (Prevention, Control, and Elimination) Act 2018 contains any provision to protect the home renters during health emergencies like the pandemic. The Act of 1991 provides ample opportunity for the house owner or the landlord to evict renters in case of renters' failure to pay the rent to the full extent allowable by this Act. However, this Act does not include any favourable provision for the renters customised in line with the right to life, right to shelter, right to health, right to work, right against inhuman or degrading treatment in case of their inability to pay the rent during emergency periods like the pandemic or on reasonable grounds. For instance, in the USA, the non-payment of house rent during the COVID-19 pandemic due to "substantial loss of household income, loss of compensable hours of work or wages, a lay-off, or extraordinary out-of pocket medical expenses", etc., are considered reasonable grounds which require the landlords not to evict their renters.[24] Such a saving

20   'Covid-19 Fallout: 68% Lost Jobs in Dhaka and Ctg' *The Daily Star*,28 September 2020, https://www.thedailystar.net/frontpage/news/68pc-lost-jobs-dhaka-and-ctg-1968641 (accessed 17 July 2021).

21   *Ibid.*

22   L Farha, 'COVID-19 Guidance Note: Prohibition of Evictions' *United Nations Human Rights Special Procedures* 2020 https://www.ohchr.org/Documents/Issues/Housing/SR_housing _COVID-19_guidance_evictions.pdf (accessed 17 July 2021).

23   Act No. 3 of 1991 http://bdlaws.minlaw.gov.bd/act-748/section-30631.html (accessed 17 July 2021); see also MT Islam, *Land Law: Text, Cases and Materials* (3rd Edition, CHRLR, Dhaka, 2023) at 561-71.

24   National Housing Law Project, 'Federal Moratorium on Evictions for Nonpayment of Rent' (2021) 3, https://nlihc.org/sites/default/files/Overview-of-National-Eviction-Mora torium.pdf (accessed 20 August 2022).

clause, i.e. "reasonable grounds", can protect the renters during crisis situations like COVID-19 pandemic. The ongoing crisis in the renters markets shows the legal vacuum in the face of human rights protection, in particular in respect of the right to housing.

Fake news also created more despair amongst the renters as the government allegedly announced a rent waiver and postponed payments of utility bills and bank loans for three months spreads[25] while the Prime Minister's Office denied those reports.[26] Though such a decision or notification could relieve the sufferings of the troubled tenants who claimed such waiver, it is merely gossip.[27] In the meantime, a Bangladesh Bank also issued its notification that loan payment would be delayed thus comforting the defaulters with relief.[28] In response to some eviction incidences,[29] the Dhaka Metropolitan Police has also said that emergency action would be taken under public nuisance provisions of section 268 of the Penal Code 1860 if any emergency service providers were to be threatened with eviction.[30] Though the law enforcement agencies have undertaken some measures in preventing the sufferings of tenants, it is very insignificant to save tenants from leaving Dhaka city.[31]

On the other side of the coin, many houses fell vacant due to the renters' removal either *sou motu* or by expulsion; causing a backlash on owners whose prime income are house rents. Some of them have built their houses with

25   'Coronavirus: Low Income People Appeal for House Rent Waiver' *Dhaka Tribune,*7 April 2020, https://www.dhakatribune.com/bangladesh/2020/04/07/coronavirus-low-income -people-appeal-for-house-rent-waiver (accessed 17 July 2021).

26   MAMI Kamal, 'House Rent Waiver, Bank Loan Postponement a Rumour: Ihsanul' *unb. com.bd,*2 April 2020, http://www.unb.com.bd/category/bangladesh/house-rent-waiver -bank-loan-postponement-a-rumour-ihsanul/48581 (accessed 17 July 2021).

27   'Tenants for Waiving House Rents for Three Months' *The Financial Express,*23 April 2020, https://thefinancialexpress.com.bd/national/tenants-for-waiving-house-rents-for-three -months-1587618296 (accessed 17 July 2021).

28   'Bangladesh Bank Further Relaxes Loan Repayment' *The Daily Star,* 1 November 2020, https://www.thedailystar.net/business/news/bangladesh-bank-further-relaxes-loan -repayment-1987593 (accessed 15 July 2021).

29   M Kabir, 'Protecting Tenants' Rights during Covid-19' *The Daily Star,* 5 May 2020, https://www.thedailystar.net/law-our-rights/news/protecting-tenants-rights-during -covid-19-1899499 (accessed 15 July 2021).

30   'Call 999 If Threatened to Be Evicted, DMP Urges Healthcare Providers' *Prothomalo,* 17 April 2020, https://en.prothomalo.com/bangladesh/call-999-if-threatened-to-be-evicted -dmp-urges-healthcare-providers (accessed 17 July 2021).

31   'Tenant Beaten for Rent, 2 Arrested Including Landlord' *Dhaka Tribune,* 20 May 2020, https:// www.dhakatribune.com/bangladesh/2020/05/20/tenant-beaten-for-rent-2-including -landlord-arrested, https://www.thedailystar.net/frontpage/police-asked-protect-tenants -106003 (accessed 17 July 2021).

bank loans and thus must pay monthly instalments with the rent. Further-more, with the rent, the house owners must pay utility bills, holding taxes, and income taxes regularly. Many owners have also repeatedly advertised for 'to-let' but failed. Thus, the pandemic causes great hardships not only to renters but also to house owners. In such situations, balancing the renters' rights with those of the owners during the ongoing pandemic appears to be essential.

In 2015, the High Court Division of Supreme Court of Bangladesh gave an order in public interest litigation directing the government to accommodate crises under existing laws, especially for regulating the house rent to fix maxi-mum and minimum amount of house rents based on areas pursuant to the Premises Rent Control Act of 1991 and gave some recommendations as direc-tives.[32] It also directed the Police to accept tenants' complaints and to take immediate action to protect tenants from eviction.[33] It also asked the govern-ment to form a seven-member commission to fix rent within six months, and to appoint the rent controller in every city.[34] However, the Government is yet to implement such recommendations and reform the laws.

3   Protection of Home Renter's Rights against Eviction: An Analysis from a Human Rights – Right to Housing – Perspective

The eviction of renters during the COVID-19 pandemic seems to have hit a plethora of human rights violations. According to article 25 of the UDHR, eve-ryone has 'right to a standard of living adequate for the health and well-being of himself and of his family' including inter alia the right to housing. Expand-ing from the UDHR, the ICESCR explicitly recognized the 'right to housing' as an essential human right. Further, article 11(1) of the ICESCR incorporated the 'right to housing' as a part of 'right of everyone to an adequate standard of living'. It also enumerated that member states will take appropriate meas-ures to ensure the realization of this right. Ensuring the housing in emergen-cies has also appeared as a reference to the UN ICESCR General Comment on the right to adequate housing inserted in article 11.[35] Moreover, the Office of

---

32   A Sarkar, 'Police Asked to Protect Tenants' *The Daily Star*, 2 July 2015, https://www
        .thedailystar.net/frontpage/police-asked-protect-tenants-106003 (accessed 14 September
        2021).

33   *Ibid.*

34   *Ibid.*

35   European Convention for the Protection of Human Rights and Fundamental Freedoms
        (adopted 4 November 1950 and entered into force 3 September 1953) 213 UNTS 222.

United Nations High Commissioner for Human Rights (OCHCR) clarified the contents of right to adequate housing in Fact Sheet No. 21/Rev. 1.[36] According to the Fact Sheet, the right to adequate housing "should be seen as the right to live somewhere in security, peace and dignity".[37] It identifies three freedoms as essential for right to adequate housing such as "Protection against forced evictions and the arbitrary destruction and demolition of one's home; the right to be free from arbitrary interference with one's home, privacy and family; and the right to choose one's residence, to determine where to live and to freedom of movement".[38] In addition to these freedoms, this Factsheet identifies several essential entitlements of the right to adequate housing, e.g., "Security of tenure; housing, land and property restitution; equal and non-discriminatory access to adequate housing; participation in housing-related decision-making at the national and community levels".[39] So, the right to adequate housing is more than "four walls and a roof".[40]

Thus, protection against forced evictions occupies as one of the essential elements of right to adequate housing.[41] The United Nations Committee on Economic, Social and Cultural Rights (CESCR) defines forced evictions as the "permanent or temporary removal against their will of individuals, families and/or communities from the homes and/or land which they occupy, without the provision of, and access to, appropriate forms of legal or other protection".[42] Evictions may also lead to human rights violation if it is unjustified, illegal, without justifiable process, unfair, etc.[43] It is to be noted here that the Factsheet 21 as mentioned above rightly discusses the safeguards against forced evictions as following:

> [even] if eviction may be justifiable, because the tenant persistently fails to pay rent or damages the property without reasonable cause, the State must ensure that it is carried out in a lawful, reasonable and

---

36   Office of the United Nations High Commissioner for Human Rights, 'The Right to Adequate Housing Fact Sheet No. 21/Rev. 1' https://www.ohchr.org/sites/default/files/Documents/Publications/FS21_rev_1_Housing_en.pdf (accessed 24 August 2022).

37   *Ibid.*, 3.

38   *Ibid.*

39   *Ibid.*

40   *Ibid.*

41   UN Committee on Economic, Social and Cultural Rights (CESCR), General Comment No. 7: The right to adequate housing (Art.11.1): forced evictions, 20 May 1997, E/1998/22, https://www.refworld.org/docid/47a70799d.html(accessed 25 August 2022).

42   *Ibid.*, para 3.

43   *Ibid.*

proportional manner, and in accordance with international law. Effective legal recourses and remedies should be available to those who are evicted, including adequate compensation for any real or personal property affected by the eviction. Evictions should not result in individuals becoming homeless or vulnerable to further human rights violations.[44]

In light of above interpretation, it may be argued that the evictions during pandemic may cause the renters homeless or may lead them to face further human rights violations and thus the government should take adequate measures to protect their right to adequate housing. Furthermore, the Report of the UN Special Rapporteur on right to adequate housing can also be taken as useful to interpret the content of article 11. In its COVID-19 Guiding Notes, the UN Special Rapporteur on right to adequate housing directed states to take essential measures as a part of their human rights obligation to declare "an end to all evictions of anyone, anywhere for any reason until the end of the pandemic and for a reasonable period of time thereafter".[45] So, home renters cannot be evicted during the pandemic and until a reasonable time after the end of the pandemic.

Now, a question may arise whether the States have any duty to prevent landlords', non-state actors, from violations of renters' rights. In this regard, it is worthy to mention that the full realization of the constitutional rights mentioned above involves tripartite obligations of the State, i.e., protect, respect, and fulfil.[46] The duty to protect consists of protecting an individual's rights against third-party nonstate actors.[47] It requires the state to prevent non-state actors or third parties from infringing constitutional rights of individuals, similar to the way the State is required to refrain itself from infringing those rights.[48] Further, the Factsheet 15 by the Human Rights Committee has made it clear that "the State party must not only refrain from violating an individual's rights itself, but it must also protect an individual from a violation of his or her rights by third parties, be they private individuals, corporations,

---

44   Office of the United Nations High Commissioner for Human Rights, *supra* note 37, 5.

45   Farha, *supra* note 22.

46   See C Soohoo and J Goldberg, 'The Full Realization of Our Rights: The Right to Health in State Constitutions' (2010) 60 *Case Western Reserve Law Review* 997, https://scholarlycommons .law.case.edu/caselrev/vol60/iss4/5 (accessed 17 July 2021).

47   *Ibid.*, 1007.

48   M Dafel, 'The Negative Obligation of the Housing Right: An Analysis of the Duties to Respect and Protect' (2013) 29 *South African Journal on Human Rights* 591, https://ssrn .com/abstract=2470388 (accessed 17 July 2021).

or other non-state actors".[49] So, the duty to protect human rights includes the states' duty to prevent third parties, including individuals, corporations, private actors, etc., from interfering in any way with the enjoyment of human rights.[50] Thus, it casts a duty upon the state to refrain third party non-state actors from interfering with individual human rights through administrative and legislative measures.[51]

Such States' duty to protect human rights from third party interferences has been reflected in several judgments. For instance, in *Velasquez-Rodriguez vs. Honduras*,[52] the Inter-American Court of Human Rights emphasized "the duty of the state to protect rights-bearers from violations of their rights, including those committed by NSA".[53] In this case, the court stated that

> This duty to prevent includes all those means of a legal, political, administrative, and cultural nature that promote the protection of human rights and ensure that any violations are considered and treated as illegal acts, which, as such, may lead to the punishment of those responsible and the obligation to indemnify the victims for damages.[54]

---

49   'Human Rights Civil and Political Rights: The Human Rights Committee' *OHCHR* 5, https://www.ohchr.org/Documents/Publications/FactSheet15rev.1en.pdf (accessed 17 July 2021).

50   See, for example, U.N. Committee on Economic, Social, and Cultural Rights, General Comment No. 19: The Right to Social Security (art. 9 of the International Covenant on Economic, Social, and Cultural Rights), 47-50, U.N. Doc. E/C.12/GC/, 9 (4 Feb. 2008); U.N. Committee on Economic, Social, and Cultural Rights, General Comment No. 15 (2002): The Right to Water (arts. 11 and 12 of the International Covenant on Economic, Social, and Cultural Rights), 41, U.N. Doc. E/C.12/2002/II (20 Jan. 2003); U.N. Committee on Economic, Social, and Cultural Rights, General Comment No. 13: The Right to Education (art. 13 of the International Covenant on Economic, Social, and Cultural Rights), 47, U.N. Doc. E/C.12/1 99 9 /jo (12 Aug. 1999); U.N. Committee on Economic, Social, and Cultural Rights, General Comment No. 14: The Right to the Highest Attainable Standard of Health (art. 12 of the International Covenant on Economic, Social, and Cultural Rights), 33, U.N. Doc. E/C.12/2000/ 4 (2 Nov. 2000); U.N. Committee on Economic, Social, and Cultural Rights, General Comment No. 18: The Right to Work (art. 13 of the International Covenant on Economic, Social, and Cultural Rights), 22, U.N. Doc. E/C.12/GC/18 (6 Feb.2006).

51   Human Rights Handbook for Parliamentarians N° 26 (United Nations Human Rights Office of the High Commissioner 2016) 32, https://www.ohchr.org/Documents/Publications/HandbookParliamentarians.pdf (accessed 17 July 2021); IT Winkler, 'Respect, Protect, Fulfil: The Implementation of the Human Right to Water in South Africa' in P Cullet et al. (eds), *Water Governance in Motion Towards Socially and Environmentally Sustainable Water Laws* (Foundation Books, 2010) 424.

52   IACtHR Series C 4 (1988).

53   See, A Nolan, 'Addressing Economic and Social Rights Violations by Non-State Actors through the Role of the State: A Comparison of Regional Approaches to the "Obligation to Protect"' (2009) 9 *Human Rights Law Review* 225, 231.

54   IACtHR Series C 4 (1988), para 175.

Thus, the observation of Nolan is relevant because he analysed different judgments and concluded, in light of their jurisprudence, that the international liability of states for the violation of human rights includes "the acts committed by third parties when the state fails to fulfil its duty to regulate and supervise them".[55]

4   Constitutional Protection of Home Renter's Rights against Eviction

Under the Constitution of Bangladesh, some human rights such as the right to life, right against inhuman or degrading treatment as inserted in Part III comprising articles 26-47A, are made judicially enforceable as per article 44. On the contrary, some rights like the right to shelter, right to work, right to health, etc., as inserted in Part II comprising articles 8-25, are not judicially enforceable as per article 8(2). Moreover, such rights are usually enforceable against the State. However, the renters' rights are found to be engrossed here by the landlords, and the State is not directly involved at this moment.

Nevertheless, Bangladesh, as a party to the international human rights instruments including the UDHR, the International Covenant on Civil and Political Rights 1966 (ICCPR),[56] and the ICESCR, has an obligation to take proactive measures to ensure that the right to housing or shelter of the misfortune renters is protected and effective remedies for the infringement of these rights must be provided with. This will ensure that individuals cannot act in such a way that makes another person homeless. Since the State fails to protect the renter's rights by preventing the landlords from evicting them, the State assumes the responsibility for such omissions.

4.1   *Eviction Curtails the Right to Life of Renters*
Though the decision of public holiday or lockdown has been undertaken to save the lives from the coronavirus, it indirectly pushes the people to unemployment, poverty, homelessness, hunger, and death. As a result, in this particular instance of the COVID-19 pandemic, renters' eviction from their houses appears to be a violation of their right to life. The evicted renters leaving Dhaka city do not know where to go and what to do for their livelihoods. It seriously impairs their right to life and livelihoods given the increased risks to exposure to the coronavirus. As per the UN Special Rapporteur on Right to

---

55   Nolan, *supra* note 44, 233.
56   International Covenant on Civil and Political Rights (adopted December 19, 1966 and entered into force 23 March 1976) 999 UNTS 171.

Adequate Housing,[57] eviction from home during the pandemic is tantamount to a probable death sentence. It goes against the WHO's direction of 'stay home, stay safe'. It causes 'overcrowded living environments, doubling up, transiency, limited access to healthcare, and a decreased ability to comply with pandemic mitigation strategies (e.g., social distancing, self-quarantine, and hygiene practices)'. Thus, it is likely to increase COVID-19 infection rates and deaths.[58] Thus, eviction that can cause renters' deaths, can endanger their 'right to life' as contained in articles 31 and 32 of Part III and can be judicially enforceable as a fundamental right as per article 44. In the past, the higher judiciary played a vital role in enforcing ESC rights through liberal interpretation of the 'right to life', making it judicially enforceable. For example, the 'right to shelter' has been included in the 'right to life' in *Ain O Shalish Kendra vs. Bangladesh* Case.[59] The fact of the case says that a large number of slum dwellers in Dhaka City was evicted by the Government without prior notice and without alternative accommodation.[60] The petitioner filed the writ petition for "for enforcement of fundamental rights of slum dwellers as guaranteed under articles 27, 31 and 32 of the constitution which includes their right to life, liberty, livelihood etc. together with articles 7, 11, 15 and 19 in particular of the chapter of fundamental state policy."[61] In this case, the petitioner put emphasis on the enforceable human right to life and livelihood of the slum dwellers putting the right to shelter in the justiciable fold. The court responded positively and upheld the claim of the petitioners. The court gave guidelines to the government to take a rehabilitation master plan "or rehabilitation schemes or pilot projects for rehabilitation of the slum dwellers and undertake eviction of the slum dwellers according to the capacity of their available abode and with option to the dwellers either to go to their village home or to stay back leading an urban life.."[62] Thus, the case appears as the landmark case protecting rights of slum dwellers against wholesale evictions.[63] Following the footsteps of the Ain O Shalish Kendra case, the High Court Division (HD) in *Kalam vs. Bangladesh* liberally interpreted "equality before law" and the "principle of non-discrimination" to protect the right to shelter of slum dwellers.[64] In this case, the court observed

---

57   Farha, *supra* note 22.

58   See for details, Benfer, *supra* note 19.

59   (1999) 19 BLD 488.

60   *Ibid.*, para 1.

61   *Ibid.*, para 5.

62   *Ibid.*, para 16.

63   SM Atia Naznin, 'Justiciability of the Basic Necessity of Housing Litigation of Forced Slum Evictions in Bangladesh' (2017) 18 Australian Journal of Asian Law 221, 230.

64   (2001) 21 BLD (HCD) 446.

that "housing is one of the bare minimum necessities of life which the state, although it may be poor and therefore cannot ensure affirmatively, must nevertheless not take away arbitrarily."[65] Justice A. B. M. Khairul Haque's observation is worth quoting here as he observed:

> The Constitution of the People's Republic of Bangladesh envisages a welfare state and makes all citizens equal in the eye of law. As such, all citizens have got equal rights in every sphere of life including food, shelter, healthcare, education, and so forth which is fundamental in nature.... After all, the slum dwellers, poorest of the poor they may be without any future dreams for tomorrow, whose every day ends with a saga of struggle with a bleak hope for survival tomorrow, but they are also citizens of this country, theoretically at least, with equal rights. Their fundamental rights may not be fully honoured, because of the limitations on the part of the state but they shall not be treated as slaves or chattels, rather as equal human beings and they have the right to be treated fairly with dignity, otherwise all commitments made in the sacred Constitution of the People's Republic shall prove to be a mere mockery.[66]

In *BLAST vs. Bangladesh and others*,[67] the HCD interpreted the relation between the right to life and right to shelter in a convincing manner. In this case, the court observed that:

> Despite being nonenforceable, these necessities [here right to shelter], which are directive principles, are as important as fundamental rights in the governance of the country. They determine state obligations, whether positive or negative. The provisions on fundamental rights express that the government has an affirmative duty to protect people's right to life and livelihood. Particularly, as a basic necessity, housing constitutes a fundamental component of the right to life and livelihood. Such a harmonious construction is significant for homeless and helpless slum dwellers, who form the most deprived part of the society. They have been forced to migrate to cities in search of a better life but end up living a subhuman life in slums. Of course. due to economic constraints and resource scarcity. the state is not in a situation to provide housing for them. But by paying regard to its negative obligation, the state must ensure that no one

---

65   Atia Naznin, *supra* note 63, 230.
66   *Kalam vs. Bangladesh* (2001) 21 BLD (HCD) 446, para 6.
67   (2008) 13 BLC (HCD) 384.

is deprived of his or her right to livelihood and life without the due process of law. Unlawful and unfair forced evictions have violated these obligations. If eviction is still necessary, there should be a prior arrangement for re-housing, keeping in mind the best interests of the slum dwellers.[68]

This approach, to uphold the right to shelter indirectly by interpreting enforceable right to life and livelihood, etc., has been reflected on other judgments.[69] Furthermore, this approach goes in line with the UNGA Guidelines for the Implementation of the Right to Adequate Housing which require states, including their judiciary, to follow this approach, meaning that "the right to adequate housing is recognized and enforceable as a fundamental human right through applicable constitutional and legislative provisions or through interpretations of interdependent rights such as the "right to life".[70] Such guidelines further require the States to "recognize the progressive realization of the right to housing as a legal obligation under domestic law",[71] to "implement comprehensive strategies for the realization of the right to housing",[72] and most importantly, to "prohibit forced evictions and prevent evictions whenever possible"[73] through national laws, etc.

4.2 Immediate Enforcement of Renter's Right to Housing as a Negative ESC Right

The Government's inaction to protect the renters from the wholesale eviction during the pandemic can result in violation of people's right to adequate housing within the meaning of article 15 embodied in Part II of the Constitution as it contains that the State shall have a responsibility to attain the basic provision of life including the right to shelter through planned economic growth. However, this right to shelter contained in the fundamental principles of state policy (FPSP) part is not judicially enforceable in Bangladesh as per article 8(2).[74]

---

68   Atia Naznin, *supra* note 63, 231.
69   See, for example, *Modhumala vs. Housing and Building Research Institute and others* (2001) 53 DLR (HCD) 540; *Aleya Begum vs. Bangladesh and Others* (2001) 53 DLR (HCD) 63.
70   UN General Assembly, 'Guidelines for the Implementation of the Right to Adequate Housing Report of the Special Rapporteur on Adequate Housing as a Component of the Right to an Adequate Standard of Living, and on the Right to Nondiscrimination in this Context' (2019) 5, Guidelines 1, paragraph 16.
71   *Ibid.*, Guidelines 2.
72   *Ibid.*, Guidelines 3.
73   *Ibid.*, Guidelines 6.
74   Article 8 (2) says that the principles contained in part II "shall be fundamental to the governance of Bangladesh, shall be applied by the State in the making of laws, shall be guide

Furthermore, the constituent assembly made such rights contained in Part II not enforceable in the court since they impose a positive obligation upon the State and are thus progressive.[75] Mr. Suranjit Sen Gupta, the lone member from the opposition in the constituent assembly vehemently criticized such a move and raised objections against the non-justiciability of ESC Rights. In reply, Dr Kamal Hossain, the then Law Minister and Chairman of the Constitution Drafting Committee keeps it on the shoulder of future parliaments considering their 'progressive realization' contingent upon availability of State resources.[76] The constituent assembly believed that the fulfilment of these rights is dependent upon socio-economic development, available resources, and technical know-how, etc. Chief Justice Mr. Shahabuddin Ahmed in *Kudrat-E-Elahi Panir vs. Bangladesh*[77] reiterated the same view. He was of the opinion that

> [S]uch principles, though fundamental to the governance of the Country, are not judicially enforceable and the reason is obvious. They are in the nature of people's program for socio-economic development in a peaceful manner, not overnight, but gradually. Implementation of these programs requires resources, technical know-how, and many other things. Whether all these prerequisites for a peaceful socio-economic revolution exist is for the State to decide.

Thus, the ESC rights as contained in Part II are judicially non-enforceable within the constitutional framework of Bangladesh since these rights can create an economic burden upon the State. This led the framers of the Constitution to look for the progressive realization or gradual implementation of these rights contingent upon the availability of resources. Further, article 2(1) of the ICESCR to which Bangladesh is a party also asks for a similar obligation

---

to the interpretation of the Constitution and the other laws of Bangladesh, and shall form the basis of the work of the State and its citizens, but shall not be judicially enforceable."

75   The debate in Constituent Assembly is relevant to reflect the original intention of the framers of the Constitution.

76   *Bangladesh Gono Parishad Bitarka, Sarkari Biboroni, 1971,* vol. 2 at 455. See also MA Ifran Hossain Mollah, 'Assessment into Feasibility of Ratifying the OP-ICESCR from the Context of the Justifiability of Economic, Social and Cultural Rights in Bangladesh' (2020) *International Human Rights Law Review* 9, 120; MF Saleh, 'ESC rights: Budding Trends in Constitutional Regimes of South Africa, India and Bangladesh' *Bangladesh Law Digest-BDLD,* 22 October 2017, http://bdlawdigest.org/economic-social-and-cultural-rights.html (accessed 6 April 2020).

77   *Kudrat-E-Elahi Panir vs. Bangladesh,* 44 DLR (AD) 319.

that is the progressive realization of the rights contained in the Covenant.[78] However, paragraph 8 of *Limburg Principle*[79] contains that "although the full realization of rights recognized in the Covenant is to be attained progressively, the application of some rights can be made justiciable immediately while other rights can become justiciable over time".[80] So, the idea that the whole content of ESC rights inflicts a positive obligation upon the State and stands as progressive in nature is not true. These rights may impose some negative obligations also, which can be fulfilled immediately, and in that case, any delay can frustrate the State's obligations to its citizens.[81]

Further, being a State party to the ICESCR, Bangladesh has the 'duty to respect'[82] denoting its duty not to be refrained from taking any action which might interfere with people's enjoyment of ESC rights. In addition, 'duty to protect' refers to the State's duty to ensure that enjoyment of ESC rights by an individual is not infringed by third parties. These two kinds of duty do not impose any budgetary obligation upon the State. They are negative in nature and can be enforced immediately. Here the 'duty to protect' requires States to take positive measures only and they can be progressive in nature.

In fact, the fulfilment of these rights is dependent upon socio-economic development, available resources, technical know-how, and other things

---

78 Bangladesh has ratified the ICESCR on 5 October 1998 https://tbinternet.ohchr.org /_layouts/15/TreatyBodyExternal/Treaty.aspx?CountryID=14&Lang=EN (accessed 17 July 2021); Article 2(1) says that "each State Party to the present Covenant undertakes to take steps, individually and through international assistance and co-operation, especially economic and technical, to the maximum of its available resources, with a view to achieving progressively the full realization of the rights recognized in the present Covenant by all appropriate means, including particularly the adoption of legislative measures".

79 UN Commission on Human Rights, 'The Limburg Principles on the Implementation of the International Covenant on Economic, Social and Cultural Rights', annexed to *Note verbale dated 5 December 1986 from the Permanent Mission of the Netherlands to the United Nations Office at Geneva addressed to the Centre for Human Rights*, 8 January 1987, E/CN.4/1987/17, https://www.escr-net.org/resources/limburg-principles-implementation -international-covenant-economic-social-and-cultural (accessed 14 August 2021).

80 *Ibid.*

81 International Commission of Jurists (ICJ), 'Courts and the Legal Enforcement of Economic, Social and Cultural Rights. Comparative Experiences of Justiciability' (2008) *Human Rights and Rule of Law Series* No. 2 https://www.refworld.org/docid/4a7840562 .html (accessed 15 August 2021), at 26.

82 'Access to justice for the right to housing' (Presented by L Farha, Special Rapporteur on the right to adequate housing, at the 40th session of the UN Human Rights Council in March 2019) https://www.ohchr.org/EN/Issues/Housing/Pages/AccessToJustice.aspx (accessed 14 August 2021).

including mass education to be fulfilled gradually but not overnight.[83] However, this may be argued that the 'progressive realization' of ESC rights is being vehemently disregarded by the State especially during the ongoing pandemic. The South African Constitutional Court has quitted from the 'progressive realization' doctrine to enforce ESC rights and has rejected the 'resource constraint' defence.[84] Here in Bangladesh, it looks awkward to sit idle in enforcing ESC rights, since the country is going to be a developing country by 2026. It also aspires to be a middle-income country by its 50th birthday.[85] Further, its yearly budget has been increased from 786 crores in 1972-73 FY[86] to 5,68,000 crores in 2020-21 FY.[87] Since the economy of Bangladesh is growing faster, it is the proper time for the court to scrutinize whether the State is due diligent in fulfilling its constitutional promises, especially during the ongoing COVID-19 crisis.

Further, to be noted that the right to adequate housing as enshrined under article 15 of the Constitution as well as article 11 of the ICESCR includes both positive and negative duties of the State. The positive duties include 'make housing accessible to the people in need' and the negative duties include not to be refrained from or refraining the third party from 'evicting persons from their housing without justification'.[88] During the ongoing pandemic, the renters' right not to be evicted from their shelter is negative in nature. States have the 'duty to respect' their right to shelter by not interfering with the peaceful enjoyment of it and the 'duty to protect' by preventing third parties, the landlord, from evicting them. It is a negative duty and can be realized immediately. The Constitutional Court of South Africa in the *Grootboom case* interpreted article 26(1) of the South African Constitution containing the right to adequate housing. The court held that this article imposed 'negative obligation on the

---

83   *Kudrat-E-Elahi Panir vs. Bangladesh,* supra note 47.
84   See Government of the Republic of South Africa and Ors v. Grootboom and Ors (2000) ZAAC 19.
85   'Bangladesh Overview: Development Research, News, Data' *World Bank* https://www .worldbank.org/en/country/bangladesh/overview (accessed 15 August 2021).
86   Online Desk, 'Chronology of Budget ince 1972' *Daily Prothom Alo English,* 4 June 2015, https://en.prothomalo.com/bangladesh/Chronology-of-budget-since-1972 (accessed 10 July 2021).
87   'Budget Traditional, Lacks Guidelines to Address Covid-19 Issues: CPD' *UNB,* 12 June 2020, https://unb.com.bd/category/Bangladesh/budget-traditional-lacks-guidelines-to-address -covid-19-issues-cpd/52932 (accessed 10 July 2021).
88   Courts and the Legal Enforcement of Economic, Social and Cultural Rights, *supra* note 51, 27.

State, other entities or persons to desist from preventing or impairing the right to access to adequate housing'.[89]

In a similar line, the Supreme Court of Bangladesh enforced one of the FPSP contained in Part II of the Constitution in *Major General KM Shafiullah (retd.) and another vs. Bangladesh*.[90] In its decision, the court focused on the distinction between negative and positive obligations and tripartite duties to protect, respect, and fulfil. Justice A. B. M. Khairul Haque liberally interpreted article 8(2) and held that

> ... it is true that Fundamental Principles of State Policies (FPSP) shall be fundamental to the governance of Bangladesh, but these are not generally enforceable in a court of law (*meaning positive enforcement*). But the Government cannot take any initiative which is in conflict with the fundamental principles contained in Part II and it if it does, the Court has the right to exercise its jurisdiction to uphold the fundamental principles (*meaning negative enforcement*).[91]

Though the judgment did not discuss the State's 'duty to protect' enjoyment of ESC rights from infringement by a third party, it is historic in the sense it opened the door to enforce the negative duty regarding the ESC rights like the right to adequate housing that can protect the evicted renters during the pandemic.

However, the Appellate Division of the High Court in *Kudrat-E-Elahi Panir vs. Bangladesh*[92] observed that the FPSPs 'are mere guidelines for State in the nature of moral precepts and not laws to be binding upon State'.[93] The court reiterated that the FPSPs are not judicially enforceable and hence according to it, in the *Major General KM Shafiullah Case* the High Court Division acted in ignorance of its upper court i.e., the Appellate Division's decision of *Kudrat-E-Elahi Panir Case*. This judgment of *Major General KM Shafiullah Case* has been

---

89   A Kucs, Z Sedlova and L Pierhurovica, 'The Right to Housing: International, European and National Perspectives' (2015) 64/65 *Cuadernos Constitucionales de la Cátedra Fadrique Furió Ceriol* 121.

90   Writ Petition No. 4313 of 2009.

91   *Major General KM Shafiullah (retd.) and another vs. Bangladesh*, Writ Petition No. 4313 of 2009, 337, para 2. See also MAU Bhuiyan, 'Comments on *Major General KM Shafiullah (retd.) and another vs. Bangladesh' Dhaka Law Review Blog*, 22 August 2016, https://www .dhakalawreview.org/blog/2016/08/comments-on-major-general-k-m-shafiullah-another -vs-bangladesh-1243 (accessed 10 August 2021).

92   *Kudrat-E-Elahi Panir vs. Bangladesh and Ors*, supra note 47, 331, para 22.

93   *Ibid.*, para 23.

criticized on the ground that the decision was given *per incuriam*, it violated article 111 of the Constitution and thus it has no precedential value.[94] So, though the decision of *Major General KM Shafiullah* raises a hope to enforce the negative obligation of the State, the decision fails to create any binding effect.

4.3   Article 7B: A Clog on Judicial Enforceability of ESC Rights like the Right to Shelter?

In 2011, the Fifteenth Amendment to the Constitution introduced an 'eternity clause' in article 7B which recognised the FPSP contained in Part II as basic structure and declared them as not amendable.[95] Thus, it has given the legislative recognition of the 'doctrine of basic structure' as spelled out in the *Constitution 8th Amendment Case (Anwar Hossain Chowdhury vs. Bangladesh, 1989)*.[96] This article provides for an inclusive list of basic structure that 'the preamble, all articles of Part I, all articles of part II, subject to the provisions of Part IXA all articles of Part III, and the provisions of articles relating to the basic structures of the Constitution including article 150 of Part XI shall not be amenable by way of insertion, modification, substitution, repeal or by any other means'.[97] The motive of the inclusion of such an 'eternity clause' in the constitution seems to preserve the core constitutional values. It intends to protect the basic structure of the Bangladeshi Constitution. However, this provision creates a barrier or hindrance on the way to change the ESC rights including the right to shelter as contained in part II from 'judicially non-enforceable' to 'judicially enforceable'.

In addition, article 7B has included more than 50 articles out of 153 articles of the Constitution directly within its reach. It further extends to the provisions of 'articles relating to the basic structures of the Constitution'. This makes almost two-third part of the Constitution unchangeable. As a result, it may lead to many problems in the future including failure to incorporate necessities or dissolution of constitutional stalemates etc. In a dynamic society, the constitutional provisions require to keep changing in order to cope with the changing

---

94   Article 111 says that "the law declared by the Appellate Division shall be binding on the High Court Division and the law declared by either division of the Supreme Court shall be binding on all courts subordinate to it."

95   Article 7B states, "Notwithstanding anything contained in article 142 of the Constitution, the preamble, all articles of Part I, all articles of Part II, subject to the provisions of Part IXA all articles of Part III, and the provisions of articles relating to the basic structures of the Constitution including article 150 of Part XI shall not be amendable by way of insertion, modification, substitution, repeal or by any other means."

96   (1989) BLD (Spl) 1, (1989) 41 DLR (AD) 165.

97   Constitution of the People's Republic of Bangladesh (1972), art. 7B.

circumstances.[98] In *A.K.M. Shafiuddin vs. Bangladesh*,[99] the HCD quoted from *Farooq Ahmed Khan Leghari vs. Federation of Pakistan*[100] which stated that '[c]onstitution is an organic document designed to cater the needs for all times to come. It is like a living tree; it grows and blossoms with the passage of time in order to keep pace with the growth of the country and its people.' In the future, if our social circumstances which we cannot foresee completely warrant any change in our constitution, this provision 'may lead to constitutional stalemate'.[101]

Suppose Dhaka, recognized as the capital city of Bangladesh by Part I of the Constitution, becomes un inhabitable at all or loses qualification to be the capital city, and thereafter the capital requires shifting; however, article 7B will be a bar to change the capital city since the part I is unamendable. Further, this article shall prevent the future parliament to include any new human rights in the constitution or make any rights contained in Part II including the right to shelter enforceable fundamental rights. In addition, this article may put a limitation on the Constitution of Bangladesh in identifying itself as the 'solemn expression of the will of the people'.[102] This is because if the people want any of these unamendable provisions to be amended in the future and if article 7B acts as a barrier, it will go against the spirit of the Constitution. So, without making these provisions completely unamendable, their amendment procedure could be made more rigid by requiring that the amendment must be passed by referendum or by the extraordinary majority.

Further, the 'amending power' is given to the parliament by the constituent assembly itself. So, any limitation upon the amending power can only be imposed by the constituent assembly itself.[103] In addition, any parliament being on equal footings cannot claim superiority over its subsequent parliaments.

---

98   LB Solum, 'Originalism versus Living Constitutionalism: The Conceptual Structure of the Great Debate' 113 *Northwestern University Law Review* 1257.

99   Writ Petition No. 9416 of 2012.

100   PLD 1999 SC 57.

101   J Ahmed, 'Article 7B and Constitutional Stalemate' *The Daily Star*, 14 March 2017, https://www.thedailystar.net/law-our-rights/article-7b-and-constitutional-stalemate-1375540 (accessed 15 August 2021).

102   See article 7 (2) which states that this Constitution is, as the solemn expression of the will of the people, the supreme law of the Republic, and if any other law is inconsistent with this Constitution that other law shall, to the extent of the inconsistency, be void.

103   Y Roznai, 'Unconstitutional Constitutional Amendments: The Migration and Success of a Constitutional Idea' (2013) 61(3) *American Journal of Comparative Law* 657; Y Roznai, 'Unconstitutional Constitutional Amendments: A Study of the Nature and Limits of Constitutional Amendment Powers' (PhD Thesis 2014) https://etheses.lse.ac.uk/915/ (accessed 11 March 2022).

However, no other amendments except the said fifteenth amendment bind the hands of its subsequent parliament to change the aforementioned provisions. So, it seems to be more than a constitutional amendment. This amendment can be compared with the making of the constitution by the explicit involvement of the people, who hold the absolute power as per article 7 of the Constitution. Further, this amendment did not even pass in the referendum as was made earlier compulsory for amending certain constitutional provisions. Further, it can be argued that as having the same status, any amendment subsequent to the fifteenth amendment can alter this provision as inserted in article 7B. For example, article 288 of the Portuguese Constitution of 1976 which contained an unamendable provision was itself amended in 1989.[104] In light of the arguments mentioned above, it may be contended that the future parliament can amend article 7B and can make the rights contained in part 11 judicially enforceable.

In addition, such 'eternity clause' as inserted in article 7B appears to be similar to holy books since only the holy books coming from the divine source are not amendable for their being originated from superhuman sources and considered as super-perfect. In consonance with this, to make any constitutional provision such 'not amendable' or 'perpetual', Benjamin Akzin suggests that it should be and must be derived from a superhuman source, not from the arrogance of the government who thinks that they are staying in the stage of super perfection.[105] The framers of the Constitution did not also intend to include such an eternity clause in the Constitution. The legislative recognition of article 7B of the Constitution for its non-amenability can be treated as the 'death of the basic feature doctrine'.[106] The inclusion of such eternity clauses can be challenged from both the originalist approach and the living constitution approach of interpretation. The originalist approach requires the interpreters to base their decision on what the framers of the constitution intend or had in mind when they wrote the constitution.[107] The living-constitution approach, on the other hand, "encourages judges to keep the Constitution relevant for contemporary concerns and purposes..."[108] Thus, it can be submitted that

---

104   S Suteu, *Eternity Clauses in Democratic Constitutionalism* (Oxford University Press, 2021) 243.

105   B Akzin, 'On the Stability and Reality of Constitutions' (1966) 3 *Scripta Hierosolymitana* 43.

106   K Ahmed, 'Article 7B, or the Death of the Basic Feature Doctrine?' *The Daily Star*, 12 June 2018, https://www.thedailystar.net/law-our-rights/article-7bor-the-death-the-basic-feature -doctrine-1589884 (accessed 10 August 2021).

107   H Gillman, 'The Collapse of Constitutional Originalism and the Rise of the Notion of the "Living Constitution" in the Course of American State-Building' (1997) 11 *Studies in American Political Development* 192.

108   *Ibid.*

freezing constitutional provisions through the eternity clause, article 7B, was not intended by the framers' of the Constitution. Furthermore, this eternity clause goes against the changing circumstances, which may include incorporating newly emerged human rights within Part III of the constitution or making the rights contained in Part III enforceable. Thus, it goes against both the originalist and the living-constitution approach to interpret the constitution. So, to make it a people's document, it should allow any positive change, including making this part "judicially enforceable" to cater to the right to shelter in a COVID-19 pandemic.

5   'Socialist Economic System' vs 'Private Ownership': A Paradox

On January 3, 1971, the elected representatives of then Pakistan led by Sheikh Mujibur Rahman took oath at the Suhrawardy Udyan before the mass people.[109] In that meeting, he presented the future economic manifesto of Bangladesh, then East Pakistan. He pledged on making a socialist society free from exploitation and particularly emphasized the distribution of *Khas* Land to the landless people.[110] Along with other reasons, this pledge played a key role later to inspire the freedom fighters to fight for the independence.

Eventually Bangladesh became an independent sovereign country in 1971 through the most brutal blood baths in history that cost millions of people's lives in the liberation war of 1971 and endured a struggle for long 24 years against the economic and social discrimination by the Pakistani rulers. To redress, the constituent assembly formed with the selective national and provincial assembly members accepted socialism as one of the four fundamental principles of the constitution of Bangladesh respecting the manifestation of popular hope and aspirations.[111] The fundamental aim of the State as pledged

---

109   See Major K.M. Shafiullah v. Bangladesh, Writ Petition No. 4313 of 2009.

110   'Speech of Bangabandhu [Sheikh Mujibur Rahman] on 3 Jan[uary] 1971' *Youtube* https://www.youtube.com/watch?v=IDy_DtRlVGg (accessed 17 July 2021 (speech delivered after the victory at the national elections of Pakistan in 1970 and before the Liberation War and Independence of Bangladesh).

111   The second paragraph of the Preamble to the Constitution of the People's Republic of Bangladesh states that "...the high ideals of nationalism, socialism, democracy and secularism which inspired our heroic people to dedicate themselves to, and our brave martyrs to sacrifice their lives in, the national liberation struggle, shall be the fundamental principles of the Constitution". Article 8 (1) says that "the principles of nationalism, socialism, democracy and secularism, together with the principles derived from those as set out in this Part, shall constitute the fundamental principles of state policy".

in the third paragraph of the preamble is supposed to attain a socialist society through the democratic process. This paragraph also asked for such a socialist society which shall be free from exploitation and 'in which the rule of law, fundamental human rights and freedom, equality, and justice, political, economic and social, will be secured for all citizens.'[112]

Further, the constitution envisioned for establishing a socialist economic system which shall help to attain a just and egalitarian society in its article 10. This egalitarian society shall also aspire to be free from the exploitation of men by men. The Constitution also imposed a fundamental responsibility upon the State to emancipate the 'toiling masses, the peasants and workers, and backward sections of the people from all forms of exploitation'.[113] Article 19 (2) says:

> The State shall adopt effective measures to remove social and economic inequality between man and man and to ensure the equitable distribution of wealth among citizens, the opportunities in order to distribute wealth among citizens, and of opportunities in order to attain a uniform level of economic development throughout the Republic.

Such provisions empowered the political branch of the government instead of empowering the judiciary to make decisions to establish a socialist society, to remove inequality, or to remove exploitation. As a result, the Government may have a moral obligation to their electorate in ensuring ESC rights including the right to shelter, but they have no legal accountability since these provisions are not judicially enforceable by dint of article 8(2).

In addition, article 13(c) acknowledges the private ownership subject to limitations imposed by any other law. Similarly, article 42 that speaks of the right to property as one of the enforceable fundamental rights, gives the citizens of Bangladesh 'right to acquire, hold, transfer or otherwise dispose of property' subject to provisions of any other law or restrictions imposed therein. Though the law-imposed restrictions on acquiring the aggregate quantity of lands, there is no such restriction on acquiring the number of flats or apartments in the urban areas.[114] Furthermore, the prestige of a man in the Bangladeshi society depends upon how many flats or apartments he owns, or how many cars he does have. In some way, it encourages or compels people to accumulate wealth, leading to inequality in the society. As a result, the ratio

---

112   See Constitution of the People's Republic of Bangladesh, para 3 of the Preamble.

113   *Ibid.*, art 14.

114   According to section 4 of the Land Reforms Ordinance 1984, a family cannot acquire more than sixty standard bighas of agricultural land. See Islam, *supra* note 23 at 123–25.

of renters and house owners in the capital city of Dhaka stands as 90:10.[115] It manifests that there are some good words regarding socialism in our Constitution, but it is ineffective in practice.

As to establishing socialism, even the opposition members of the constituent assembly were of the view that the provisions regarding socialism in the Constitution are meaningless for several reasons including retaining private ownership or keeping FPSPs including the right to housing out of judicial review etc. Opposition members of the constituent assembly, even some members of the ruling Awami League opposed the decision to recognize the private ownership as inserted in article 13 and advocated for the nationalization of property that could ensure ESC rights, especially the right to housing.[116] Further, article 8(2), which keeps FPSPs out of judicial review, was also seriously attacked by opposition members. They were of the view that it made the objectives of establishing socialism meaningless.[117] Mr. Tajuddin Ahmed, the then Finance Minister, advocated for non-justiciability of FPSPs and said that 'the Parliament democratically elected by a politically conscious people, would determine the priorities based on objective conditions obtaining in the country at a particular phase and would implement the Fundamental Principles following the wishes of the people.'[118] For these reasons, the opposition members doubted that the Constitution would not help transition to socialism.[119]

6   Ways Onward Considering the Global Best Practices to Protect the Interests of Renters during the Pandemic

During the ongoing pandemic, the State should be due diligent in protecting the interests of both house owners and renters. Many countries have adopted various economic, fiscal, or financial measures to suspend house evictions for unpaid rents during the ongoing crisis by providing stimulus packages to all

---

115   'Coronavirus: Tenants for Waiving House Rents for 3 Months' *UNB*, 20 April 2020, https://
       www.unb.com.bd/category/Special/coronavirus-tenants-for-waiving-house-rents-for-3
       -months/50302 (accessed 14 August 2021).
116   AF Huq, 'Constitution-Making in Bangladesh' (1973) 46 *Pacific Affairs* 73.
117   See Constituent Assembly Debates, October 30, 1972, published in *The Bangladesh
       Observer*, 31 October 1972; see also Huq, *supra* note 84.
118   See CA debates, 30 October 1972, published in *The Bangladesh Observer*, 31 October 1972;
       see also AF Huq, 'Constitution-Making in Bangladesh' (1973) 46 *Pacific Affairs* 73.
119   Huq, *supra* note 84.

concerned.[120] They have taken some temporary emergency measures to prevent homelessness and to protect renters from eviction during a pandemic.

For example, Portugal has announced a National Fund for Urgent Housing; Indonesia designated sports centres and public halls to accommodate homeless people temporarily; and the UK government offered emergency accommodation to the rough sleepers and announced £105 million to support people who are at the risk of homelessness. France also accommodates new houses for homeless people; Italy, Spain, and Sweden also offered emergency housing for homeless people;[121] and the President of Kenya prohibited eviction during a pandemic. In addition, the UK enacted the Coronavirus (Scotland) Act 2020 to protect renters eviction up to six months and Austria and Spain has also prohibited eviction for unpaid rent due to lockdown.[122] Similarly, the US government has enacted the American Rescue Plan Act 2021 which is also known as COVID-19 stimulus package.[123] It announced funding for both renters and the house owners, e.g. it declared $21.6 billion for rental assistance programs and $10 billion for the Homeowner Assistance Fund.[124]

Furthermore, the Special Rapporteur on the right to adequate housing has also adopted the COVID-19 guidance note to protect renters and mortgage payers.[125] This guidance suggests three principles to be undertaken to address the issue which are:

i.   the burden of the response to the pandemic must be shared across the society in a fair and equitable manner;
ii.   renters and homeowners-whether in informal or formal markets-must not emerge from the pandemic overburdened with housing related debt as a result of financial and economic circumstances created by the pandemic; and

---

120   UN, 'COVID 19 and Human Rights We Are all in This together' (April 2020) https://www .un.org/victimsofterrorism/sites/www.un.org.victimsofterrorism/files/un__human _rights_and_covid_april_2020.pdf (accessed 17 July 2021).
121   'COVID-19 and the Right to Housing – a Submission to the UN Special Rapporteur on Adequate Housing' *Amnesty International*, June 2020, https://www.amnesty.org/download /Documents/IOR4026262020ENGLISH.PDF (accessed 14 August 2021).
122   *Ibid.*
123   It is a $1.9 trillion stimulus package to speed up the US's recovery from economic and health effects of the pandemic.
124   'Analysis: Congress Passes $1.9 Trillion COVID-19 Relief Package' *Buchanan Ingersoll & Rooney PC* https://www.bipc.com/analysis-congress-passes-covid-19-relief-package-ameri can-rescue-plan-of-2021#bookmark2 (accessed 14 August 2021).
125   L Farha, 'Protecting Renters and Mortgage Payers' (COVID-19 Guidance Note:1, prepared by the Special Rapporteur on the right to adequate housing, OHCHR, 8 April 2020) https://www.ohchr.org/Documents/Issues/Housing/SR_housing_COVI9_guidance_rent _and_mortgage_payers.pd (accessed 14 August 2021).

iii. the financial burden shouldered by banks, financial institutions, corporate landlords, and other financial actors must be proportionate to their resources.

To protect the interests of renters and homeowners, this guidance asks the states to undertake some specific measures immediately.[126] During the pandemic period and for a reasonable period thereafter, states must prohibit evictions or the threat of evictions due to rental arrears, arrears of utility bills, etc.[127] Even the eviction scheduled before the pandemic is required to be suspended.[128] This guidance further requires establishing monitoring mechanisms to ensure those prohibitions are adhered to.[129] It also requires the states to prohibit rental increases, cancelling rental contracts except on the grounds of criminal behaviour, etc.[130] This guidance suggests the government consider the income decline situation of the tenants due to the COVID-19 and legislate a mandatory rent recalculation which ensures that the tenant will have not to pay 30 percent of the total income of the tenants during a pandemic, including other social benefits received.[131] In this situation, to protect the interests of the house owners, the guidance asks for compensatory schemes as well.[132]

In this regard, the State can consider the circumstances of particular landlords on a case-by-case basis. This guidance further suggests establishing a "social solidarity fund" funded through taxation and revenues earned from corporate landlords, which will be given to smaller landlords.[133] The State may also require the banks and other financial institutions, or other lenders "to renegotiate mortgage payments with those affected by the COVID-19, so that no more than 30 percent of household income is devoted to servicing during a pandemic and for a reasonable time thereafter".[134] It also suggests the states provide tax credits or other financial easing tools to those homeowners, financial institutions, banks, etc.[135] It also advises the State to ensure that the homeowners and tenants do not have to accrue unsustainable rents because of the aforementioned guidelines.[136] To ensure the better implementation of

---

126 *Ibid.*
127 *Ibid.*, para 1.
128 *Ibid.*
129 *Ibid.*
130 *Ibid*, para 3.
131 *Ibid.*, para 4.
132 *Ibid.*, para 5.
133 *Ibid.*
134 *Ibid.*, para 7.
135 *Ibid.*, para 10.
136 *Ibid.*, para 11.

the guidance, the State is required to establish an implementation or oversight body as well.[137] To this end in view, the Government of Bangladesh could make a law incorporating all this guidance to ensure renters' right to shelter during the pandemic. By following such best practices and undertaking similar measures within its available resources, the country can mitigate the negative impact of the COVID-19, especially in cases of homelessness.

7   Conclusion

The Government of Bangladesh tends to play a passive role in protecting renters evicted for non-payment due to the lockdown or shutdown. In addition, its Premises Rent Control Act 1991 or the Communicable Disease (Prevent, Control, and Elimination) Act 2018 does not contain any provision to protect renters during health emergencies like the COVID-19 pandemic. Since staying at home has been considered as the frontline defence against the pandemic and being outside the home is tantamount to probable death, renters' eviction seems to have violated their right to life which is a fundamental enforceable right under the Constitution of Bangladesh. Further, since renters' protection during the pandemic casts a negative obligation, the government can enforce it following the interpretation of the provisions of the Constitution. Against this background, Bangladesh can follow the guidelines provided by the UN Special rapporteur and the global best practice to fulfil its constitutional mandate.

Note on the Contributors

Mohammad Towhidul Islam
Professor, Department of Law, University of Dhaka.

Md Jahid Al-Mamun
Lecturer, Department of Law, University of Dhaka.

---

137   *Ibid.*, para 12.

CHAPTER 4

COVID-19, Inter-Religious Strife and the Erosion of Human Rights in India

Nafees Ahmad

Abstract

The Constitution of India promises a brolly of fundamental rights available to all, including minorities. In the pandemic proscenium, the right to religion has become more pertinent than ever to prevaricate parochial pursuits and equivocate the diversity jabberwockies in India. The right to religion is for all, and it transcends all socio-political binaries and religious-cultural dichotomies. But the religious attitudes of We, the People of India, are incompatible with the inclusive interpretation of the Constitution. If a right is pleaded, it is not a right but exclusion. Pandemics do not discriminate between barbed boundaries, geostrategic visions, and ideological idiosyncrasies. In India, all religions propel people's lives and invoke religions to redress misfortunes such as the COVID-19 pandemic. The religious precepts glazed with biases, bigotry, and prejudices were part of the structural justice machinery during the pandemic scenario aggravated by India's irresponsible and irreversible role of media outlets. The mainstream media has been violating fundamental principles of non-discrimination, and impartial journalism and has become propaganda machinery blaming the Muslims for spreading coronavirus with no such evidence. The Muslim clergy too has constructed the religious precepts of Indian Muslims for centuries as Islamic injunctions and usages. The Muslim clergy has embezzled the Islamic illiterateness of Muslims and steered them into an imaginative interpretation of Islam during the pandemic. Based on the illiberal construction of Islam and Hinduism, the media has presented the global pandemic as a religious rivalry between Islam and Hinduism that has acquiesced both Hindus and Muslims.

Keywords

freedom of religion – right to health – hate speech – social media – constitutionalism

1   Introduction

Globally, as of 10 January 2023, there have been 660,131,952 confirmed cases of COVID-19 pandemic, including 6,690,473 deaths, reported to the World Health Organization (WHO) and as of 21 December 2022, a total of 13,073,712,554 vaccine doses have been administered as per the data[1] and documentation compiled by the WHO. There is no second opinion that we confront a global public health emergency. Medical infrastructures have proved inadequate and are in bad shape in many countries. People die at an unprecedented rate if measured against technological advancement and scientific research. The total rate of identified contagious cases and deaths is a significant concern. All reasonable people understand the need for drastic measures to combat and curtail our accustomed and acclimatized freedoms and rights. The curtailment of the rights and liberties of the citizens and people under the law during pandemics, however, is seriously unacceptable and disturbing. Efforts of curtailments have proved imperfect due to a lack of medical and administrative preparedness to cope with the pandemic. However, world history is testimony to this fact and has repeatedly demonstrated that it has never been prepared to confront such global epidemics since their germination and gestation.

The COVID-19 crisis amplifies current inequalities and discrimination and makes the fight of 'leaving nobody behind' all the more problematic. The inequalities and discrimination know no borders, and as such, these exist in various forms and across social contexts. The deepening inequality gaps brought about by COVID-19 have profound implications for fundamental human rights like the right to health, the right to ethical care, the right to human dignity, the right to education, the right to work, and most importantly, the right to life. Fear and indecision about the pandemic have equally fuelled the so-called "Coronavirus stigma" based on racial, religious, and gender grounds, and laid bare, specifically, the vulnerability of those living in precarious situations and marginalized groups, including persons with disabilities, women, and children, refugees and migrants. Their discrimination is lasting beyond the pandemic.

History repeats itself in many ways, including blame-shifting[2] in the matters of pandemic diseases in every nook and corner of the world. The blame-shifting or attribution has been a universal phenomenon in all the socio-cultural and political discourses worldwide. Blame attribution results from biases, bigotry,

---

1   WHO Coronavirus (COVID-19) Dashboard https://covid19.who.int/ (accessed 16 January 2023).
2   D Nelkin and SL Gilman, 'Placing Blame for Devastating Disease' (1988) 55 *Social Research* 361–378.

and prejudices indoctrinated and harboured by adversaries in different geo-political entities worldwide. Presently, it turns its tentacles on India and other countries gripped with coronavirus that got acquiesced in the quagmire of blame politics in the current milieu of a devastating disease. In this regard, media houses in India identified one religious group of Muslims whose religious precepts have been blamed for the COVID-19 crimes and contagion by raising a fallacious bogey of Islamophobia. In India, alleged COVID-19 violations by Muslims are an extension of perennial hate crimes against them and so-called mainstream media has been adding fuel to the fire and now many social media outlets have stoked it further. Conversely, the Muslim clergy too performs erroneous interpretation of the sacred texts and manipulate their followers into refusing to comply with the governments' health measures since those were adopted on Hindu ethnonationalist grounds. The resulting human rights, including the right to health and religion, have suffered by this pernicious inter-religious strife while a unified and concerted effort would have been required to fight the virus and save human lives irrespective of belief.

This chapter addresses in the following section the presence of inter-religious strife between Hindu and Muslim communities which operate in the background of the COVID-19 pandemic in India. The third section looks how the COVID-19 pandemic has been instrumentalised by Hindu ethnonationalism to advance Islamophobic discourses aimed at targeting and blaming the Muslims in India for the health crisis undermining the right to religion. The fourth section addresses the attitude of Muslim clerics in India to pursue an equally reactionary stance in handling the health crisis thus undermining basic human rights such as the right to health.

2 Inter-Religious Strife in India Operating in the Background of the COVID-19 Pandemic

Since November 2019, the world has been experiencing and enduring the most dangerous global health events of the present era, i.e. the COVID-19 or coronavirus pandemic or epidemic,[3] that has been gobbling people like carnivorous. Currently, there are no answers to COVID-19 as to how to cope with this pandemic holistically. Deadly virus-driven epidemics have existed in different regions of the world, and religions have played both negative and positive roles. During pandemics or otherwise, religion is regarded as the last

---

3   Staff Writer, 'What's the Difference between an Epidemic and a Pandemic?' *MPHonline*, https://www.mphonline.org/epidemic-vs-pandemic/ (accessed 2 March 2022).

hope in the absence of no solutions or cures. Thus, the religious and spiritual institutions have been readjusting, adapting, and re-shaping their responses to the coronavirus pandemic. In India, the so-called "Religion-Induced Politics for Everything" (RIPE) syndrome has immensely weakened social cohesion, political stability, and economic equality in India. Conversely, constitutional politics in societies comprising social, cultural, religious, economic diversity such as India, is needed. But, unfortunately, these diversity dimensions are not reflected in the social histories of pandemics, and the role played by religion without any scientific evidence quagmire the national and regional politics in South Asia. Therefore, lessons from the history of epidemics must be learned to re-conceive best strategies and innovative practices for combating the current virus without religionizing it.

As an assortment of multi-religious, multi-cultural, and multi-lingual geopolitical identities,[4] India been emerging as a potential game-changer[5] in the global power structure. However, this multitude of identities is resented by the current popular nationalist leadership in the name of integration, assimilation, and patriotization of Muslims, while discarding their sacrifices[6] in the freedom struggle of India. Religious minorities constitute approximately 20% of the total population of India, out of which Muslims account for 14.2% who feel deprived,[7] dehumanized,[8] neglected, threatened, and unwanted. The concept of 'unity in diversity' has always been a unifying force in India since antiquity. Integration does not ensure assimilation of any religious group in any geopolitical entity if it predominantly remains a cluster of identities. However, Muslims are vertically well integrated and horizontally well-assimilated in the reservoir of *We, the People of India*,[9] consistent with

---

4   D Beland, C Howard and KJ Morgan, *The Oxford Handbook of Transnational Feminist Movements* (Oxford University Press, 2015); *See also*: Ek Bharat Shreshtha Bharat, https://www.in*dia.gov.in/spotlight/ek-bharat-shreshtha-bharat (accessed 12 January 2023).

5   'India's Diversity is a Strategic Asset' *Greater Pacific Capital*, https://www.greaterpacificcapital .com/thought-leadership/indias-diversity-is-a-strategic-asset (accessed 12 January 2023).

6   C Rammanohar Reddy, 'Why the Sacrifices of Abdul Khader and the Penang 20 Freedom Fighters Bear Special Relevance in 2022' *Scroll.in*, 12 August 2022, https://scroll.in/article /1030295/why-the-sacrifices-of-abdul-khader-and-the-penang-20-freedom-fighters-bear -special-relevance-in-2022 (accessed 16 January 2023).

7   Sachar Committee Report on Social, Economic and Educational Status of the Muslim Community of India, Prime Minister's High Level Committee, Cabinet Secretariat, Government of India, November 2006, https://www.minorityaffairs.gov.in/en/document/sachar-committee-report/complete-sachar-committee-reportenglish-2006-6655-kb (accessed 12 December 2022).

8   DR Chowdhury, 'Is India Headed for an Anti-Muslim Genocide?' *Time*, 4 October 2021, https:// time.com/6103284/india-hindu-supremacy-extremism-genocide-bjp-modi/ (accessed on 12 December 2022).

9   Preamble, The Constitution of India, 1950.

the Preamble[10] to the Constitution of India. The contemporary socio-political orientation in India does not have space for demurring, or divulging alternative views and vision. At the heart of the discussion is the inter-religious strife which has harmed the People of India irrespective of which belief they have. Harvard University Nobel Laureate Professor Amartya Sen in his interview to French newspaper *La Monde* observed:

> India has always been a multi-ethnic country, it treats its own people in such a nasty way, the Indian government's record has been really rather terrible, the word barbaric comes to my tongue because it's not just unjust and wrong but it makes people's lives totally precarious and makes India's culture limited, it is communitarian in the narrowest sense of the term, attacking Muslims and propagating the idea that Hindus form a nation and majoritarian policies are a reduction of India, a demolition of part of the country, a national disaster, a matter of horrendous potential of nastiness. I am not only worried; I am terrified that a nation with different components is suddenly in a state of catastrophic isolation. The ill-treatment of minorities is one of the major follies of the nation; it is a fantastic denigration and demolition of the country's history and its present.[11]

Indeed, the manufacturing of religious identities and the roots of religious antagonisms in India are not only colonial but also have a pre-colonial genesis, for example; the 17th century battles between Aurangzeb and Shivaji. Throughout the Middle Ages, Muslim expansion into the Indian Peninsula endangered the Hindu way of life leading to some Hindus embracing Islam. Thus, the Hindu-Muslim schism dates back to the 1679 decision of the Mughal Emperor Aurangzeb, re-imposing the abhorrent *Jizyah* (tax) on all non-Muslims in his reign. Muhammad Saqi Musta'id Khan, an employee in the Court of Aurangzeb who recorded an authoritative account of the Aurangzeb's life in the following words:

> As all the aims of the religious Emperor were directed to the spreading of the law of Islam and the overthrow of the practice of the infidels, he issued orders... [that in] agreement with the canonical traditions, *Jizyah* should be collected from the infidels... of the capital and the provinces.[12]

---

10   *Ibid.*

11   K Thapar, 'Interview 'Modi Govt Is One of the Most Appalling in the World,' Says Amartya Sen' *The Wire*, 14 January 2023, https://thewire.in/rights/interview-modi-govt-is-one-of-the-most-appalling-in-the-world-says-amartya-sen (accessed 16 January 2023).

12   S Chandra, 'Jizyah and the State in India During the 17th Century' (1969) 12 *Journal of the Economic and Social History of the Orient* 322–323

A Hindu prominent chieftain Shivaji Bhonsle in the Deccan fustigated the decision and rebelled against the Mughal Empire and founded the Maratha Empire in 1674. The death of Aurangzeb in 1707 paved the way for Maratha conquests of Mughal territories across India and often retaliated against local Muslim populations in the process. It is axiomatic from such instances that Hindu-Muslim conflict has a prolonged pedigree in India. However, over the course of time there are many recondite facts to the communal crevasse between the two largest religious communities in India. In 1871, British Raj carried out first census in India that provided an opportunity to the colonial rule to consolidate Hindu-Muslim division for the perennial perpetuation of imperial rule. Subsequently, the Partition of Bengal in 1905 and the creation of separate religious electorates in 1909 germinated the seeds of religion-driven hatred and hostility resulting into blood-spattered partition of the Indian subcontinent into a Hindu India and a Muslim Pakistan in 1947.

This Hindu-Muslim clash is a relatively recent phenomenon that has been exploited by the current nationalist leadership[13] for political power and which is known as inter-religious domination. There is forging of privatization of public, the economization of *Hindutva*,[14] the medialization of hate, and geopolitics of identity othering by pursuing "the communitarian and majoritarian policies"[15] against the fundamental human rights[16] and basic human freedoms enunciated in its Constitution for minorities. The Supreme Court (SC) of India, however, observed in a catena of cases, particularly in *S.R. Bommai v. Union of India*[17] that secularism is an inalienable part of the basic structure[18] of the Constitution of India. The SC, time and again, in *Ayodhya case*[19] opined that the secular character is the foundation of the Constitution even if it hadn't been conspicuously spelt out. But, in 1976, the Constitution of

13   G Shih and A Gupta, 'Religious Clashes across India Spark Fears of Further Violence' *The Washington Post*, 20 April 2022, https://www.washingtonpost.com/world/2022/04/20/india-hindu-muslim-communal-violence/ (accessed 10 December 2022).

14   J Ghosh, 'Hindutva, Economic Neoliberalism and the Abuse of Economic Statistics in India' (2020) 24–25 *South Asia Multidisciplinary Academic Journal* 1–7.

15   J Bouissou, 'Amartya Sen: 'The Indian Government Is One of the Most Appalling in the World' *Le Monde* interview published on 19 December 2022 at 12:00 p.m., updated on 6 January 2023, https://www.lemonde.fr/idees/article/2022/12/19/amartya-sen-le-gouvernement-indien-est-l-un-des-plus-epouvantables-au-monde_6155041_3232.html (accessed 16 January 2023).

16   *Golaknath v. State of Punjab*, 1967 AIR 1643.

17   1994 AIR 1918, 1994 SCC (3), 1, JT (Decided: 11 March 1994).

18   *Kesavananda Bharti v. State of Kerala* AIR 1973 SC 1461.

19   *M Siddiq (D) Thr Lrs v. Mahant Suresh Das & Ors* (Civil Appeal Nos 10866–10867 of 2010) (Decided: 9 November 2019).

India was amended[20] and the word "secular" was inserted in the Preamble that recognized India as a secular nation-state. Secularism is the first and foremost doctrine that opposes all forms of inter-religious domination and functions as a firewall safeguarding minorities and other vulnerable victims of inter-religious discriminations.

To the contrary, the constitutional right of the freedom of speech[21] determines the civility of the modern life in all liberal and secular democracies, including India. Free speech is a firewall that protects constitutional trust, public morality, and the rule of law in a plural society and identifies the violation of principle of non-discrimination. The basic structure of freedom of speech rests on freedom of dissent, public order, political equality, constitutional morality,[22] transformative constitutionalism, and secular democracy. Therefore, the role of media in democratic political governance is central, and it derives its legitimacy and validity norms from a grand model called the Constitution.[23] Therefore, any deviation from this path is dangerous and destructive to the fabric of democratic liberalism, secular pluralism, composite culture, co-existence, and unity in diversity.

But vulpine media has become misanthropic towards minorities in violation of its constitutional obligations. Media has deliberately created a sense of Islamophobia[24] among the people of India to satisfy the so-called "Far-Right-Anti-Muslim-Elements"[25] (FRAME) who enjoy the institutional patronage. Islamophobia is the most abused expression describing negative sentiments, prejudices and animosity against Islam and its adherents. Islamophobia could be based on opaque opinions and flawed understandings about Muslims as a socio-cultural and ethno-racial group in any geopolitical entity or region. Islamophobic ideas are misanthropic depicting Islam and Muslims as an existential danger to non-Muslims worldwide. Some scholars[26] argue that

---

20   42nd Amendment of the Constitution of India enacted in 1976.

21   Article 19 (1) (a), the Constitution of India, 1950.

22   BR Ambedkar, 'Speech Delivered on 25 November 1949' in *The Constitution and Constituent Assembly Debates* 174.

23   Preamble, The Constitution of India, 1950.

24   G Conway, *Islamophobia: A Challenge for Us All* (Runnymede Trust, 1997) https://www .runnymedetrust.org/companies/17/74/Islamophobia-A-Challenge-for-Us-All.html (accessed 10 January 2023).

25   JP Zúquete, 'The European Extreme-Right and Islam: New Directions?' (2008) 13 *Journal of Political Ideologies* 321–344, Far-Right-Anti-Muslim-Elements (F.R.A.M.A. or FRAME) is a community of people believing in Majoritarian political narrative that excludes Muslims from the mainstream India.

26   S Bangstad, 'Eurabia Comes to Norway' (2013) 24 *Islam and Christian–Muslim Relations* 369–391.

Islamophobia is the straight counterpart of antisemitism and Muslim are the new Jews who are most persecuted, hounded and hated minority. The expression Islamophobia combines antagonism to Islam with bias and bigotry that might translate bias into hate towards Muslims.[27] To intensify the threshold of exactitude and derogate the omphalos on fallacy of Islamophobia, some scholars[28] supplant Islamophobia with two analytically conspicuous classification of Anti-Islam and Anti-Muslim premises. Anti-Islam can be defined as "framing Islam as homogenous, totalitarian ideology which threatens western civilization".[29] Anti-Muslim can be defined as "oversimplified beliefs, negative feelings and evaluations of Muslims as group".[30]

Furthermore, some scholars argue that "counter-terrorism" policies of Western states are inherently Islamophobic and branded Muslims populations as potential terrorists.[31] In the non-Western societies, multiple varieties of Islamophobia buttress the enforcement of policies of othering of Muslims such as far-right nationalism in India[32] where the framing[33] of Muslims by the electronic media, mainstream media, and social media in India has been driven by the FRAME trajectory and they have seeped deep into the Indian State's hierarchical structures and institutional responses. The inflammatory social media rhetorical charades have been responsible for violence against Muslim populations. The impact of disinformation, misinformation, and hate speech on civilians in diversity settings has become *cause celebre* in India.

In India, people are the prisoners of their religious consciousness that guide their religious attitudes towards everything under the sun and Muslims are not an exception either. Muslims constitute the most prominent religious group after Hindus. Once upon a time, Muslims were the rulers[34] of the Indian

27   M Helbling and R Traunmüller, 'What is Islamophobia? Disentangling Citizens' Feelings toward Ethnicity, Religion and Religiosity Using a Survey Experiment' (2018) 50 *British Journal of Political Science* 1–18.
28   LE Berntzen, *Liberal Roots of Far Right Activism: The Anti-Islamic Movement in the 21st Century* (Routledge, 2019).
29   *Ibid.*
30   N Lean, 'The Debate over the Utility and Precision of the Term "Islamophobia' in I Zempi and I Awan (eds.) *The Routledge International Handbook of Islamophobia* (Routledge, 2019) 11–17.
31   N Massoumi, T Mills and D Miller (eds.) *What Is Islamophobia? Racism, Social Movements and the State* (Pluto Press, 2017).
32   D Anand, *Hindu Nationalism in India and the Politics of Fear* (Palgrave Macmillan, 2011).
33   D Müller, 'Coronavirus in India: Muslims as Scapegoats' https://en.qantara.de/content/coronavirus-in-india-muslims-as-scapegoats (accessed 24 April 2022).
34   Encyclopædia Britannica, 'The Mughal Empire, 1526–1761: The Significance of Mughal Rule' https://www.britannica.com/place/India/The-Mughal-Empire-1526-1761 (accessed 10 February 2022).

sub-continent and enriched the history, civilization, and culture of the region. They had provided many novel methods of administration, agricultural and land management techniques, artworks, architecture, construction methods, canals, navigation, trade and sports.[35] Today, their heritage and legacy have become the primary source of tourism and hospitality industries, generating a lot of revenue. Despite the fact of having a glorious and rich past, today, their actions doomed them and they always blame the government and the majority community for their exclusion and discriminatory treatment.

Yet, Muslims must fully reconcile their Islamic-oriented past with their secularism-dominated present. Some conservative Muslims nostalgically glorify Muslim rule based on the amalgamation and interconnection of Islam and politics. However, the progressive Muslims take a liberal approach based on secularism[36] while considering education, measures within the gamut of contemporary political frameworks and Muslim community services might precipitate to help generate the liberal orientation of Islam. Thus, Muslim society is divided over the role of Islam today in India and elsewhere. In recent years, the Arab Spring[37] and succeeding disorder in Egypt, Tunisia, and Syria have exposed these two contesting contentions' apparent inconsistency and discordancy. In India, Muslims are at the crossroads between constitutional secularism[38] and liberal Islam, and the far-right nationalist government is adamant about reversing the decades of India's state practice of secularism.[39] Such a dichotomy raises some pertinent questions: Will far-right nationalism and constitutional secularism be the new contesting ideologies in India? Is any reconciliation between far-right nationalism and constitutional secularism acceptable to all in the coming decades? These questions have been hovering since the partition of the Indian sub-continent in 1947 for all and sundry. The fate of secularism[40] is contingent upon the commitment to unity in diversity and the dilution of the far-right brand of religious nationalism and Islamic conservatism.

---

35   Encyclopædia Britannica, 'Islamic History from 1683 to the Present: Reform, Dependency, and Recovery' https://www.britannica.com/topic/Islamic-world/Islamic-history -from-1683-to-the-present-reform-dependency-and-recovery (accessed 10 February 2022).

36   DD Acevedo, 'Secularism in the Indian Context' (2013) 38 *Law & Social Inquiry* 138–167.

37   A Roberts, 'The Arab Spring: Why Did Things Go So Badly Wrong?' *The Guardian*, 15 January 2020, https://www.theguardian.com/commentisfree/2016/jan/15/arab-spring-badly -wrong-five-years-on-people-power (accessed 12 January 2023).

38   VM Tarkunde, 'Secularism and the Indian Constitution' (1995) 22 *India International Centre Quarterly* 143–152.

39   PR Brass, 'Indian Secularism in Practice' (2006) 9 *Indian Journal of Secularism* 115–132.

40   C Jaffrelot, 'The Fate of Secularism in India' *Carnegie Endowment for International Peace*, 4 April 2019, https://carnegieendowment.org/2019/04/04/fate-of-secularism-in-india-pub -78689 (accessed 4 January 2023).

3   The COVID-19 Pandemic in India: The Latest Pretext for Hindu
       Islamophobia

Muslim-bashing and hate speech[41] have become the new normal in the contemporary socio-political life of India. As the most significant minority in
India, it experienced and endured media-generated stigma,[42] state-tolerated
violence, and mental health challenges. The people of the FRAME community assert their ethnonationalism[43] by hurling expletives and vituperations
and using slanderous language[44] against the Muslims. In achieving this,
social media has played a dangerous and religiously very provocative role in
disturbing the socio-religious stability of different religions and their followers.
To be liberal,[45] secular[46] and progressive[47] has become an offense in India.
The FRAME community does not recognize liberal, rational and progressive
Muslims in India; instead, it treats and targets all Muslims equally if their
identity[48] is Muslim.

Media reportage focused more on tarnishing and targeting Muslims who
have become new scapegoats[49] for spreading coronavirus rather than highlighting the urgent need for sufficient protective gear and facilities for across-the-
board treatment of pandemic patients. The COVID-19 pandemic emergencies
witnessed the manufacturing of a new derogatory discourse called "Corona
Jihad"[50] that can be construed as a central element of disjunctive politics of

41   Section 153 A, Indian Penal Code, 1860.
42   R Barrett and PJ Brown, 'Stigma in the Time of Influenza: Social and Institutional
     Responses to Pandemic Emergencies' (2008) 197 *Journal of Infectious Diseases* 34–37.
43   MS Prabhakara, 'Ethno-Nationalism: Theory and Practice' *The Hindu*, 28 October 2009,
     https://www.thehindu.com/opinion/lead/Ethno-nationalism-theory-and-practice
     /article16888924.ece (accessed 4 January 2023).
44   D Basu, 'Dominance of Majoritarian Politics and Hate Crimes Against Religious Minori-
     ties in India, 2009–2018' (2019) 272 *UMass Amherst Economics Working Papers*, https://
     scholarworks.umass.edu/econ_workingpaper/272 (accessed 11 January 2023).
45   Preamble, the Constitution of India, 1950.
46   Preamble, the Constitution of India, 1950.
47   AAA Fyzee, *Outlines of Muhammadan Law* (Oxford University Press, 1949). It gives a
     comparatively modern treatment of the application of Islamic law in the Indian subcon-
     tinent.
48   HT Blom, *The Saffran Wave: Democracy and Hindu Nationalism in Modern India* (Princeton
     University Press, 1999).
49   S Varadarajan, 'In India, a Pandemic of Prejudice and Repression' *The New York Times*,
     21 April 2020, https://www.nytimes.com/2020/04/21/opinion/coronavirus-india.html
     (accessed 22 April 2022).
50   MT Joseph, 'Religion in Times of COVID-19' (2021) 56 *Engage-EPW* https://www.epw.in
     /engage/article/religion-times-covid-19 (accessed 28 January 2023).

metonymic representation within the ambit of Islamophobia that was used to subdue Muslims by the mainstream media. The FRAME community has been fighting[51] with Muslims instead of the coronavirus. Consequently, Muslims were left to confront their dehumanization, stigmatization, regression, and ostracization to the hilt.

In reality, the peoples of India – irrespective of their beliefs – are not bothering about the preventative methods and Physical Distancing Measures (PDMs) such as lockdowns, quarantine, *Janata Curfew*,[52] restrictions, regulations, constitutional rights, and freedoms' curtailments[53] and health advisories issued by the government, the WHO and other agencies. Further, the religious gatherings[54] of Muslims and their religious practices were flagrantly devastated by discriminatory lockdowns, unlawful arrests, and economic boycotts due to their membership to the religion of Islam. Such politics contravenes the WHO procedure on designating new human contagious diseases. It also incubated lasting socio-political ramifications for Muslims that enfeebled the national solidarity to combat the COVID-19 pandemic as a collective project.

In a constitutional democracy, every individual, regardless of their adherence to a specific religion, allegiance to a particular ideology, or affiliation to a political outfit, is not the determinant to assess patriotism, nationalism, and citizenship. In the constitutional sense, no minority before institutional integrity must be the pervading thread of Indian state functionalism. The Constitution of India discreetly mandates all state institutions to respect every individual idea and opinion as per the established law. But in the case of Muslims in India, all these factors have become irrelevant, and they do not dare to demand constitutionally-ordained treatment from the state institutions. The state institutions have changed the constitutional norms of engagement and tightened their noose around the gasping of Muslims and other vulnerable sections of society. Therefore, the question of a minority does not arise in doing justice and providing constitutional rights to every section of society.

---

51   C Kapoor, 'Fight Virus not Muslims, Plead Indian Muslim Leaders' *Anadolu Agency*, 1 April 2020, https://www.aa.com.tr/en/asia-pacific/fight-virus-not-muslims-plead-indian -muslim-leaders/1788412 (accessed 5 April 2022).

52   Shri Narendra Modi, the Prime Minister of India who coined the expression "Janata Curfew" in his televised address to the people of India on March 20, 2020 at around 08.00 p.m. https://www.youtube.com/watch?v=8aD9-Y4EHhc (accessed 20 March 2022).

53   The fundamental freedoms such as the freedom of movement, right to recognized in the Constitution of India

54   Z Ahmed, 'Tablighi Jamaat: The Group Blamed for New COVID-19 Outbreak in India' *BBC News*, 2 April 2020, https://www.bbc.com/news/world-asia-india-52131338 (accessed 28 January 2023).

It is, unfortunately, a fashionable and inalienable part of political discourse in post-colonial India to adopt communal narratives and give divisive shapes to every contention, if it is between Hindus and Muslims, while putting aside its constitutional, administrative, and legal merits. The governmental measures against the COVID-19 pandemic, invariably in all liberal democracies, have raised vital concerns regarding the proportionality of limitations on fundamental human rights and human freedoms, including the right to religion. The right to religion ordains the righteousness to humanize all humanities beyond current majoritarian narratives. However, the tentacles of the COVID-19 pandemic lachrymosed society irrespective of the contours of global health constitutionalism based on medical equality, health civility, restorative justice, the right to health, and the right to healthcare democracy.

Such discriminatory state practices have rekindled and rejuvenated curiosity in the potential role of religion in COVID-19 crises worldwide, including in India. Its implications during the COVID-19 pandemic have been resulting in the denial of a Muslim pregnant[55] woman admission to hospitals, the banning of Muslim vegetable vendors' entry into Hindu colonies,[56] the sprinkling of urine[57] on fruits, ascribing stigmatization[58] to Muslims for the coronavirus and attributing radicalization[59] of Muslims as a whole consistent with ethnonationalism[60] and autochthonic[61] majoritarianism. By the mere fact of being a

---

55   DA Wadhawan, 'Rajasthan: Doctor Refuses to Admit Pregnant Woman Because She's Muslim, Her Child Dies after Delivery' *India Today*, 4 April 2020, https://www.indiatoday.in/india/story/rajasthan-doctor-refuses-to-admit-pregnant-woman-because-she-s-muslim-her-child-dies-after-delivery-1663352-2020-04-04 (accessed 8 April 2022).

56   Special Reporter, 'Activists Condemn Discrimination against Muslim Vendors' *The Hindu*, 15 April 2020, https://www.thehindu.com/news/national/other-states/activists-condemn-discrimination-against-muslim-vendors/article31349219.ece (accessed 18 April 2020).

57   P Jha, 'Video from Bijnor Viral with False Allegation that Elderly Muslim Vendor Sprinkled Urine on Fruits' *Altnews*, 24 April 2020, https://www.altnews.in/video-shared-with-false-claim-that-muslim-fruit-seller-caught-contaminating-bananas-with-his-urine-in-bijnor-up/ (accessed 25 April 2020).

58   WHO and Johns Hopkins Center for Communication Programs, READY Network, 'Social Stigma associated with COVID-19' 24 February 2020, https://www.who.int/docs/default-source/coronaviruse/covid19-stigma-guide.pdf (accessed 28 February 2022).

59   V Mazzoni, 'Coronavirus: How Islamist Militants Are Reacting to the Outbreak' *European Eye Radicalization*, 30 March 2020, https://eeradicalization.com/coronavirus-how-islamist-militants-are-reacting-to-the-outbreak/ (accessed 2 April 2022).

60   S Deb, 'India's Looming Ethno-Nationalist Catastrophe' *The New Republic*, 7 August 2019, https://newrepublic.com/article/154682/india-looming-ethno-nationalist-catastrophe (accessed 2 January 2023).

61   J Habermas, 'Citizenship and National Identity: Some Reflections on the Future of Europe' in R Beiner (ed.) *Theorizing Citizenship* (SUNY Press, 1995) 255–282.

Muslim, Muslims have been enduring, convulsing, and reeling under incessant religious inequality.[62] This so-called "Discrimination Against Religious Distinction" (DARD)[63] in every walk of life means "pain" in Hindi and Urdu which Muslims have been experiencing in their interaction with the Indian State and its instrumentalities. DARD is omnipresent and pervasive worldwide as opposed to constitutional trust, institutional accountability, and non-discrimination guarantees engrafted in international human rights law.

A US government commission[64] has critically evaluated the role of India for failing to safeguard religious minorities and advocated "targeted sanctions"[65] on government officials responsible for violating religious freedoms[66] treasured in the Constitution of India. The commission further recommended that India should be put in the category of "country of particular concern" (CPC). This is the worst category that has already designated 14 countries as the most egregious religious freedom offenders[67] in the CPC category and prominent among them are China, Iran, Myanmar, Nigeria, Pakistan, Russia, Syria, and Vietnam, while proposing the exclusion of Sudan and Uzbekistan from the CPC list and recommending the inclusion of 11 countries such as Afghanistan, Algeria, Azerbaijan, Bahrain, the Central African Republic, Egypt, Indonesia, Iraq, Kazakhstan, Malaysia and Turkey in the CPC category for widespread religious freedom infringements.

4   Exploitation of the COVID-19 Pandemic by the Muslim Clergy

The discriminatory practices vis-à-vis the Muslim community in India during the COVID-19 pandemic is not the only reason why the government failed to

---

62   Report of the Sachar Committee.

63   DARD as I refer it means "pain of discrimination and deprivation" in Hindi and Urdu languages form lawful claims and entitlements under the Constitution of India that Muslims have been experiencing in their interaction with the Indian state and its instrumentalities on daily basis.

64   Reuters, 'U.S. Panel on Religious Freedom Urges Targeted Sanctions on India' *The New York Times*, 29 April 2020, https://www.nytimes.com/reuters/2020/04/29/world/asia/29reuters -india-usa-religion.html (accessed 30 April 2022).

65   E Schor, 'Religious Freedom Watchdog Pitches Adding India to Blacklist' *AP News*, 28 April 2020, https://apnews.com/0c8e54f35e1b5739cfd6787d4655a519 (accessed 29 April 2022).

66   Article 25, 26, 29, and 30 of the Constitution of India, see also Article 27 of the ICCPR, 1966.

67   T Gjelten, 'Religious Freedom in India Takes "Drastic Turn Downward"' *NPR*, 28 April 2020, https://www.npr.org/2020/04/28/847373064/religious-freedom-in-india-takes-drastic -turn-downward-u-s-commission-says (accessed 29 April 2022).

deliver on the right to health of all Indians irrespective of their beliefs. Religion is alleged to have been playing a role in spreading COVID-19.[68] Religious congregations like *Tablighi Jamaat* (Outreach Society or TJ) in India, religious engagements of Christians in Korea,[69] and religious activities in China and elsewhere have been linked to the spread of the coronavirus. To stop the virus from spreading, pastors have readjusted their religious obligations in the US in conformity with COVID-19 requirements. The catholic priests[70] in Israel have adopted new methods of delivering sacraments. The annual Haj pilgrimage and other Islamic congregational worships in Saudi Arabia have been put on hold. The WHO and Ministry of Health-Iran have linked[71] COVID-19 in Iran to Shia's Holy places in Qom.

In India and SAARC countries, the religion of Islam has also become the personal fiefdom of a majority of *Imams* (Muslim religious leaders) and *Muftis* (Islamic jurists) who are opposed to modern logical thinking, rational arguments and scientific temperament. In Pakistan, one Mufti Muneeb Ur Rehman[72] resented the implementation of PDMs on Islamic places of worship by the policemen and called physical distancing anti-Islamic and advocated that *Imams* cannot stop people from entering into *Masjids* (Mosques) for offering *Namaz* (Prayers) and other forms of Islamic rituals. In India, the chief of TJ, Maulana Mohammad Saad, has followed an un-Islamic path and violated the PDMs and other guidelines ordained in *Sunnah* and *Hadith*. He undermined the law of the land and did not provide sensible guidance to the TJ people.

These PDMs, however, are consistent with the religion of Islam, but, unfortunately, Indian Muslims hell-bent not to adhere even to the Islamic traditions and preventive measures in the wake of pandemics due to their indoctrination with a wrong interpretation of the Prophetic traditions. Prophet Muhammad

---

68   E Pennisi, 'Does Religion Influence Epidemics?' *Science*, 23 August 2011, https://www
      .sciencemag.org/news/2011/08/does-religion-influence-epidemics (accessed 22 January
      2023).
69   SN Park, 'Cults and Conservatives Spread Coronavirus in South Korea' *Foreign Policy*,
      27 February 2020, https://foreignpolicy.com/2020/02/27/coronavirus-south-korea-cults
      -conservatives-china/ (accessed 7 March 2022).
70   R Ayyub and S Farrell, 'Coronavirus Fears Lead Holy Land Catholic Churches to Give
      Communion by Hand Only' *Reuters*, 28 February 2020, https://www.reuters.com/article
      /us-china-health-religion-jerusalem/coronavirus-fears-lead-holy-land-catholic-churches
      -to-give-communion-by-hand-only-idUSKCN20M20K (accessed 2 March 2022).
71   SE Rasmussen, 'Pilgrims to Muslim Holy Sites Risk Spreading Coronavirus' *The Wall
      Street Journal*, 27 February 2020, https://www.wsj.com/articles/pilgrims-to-muslim-holy
      -sites-risk-spreading-coronavirus-11582800152 (accessed 2 March 2022).
72   Mufti Muneeb Ur Rehman Press Conference, 14 April 2020, https://www.youtube.com
      /watch?v=D9Z7bGhBzkM (accessed 15 April 2022).

(PBUH) commanded on the matter of on physical distancing that "those with contagious diseases should be kept away from those who are healthy".[73] But Indian Muslims have not been adhering to the command of Prophet and bringing the Islamic traditions in disrepute and controversy. In the case of COVID-19 symptoms, the Prophet (PBUH) stated that "do not cause harm or return harm",[74] but Muslims have caused harm to others by avoiding, hiding, and quarrelling with medical personnel and law enforcement agencies. Muslims associated with *Tablighi Jamat* have significantly contributed to the spread of coronavirus.

In this regard, there is Prophetic teaching on travel bans where he said that "do not enter a land where the plague (a contagious ailment) has broken out; don't leave from where it has broken out".[75] Another Prophetic command is there on staying at home: "those stay at home to protect themselves and others are under the protection of Allah."[76] But Muslims have not been following these Prophetic commands; rather, they have allowed themselves to be the pawn in the hands of politico-religious cocktail operating within the Muslim community. In addition, the Prophet (PBUH) commanded that, if required, "the entire earth has been made a Masjid, except graveyards and washrooms",[77] therefore, Muslims' insistence of offering prayers only in Masjid during a pandemic is misplaced and violation of Prophetic Hadith (tradition). But there is cure and patience is the virtue as Prophet (PBUH) says that "there is no disease that Allah sent without sending for it a cure".[78] Still many Muslims in their localities have registered their desperation for vagrant behaviour throughout India. Face-masking is a Prophetic teaching that says "while sneezing, would cover his face with hand or with his garment"[79] and it further says that "every time you enter the home you must follow it as cleanliness is half of the faith"[80] but Muslims do not practice cleanliness as ordained and commanded in Islam.

Even the origin of the word "quarantine"[81] can be traced back to Islamic roots, namely to Prophetic guidance that says, "run away from the leper (the

---

73 Bukhari (6771) and Muslim (2221).
74 Sunnah Ibn Majah (2340).
75 Bukhari (5939) and Muslim (2340).
76 *Ibid.*
77 Tirmidhi (al-Salaah, 291).
78 Bukhari Vol. 7 Book 71 No. 582.
79 Abu Dawud, Tirmidhi Book 43 Hadith 2969, Muslim Sahih.
80 Muslim Sahih (223).
81 R Hashmi, 'Muslim Scholar Ibn Sina First Came up with Idea of Quarantine' *The Siasat Daily*, 6 April 2020, https://www.siasat.com/muslim-scholar-ibn-sina-first-came-idea -quarantine-1870313/ (accessed 7 April 2022). Ibn Sina was a Persian polymath who is

one with contagious ailment) as would you run away from a lion".[82] This is consistent with the state PDMs imposed in India. In case of home-quarantine, Prophet (PBUH) guided that "the plague (contagion) patient who remains in his home with patience and expectation of reward; knowing that nothing will befall him other than Allah's decree will attain the reward of a martyr".[83] It is here established that if humans are safe, then religion is also reliable. Thus, the state regulations under the EDA require mandatory quarantining of individuals having travel histories and people with COVID-19 symptoms. But there have been reports of jumping quarantine from many quarantine facilities even though state governments have applied innovative techniques[84] in implementing the quarantine and other PDMs. One of the methods could be an ink-stamp on the body of a quarantined person that can be erased after the termination of the forty-day quarantine period.

The *Imams* too are not interested in having the modernization of religious education imparted in the Madrassa system and they do not have any liking for modern English education for the Muslims in India – except for Sir Syed Ahmad Khan.[85] The political ambitions and vested interests of a few Muslim leaders and *Imams* are responsible for the Muslim community's educational, socioeconomic, and political disempowerment. These few individuals want to perpetuate and protect their political affairs at the expense of ordinary illiterate Muslims. Thus, these clerics have shaped the theological attitudes of vulnerable, marginalized, and defenceless Muslims who do not understand the real message of Islam. Ordinary Muslims do not understand the Arabic language, and they memorize the semantics[86] of the *Holy Quran* in Arabic verbatim without following its intent, message, and direction in a specific situation. Similarly, all *Hadith* are in Arabic and are explained in Urdu as per the

---

       regarded as one of the most significant physicians, astronomers, thinkers and writers of the Islamic Golden Age, and the father of early modern medicine.

82   Bukhari Vol. 7 Book 71 No. 608.

83   Musnad Ahmad, Muslim Sahih (1914); Bukhari (2829).

84   COVID-19 State-wise Status of Information available at https://www.mohfw.gov.in / (accessed 31 March 2022).

85   Sir Syed Ahmed Taqvi bin Syed Muhammad Muttaqi KCSI, commonly known as Sir Syed Ahmed Khan (October 17, 1817 – March 27, 1898) was an Educationist, Islamic pragmatist, Islamic reformer, and philosopher of 19th century British India. Born into a family with strong bonds with the Mughal court, Ahmed studied the Quran and Sciences within the court. Sir Syed Ahmed Khan was a social reformer, an architect of modern English education among the Muslims and founder of Aligarh Muslim University in British India in 1875 where he welcomed students from all religions.

86   M Alhawarat, 'Extracting Topics from the Holy Quran Using Generative Models' (2015) 6 *International Journal of Advanced Computer Science and Applications* 288–294.

understanding and wisdom of these *Imams* and other clerics. Their teachings are based on misplaced political perceptions against Hindus and Hinduism.

Unfortunately, most Muslim clerics in the Indian context are not well-versed in Islamic *Fiqah* (jurisprudence) principles and *Sunnah* (Prophetic conduct), and they have been indoctrinating, injecting, and influencing ordinary Muslims with the illiberal and puritan[87] interpretation[88] of Islam. In this regard, these *Imams* or *Maulvis* of the 21st century have created a division of Islam between *Allah's* (God) Islam and *Maulvis'* Islam and presented a dichotomy of preferences before the ordinary Muslims in India. *Allah's* Islam guides ordinary Muslims to follow all PDMs and other forms of governmental measures to combat the spread of COVID-19 in the light of Prophetic *Hadiths* (Traditions). In contrast, *Maulvis'* Islam is hate-driven against *Kafirs* (non-believers in Islam) and gives an opposite interpretation of all governmental guidelines and PDMs. *Maulvis* preach a reactionary and exclusive patriarchal orientation of Islam to ordinary Muslims.

Such preaching does not convey an inclusive interpretation of Islam that incorporates gender justice, coexistence, diversity and multiculturalism. Consequently, the idea of the unity of *Allah* has become subservient to these divisions that do not provide any uniformity, equality, or interpretive equilibrium in understanding the fundamentals of the *Holy Quran*. However, limiting the Holy Quran to religion alone will be an injustice to Islam as *Holy Quran* is a collection of all disciplines touching the human existence under the sun, and it provides divine guidance on health[89] to the entire Muslim *Ummah* (community). The Maulvis have bypassed these traits of Islam at the cost of socialization and international reciprocity in human interactions. It is said that adversities and calamities make people more sensible and humane in their deeds. But unfortunately, the coronavirus has not successfully transformed human beings into a better version.

---

87   EB Brown, 'After the Ramadan Affair: New Trends in Islamism in the West: Current Trends in Islamist Ideology' *Hudson Institute*, 12 September 2005, https://www.hudson.org /research/3780-after-the-ramadan-affair-new-trends-in-islamism-in-the-west (accessed 8 January 2022).

88   Al-Fatāwā al-ʿālamgīrīyah, Translated by Neil B. E. Baillie as A Digest of Moohummudan Law (1865), Reprint, Lahore, 1957. This is the work ordered by Sultan Awrangzib and based on the most famous Ḥanafī texts. It is also called Al-Fatāwā al-hindīyah.

89   SH Saadat, AA Chavoshi and K Ahmadi, 'A Brief Survey on Medical Ethics Regarding the Holy Quran and Isalmic Hadith' (2014) 1 *International Journal of Medical Reviews* 9–12.

5   Conclusion

Nature has taken humankind by the scruff of the neck and doomed it in the nethermost crust of boorishness. While COVID-19 pandemic could have been the 'universal equalizer' that has removed all kinds of distinction and discrimination in treating people of all ages, castes, creeds, gender, origin, races, religion, regions, opinions, and ideologies and serve as a catalyst to reassert the importance of humanity based on compassion, communal stability, social harmony, and (inter)national solidarity, it has been exploited along religious lines India. Hindu ethnonationalism alone did not undermine secularism[90] in post-colonial multireligious societies such as in India where neutral political discourse has increasingly been under threat. Any religion (Hinduism and Islam) itself – whether exploited for terrorist and radicalization ends – is equally infectious and effective[91] when used to distort secular democracy and disturb peaceful social stability.

On the one hand, the COVID-19 pandemic presented an opportunity for the FRAME community to target the entire Muslim community of India. Once-fringe elements of FRAME have occupied the liberal political space in India, but, unfortunately, FRAME-induced political discourse is the new normal. FRAME has even been questioning Muslims' nationality and citizenship credentials on religious lines. Yet, the Hindu community is unaware of the intersectionalities, dichotomies and intra-fragmentary dimensions of Islam in India and elsewhere. Therefore, all Indian Muslims cannot be clubbed with Muslims associated with *Tablighi Jamat* (TJ). They do not represent all Muslims in India and elsewhere.[92] On the other hand, *Tablighi Jamat* Muslims armed with the illiberal interpretation of Islamic norms were not amenable to adjust their religious preferences and choices in conformity with Prophetic teachings. Instead, they have brought the whole Muslim community into disrepute and stigmatization. Laws could never be complete at the time of their promulgation because future adverse situations cannot be reflected upon comprehensively. The propagation of theological perception by the FRAME community, on the one hand, and Maulvis, on the other hand, goes against the Indian constitutional values and the IHRL framework.

---

90   J Assayag, 'Spectral Secularism Religion, Politics and Democracy in India' (2003) 44 *European Journal of Sociology* 325–57.

91   R Saeidi, 'The Dialectic of Secularism and Religionism: Prof. Elizabeth Shakman Hurd' *Tehran Times*, 25 April 2020, https://www.tehrantimes.com/news/435030/The-dialectic -of-secularism-and-religionism-prof-Elizabeth (accessed 25 April 2022).

92   TJ has long been banned in Saudi Arabia due to its propagation of the Hanafi version of Islam, whereas Saudi Arabia follows the Shafi version of Islam.

Contrary to the blame-shifting on both sides of the divide and creation a communal narrative from a pandemic, a flexible, liberal, and accommodative construction of legislative language empowers states to recalibrate domestic laws in tune with the IHRL framework for addressing crises like COVID-19. If not, the health crisis can become an existential one and further erode secular democracy and disturb peaceful social stability. To secure those constitutional and societal ends, one must review the role of any religion that gives rise to discriminatory practices on their respective religious grounds that undermine basic human rights including the right to religion and the right to health. The COVID-19 pandemic in India presents an opportunity for researchers to envision critical ways out of the undeniable erosion of human rights due to inter-religious strife.

Note on the Contributor

Nafees Ahmad
Associate Professor, Faculty of Legal Studies, South Asian University, New Delhi. PhD (International Refugee Law and Human Right), LLM (International Law). Contact: drnafeesahmad@sau.ac.in

Humanitarian Relief from COVID-19: The Treatment of Iran under the U.S. Unilateral Sanctions

Zeynab Malakouti Khah and Clive Walker

Abstract

The Iranian population faces multiple dangers from COVID-19. Although COVID-19 is a global pandemic which must be countered through global cooperation, Iran experiences more intense harms due to the imposition of unilateral economic sanctions by the U.S. even though other factors such as the policies and actions of the Iranian government are also significant in alleviating the pandemic's impacts. Global cooperation with Iran is paralysed because of the unilateral sanctions imposed by the U.S., based on allegations of supporting terrorism, violating human rights, and developing nuclear weapons, with impact well beyond U.S. traders. Even though the U.S. has declared that humanitarian goods are exempt from sanctions, Iran has received limited humanitarian aid. As a result of the restraints on international transactions, Iran has the highest mortality rate due to COVID-19 in the Middle East and more limited health services than neighbouring countries. Global cooperation to combat COVID-19 conflicts with the 'maximum pressure' strategy adopted by the U.S. administration through withdrawal from the Joint Comprehensive Plan of Action ("JCPOA") in 2018. This article's unique contribution to the critique of sanctions is to explain and analyse from an Iranian perspective how the U.S. unilateral sanctions imposed on Iran have created impediments for Iran in accessing humanitarian goods, in particular medicine and medical devices, during the time of the COVID-19 pandemic. To this end, this article is divided into three sections. The first explores the legal rights of Iranians to access medicine, medical supplies and general humanitarian goods. The second explains and illustrates the failures of the U.S. humanitarian concessions, and in particular general licenses, due to Iran's lack of access to the international financial system. The third is also related to the failure of the U.S. humanitarian exemptions and points to bureaucratic impediments, particularly because of the need for specific authorisation from Office of Foreign Assets Control ("OFAC") in the U.S. Department of Treasury.

Keywords

humanitarian exemption – COVID-19 – unilateral sanctions – international financial system – right to health

1   Introduction

International and unilateral sanctions have been imposed on Iran since 1979 for several reasons, including the deterrence of nuclear proliferation, the violation of human rights and support for terrorism. Unilateral sanctions are used as a tool for foreign policy and are imposed through the application of several states' own domestic legislation, which may have national and extraterritorial aspects, and may be the subject of state pressure for enforcement through international instruments.[1] The focus of this article is on the effects of unilateral sanctions upon the civilian population as principally imposed by the United States, and but with the backing of some other jurisdictions, especially the European Union.[2] The comprehensive sanctions imposed by the United Nations Security Council ("UNSC") are also under scrutiny. The paper does not consider the extent to which the policies and actions of the Iranian government exacerbate the pandemic's impacts, whether in terms of inefficiencies in public health or in terms of domestic and foreign policies which have triggered sanctions.

The U.S. has unilaterally imposed sanctions on Iran since the hostage-taking crisis in 1979[3] and has expanded them since then. They currently comprise

---

1   See R Mohamad, 'Unilateral Sanctions in International Law: A Quest for Legality' in AZ Marossi and MR Bassett, *Economic Sanctions Under International Law: Unilateralism, Multilateralism, Legitimacy and Consequences* (Asser Press 2015); and R Barnes, 'U.S. Sanctions: Delisting, Applications, Judicial Review and Secret Evidence' in M Happold and P Eden (eds.), *Economic Sanctions and International Law* (Bloomsbury Publishing 2016); I Bogdanova, *Unilateral Sanctions in International Law and the Enforcement of Human Rights* (Brill 2022).

2   Note that Iran itself maintains an autonomous sanctions regime which it has invoked against U.S. persons allegedly involved in the killing of General Ghasem Soleimani, including Donald Trump and others, under the Act on Countering Violations of Human Rights and Adventurist and Terrorist Actions of the United States of America in the Region, https://en.mfa.ir/portal /NewsView/665556, 8 January 2022.

3   The US Sanctions: EO 12170, 12205 and 12211 (1979-1980), State Sponsor of Terror Designation (January 1984), EO 12613 (1987), EO 12938 (1994), EO 12957 and 12959 (1995), Iran and Libya Sanction Act of 1996, Pub.L. 104-172, 110 Stat. 1541, codified as amended at 50 U.S.C. ch. 35 s 1701 et seq., Iran Non-proliferation Act of 2000, Pub.L. 106-178, 114 Stat. 38, codified as amended at 50 U.S.C. ch. 35 s 1701, EO 13224 (2001), EO 13382 (2005), Iran Freedom Support Act of 2006, Pub.L. 109-293, 120 Stat. 1344, EO 13438 (2007), Comprehensive Iran Sanctions

'primary' and 'secondary' sanctions, with the result that both U.S. and non-U.S. citizens and companies that have 'substantial connections'[4] with the U.S. are expected to comply. The U.S. secondary sanctions restrict the third party's access to the U.S. markets if they have impugned business with Iran.[5] The U.S. is the most powerful enforcer of sanctions, but it is not unique since several other states have devised unilateral sanction regimes too.[6] The European Union ("EU") for its part imposes sanctions in pursuit of its Common Foreign and Security Policy.[7] Unlike the U.S., which applies the policy of containment, the European states had no intention of abandoning all links with Iran, so they continue to embrace the policy of some engagement with Iran. This stance has culminated in the Joint Comprehensive Plan of Action ("JCPOA") (2015–present).[8] Following the JCPOA, the UNSC issued resolution 2231 (2015) which terminated the ongoing UN Security Council Resolutions ("UNSCRs") against Iran which had related to arms sales and nuclear proliferation.[9] The UNSCR 2231 (2015), issued

---

Accountability and Divestment Act of 2010, Pub.L. 111–195, 124 Stat. 1312, EO 13553 (2010), EO 13572 (2011), EO 13590 (2011), USA PATRIOT ACT of 2011, Pub.L. 107-56, 115 Stat. 272, Section 1245, EO 13599 (2012), EO 13606 (2012), EO 13608 (2012), EO 13622 (2012).

4 For relevant factors in relation to Iranian sanctions, see U.S. Department of Treasury, 'FAQs: Iran Sanctions', https://home.treasury.gov/policy-issues/financial-sanctions/faqs/154 (accessed 17 March 2022).

5 B Han, 'The Role and Welfare Rationale of Secondary Sanctions: A Theory and a Case Study of the U.S. Sanctions Targeting Iran' (2018) 35(5) *Conflict Management and Peace Science* 474, 476; Pardis *Gheibi, 'The rise and fall of U.S. secondary sanctions'* (2022) 50 *Georgia Journal of International and Comparative Law* 389.

6 For example, UK sanctions arise under the Counter-Terrorism (International Sanctions) (EU Exit) Regulations (S.I. 2019/573), Iran (Sanctions) (Nuclear) (EU Exit) Regulations 2019 (S.I. 2019/461) and the Iran Human Rights (Sanctions) (EU Exit) Regulations 2019 (S.I. 2019/134), as issued under the Sanctions and Anti-Money Laundering Act 2018.

7 EU Council, 'Basic Principles on the Use of Restrictive Measures (Sanctions)', Doc. No. 10198/1/04 REV 1,7 June 2004, https://data.consilium.europa.eu/doc/document/ST-10198 -2004-REV-1/en/pdf (accessed 10 April 2023).

8 P Seeberg, 'The EU and the International Sanctions against Iran: European and Iranian Foreign and Security Policy Interest, and a Changing Middle East' (2016) 16080 *Nature*, https://doi.org/10.1057/palcomms.2016.80, 4–5 (accessed 10 April 2023).

9 UNSCRs 1696 (2006), 1737 (2006), 1747 (2007), 1803 (2008), 1835 (2008), 1929 (2009), 1984 (2011), 2049 (2012), 2105 (2013), 2159 (2014). See D Esfandiary and M Fitzpatrick, 'Sanctions on Iran: Defining and Enabling "Success"' (2011) 53 *Survival* 143; PE Dupont, 'Countermeasures and Collective Security: The Case of the EU Sanctions Against Iran' (2012) 17 *Journal of Conflict and Security Law* 301; H Nakanishi, 'The Construction of the Sanctions Regime Against Iran: Political Dimensions of Unilateralism' in AZ. Marossi and MR. Bassett (eds.), *Economic Sanctions under International Law* (Springer 2015) 23-41; O Borszik, 'International Sanctions against Iran and Tehran's Responses: Political Effects on the Targeted Regime' (2016) 22 *Contemporary Politics* 20.

in part under Article 41 of the UN Charter,[10] endorsed the JCPOA and terminated the provisions of the previous UNSCRs against Iran. Thereafter, the EU and the U.S. lifted nuclear-related economic and financial sanctions against Iran; however, some restrictions remain in force.[11] Furthermore, the U.S., under the Trump administration, withdrew from the JCPOA on 8 May 2018 and unilaterally reinstated highly restrictive sanctions against Iran.[12]

The purpose of sanctions is to coerce a change in the target state's behaviour; thus, sanctions weaken a target by denying access to economic and military resources and by growing public deprivation related to a detrimental economic situation and by causing political instability.[13] Based on the 'naïve theory' of sanctions explained by Johan Galtung, the more value-deprivation which is caused by the system, the more political disintegration occurs, and then the greater chance that disintegration will lead to negotiation.[14] However, this theory might not be pursued or secured in all cases. Sometimes, sanctions barely impact upon the capacity, stability or power of the targeted political regime. Yet, even if the target state remains resilient against sanctions, populations may become vulnerable because of economic pressures and also, due to the regime's policy of resistance to the sanctions, because residents try to comply with their government's policy rather than protest against it. This outcome has arguably applied to Iran after the U.S. withdrawal from the JCPOA in 2018, whereby Iran's behaviour did not change and Iran gained more power in the

---

10   UNSCR 2231 (2015), Arts 7, 8, 9, 11, 12, 13, 16, 21, 22 and 23. See: M Rosenthal, 'United Nations Security Council 2231 and Joint Comprehensive Plan of Action' (2016) 55(1) *International Legal Materials* 98; DR Haupt, 'Legal Aspects of the Nuclear Accord with Iran and Its Implementation: International Law Analysis of Security Council Resolution 2231 (2015)' in JL Black-Branch and Dieter Fleck (eds.), *Nuclear Non-Proliferation in International Law - Volume III* (Springer 2016); ZS Sharegh and A Abedini, 'The Relationship between Sanction Committee 1737 and Joint Commission in Light of Implementation of Joint Comprehensive Plan of Action: Terminating or Suspending?' (2017) 18(53) *Pizhūhish-i ḥuqūq-i 'umūmī* 149; O Irani, 'The Joint Comprehensive Plan of Action and its Looming Shadow on American-Iranian Relations' (2017-2018) 42 *Seton Hall Legislative Journal* 401.

11   European Council, 'EU Restrictive Measures against Iran', https://www.consilium.europa .eu/en/policies/sanctions/iran/ (accessed 10 April 2023).

12   White House, 'President Donald J. Trump is Ending United States Participation in an Unacceptable Iran Deal' (Fact Sheet, 8 May 2018), https://trumpwhitehouse.archives.gov /briefings-statements/president-donald-j-trump-ending-united-states-participation -unacceptable-iran-deal (accessed 10 March 2022).

13   D Peksen, 'Political Effectiveness, Negative Externalities, and the Ethics of Economic Sanctions' (2019) 33 *Ethics & International Affairs* 279, 281.

14   J Galtung, 'On the Effects of International Economic Sanctions: With Examples from the Case of Rhodesia' (1967) 19 *World Politics* 378, 388.

region.[15] The sanctions have not seriously undermined Iran's political stability, despite the decline in the economic situation of the population, nor have Iran's foreign policies markedly shifted,[16] although the protests following the death of Mahsa Amini while she was under arrest by the Morality Police in September 2022, have been strengthened by other factors, such as economic pressures due to the imposed sanctions, Conversely, based on the literature about various sanctions regimes operative in the 1990s and 2000s (including against Iraq), links were found between the imposed sanctions and a deterioration in the health and well-being of populations living in targeted countries.[17] This tendency also applies in the case of Iran.[18]

There is no doubt that economic sanctions not only cause socio-economic and political damage to the targeted state,[19] but they also have adverse effects on the human rights. Although there is a distinction between international and unilateral sanction regimes, the unilateral sanctions regime against Iran can be considered as 'comprehensive' in impact, similar to the previous UNSC sanction regime imposed on Iraq.[20] The adverse effect of economic sanctions on human rights, as both intended and unintended consequences, are well-documented and have a negative effect on public health, economic conditions,

---

15   H Rome, 'Iran Is Doing Just Fine' (*Foreign Affairs*, 5 November 2019), https://www.foreig naffairs.com/articles/iran/2019-11-05/iran-doing-just-fine (accessed 10 October 2021). See also: F Bagherzadeh, 'Unilateral Economic Sanctions and Protecting US National Security' (2021) 44(2) *Hastings International and Comparative Law Review* 168.

16   See SF Dizaji and MR Farzanegan, 'Do Sanctions Constrain Military Spending of Iran?' (2021) 32 *Defence and Peace Economics* 125–150; S Ghasseminejad and MR Jahan-Parvar, 'The Impact of Financial Sanctions: The Case of Iran' (2021) 43 *Journal of Policy Modeling* 601-621; AM Kelishomi and R Nisticò, "Employment Effects of Economic Sanctions in Iran' (2022) 151 *World Development* 105760; IMF, Regional Economic Outlook, https://data.imf .org/?sk=4CC54C86-F659-4B16-ABF5-FAB77D52D2E6&sId=1390030109571 (accessed 10 March 2022).

17   E Moret, 'Humanitarian Impacts of Economic Sanctions on Iran and Syria' (2015) 24 *European Security* 120 at 123. See also A Shehabaldin and WM Laughlin Jr, 'Economic Sanctions against Iraq: Human and Economic Costs' (1999) 3(4) *International Journal of Human Rights* 1; SH Allen and DJ Lektzian, 'Economic Sanctions: A Blunt Instrument?' (2013) 50 *Journal of Peace Research* 121.

18   See: A Omidi, 'The United States' Breaching of the Iranian People's Right to Health and Its Legal Liability in Donald Trump's Administration' (2021) 27(2) *Australian Journal of Human Rights* 249; P Bastani and et al., 'Universal Health Coverage under the Joint Comprehensive Plan of Action's Sanctions: Strategic Purchasing Approach in the Iranian Health System' (2021) 36 *Health Promotion International* 693-702; and G Danaei and et al., 'The Harsh Effects of Sanctions on Iranian Health' (2019) 394(10197) *The Lancet* (*British edition*) 468.

19   D Peksen, 'Better or Worse? The Effect of Economic Sanctions on Human Rights' (2009) 46 *Journal of Peace Research* 59.

20   M Happold, 'Targeted Sanctions and Human Rights' in M Happold and P Eden (eds.), *Economic Sanctions and International Law* (Hart Publishing 2016) 87.

civil society, development, employment, gender equality and the education of the population of the targeted state.[21] Even with humanitarian exemptions, the negative humanitarian impacts of sanctions can be directly and indirectly observed.[22]

The current UN Special Rapporteur on unilateral sanctions, Alena Douhan, after visiting Iran in May 2022, has mentioned that "the weight of secondary sanctions deepened the negative impact of sanctions, undermining the economy, increasing poverty and threatening the health and nutrition of the most vulnerable".[23] The former UN Special Rapporteur on unilateral sanctions imposed upon Iran, Idriss Jazairy, underlined that "the unjust and harmful sanctions are destroying the economy and currency of Iran, driving millions of people into poverty and making imported goods unaffordable".[24] Iranian officials have called the unilateral U.S. sanctions acts of "economic terrorism/ economic war", because they target innocent people through the curbing of trade and investment with other countries.[25] In October 2011, the U.S. Republican Senator, Mark Kirk said that it was "okay to take the food out of the mouths of the citizens from a government that's plotting an attack directly on American soil".[26] Such a statement illustrates that the U.S. authorities know about the intended and unintended damaging consequences of unilateral sanctions on the health of the population of Iran. This U.S. stance on sanctions have been criticised by prominent figures in third countries. Senior diplomats and defence officials from around the world—including former chief European Union diplomat, Federica Mogherini, and former Director General of the

---

21 See: J Galtung, 'On the Effects of International Economic Sanctions: With Examples from the Case of Rhodesia' (1967) 19 *World Politics* 378; T Weiss et al. (eds.), *Political Gain and Civilian Pain: Humanitarian Impacts of Economic Sanctions* (Rowman and Littlefield, 1997); T Weiss, 'Sanctions as a Foreign Policy Tool: Weighing Humanitarian Impulses' (1999) 36 *Journal of Peace Research* 499.

22 Moret, *supra* note 17, 123-4.

23 See: https://www.ohchr.org/sites/default/files/2022-05/Iran-country-visit-conclusions-SR -UCM-17May2022%20-EnglishPersian.docx (accessed 11 June 2022).

24 I Jazairy, United Nations Special Rapporteur, 'Iran Sanctions are Unjust and Harmful, Says UN Expert Warning against Generalised Economic War' (OHCHR, 22 August 2018), https:// www.ohchr.org/en/press-releases/2018/08/iran-sanctions-are-unjust-and-harmful-says -un-expert-warning-against?LangID=E&NewsID=23469 (accessed 16 March 2022).

25 M J Zarif, Iran Foreign Minister, 'امریکا اقتصادی تروریسم درمورد ظریف توییت Zarif's Tweet on the US Economic Terrorism', (*Mashregh News*, 14 June 2019), https://www.mashreghnews .ir/news/966614/امریکا-اقتصادی-تروریسم-درباره-ظریف-توییت accessed 21 June 2019; H Rouhani, Iran President, 'Sanction is Economic Terrorism اقتصادی تروریسم یعنی تحریم' (*Donya-e-eqtesad*, 22 November 2018), https://donya-e-eqtesad.com (accessed 21 June 2019).

26 J Rogin, 'Kirk: Time to Collapse the Central Bank of Iran' (Foreign Policy, 11 October 2012), https://foreignpolicy.com/2011/10/11/kirk-time-to-collapse-the-central-bank-of-iran/ accessed 10 April 2023.

International Atomic Energy Agency, Ambassador Hans Blix—signed a letter in 2020 calling for the Trump administration to ease immediately sanctions against Iran.[27] The EU also called upon other jurisdictions, such as the U.S., to ensure that the sanctions do not obstruct the global fight against COVID-19.[28]

Even before the COVID-19 pandemic, Iran faced barriers to providing required medicine and medical equipment due to the U.S. unilateral sanctions.[29] In the pending case before the International Court of Justice ("ICJ"), with regard to the claim of Iran concerning the alleged violations of the Treaty of Amity, Economic Relations and Consular Rights between The United States of America and Iran (1955) ("the Treaty of Amity") because of the U.S. decision to reimpose sanctions after the withdrawal from the JCPOA,[30] the ICJ considered that the restriction on the purchase and importation of goods relating to humanitarian needs may have a serious impact on the health and lives of individuals in Iran.[31] Moreover, the ICJ ordered that the U.S. must remove any impediments from the measures taken by them on 8 May 2018 relating to the free exportation of medicines, medical devices, foodstuffs, agricultural commodities, and goods and services for the safety of aviation. The U.S. must also ensure that the transfer of funds related to humanitarian needs is not subject to any restrictions.[32] The immediate response of the U.S. to the judgment was

27   European Leadership Network, The Iran Project, 'Transatlantic Call to Ease Humanitarian Trade with Iran due to the COVID-19 Pandemic', https://www.europeanleadershipnetwork .org/wp-content/uploads/2020/04/06042020-ELN-IP-US-Sanctions-Iran-Humanitarian -Trade-Statement-FINAL.pdf (accessed 16 June 2021).

28   European Parliament, 'EU-Iran: The Way Forward, Can the JCPOA Survive the Trump Presidency? (July 2020), https://www.europarl.europa.eu/RegData/etudes/BRIE/2020/652001 /EPRS_BRI(2020)652001_EN.pdf (accessed 20 September 2021).

29   UN Country Team in Iran, 'Building Back Better: UN Iran Socio-Economic Recovery Programme Against the Impact of COVID-19' (June 2020), https://reliefweb.int/report /iran-islamic-republic/building-back-better-un-iran-socio-economic-recovery -programme-against (accessed 28 February 2021).

30   UNTS 284 (p. 93), https://treaties.un.org/pages/showdetails.aspx?objid=080000028014 2196 (accessed 10 June 2022).

31   *Islamic Republic of Iran v. United States of America, Alleged Violations of the 1955 Treaty of Amity, Economic Relations, and Consular Rights: Request for the Indication of Provisional Measures*, No. 175, ICJ, para 91, 3 October 2018. See also the earlier and narrower application, *Certain Iranian Assets (Islamic Republic of Iran v. United States of America)*, https:// www.icj-cij.org/en/case/164, which commenced on 14 June 2016, also based on violation of Treaty of Amity, Economic Relations and Consular Rights and in response to the judgment of the U.S. Supreme Court in *Bank Markazi aka The Central Bank of Iran v. Peterson* 578 US 948 (2016) in which assets were seized from the Iranian national bank to compensate victims of the 1983 bombing of a U.S. military base in Beirut; the case has not advanced since 2019.

32   *Ibid*, para 98.

to announce its withdrawal from the 1955 Treaty, and the former U.S. Secretary of State under the Trump administration, Mike Pompeo, said the U.S. would ignore the ruling.[33] Formal renunciation was issued on 3 October 2018 (with effect a year later),[34] but, though the U.S. withdrawal did not affect the Treaty of Amity's applicability in the cases currently pending before the ICJ,[35] the litigation before the ICJ has not yet advanced beyond the rejection of preliminary objections to jurisdiction.[36] Aside from the obstacles to the operation of the ICJ which resulted from COVID precautions applied between 2020 to 2022,[37] this limited activity in the litigation might suggest that attention is being focused on the renegotiation of the JCPOA rather than this indirect avenue for disputation. The prospects for Iran at the merits stage of the case may also be clouded since the ICJ has accepted in preliminary rulings that the scope of the national security exception in Article XX(1) of the 1955 Treaty, which excludes national security action from its purview, might be considered in the light of U.S. domestic law on sovereign immunity.[38]

Although the U.S. has inserted some humanitarian exemptions within its sanction regime in order to alleviate the humanitarian impacts of the sanctions (as described further below), in practice the General Licenses issued to

---

33   C Morello, 'U.S. Terminates 1955 Treaty with Iran, Calling it an 'Absolute Absurdity' (*Washington Post*, 3 October 2018), https://www.washingtonpost.com/world/national -security/us-terminates-1955-treaty-with-iran-calling-it-an-absolute-absurdity /2018/10/03/839b39a6-3bcf-42b1-a2d5-04bfe1c5f660_story.html (accessed 16 June 2021).

34   Preliminary Objections: Judgment of 3 February 2021, https://www.icj-cij.org/public /files/case-related/175/175-20210203-JUD-01-00-EN.pdf, para 24 (accessed 10 June 2022).

35   See *Certain Iranian Assets (Islamic Republic of Iran v. United States of America)* Judgment of 13 February 2019: Preliminary objections, https://www.icj-cij.org/public/files/case-related /164/164-20190213-JUD-01-00-EN.pdf, para 30 (accessed 10 June 2022).

36   Preliminary Objections: Judgment of 3 February 2021, https://www.icj-cij.org/public /files/case-related/175/175-20210203-JUD-01-00-EN.pdf (accessed 10 June 2022).

37   See Press Release 2022/20, https://www.icj-cij.org/public/files/press-releases/0/000-2022 0603-PRE-01-00-EN.pdf (accessed 10 June 2022).

38   See E Chachko, 'Certain Iranian Assets: The International Court of Justice Splits the Difference between the United States and Iran' *Lawfare* 14 September 2019, https://www .lawfareblog.com/certain-iranian-assets-international-court-justice-splits-difference -between-united-states-and-iran (accessed 10 June 2022). See also SMH Razavi and F Zeynodini, 'Economic Sanctions and Protection of Fundamental Human Rights: A Review of the ICJ's Ruling on Alleged Violations of the Iran-U.S. Treaty of Amity' (2020) 29 *Washington International Law Journal* 303; A Alexander and S Sarkar, 'Shifting Interpretation in International Court of Justice's Decision in the Islamic Republic of Iran v. United States of America: A Deliberate Step?' (2022) 43 *Liverpool Law Review* 97; and JR Harper, 'U.S. Sanctions Policy on Trial: The Alleged Violations Litigation and Opportunities for Other States to Follow this Strategy' (2022) 62 *Virginia Journal of International Law* 463.

allow export and reexport of the humanitarian goods (explained in Section 3.1) are subject to three major obstacles which have not been substantially alleviated in reaction to the COVID pandemic. One is an exhaustive number of conditions imposed on exporters, which are difficult to verify. Another is the difficulty of transacting financial arrangements when Iran does not have access to the international financial payment systems, such as the Society for Worldwide Interbank Financial Telecommunication ("SWIFT").[39] The third problem is related to the need for specific bureaucratic authorisation to export and reexport some goods (explained in Section 3.2).

Not surprisingly, Javaid Rehman, the current UN Special Rapporteur on the Situation of Human Rights in Iran, noted that many humanitarian organisations still encounter difficulties in obtaining the cash and supplies needed to carry out their work.[40] After the outbreak of COVID-19 in early 2020, the imposed sanctions cause more problems for Iran compared to other countries facing the same threat.[41] As mentioned previously, the analysis of the state's management of the COVID-19 is beyond the scope of this paper. As for sanctions, Javad Zarif, a former Iranian Foreign Minister, in a letter to the Secretary General of the UN, stated that due to the illegal secondary sanctions of the U.S., even if suitable foreign medical suppliers were found, potential transactions were impossible because of the imposed sanctions on shipping, insurance and financial transactions.[42]

The sanctions imposed on Iran have both direct and indirect humanitarian impacts. The U.S. sanctions directly interfere with the international trade in vital goods, resulting in the shortage of medical supplies and medicine. As an example, in 2018, the MAHAK charity, which is the only Iranian charity dedicated to the treatment of cancer in children, revealed a shortage of oncology drugs.[43] In addition, the Iranian Centre for International Criminal Law ("ICICL") filed a complaint against a Swedish Company, Molnlycke, for

---

39   K Katzman, *Iran Sanctions* (Congressional Research Service RS20871, 2022) 45.

40   UNGA, 'Report of the Special Rapporteur on the Situation of Human Rights in the Islamic Republic of Iran', HRC, UN Doc. A/HRC/43/61, 28 January 2020.

41   PE Dupont, 'Unilateral Sanctions as Unilateral Coercive Measures: Discussing Coercion at the UN Level' in C Beaucillon, *Research Handbook on Unilateral and Extraterritorial Sanctions* (Edward Elgar 2021) 375.

42   'Letter to the Secretary General of the UN,' 12 March 2020, https://www.presstv.com /Detail/2020/03/12/620709/Iran-letter-United-Nations-US-sanctions-medicine-medical -coronavirus-epidemic (accessed 14 March 2020).

43   G Mallard, F Sabet, and J Sun, 'The Humanitarian Gap in the Global Sanction Regime' (2020) 26 *Global Governance* 121. See further https://mahak-charity.org/ (accessed 12 March 2022).

stopping exports of life-saving medical dressings to Iran due to the unilateral sanctions which it claimed caused the death of children with rare diseases.[44] As for indirect impacts, the drop in oil sales and other related raw materials,[45] together with penalties for foreign investments[46] and obstructions to international financial institutions, have led to a prolonged decline in the Iranian government's budgetary capabilities to prepare for the humanitarian needs of the people.[47] Furthermore, the purported humanitarian exemptions in U.S. policy have not alleviated the severe difficulties for Iran to access to humanitarian goods, especially medicine and medical devices in response to COVID-19.[48] The evidence to hand is the COVID was not a watershed in ameliorating sanctioning practices. In this regard, the UN Special Rapporteur, Alena Douhan, stated that regardless of the previous or new exemptions, 'the vagueness and complexity of the licensing processes, the persistent fear among producers and suppliers, the restrictions in the processing of payments, and the obstacles to shipping these goods have rendered medicine and medical devices inaccessible to the Iranian public'.[49]

The three major issues with regards to unilateral sanctions are as follows: whether the imposition of sanctions by one country or a group of countries is lawful; whether those countries should seek to impose extraterritorial effects of their sanctions on a third country; and whether there have been violations of individual human rights of the population of the sanctioned state. The lawfulness of the device of unilateral sanctions is beyond the aim of this paper,[50] so the extraterritorial effect and the violation of human rights in association with the humanitarian aid during the COVID-19 pandemic in Iran will

---

44 M Gadzo, 'Iranians with Rare Disease are Dying under US Sanctions' *Aljazeera*, 28 May 2021, https://www.aljazeera.com/news/2021/5/28/iranians-with-epidermolysis-bullosa-dying -under-us-sanctions (accessed 12 October 2021).

45 International Monetary Fund, Crude Oil Exports for Iran, Islamic Republic of [IRNNX-GOCMBD], retrieved from FRED, Federal Reserve Bank of St. Louis, https://fred.stlouisfed .org/series/IRNNXGOCMBD 28 December 2021 (accessed 10 April 2023).

46 Moret, *supra* note 17, 126.

47 See further JM Jeong, 'Coercive Diplomacy and Foreign Supply of Essential Goods: Effects of Trade Restrictions and Foreign Aid Suspension on Food Imports' (2021) 32 *Defence and Peace Economics* 989.

48 See: A Takian, A Raoofi, and S Kazempour-Ardebilid, 'COVID-19 Battle during the Toughest Sanctions against Iran' (2020) *Lancet* 28 March-3 April 395 (10229) 1035.

49 See: https://www.ohchr.org/sites/default/files/2022-05/Iran-country-visit-conclusions-SR -UCM-17May2022%20-EnglishPersian.docx> (accessed 11 June 2022).

50 See: A Almutawa, 'The Qatar Crisis, Legitimacy, and the Use of Sanctions against Terrorist Financing' in K Benson, C King, and C Walker (eds), *Assets, Crimes, and the State: Innovation in 21st Century Legal Responses* (Routledge, 2020).

be examined. In this regard, two main aspects will be evaluated. Firstly, some medical supplies related to COVID-19 apparently qualify as permissible exports under the General Licenses within U.S. sanctions regimes, but the attendant financial transactions cannot be secured as Iran is barred from accessing the international financial system. Secondly, other medical supplies and devices need authorisation from the U.S. Office of Foreign Assets Control (OFAC – an agency of the Department of Treasury),[51] but the process is burdensome for applicants.

This article's original contribution to the critique of sanctions is to explain and analyse from an Iranian perspective how the U.S. unilateral sanctions on Iran have created impediments for Iran in accessing humanitarian goods, in particular medicine and medical devices, during the COVID-19 pandemic. To this end, the remainder of this article is divided into two sections. The first explores the rights of Iranians to access medicine, medical supplies and general humanitarian goods. The second explains and illustrates the failures of the U.S. humanitarian concessions and divided into two sub-sections: failure in the provision of medicines and other aid under general licenses due to Iran's lack of access to the international financial system; and failure in medicine and aid requiring specific authorisation due to the problems of bureaucracy.

2 The Right to Health

Although direct references to access to humanitarian assistance in human rights treaties are limited, a wide range of basic human rights are of relevance to its fulfilment, such as the right to life, the right to food, the right to water, the rights of the child, the rights of people with disabilities and the right to health.[52] The focus of this paper relates to the consequences of sanctions on the right to health due to the lack of access to medicine and medical devices, particularly to combat COVID-19.

With that focus in mind, the UN Universal Declaration of Human Rights (Article 25), the UN International Covenant on Economic, Social and Cultural Rights ("ICESCR") (Article 12) and the International Convention on the

---

51   U.S. Department of Treasury, 'Sanction Program and Information', https://home.treasury
     .gov/policy-issues/office-of-foreign-assets-control-sanctions-programs-and-information
     (accessed 16 June 2021).

52   See Swiss Federal Department of Foreign Affairs, 'Humanitarian Access: Handbook on
     the International Normative Framework' (2014) 40; PE Dupont, 'Human Rights Implica-
     tions of Sanctions' in M Asada (ed.), *Economic Sanctions in International Law and Practice*
     (Routledge 2020) 43–47.

Elimination of All Forms of Racial Discrimination (Article 5 (e) (iv)) all mention the right to health. Article 12(2) of the ICESCR also specifies that every state must take the necessary steps for "the prevention, treatment and control of epidemic, endemic, occupational and other diseases". Thus, State parties to the ICESCR have obligations to respect, protect and fulfil the right to health which includes refraining from interfering directly or indirectly with the enjoyment of this right and adopting the required measures towards the full realisation of the right to health.[53] According to the Committee on Economic, Social and Cultural Rights ("CESCR"), the state should "refrain at all times from imposing embargoes or similar measures restricting the supply of another state with adequate medicines and medical equipment".[54] The deleterious impact of sanctions on the right to health of people in targeted states has been highlighted in the resolutions and documents of the United Nations General Assembly ("UNGA")[55] and the Human Rights Council.[56]

As declared by the International Court of Justice, access to required medicine and medical devices is categorised as access to humanitarian goods, and there should occur no restriction on the importation and purchase of goods relating to humanitarian needs because the lack of access to such facilities may have a serious impact on the health and lives of individuals in Iran.[57]

Yet, in response to these international standards, Iran is not able to protect and fulfil the right to health[58] for the Iranian population because its ability is undermined due to the U.S. sanctions. The situation is becoming more dire, and Iran's confirmed deaths due to COVID-19 as of 24 March 2022 was 139,865, and it is believed the real number of deaths is four to seven times higher, which is one of the highest in the Middle East.[59] The rates in Iran reflect, at least in part, the adverse effects of the unilateral sanctions of the U.S.[60]

---

53   OHCHR, 'CESCR General Comment No. 14: The Right to the Highest Attainable Standard of Health (Art. 12)' E/C.12/2000/4, 11 August 2000, para 33.

54   *Ibid.*, para 41.

55   See UNGAR 66/156 (2011); UNGAR 68/162 (2013).

56   See Human Rights Council Resolution 15/24 (2011); Human Rights Council Resolution 27/21 (2014).

57   *Islamic Republic of Iran v. United States of America, Alleged Violations of the 1955 Treaty of Amity, Economic Relations, and Consular Rights: Request for the Indication of Provisional Measures*, No. 175, ICJ, para 91, 3 October 2018.

58   Javan Newspaper, (We have to control the corona in 4 months) کرونا را باید در ۴ ماه مهار کنیم, No. 23 (6283), 23 August 2021, p. 3.

59   https://ourworldindata.org/coronavirus/country/iran#what-is-the-cumulative-number -of-confirmed-deaths (accessed 25 March 2022).

60   UN Country Team in Iran, 'Building Back Better: UN Iran Socio-Economic Recovery Programme Against the Impact of COVID-19' (June 2020), https://reliefweb.int/report

The Iranian President and the Foreign Minister have repeatedly condemned the U.S. unilateral sanctions. Javad Zarif, the Iranian Foreign Minister, has commented that "This is the ugliest face of a government addicted to sanctions which wants to revive its abortive maximum pressure campaign through weakening Iran in the face of the corona."[61] As a result, the number of deaths due to COVID-19 in Iran, as of 31 May 2022, is higher in comparison to neighbouring states; total deaths then stood as follows: Saudi Arabia, 9,156; Kuwait 2.555; Turkey 98,969; Iraq 25,221; and Iran 141,331.[62]

Another important consideration here relates to extraterritorial obligations for the protection of human rights. It should be assessed as to whether state parties to the ICESCR have extraterritorial obligations to respect, protect and fulfil the rights under the ICESCR. The moral reason for extraterritorial obligations of the state is that the state should not violate human rights abroad, whilst they are prohibited from doing so at home.[63] Inhabitants of a targeted state should not lose their basic economic, social and cultural rights simply because their leaders have violated (allegedly) some norms relating to international peace and security.[64] Such a broad, cross-border concern for the well-being of human beings in other polities is at the heart of cosmopolitanism which underlies human rights.[65]

In more legal detail, Article 2(1) of the ICESCR states that "each State Party to the present Covenant undertakes to take steps, individually and through international assistance and cooperation, especially economic and technical, to the maximum of its available resources, with a view to achieving progressively the full realisation of the rights recognised in the present Covenant".[66] The article does not limit the obligations to the state's own territory or jurisdiction. In addition, General Comment 3 on the ICESCR states that the international cooperation for the realisation of the economic, social and cultural

/iran-islamic-republic/building-back-better-un-iran-socio-economic-recovery -programme-against (accessed 12 October 2021).

61 'Zarif on COVID-19 and Sanctions', https://iranprimer.usip.org/blog/2020/mar/31/zarif -covid-19-and-sanctions 30 March 2021 (accessed 7 June 2022).

62 See WHO, https://covid19.who.int/ (accessed 7 June 2022).

63 F Coomans, 'The Extraterritorial Scope of the ICESCR in the Work of the UN Committee on Economic, Social and Cultural Rights' (2011) 11 *Human Rights Law Review* 1, 6.

64 UN Committee on CESCR, 'General Comment No. 8: The Relationship Between Economic Sanctions and Respect for Economic, Social and Cultural Rights', E/C.12/1997/8, para 16, 12 December 1997.

65 See KA Appiah, *Cosmopolitanism: Ethics in a World of Strangers* (Allen Lane, 2006); R Fine, *Cosmopolitanism* (Routledge 2007).

66 See S Joseph, 'International Human Rights Law and the Response to the COVID-19 Pandemic' (2020) 11 *Journal of International Humanitarian Legal Studies* 249.

rights is an obligation of all states.[67] In short, the provisions of the ICESCR cannot be ignored, even in the case of economic sanctions due to international peace and security; under all circumstances, the human rights of people must be respected.[68] Even if it is supposed that the state of Iran has violated international laws (relating to nuclear proliferation or support for terrorism) and deserves sanctions, 'lawlessness of one kind should not be met by lawlessness of another kind, which pays no heed to the fundamental rights that underlie and give legitimacy to any such collective action'.[69] If the extraterritorial obligation of the states is accepted, the states which enforce unilateral sanctions, which diminish the economic, social and cultural rights of the Iranian people, are responsible for the violation of human rights, in particular, under the ICESCR. Generally, by using the Human Rights Impact Assessments tool ("HRIA"), sanctions are shown to have resulted in deteriorating overall welfare and lower access to necessities such as nutritious food, healthcare and medicine.[70]

An important countervailing argument to this more legalistic approach to human rights is that the U.S. has not ratified the ICESCR, so has no obligation to promote the enjoyment of the right to health of Iranians. However, this form of denial of responsibility may not be determinative since, at least in the context of the right to health as an aspect of the right to life in a pandemic, it is arguably contrary to the provisions of the UN Charter, the UDHR,[71] and the Articles of State Responsibility,[72] which are often recognised as international customary law.[73] For example, Art 1(3) of the UN Charter states that "to achieve international co-operation in solving international problems of an economic, social, cultural, or humanitarian character". Article 56 of the UN Charter obliges States to take 'joint and separate action' for the promotion of "solutions of international, economic, social, health". Article 25 of the UDHR asserts more directly that "everyone has the right to a standard of living adequate for the health and well-being of himself and of his family, including medical care".

---

67 OHCHR, 'CESCR General Comment No. 3: The Nature of States Parties' Obligations (Art. 2, Para. 1, of the Covenant)', E/1991/23, para 14, 14 December 1990.

68 UN Committee on CESCR, 'General Comment No. 8: The Relationship Between Economic Sanctions and Respect for Economic, Social and Cultural Rights', E/C.12/1997/8, para 7, 12 December 1997.

69 *Ibid*, para 16.

70 F Kokabisaghi, 'Assessment of the Effects of Economic Sanctions on Iranians' Right to Health by Using Human Rights Impact Assessment Tool: A Systematic Review' (2018) 7(5) *International Journal Health Policy Management* 374.

71 UDHR, Arts. 22, 28.

72 The Articles on State Responsibility of the International Law Commission, Arts. 16–18.

73 S Joseph, *Blame it on the WTO? A Human Right Critique* (Oxford University Press, 2011) 246–248.

These are strong foundations for the extraterritorial obligation to respect the right to health, including under customary international law. In addition to the above-mentioned reasons, the right to health can be categorised as a *jus cogens* norm which results in obligations *erga omnes*. The concept of *jus cogens* can be applied to the right to health because it is an integral aspect of the protection of other *jus cogens* rights, such as the right to life.[74]

A more expansive view of state responsibility regarding the right to health may also be warranted because of the differences in enforcement and potential limitation of rights between the International Covenant on Civil and Political Rights ("ICCPR") and the ICESCR cannot be ignored. The provisions of ICESCR leave more room for potential restrictions, and the existing procedures of the ICESCR rely on persuasion rather than adjudication. Due to the lack of provisions that allow states or individuals to complain under the ICCPR to a review body equivalent to the Human Rights Committee, the ICESCR Committee has noted that the absence of the procedures "places significant constraints on the ability of the Committee to develop jurisprudence or case-law and, of course, greatly limits the chances of victims of abuses of the ICESCR obtaining international redress."[75]

In summary, the production, availability and distribution of essential medical and pharmaceutical equipment and supplies are hindered by the economic sanctions against Iran. The situation has become worse because of COVID-19 with very limited concessions being made for the deadly threat caused by the pandemic, as will now be further explored.

3   Failure of U.S. Humanitarian Concessions

3.1   *Medicines and Aid Under General Licences and the Problems of Finance*

3.1.1   Humanitarian Exemptions

Humanitarian exemptions carve out a space in sanction regimes to allow humanitarian actors to deliver their services without the risk of contravening the regimes. One of the reasons for changing the international policy from comprehensive sanctions to targeted or smart sanctions was the dire humanitarian

---

74   P Zenovic, 'Human Rights Enforcement via Peremptory Norms: A Challenge to State Sovereignty' (RGSL Research Paper 2012), 37.

75   United Nations Committee on Economic, Social and Cultural Rights, Fact Sheet No. 16 (Rev.1) (1991), https://www.ohchr.org/Documents/Publications/FactSheet16rev.1en.pdf (accessed 22 March 2022).

consequences of earlier sanction regimes, in particular those imposed on Iraq during the time of Saddam Hussein.[76] In response, humanitarian exemptions have been devised to help good-faith humanitarian actors avoid punishment.[77] Yet, criticisms remain that humanitarian exemptions are not fit for their intended purpose and even help to sustain unpalatable regimes.[78] The concerns about the limitations imposed on humanitarian actions are strong in the case of Iran, as discussed below.

Trade sanctions can prevent countries from importing or exporting goods or services in certain sectors. Humanitarian exemptions now commonly moderate trade sanctions in different sanctions regimes.[79] The existing U.S. regime against Iran provides humanitarian exemptions for the supply of medicine, medical devices, food and agricultural commodities.[80] The OFAC has issued several general medical licenses to allow for the export of medicine and medical devices to Iran.[81] However, there remain three salient barriers against Iran's access to humanitarian goods to combat COVID-19. They include: an exhaustive number of conditions imposed on exporters, which are difficult to verify; the difficulty of transacting financial arrangements when Iran does not have access to the international financial system; and the requirement for a specific authorisation from the OFAC for medicine and medical devices which are not

---

76   M Happold, 'Targeted Sanctions and Human Rights' in M Happold and P Eden (eds), *Economic Sanctions and International Law* (Hart Publishing, 2016) 87.

77   K King, N Modirzadeh and D Lewis, 'Understanding Humanitarian Exemptions: UN Security Council Sanctions and Principled Humanitarian Action' (Harvard Law School Program on International Law and Armed Conflict Counterterrorism and Humanitarian Engagement Project 2016), https://dash.harvard.edu/bitstream/handle/1/29998395/Understanding_Humanitarian_Exemptions_April_2016.pdf?sequence=1 (accessed 29 November 2022).

78   *Ibid.*

79   B Smith, 'Coronavirus: Sanctions and Humanitarian Crises' (House of Commons Library, Number CBP 8913, 13 May 2020) 5.

80   See *Guidance on the Sale of Food, Agricultural Commodities, Medicine, and Medical Devices by Non-U.S. Persons to Iran*, (https://ofac.treasury.gov/media/7846/download?inline, 25 July 2013, as amended. A full list of advisories, guides, and licenses can be found at https://ofac.treasury.gov/sanctions-programs-and-country-information/iran-sanctions) (accessed 10 April 2023).

81   The Iranian Transaction and Sanctions Regulations, 31 C.F.R. Part 560, is comprised of two parts: (i) an authorization to conduct commercial sales, exports or reexports of qualifying goods, at 31 C.F.R. s 560.530; and (ii) an authorization to engage in transactions for the payment of exports and reexports of qualifying goods, (31 C.F.R. ss 560.532, 560.533). General License 8. issued pursuant to the Global Terrorism Sanctions Regulations (GTSR) and the ITSR, by s.560.545, describes a specific licensing policy to authorize non-governmental organizations and other entities to engage in certain projects or activities in or related to Iran that are designed to directly benefit the Iranian people.

categorised as having a standard exemption under rule "EAR99" in the Commerce Control List under the Export Administration Regulations ("EAR").[82] This section will examine the first and second barriers, and the next section will examine the specific authorisation needed for some humanitarian goods and its consequences.

As for conditions imposed on exporters, due to the COVID-19 outbreak, alongside the existing general licenses, the U.S. has taken some extra steps to allow humanitarian aid even though they are not very effective or reasonable in solving the problem.[83] Firstly, in a Fact Sheet published by the OFAC in 2020, it is emphasised that "for COVID-19 related support, the Treasury continues to stress that U.S. and non-U.S. persons may provide such humanitarian goods— including medicine and medical devices—to Iran under the existing exemptions, exceptions and authorisations in U.S. sanctions laws and regulations".[84] Moreover, there are exemptions for humanitarian goods in the trade sanctions in relation to combating COVID-19. For example, most medicine and medical devices, including certain personal protective equipment and other items used for COVID-19 related treatment, such as medical gowns, eye shields and goggles, surgical gloves, face shields, certain respirators and masks, and some types of ventilators, already qualify for export and reexport to Iran under general licenses, without the need for further authorisation from OFAC.[85]

Aside from these technicalities, the Trump administration offered Iran assistance via the World Health Organisation (WHO), to help it battle the COVID-19 outbreak in early 2020, though Iran refused the aid.[86] The offer and refusal must be seen in the context of the designation of the Central Bank of Iran as a terrorist entity under Executive Order 13224 on 9 September 2019.[87] This designation restricted Iran's ability to use its Central Bank accounts abroad to pay for imports of humanitarian items because the terrorism designation does not

---

82   15 CFR ss 730-774, issued by the United States Department of Commerce, Bureau of Industry and Security (BIS) under the Export Administration Act of 1979 (as amended at 50 U.S.C. ch. Appendix - Export Regulation s.2401).

83   See: M Fitzpatrick, 'Sanctioning Pandemic-Plagued Iran' (2020) 63 *Survival* 93–102.

84   U.S. Department of Treasury, 'Publication of a Fact Sheet on the Provision of Humanitarian Assistance and Trade to Combat COVID-19' (Fact Sheet, 16 April 2020), https://ofac. treasury.gov/recent-actions/20200416 (accessed 10 April 2023).

85   *Ibid.*

86   Katzman, *supra* note 39.

87   https://home.treasury.gov/news/press-releases/sm780 (accessed 1 October 2021). The Executive Order was issued under the International Emergency Economic Powers Act (50 U.S.C. s 1701 et seq.), the National Emergencies Act (50 U.S.C. s 1601 et seq.), the United Nations Participation Act 1945 (22 U.S.C. s 287c), and 3 U.S.C. 301.

allow for a humanitarian exception. Following some criticism against the U.S. policy in February 2020, and as the COVID-19 pandemic grew in Iran, the Treasury Department issued General License 8 to permit transactions with Iran's Central Bank for the purchase of humanitarian items; the General License exempts any transactions from sanctions that are with Iran's Central Bank and are for "the sale of agricultural commodities, food, medicine, or medical devices to Iran".[88]

Despite this apparent concession, doubts remain about whether the U.S. authorities truly intend to help or hinder the response to COVID-19 in Iran. The first reason is that the U.S. has not entered into any discussion about the design or procedures of the temporary sanctions relief. The second is that the U.S. State Department has issued claims that the Iranian government exaggerates reports of the effects of U.S. sanctions on its medical imports.[89] Thirdly, the U.S. believes that the Iranian government is exaggerating the impacts of the sanctions[90] and so opposed the request of Iran for a $5 billion dollar loan from the International Monetary Fund ("IMF") on the grounds that Iran has sufficient funds to properly respond to the COVID-19 pandemic.[91] Under such pressure, the World Bank has accepted the request of Iran to receive a loan (albeit for just $50m) under the Fast-Track COVID-19 Facility ("FTCF"). The loan has been given to Iran under Article 12 of the Word Bank procedure, "Preparation of Investment Project Financing—the Situation of Urgent Need of Assistance or Capacity Constraint".[92] The fourth reason is that the U.S. claims that sanction relief for Iran will be diverted toward the sponsorship of terrorism and away from the support of humanitarian activities.[93] Even after the change of the U.S. President, on 5 March 2021, the Biden administration extended the U.S. national emergency declared in EO 12957 in respect to Iran in order to

---

88   OFAC, Global Terrorism Sanctions Regulations 31 C.F.R. Part 594 Iranian, Transactions and Sanctions Regulations 31 C.F.R. Part 560, General License No. 8, 27 February 2020. See now General License 8A, https://ofac.treasury.gov/media/48841/download?inline (accessed 10 April 2023).

89   Katzman, *supra* note 39, 55.

90   *Ibid*, 55.

91   *Ibid*, 49.

92   World Bank, 'Project Appraisal Document for Proposed Loan', (Report No: PAD3899, 18 May 2020). http://documents1.worldbank.org/curated/en/420761590804103722/pdf/Iran -COVID-19-Emergency-Response-Project.pdf (accessed 12 October 2021).

93   U.S. Department of State, Office of the Spokesperson, 'Iran Sanction Relief Scam', https://2017-2021.state.gov/irans-sanctions-relief-scam/index.html, 6 April 2020. See also: ZM Khah, 'Iran: Sponsoring or Combating Terrorism?' (2020) 43 *Studies in Conflict and Terrorism* 913.

keep in force and maintain the comprehensive sanctions against Iran.[94] These actions and behaviours of successive U.S. administrations demonstrate that there is limited will to enforce humanitarian exemptions or to eliminate the barriers caused by the sanctions for Iran. Despite humanitarian exemptions, the U.S. sanctions constrain Iran's procurement of essential medical goods, thereby hindering access to life-saving treatments.[95]

3.1.2   Lack of Access to the International Financial System

A major obstacle which prevents Iran from availing itself of humanitarian exemptions to the sanction regime derives from the sanction regime itself. The essence of the problem is that Iran does not have access to the international financial system because of the direct and indirect sanctions.[96] In addition, owing to years of sanctions, Iran suffers from a fragile banking system which lacks the most recent facilities and technologies.[97] Prior to explaining this blockage, the international financial stance against Iran must be briefly explained.

The global fight against terrorism financing was launched with reference to the International Convention for the Suppression of the Financing of Terrorism (1999) (the "Financing Convention"), followed by the UNSCR 1373 (2001)[98] and the special recommendations issued by the Financial Action Task Force

---

94   The White House, 'Notice on the Continuation of the National Emergency with Respect to Iran,' 5 March 2021, https://www.whitehouse.gov/briefing-room/presidential-actions/2021 /03/05/notice-on-the-continuation-of-the-national-emergency-with-respect-to-iran/ (accessed 22 March 2022).

95   European Civil Protection and Humanitarian Aid Operations, 'Iran' (Fact Sheet, January 2021), https://ec.europa.eu/echo/where/asia-and-pacific/iran_en (accessed 12 October 2021).

96   See: K Suzuki, 'Iran: The Role and Effectiveness of UN Sanctions' in M Asada (ed.), *Economic Sanctions in International Law and Practice* (Routledge 2020) 193.

97   For more information see: A Mazarei, 'Iran Has a Slow Motion Banking Crisis' *Peterson Institute for International Economics*, June 2019, https://www.piie.com/publications/policy -briefs/iran-has-slow-motion-banking-crisis (accessed 10 April 2023).

98   UNGA International Convention for the Suppression of the Financing of Terrorism (adopted 9 December 1999, (2000) 39 ILM 270. See further I Bantekas, 'The International Law of Terrorist Financing' (2003) 97 *American Journal of International Law* 315; A Bianchi, *Enforcing International Norms against Terrorism* (Hart Publishing 2004); PA Schott, *Reference Guide to Anti-Money Laundering and Countering the Financing of Terrorism* (2nd supp edn, World Bank Publications 2006); CH Powell, 'The United Nations Security Council Sanctions Regime Against the Financing of Terrorism' in C King, C Walker, and J Gurulé, (eds.), *The Palgrave Handbook of Criminal and Terrorism Financing Law* (Palgrave MacMillan 2018); Gavin Sullivan, *The Law of the List* (Cambridge University Press 2020).

("FATF") (2001).[99] Iran is not a member of the Financing Convention and has been condemned as a high-risk and non-cooperative jurisdiction by the FATF; as a result, the FATF has called upon its members to apply counter-measures against Iran under Recommendation 19.[100] The resulting limitation of access by Iran to the international financial system, augmented by U.S. secondary sanctions, significantly hampers access by Iran to humanitarian goods in the time of COVID-19 even through the importance of humanitarian exemptions in domestic terrorism laws has been emphasised by the United Nations.[101]

Based on FATF Recommendation 1, the banks must perform their tasks based on the risk-based approach ("RBA"); in other words, the banks must assess the threat, vulnerability and consequences for customers and transactions. Banks should create a risk profile for each customer based on the individual customer's risk level and, dependent upon this level, banks can adopt either enhanced due diligence ("EDD") or simplified due diligence ("SDD"). The EDD process is conducted when the customer, product or service rendered is regarded as a high-risk.[102] Several factors must be taken into account when assessing a jurisdiction, including geographical factors, the membership of groups that reflect certain benchmarks, contextual factors, evidence of relevant official criticism, mutual evaluation reports, the implementation standards and the incidence of trade with the jurisdiction.[103] In accordance with these elements, Iran is categorised as a high-risk country based on several reasons: Iran does not have an effective Anti-Money Laundering ("AML") or Counter Terrorism Financing ("CTF") regime in place; it has been recognised as a country with significant levels of money laundering (placed worst out of 146 by the Basel Committee in

---

99   The Special Guidelines were incorporated into a 2012 revision of the entire Guidelines: FATF, *International Standards on Combating Money Laundering and the Financing of Terrorism & Proliferation: The FATF Recommendations* (FATF/OECD 2012) (updated in October 2016) 13. See further FATF, *Best Practices: Combating the Abuse of Non-Profit Organisations (Recommendation 8)* (2015).

100 See: http://www.fatf-gafi.org/publications/high-risk-and-other-monitored-jurisdictions /documents/call-for-action-february-2020.html#fn2 (accessed 12 October 2020).

101 UN Counter-Terrorism Committee Executive Directorate, *The Interrelationship between Counter-Terrorism Frameworks and International Humanitarian Law*, https://www.us2 .list-manage.com/track/click?u=8343c3b932a7be398ceb413c9&id=d3d5c82fc4&e =1bbe80e20d, 2022 (accessed 10 April 2023).

102 Financial Conduct Authority, 'High-Risk Customers, Including PEPs,' 16 August 2021, https://www.fca.org.uk/firms/money-laundering-terrorist-financing/high-risk-customers -politically-exposed-persons (accessed 12 March 2022).

103 Joint Money Laundering Steering Group (JMLSG), 'Prevention of ML/TF, Guidance for UK Financial Sector, Part.I' (December 2017) 59.

2017);[104] the Iranian authorities are judged not to have fully cooperated with the FATF; no mutual evaluation has been undertaken; and, finally, Iran is subject to severe secondary sanctions by the U.S.

Despite these misgivings, EDD should not lead to absolute financial exclusion and hence cause violations of human rights. Financial institutions should not refuse to open accounts or enter business relationships only because the customer is high risk. Only in a situation where a party cannot satisfy itself as to the identity, the verification of the identity, or be able to obtain sufficient information to mitigate risk should it not enter into, or terminate, a business relationship.[105] In reality, due to the threat of sanctions and penalties being applied to banks that fail to apply and monitor situations using the RBA, the banks especially tend not to enter into a business relationship with high-risk customers, such as those in Iran.[106] Thus, due to over-compliance and risk aversion, strict regulations, potential reputational damage and, above all, fear from being penalised because of the violation of sanction regimes, banks have a low risk-appetite for engaging with high-risk countries.[107] As already described, the secondary sanctions of the U.S. are also broad, comprehensive and vague, and so deter transactions in general, including those which might rely on humanitarian exemptions,[108] even though General License E of the Iranian Transactions and Sanctions Regulations ("ITSR") allows non-governmental organisations ("NGOs") to provide humanitarian goods, including medicine.[109]

The bite of sanctions also affects non-profit organisations ("NPOs"). Generally speaking from the banking perspective, charities are unattractive institutions for banks because of the combination of risks, the fear of fines

---

104   Basel Committee on Banking Supervision, 'Basel AML Index 2017, Report', https://www
       .baselgovernance.org/sites/default/files/2020-06/2017_report.pdf (accessed 10 October
       2021). Due to a lack of data the Basel Committee did not rank Iran in 2018–2020.
105   JMLSG, 'Prevention of ML/TF, Guidance for UK Financial Sector, Part.I' (December 2017) 49.
106   N Goodway, 'Paying the Price for Sanctions' *The Independent*, 14 August 2014, https://
       www.independent.co.uk/news/business/analysis-and-features/paying-the-price-for
       -sanctions-the-customers-with-iranian-links-being-ditched-by-british-banks-9679692
       .html (accessed 22 May 2021).
107   See: V Ramachandran, M Collin, and M Juden, 'De-risking: An Unintended Negative
       Consequence of AML/CFT Regulation' in C King, C Walker, and J Gurulé, J. (eds.), *The
       Palgrave Handbook of Criminal and Terrorism Financing Law* (Palgrave 2018); I Prezas,
       'From Targeted States to Affected Populations: Exploring Accountability for the Nega-
       tive Impact of Comprehensive Unilateral Sanctions on Human Rights' in C Beaucillon,
       Research Handbook on Unilateral and Extraterritorial Sanctions (Edward Elgar 2021) 388.
108   See Smith, *supra* note 82, 8.
109   *Authorizing Certain Services in Support of Nongovernmental Organizations' Activities
       in Iran*, https://ofac.treasury.gov/media/7996/download?inline, 10 September 2013
       (accessed 10 April 2023).

and their low profitability as customers.[110] Banks are cautious in transferring funds to countries which are labelled as risky by the FATF, even for humanitarian aid.[111] Banks will want to be sure how humanitarian agencies will use the funds and who will handle them.[112] Based on a survey conducted in 2017 by the Charity Finance Group, 79% of 34 charity respondents had problems in accessing or using the banking system, such as transfer delays, closed accounts and frozen funds.[113] As private sector bodies, banks can choose their clients, even if NPOs and others rely upon them as common utilities which are licensed by society to render services which are for the public good, and not just to make profits.[114] Limits on access to the formal financial systems will undermine both the delivery of charitable work and public trust in banks. The charities most at risk are those who work in the high-risk jurisdictions, such as Iran.[115] The counter-terrorism measures, including sanctions, have a negative impact on their activities, and, consequently, some have had to suspend humanitarian operations because of fear of violating domestic and international laws and because of impediments to financial services.[116]

Volunteers and charities providing humanitarian assistance are in turn often unwilling to accept the legal risks.[117] In a statement released by the major humanitarian organisations in 2020 in the light of COVID-19, they stated that "we particularly call on the government of the U.S. to provide assurances to financial institutions that they will not be subjected to U.S. sanctions for facilitating transfers of Iran's foreign currency for the purpose of purchasing

---

110   T Keatinge, *Counter Terrorist Regulation Restricts Charity Worldwide: Uncharitable Behaviour* (2014) 58.

111   Disaster Emergency Committee, 'Getting Aid to Syria: Sanctions Issue for Banks and Humanitarian Agencies', https://www.dec.org.uk/sites/default/files/pdf/getting_aid_to _syria.pdf (accessed 12 October 2021).

112   *Ibid.*

113   Charity Finance Group, 'Impact of Money Laundering and Counter-Terrorism Regulations on Charities', March 2018, https://cfg.org.uk/userfiles/documents/Policy%20documents /Impact%20of%20money%20laundering%20and%20counter-terrorism%20regulations %20on%20charities.pdf (accessed 10 April 2023).

114   See: C Walker, 'Terrorism Financing and the Governance of Charities' in C King, C Walker, and J Gurulé (eds.), *The Palgrave Handbook of Criminal and Terrorism Financing Law* (Palgrave 2018).

115   Keatinge, *supra* note 114, 35.

116   V Metcalfe-Hough, T Keatinge and S Pantuliano, 'UK Humanitarian Aid in the Age of Counter-Terrorism: Perceptions and Reality' (Working Paper, Overseas Development Institute, March 2015), https://www.odi.org/documents/4740/9479.pdf 5 (accessed 1 October 2021).

117   *Ibid.*, 11.

COVID-19 vaccines".[118] Thus, it can be concluded that individuals, companies, financial institutions and humanitarian organisations are scared of the violation of the U.S. sanctions, in particular the secondary sanctions with their extraterritorial effects. They have a low appetite risk that subsequently causes de-risking and de-banking and ultimately the financial exclusion of Iran at an international level.[119]

3.1.3 European Reactions to the U.S. Extraterritorial Sanctions

To decrease the commercial effects of U.S. extraterritorial sanctions, the EU inaugurated a "Blocking Statute" in 1996 as a countermeasure to what the EU considered to be the unlawful effect of extraterritorial U.S. sanctions regimes.[120] It was not implemented while negotiations on nuclear proliferation were conducted with Iran and the U.S., culminating in the JCPOA in 2015.[121] In August 2018, the Blocking Statute took effect and sought to protect EU firms from re-imposed U.S. sanctions after withdrawal from the JCPOA by the adoption of a "Delegated Regulation".[122] The Delegated Regulation lists five U.S. Acts, including the Iran Sanctions Act 1996, the Iran Freedom and Counter-Proliferation Act 2012, the National Defence Authorisation Act for Fiscal Year 2012, the Iran Threat Reduction and Syria Human Rights Act 2012, and the Iranian Transactions and Sanctions Regulations.[123] The Blocking Statute has

118   Center for Human Rights in Iran, 'Major Humanitarian Organisations Call for Access to COVID-19 Vaccines for Iranians', https://iranhumanrights.org/2020/12/major-humanitarian-organizations-call-for-access-to-covid-19-vaccines-for-iranians/ (accessed 10 October 2021).

119   See further: Z Malakoutikhah, 'Financial Exclusion as a Consequence of Counter-Terrorism Financing' (2020) 27(2) *Journal of Financial Crime* 663.

120   Council Regulations (EC) No.2271/96 'Protecting against the Effects of the Extraterritorial Application of Legislating Adopted by a Third-Country, and Actions based on thereon or Resulting therefrom', 22 November 1996, art 1. The measure has been adapted in the UK for continuance after Brexit: Protecting Against the Effects of the Extraterritorial Application of Third Country Legislation (Amendment) (EU Exit) Regulations 2020, S.I. 2020/1660.

121   Joing Comprehensive Plan of Action, Vienna, 14 July 2015, https://www.europarl.europa.eu/cmsdata/122460/full-text-of-the-iran-nuclear-deal.pdf (accessed 29 November 2022).

122   Commission Delegated Regulation (EU) 2018/1100, Amending the Annex to Council Regulation (EC) No 2271/96 Protecting against the Effects of Extra-Territorial Application of Legislation Adopted by a Third Country, and Actions based Thereon or Resulting Therefrom, 6 June 2018. See: M Jennison, 'The More Things Change, the More They Stay the Same: The United States, Trade Sanctions, and International Blocking Acts' (2020) 69 *Catholic University Law Review* 163.

123   See: 50 U.S.C. Ch. 35 s 1701 et seq; 22 USC Ch. 95 s 8801 et seq; 22 USC s 8513a (Pub.L. 112-81 s 1245); 22 USC Ch. 94 s 8701 et seq; 31 CFR Part 560.

four consequences.[124] Firstly, it requires any person to notify the European Commission of impacts on the economic and financial interests caused by a blocked measure. Secondly, no judgment of a court or tribunal within the EU and no decision of an administrative authority located outside the Community giving effect to U.S. secondary sanctions shall be recognized or be enforceable in any manner. Third, no EU person shall comply with any requirement or prohibition, including the requests of foreign courts. Fourth, an EU person shall be entitled to recover any damages, including legal costs, caused to that person by the application of the measures. Under this measure, the EU Commission received 28 Iran-related notifications from 1 August 2018 to 1 March 2021 regarding the adverse effects of the U.S. extraterritorial sanctions, which mainly arise in four categories, including banking activities and other financial services, effects caused by several business partners, administrative and judicial proceedings in the U.S., and reluctance to invest in the targeted states.[125]

Despite these arrangements, the risks associated with the violation of the U.S. sanctions involve civil, criminal and administrative penalties.[126] So, the prospect of OFAC attention has been enough to deter the global banks and even humanitarian aid exporters from working within Iran. As an example, from 2009 to 2018, some banks such as Barclays, HSBC, Standard Chartered and the Royal Bank of Scotland, were fined by the U.S. due to violations of Iran-related sanctions.[127] Banking systems fall under U.S. control because of the dominance of the dollar in international trade, which creates the territorial authority of the U.S. to apply sanctions, even outside its territory.[128] In terms of exporters, they are responsible for undertaking due diligence to ensure that: the items qualify under general licenses; screening is completed before shipments are made; all parties to the transactions are acceptable to the same extent as required when engaging business under a specific license; and the identities of end users and customers are known and are acceptable.[129]

---

124   Council Regulation (EC) No.2271/96, Protecting against the Effects of the Extraterritorial Application of Legislating Adopted by a Third-Country, and Actions based on thereon or Resulting therefrom, 22 November 1996, arts. 3–6.

125   European Commission, Report from the Commission to the European Parliament and the Council relating the Article 7(a) of the Council Regulation (EC) No.2271/96 ('Blocking Statute) COM (2021) 535 Final, https://eur-lex.europa.eu/legal-content/EN/TXT/PDF/?uri =CELEX:52021DC0535&from=EN (accessed 10 October 2021).

126   *Ibid.*

127   Mallard, *supra* note 43, 131.

128   *Ibid.*

129   S Flicker and et al., 'Humanitarian Aid to Iran under Existing Sanctions' (21 April 2020), https://www.paulhastings.com/insights/client-alerts/humanitarian-aid-to-iran-under

Consequently, although the EU's Blocking Statute "appears at first sight to be a powerful tool", it has failed both in the past and at present, to protect EU businesses, including banks, from penalties on the grounds of non-compliance with U.S. sanctions.[130] Furthermore, the conflict between the two competing legal regimes of the U.S. secondary sanctions and the EU's Blocking Statute causes enduring uncertainty for companies and banks. The financial clout of the U.S. in the international financial system is the ultimate reason for nullifying the EU's efforts. As the European Commission itself recognises, sometimes not engaging in business with a specific country is not the direct result of the U.S. sanctions, but rather that of commercial considerations.[131] It might be said that it is an indirect result of the listed persons and asset freeze because a company must carry out due diligence due to there being different sanctions by different countries with different parameters and sometimes the sanctions regimes are vague.[132] This risk results in traders not wanting to conduct business with a particular country due to the cost of compliance with the sanctions regime and due to the uncertainty as to the impact of U.S. and EU laws and enforcement practices.[133]

As a result of the limited effectiveness of the EU Blocking Statute, in 2021, the European Commission considered the amendment of the the Blocking Statute (Regulation 2271/96) in order to deter and counteract the unlawful extraterritorial application of sanctions to EU operators.[134] Furthermore, specifically in terms of Iran, in 2019 the EU announced the creation of the Instrument for Supporting Trade Exchanges ("INSTEX"), a special purpose vehicle in order

---

-existing-sanctionsan-important-reminder-in-a-time-of-pandemic (accessed 12 October 2021).

130   Special Rapporteur on the Negative Impact of the Unilateral Coercive Measures on the Enjoyment of Human Rights, *Report 2016–17* (UN Doc. A/HRC/36/44, 26 July 2017), para 32. See also the negative verdict in European Commission, *Summary of Results of the Open Public Consultation on the Review of the Blocking Statute* (Ref. Ares (2021)7829130 - 17/12/2021).

131   European Parliament, Answer given on 1 April 2015 by Vice-President Mogherini on behalf of the Commission to Parliamentary questions E- 007804/2014, https://www.europarl .europa.eu/doceo/document/E-8-2014-007804-ASW_EN.html (accessed 12 October 2021).

132   J Gordon, 'The Not So Targeted Instrument of Asset Freezes' (2019) 33 *Ethics & International Affairs* 303.

133   H Territt et al., 'US Sanctions and the EU Blocking Regulation: Issue of Legal Uncertainty' (Financial Market Law Committee, June 2019) para 3.18.

134   European Commission, 'Amendment of the Blocking Statute', https://ec.europa.eu/info /law/better-regulation/have-your-say/initiatives/13129-Unlawful-extra-territorial -sanctions-a-stronger-EU-response-amendment-of-the-Blocking-Statute-_en; European Commission, *Summary of Results of the Open Public Consultation on the Review of the Blocking Statute* (Ref. Ares (2021)7829130 - 17/12/2021) (accessed 10 June 2022).

to alleviate the extraterritorial effects of the U.S. unilateral sanctions and to facilitate legitimate trade between European economic operators and Iran. The focus of INSTEX is on the humanitarian non-sanctioned goods needed for Iran, such as medicines, medical devices, food and agricultural commodities.[135] It is declared that INSTEX would not be a tool for circumventing sanctions nor will it undermine transparency and due diligence for the standards of AML and CTF.[136] On 31 March 2020, INSTEX completed its first transaction for about $540,000 worth of medical equipment.[137] Nevertheless, it seems that caution still prevails; although the European Union claimed that the FATF's recommendations are not a prerequisite for INSTEX,[138] the lack of laws and regulations within the Iranian legal system concerning AML/CTF might remain one highly persuasive factor for hesitancy over INSTEX transactions.

Another obstacle to INSTEX is once again the dominant U.S. commercial importance. Major companies are unlikely to engage in trade with Iran because of their far greater dependence on U.S. businesses and, therefore, ongoing connections with the U.S. jurisdiction.[139] In response, Iran established a Special Trade and Finance Institute ("STFI") as a financial mechanism equivalent to INSTEX.[140] However, as the SIFI is monitored and supervised by the Central Bank of Iran, it might be sanctioned by the U.S. To date, only two

---

135   Foreign and Commonwealth Office, 'Joint Statement on the Creation of INSTEX, the Special Purpose Vehicle Aimed at Facilitating Legitimate Trade with Iran in the Framework of the Efforts to Preserve the JCPOA', 31 January 2019, https://assets.publishing.service.gov.uk/government/uploads/system/uploads/attachment_data/file/775681/19_01_31_Joint_Statement_E3.pdf (accessed 12 October 2021).

136   EU, European External Action Service, 'Speech on the Extraterritorial Effects of US Sanctions on Iran for European Companies, at the European Parliament,' 14 November 2018, https://eeas.europa.eu/headquarters/headquarters-homepage/53860/speech-extraterritorial-effects-us-sanctions-iran-european-companies-european-parliament_en (accessed 2 April 2020).

137   'EU Ramps up Trade System with Iran despite U.S. Threats' *Wall Street Journal*, 31 March 2020.

138   J Irish, 'No Trade Mechanism until Iran Passes Terrorism Financing Laws' *Reuters*, 4 September 2019, https://uk.reuters.com/article/uk-iran-nuclear-europe-trade/no-trade-mechanism-until-iran-passes-terrorism-financing-laws-french-diplomat-idUKKCN1VP1N2 (accessed 12 October 2021).

139   B Cova and F Cozzi, 'The EU is Launching "INSTEX" to Support Trade with Iran Despite U.S. Sanctions' (January 2019), http://www.paulhastings.com/docs/default-source/default-document-library/stay-current-the-eu-is-launching-instex-to-support-trade-with-iran-despite-u-s-sanctions.pdf (accessed 10 October 2021).

140   ISNA, 'شرکت ایرانی متناظر با اینستکس به ثبت رسید STFI Is Registered' (*ISNA*, 20 February 2019), https://www.isna.ir/news/97122915370/شرکت-ایرانی-متناظر-با-اینستکس-به-ثبت-رسید (accessed 2 April 2020).

or three transactions have been undertaken,[141] and because of the Iranian officials' insistence that INSTEX must encompass oil transactions,[142] as oil sales
are the primary source of foreign income for Iran, the prospects for progress
are remote. Finally, on 9 March 2023, INSTEX was terminated by the Europe-
ans, the reason cited was that Iran has systematically prevented INSTEX from
fulfilling its humanitarian goals.[143]

Besides INSTEX, the U.S. and Swiss governments finalised the conditions
for the operation of the Swiss Humanitarian Trade Arrangement (SHTA) in
February 2020. The SHTA is intended to facilitate the flow of humanitarian
goods to Iran, such as food and medical supplies. The first transaction was conducted in January 2020 to show the effectiveness of the channel. The SHTA
specifies that the humanitarian goods must not be misused by the Iranian government, and all participating financial institutions must conduct EDD for all
transactions.[144] As the SHTA is in its early stages, its effectiveness is unclear,
but already it has been reported that a delay can be observed in the process of
the SHTA because "the pharmaceutical sector was faced with other priorities
overnight [COVID-19]".[145]

The next blow in the contest between global trading powers was delivered
in May 2021 by the then Advocate General of the Court of Justice, Gerard
Hogan, who rendered an Opinion in the first case before the Court of Justice of
the European Union on the interpretation of the EU Blocking Statute.[146] The
case concerns Bank Melli Iran, which is Iran's largest commercial retail bank
and which trades in Germany.[147] Bank Melli Iran claimed that a notice of termination issued by Telekom Deutschland with respect to their contracts for
telecommunication services was triggered solely by the desire to comply with

141   Iran Press, 'Mogherini: First Transaction being Processed by INSTEX' *Iran Press*, 30 June 2019,
       http://iranpress.com/en/europe-i136184-mogherini_first_transaction_being_processed
       _by_instex (accessed 10 October 2021).
142   Financial Tribune, 'INSTEX Close to 1st Deal in Days' *Financial Tribune,* 5 July 2019, https://
       financialtribune.com/articles/business-and-markets/98770/instex-close-to-1st-deal-in
       -days (accessed 12 October 2021).
143   https://www.gov.uk/government/news/the-10-instex-shareholder-states-have-decided
       -to-liquidate-instex-due-to-continued-obstruction-from-iran (accessed 10 April 2023).
144   U.S. Department of Treasury, 'United States and Switzerland Finalise the Swiss Human-
       itarian Trade Arrangement' (Press Release, 27 February 2020), https://home.treasury.gov
       /news/press-releases/sm919 (accessed 11 October 2021).
145   J Crawford, 'Swiss Humanitarian Trade Deal with Iran Faces Delay, Questions,' (22 July 2020,
       https://www.swissinfo.ch/eng/swiss-humanitarian-trade-deal-with-iran-faces-delays
       --questions--/45906142 (accessed 8 March 2021).
146   Case C-124/20, 12 May 2021.
147   See http://bmi.ir/ (accessed 10 October 2021).

U.S. sanctions legislation. Bank Melli Iran claims that this action breaches of the EU Blocking Statute. The Advocate General Hogan argued that an EU business seeking to terminate an otherwise valid contract with an Iranian entity must demonstrate to the satisfaction of the national court that it did not do so by reason of its desire to comply with U.S. sanctions (and thereby to defy the Blocking Statute) rather than, say, as part of a coherent and systematic corporate social responsibility policy such as refusal to deal with any company linked to the Iranian state. If in breach of this legal interpretation, a national court could order the restitution of contractual relationships. However, in *Bank Melli v Telekom Deutschland*,[148] the European Court of Justice backed down from the strict interpretation of the Advocate General. It does not infringe the EU Blocking Statute where compliance would cause disproportionate economic loss; in most cases one can expect major corporations to claim that compliance would have such impact because the dominant economic market and regulatory risk derived from the U.S. As a result, sanctions compliance will prevail.

3.2 Medicines and Aid Requiring Specific Authorisation and the Problems of Bureaucracy

The humanitarian exemptions under U.S. law are determined both by general licenses, which were examined earlier, and by the mechanism of specific authorisation, which is required for the export of specific humanitarian goods to Iran. Under Iran General License – Authorizing the Exportation or Reexportation of Replacement Parts for Certain Medical Devices, the OFAC must review license applications for some types of medical equipment which are required for the treatment of COVID-19, such as HEPA filters, full face mask respirators, diagnostic medical imaging equipment, oxygen generators, decontamination equipment and pumps, and on a case-by-case basis because these might be dual-used.[149] In this way, the requirements for specific authorisation by the OFAC have created further obstacles. These obstacles contrast with the call for "broad, practical effect with prompt, flexible authorisation for essential medical equipment and supplies".[150] After criticism of the US humanitarian exemption policy, on 17 June 2021, the US Treasury issued "Iran General Licence N: Authorising Certain Activities to Respond to the

---

148   C124/20, ECLI: EU:C:2021:1035, 21 December 2021.

149   Iranian Transactions and Sanctions Regulations, 31 C.F.R. Part 560.

150   OHCHR, 'Bachelet Calls for Easing of Sanctions to Enable Medical Systems to Fight COVID-19 and Limit Global Contagion', 24 March 2020, https://www.ohchr.org/en/2020/03/bachelet-calls-easing-sanctions-enable-medical-systems-fight-covid-19-and-limit-global (accessed 10 April 2023).

Coronavirus Disease 2019 Pandemic". The General License N expands authorisation to cover certain items that previously would have required a specific license for exportation or re-exportation to Iran, such as certain COVID-19 testing or vaccine manufacturing equipment. The License N authorises exportation of goods and technology; importation of or dealings in certain COVID-19-related goods; importation or exportation of services; certain transactions involving the Central Bank; and other specified financial transactions.[151] Even this further License may not prove to be effective as it has been issued under the process and policy similar to the previous failed exemptions. In addition, it is time-limited and might be renewed year by year; recently the General License was renewed and will be expired on 17 June 2023.[152]

Under the Trump administration, the OFAC issued a declining number of special licenses for medicine and medical devices exported to Iran — down from more than 50% approved during the first quarter of 2016 to 10% during the same period of 2019.[153] No report has been published to show the number of authorisations during COVID-19.

The need for specific authorisation for humanitarian goods causes four main problems which further inhibit the U.S. humanitarian exemption policy. Firstly, the humanitarian exemption items are very limited, so, for the rest of the required medical devices and medicines, specific authorisation is needed. This means that even when there is no U.S. connection, these items are nevertheless not covered by the humanitarian exemption under General License 8.

Secondly, the specific authorisation process is very slow and complex and can take several months to navigate.[154] The process should be fast and reasonable to enable humanitarian organisations and other companies to supply the goods to Iran's health system during the time of the pandemic, which would also be assisted by allocating more staff and resources.[155]

---

151   OFAC, 'Iran General Licence N: Authorising Certain Activities to Respond to the Coronavirus Disease 2019 Pandemic', https://ofac.treasury.gov/media/99261/download?inline (accessed 10 April 2023).

152   U.S. Department of Treasury, 'Frequently Asked Questions' No. 906, https://ofac.treasury .gov/faqs/906 (accessed 10 April 2023).

153   D Benger, T Carney, and M Lorenzini, 'Challenges to U.S. Sanctions Against Iran During the Coronavirus Pandemic' *Lawfare*, 30 April 2020, https://www.lawfareblog.com/challenges -us-sanctions-against-iran-during-coronavirus-pandemic (accessed 10 October 2021).

154   Fitzpatrick, *supra* note 86.

155   The statement was organised by the European Leadership Network and The Iran Project, 'Transatlantic Call to Ease Humanitarian Trade with Iran due to the COVID-19 Pandemic' (6 April 2020), https://www.europeanleadershipnetwork.org/wp-content/up loads/2020/04/06042020-ELN-IP-US-Sanctions-Iran-Humanitarian-Trade-Statement -FINAL.pdf (accessed 12 October 2021).

Thirdly, the specific authorisation is only allowed for U.S. persons and is out of reach for non-U.S. firms, companies and humanitarian organisations.[156] Thus, the sanctions of the U.S. have extraterritorial impacts, but the humanitarian exemption policy is confined to U.S. persons.

Fourth, the applicants requesting specific licenses have overall responsibility which impedes them in applying for specific licenses. For example, the applicant must have information on: "the full names and addresses of all parties involved in the transactions and their roles, including financial institutions and any Iranian broker (identify company principals), purchasing agent (identify company principals), end-user(s) (full contact name), or other participants involved in the purchase of the proposed export items; and b) if applicable, the commodity classification numbers that are associated with the proposed export items".[157]

In summary, as Mallard explained, the governance arrangements of sanctions can be divided into three types: transnational, hegemonic and hybrid. The failure of U.S. exemption system can be explained by the hegemonic governance arrangements because the U.S. sanctions system is only governed by U.S. public authority as an uncontested hegemon.[158] If the request for the license is rejected by the OFAC then no appeal process is available.[159] The OFAC will decide all aspects of sanctions and licensing primarily in the interests of the U.S. Thus, highly complex, time-consuming, and overlapping regulatory frameworks for granting licenses leads to the ineffectiveness of the humanitarian exemption.[160]

4   Conclusion

The COVID-19 pandemic amounts to "the worst combined health and socio-economic crisis in living memory, and a catastrophe at every level:[161] on a scale which is unprecedented outside of wartime.[162] However, this paper

---

156   Fitzpatrick, *supra* note 86.
157   U.S. Department of Treasury, FAQ, https://ofac.treasury.gov/faqs/topic/1506 (accessed 10 April 2023).
158   Mallard, *supra* note 43, 127–128.
159   *Ibid.*
160   I Prezas, 'From Targeted States to Affected Populations: Exploring Accountability for the Negative Impact of Comprehensive Unilateral Sanctions on Human Rights' in C Beaucillon, *Research Handbook on Unilateral and Extraterritorial Sanctions* (Edward Elgar 2021) 388.
161   Independent Panel, *COVID-19: Make It the Last Pandemic* (WHO, 2021) 4.
162   UNSCR 2532 on cessation of hostilities in the context of the coronavirus disease (COVID-19) pandemic (2020) calls for an end to all hostilities so as to facilitate humanitarian aid

has demonstrated that the Iranian population has experienced exceptional harms due to the imposition of unilateral economic sanctions by the U.S. before, during and after the Covid-19 global health crisis. Global aid and cooperation with Iran has been blocked, and exemptions for humanitarian goods are wholly inadequate. It appears that Iran has become subject to the vagaries of multiple discordant power-blocks. Within the U.S., there has been competition between the Obama, Trump and Biden administrations as to policy towards Iran. Within the EU, calculations are made with regard to the policy priority to be accorded to U.S. trade harmony or the importance of Iran as a trading partner, both compared to other negotiations about tariffs and subsidies and wider foreign policy interests in the Middle East. As a result of the prevailing of U.S. unilateral sanctions, the right to health and specifically the right to access humanitarian goods in the time of COVID-19 is relegated in importance and violated. Although the humanitarian exemption has been adopted as a policy to alleviate the human rights and humanitarian impacts of the unilateral sanction, in practice the failure of humanitarian exemption is evident. Alongside the vagueness of the issued general licenses with extensive conditions, the main obstacle for Iran is the lack of access to international financial system for financial transactions. The complication stems both from direct and indirect effects of sanctions on financial institutions; apart from some Iranian financial institutions which are under the direct sanctions, the overcompliance, risk aversion, strict regulations, potential reputational damage and, above all, fear from being penalised because of the violation of sanction regimes have raised barriers for Iran in funding humanitarian goods. The humanitarian exemption is not limited to failure of general licenses, for even the mechanism of specific authorisation for some COVID-19 related goods has not been successful. Here, the problems consist of the limitation of the goods under specific authorisation, very slow and complex processes which can take several months to navigate, specific authorisations only allowed for U.S. persons. Thus, secondary sanctions with exterritorial impacts impede Iranian access to humanitarian goods.

In these circumstances, the only plea that can be firmly endorsed is for international engagement, including in the application of sanctions,[163] towards the alleviation of the consequences of COVID-19 as experienced by the

---

delivery. See M Arcari, 'Some Thoughts in the Aftermath of Security Council Resolution 2532 (2020) on Covid-19' (2020) 70 *Questions of International Law* 59.

163   See UN Secretary-General, *Negative Impact of Unilateral Coercive Measures on the Enjoyment of Human Rights* (A/75/209, 2020) paras. 14–20.

Iranian population.[164] More specific reforms have also been suggested for the U.S.[165] and EU[166] sanctions regimes. Cosmopolitan solidarity demands more than negative respect for universal rights of one's own neighbours, and every country should seek to promote the value of collective "human security" in the interests of all.[167]

Postscript: UN Security Council Resolution 2664 of 9 December 2022 creates a carve-out across most UN sanctions regimes for the provision, processing or payment of funds, other financial assets or economic resources or the provision of goods and services necessary to ensure the timely delivery of humanitarian assistance or to support other activities that support basic human needs. Such activity will not violate asset freezes even if designated persons are involved so long as providers use reasonable efforts to minimize the accrual of any benefits to designated individuals or entities, including by strengthening risk management and due diligence strategies and processes. The concession affects UN sanctions but need not be applied to unilateral sanctions. For US application, see 31 CFR Parts 510, 525, 536, 539, 541, 542, 544, 546, 547, 548, 549, 551, 552, 555, 558, 560, 561, 562, 569, 576, 579, 582, 583, 584, 585, 591, 594, 596, 597, and 598 (Federal Register Vol. 87, No. 244 21 December 2022, 78484, 78470).

Note on the Contributors

Zeynab Malakouti Khah
UNESCO Chair for Human Rights, Peace and Democracy, Shahid Beheshti University, Tehran, z.malakotikhah@gmail.com.

Clive Walker
Professor Emeritus of Criminal Justice Studies, School of Law, University of Leeds, Leeds, law6cw@leeds.ac.uk.

---

164 A wider agenda is suggested by the House of Commons Foreign Affairs Committee, *No Prosperity without Justice: the UK's Relationship with Iran* (2019–21 HC 415) para. 46. See also Government Reply (2019-21 HC 1263).

165 See: A Boyle, *Checking the President's Sanctions Powers* (Brennan Center for Justice, 2021), 23.

166 See: K Brockmann and KA Preble, *Mitigating Humanitarian Impact in a Complex Sanctions Environment: The European Union and the Sanctions Regimes against Iran* (SIPRI, 2020).

167 See: UN Commission on Human Security, *Human Security Now*, <https://digitallibrary. un.org/record/503749/files/Humansecuritynow.pdf, 2003; A Zwitter, *Human Security, Law and the Prevention of Terrorism* (Routledge, 2010).

PART 2

Economic, Social and Environmental Rights Contestation and Evolution

∵

CHAPTER 6

The Imperative for Justiciability of Economic, Social, and Cultural Rights in Post-Civil War Sri Lanka

Muttukrishna Sarvananthan and Navaratnam Sivakaran

Abstract

Between 2015 and 2019 Sri Lanka has been in the process of drafting a new Constitution in the aftermath of the civil war that lasted from 1983 to 2009. In spite of the very high human development in Sri Lanka, public expenditures on education and health as a proportion of the GDP have declined since the 1960s. Besides, it is argued that democracy in Sri Lanka is patronage cum greed based, and hence a case is made for inculcating a merit cum need based democracy for which justiciability of Economic, Social, and Cultural Rights (ESCR) is a *sine qua non*. Moreover, we argue a case for incorporating ESCR as justiciable rights in the proposed new Constitution not only on its own right but also as a means of durable peace-building in the aftermath of a savage civil war.

Keywords

ESCR – human rights – peace-building – rights based development – Sri Lanka – transitional Justice

1   Introduction

The year 2019 marked the tenth anniversary of the end of the long drawn out civil war in Sri Lanka (1983–2009) that ended in May 2009, after the total military defeat of the Liberation Tigers of Tamil Eelam (LTTE – aka Tamil Tigers) by the security forces. For the first five and a half years after the end of the civil war (i.e. until December 2014) there was no serious attempt to address the abuses endured by the victims of the civil war on all sides of the Sri Lankan society (especially civilians), simply because the then government had the audacity to deny that abuses ever took place (for example, "zero civilian casualties" has been the oft repeated mantra of the then government).

In spite of the fact that the Government of Sri Lanka set up a Lessons Learnt and Reconciliation Commission (LLRC)[1] in May 2010 in response to intense pressure from the United Nations and the wider international community, there was no serious attempt of introspection or rectification on the part of the perpetrators of unbridled violence on all sides, including by the then Government of Sri Lanka.

Since the change of government in January 2015, there has been limited attempt to institute Transitional Justice[2] mechanisms (e.g. setting-up of the Office on Missing Persons and the Office for Reparations to address the past abuses and draw lessons therefrom in order to prevent recurrence of such abuses in the future.

Sri Lanka has been in the process of drafting its third Constitution since independence from the British colonial rule on February 04, 1948; the first being the Republican Constitution of 1972 and the second being the 1978 Constitution. The process of Constitution drafting between 2015 and 2019 has been unique because of its public consultations throughout the country. There has been a groundswell of support for the incorporation of Economic, Social, and Cultural Rights (ESCR) in the proposed new Constitution as a justiciable right (with judicial enforcement) during the course of these public consultations by the Public Representations Committee on Constitutional Reform. The specific rights incorporated in the ESCR are the (1) right to education, (2) right to health, (3) right to housing, (4) right to food, and the (5) right to work.

However, a small but vociferous group of legal professionals and scholars in Sri Lanka have been publicly campaigning against the incorporation of the ESCR in the proposed new Constitution. The objections for inclusion of ESCR are that (1) the enforcement and fulfillment of the ESCR is best left to the democratic processes through the elected Executive and Legislature branches of the government and not through the unelected Judiciary branch of the government, (2) the unelected judiciary should not be allowed to trespass into policy making process of a democratic polity, (3) incompetence of the judiciary to adjudicate on fiscal and monetary policies of the government, and (4) the legal enforcement of ESCR would be financially costly to the exchequer. (See also

---

1 Government of Sri Lanka, 'Report of the Commission of Inquiry on Lessons Learnt and Reconciliation' http://www.slembassyusa.org/downloads/LLRC-REPORT.pdf (accessed 23 August 2018).

2 International Center for Transitional Justice, 'What is Transitional Justice?' https://www.ictj .org/about/transitional-justice (accessed 23 August 2018).

Landau, 2012: 221, for similar grounds for opposition to ESCR in Colombia, for example).[3]

2   A Framework for Analysis

2.1   The Intersectionality of Transitional Justice and Economic, Social, and Cultural Rights

The United Nations has defined 'Transitional Justice' as "the full range of processes and mechanisms associated with a society's attempt to come to terms with a legacy of large-scale past abuses, in order to ensure accountability, serve justice and achieve reconciliation".[4]

The former United Nations High Commissioner for Human Rights, Louise Arbour, had observed that "transitional justice must have the ambition to assist the transformation of oppressed societies into free ones by addressing the injustices of the past through measures that will procure an equitable future. It must reach to—but also beyond—the crimes and abuses committed during the conflict that led to the transition, and it must address the human rights violations that predated the conflict and caused or contributed to it".[5]

The four pillars of the Transitional Justice processes are: (1) ACCOUNTABIL-ITY to the abuses of human rights during the course of the conflict by investigating and punishing the perpetrators of such abuses (the right to accountability), (2) TRUTH SEEKING to identify the root causes as well as the consequences of the conflict (the right to the truth), (3) REPARATIONS should be provided to partially compensate for the material losses incurred by the victims of the conflict (the right to reparations), (4) ENSURING NON-RECURRENCE of the conflict by various means of reconciliation efforts and enshrining legal guarantees to ensure non-recurrence (the right to non-recurrence).[6]

Although, the Truth Commissions (beginning with the establishment of the Truth and Reconciliation Commission (TRC) in South Africa in 1996) until 2005 have primarily or solely focused on the violations of civil and political rights (prior to the conflict as well as during the course of the conflict), the Commission for Reception, Truth and Reconciliation in Timor-Leste (formerly

3   D Landau, 'The Reality of Social Rights Enforcement' (2012) 53 *Harvard International Law Journal* 190.
4   Office of the High Commissioner for Human Rights (OHCHR), *Transitional Justice and Economic, Social, and Cultural Rights* (United Nations, 2014) 5.
5   Arbour, 2007, quoted in *ibid.*, 1.
6   *Ibid.*N 5.

known as East Timor) in its report dated 2005 has for the first time embedded the violations of economic, social, and cultural rights (predating the conflict as well as during the course of the conflict; that is, the causes and the consequences of the conflict) as well into its remit.[7] For example, the Commission for Reception, Truth and Reconciliation in Timor-Leste discovered that out of the total of 102,800 deaths caused as a result of the conflict during the period between April 25, 1974 and October 25, 1999, only 18,600 (mere 18%) was due to killings while the overwhelming majority (82%) was due to "hunger and illness", especially during the famine of 1978–1979.[8] Whilst the former (killings) constitutes violations of the right to life (a civil and political right), the latter (deaths due to hunger and illness), of course, constitutes violations of economic and social rights.

2.2   *The Indivisibility of Civil and Political Rights (CPR) and the Economic, Social, and Cultural Rights (ESCR)*

In order to transform provisions of the Universal Declaration Human Rights (UDHR) into legally binding obligations, the United Nations adopted two International Covenants, namely, the International Covenant on Civil and Political Rights (ICCPR) and the International Covenant on Economic, Social, and Cultural Rights (ICESCR) in 1966. The CPR as incorporated in the ICCPR are referred to as the first-generation rights and the ESCR incorporated in the ICESCR are referred to as the second-generation rights. These two types of rights are fundamentally interdependent and are *sine qua non* for the functional fulfilment of both types of rights.

The ICESCR addresses a number of specific rights, including the right to an adequate standard of living, to education, to self-determination, and to participation in cultural life. Further, it specifies equal rights for women and men, the right to work, to form and join trade unions, to have just and favourable conditions for work, the right to the best standards of physical and mental health, to social security and social insurance, and to enjoy the benefits of scientific progress.[9]

3   Objectives

The overall objective of this policy research paper is to advance evidence-based analyses and critically informed arguments in favour of the incorporation

---

7   *Ibid.*, 17–18.
8   *Ibid.*, 18.
9   S Leckie and A Gallagher, *Economic, Social, and Cultural Rights: A Legal Resource Guide* (University of Pennsylvania Press, 2006) 3.

of economic, social, and cultural rights in the proposed new Constitution of Sri Lanka towards building an inclusive society promoting shared prosperity grounded on meritocracy cum needs based democracy (as opposed to the present matronage/patronage cum greed based democracy – further on this below) after a quarter-century of savage civil war. Thus, we aim to argue a case for the inclusion of ESCR in the proposed new Constitution not only on its own right, but also as a means of transitional justice and peace-building in a war-torn country. Specifically, the justiciability of ESCR is proposed as a means of ensuring non-recurrence of the past armed conflict (the fourth pillar of the transitional justice processes).

The specific objectives of this policy research paper are to: (1) firstly, outline the status of Sri Lanka vis-à-vis ESCR as reflected in the Social and Economic Rights Fulfillment (SERF) Index compiled by the University of Connecticut in the United States of America, (2) secondly, to provide statistical and other evidences pertaining to Sri Lanka to demonstrate the inadequacy of SERF Index to gauge the real status of a country in terms of realisation of ESCR, (3) thirdly, to provide evidences of greed cum matronage/patronage based practices of democratic governance in Sri Lanka, and (4) finally, to counter the arguments advanced by the antagonists of incorporation of ESCR as a justiciable right in the proposed new Constitution of Sri Lanka, drawing from the international experiences on the judicial enforcement of ESCR.

4   Social and Economic Rights Fulfillment Index

The Social and Economic Rights Fulfillment (SERF) Index is compiled at the University of Connecticut in the United States of America (USA). The SERF Index was pioneered by a Development Economist Prof. Sakiko Fukuda-Parr and her colleagues.

The SERF Index, perhaps useful for bench-marking fulfillment of social and economic rights in a country as a whole, may not capture the intra-country imbalances in such fulfilment. Therefore, the SERF Index should not be construed as an all-encompassing indicator of the realisation of social and economic rights of ALL the citizens of any country. Moreover, the quality of educational, health, housing, food, and employment rights enjoyed by the citizens could not be captured by the SERF Index for understandable reasons, which is a drawback of this measure. However, the SERF Index is a reasonably indicative measure for policy analyses and discourses.

The SERF Index for Sri Lanka has increased from 70.48 in 1985 to 86.70 in 2015. While the improvement or rise in SERF Index has been phenomenal between 1985 and 2005 (rising from 70.48 in 1985 to 82.01 in 1995, and 85.17 in

2005), the rise has moderated between 2005 and 2015 (marginally increasing from 85.17 in 2005 to 86.70 in 2015), most likely because of the effect of higher base. (See Figure 6.1 and Table 6.1)

According to the latest available data, Sri Lanka ranked fifteenth out of seventy-nine developing countries in terms of SERF Index in 2015. (See Table 6.1)

The sub-components of the SERF Index for Sri Lanka are catalogued in Table 6.2. Accordingly, the indices for education and housing rights fulfillment are the greatest out of the five sub-components such as the right to education, health, housing, food, and work.

The universal free education and universal free public health services coupled with many economic and social welfare programmes throughout the post-independence period have elevated Sri Lanka to such a high ranking on its own right and more so in comparison to other South Asian countries. (See Figure 6.2 and Table 6.3)

5   Inadequacy of SERF Index for Policy

5.1   *Progressive Decline in Public Expenditure on Education and Health*
The average annual public expenditure on education as a percentage of the Gross Domestic Product (GDP) has been progressively declining from the peak of 4.24% during the decade 1960–1969 to just 1.76 during the eight-year period 2010–2017. The average annual public expenditure on education as a percentage of the GDP has nearly halved from 3.14% during the first decade after

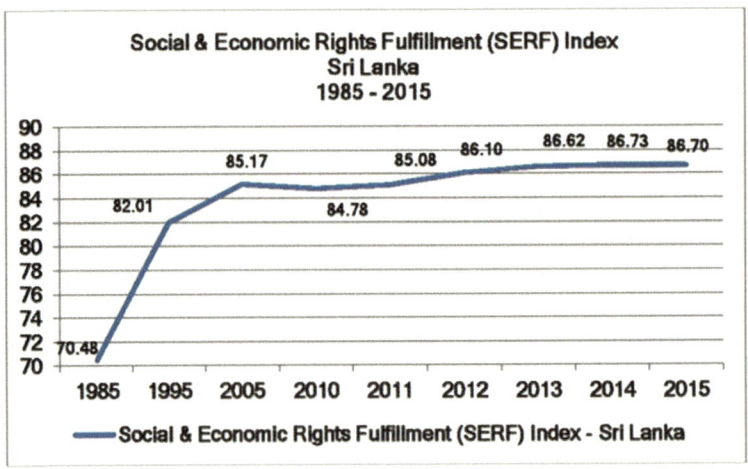

FIGURE 6.1   Social and Economic Rights Fulfillment (SERF) index of Sri Lanka
                1985–2015
                SOURCE: DERIVED FROM TABLE 6.1

TABLE 6.1   Social and Economic Rights Fulfillment (SERF) Index of Sri Lanka 1985–2015

SRI LANKA (LKA)	1985	1995	2005	2010	2011	2012	2013	2014	2015
SERF Index	70.48	82.01	85.17	84.78	85.08	86.10	86.62	86.73	86.70
Rank	N.A	N.A	15	19	21	20	19	19	15
			(out of 76)	(out of 86)	(out of 88)	(out of 90)	(out of 87)	(out of 85)	(out of 79)
GDP Per Capita (2011 PPP) USD	N.A	N.A	6527	8563	9213	9980	10239	10642	11048

SOURCE: ECONOMIC AND SOCIAL RIGHTS EMPOWERMENT INITIATIVE, UNIVERSITY OF CONNECTICUT, CONNECTICUT, USA. HTTP://SERFINDEX.
UCONN.EDU/WP-CONTENT/UPLOADS/SITES/1843/2017/04/CORE_2005TO2015.PDF
HTTP://SERFINDEX.UCONN.EDU/WP-CONTENT/UPLOADS/SITES/1843/2016/08/SERF-HISTORICAL-TRENDS-CORE-COUNTRIES.PDF

TABLE 6.2   Sub Components of the Social and Economic Rights Fulfillment (SERF) Index of Sri Lanka 1985–2015

SRI LANKA (LKA)	1985	1995	2005	2010	2011	2012	2013	2014	2015
Right to Education Index	N.A	N.A	N.A	90.81	91.54	89.26	90.48	90.00	90.00
Right to Health Index	91.36	91.98	83.19	83.96	83.80	83.64	83.72	83.78	83.78
Right to Housing Index	N.A	N.A	85.15	89.83	90.73	91.82	93.08	94.04	93.93
Right to Food Index	N.A	N.A	79.82	76.52	76.52	82.44	82.44	82.44	82.44
Right to Work Index	61.49	58.38	67.91	82.78	82.78	83.37	83.37	83.37	83.37

SOURCE: ECONOMIC AND SOCIAL RIGHTS EMPOWERMENT INITIATIVE, UNIVERSITY OF CONNECTICUT, CONNECTICUT, USA. HTTP://SERFINDEX.
UCONN.EDU/WP-CONTENT/UPLOADS/SITES/1843/2017/04/CORE_2005TO2015.PDF
HTTP://SERFINDEX.UCONN.EDU/WP-CONTENT/UPLOADS/SITES/1843/2016/08/SERF-HISTORICAL-TRENDS-CORE-COUNTRIES.PDF

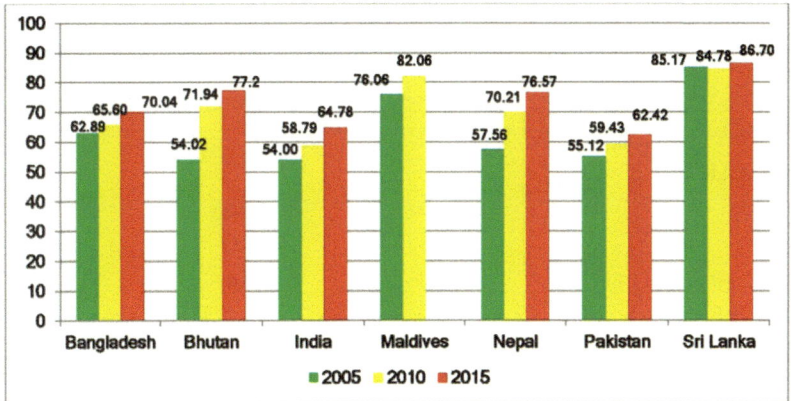

FIGURE 6.2   Social and Economic Rights Fulfillment (SERF) Index of South Asian
Countries 2005–2015
SOURCE: DERIVED FROM TABLE 6.3

TABLE 6.3   Social and Economic Rights Fulfillment (SERF) Index of South Asian Countries
2005–2015

	2005	2010	2015
Bangladesh (BGD)			
SERF Index	62.89	65.60	70.04
Rank	(46)	(54)	(43)
GDP Per Capita (2011 PPP) $	1937	2451	3137
Bhutan (BTN)			
SERF Index	54.02	71.94	77.20
Rank	(63)	(41)	(34)
GDP Per Capita (2011 PPP) $	4560	6486	7861
India (IND)			
SERF Index	54.00	58.79	64.78
Rank	(64)	(66)	(57)
GDP Per Capita (2011 PPP) $	3213	4405	5730
Maldives (MDV)			
SERF Index	76.06	82.06	N.A
Rank	(31)	(26)	N.A
GDP Per Capita (2011 PPP) $	7961	10514	11994
Nepal (NPL)			
SERF Index	57.56	70.21	76.57
Rank	(57)	(44)	(35)
GDP Per Capita (2011 PPP) $	1693	1997	2312

TABLE 6.3   Social and Economic Rights Fulfillment (SERF) Index of South Asian Countries
2005–2015 (cont.)

	2005	2010	2015
Pakistan (PAK)			
SERF Index	55.12	59.43	62.42
Rank	(60)	(62)	(62)
GDP Per Capita (2011 PPP) $	4028	4297	4706
Sri Lanka (LKA)			
SERF Index	85.17	84.78	86.70
Rank	(15)	(19)	(15)
GDP Per Capita (2011 PPP) $	6527	8563	11048

SOURCE: ECONOMIC AND SOCIAL RIGHTS EMPOWERMENT INITIATIVE, UNIVERSITY OF
CONNECTICUT, CONNECTICUT, USA.
HTTP://SERFINDEX.UCONN.EDU/2017-INTERNATIONAL-SERF-INDEX-DOWNLOADS/

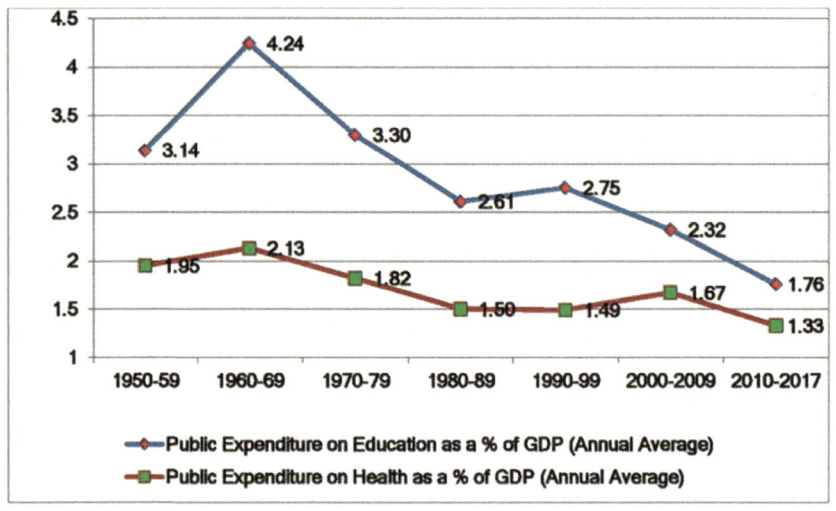

FIGURE 6.3   Public Expenditure on Education and Health as a percentage of GDP in
Sri Lanka 1950–2017
SOURCE: DERIVED FROM TABLE 6.1

independence (1950–1959) to just 1.76% during the eight years of post-civil-war
period (2010–2017). (See Figure 6.3 and Table 6.4)

Similarly, the average annual public expenditure on health as a percentage
of the GDP has declined from the peak of 2.13% during 1960–1969 to 1.33%
during 2010–2017. The average annual public expenditure on health as a

TABLE 6.4   Public Expenditure on Education and Health as a percentage of GDP in
Sri Lanka 1950–2017

Annual average for the ten-year period	Expenditure on education as a percentage of the GDP (annual average)	Expenditure on health as a percentage of the GDP (annual average)
1950–59	3.14	1.95
1960–69	4.24	2.13
1970–79	3.30	1.82
1980–89	2.61	1.50
1990–99	2.75	1.49
2000–2009	2.32	1.67
2010–2017 (Eight Years)	1.76	1.33

SOURCE: CENTRAL BANK OF SRI LANKA, ONLINE DATA LIBRARY. HTTPS://WWW.CBSL.LK
/ERESEARCH/ ACCESSED ON JULY 14, 2018.

percentage of the GDP dropped from 1.95% during the first decade after independence (1950–1959) to 1.33% in the first eight years after the end of the civil war (2010–2017). The average annual public expenditure on health as a percentage of the GDP has dropped significantly from 2.13% during the second decade after independence (1960–1969) to just 1.33% during the eight years of post-civil-war period (2010–2017) (See Figure 6.3 and Table 6.4)

It is also noteworthy that the public expenditure on education has always been significantly greater than the public expenditure on health, especially during the four decades between 1960 and 1999. However, the gap between the public expenditures on education and health has significantly narrowed in the new millennium; i.e. from 2000 to 2017. (See Figure 6.3 and Table 6.4)

In spite of the progressive decline in public expenditures on education and health since independence, the SERF Index of Sri Lanka has continued to rise, especially between 1985 and 2005.

There are inequalities in public expenditures on health in different provinces. According to Fernando, et al, (2009: 38),[10] the per capita public health expenditure in 2006 was lowest in the Sabaragamuwa Province (LKR (Lankan rupees) 1,643); followed by Eastern (LKR 1,717), North Central (LKR 1,768), and Southern Province (LKR 1,907), whereas the highest expenditure was in

10   T Fernando, RP Rannan-Eliya, and JMH Jayasundara, *Sri Lanka Health Accounts: National Health Expenditures 1990–2006* (Institute for Health Policy, 2009).

the Central Province (LKR 2,537) followed by in the Western Province (LKR 2,318). However, the foregoing discrepancies in per capita public expenditures on health could be due to the different health conditions of the populations in different provinces rather than due to deliberate discrimination by the government.

5.2   Gender Deficit

In spite of the relatively higher educational levels of women in comparison to men in Sri Lanka and higher educational levels of Sri Lankan women in comparison to women in other South Asian countries, the labour force participation rate of women in Sri Lanka is one of the lowest in South Asia.[11] Further, the labour force participation of women in the Eastern and Northern Provinces are the lowest within the country.[12]

We accept the fact that labour force participation rate is not the only criterion by which the impediments to upward mobility of women in the economy and society should be judged. However, due to brevity of space, it is the only impediment highlighted here as an example.

5.3   Unequal Human Development

In spite of the highest human development in Sri Lanka compared to rest of South Asia, malnutrition/undernourishment are very high among children and lactating women across the country, and the human development is far below the national average in the hill-country among the plantation Tamil community, among the Muslim minority community throughout the country, and in the former armed conflict-affected provinces and the adjacent districts.[13]

5.4   Democratic Deficit

Although Sri Lanka was the first country in South Asia to have exercised universal franchise in 1933 and one of the first countries in the world to let women exercise their franchise in the democratic process under colonial rule as well

---

11   R Nayar, P Gottret, P Mitra, G Betcherman, YM Lee, I Santos, M Dahal and M Shrestha, *More and Better Jobs in South Asia* (The World Bank, 2012).

12   M Sarvananthan, 'Impediments to Women in Post-Civil War Economic Growth in Sri Lanka' (2015) 2 *South Asian Journal of Human Resources Management* 23.

13   See United Nations Development Programme (UNDP), *Sri Lanka National Human Development Report 2012: Bridging Regional Disparities for Human Development* (United Nations Development Programme, 2012); United Nations Development Programme (UNDP), *Sri Lanka National Human Development Report 1998: Regional Dimensions of Human Development* (United Nations Development Programme, 1998).

as during the post-colonial native rule (including the election of world's first woman Prime Minister in 1960), the democratic governance in Sri Lanka has been by and large based on matronage/patronage (in terms of caste, class, ethnicity, family, gender, religion, etc.) cum greed as opposed to one based on merit cum need. See Kumarasingham 2014 for the politics of patronage in Ceylon; that is, during the early post-independence period.[14]

Democracy in South Asia appears to be paradoxical, and in its infancy so to speak. Andrew Roberts Wilder (1999)[15] argued that the voters at elections in the Punjab Province in Pakistan perceived that the prospective most effective deliverer of patronage (either the candidate and/or the political party) is the main criteria on which their voting is based.

"Look, we get elected because we are *ba asr log* [effective people] in our area. People vote for me because they perceive me as someone who can help them. And what help do they seek from me? Somebody's brother has committed a murder and he comes to me and I protect him from the authorities. Somebody's son is a matric fail and I get him a job as a teacher or a government servant. Somebody's nephew had been caught thieving and I protect him. This sort of thing. That is my power. This is what they perceive as power. You know, somebody has not paid up their loan and I try to have the payment delayed, etc. That means that I get elected because I am doing all the wrong things ... My skill is that laws don't mean anything to me, and that I can cut right across them and help people whether they are in the right or in the wrong. If somebody's son is first class, he's not coming to me to get him a job. If somebody has merit they very rarely come to me – occasionally they come to me. But it's the real wrongdoers who come to me."[16]

It is not just in Pakistan, most likely in other South Asian countries as well, the democratic franchise is exercised by the voters based on the perception which political party or the politician could potentially afford most patronage to the voters. The British High Commissioner in Ceylon in 1955 had succinctly observed that "elections are very largely a conflict of personalities over the distribution of government patronage and services" (quoted in Kumarasingham 2014: 181[17]), which is most likely the case even today (see below).

---

14   See H Kumarasingham, 'Elite Patronage over Party Democracy-High Politics in Sri Lanka Following Independence' (2014) 52 *Commonwealth & Comparative Politics* 166.

15   Anonymous politician quoted by AR Wilder, *The Pakistani Voter, Electoral Politics and Voting Behaviour in the Punjab* (Oxford University Press, 1999) quoted in N Martin, 'The Dark Side of Political Society: Patronage and the Reproduction of Social Inequality' (2014) 14 *Journal of Agrarian Change* 419.

16   *Ibid.*, 419.

17   Kumarasingham, *supra* note 14, 181.

The art and science of politics in Sri Lanka in the early independence period as well as today were/are personalities and patronage (patron-client or "leader-patron" or "leader-follower") underpinned by "blood and interests" in lieu of political philosophy and policies.[18] The "leader-centric" politics permeated all political parties - left to right, majority community parties to minority communities' parties – where policy was secondary.[19] Thus, "a parochial political class solidified by kinship and patronage rather than political party and professionalism" has hijacked the body politics of Ceylon (1948–1972)[20] and Sri Lanka (1972 – to date).

Whilst political philosophy and policies-based politics would represent competitive or deliberative or discursive democracy, personalities and patronage-based politics represent authoritarian or feudal or oligarchic democracy.

Sri Lanka is a majoritarian democracy with very little protections to the interests of the minority communities or marginalised groups of people (including in terms of gender and sexuality). The majoritarian democracy was first enshrined in the Constitution of 1972 (undoing the Constitutional safeguards afforded to the minority communities in the first Constitution enacted during the colonial rule) and retained in the Constitution of 1978 that is in operation until today. Sri Lanka should transform into a constitutional democracy where Constitution becomes supreme and not the elected majoritarian legislature or the executive which are structurally biased in favour of the majority community, majority decision-making, and the rule of patronage.

5.5   The Rule by Patronage

The very foundation of Sri Lankan society is based on patronage (especially elite) and social relationships[21] and personal followings which mirror the eighteenth-century British society and the then Westminster.[22] Patronage is the source of administrative and political power today, throughout the country, cutting across ethnicities, geographies, and gender.[23]

The nefarious history of matronage/patronage based partisan policy making (in terms of caste, class, ethnicity, family, gender, geography/place of origin, religion, etc.) in the democratic processes of Ceylon led to the first-ever armed rebellion in South Asia and the attempt to overthrow the democratically elected government in then Ceylon in 1971. The popular slogan of rural youths

---

18   Kumarasingham, *supra* note 14, 166–167.
19   *Ibid.*, 182.
20   *Ibid.*, 181.
21   *Ibid.*, 166.
22   *Ibid.*, 180.
23   See also K Hogland and A Piyarathne, 'Paying the Price of Patronage: Electoral Violence in Sri Lanka' (2009) 47 *Commonwealth and Comparative Politics* 287.

at that time was *"Colombata kiri* (milk) *apata kakiri* (marrow/cucumber)" (which is translated as, milk for Colombo (folks), but marrow/cucumber for village (folks). Subsequently, the youths of the largest ethnic minority community rebelled against the Sri Lankan state (beginning 1972) because of the systematic marginalisation of their educational, employment, land, and language rights since 1956 (if not before).

It is not only the governance of the state in Sri Lanka is grounded on matronage/patronage; professional associations, trade unions, past pupils' associations of schools, co-operatives, non-governmental organisations (NGOs), private sector firms, think thanks, religious organisations, media institutions, and the wider civil society (indeed uncivil society) are all governed by matronage/patronage, nepotism, and favouritism (*panthangkarayos*) as opposed to the governance by competence/efficiency criteria based on merit and equality of opportunities.

There are numerous heads of co-operatives (e.g. fisheries cooperatives in the north), NGOs/think tanks (e.g. Sarvodaya, MARGA Institute, the recent past Institute of Policy Studies), trade unions (e.g. Ceylon Teachers' Union, the recent past Ceylon Mercantile Union (CMU), Nurses' Union, religious organisations (e.g. the recent past All Ceylon Hindu Congress), newspaper editors (e.g. editors of the *Sunday Times* and *Sunday Island*), as well as heads of professional associations (e.g. the recent past Government Medical Officers' Association (GMOA), the recent past Sri Lanka Economic Association (SLEA) who remain or have remained in power for well over a decade (sometimes for many decades – e.g. recent past CMU President was in power for more than fifty years), ostensibly re-elected perpetually.

Moreover, employment opportunities in large private companies in Colombo and other metropolitan cities and towns are overwhelmingly favoured for school leavers from the prominent/prestigious schools in the respective cities and towns thereby structurally hindering the upward mobility of rural youths and youths from underprivileged backgrounds or communities who largely attend lesser known schools. Because of this structural bias in the employee recruitment practices of the private corporate sector (e.g. the stranglehold of Royal/Thomian fraternity in Colombo), there is cut-throat competition for admissions to prominent/prestigious schools in the cities and towns across the country involving widespread bribery and corruption[24] thereby permanently disadvantaging and dispossessing numerous communities of ordinary citizens.

---

24   See Transparency International Sri Lanka, https://www.tisrilanka.org/ (accessed 30 November 2022).

It is NOT a coincidence that numerous Ministers, Deputy Ministers, and State Ministers in the immediate past government (2015–2019) are alumni of the Royal College in Colombo (a prestigious boys' school representing the affluent and politically powerful classes). Indeed, all the members (except one) of the very first cabinet of independent Ceylon were either educated at Royal College (City of Colombo) or the St. Thomas College (Mount Lavania, a suburb of the City of Colombo). Moreover, the very first cabinet of independent Ceylon comprised two graduates of the University of Oxford, four graduates of the University of Cambridge, and six graduates of the University of London.[25] It is this pathological crony capitalism that is holding back Sri Lanka from realising its full potential and not capitalism *per se*. Moreover, the non-competitive employee recruitment practices of several agencies of the United Nations as well as the diplomatic missions of foreign countries in Sri Lanka are also structurally in favour of the elites of Colombo, Kandy, other urban centres, and the rural elites.

In sum, matronage/patronage is the bloodline and the breadline of the economy, polity, and the society of Sri Lanka (and the erstwhile Ceylon).

6   Directive Principles versus Justiciable Rights

The legal (and other) professionals who oppose the incorporation of the ESCR in the proposed new Constitution of Sri Lanka argue that the ESCR should be realised through directive principles of the government/s rather than through enshrining ESCR as justiciable rights in the Constitution. However, the antagonists of ESCR do not seem to realise that the Official Languages Act of 1987 in Sri Lanka (proclaiming Tamil as an official language in addition to Sinhala) is not fully implemented even today after thirty years of its enactment.

Argentina, Bangladesh, Colombia, Finland, Hungary, India, Ireland, Kenya, Latvia, the Philippines, South Africa, Switzerland, USA, and Venezuela are some countries where the justiciability and judicial enforce-ability of economic and social rights have been upheld by the judiciary.[26]

---

25   AJ Wilson 1960 'Ceylon Cabinet Ministers 1947–1959 – Their Political, Economic and Social Background' (1960) 5 *The Ceylon Economist* 1 quoted in Kumarasingham, *supra* note 14, 177.

26   A Nolan, B Porter and M Langford, *The Justiciability of Economic, Social and Cultural Rights: An Updated Appraisal* (Human Rights Consortium, 2007) 4.

Verma (2005)[27] has catalogued numerous case law in a number of countries in all the continents of the world where the judiciary has taken a proactive stance as regards upholding the economic, social, and cultural rights of its citizens; even in many countries where economic, social, and cultural rights are not incorporated into their respective Constitution.

In the circumstance of the Official Languages Act of 1987 not being implemented due to administrative and political apathy, how can the citizens of Sri Lanka expect or trust the directive principles of the state to be implemented faithfully in the case of ESCR? Whilst we do accept that enshrining ESCR as justiciable rights in the proposed new Constitution would not guarantee sincere implementation of the same,[28] we would argue that enshrining ESCR as justiciable rights is necessary but not sufficient.

7   Alleged Incompetence of the Judiciary

The antagonists of the ESCR as justiciable rights claim that the judiciary in Sri Lanka does not have the competencies to adjudicate on economic policies of the government. While we partially agree with such claim, we would argue that the judiciary is relatively much better educated, and relatively much more level-headed and rational than most of the politicians and legislators in Sri Lanka. Moreover, judges usually learn a lot on the job and through judicial education, especially on the matters of commercial law and intellectual property rights. Furthermore, the judges do weigh-in intricate technical and medical evidences in many criminal cases in all countries; similarly, it would not be difficult to weigh-in fiscal and monetary policy intricacies, even if that requires seeking outside expertise or delegating certain judicial tasks to outside experts.[29]

The separation of powers (among the three branches of a government; executive, judiciary, and the legislature) argument[30] and the alleged incompetence of the judiciary argument[31] are very common among people who are opposed to the justiciability of ESCR in many countries, which have been debunked by

---

27   S Verma, *Justiciability of Economic, Social, and Cultural Rights: Relevant Case Law*, Working Paper (International Council on Human Rights Policy, 2005).

28   See E Kaletski, L Minkler, N Prakash and S Randolph, 'Does Constitutionalizing Economic and Social Rights promote their fulfillment?' (2016) 15 *Journal of Human Rights* 433.

29   Nolan et al., *supra* note 26, 17.

30   *Ibid.*, 194.

31   Nolan et al., *supra* note 26, 16–20; Landau, *supra* note 3, 194.

the judiciary in many countries, including in Canada, France, Ireland, South Africa, and the United States.[32]

Probably, exclusive (or special) courts could be set-up with specially trained justices to adjudicate on the matters of ESCR (*ala* consumer affairs courts in India and other countries). Furthermore, the proposed constitutionalisation of economic, social, and cultural rights has to be specific as much as practically possible, in order not to give leeway to the judiciary as well as the wider legal fraternity to arbitrarily interpret the law.

For example, the International Covenant on Economic, Social and Cultural Rights (ICESCR) mandates or obligates signatory countries towards "progressive realization (of the rights) utilizing the maximum of available resources". In the view of this author, "maximum" in the foregoing could be interpreted in law arbitrarily, and therefore needs to be more specifically defined.

8   The Cost of Legal Enforcement of the ESCR

The argument advanced by the antagonists of the justiciable ESCR that the legal enforcement of ESCR will be costly to the exchequer is untenable because public investments in education (for example) will certainly contribute to higher economic growth and public investments in primary health-care (preventive health-care) will reduce the cost of secondary and tertiary health-care (curative health-care).[33] Moreover, the enforcement of the civil and political rights also requires substantial public funding by way of maintaining a police force, penal system, and an independent judiciary.[34] If the legal enforcement of the civil and political rights is affordable, why not the legal enforcement of the economic, social, and cultural rights?

The very high SERF Index of Sri Lanka is an indication that legal enforcement of ESCR would not be costly to the exchequer (because of its already higher position) and therefore the contrived fear/s of the antagonists for enshrining ESCR as justiciable rights is unwarranted and unjustified.

As noted above, the fact that, in spite of progressive decline of public expenditures on education and health since independence, the SERF Index of Sri Lanka has continued to rise, especially between 1985 and 2005, is an indication

---

32   *Ibid.*

33   For example see D Seymour and J Pincus, 'Human Rights and Economics: The Conceptual Basis for their Complementarity' (2008) 26 *Development Policy Review* 399.

34   For example, see JK Mapulanga-Hulston, 'Examining the Justiciability of Economic, Social and Cultural Rights' (2002) 6 *International Journal of Human Rights* 40–41.

that the financial cost of fulfillment of economic, social, and cultural rights through judicial action need not be excessive. In any case, the civil, cultural, economic, political, and social rights of the citizens cannot and should not be deprived because of the financial cost involved. In a landmark judgment issued in 1997, the Brazilian Federal Supreme Tribunal held that "the right of the individual ("protection of the inviolable rights to life and health") must always prevail, irrespective of its costs".[35]

The present Sri Lankan Constitution enacted in 1978, for the first time, provided constitutional guarantees to foreign investors against expropriation or nationalisation of their investment by the government. If the Sri Lankan Constitution could guarantee the economic/financial rights of foreign investors, why not guarantee the economic rights of its citizens? Most trade and investment agreements between different governments do provide mechanisms for adjudication of economic/financial rights of the foreign investors. If such judicial guarantees are necessary to secure foreign trade and investments, why not provide bare minimum judicial guarantees to the economic rights for its citizens?

Moreover, successive governments of Sri Lanka since 1977 have given excessive tax holidays and tax incentives to national and international businesses in order to attract foreign direct investments and joint ventures to fill the growing gap between savings and investments in the country. As a direct consequence of these lavish tax exemptions, holidays, and incentives, the total tax revenue of the government progressively shrunk from 18% of the Gross Domestic Product (GDP) in 1987 to 13% in 2017, and just 7% in 2021.[36]

If the successive Sri Lankan governments could afford to incur progressive significant decline in the total tax revenue, why not bear the cost of basic educational and health needs of its citizens, which is expected to be far less than the lost tax revenue over a period of thirty-five years?

9   ESCR as a Means of Transitional Justice and Peace-Building

Ceylon and its successor Sri Lanka has undergone fractures between different ethnic communities from time to time, especially between its majority Sinhalese community and the single largest minority community; the Tamils of eastern and northern heritage. The educational, employment, land, and

---

35   See Landau, *supra* note 3, 231.
36   See Central Bank of Sri Lanka, *Annual Report 2017* (Central Bank of Sri Lanka, 2018), special statistical appendix tables 2&6.

language rights of the Tamils, hailing from the Eastern and Northern Provinces of Sri Lanka, have been at the forefront of the ethnic conflict in Sri Lanka since its independence from Great Britain in 1948.

The foremost demand of the democratic political leaders of the Tamil community, since independence, has been to transform the country into a federal state from the unitary state enshrined in the Constitutions of Ceylon and its successor Sri Lanka. The Tamil youths, since 1972, took up arms to carve out a separate sovereign state encompassing the eastern and northern parts of Sri Lanka, which was militarily defeated by the armed forces of Sri Lanka in May 2009.

Several governments and democratic political leaders of the Tamils, since 1956, have attempted to arrive at a mutually agreeable solution to the enduring ethnic conflict in the country. A partial devolution of administrative and political power to the nine provinces of the island nation has been in force to date as a result of the Thirteenth Amendment to the 1978 Constitution of Sri Lanka brokered by the Government of India in 1987. However, in practice certain critical administrative and political powers have not been devolved to the provinces to date; two of which are the administration of lands and the law and order (by way of setting-up provincial police force).

As of 2020, there appears to be no sufficient political will among the majority Sinhalese community or its political leaderships to grant the powers of administration of lands and the law and order to the Provincial Councils set-up under the Thirteenth Amendment to the Constitution.

It is thirteen years since the end of the civil war in 2009 and there appears to be no workable political solution to the enduring ethnic conflict in Sri Lanka. Whilst the ultimate goal of the democratic political leadership of the Tamils remains a federal solution, there is an urgent need to work out interim solutions to address the long simmering legitimate grievances of the Tamil minority community.

One such interim solution proposed by this author was fiscal devolution to the Provincial Councils.[37] In this present policy research paper we would like to propose strictly enforceable economic, social, and cultural rights as another means of an interim solution to the long simmering ethnic conflict in the country. Whereas federalism is a taboo subject in the democratic politics of Sri Lanka, fiscal devolution and constitutionally enforceable economic, social, and cultural rights coupled with an equal opportunities law could be politically palatable to a critical mass of the Sri Lankans.

---

37   M Sarvananthan, 'Fiscal Devolution: A Stepping Stone towards Conflict Resolution in Sri Lanka' (2000) 19 *South Asian Survey* 101.

Transitional justice and peace-building are long processes, and there are different pathways to the realisation of enduring peace in any post-conflict country. Hence, the enshrining of ESCR as justiciable rights in the proposed new Constitution is proposed not only in its own right, but also as a means of conflict resolution in Sri Lanka (i.e. ensuring non-recurrence of the past armed conflict, which is the fourth pillar of the transitional justice processes).

Thus, justiciable ESCR could be an incremental fulfilment of the aspirations of not only the Tamil minority community, but also other minority communities as well as the marginalised segments of the majority Sinhalese community, and other marginalised segments of the Sri Lankan population such as women and the members of the dispossessed castes.

Moreover, whereas a federal politico-administrative system and fiscal devolution could satisfy the aspirations of the majority of the people of Eastern and Northern Provinces of Sri Lanka, viz. the Tamils, the justiciability of ESCR could provide guarantees to the minority communities within the eastern and northern provinces, viz. the Muslims and the Sinhalese, against any reverse discrimination. Furthermore, constitutionally guaranteed ESCR could address the marginalisation and the grievances of the hill-country Tamils (mostly working in the tea and rubber plantations without adequate educational, health, and housing facilities for over one-hundred-and-fifty years), the Tamils originating from Eastern and Northern Provinces and the Muslims spread throughout the country, and of course the marginalised segments of the Sinhalese community as well.

Whilst a federal politico-administrative system of government and fiscal devolution could address the inequality between different ethnic/religious communities in the country, the constitutionally guaranteed ESCR rights coupled with strictly enforceable equal opportunities law could address the inequalities based on caste, class, and gender as well (irrespective of one's ethnicity).

There are considerable case law evidences from Brazil, Colombia, and South Africa (for example) that reveal that the greatest beneficiaries of the justiciable ESCR are the middle and upper classes of the society than the poorer classes because of the former's greater ability to resort to judicial action and individualised enforcement of the law.[38] However, in Colombia there have been instances when justices have used the ESCR law to help more people from the poorer classes by resorting to structural enforcement/injunctions.[39]

---

38   Landau, *supra* note 3, 199–201, 209, 214, 218, 219–220, 230.
39   *Ibid.*, 202–203, 205–206, 208, 210.

10   Conclusions

According to the Freedom in the World 2013 compiled by the Freedom House in the United States of America (USA), Sri Lanka was one of the fourteen countries which had experienced negative growth in the aggregate score (incorporating political rights and civil liberties) during the five-year period between 2009 and 2013 and was at high risk of social unrest among sixty-five such countries.[40]

The ratings for Political Rights (PR) and Civil Liberties (CL) range from 1 to 7, whereby 1 denotes "greatest degree of freedom" and 7 denotes "smallest degree of freedom". The combined average of the PR and CL ratings determines the status of country whether they are free (1.0–2.5), partly free (3.0–5.0), or not free (5.5–7.0).[41]

During the 2006 to 2014 period, Sri Lanka's Political Rights (PR) rating was 4 (out of 7) between 2006 and 2010, which deteriorated to 5 (out of 7) between 2011 and 2014. However, the PR rating has improved to 4 during 2015 and further to 3 in 2016. Similarly, the Civil Liberties (CL) rating remained flat at 4 between 2006 and 2013, but deteriorated to 5 in 2014. However, the CL rating has improved to 4 in 2015 and remains the same in 2016.[42]

Although there have been marginal improvements in both the political rights and civil liberties ratings of Sri Lanka in 2015 and 2016, it continues to be only a "partly free" country according to the Freedom of the World ranking.

The Civil and Political Rights (CPR) of human beings are intrinsically interconnected with Economic, Social, and Cultural Rights (ESCR); which is what the human rights scholars term "indivisibility of rights" (or "interdependence of rights") or "intersectionality" (of rights) in terms of feminist theory. There is a two-way relationship between the CPR and ESCR; the former rights cannot be fully realised without the realisation of the latter and vice versa.

Therefore, an enforceable equal opportunities law (in terms of caste, class, ethnicity, gender, religion, sexuality, etc.) and enshrining of ESCR as justiciable rights in the proposed new Constitution of Sri Lanka are *sine qua non* for developing a perfectly competitive market economy, in addition to fostering an inclusive economy and shared prosperity for ALL the citizens of the country.

---

40   Freedom House, 'Freedom in the World 2017' https://freedomhouse.org/report/fiw-2017
      -table-country-scores (accessed 23 August 2018).
41   *Ibid.*
42   *Ibid.*

Note on the Contributors

Muttukrishna Sarvananthan
Founder cum Principal Researcher of the Point Pedro Institute of Development, Point Pedro, Northern Province, Sri Lanka (PhD Wales, MSc Bristol, MSc Salford & BA (Hons) Delhi)) Corresponding author sarvi@pointpedro.org
ORCID 0000-0001-6443-0358

Navaratnam Sivakaran
Senior Lecturer in Philosophy in the Department of Philosophy, University of Jaffna, Northern Province, Sri Lanka (BA (Special) and MPhil in Philosophy, University of Jaffna; MA in Philosophy, University of Peradeniya, Sri Lanka. This article was first published in *The Journal of Law, Social Justice & Global Development*, 25 December 2020, 46–59. DOI: 10.31273/LGD.2019.2504

Just Transition on the Margins of Labour Law: Integrating Legal Adaptive Capacity and Philippine Administrative Legal Framework

Jayvy R. Gamboa

Abstract

Achieving global climate targets is tied to the shift to a low-carbon economy, but such shift may entail unequitable sharing of costs to the detriment of workers and front-line communities who depend on carbon-intensive industries, such as coal and fossil fuel. Similar to any disruption or new phenomena, legal systems, including laws and institutions, respond in a regulatory or clinical manner, yet such attempts are constantly hindered by bureaucratic rigidity. Provided that Philippine labour policy thus far lacks an actionable just transition aspect, this exploratory research confronts the problem by inquiring into the ability of *existing* Philippine labour legal mechanisms (Department of Labor and Employment, Employees' Compensation Commission, and Social Security Commission) to adopt and implement just transition measures within the bounds of lawful authority, assessed through the prevailing administrative legal framework and the legal adaptive capacity (LAC) analysis as adopted from Camacho and Glicksman (2016). Besides forwarding the academic, policy, and legal discourse on just transition in the Philippines, it further contributes by integrating a contemporary viewpoint to the study of Philippine administrative law and by building on the methodological soundness and applicability of the LAC analysis for future research.

Keywords

legal adaptive capacity – just transition – low-carbon economy – adaptive law – disruption – labour law – administrative law – Philippines

1 Introduction

Disruptions, whether technological, industrial, cultural, social, political, or economic, have their ways of influencing—at best—and leading towards obsolescence—at worst—structures and systems. Historically, societies saw how massive and intrusive changes have loosen the weave of social fabrics, such that prevailing frameworks and psyches of a particular era were challenged to fit and respond to such changes.[1] Today, in fact, the world faces no shortage of disruptions, the largest and most recent of which is the COVID-19 pandemic that has not spared any country in the planet. The fourth industrial revolution (4IR) is also looming. Artificial intelligence, blockchain, cryptocurrency, social media, and digital economy are here to pervade people's daily lives from hereon. Climate change has been made known to the global community for decades already, yet it still remains as one of the biggest disruptions felt by communities, especially the most vulnerable, now more than ever. The particular disruption studied by this paper, which will be further explained in the succeeding sections, is the shift to a low-carbon economy driven by the global climate targets and more specifically by the Philippines' commitments to achieve such targets.

The shift to a low-carbon economy demands, among other efforts, a shift to renewable energy and away from energy sources linked to high emissions, such as coal. *Suppose* that a systemic and widespread shift was started; *imagine* that coal-fired power plants were ordered to shut down. Although the timelines for closure differ from plant to plant—may it be three, five, or ten years—one thing is certain. Closure is inevitable.[2] Without any safeguard measures in place, the workers and frontline communities who depend on such plants will definitely be left behind. It is not unreasonable to assume that workers will be terminated, and frontline communities will be forced to live in a void of economic activity.[3] *How can then this tragic outcome be avoided?*

---

1   *See, generally* RS Cowan, 'The "Industrial Revolution" in the Home: Household Technology and Social Change in the 20th Century' (1976) 17 *Technology & Culture* 1 ; KJ Bindas, *Modernity and the Great Depression: The Transformation of American Society, 1930 – 1941* (2017); JL Collins and B Wellman, 'Small Town in the Internet Society: Chapleau Is No Longer an Island' (2020) 53 *American Behavioral Scientist* 1344.

2   Closure is inevitable, assuming that fossil fuel lobbied interests and investment would relent. *See, e.g.* People for Power Coalition, 'Philippine Civil Society Position on the Energy Legacy and Energy Policy Update of the Asian Development Bank' Center Energy Ecology and Development, 30 April 2021, https://ceedphilippines.com/philippine-civil-society-position -on-the-energy-legacy-and-energy-policy-update-of-the-asian-development-bank/ (accessed 4 January 2022).

3   See International Labour Organization, Guidelines for a Just Transition Towards Environmentally Sustainable Economies and Societies for all (2015). The International Labour Organization recognizes as economic structuring as a major challenge, "resulting in the displacement of workers and possible job losses and job creation attributable to the greening

A just transition can address such an outcome.[4] For every systemic change—or transition, there will definitely be costs incurred and opportunities lost. A just transition ensures that such costs are equitably distributed to stakeholders and that workers and frontline communities do not carry said burden *alone*. Ensuring just transition in the middle of the shift to a low-carbon economy seems a tall order to hurdle, because, as many have argued, it will make the shift more thorough—thus, costlier and slower. However, the fundamental premise that this paper establishes is that just transition, and its demands of equity and social protection, must never be a reason for further delay in the shift to a low-carbon economy.[5] The challenge for the public sector therefore is to adopt and implement just transition measures in an immediate, yet neither arbitrary nor unreasonable, manner while being consistent with climate change science. Among those measures are legislative ones. But the question remains whether *the legal system and its mechanisms are capable of adapting to those constraints and of delivering effective intervention to meet societal needs.*

With these, the research question presented by this paper is *whether or not existing Philippine labour legal mechanisms (instruments and institutions) have sufficient ability to adopt and implement just transition measures in response to the shift to a low-carbon economy within the bounds of lawful authority.* Correspondingly, this is answered through an examination of labour legal mechanisms (i.e. Department of Labor and Employment, Employees' Compensation Commission, Social Security Commission) using the prevailing administrative legal framework and the legal adaptive capacity (LAC) analysis adopted from Camacho and Glicksman (2016), which refers to "the formal regulatory or management [or administrative] regime's capacity to adapt to new phenomena that affect the resource or activity it regulates or manages."[6]

A caveat, however, is that just transition is not yet as pronounced as a policy agenda in the Philippines, which is why the results of this paper will remain illustrative rather than conclusive. Nonetheless, it starts the much-needed

---

of enterprises and workplaces". *See also* A Bowen, "'Green' Growth, 'Green' Jobs and Labor Market' *World Bank Policy Research Working Paper* 5990 (2012).

4   See Just Transition Research Collaborative, *Mapping Just Transition(s) to a Low-Carbon World* (United Nations Research Institute for Social Development, 2018).

5   See IPCC, *Summary for Policymakers in* Climate Change 2021: The Physical Science Basis. Contribution of Working Group I to the Sixth Assessment Report of the Intergovernmental Panel on Climate Change (2021).

6   AE Camacho and RL Glicksman, 'Legal Adaptive Capacity: How Program Goals and Processes Shape Federal Land Adaptation to Climate Change' (2016) 87 *University of Colorado Law Review* 711, 722.

academic discourse on this matter. Further, this paper decides to take an unconventional path in legal research. Instead of problematizing the co-existence of two (or more) competing rights in a legal system, which often requires a reconciliation of particular doctrines within a legal hierarchy—and a prevailing right, this paper avoids the dangerous slippery slope of nitpicking the intrinsic worth of the shift to a low-carbon economy, on the one hand, and just transition, on the other. Informed by the historical roots of the dilemma at hand that has been characterized for so long as jobs versus environment,[7] the legal question on which this paper is grounded acts as an *antithesis* to such false dichotomy.

This exploratory research thus has a three-pronged objective: *first*, to initiate legal research on just transition in light of Philippine labour legal mechanisms; *second*, to shape the further development of Philippine administrative legal framework by integrating contemporary theory, such as LAC; and *third*, to extend the LAC analysis by introducing a conceptual framework and a scalable multi-step process in adopting the LAC analysis to various legal jurisdictions, fields of law, and other forms of disruptions.

The paper is divided into five more parts. Part 2 probes the complex problem by understanding the relationship between disruptions and legal systems and by discussing the literature on the shift to a low-carbon economy, just transition, and labour law, in general. The *margins* of legal mechanisms are identified as a starting point to which administrative law presents a necessary yet inadequate opening for further analysis. Part 3 sets up the framework of analysis to be used in this paper by looking at the theoretical origins of the LAC analysis. These will serve as steppingstone in developing a counterpart conceptual framework of the LAC analysis and a multi-step process in adopting the LAC analysis to other cases and examples with an aim of a more scalable tool of analysis for future research. Furthermore, this paper extends the LAC analysis by introducing what this paper calls as *absolute* and *relative* LAC. Part 4 then examines the Philippine legal system, including its administrative regime, and its major legal doctrines to determine its potential intersection with the LAC analysis. Through this, the LAC analysis will be properly grounded in the nuances of Philippine law yet recognizing the gaps of the latter by offering an alternative method to answer the research question. Part 5 proceeds to the analysis proper of the Philippine labour legal mechanisms in relation to just transition measures by applying the LAC analysis through the earlier

---

7   D Stevis, E Morena and D Krause, 'Introduction: The Genealogy and Contemporary Politics of Just Transitions' in E Morena, D Krause and D Stevis (eds.) *Just Transitions: Social Justice in the Shift Towards a Low-Carbon World* (Pluto Press, 2020) 21–23.

crafted multi-step process. Part 6 concludes by summarizing the milestones reached by this paper, presenting emerging issues, and proposing questions for future research on the topic from academic, policy, and legal perspectives both in the Philippines and globally.

2   Understanding the Problem

2.1   *Law and Disruptions*

Disruptions come in many forms and in different ways at various points of history. For every disruption, legal responses emerge. In one way or another, generally, law regulates—or is expected to regulate—these and the consequences that come along with them. It is thus imperative to inquire first on the role of law within and beyond these disruptions and new phenomena.

In a broader perspective, a modern legal system's primary purpose is "to create and sustain certainty and security in the distribution of resources among humans in society".[8] Legal systems are also structured to prefer the status quo.[9] Conversely, history and human experience have shown that disruptions require institutions, including the legal system, that are flexible and adaptive. Some have even described the law as "brittle"[10] if it cannot keep up with the pace, scale, and direction of disruptions, despite its noble goals of stability and certainty. "All regulators must adapt to change in order to remain effective."[11]

This then justifies the greater need to understand the law in light of new scholarly developments. In this section, two strands of studies on the relationship of law and disruptions are explored: *first*, the role of law as an adaptive tool, particularly in governance; and *second*, law as a complex adaptive system that itself requires adaptation or resilience.[12]

---

8   CA Arnold and LH Gunderson, 'Adaptive Law and Resilience' (2013) 43 *Environmental Law Report* 10427.

9   *Ibid.*, 10428. "The basic features of the U.S. legal system that are maladaptive fall into four large categories: (1) systemic goals that are narrow; (2) a structure that is monocentric (i.e., centralization of authority to solve problems), unimodal (i.e., the use of single, uniform models as solutions to problems), and fragmented; (3) inflexible methods that employ rules, legal abstractions, and promote resistance to change; and (4) rational, linear, legal-centralist processes that assume away uncertainty."

10   Arnold and Gunderson, *supra* note 8, 10427.

11   Camacho and Glicksman, *supra* note 6, 722, *citing* B McDonnell and D Schwarcz, 'Regulatory Contrarians' (2011) 89 *N.C. Law Review* 1629, 1635.

12   Without preempting the discussion of legal adaptive capacity as adopted by this present paper, both of these strands of studies on law and disruptions seem to be integrated in the study and use of LAC. On the primary level, LAC refers to the flexibility of law or resilience

2.1.1 Adaptive Governance and Law

In the past decade, scholarly studies have examined the role of law in adaptive governance, which owes its conceptual roots to ecological and subsequently climate change literature. Adaptive governance is understood to incorporate "formal organizations, informal groups, and individuals at multiples scales and requires collaboration, communication, and adaptation in response to social and ecological monitoring."[13]

It is crucial to note, however, that governance is not limited to matters of law. Instead, other aspects that influence the system such as socio-cultural factors and historical context are also essential to such an appreciation. This paper also deems adaptive governance as equally applicable to other types of phenomena besides ecological and environmental issues, perhaps only requiring slight modifications in its operational definition and outcomes.

Adaptive management's[14] legal barriers include narrow and prescriptive rules that tend to limit the application of laws to particular categories of the regulated property or transaction; jurisdictional and legal boundaries, fragmentation, and division that are inconsistent with those of ecosystems; extensive legal requirements in public participatory processes; liberal exercise of judicial review that tend to unduly control the discretion of public officials and agencies in implementing adaptive measures;[15] and inflexible and outdated goals that require very specific outcomes.[16]

Focus has since shifted in favor of analyzing adaptive governance, because any legal reform that seeks to accommodate adaptive management is linked to the legal system's governance structure, including its laws, regulations, and

---

of such a system. On a deeper level, this flexibility of law itself can also be further used for adaptive governance.

13   LH Gunderson, A Garmestani, KW Rizzardi, JB Ruhl and A Light, 'Escaping a Rigidity Trap: Governance and Adaptive Capacity to Climate Change in the Everglades Social Ecological System' (2014) 51 *Idaho Law Review* 127, 149, *citing* AS Garmestani and MH Benson, 'A Framework for Resilience-Based Governance of Social-Ecological Systems' (2013) 18 *Ecology and Society* art. 9.

14   MF Frohlich, C Jacobson and P Fidelman, 'The Relationship Between Adaptive Management of Social-Ecological Systems and Law: A Systematic Review' (2018) 23 *Ecology and Society*. It is defined as a "framework designed for managing complex and dynamic social-ecological systems, in which decision making follows a structured and iterative process aiming to reduce uncertainties over time through monitoring and evaluation of management actions."

15   *Ibid*. "[T]his encourages a management approach more concerned with avoiding legal disputes rather than engaging in experimentation and monitoring."

16   *Ibid*. "[L]egal barriers to adaptive management are usually related to one or more of the following legal values: (i) stationarity; (ii) certainty; and (iii) finality."

other legal instruments.[17] Moreover, it has been recognized that, in a reality where there are multiple goals, scales, and authorities involved in governance that need to be negotiated, adaptive governance, instead of mere management, is required.[18]

Recognizing that fast-paced change, high uncertainty, and an intergenerational timeframe exacerbate the nature of value-laden problems resulting from disruptions, adaptive governance is explored as a possible tool and a "promising means to manage modern problems."[19] *What then is the role of law in this?* It need not be stated that all discourses on governance have a strong connection, although not an exclusive one, with the legal system where such governance ensues.[20]

Setting aside the non-legal aspects of adaptive governance, Cosens et al. argue that adaptive governance is facilitated, not controlled, by formal law and government.[21] They then identified steps how to maximize the potential of law and government in adaptive governance. As to the *government structure*, the authority to adaptively manage must be delegated to the level of government closest to the problem without dismissing the broad goals and standards established in the higher level of government. As to the *government's role in capacity building*, the government must lead in focusing, catalyzing, and accelerating innovation that ensures public and private participation. As to the *governmental adaptive capacity*, agencies must have the authority to implement adaptive management, the resources to initiate monitoring, and the

---

17   See JB Ruhl, B Cosens and N Soininen, 'Resilience of Legal Systems: Toward Adaptive Governance' in M Ungar (ed.) *Multisystemic Resilience: Adaptation and Transformation in Contexts of Change* (Oxford University Press, 2021) 509, 523. "Whereas adaptive management focuses on *instrument* design for decision- making at the microscale, this new movement focused on *governance* design to promote adaptive capacity at the macroscale of social- ecological system management more broadly. [...] They referred to this new configuration of institutional design and capacity as adaptive governance[.]"

18   *See* Ruhl et al., *supra* note 17. "Although achieving adaptive governance does not necessitate employing adaptive management and employing adaptive management does not guarantee achieving adaptive governance, most theorists and practitioners suggest that the two are reinforcing and should go hand in hand [...]."

19   BA Cosens, JB Ruhl, N Soininen and L Gunderson, 'Designing Law to Enable Adaptive Governance of Modern Wicked Problems' (2020) 73 *Vanderbilt Law Review* 1687, 1690.

20   *See* BA Cosens, RK Craig, SL Hirsch, CT Arnold, MH Benson, DA DeCaro, AS Garmestani, H Gosnell, JB Ruhl and E Schlager, 'The Role of Law in Adaptive Governance' (2017) 22 *Ecology and Society*. "For example, how is authority distributed among local, state, tribal, and federal authorities; what authority do governmental agencies have to act in a particular situation; and what processes are agencies required to follow in taking that action? All of these processes are governed by law."

21   Cosens et al., supra note 19, 1727.

authority to change course if scientific knowledge indicate a need to do so. As to the *government process and oversight*, the government must provide oversight on agency actions and accountability measures for good governance.[22]

Besides these interventions, it is concluded as well that law and government, to fully facilitate adaptive governance, are required to be adaptive themselves, or what is known in literature as *adaptive law*.

2.1.2   Adaptive Law

Before exploring the literature on adaptive law, it is significant to note the fundamental difference in perspectives between the first strand on adaptive governance and the second strand on adaptive law. Not only does the study of adaptive law draw from ecological literature when it refers to the concepts of resilience and adaptive capacity, it also involves complexity science or the study of complex adaptive systems in its framework.

Ruhl et al. presents a tall order of goals in their article, *Resilience of Legal Systems*, which include how to contextualize resilience for legal systems, recognizing that legal systems are situated within a vast co-evolving system of systems.[23] A critical observation in considering a *legal system* as a *complex system* is that "[l]egal regimes must therefore not only consider the complex adaptive qualities of social-ecological systems, but also must themselves achieve appropriate resilience and adaptive capacity".[24] Instead of thinking about the law as a purely normative, independent, and insulated amalgamation of rules and processes, this view instead presents law as something within and interacts with other social systems.[25]

From this perspective, a legal system is defined as "a complex adaptive system comprised of numerous interacting and even nested systems of international law, regional law (e.g. the EU), as well as national and subnational systems (i.e. a system of systems), all of which exhibit varying degrees of resilience."[26] Such legal system then responds to internal (e.g. changes within the law) and external forces (e.g. changes from other social systems that impact the law) for which resilience is necessary.

---

22   *Ibid.*, 1727–1731.

23   Ruhl et al., *supra* note 17, 509.

24   *Ibid.*, 521.

25   See J Murray, TE Webb and S Wheatley, 'Encountering Law's Complexity' in J Murray, TE Webb and S Wheatley (eds.) *Complexity Theory and Law: Mapping an Emergent Jurisprudence* (Routledge, 2018) 6–8. The chapter distinguishes the complexity theory and the autopoietic theory, which was earlier forwarded by Teubner, and argues that the former "significantly enhances the value of systems theory thinking in law".

26   Ruhl et al., *supra* note 17, 514

After laying the basis for a view of the legal system as resilient and adaptive, adaptive law is then defined as "refer[ing] to the design of legal systems, institutions, and instruments intended to facilitate flexibility, resilience, and dynamism in the management of complex social-ecological systems."[27] It is a counternarrative to conventional regulatory law, which has been characterized as centralized, rigid, heavily skewed on front-end assessment, litigation, and limited opportunity for administrative adjustment.

Another study has deconstructed the features of adaptive law into the following: (1) adaptive goals, which aim to achieve multiple coexistent forms of resilience (or poly-resilience) that strengthen the adaptive capacity of both social systems, including institutions and communities, and ecological systems; (2) adaptive structure, which spreads power and authority among multiple centers (or polycentric) that avoid a cascade of failure, and uses multiple modes, methods, or instruments to address problems at multiple scales; (3) adaptive methods, which use context-regarding standards and flexible discretionary decision making; and (4) adaptive processes, which recognize iterative processes among multiple participants.[28]

2.1.3   Rigidity and Responses

With these two strands of research, legal systems can either be viewed as the structure that merely provides a platform for adaptive governance that ultimately addresses the disruption; or as complex adaptive systems in themselves that require to be resilient and adaptive—not only for setting up adaptive governance, but also for one that is rigid if need be. Law therefore is not only in the sidelines of addressing disruptions; it is well within the playing field or battleground, depending on the disruption at hand.

As mentioned earlier, legal systems are much like any other complex adaptive system in that they absorb impacts brought by disruptions and they devise ways of responding to these. The *conventional* response to any new phenomenon usually takes either of two forms: legislation by congress or parliament or adjudication on an actual case or controversy by courts or tribunals.[29]

---

27   *Ibid.*, 521.
28   CA Arnold, 'Resilient Cities and Adaptive Law' (2014) 50 *Idaho Law Review* 245, 252–254. See also Ruhl et al., *supra* note 17, 524. "Adaptive law promotes process that is legitimate, just, problem- solving, reflective, dispute resolving, and balanced between stability and flexibility. The latter quality— the optimal trade- off between stability and flexibility that produces neither too much rigidity nor too much room for arbitrary decision- making— is perhaps the one that will be most vexing for legal theorists and practitioners to design and implement [...]."
29   Cosens et al., *supra* note 20.

Regardless of the constitutional order that a state adopts, law-making is a central part of responding to disruptions. For those that follow a civil law tradition, disruptions are addressed by codifying norms through statutes passed by a national or local legislature, depending on the level of government. On the other hand, for those that subscribe to common law tradition, judge-made law and judicial precedents pervade law-making.[30]

Electoral and democratic exercises—the processes of which are also governed by laws—can also be considered as *conventional* responses. Should disruptions be so fundamental and polarizing, a change in the ruling government, especially in countries where ideology-based party system exists, may be required to address a disruption.[31] However, this pattern causes a gap between the time when the disruption arose and when actual and functional measures are institutionalized. Otherwise stated, legal systems, to *conventionally* respond to disruptions, take time. Unfortunately, this results in the detriment of stakeholders who are left exposed and vulnerable to the impacts of disruption that unfortunately *do not* and *cannot wait.*

Notwithstanding the bureaucratic rigidity of the legal system, it remains a potent tool in responding to disruptions, primarily due to its ability—no matter how slow—to bring stability and predictability in the newly created spaces of relations. While it is apparent that the logical step for a legal system when faced by a disruption is to take the *conventional responses* of letting the legal mechanisms run its course, the discussion of an adaptive legal system or adaptive law shows their limitations.

This paper argues that, to overcome these, there must be *alternative responses* that are equally valid and lawful yet significantly more adaptive. Its key challenge however is its evasive position *on the margins* of existing law, which is attempted to be explored in this paper.

2.2   *Shift to a Low-Carbon Economy and Just Transition*
After grasping the wider context on how disruptions affect legal systems and how legal systems consequently play a role in adapting to such disruptions, this section explains the shift to a low-carbon economy and just transition.[32] Further, connecting the technical discussions herein and the concept of adaptive

---

30   A state that has hybrid legal system, such as the Philippines, may also present a unique situation, where the legal system is neither fully civil law nor fully common law—but a class of its own. See *infra* Part 4. for discussion on the Philippine legal system and its hybridity.

31   Cosens et al., *supra* note 20.

32   It must be noted that such topics of shift to a low-carbon economy and just transition are generally discussed to avoid preempting the analysis in Part 5.

law, an argument is made on how the problem presented in this research may be addressed from a legal perspective.

2.2.1   Shift to a Low-Carbon Economy

There is no more resounding alarm than the recent 6th Assessment Report of the Intergovernmental Panel on Climate Change – Working Group 1 (2021), which states that "[h]uman-induced climate change is already affecting many weather and climate extremes in every region across the globe. Evidence of observed changes in extremes such as heatwaves, heavy precipitation, droughts, and tropical cyclones, and, in particular, their attribution to human influence, has strengthened since AR5 [the 5th Assessment Report of 2014]."[33] Not only are extreme weather events more intense, they have also become more frequent; thus, more destructive in terms of resources and more deadly in terms of human lives.

The shift to a low-carbon economy can be traced back to the United Nations Framework Convention on Climate Change (UNFCCC) in 1992.[34] Through the years and climate conferences, the concept of a low-carbon economy has evolved, even including how it is used in practice, but its core remained intact, which is climate change mitigation and sustainable development. The most recent reference to the low-carbon economy is the "low greenhouse gas emission and climate resilient development," which is integrated into the Paris Agreement in 2015 and the Glasgow Climate Pact in 2021.[35]

Science and policy have concurred that keeping the average global temperature well below 2.0 °C is necessary to reduce the impacts of climate change, although climate science does emphasize that 1.5 °C is the more ambitious target.[36] Much more is required if the global community is keen on reversing the trend.

---

33   IPCC, *supra* note 5, 8.

34   UN General Assembly, United Nations Framework Convention on Climate Change, A/RES/48/189 (1994) [hereinafter "UNFCCC"].

35   Conference of the Parties, Adoption of the Paris Agreement, at art. 2, para 1(c), U.N. Doc FCCC/CP/2015/L.9/Rev/1 (2015) [hereinafter "Paris Agreement"]; Conference of the Parties, Glasgow Climate Pact, para 52, U.N. Doc FCCC/PA/CMA/2021/L.16 (2021) [hereinafter "Glasgow Climate Pact"].

36   *See Glasgow Climate Pact*, para 22. "*Recognizes* that limiting global warming to 1.5 °C requires rapid, deep and sustained reductions in global greenhouse gas emissions, including reducing global carbon dioxide emissions by 45 per cent by 2030 relative to the 2010 level and to net zero around mid-century, as well as deep reductions in other greenhouse gases;"

Definitely, climate change mitigation is easier said than done; all the more for the shift to a low-carbon economy. It is granted that the developed countries will have to pay the price of their economies' unabated dependence to fossil fuels by channeling resources to developing and most vulnerable countries— that have the dual burden of facing the most extreme climate events and of striving for economic development.[37] The intersectionality of vulnerability to the impacts of climate change and of the lack of human development in these countries makes it even more difficult to address.

An approach of the Paris Agreement in operationalizing this is for Parties to create "long-term low greenhouse gas emission development strategies"[38] in the national level. This has not prevented the European Union to as well adopt such long-term strategies for its Member States to follow. In 2020, EU's *Long-term low greenhouse gas emission development strategy* was adopted to "[achieve] a climate-neutral EU by 2050".[39]

The Glasgow Climate Pact presents a more aggressive and concrete low-emission development strategy. The agreement calls upon the Parties to "transition towards low-emission energy systems, including by rapidly scaling up the deployment of clean power generation and energy efficiency measures, including accelerating efforts towards the phasedown of unabated coal power and phase-out of inefficient fossil fuel subsidies, while providing targeted support to the poorest and most vulnerable in line with national circumstances and recognizing the need for support towards a just transition".[40] For the first time, language specifically pertaining to fossil fuel and coal power are integrated, which is hoped to increase efforts in this area.

If this will be situated in the disruptions discourse, it can be argued that the shift to a low-carbon economy is not entirely a disruption; instead, it is only a response—a wide-scale global response—to climate change. While this may hold true, this paper intends to present an example where a response to a primary disruption (i.e. shift to a low-carbon economy vis-à-vis climate change) that is so fundamental can itself be a secondary disruption.

---

37   See UNFCCC, art. 11, para 5. "The developed country Parties may also provide and develop-
      ing country Parties avail themselves of, financial resources related to the implementation
      of the Convention through bilateral, regional and other multilateral channels." This has
      ripened into an obligation through the official adoption of the Green Climate Fund in
      COP 17 (Durban, South Africa).
38   Paris Agreement, art. 4, para 19.
39   European Union, *Long-term Low Greenhouse Gas Emission Development Strategy of the
      European Union and its Member States* (European Union, 2020).
40   Glasgow Climate Pact, para 20.

The global scientific community has declared that "human influence has warmed the atmosphere, ocean and land."[41] Thus, there should be no doubt as to the pressing, unqualified, and existential need to pursue low-emission and climate-resilient development. This is both a national commitment to ensure the well-being of a country's own citizens and a collective commitment to do what is scientifically sound for peoples of other nations, especially those most vulnerable to extreme weather events.[42]

2.2.2   Just Transition

The term "just transition" was officially integrated into the climate change discourse through the Paris Agreement, where it states that Parties "[takes] into account the imperatives of a just transition of the workforce and the creation of decent work and quality jobs in accordance with nationally defined development priorities."[43] Notably six years after Paris, the historic COP in Glasgow expanded what just transition entails.[44]

The expansion of just transition's meaning in the major climate change agreements signals the flexibility that the concept has at this point of history. Such flexibility has even made itself a target of appropriation[45] like any newly minted concepts. In fact, the use of just transition in the Paris and Glasgow agreements can even be argued as appropriation. Although to a lesser extent, non-governmental organizations, private corporations, business associations, lobbying and advocacy groups, and other institutions have started exploring

---

41   IPCC, *supra* note 5, 4.

42   See E BC Novio, 'Climate Change and Disasters in the Philippines' *Heinrich Böll Stiftung Southeast Asia* (2022) https://th.boell.org/en/2022/01/21/climate-disasters-philippines (accessed 5 December 2022), for a brief overview of the increased frequency and intensity of extreme climate events in the Philippines. See also Commission of Human Rights of the Philippines, National Inquiry on Climate Change Report (2022), for the nexus between climate change and human rights in the Philippine context.

43   Paris Agreement, preamble.

44   Glasgow Climate Pact, para 52. "*Recognizes* the need to ensure just transitions that promote sustainable development and eradication of poverty, and the creation of decent work and quality jobs, including through making financial flows consistent with a pathway towards low greenhouse gas emission and climate-resilient development, including through deployment and transfer of technology, and provision of support to developing country Parties;"

45   This paper avoids to categorically use *misappropriation* to avoid a normative determination of what is a correct and incorrect meaning of just transition, although one can reasonably make a judgment whether a particular meaning is a misuse or abuse of just transition.

the concept and how it could best fit their vision and, of course, their respective interests.[46]

Moreover, Stevis, Morena, and Krause, in *Introduction: The genealogy and contemporary politics of just transition*,[47] present the historical development of the concept of just transition, which traces its origins to Tony Mazzocchi, an American trade unionist in the 1970s. At that time, the labour movement called for a review of industry practices to protect the health and safety of workers. Later on, the Superfund for Workers, or a just transition fund, was established to fund the clean-up of hazardous industrial sites, such as manufacturing and processing plants, mines, and landfills.[48] While the struggle of the labour movement has not wavered in any way, the rise of climate change as a global threat in the following decades saw the potential of just transition as a guiding principle.

This paper, although not exclusively, adopts the following definition of just transition: "a policy platform that advocates legal and policy responses and planning that recognizes the need for economies to transition to lower carbon economic activity, while at the same time respects the need to promote decent work and a fair distribution of the risks and rewards associated with this transition."[49] This formulation seems appropriate to how the research problem herein is purposely framed: one that does not perpetuate the jobs versus environment dichotomy, but instead focuses on the most equitable way

---

46   Stevis et al., *supra* note 7, 4–6. See also Just Transition Research Collaborative, *supra* note 4. This groundbreaking research among climate change, labour, environmental, social justice, and political science scholars maps the just transition framings of selected organizations as used in official communications, projects, and other materials—from those that merely forward green growth and green industries to those that demand a necessary rethinking of economic and social systems to address injustice.

47   *Ibid.*

48   *See* Stevis et al., *supra* note 7, 11, *citing* L Leopold, *Statement at the International Joint Commission's 1995 Biennial Meeting on Great Lakes Water Quality* (International Joint Commission, 1995) 83, https://legacyfiles.ijc.org/publications/C46.pdf (accessed 5 January 2022). "We propose that a special fund be established; a just-transition fund which we've called in the past a superfund for workers. Essentially this fund will provide the following: full wages and benefits until the worker retires or until he or she finds a comparable job; two – up to four years of tuition stipends to attend vocational schools or colleges plus full income while in school; three – post-educational stipends or subsidies if no jobs at comparable wages are available after graduation; and four – relocation assistance."

49   DJ Doorey, 'Just Transitions Law: Putting Labour Law to Work on Climate Change' (2017) 30 *Journal of Environmental Law and Practice* 201, 207. See also AM Eisenberg, 'Just Transitions' (2019) 92 Southern California Law Review 273.

of pursuing a shift to a low-carbon economy without sacrificing the well-being of workers and frontline communities.[50]

Proceeding to the legal perspective of this problem, Doorey presents the novel impasse for just transition in the context of climate change and shift to a low-carbon economy. In this regard, there is simply no particular field of law that entirely governs it, such as labour law or environmental law.[51] As he says, "[a] legal field organized around the idea of just transitions would require lawyers, legal scholars, and policy-makers to expand their areas of expertise, and for experts from different legal fields to converge and coordinate around a new narrative."[52] He then proceeds in introducing the concept of *just transitions law*, or *law of just transitions*, that combines insights from environmental law, environmental justice, and labour law.[53]

However, *just transitions law*—no matter how noble the idea is, to which this paper is more than honored to contribute—would take years, if not decades, of legal practice, scholarship, and demand-driven legal development to build. While there is no distinct field of law that fully encapsulates the nature and character of relations and transactions involved in just transition, it does not necessarily mean that the law has no potential of regulating or facilitating just transition at all.

This paper determines that labour and employment law (or briefly as "labour law") and social welfare legislation (or briefly as "social legislation") have key regulatory and clinical functions in effectively facilitating just transition in the

---

50   See JM Cha, 'A Just Transition: Why Transitioning Workers into a New Clean Energy Economy Should Be at the Center of Climate Change Policies' (2017) 29 *Fordham Environmental Law Review* 196, 198. "[J]ust transition must be at the center of any climate change efforts. Without transitioning fossil fuel communities and workers, climate change advocates will continue a pattern of exploitation and exacerbate existing inequalities that will ultimately hinder efforts to abate the worst impact of climate change. In fact, inequality and climate change are inextricably intertwined and one cannot be solved without addressing the other."

51   Doorey, *supra* note 49, 238–239.

52   *Ibid.*, 239.

53   *Ibid.*, 206. *See also* Doorey, *supra* note 49, 234. Guided by a theory of justice, Doorey's proposed novel field of law has the following normative claims adopted from climate science, environmental law, environmental justice, and labour law:
      - States should respond to climate change through public policy and law.
      - Public policy should encourage a transition towards "greener", lower carbon economies.
      - Governments should seek to minimize the economic and social harms associated with the desired transition to a greener economy, and attempt, through law and policy, to distribute those harms and any resulting benefits in an equitable manner.

context of a shift to a low-carbon economy.[54] It is also consistent with Stevis et al.'s argument that any research or discourse on just transition must, at the very least, acknowledge its roots in labour policy and labour environmentalism.[55] It is sufficient at this point to be reminded of what Professor Azucena, an authority in Philippine labour law, writes: "[Labour laws] explain, albeit partly, why a nation is poor or otherwise [...]. Thus, the needs, the faults, and the goals of the economy cannot be ignored in formulating the labor laws, otherwise the labor laws become purposeless, socially irrelevant, or economically damaging pronouncements."[56] The same is true for climate change and low-carbon development.

2.2.3 Margins of Law

With the elements of the analysis herein already mapped, the similar question of how Philippine labour legal mechanisms – discussed in Part 5 – respond to the disruption of a shift to a low-carbon economy through just transition measures must be asked. Definitely, the *conventional* responses are on the table.[57] The Labor Code of the Philippines may be amended to include workers in carbon-dependent industries in the special groups of employees recognized in the Code.[58] Consider as well an amendment that identifies closures due to decarbonization as an authorized cause for termination and consequently mandates a higher amount of separation pay and benefits for terminated employees of such industries.[59] Earlier retirement ages may be legislated, similar to the racehorse jockeys[60] and underground and surface mining workers.[61] A special

---

54   See CA Azucena, Jr., *The Labor Code with Comments and Cases* (Rex Book Store 2010) 7, 9. Labour law is defined as "governing the relations between capital and labor, by providing for certain employment standards and a legal framework for negotiating, adjusting and administering those standards and other incidents of employment." On the other hand, social legislation is defined as those that "provide particular kinds of protection or benefits to society or segments thereof in furtherance of social justice."

55   Stevis et al., *supra* note 7. See also D Stevis and R Felli, 'Global Labour Unions and Just Transition to a Green Economy' (2015) 15 *International Environmental Agreements* 29–43.

56   Azucena, *supra* note 54, 24–25.

57   See, e.g. L Raitbaur, 'The New German Coal Laws: A Difficult Balancing Act' (2021) 11 *Climate Law* 176–194.

58   Lab. Code, Book Three, Title III (Working Conditions for Special Groups of Employees). Labor Code of the Philippines or Pres. Dec. No. 442 (1974), as amended.

59   Art. 298. See also Dep't of Lab. and Employment (DOLE) Dep't Order No. 147-15 (2015). Amending the Implementing Rules and Regulations of Book VI of the Labor Code of the Philippines, as Amended.

60   Rep. Act No. 10789 (2016). Racehorse Jockey Retirement Act.

61   Rep. Act No. 10757 (2016). An Act Reducing the Retirement Age of Surface Mine Workers from Sixty (60) to Fifty (50) Years, Amending for the Purpose Article 302 of Presidential Decree No. 442, as Amended, Otherwise Known as the "Labor Code of the Philippines".

division of the National Labor Relations Commission (NLRC) may be vested with special jurisdiction to adjudicate labour disputes arising from sunsetting or closure of industries pursuant to the national emissions reduction targets.[62]

The list can go on, but it must be noted that *conventional* responses take time, which both management and workers do not have. Nor can the Philippines afford to wait when emissions are at stake.[63] Also, they seem contrary to the nature of contemporary disruptions, which are fluid and ever-changing—a stark contrast to the legal system's rigidity.

Taking a step back and moving towards the *alternative* responses, the preceding sections hinted on a possible headroom in this analysis, which is to examine the *margins* of existing law and find space for responses that address the disruption. As applied, the *margins* of Philippine labour law as it now exists must be examined to see whether there is space to adopt and implement just transition measures, although admittedly not as potent and robust as the *conventional* responses mentioned above. A possible illustration of this approach can be seen in Figure 7.1.

The Figure shows that the *existing* legal mechanisms have *margins* that can possibly accommodate *alternative* responses, which do not require the grueling enactment of laws or the waiting of a court decision.[64] The unshaded area represents the known and clear scope of the law, while the shaded area represents the *margins* of law. The dashed line represents the substance of the law, which is often provided through the text of the statute. On the other hand, the solid line represents the extreme bounds of lawful authority, such that any act that goes beyond it would be contrary to law. What this Figure represents is that there can be valid acts of related nature, but are not specifically provided for in the text of the statute—which are *on the margins* or the shaded area. However, the question remains how does one exactly look at this margin: *what is there to look for and how does one look for it?* Administrative law may offer an answer to explore those margins.

2.3   *Is Administrative Law the Way Forward?*

The proliferation of administrative agencies is most often attributed to socio-political factors such as "the growing complexity of modern life."[65] Undoubtedly,

---

62   Lab. Code, art. 224.

63   But see Rep. Act No. 10771 (2016). Philippine Green Jobs Act of 2016.

64   There is really no substantial difference in the interpretation of A. and B. They simply differ in the manner of illustration.

65   *Pangasinan Transportation Co., Inc. v. Public Service Comm'n*, G.R. No. 47065, 70 Phil. 221, 229 (1940).

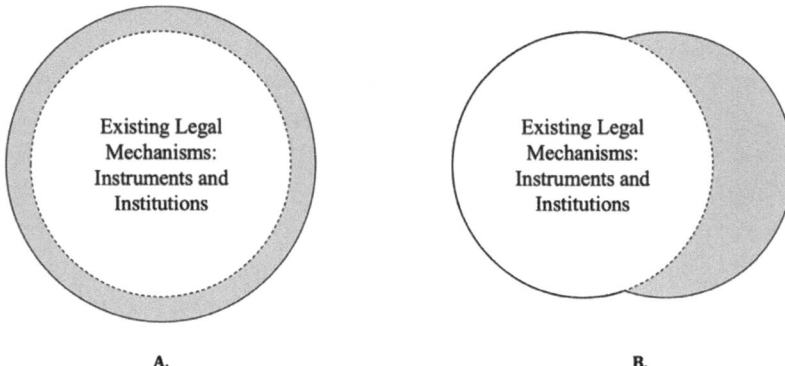

FIGURE 7.1   Margins of existing law

one of the fields of law that have been historically used to address bottlenecks, not only in the form of disruptions, but also in governance, bureaucracy, and technical capability and expertise is *administrative law.*

A deeper probe would however reveal, as Agabin argues, that the reliance for administrative agencies is a manifestation of the new role taken by the state amid the witnessed lapses of *laissez faire,* or a market-driven economy and public affairs.[66] To pursue such new role, "administrative agencies actively took over jurisdiction of narrow areas of the law within their specialized field"[67] and "performed licensing, rule-making, investigating, prosecuting, and other related functions, with corollary power to grant provisional and final remedies, including awarding of damages."[68]

For instance, in Philippine administrative law, various methods of legal analysis involving the extent of powers that may be delegated and exercised by administrative agencies have developed through the years such as the doctrine of permissible delegation as an exception to the constitutional principle of non-delegation and separation of powers,[69] the valid exercise of the powers of administrative rulemaking and administrative adjudication,[70] the administrative due process,[71] the doctrine of exhaustion of administrative

---

66   PA Agabin, *Mestizo: The Story of the Philippine Legal System* (Lap Lambert, 2011) 217.

67   *Ibid.,* 218.

68   *Ibid.,* 218–219.

69   See HS De Leon, *Administrative Law: Text and Cases* (Rex Book Store, 2010) 170–172. See also *infra* Part 4 4.2.1.

70   *Ibid.,* Chapter III, C. Rule-Making Powers and D. Adjudicatory Powers. *See also infra* Part 4 4.1.3.

71   *Ibid.,* 245–252. See also *Ang Tibay v. Court of Industrial Relations,* G.R. No. 46496, 69 Phil. 635 (1940).

remedies,[72] and the doctrine of primary jurisdiction,[73] among others. While these doctrines have been successful in addressing every administrative legal problem that have faced the Philippine courts thus far—which is a fact this paper does not dispute, the practice and the scholarly study of administrative law are not static. There are new questions—and disruptions—that will arise; administrative law cannot be stagnant.

It is from such gap that this research presents an approach in understanding what could be *on the margins* of law or, as what has been previewed earlier, its *legal adaptive capacity*. While this paper does not try to bolster administrative law *per se*, it does attempt to build on the gains of administrative law as currently theorized and use it in conjunction with much contemporary theories, namely the legal adaptive capacity analysis from Camacho and Glicksman as adopted in this paper.

3   Legal Adaptive Capacity Analysis

This section explores the theoretical background of the LAC analysis and the various scholarly research that adopted such framework. These serve as a starting point for this paper's critique on the methodological soundness of the framework, especially in applying such to jurisdictions beyond the United States as well as in fields of law beyond natural resources and environmental law. After such examination, a conceptual framework is introduced in attempting to systematically understand the elements at play in the LAC analysis. With this, a proper and standardized adoption of the LAC analysis is ensured. Lastly, a multi-step process on how to operationalize the LAC analysis complements the earlier critiques and contributions made by this paper to the theory.

As pointed in the preliminary part of the paper, the legal research method herein is purposefully adopted to consider the broader sensibilities of the issues involved, which will not force a strictly doctrinal legal research method that would reinforce a conflict of interest (i.e. jobs versus environment)—when in reality there must be none. Legal research does not exist in a vacuum.[74]

---

72   *Ibid.*, 360–381.

73   *Ibid.* 355–360.

74   See S Taekema, 'Theoretical and Normative Frameworks for Legal Research: Putting Theory into Practice' (2018) *Law and Method* 13. "Thus, a crucial connection made between factual and normative aspects of scholarship is the need for context (Del Mar 2016, p. 235): we cannot understand values without investigating the concrete pursuit of those values in practice, i.e., without an understanding of the factual contexts in which values operate."

3.1 *Theoretical Origins and Applications*

In their law review article *Legal Adaptive Capacity: How Program Goals and Processes Shape Federal Land Adaptation to Climate Change*, Alejandro E. Camacho and Robert L. Glicksman examine the LAC of US federal land agencies in relation to climate change adaptation measures.[75] The study streamlines the use of legal adaptive capacity in legal and policy research, such that they are able to make the key distinction between what they termed *procedural legal adaptive capacity* and *substantive legal adaptive capacity*.[76] The extension to include the *substantive*, despite the trend of focusing on the *procedural* aspect, in the LAC analysis paved the way, in what this paper would argue, for a more foundational LAC analysis and the broader study of adaptive law.

Camacho and Glicksman express the shortcomings of the *procedural* LAC by stating that "a regulatory or management regime's [LAC] is not only influenced by the extent of *procedural flexibility* the implementing agency enjoys under its organic statute and other sources of law."[77] This breakthrough allows them to establish that "[LAC] is also affected by the degree to which the underlying program's substantive goals are *capable of accommodating shifts* in management approaches in response to change."[78]

For a clearer appreciation of the theory and its extension, the succeeding points are directly derived from Camacho and Glicksman's article.

Their article adopts the following definition of LAC: "the formal regulatory or management regime's capacity to adapt to new phenomena that affect the resource or activity it regulates or manages."[79] Regime then refers "rules promulgated by public legal institutions, including legislatures, courts, and administrative agencies (including agency regulations, manuals, plans, and guidance)."[80] It then clarifies that the LAC analysis excludes consideration of "other factors, such as resource constraints or agency culture, which may nonetheless influence the adaptive capacity of a regulatory regime."[81]

From this definition, the gateway in discovering the LAC is the "regime", or statutes, rules, or regulations, regardless of source. Whether examining the *substantive* or *procedural* LAC, the LAC analysis reveals the capacity to adapt to new phenomena through a probe into such statutes, rules, or regulations.

---

75   Camacho and Glicksman, *supra* note 6.

76   *Ibid.*

77   *Ibid.*, 713–714. (Emphasis supplied.)

78   *Ibid.*, 714. (Emphasis supplied.)

79   *Ibid.*, 722.

80   *Ibid.*

81   *Ibid.*

Camacho and Glicksman make a distinction between *substantive* and *procedural* LAC, which they considered as the two axes of LAC. Drawing from the earlier study of J.B. Ruhl, a renowned scholar of administrative law, it is "important to distinguish between the resilience of the legal system's underlying structure and processes and the stability of the substantive content of the law."[82]

Substantive LAC is "the extent to which a legal regime's goals are capable of responding to changed conditions."[83] Camacho and Glicksman characterize LAC as a spectrum, where a high degree of *substantive* LAC corresponds to "[a]n agency [that] has the authority under its organic legislation to adjust its interpretation of regulatory goals or the means of pursuing them to meet new challenges or accommodate changed circumstances[;]"[84] while a limited degree corresponds to "relatively rigid goals that do not allow agencies to alter regulatory or management approaches, notwithstanding changed conditions."[85] A visual illustration of such spectrum is shown in Figure 7.2.

On the other hand, *procedural* LAC is "the degree to which a legal regime's process is able to adjust to new policy directions or information or changed factual circumstances."[86] From a spectrum, a high degree of *procedural* LAC

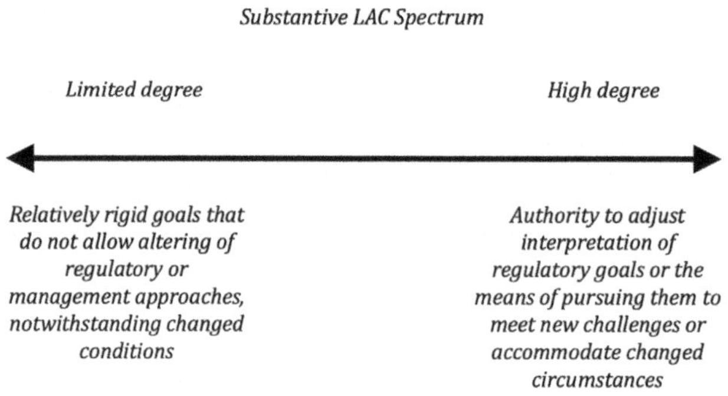

Substantive LAC Spectrum

Limited degree   High degree

←——————————————————————————————→

Relatively rigid goals that   Authority to adjust
do not allow altering of   interpretation of
regulatory or   regulatory goals or the
management approaches,   means of pursuing them to
notwithstanding changed   meet new challenges or
conditions   accommodate changed
                                                              circumstances

FIGURE 7.2   Substantive legal adaptive capacity spectrum

---

82   *Ibid.*, 723, *citing* JB Ruhl, 'General Design Principles for Resilience and Adaptive Capacity in Legal Systems - with Applications to Climate Change Adaptation' (2011) 89 *North Carolina Law Review* 1373, 1383.
83   *Ibid.*, 724.
84   *Ibid.*
85   *Ibid.* See also Camacho and Glicksman, *supra* note 6, 728–729, for the discussion of rules and standards in terms of *substantive* LAC.
86   *Ibid.*, 729.

corresponds to regimes with a "capacity to distinguish previous cases when addressing new factual circumstances"[87] or a process "to address a new situation not covered by existing law, or because changed circumstances have undercut the effectiveness of existing law[;]"[88] while there is a limited degree where there is "a rigorous process for amendment" or "little tolerance for structural or process change[.]"[89] A visual illustration of such spectrum is shown in Figure 7.3.

These two axes, the *substantive* and *procedural* LAC, complement each other, because there are a variety of insights learned from either. While it is ideal that they is examined together simultaneously, there is nothing inherently lacking if an examination of only one axis is conducted.

The studies that applied LAC as a framework of analysis are also crucial in seeing the scholarly development of the theory.[90]

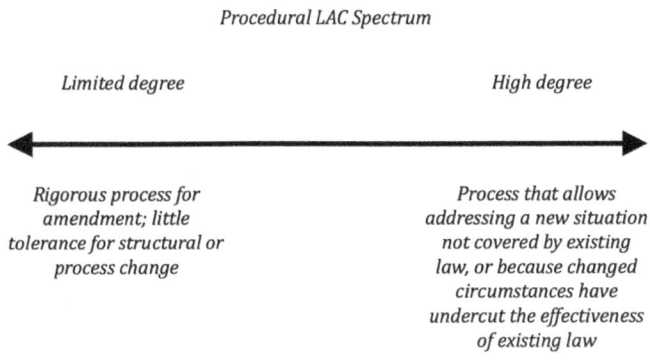

Procedural LAC Spectrum

Limited degree   High degree

Rigorous process for   Process that allows
amendment; little   addressing a new situation
tolerance for structural or   not covered by existing
process change   law, or because changed
                                          circumstances have
                                  undercut the effectiveness
                                            of existing law

FIGURE 7.3   Procedural legal adaptive capacity spectrum

---

87   *Ibid.*

88   *Ibid.*, 730.

89   *Ibid.*, 729. See also the discussion of front-end and back-end mechanisms in terms of *procedural* LAC.

90   See J Similä, N Soininen and E Paukku, 'Towards Sustainable Blue Energy Production: An Analysis of Legal Transformative and Adaptive Capacity' (2021) *Journal of Energy and Natural Resources* on sustainable production of blue renewable energy in Finland; AE Camacho, 'De- and Re-Constructing Public Governance for Biodiversity Conservation' (2020) 73 *Vanderbilt Law Review* 1585 on public biodiversity governance in United States; L Greenhill, J Kenter and H Dannevig, 'Adaptation to Climate Change – Related Ocean Acidification: An Adaptive Governance Approach' (2020) 191 *Ocean and Coastal Management* on ocean acidification in Scotland; L Greenhill, *An Analysis of the Emergence of Adaptive Governance for Sustainable Management of Marine Resources* (May 2020) (thesis for Doctor of Philosophy, University of Aberdeen), https://pure.uhi.ac.uk/en/studentTheses

3.2 Conceptual Framework

The previous section discussed the LAC analysis as originally conceptualized and applied by Camacho and Glicksman. There remains the question for other researchers seeking to adopt the LAC analysis. *Is the LAC analysis applicable in my jurisdiction and in my field of law? Or was it envisioned to cater only to the US legal system and natural resources and environmental law?* These questions also hound this present paper.

This paper humbly contributes in answering these by laying the groundwork for what may eventually be developed as a conceptual framework for the LAC analysis.[91] This approach is chosen to primarily address the lack of substantial entry point for the adoption of the LAC analysis in research questions that are distant from its original use.

The proposed conceptual framework, as seen in Figure 7.4, is a product of the deconstruction of the various components, elements, and concepts involved in the LAC analysis. There is a notable resemblance between what Camacho and Glicksman explained and the elements of the proposed conceptual framework, but there are insights derived and reflected therein as well to create a more general understanding of what the LAC analysis entails. This veers away from the agency-specific understanding of LAC.[92]

A caveat, however, is that this proposed conceptual framework does not claim to incorporate all existing conceptions of LAC. Instead, it mainly draws from the LAC analysis as forwarded by Camacho and Glicksman.

Before discussing the different elements of the conceptual framework, some assumptions that are not illustrated therein must be first expressed. *First*, the conceptual framework does not indicate nor refer to any legal jurisdiction in particular, because this paper argues that the LAC analysis must be equally yet differently applicable to various jurisdictions (e.g. countries) and to varying

---

/an-analysis-of-the-emergence-of-adaptive-governance-for-sustainab (accessed 5 January 2022) on sustainable management of marine resources in Scotland; A Garmestania, JB Ruhl, BC Chaffin, R K Craig, HFMW van Rijswick, DG Angeler, C Folke, L Gunderson, D Twidwell and CR Allen, 'Untapped Capacity for Resilience in Environmental Law' (2019) 116 *Proceedings of the National Academy of Sciences of the United States of America* 19899 on fostering resilience in social-ecological systems in United States and European Union; RL Glicksman, 'Management of Federally Owned Grasslands in the Climate Change Era' (2017) 26 *Kansas Journal of Law and Public Policy* 324 on management of grasslands in United States.

91   *See* Y Jabareen, 'Building a Conceptual Framework: Philosophy, Definitions, and Procedure' (2009) 8 *International Journal of Qualitative Methods* 49, 51. A conceptual framework is "a network, or 'a plane,' of interlinked concepts that together provide a comprehensive understanding of a phenomenon or phenomena."

92   Another contribution by this paper to this effect will be discussed *infra* Part 4.

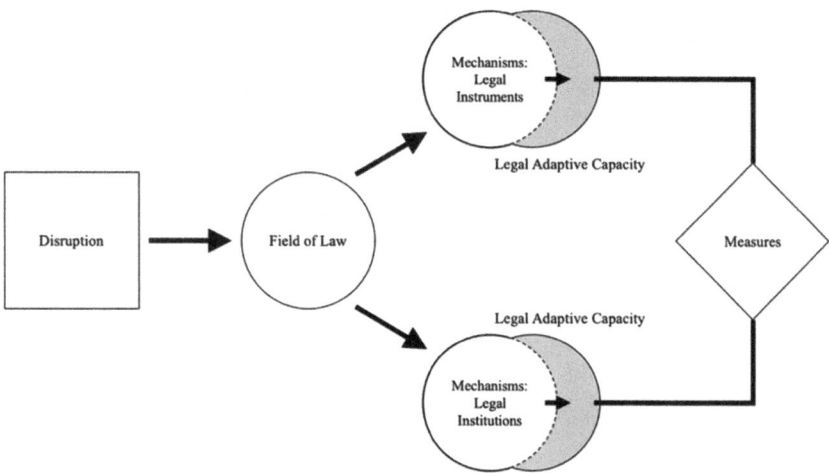

FIGURE 7.4   Legal adaptive capacity (LAC) analysis conceptual framework

levels of governance (e.g. states, regions, and cities). This framework assumes that it applies to a particular jurisdiction.

Second, the conceptual framework assumes a certain level of rigidity of the legal system. This means that the framework may only prove useful to jurisdictions where there are constitutional or statutory processes and safeguards for institutionalizing new mechanisms and for implementing new measures. Otherwise, should the legal system have close to none, or none at all, of any such process (e.g. authoritarian regime, where executive, legislative, and judicial powers, or a combination of these, are held only by one person or body), then there is no foreseeable need for the LAC analysis. It may be argued that when there is not so much rigidity, it is inefficient or even futile to examine the LAC.

Third, the conceptual framework does not consider the possible consequent effects of adjustments in the mechanisms and measures arising from the disruption to such disruption itself. While some disruptions (e.g. climate change) may need a considerable length of time and major policy changes to actually influence such disruption, other kinds of disruptions may be more susceptible to mitigating effects within a short-term timeframe. Nonetheless, this conceptual framework does not foresee neither of these circumstances, but instead focuses on the initial adjustments made to the mechanisms to address the disruption and its impact rather than alter the disruption itself.

The different elements of the conceptual framework are as follows: (a) Disruption; (b) Field of Law; (c) Mechanisms; (d) Measures; and (e) Legal Adaptive Capacity. At this point, only a brief definition of each element will be provided. Details on how such can be operationalized will be discussed in the succeeding section.

a. *Disruption* – the new phenomenon, innovation, event or a series thereof, or systemic change that drastically impacts an existing, or causes the creation of a new, unregulated social behavior or relation

b. *Field of Law* – the substantive law that is likely to be affected by the disruption, that could regulate the social behavior or relation affected or created by the disruption, or that has the potential of addressing the disruption

c. *Mechanisms* – the *existing* legal instruments (i.e. constitution, organic law, statute, judicial decisions, rules, regulations, administrative rulings) and legal institutions (i.e. executive offices, legislative bodies, courts, independent offices, local governments, administrative agencies, bodies, and tribunals), institutionalized and constituted in accordance with legal processes

d. *Measures* – the executive actions, orders, and programmes, administrative rules and regulations, administrative rulings, and judicial decisions that are adopted and implemented by legal institutions in accordance with and within the lawful bounds of *existing* legal instruments, which address the disruption and its impact

e. *Legal Adaptive Capacity* – the formal regulatory or management regime's capacity to adapt to new phenomena that affect the resource or activity it regulates or manages, which may either be *substantive* or *procedural*[93]

The arrows in the conceptual framework denote the expected relationship among the elements. To start, *Disruption* serves as the starting point, because once a disruption arrives in society there is a consequent effect and impact to a social behavior or relation that ought to be regulated by a particular *Field of Law*. The existing *Mechanisms* belonging to the *Field of Law* are then examined as to their capacity to adapt to such disruption by adopting and implementing *Measures*, which directly address the disruption and its impact. The arrow from the *Mechanisms* to the *margins* signify the space for implementing *Measures* within the framework and lawful bounds of existing *Mechanisms* composed of legal instruments and legal institutions. While the area of the *margins* differs on a case-by-case basis, this paper argues that such *margins* correspond to the LAC. Essentially, the LAC analysis, using this conceptual framework, is an inquiry on the *margins* of existing legal mechanisms.

---

93   Camacho and Glicksman, *supra* note 6, 722.

3.3   *Multi-step Process in Adopting the LAC Analysis*

With the conceptual framework for the LAC analysis discussed, the next step is to operationalize such framework through a multi-step process. Without concrete steps on how to adopt the LAC analysis for other types of research questions, this paper is bound to repeat what was lacking in the earlier study of Camacho and Glicksman.[94]

The main purpose of creating a multi-step process is to aid researchers who are interested to adopt the LAC analysis in examining other legal jurisdictions, disruptions, and fields of law. It becomes an invitation for scholars to use the theory, and in doing so, hopefully enrich the theory itself similar to what the present paper aims to achieve.

There is much to adopt from the preceding section's discussion of the conceptual framework. In particular, the assumptions behind the framework and the definitions of the elements therein also inform the multi-step process, such that both must be used together. For instance, the multi-step process also assumes that the jurisdiction and level of governance were already determined prior to the analysis. *Will the LAC analysis cover assessments of legal mechanisms in the national level, state level, or local government level?* This resides in the good judgment of the researcher. Further, the definitions of *Disruption, Field of Law, Mechanisms, Measures,* and *Legal Adaptive Capacity* in the preceding section are key in applying the multi-step process.

The multi-step process crafted by this paper is shown in Table 7.1. It is composed of seven steps, which are correspondingly divided into three categories. The first category, *Inclusion Criteria,* covers the first four steps, namely (1) *Disruption,* (2) *Field of law,* (3) *Mechanisms,* and (4) *Measures.* This category is concerned with identifying the elements for the proper application of the LAC analysis. The second category, *Point of Analysis,* covers the fifth step, namely (5) *LAC.* It sets the parameters of the study by identifying the axes of LAC to be used in the LAC analysis. Lastly, the third category, *Analysis Proper,* covers the sixth and seventh steps, namely (6) *Absolute LAC* and (7) *Relative LAC.* It is the last part of the multi-step process where the elements identified in steps (1) to (4) are analyzed using the point of analysis identified in step (5). At this point, the only part of the multi-step process that requires further explanation is the meaning of *absolute* LAC and *relative* LAC in steps 6 and 7, respectively. While Camacho and Glicksman emphasized the significant difference between *substantive* and *procedural* LAC, this paper offers another plane of distinction in analysis, *absolute* and *relative* LAC, such that there could

---

94   *Ibid.*

TABLE 7.1   Multi-step process in adopting the Legal Adaptive Capacity (LAC) analysis

Category	Step	Description
INCLUSION	Step 1. Disruption	Identify the disruption or new phenomenon .
CRITERIA	Step 2. Field of law	Identify the field of law using the following guide questions:
		a. Which field of law is most likely to be affected by such disruption?
		b. Which field of law could regulate the social behavior or relation that is most likely to be affected by such disruption?
		c. Which field of law has the potential of addressing such disruption?
	Step 3. Mechanisms	Within the identified field of law in (2), identify existing legal mechanisms (instruments and institutions) using the same guide questions in (2):
		a. Which legal instruments and institutions are most likely to be affected by such disruption?
		b. Which legal instruments and institutions could regulate the social behavior or relation that is most likely to be affected by such disruption?
		c. Which legal instruments and institutions have the potential of addressing such disruption?
	Step 4. Measures	Within the identified legal instruments and institutions in (3), identify current and future measures that may respond to the disruption.
POINT OF ANALYSIS	Step 5. LAC	Identify the axis of LAC (i.e. *substantive ,procedural*) to be used in the analysis.
ANALYSIS PROPER	Step 6. *Absolute* LAC	Apply the identified LAC analysis in (5) to determine the *absolute* LAC of legal instruments and institutions in (3).
	Step 7. *Relative* LAC	Apply the identified LAC analysis in (5) to determine the *relative* LAC of legal instruments and institutions in (3) in relation to current and future measures in (4).

be a resulting *absolute substantive LAC* and *relative substantive LAC*, or *absolute procedural LAC* and *relative procedural LAC*.

On the one hand, *absolute* LAC is the legal mechanisms' capacity to adapt to new phenomena, without any specific disruption or new phenomenon considered in the analysis. It is absolute, because it gauges the adaptive capacity *per se* of the legal mechanisms regardless of any disruption that may impact the social behavior or relation that such mechanisms regulate. It is expected to give insights on the long-term adaptive capacity, especially when faced by totally novel disruptions in the future. More focus is given instead to the broader nature and structure of legal mechanisms that allows or restricts adaptive capacity.

On the other hand, *relative* LAC is the legal mechanisms' capacity to adapt to new phenomena, with particular consideration of a specific disruption or new phenomenon. It is relative, because it considers the specific nuances and the directed impacts of such disruption to the social behavior or relation regulated by the legal mechanisms. Focus is aimed at specific provisions of legal instruments or processes of legal institutions that are directly related to the disruption. This is the type of LAC analysis usually conducted by previous studies.

In this section, LAC as a legal research method was explored starting from the milestone research of Camacho and Glicksman. Its efficacy in facing not only novel questions of law but also looming disruptions in society was established. However, the existing conception and scholarly use of the LAC analysis have major gaps, which were attempted to be addressed herein. The conceptual framework proposed herein responds to the lack of model to enable the systematic application of the LAC analysis by other researchers in other jurisdictions, fields of law, and disruptions. Further, the multi-step process then operationalizes such conceptual framework by setting a guide in identifying the essential elements and the point of analysis for a more stable and replicable LAC analysis.

4   LAC Analysis and Philippine Legal System

With both the theoretical and analytical approaches explained in Part 3, the next step is to inquire into the efficacy of the LAC analysis as a legal research method in the Philippine jurisdiction. The key elements of the Philippine legal system, from constitutional and administrative law perspectives, are identified and derived from the authoritative works of Pacifico A. Agabin in *Mestizo: The Story of the Philippine Legal System*,[95] Myrna S. Feliciano in *Philippine Legal System*,[96] and Salvador T. Carlota in *Philippine Administrative Rulemaking and Adjudication in the Twentieth Century: Issues, Trends, and Perspectives*.[97]

---

95   Agabin, *supra* note 66.
96   MS Feliciano, *Philippine Legal System* (UP Law Complex, 2015).
97   ST Carlota, 'Philippine Administrative Rulemaking and Adjudication in the Twentieth Century: Issues, Trends, and Perspectives' in DB Gatmaytan (ed.) *Grandeur: Lectures*

Further, key legal principles derived from Supreme Court decisions are enumerated as well. Within said discussions are annotations on how the LAC as a concept may complement the existing concepts in the Philippine legal system—or bridge any gap the latter may have. This serves as a preliminary necessary work for the more specific analysis to be undertaken in Part 5.

4.1   *Structural Elements of the Philippine Legal System*
This paper discusses a selection of key elements that are essential to understand the fundamental and basic underpinnings of the Philippine legal system, namely (1) legal tradition; (2) government structure; and (3) administrative regime.

4.1.1   Legal Tradition
The colonial experience of the Philippines permeates its legal system. The centuries of Spanish rule imposed the civil law tradition that originated from Roman law.[98] After a brief moment of Philippine independence, where the Malolos Constitution—the first Constitution in Asia—was adopted by a representative democracy, the Americans took over and imposed a common law tradition that originated, on the other hand, from Anglo-American law.[99]

As Agabin argues, "[the Philippine] legal system, in brief, is a *mestizo*, the result of cross-breeding the common and the civil law systems."[100] Where *mestizo* often refers to a person of mixed-race, a *legal mestizo* then is "basically a civilian system that had been under pressure from the Anglo-American common law and has in part been overlaid by that rival system of jurisprudence."[101] It must be noted as well that, while the hybridity usually only refers to the

<hr>

Delivered on the Occasion of the Centennial of the University of the Philippines, College of Law (UP Law Complex, 2013) 71–89.
98   ST Carlota, 'The Three Most Important Features of the Philippine Legal System that Others Should Understand' in *International Association of Law Schools Conference Learning from Each Other: Enriching the Law School Curriculum in an Interrelated World* (International Association of Law Schools 2007) 177–178, 177. Carlota identifies these features, which are discussed separately in this section, as: "[t]he harmonious blending of common law and civil law in one legal system[;]" "[t]he doctrine of Separation of powers between the Executive, Legislative, and Judicial branches of government[;]" and "[t]he power of Judicial Review and the Bill of Rights in the Constitution[.]"
99   *Ibid*.
100   Agabin, *supra* note 66, 2. See also AB Lorca, *Mestizo International Law: A Global Intellectual History* (Cambridge University Press 2014) 1842–1933.
101   *Ibid*.

"cross-breeding" of civil and common law, there are customary laws, indigenous laws, and Islamic laws that co-exist with the usual suspects of hybridity.

Presently, there are areas of Philippine law that are traceable to a particular legal tradition. Feliciano states that "[t]he civil law operates in areas such as family relations, property, succession, contract and criminal law[.]"[102] On the other hand, common law is "evident in such areas as constitutional law, procedure, corporation law, negotiable instruments, taxation, insurance, labor relations, banking and currency."[103] In practice and development of Philippine law, identifying a corresponding legal tradition for a field of law is not as easy as it seems. More often, the principles are intertwined and consequently give birth to new dynamics.[104]

Further, the sources of law also illustrate the hybridity. According to Feliciano, the main sources of Philippine law are the Constitution, statutes, treaties and conventions, and judicial decisions.[105] At first glance, the hybridity is already apparent. Statutes are exhibits of the civil law tradition, where norms are codified and then applied based on the independent facts of each case; judicial decisions are reflective of the common law tradition, where the doctrine of stare decisis is adopted. In addition, the legislative rules and regulations validly adopted by administrative agencies also have the force and effect of law.[106]

4.1.1.1   *LAC Insight: Diversity*

The legal tradition of a legal system informs the LAC of such system. This does not end however with the legal tradition; it continues with the particular field of law, source of law, and the interplay of these elements. Without saying that a legal system that subscribes only to a single legal tradition is easier to analyze, the discussion above just emphasizes the point that hybridity indeed adds another level of complexity in any analysis such as the LAC analysis. There is a diversity of legal aspects that may affect the LAC.[107] The interplay of the

---

102   Feliciano, *supra* note 96, 1.
103   *Ibid.*
104   For example, in criminal law, while the Revised Penal Code, where felonies are defined and punished, traces its roots to the *Codigo Penal de* 1870 of Spain, the special penal laws, or those enacted by the Philippine legislature either in addition or as an extension of the acts punishable under the Revised Penal Code, adopt the nomenclature and principles of common law.
105   Feliciano, *supra* note 96, 14.
106   *Cebu Institute of Technology v. Ople*, G.R. No. L-58870, 156 SCRA 629, 658 (1987).
107   To illustrate, consider the Securities and Exchange Commission, whose mandate include the regulation of corporations. The LAC analysis of SEC thus will require a look into the

sources of law combined with their actual legal authority within the field of law makes the successful application of the LAC analysis more challenging. This then stresses the fact that the LAC analysis must consider the totality of the legal system's nuances.

4.1.2 Government Structure

The constitution or an organic act defines the structure of the government of any modern society. In fact, aside from citizens' rights, the government's form and structure are expected to be a few of the most crucial components of the fundamental law. However, for purposes of analysis such as in this paper, there are criticisms that must be immediately addressed so as to not dilute the significance of this section. One of these is the legal structuralism critique, which states that any analysis is constrained by and within the government structure and thus leaves no space for analysis beyond it. This is addressed by acknowledging that there are certain issues, even legal issues, that necessitate an analysis of the government structure, especially for those that are extremely rigid such as the Philippines'.[108]

The Philippine government as adopted in the 1987 Constitution is republican in form and under a presidential system.[109] It is characterized as a unitary, centralized government with the principle of separation of powers as a basic feature.[110] The government has three main branches that correspond to the powers granted to each: the executive, the legislative, and the judiciary.[111]

The Constitution also establishes three constitutional commissions, which are independent from control of any of the three branches mentioned above: Commission on Elections, Civil Service Commission, and Commission on

---

Revised Corporation Code and Securities Regulation Code, both of which were enacted by Congress, into the Supreme Court decisions that in effect widened or restricted the SEC's jurisdiction, into the administrative rules adopted by the SEC in exercise of its rulemaking power, and into the constitutional limitations, among others.

108   The present 1987 Constitution of the Philippines remain unamended for more than 30 years, despite calls from every new administration. *See* M H Yusingco and S Navarro, 'Why the 1987 Constitution has Endured for 32 Years Without Amendment' ASOG Working Paper 19-004, Ateneo Sch. Govt, 12 March 2019, https://papers.ssrn.com/sol3/papers .cfm?abstract_id=3350888.

109   Const. art. II, § 1; Const. art. VII, § 1.

110   Feliciano, *supra* note 96, 33.

111   Const. arts. VI-VIII. The doctrine of separation of powers will be discussed further in the next section.

Audit.[112] Another independent office is the Ombudsman, which is focused on offenses committed by any public official, employee, office, or agency.[113]

Local governments are also an essential part of Philippine government structure. The Constitution states two broad categories of local governments: the territorial and political subdivisions or more commonly known as local government units (LGUs) and autonomous regions.[114]

Although not expressly provided in the Constitution, jurisprudence and the structural limitations in addressing the demands of modern society have justified the establishment of administrative agencies in the modern legal system, which will be discussed in the next section.

4.1.2.1   LAC Insight: Rigidity

The government structure has a large impact on the LAC of a legal system. As briefly discussed in Part 2, the legal mechanisms' rigidity—whether substantively or procedurally—determines the pace by which the government structure can churn out appropriate laws and regulations and adjudicate actual cases. The rate at which a legal system is able to do these things influences the need for LAC, because such rigidity is the primary reason why the LAC is examined and made a subject of interest. Thus, it can be said that a highly rigid government structure presents a greater need for the LAC. Conversely, a government structure with low rigidity may not need LAC at the first place, because it is able to *adapt* through the conventional methods provided by law.

This paper also argues that the level of government also plays a role in determining the LAC. The LAC analysis as applied in the United States should consider the intergovernmental relationship between the federal and state governments—together with the rich jurisprudence on this matter. If this will be seen in the Philippine context, the intergovernmental relationship between the national and local governments must be considered. The power dynamics between or among levels of government must be considered in examining the LAC of a particular agency or unit of governance.

Independently, the level of government may be the subject of the LAC analysis in itself. For example, if a study intends to look at the LAC of *barangays*, the smallest political unit in the Philippines governed by the *Punong Barangay*

---

112   Art. IX-A, § 1.

113   Art. XI, §§ 5, 13. See also Rep. Act No. 6770 (1989). The Ombudsman Act of 1989.

114   Art. X, § 1. See also Rep. Act No. 7160 (1991), § 25 (a). Local Government Code of 1991. "Consistent with the basic policy on local autonomy, the President shall exercise general supervision over local government units to ensure that their acts are within the scope of their prescribed powers and functions."

or Barangay Chairman and the *Sangguniang Barangay*, in addressing climate change, this paper does not see any hindrance in such an attempt. Further, the legislative power of the local *Sanggunian* or the power of the local government offices to implement programmes as they see fit to address a disruption may be examined as well.

It must be noted, however, that this is not imperative in all cases. The decision whether to incorporate the intergovernmental aspect into the LAC analysis depends on the issue, field of law, and the scope of the study itself. For instance, if the issue exclusively lies with the national government, then it would be pointless to consider whether the local governments have the necessary LAC to address a particular disruption. The bottom-line is still rigidity, especially if the capacity to address an issue is restricted to a particular agency or office.

4.1.3   Administrative Regime

While the administrative legal regime of the Philippines drew its basics as well as some of its agencies from the US administrative experience,[115] it can be argued that the Philippine administrative law has already developed into a field of law entirely separate from the doctrines of US law. In this part, the two most contentious and highly litigated powers granted to administrative agencies will be discussed herein: administrative rulemaking and administrative adjudication. For purposes of this section, it is assumed that these powers were validly and lawfully granted to an administrative agency.[116]

Administrative rulemaking is legislative in character, or "subordinate legislation". According to a landmark decision of *People v. Que Po Lay*,[117] which exonerated a supposed offender due to non-publication of an administrative rule with penal provisions for which the offender was being held liable, administrative rules "being issued for the implementation of the law authorizing its issuance [...] has the force and effect of law."[118] A necessary condition for its effectivity, however, is that the "the legal requirements for the valid exercise of the rulemaking power are observed."[119]

---

115   See, e.g. Pangasinan Transportation Co., Inc. v. Public Service Comm'n, G.R. No. 47065, 70 Phil. 221, 229 (1940); Ang Tibay v. Court of Industrial Relations, G.R. No. 46496, 69 Phil. 635 (1940). See also Agabin, *supra* note 66, 219–224.

116   The doctrine of separation of powers and the doctrine of non-delegation of powers, which is an essential component of administrative law discourse, will be discussed in *infra* Part 4 4.2.1

117   G.R. No. 6791, 94 Phil. 640 (1954).

118   *Ibid.*, 642.

119   Carlota, *supra* note 97, 75.

Carlota summarizes the guidelines for valid administrative rulemaking as follows:

> Being in the nature of subordinate legislation, administrative rulemaking is subject to certain limitations. The rulemaking grant is not a license for the agency to promulgate any rule. Aside from being authorized by law, the rule must not be inconsistent with the law or the Constitution. It must likewise be reasonable and germane to the purpose of the law. Agency perception regarding the desirability of the rule or its possible beneficial effects is immaterial where the rule is shown to be inconsistent with the law. The rule is void and can be successfully challenged in court.[120]

As to administrative adjudication, such function is known as *quasi-judicial*. Carlota observes that, while it is termed quasi-judicial, administrative agencies do in fact exercise a "judicial function just like the regular courts."[121] Notwithstanding this, the use of quasi-judicial power is still justified by the stark differences in how such judicial function, as described, is exercised. Carlota identifies four distinctions: (1) administrative agencies are not regular courts; nor are they part of the judiciary; (2) the quantum of evidence in an administrative proceeding is mere substantial evidence; (3) administrative proceedings do not strictly observe technical rules of evidence and procedure, and are actually frowned upon if they adhered to such; and (4) adjudicators are not all required to be members of the bar, since technical expertise on the specialized field is given priority.[122] Another important aspect of administrative adjudication is procedural due process, or the cardinal primary rights in administrative proceedings, as affirmed by the case of *Ang Tibay v. Court of Industrial Relations*.[123]

4.1.3.1   *LAC Insight: Domestic Administrative Law as Guide*
Every LAC analysis must ground itself on the administrative law of the jurisdiction sought to be examined. While the LAC as conceptualized by Camacho and Glicksman does not expressly state its connection with administrative law, such connection is apparent. For instance, administrative law is concerned about the valid exercise of power and jurisdiction of agencies over transactions, relations, and behavior sought to be regulated. LAC, on the other hand, is

---

120   *Ibid.*, 79.
121   *Ibid.*, 81.
122   *Id.* at 82–83.
123   G.R. No. 46496, 69 Phil. 635, 642–644 (1940).

concerned about how capable such agencies of are adapting to new phenomena. It can be understood that LAC still concerns itself with the agency's exercise of power—just like administrative law—but does not make the validity of such exercise the end-all-be-all of analysis. In a way, LAC seems to set aside, just for a while, the issues of abuse of power and authority, and focuses instead on *what could be possible in the margins of the law*.

Using the illustration of *margins* of law discussed earlier in Figure 7.1, administrative law may be said to be too fixated on the borders—where another step would make the agency's exercise of power *ultra vires*. Otherwise stated, *did the agency by doing such act went overboard?* On the other hand, unlike administrative law's focus on the legal issue of validity of exercise, LAC instead tries to map the plane, the space, or the *margins* between what is expressly stated in the law or what is deemed conventional and what is deemed unlawful already. Referring to the illustration, yes, LAC still minds the border, but focuses more on the exercise of power within the *margins*.

This paper suggests that the proper way to settle this seeming incompatibility between administrative law and LAC is for the LAC analysis to use the domestic administrative law as a guide in examining the legal mechanisms. After all, no matter how sophisticated the LAC analysis is, once the agency's rules or programme is challenged before the courts, the courts will still refer to administrative law for standards of valid exercise of authority.[124]

To conclude the discussion herein, provided with the principles of Philippine administrative law above, the LAC analysis must consider the issues of permissible delegation, subordinate legislation, and administrative due process, among others, in determining how these affect the LAC of a certain agency or office.

4.2   Key Legal Principles and Judicial Doctrines

After discussing the broad structural elements of the Philippine legal system, a selection of key legal principles and judicial doctrines are examined herein. These include the two of the most fundamental principles of Philippine constitutional law: (1) the doctrine of separation of powers in relation to doctrine of non-delegation of powers; and (2) the power of judicial review. In addition, this paper adopts the three constitutional rights discussed in the case of *Provincial Bus Operators Ass'n of the Phil. v. DOLE*:[125] (1) due process of law, (2) equal protection of the laws, and (3) non-impairment of obligation of contracts.

---

124   If this is the case, *what then is the contribution of the LAC in terms of administrative litigation?* The proposed answer to this will be explored in Part 6.

125   G.R. No. 202275, 872 SCRA 50 (2018).

4.2.1   Doctrine of Separation of Powers and Doctrine of
          Non-delegation of Powers

It is essential that the doctrine of separation of powers and the doctrine of non-delegation of powers are discussed in relation to administrative law, and now to LAC, because Carlota argues that "[t]he nature and scope of administrative rulemaking and adjudication can be better appreciated when viewed in the light of the doctrine of separation of powers and its corollary doctrine of non-delegation of powers."[126]

The landmark case of *Angara v. Electoral Commission*[127] illuminates on the doctrine of separation of powers:

> The separation of powers is a fundamental principle in our system of government. It obtains not through express provision but by actual division in our Constitution. Each department of the government has exclusive cognizance of matters within its jurisdiction, and is supreme within its own sphere. But it does not follow from the fact that the three powers are to be kept separate and distinct that the Constitution intended them to be absolutely unrestrained and independent of each other.[128]

Not only is there a *separation*, there is also an expectation that, whatever power has been granted by the Constitution to the three great branches, they may not further delegate the same. "*Potestas delegata non delegari potest*. What has been delegated cannot be delegated. [...] A further delegation of such power would indeed constitute a negation of the duty in violation of the trust reposed in the delegate mandated to discharge it directly."[129] This is most prevalent in legislative delegation of power.

Does a grant of seemingly legislative and judicial power to statutory agencies transgress the separation of powers? Carlota steers the discourse away from this myopic and simplistic view, and instead offers an alternative by saying that "if there are existing control or checking mechanisms that can keep the regulatory agencies within legal bounds in the exercise of their hybrid functions, then the existence of such agencies can be reconciled with the doctrine of separation of powers under our constitutional framework."[130] Similar to what *Angara* stated,

---

126   Carlota, *supra* note 97, 73.
127   G.R. No. 45081, 63 Phil. 139 (1936).
128   *Ibid.*, 156.
129   *Kilusang Mayo Uno v. Garcia*, G.R. No. 115381, 239 SCRA 386, 405–406 (1994).
130   Carlota, *supra* note 97, 74.

the grant of powers—whether executive, legislative, or judicial in nature—are not intended to be absolutely unrestrained.

One of these "control or checking mechanisms" is the test of permissible delegation of power to administrative agencies, which was adopted and repeatedly affirmed as effective by the Supreme Court. The completeness test and sufficient standards test require "that said law [which grants power to an agency]: (a) be complete in itself – must set forth therein the policy to be executed, carried out or implemented by the delegate – and (b) fix a standard – the limits of which the delegate must conform in the performance of his functions."[131] Carlota however notes the problematic application of the latter, the sufficient standards test, which have affirmed broad statutory standards such as interest of law and order[132] and public interest.[133] With standards so broad yet deemed sufficient, unbridled discretion is not too farfetched of an idea.

4.2.1.1   LAC Insight: Implied Grant

From the much litigated and researched doctrine of separation of powers, there definitely is a gamut of possible insights from the perspective of LAC, which may itself warrant a research independent from the present paper. At this point, it is sufficient to focus on how the LAC figures itself in a permissible delegation of power, for example, to administrative agencies. This paper argues that with the valid grant of power—whether rulemaking or adjudicatory—to administrative agencies through a legislative act, there is a simultaneous yet implied grant of LAC.

It has been argued earlier that there are *margins* of law, to which the LAC is akin. If one is to think about the illustration of such *margins*, it is within the bounds of lawful authority or grant of power. If such is the case, then it would be uncontentious to state that once the power is expressly granted to administrative agencies so that they may have jurisdiction and supervision of certain areas of social behavior and relations, or transactions, the LAC is tucked into such grant.

Such, however, may be confused with the *implied powers* as understood in Philippine administrative law jurisprudence, which states that "[s]tatutes conferring powers on administrative agencies must be liberally construed to enable them to discharge their assigned duties in accordance with the

---

131   *Pelaez v. Auditor General*, G.R. No. L-23825, 15 SCRA 569, 576–577 (1965).
132   Carlota, *supra* note 97, 77, *citing Rubi v. Provincial Board*, G.R. No. 14078, 39 Phil. 660 (1919)).
133   *Ibid.*, *citing People v. Rosenthal*, G.R. No. 46076, 68 Phil. 328 (1939).

legislative purpose."[134] While the two may seem similar, the *implied powers* currently in jurisprudence and the *implied grant of* LAC as this paper suggests are different. The former refers to ancillary powers that can be exercised by the agency in pursuing the state policy in its statute, while the latter instead refers to the power itself to pursue the state policy—although not categorically provided therein.

Nonetheless, such recognition of an implied grant is crucial in the LAC analysis, because it affirms the assumption that there indeed are *margins* and that the LAC can exist within lawful bounds.

4.2.2   Power of Judicial Review

The power of courts, including the Supreme Court and all the lower courts, to adjudicate cases brought before them, subject to the requirements of law, is enshrined in the Constitution as judicial power.[135] The expansion of the concept of judicial power, as declared in the case of *Angara*, vests the courts with the power of judicial review.

It is now the courts' duty to look into the lack or excess of jurisdiction brought by grave abuse of discretion; and not reject passing upon the case on the ground of such act or omission being a 'political question'.[136] For instance, the delegation of rulemaking and quasi-judicial powers administrative agencies are generally included herein. However, the Supreme Court has embodied the philosophy of judicial restraint even as to acts of administrative agencies themselves, provided they are not contrary to the Constitution and statutes, particularly the statute which grants their authority.[137]

---

134   Solid Homes, *Inc. v. Payawal*, G.R. No. 84811, 177 SCRA 72, 79 (1989). See also De Leon, *supra* note 69, 57: "While it is the fundamental rule that an administrative agency has only such powers as are expressly granted to it by law, it is likewise the rule that it has also such powers as are necessarily implied in the exercise of its express powers. Accordingly, where a general power is conferred or duty is enjoined by law, every particular power necessary for the exercise of one or the performance of the other is also conferred."

135   Const. art VIII, § 1.

136   *Ass'n of Medical Clinics for Overseas Workers, Inc. v. GCC Approved Medical Centers Ass'n*, G.R. No. 207132, 812 SCRA 452, 478 (2016): "[C]ourts of justice determine the limits of power of the agencies and offices of the government as well as those of its officers. In other words, the judiciary is the final arbiter on the question whether or not a branch of government or any of its officials has acted without jurisdiction or in excess of jurisdiction, or so capriciously as to constitute an abuse of discretion amounting to excess of jurisdiction or lack of jurisdiction. This is not only a judicial power but a duty to pass judgment on matters of this nature."

137   See *Kilusang Mayo Uno v. Garcia*, G.R. No. 115381, 239 SCRA 386, 411 (1994).

When the validity of an administrative act is involved, the constitutional grant of power of judicial review limits the determination as to whether there has been grave abuse of discretion amounting to lack or excess of jurisdiction on the part of the official whose action is being questioned.[138] As pointed out in *Zamora*, "while this Court has no power to substitute its judgment for that of Congress or of the President, it may look into the question of whether such exercise has been made in grave abuse of discretion."[139]

However, there is a burden on the part of the plaintiff to clearly prove such grave abuse of discretion, because of the presumption that "that official acts of the other branches of government are constitutional."[140] In this regard, according *to Sec. of Agrarian Reform*, "before the act was done or the law was enacted, earnest studies were made by Congress or the President, or both, to insure that the Constitution would not be breached."[141]

4.2.2.1   *LAC Insight: Grave Abuse of Discretion as Limit*

Judicial review will be as potent as a safeguard to LAC as it is currently with administrative rulemaking and administrative adjudication. The clincher, however, is that the use (or abuse) of discretion must be grave—capricious or whimsical. As have been observed in Supreme Court decisions as well as by scholars, such bar is not easy to hurdle. Many administrative acts have been challenged before the courts, but only few have clearly proven that there was grave abuse of discretion on the part of the agency that would warrant a declaration of nullity of said act or decision.

Nevertheless, despite the very high bar of grave abuse of discretion, the power of judicial review is still effective as it was developed. In particular to LAC, the fundamental question is *whether an agency's exercise of its power*

---

138   *Land Bank of the Phil. v. Ct. of Appeals*, G.R. No. 129368, 409 SCRA 455, 481 (2003).

139   *Integrated Bar of the Phil. v. Zamora*, G.R. No. 141284, 338 SCRA 81, 106 (2000).

140   *Provincial Bus Operators Ass'n of the Phil. v. DOLE*, G.R. No. 202275, 872 SCRA 50 (2018).

141   *Ass'n of Small Landowners in the Phil., Inc. v. Sec. of Agrarian Reform*, 256 Phil. 777, 798 (1989). See also Estrada v. Sandiganbayan, G.R. No. 148560, 369 SCRA 394, 431 (2001). "If there is any reasonable basis upon which the legislation may firmly rest, the courts must assume that *the legislature is ever conscious of the borders and edges of its plenary powers*, and has passed the law *with full knowledge of the facts and for the purpose of promoting what is right and advancing the welfare of the majority*. Hence, in determining whether the acts of the legislature are in tune with the fundamental law, courts should proceed with judicial restraint and act with caution and forbearance. Every intendment of the law must be adjudged by the courts in favor of its constitutionality, invalidity being a measure of last resort. In construing therefore the provisions of a statute, courts must first ascertain whether an interpretation is fairly possible to sidestep the question of constitutionality." (Emphasis added)

in relation to its LAC *would amount to a grave abuse of discretion.* This paper argues that, with the presumption of constitutionality on official acts, grave abuse of discretion cannot be attributed indiscriminately to all acts pertaining to LAC. So long as the act is on the *margins* of law and it is not unreasonable or unlawful, then it must persist. On the other hand, acts done pursuant to LAC are not isolated, but arguably even more exposed, to such attacks.

It can be noted that, in the research of Camacho and Glicksman, they argued that the LAC is not equivalent to agency discretion.[142] This paper does not disagree with this point. However, it must be clarified that the discretion as discussed therein and the discretion within the context of judicial review are not quite the same. The former considers the situation where an agency has sufficient LAC, but such agency and its leadership may or may not have the choice—or discretion—to use the flexibility granted to it.

4.2.3 Fundamental Rights and Police Power

The recent case of *Provincial Bus Operators Ass'n of the Phil. v. DOLE*[143] is a landmark case in administrative law. The Supreme Court upheld the Department Order and Memorandum Circular issued by the DOLE and the LTRFB, respectively, and declared such as valid exercise of administrative rulemaking pursuant to the State's police power in relation to constitutional rights.[144] As summed by the decision, "all these constitutional limits [referring to the due process clause, the equal protection clause, and the non-impairment clause] are subject to the fundamental powers of the State, specifically police power. As such, the burden of proving that the taking is unlawful rests on the party invoking the constitutional right."[145]

Police power,[146] one of the inherent powers of the State, is primarily vested in the legislative branch of government, which it may then delegate to persons and bodies such as the President, local government units, and of course administrative agencies in its exercise of rulemaking power.[147] The valid exercise of police power is thus measured through the standard of *reason*. "The police

---

142   Camacho & Glicksman, *supra* note 6, at 824–826.
143   G.R. No. 202275, 872 SCRA 50 (2018).
144   *Ibid.*
145   *Ibid.*
146   *Phil. Ass'n of Service Exporters, Inc. v. Drilon*, G.R. No. L-81958, 163 SCRA 386, 390 (1988), *citing Edu v. Ericta*, G.R. No. L-32096, 35 SCRA 481, 487 (1970). Police power is defined as the "state authority to enact legislation that may interfere with personal liberty or property in order to promote the general welfare."
147   See *City of Batangas v. Phil. Shell Petroleum Corp.*, G.R. No. 195003, 826 SCRA 297, 318 (2017).

power legislation must be firmly grounded on public interest and welfare, and a reasonable relation must exist between purposes and means."[148]

First, the right to due process of law is enshrined in Article III, Section 1 of the Constitution,[149] which requires that "official action [...] must not outrun the bounds of reasons and result in sheer oppression[,]"[150] or simply "freedom from arbitrariness."[151] *Second*, the right to equal protection of the laws is also enshrined in Article III, Section 1 of the Constitution,[152] which does not prohibit the State in making valid classifications, provided that persons under like circumstances and conditions are treated alike in terms of privileges and burdens.[153] *Third*, the right to non-impairment of obligation of contracts is enshrined in Article III, Section 10 of the Constitution,[154] the primary purpose of which is to "protect purely private agreements from State interference."[155]

4.2.3.1   *LAC Insight: Constitutional Rights as Limit*

The primacy of citizens' constitutional rights needs no further emphasis when government acts, and administrative acts in particular, are involved. It has been well-settled in jurisprudence that, while constitutional rights are indeed protected, there are valid limitations to such rights as briefly discussed above. Different standards and tests are used by courts to determine whether a government act has transgressed these standards.

---

148   *Ichong v. Hernandez*, G.R. No. L-7995, 101 Phil. 1155, 1165 (1957).

149   Const. art. II, § 1. "No person shall be deprived of life, liberty, or property without due process of law [...]."

150   *Ermita-Malate Hotel and Motel Operators Ass'n, Inc. v. City Mayor of Manila*, G.R. No. L-24693, 20 SCRA 849, 860 (1967).

151   Ibid. See also *White Light Corp. v. City of Manila*, G.R. No. 122846, 576 SCRA 416, 435–436 (2009). Due process has *procedural* and *substantive* aspects. *Procedural* due process entails the government's compliance with "established process when it makes an intrusion into the private sphere[,]" where such process refers to notice and hearing. On the other hand, *substantive* due process demands from the government "sufficient justification for depriving a person of life, liberty, or property."

152   Const. art. II, § 1. "[...] [N]or shall any person be denied the equal protection of the laws."

153   *People v. Vera*, G.R. No. 45685, 65 Phil. 56, 126 (1937). To create a valid classification, the following requisites must be met: (1) substantial distinctions; (2) germane to the purposes of the law; (3) not limited to existing conditions only; and (4) applicable to each member of the class.

154   Const. art. II, § 10. "No law impairing the obligation of contracts shall be passed."

155   *Provincial Bus Operators Ass'n of the Phil. v. DOLE*, G.R. No. 202275, 872 SCRA 50 (2018). But see *Phil. Ass'n of Service Exporters, Inc. v. Drilon*, G.R. No. L-81958, 163 SCRA 386, 397 (1988). "Freedom of contract and enterprise, like all other freedoms, is not free from restrictions, more so in this jurisdiction, where laissez faire has never been fully accepted as a controlling economic way of life."

In considering the LAC, constitutional rights must also play a role. The previous studies on LAC, which were heavily skewed in examining climate change and environmental issues, lack thorough discussions of constitutional rights as to LAC. Perhaps, a reason for that is that climate change measures are not necessarily situated at odds with constitutional rights. However, as suggested by this paper, this may not be the case when other fields of law are considered, especially those areas that have a high chance of interfering with private rights such as labour law. Further, each jurisdiction has different rights or different standards on how those rights may be justifiably limited.

Consider the following questions. How can an agency ensure that, in adopting measures, no constitutional rights are violated? If there indeed is an unavoidable conflict, how can an agency then adopt measures that are justified in interfering with constitutional rights, considering the State's police power and the standards for a valid limitation of rights? Adding the LAC element, *can an agency act done pursuant to LAC withstand judicial standards should it be in conflict with constitutional rights?* This is only an example of how the discourse of constitutional rights can be integrated into the LAC analysis.

To conclude this section, the insights considering LAC derived from the review of key elements of the Philippine legal system and of key legal principles and judicial doctrines undertaken in this section are summarized in Table 7.2.

These insights will take no indispensable part in the LAC analysis proper in Part 5. It is sufficient at this point that this paper has articulated the relationship of LAC with the Philippine legal system. Moreover, it may also be a preview to the efficacy of the LAC analysis within Philippine law by knowing its nuances and history. As observed in the discussion herein, there is so much more to unpack from LAC, especially when it is applied to broader structures of a legal system, which could as well be the subject of future research. Consistent with a point raised earlier, the LAC analysis developed herein veers away from an agency-specific understanding of LAC.[156] Instead of zooming only into a single agency or a group of agencies, the broader legal structures and even the legal history of a jurisdiction is given much importance. All of these are done in the hope of reaching a more accurate picture of LAC as a concept and as a legal research method.

---

156   See, e.g. Camacho and Glicksman, *supra* note 6.

TABLE 7.2   Summary of LAC insights on Philippine legal system

Category	Key Elements of Philippine Law	LAC Insight
PHILIPPINE LEGAL SYSTEM	Legal Tradition	Diversity
	Government Structure	Rigidity
	Administrative Regime	Domestic Administrative Law as Guide
LEGAL PRINCIPLES AND JUDICIAL DOCTRINES	Doctrine of Separation of Powers and Doctrine of Non-delegation of Powers	Implied Grant
	Power of Judicial Review	Grave Abuse of Discretion as Limit
	Fundamental Rights and Police Power – Due Process of Law – Equal Protection of the Laws – Non-impairment of Obligation of Contracts	Constitutional Rights as Limit

5   LAC Analysis of Philippine Labour Law in Relation to Just Transition Measures

This section contains the LAC analysis proper as applied to the research question considered in this paper. After laying the groundwork in the earlier sections, including the context of the problem (Part 2), theory and methods (Part 3), and nuances of the Philippine legal system in relation to LAC (Part 4), the stage is now reached for an application and integration of all these factors into a structured analysis.

To restate, the problem arises from the recognition that the disruption brought by the global trend of a shift to a low-carbon economy has corresponding costs that must be equitably distributed to prevent workers and frontline communities in carbon-intensive industries from being left behind, as well as that the *conventional* legal responses are marred by bureaucratic rigidity. Essentially, there has to be a way—a legal way—to timely address such disruption and the inequality it may produce.

Thus, the research question herein is *whether or not existing Philippine labour legal mechanisms (instruments and institutions) have sufficient ability,*

otherwise known as legal adaptive capacity, to adopt and implement just transi-
tion measures in response to the shift to a low-carbon economy within the bounds
of lawful authority.

In confronting such problem, this section adopts the multi-step process
created in Part 3. The process is generally divided into *Inclusion Criteria* (Steps
1–4), *Point of Analysis* (Step 5), and *Analysis Proper* (Steps 6–7). Each of these
steps will be discussed and applied in relation to the research question. This is
a necessary undertaking to see the efficacy of a more structured LAC analysis.

5.1   Step 1: Disruption – Shift to a Low-Carbon Economy

Identify the disruption or new phenomenon.

The disruption to be considered here is the shift to a low-carbon economy.[157] An insight that must be reiterated is that a response that was originally
intended to address a disruption may itself become a disruption, especially if
the change that it requires is so fundamental. In this case, the shift to a low-
carbon economy may be considered as a response to a primary disruption
(climate change), which this paper does not dispute. However, the shift to a
low-carbon economy, with its necessary incidents, has the character of being
a disruption itself.[158] While it is named to be a key effort in addressing climate
change, low-carbon development definitely has unintended consequences to
other sectors that themselves must be addressed.

Aside from the international agreements, Paris Agreement and the Glasgow Climate Pact, the Philippines has reflected its commitment to the shift
to a low-carbon economy through the Nationally Determined Contributions
(NDCs)[159] and the National Climate Change Action Plan 2011–2028.[160] A House

---

157   See *supra* Part 2 2.2.1 for the background of the shift to a low-carbon economy.

158   It should be remembered that a considering a phenomenon a *disruption* is not a norma-
       tive statement on the phenomenon's positive or negative impact to society. See Part 3 3.2
       for definition of disruption: "the new phenomenon, innovation, event or a series thereof,
       or systemic change that drastically impacts an existing, or causes the creation of a new,
       unregulated social behavior or relation".

159   Republic of the Philippines, Nationally Determined Contribution 2 (2021): "The Philip-
       pines, in line with its national security policy and its sustainable development aspirations
       and in solidarity with ASEAN Member States, shall endeavor to peak its emissions by 2030
       in the context of accelerating the just transition of its sectors into a green economy and
       the delivery of green jobs and other benefits of a climate and disaster-resilient and low
       carbon development to its people, among others."

160   Climate Change Commission, *National Climate Change Action Plan 2011–2028* (Climate
       Change Commission 2011) 20: "The second focus of the NCCAP is the creation of green

Bill was also filed in 2019 during the 18th Congress to institutionalize a system of carbon credits pursuant to a low-carbon economy, but did not reach the plenary.[161]

One of the sectors expected to be most affected by this disruption is the energy sector.[162] According to the Department of Energy, coal remains the major energy source in the country's installed capacity mix with 41.6% share. Other carbon intensive sources include oil-based with 16.1% and natural gas with 13.1%.[163] If there is any effort to reduce emissions at the rate required, there must be an active effort and government policy to shift the country's dependence from coal to renewable energy.[164]

However, the state must not only give importance to fighting climate change while simultaneously ensuring energy security and access to meet market demands, whether industrial or residential. It must also consider the workers and frontline communities at risk in every individual plant closure. To illustrate the extent of those impacts, data show that, as of December 2020, there are 86 grid-connected coal, oil-based, and natural gas power plants nationwide (52 coal, 29 oil-based, and 5 natural gas), which vary in size, capacity, and of course labour force.[165]

----

jobs. The plan adheres to the United Nations Environment Program and International Labor Organization's definition of Green jobs as decent jobs, which help protect the environment, ensure a shift to a low carbon development and adapt to the effects of climate change."

161   H. No. 2184, 18th Cong., 1st Sess. (2019). An Act to Promote a Low Carbon Economy Establishing for this Purpose the Emission Cap-and-trade System in the Industry Sector to Reduce Greenhouse Gas Emissions and Protect the Climate. See also H. No. 4050, 14th Cong., 1st Sess. (2008); H. No. 6997, 14th Cong., 3rd Sess. (2009).

162   It must be noted that there are still other industries such as transportation, agriculture, and mining that have the tendency to be carbon-dependent. *See* United States Environmental Protection Agency, *Sources of Greenhouse Gas Emissions*, https://www.epa.gov /ghgemissions/sources-greenhouse-gas-emissions (accessed 5 January 2022).

163   Department of Energy - Electric Power Industry Management Bureau, 2020 *Power Situation Report* (2021) 5.

164   See K Crismundo, 'DOE Stops Endorsements for New Coal Power Projects' *Philippines News Agency*, 27 October 2020, https://www.pna.gov.ph/articles/1119918 (accessed 5 January 2022). But see People for Power Coalition, 'P4P on the DOE Moratorium on New Coal Plants' *Center Energy, Ecology & Development*, 30 October 2020, https://ceedphilippines .com/p4p-on-the-doe-moratorium-on-new-coal-plants/ (accessed 5 January 2022).

165   Department of Energy, *List of Existing Power Plants (Grid-Connected) as of December 2020 – Luzon Grid*; Department of Energy, *List of Existing Power Plants (Grid-Connected) as of December 2020 – Visayas Grid*; Department of Energy, *List of Existing Power Plants (Grid-Connected) as of December 2020 – Mindanao Grid*.

5.2   *Step 2: Field of Law – Philippine Labour Law and Related Social*
        Legislation

> *Identify the field of law using the following guide questions:*
> a.   *Which field of law is most likely to be affected by such disruption?*
> b.   *Which field of law could regulate the social behavior or relation that is*
>   *most likely to be affected by such disruption?*
> c.   *Which field of law has the potential of addressing such disruption?*

After identifying the disruption, the next step is determining the field of law that will be the subject of the analysis. Using these guide questions from the multi-step process, this paper identifies labour law as one of the major fields of law that is relevant to the shift to a low-carbon economy.[166] The termination of employment is a natural consequence of the closure of carbon-intensive industries. Whether the closure is government-mandated, government-incentivized, or private sector-led, employment will always be at stake. Thus, this issue is under the purview of labour law, although there may not be a specific regulation currently enforced for termination pursuant to a low-carbon development. In addition, social legislation that seeks to address a citizen's transition out of employment, or otherwise stated to unemployment, may be included as well.

It must be noted, however, that there are usually varied fields of law that are relevant to a disruption, because of the latter's extremely pervasive nature. In the case considered herein, there are the fields of energy law, public utilities law, and even competition law that may also be examined, aside from the usual suspects of environmental and natural resources law.

5.3   *Step 3: Mechanisms*

> *Within the identified field of law in (2), identify existing legal mechanisms*
> *(instruments and institutions) using the same guide questions in (2):*
> a.   *Which legal instruments and institutions are most likely to be affected*
>   *by such disruption?*
> b.   *Which legal instruments and institutions could regulate the social*
>   *behavior or relation that is most likely to be affected by such disruption?*
> c.   *Which legal instruments and institutions have the potential of*
>   *addressing such disruption?*

---

166   See *supra* Part 2 2.2.2 for discussion on labour law.

Labour law and related social legislation were identified as the general field of law in this analysis. Similar guide questions will be used to determine the existing legal mechanisms, composed of legal instruments and legal institutions, that may be used to address the disruption.

The legal instruments are identified as Presidential Decree No. 442, otherwise known as the Labor Code of the Philippines, as amended, particularly the provisions under Book Six (Post-Employment)[167] and Book Four (Health, Safety, and Social Welfare Benefits), Title II – Employees Compensation and State Insurance Fund,[168] and Republic Act No. 11199, otherwise known as the Social Security Act of 2018, particularly the provisions on unemployment insurance.[169] The relevant implementing rules and regulations issued by the government agency vested with the power to adopt such are also considered herein. Furthermore, the 1987 Constitution, particularly the labour and social justice provisions in Articles II and XIII, as the fundamental source of state policy is crucial as well in contextualizing these legal instruments.[170] Lastly, relevant legal and judicial doctrines are also included.

In addition, the legal institutions identified here are the Department of Labor and Employment,[171] the Employee's Compensation Commission,[172] and the Social Security Commission.[173] Since this paper is concerned about the capacity of these existing mechanisms to adopt and implement just transition measures, only the executive or implementing and quasi-legislative or rulemaking powers of such agencies will be examined.[174] Similar to the legal

---

167   Lab. Code, arts. 293–302.

168   Arts. 172–215.

169   See also Rep. Act No. 10771 (2016). Philippine Green Jobs Act of 2016. This paper does not subscribe to the view that the Philippine Green Jobs Act of 2016 is consistent with the meaning of just transition espoused in this paper. For instance, while the statute provides incentive mechanisms for private actors that create green jobs as defined therein, there is a wide gap on the steps to safeguard the workers and frontline workers of carbon-intensive industries.

170   Const. art. II, § 18. "The State affirms labor as a primary social economic force. It shall protect the rights of workers and promote their welfare." Const. art. XIII, § 3. "The State shall afford full protection to labor, local and overseas, organized and unorganized, and promote full employment and equality of employment opportunities for all."

171   Rev. Adm. Code, Title VII. Administrative Code of 1987 or Exec. Order No. 292 (1987); Lab. Code, art. 5.

172   Lab. Code, *amended by* Pres. Dec. No. 626 (1974).

173   Rep. Act No. 11199 (2019). Social Security Act of 2018.

174   While it can be argued that the exercise of quasi-judicial or adjudicatory powers may also contribute to the adoption and implementation of such measures, this paper expressly reserves discussion of such aspect to a future research.

instruments, relevant legal and judicial doctrines on the extent of authority and exercise of powers of said legal institutions are also considered.

5.4   Step 4: Measures – Just Transition

Within the identified legal instruments and institutions in (3), identify current and future measures that may respond to the disruption.

The last step in completing the inclusion criteria is identifying the types of measures that the agency implements or may implement to address the disruption. The measures are important, because they act as test points in determining the LAC of legal mechanisms. In this case, the *potential* measures to ensure just transition within the realm of labour law and related social legislation must be identified, or at least approximated.

As mentioned earlier, just transition is not yet as pronounced as a policy agenda in the Philippines, which also means that the existing just transition measures — if there is any to begin with — are limited. Such may not even include just transition language or any reference to the shift to a low-carbon economy, which makes it even more challenging to identify them for an analysis such as this one. Moreover, the analysis does not get any easier when future measures, or those which have not yet been adopted *but may be adopted*, are considered within the margins.

To illustrate, this paper refers to academic literature that surveys just transition measures in other jurisdictions to show the extent of what such measures may cover. One study includes temporary financial support for displaced workers, employment services, social insurance/unemployment support, and pension support under the broad area of social supports; and employment and skills strategies, training and education programmes, job databases and labour market information under workforce development.[175] Another study identifies just transition initiatives such as worker pensions, job guarantees and compensation, worker transition service, and retraining of workers, among others.[176]

While the aforementioned may serve as a guide for policy-setting, again, this paper does not make a normative input on *what law, programmes, and policies*

---

175   TA Krawchenko and M Gordon, 'How Do We Manage a Just Transition? A Comparative Review of National and Regional Just Transition Initiatives' (2021) 13 *Sustainability* 6070.

176   S Pai, K Harrison and H Zerriffi, 'A Systematic Review of the Key Elements of a Just Transition for Fossil Fuel Workers' *Clean Economy Working Paper Series, Smart Prosperity Institute* (2020).

ought to be adopted, but only as to whether they may be adopted within the bounds of the existing mechanisms' lawful authority.

5.5   Step 5: LAC – Substantive

> *Identify the axis of* LAC *(i.e. substantive, procedural) to be used in the analysis.*

Once the elements of the analysis are determined through the inclusion criteria, the next step is to set the parameters or point of analysis. A researcher may either choose *substantive* LAC, *procedural* LAC, or both. As mentioned, while it is ideal to use both parameters, there is nothing inherently lacking if an examination of only one axis is conducted, such as in this present paper.

Consistent with the illustrations of *margins* of law and the assumption that *conventional* responses are not the priority when a disruption hits—although if given more time, those may also prove useful, the point of analysis in this paper is *substantive* LAC, which is "the extent to which a legal regime's goals are capable of responding to changed conditions."[177] A high degree of *substantive* LAC corresponds to an agency's authority to adjust interpretation of regulatory goals or the means of pursuing them to meet new challenges or accommodate changed circumstances, while a limited degree corresponds to relatively rigid goals that do not allow altering of regulatory or management approaches, notwithstanding changed conditions.[178] Such an approach is consistent with the research question presented herein, which is not concerned with the procedural rigidity (as it was already assumed as a fact) but with substantive rigidity as to statutory goals and grant of authority relating to the pursuance of such state policy.

5.6   Step 6: Absolute LAC

> *Apply the identified* LAC *analysis in (5) to determine the absolute* LAC *of legal instruments and institutions in (3).*

Absolute LAC is the legal mechanisms' capacity to adapt to new phenomena, without any specific disruption or new phenomenon considered in the

---

177   Camacho and Glicksman, *supra* note 6, 724.
178   See Part 3.1, for the discussion of *substantive* LAC.

analysis. Focus is directed to the broader nature and structure of legal mechanisms that allow or restrict adaptive capacity.[179]

Similar to the approach of previous studies, the legal institutions determined in Step 3 shall primarily guide the analysis proper moving forward. The discussion of such agencies is then supported by the legal instruments likewise identified. The substantive goals and the agencies' powers in pursuing such goals are examined to determine the degree of *absolute substantive* LAC.

5.6.1   Department of Labor and Employment

The Department of Labor and Employment (DOLE) was created by Executive Order No. 292, otherwise known as the Administrative Code of 1987.[180] With the post-Marcos regime change and the new constitutional order, it was imperative to overhaul the administrative and bureaucratic structure of the Philippine government. Under the Administrative Code, the DOLE shall be the "primary policy-making, programming, coordinating and administrative entity of the Executive Branch of the government in the field of labor and employment."[181]

The Administrative Code also vests extensive powers and functions to the DOLE, which include "[enforcing] social and labor legislation to protect the working class[,]" "[providing] for safe, decent, humane and improved working conditions and environment for all workers[,]" and "[maintaining] a harmonious, equitable and stable labor relations system[,]" among others.[182]

These broad substantive goals and powers in pursuing labour protection must be understood in the context of the 1987 Constitution. One of the hallmarks of the 1987 Constitution is its stand-alone Article on Social Justice,[183] which is the first in Philippine constitutional history.[184] Generally, the Constitution imposes on Congress the duty to "give highest priority to the enactment

---

179   See *supra* Part 3. 3.3 for the discussion of *absolute* LAC.

180   Rev. Adm. Code, Title VII.

181   Title VII, § 2. The DOLE shall assume primary responsibility on the following matters:
       "(1)   The promotion of gainful employment opportunities and the optimization of the development and utilization of the country's manpower resources;
       (2)   The advancement of workers' welfare by providing for just and humane working conditions and terms of employment;
       (3)   The maintenance of industrial peace by promoting harmonious, equitable, and stable employment relations that assure equal protection for the rights of all concerned parties."

182   Rev. Adm. Code, Title VII, § 3.

183   Const. art. XIII.

184   SM Candelaria & JL Sy, 'Social Justice: Strengthening the Heart of the 1987 Constitution for Those at the Margins of Philippine Society' (2020) 64 *Ateneo Law Journal* 1412, 1416. See also CS Monsod, 'Social Justice' (2014) 59 *Ateneo Law Journal* 691, 697–700.

of measures that protect and enhance the right of all the people to human dignity, reduce social, economic, and political inequalities, and remove cultural inequities by equitably diffusing wealth and political power for the common good."[185]

More specifically, on labour, the Constitution mandates "full protection to labor, local and overseas, organized and unorganized[.]"[186] The State shall also "promote full employment and equality of employment opportunities for all."[187] The following rights are also guaranteed: self-organization, collective bargaining and negotiations, peaceful concerted activities, strike in accordance with law, security of tenure, humane conditions of work, and living wage.[188] Clearly, the mandate of the DOLE must be situated within these higher-order constitutional policy.

Another crucial legal instrument in this discussion is the Labor Code of the Philippines.[189] Although promulgated prior to the 1987 Constitution, numerous amendments were introduced thereto to make it consistent with the Constitution. While the Labor Code enumerates the various standards of employment such as hours of work,[190] overtime,[191] and statutory leaves[192] to name a few, it also expands the power of the DOLE to include visitorial power,[193] enforcement power,[194] adjudicatory power,[195] and rulemaking power,[196] among others. The Labor Code also creates and defines the mandate of other DOLE-attached agencies attached, such as the Employees' Compensation Commission and the National Labor Relations Commission.[197]

Of particular interest in this analysis is the rulemaking power vested by Article 5 of the Labor Code to the DOLE, which states "The Department of

---

185   Const. art. XIII, § 1.
186   Art. XIII, § 3. See Phil. Ass'n of Service Exporters, Inc. v. Drilon, G.R. No. L-81958, 163 SCRA 386, 397 (1988). The Supreme Court characterized that ""[p]rotection to labor" does not signify the promotion of employment alone. What concerns the Constitution more paramountly is that such an employment be above all, decent, just, and humane."
187   Const. art. XIII, § 3.
188   Art. XIII, § 3.
189   Pres. Dec. No. 442 (1974), as amended.
190   Lab. Code, arts. 83–85.
191   Arts. 87–89.
192   Art. 95.
193   Art. 128; DOLE, Omnibus Rules Implementing the Labor Code (1989) [hereinafter "Omnibus Rules"], Book Three, Rule X, § 1.
194   Art. 128; *Omnibus Rules*, Book Three, Rule X, §§ 2–3.
195   Art. 129; *Omnibus Rules*, Book Three, Rule XI, §§ 1–4.
196   Art. 5.
197   Book Four, Title II; Book Five, Title II.

Labor and other government agencies charged with the administration and enforcement of this Code or any of its parts shall promulgate the necessary implementing rules and regulations. Such rules and regulations shall become effective fifteen (15) days after announcement of their adoption in newspapers of general circulation."[198]

Further, the Supreme Court decisions that directly confront such rulemaking power is illustrative of its nature. The following issuances were held as valid by the Supreme Court: Department Order temporarily suspending the overseas deployment of Filipino female domestic and household workers;[199] Administrative Order providing for the NLRC's exercise of adjudicatory powers through divisions, instead of *en banc*;[200] Department Order temporarily suspending the recruitment by private employment agencies of Filipino domestic workers and vesting in the DOLE the task of processing and deploying such workers;[201] Department Order simplifying the requirements for the establishment of locals of chapters compared to that of independent labour organizations;[202] and Department Order providing for the rule for computing the fixed and the performance-based component of a public utility bus driver's or conductor's wage.[203]

There is a clear trend of upholding the DOLE's exercise of quasi-legislative powers. The constitutional policy of social justice and the legal principles of presumption of constitutionality and the valid exercise of the State's police power remain to be the cornerstone of labour regulation in the Philippines.

The DOLE has a high degree of *absolute substantive* LAC, which is manifested through its authority to adjust interpretation of regulatory goals or the means of pursuing them to meet new challenges or accommodate changed circumstances. This is supported by the broad substantive goals mandated by statute and the Constitution, combined with the wide latitude given by the courts on rules and regulations issued pursuant to its rulemaking power.

---

198   Art. 5.
199   *Phil. Ass'n of Service Exporters, Inc. v. Drilon*, G.R. No. L-81958, 163 SCRA 386 (1988).
200   *Union of Filipro Employees v. Nat'l Lab. Rel. Comm'n*, G.R. No. 91025, 192 SCRA 414 (1990). An en banc decision is where a case is heard, tried, and decided by the full complement of judges of a court, rather than by its divisions composed of a smaller group of judges.
201   *Phil. Ass'n of Service Exporters v. Torres*, G.R. No. 101279, 212 SCRA 298 (1992). It, however, failed to comply with the publication requirement.
202   *Electromat Manufacturing and Recording Corp. v. Lagunzad*, G.R. No. 172699, 654 SCRA 633 (2011).
203   *Provincial Bus Operators Ass'n of the Phil. v. DOLE*, G.R. No. 202275, 872 SCRA 50 (2018).

5.6.2   Employees' Compensation Commission

The Employees' Compensation Commission (ECC) was created by the Labor Code "[t]o initiate, rationalize, and coordinate the policies of the employees' compensation program[,]"[204] which mandates that "employees and their dependents, in the event of work-connected disability or death, may promptly secure adequate income benefit and medical related benefits."[205] Its predecessor, the Workmen's Compensation Commission, together with the statutory presumption of compensability and theory of aggravation, was abolished in 1975.[206]

Some of the powers and duties of the ECC include "[assessing] and [fixing] a rate of contribution from all employers[,]" "[approving] rules and regulations governing the processing of claims and the settlement of disputes[,]" and "[performing] such other acts as it may deem appropriate for the attainment of the purposes of the Commission and proper enforcement of the provisions [related to employees' compensation program]."[207] Moreover, the ECC has the power "[t]o initiate policies and programs toward adequate occupational health and safety and accident prevention in the working environment, rehabilitation [...], and other related programs and activities, and to appropriate funds therefor."[208] It also has an adjudicatory power to review cases appealed from the Social Security System (SSS) or Government Service Insurance System (GSIS) on matters of "coverage, entitlement to benefits, collection and payment of contributions and penalties thereon, or any other matter related thereto[.]"[209]

Aside from the general rulemaking power granted by Article 5 of the Labor Code, the ECC also has the power "to determine and approve occupational diseases and work-related illnesses that may be considered compensable based on peculiar hazards of employment."[210] Such list of occupational diseases and conditions required for compensability is significant in determining a claim's success. Otherwise, the employee has the burden to prove that the risk of contracting such illness is increased by the working conditions. For example, the

204   Lab. Code, art. 182.
205   Art. 172.
206   Act No. 3428 (1927). Workmen's Compensation Act. *See also* Pres. Dec. No. 626 (1974), § 4; Lab. Code, art. 311.
207   Lab. Code, art. 183.
208   Art. 183 (d).
209   Art. 186.
210   Art. 173 (*l*).

ECC through its rulemaking power recently included COVID-19, subject to certain conditions, as a compensable sickness.[211]

To contrast, in terms of compensable injury, the *proviso* "arising out of and in the course of employment" has been well litigated in administrative bodies and courts to rule on the compensability of injuries considering the varied circumstances of each case.[212]

Moreover, despite the silence of the Constitution on matters of employees' compensation, it is argued that the broad constitutional policy of "full protection to labor" covers compensation arising from injury and illness.

The ECC has a high degree of *absolute substantive* LAC, which is manifested through its authority to adjust interpretation of regulatory goals or the means of pursuing them to meet new challenges or accommodate changed circumstances. This is supported by the statutory grant of regulatory and enforcement powers by allowing the ECC to determine conditions of compensability and to identify employers or industries that have high frequency of work accidents or occupational diseases.

5.6.3   Social Security Commission

The Social Security System which is directed and controlled by the Social Security Commission (SSC), while originally created in 1954 through Republic Act No. 1161,[213] has since evolved to enforce an effective social security programme in the Philippines. Republic Act No. 11199,[214] otherwise known as the Social Security Act of 2018, expanded the powers of the SSC, among other things.

Briefly stated, the state policy and substantive goals pursued by the SSC are summarized into establishing, developing, promoting and perfecting a sound and viable tax-exempt social security system suitable to the needs of the people throughout the Philippines.[215] It must be noted that the social security programme aims to protect Filipinos not only from the hazards of "disability,

---

211   Employees' Compensation Commission (ECC), Board Resolution No. 21-04-14 (2021). Conditions for the Compensability of COVID-19 under the ECC List of Occupational and Work-related Disease or Annex A of the Amended Rules on Employees' Compensation (EC).

212   Lab. Code, art. 173 (k). See *Belarmino v. Employees' Compensation Comm'n*, G.R. No. 90104, 185 SCRA 304 (1990).

213   Rep. Act No. 1161 (1954), § 3–4. Social Security Law.

214   Rep. Act No. 11199 (2019), § 3–4. Social Security Act of 2018.

215   § 2.

sickness, maternity, old age, [and] death[,]"[216] but also from "other contingencies resulting in loss of income or financial burden."[217]

From a constitutional perspective, social security may not be considered as a necessary incident of the labour provisions in the Constitution, because social security functions beyond labour protection and covers a broader segment of society. In fact, the 1987 Constitution speaks of social security not in terms of a guarantee, but an optional state action, and only in terms of caring for the society's elderly.[218] On the other hand, it may be argued that the broad theme of social justice incorporates social security in it as well.

Consistent with the SSC's expansion of powers, it now has the power to "formulate, adopt, amend and/or rescind such rules and regulations as may be necessary to carry out the provisions and purposes of [the Social Security Act of 2018]"[219]—which is a significant leap from the previous statute that subjects such rulemaking power to the approval of the President of the Philippines. Further, the SSC is empowered now as well to "develop and administer a special social security program for workers, with unique economic, social, and geographic situations[.]"[220] Conditions for such special programme require that should such have different contributions and benefits, they are proportionately calculated and must be fair, equitable, actuarially sound and viable.

Similar to the DOLE and the ECC, the SSC has a high degree of *absolute substantive* LAC, which is manifested through its authority to adjust interpretation of regulatory goals or the means of pursuing them to meet new challenges or accommodate changed circumstances. This is supported by the statutory grant of expanded powers by allowing the SSC adopt rules, regulations, and programmes that it may deem necessary and in favor of a certain group of workers. Despite lack of clear constitutional mandate, the statute itself provides a wide leeway for the SSC to respond to new phenomena.

5.7   *Step 7: Relative LAC*

> *Apply the identified LAC analysis in (5) to determine the relative LAC of legal instruments and institutions in (3) in relation to current and future measures in (4).*

---

216   § 2.

217   § 2.

218   Const. art. XV, § 4. But see Const. (1973), art. II, § 7. "The State shall establish, maintain, and ensure adequate social services in the field of education, health, housing, employment, welfare, and social security to guarantee the enjoyment of the people of a decent standard of living."

219   Rep. Act No. 11199 (2019), § 4(a)(1).

220   § 4(a)(10).

Relative LAC is the legal mechanisms' capacity to adapt to new phenomena, with particular consideration of a specific disruption or new phenomenon. Attention is paid at specific provisions of legal instruments or processes of legal institutions that are directly related to the disruption.[221]

This step will follow a similar approach as the preceding step. The legal institutions and instruments identified in Step 3 will be examined in relation to the measures identified in Step 4, or just transition measures. To keep the discussion concise, current measures related to transition of workers (e.g. termination of employment, suspension of employment) are first considered and then just transition measures, as defined in Step 4, connected to such current measures—most of which are not yet adopted—are subsequently examined. Although this step focuses more on the capacity of the legal institutions to adopt and implement particular measures, the analysis in Step 6 on the *absolute* LAC must also be taken into consideration in this step,

5.7.1   Department of Labor and Employment

The Labor Code presents two categories of concluding an employment relationship: termination of employment (Book Six, Title I)[222] and retirement from the service (Book Six, Title II).[223] These are the statutorily recognized means of transitioning out of employment. Of course, there are significant differences among the causes and effects of each of these means.

To illustrate, the termination of employment may be understood as either termination by the employer[224] or termination by the employee.[225] Termination by the employer is further divided into just causes,[226] or those attributable to the fault or negligence of the employee, and authorized causes,[227] or those brought by the necessity and exigencies of business, changing economic conditions, or illness of the employee. There is also the concept of constructive dismissal,[228] which is a form of termination by the employer, although not specifically mentioned in the Labor Code.

For purposes of the research problem herein, which is the shift to a low-carbon economy and the corresponding just transition measures, the authorized causes are considered. This is the most relevant and foreseeable

---

221   See *supra* Part 3 3.3 for the discussion of *relative* LAC.
222   Lab. Code, arts. 293–301.
223   Art. 302.
224   Arts. 297–299.
225   Art. 300.
226   Art. 297; DOLE Dep't Order No. 147-15 (2015), §§ 5.1–5.2.
227   Lab. Code, arts. 298–299; DOLE Dep't Order No. 147-15 (2015), §§ 5.3–5.4.
228   *Philippine Japan Active Carbon Corp. vs. Nat'l Lab. Rel. Comm'n*, G.R. No. 83239, 171 SCRA 164, 167–168 (1989).

form of termination in a low-carbon development situation, because the business closure is expected to be driven by the employer's decision, whether there is government incentive or not. In the current measure, there are five authorized causes: (1) installation of labour-saving device; (2) redundancy; (3) retrenchment or downsizing; (4) closure or cessation of operation; and (5) disease. Pursuant to the DOLE's rulemaking power, Department Order No. 147-15 provides the substantive and procedural due process standards for a valid termination as well as the corresponding separation pay.[229]

If a termination of employment arising from the shift to a low-carbon economy is situated within these authorized causes, the most likely cause is *closure or cessation of operation*, which requires that there must be a decision to close by the management, that such decision be done in good faith, and that there exists no other option but to close.[230] According to the Labor Code, the separation pay entitlement of an employee terminated due to closure is "equivalent to one (1) month pay or at least one-half (1/2) month pay for every year of service, whichever is higher, a fraction of six (6) months service is considered as one (1) whole year."[231] If the employer argues that the closure is due to serious business losses, the terminated employee shall have no separation pay at all.

Definitely, some employers would instead offer separation packages that may be more generous than what the law provides to workers to be terminated due to closure of a carbon-intensive enterprise, but that is besides the point. What is at issue herein is the legally demandable separation benefit due to the worker.

Without opening the pandora's box of determining the *correct* amount of separation pay, it is merely assumed for the purposes of discourse that the DOLE deems the separation pay required for the authorized cause of closure or cessation of operation would not fulfill the ideal of social justice for fossil-fuel workers who have sacrificed their prime years and health working for a hazardous industry only to be unceremoniously let go after five, ten, or fifteen years of service and way ahead before retirement. The question then is, *does the DOLE with its existing powers have the authority to increase the separation pay due to such workers by way of quasi-legislative rules and regulations?*

It is argued that, despite the constitutional precept of social justice and the broad substantive goals in favor of labour, the DOLE would violate the bounds of its statutory authority should it promulgate a Department Order increasing the separation pay for terminated fossil-fuel workers. The clear language

---

229   DOLE Dep't Order No. 147-15 (2015).
230   § 5.4(d).
231   Lab. Code, art. 298; DOLE Dep't Order No. 147-15 (2015), § 5.5.

of this part of the law—probably a product of lobbied interests or an intended safeguard against *back-end* interpretation—prevails and cannot be overridden by administrative rulemaking. In this respect, the DOLE has a limited degree of *relative substantive* LAC.

However, the DOLE has a medium degree of *relative substantive* LAC if the DOLE, through an issuance, amends the requisites for an authorized cause to be a valid ground for termination. As shown in Department Order No. 147-15, the DOLE was able to create a list of requisites—although not specifically provided in the Labor Code—that will guide the quasi-judicial and judicial bodies in determining the validity of termination. Such requisites may still be struck down by the courts should they be unreasonable or beyond the lawful bounds of the Labor Code.

On retirement, there are conditions provided for by the Labor Code, or by a collective bargaining agreement or by an employment contract provided that these do not provide less than what is statutorily guaranteed, for an employee to undertake voluntary retirement or compulsory retirement.[232] Similar to the exercise above, suppose as well that the DOLE deems that the statutory voluntary retirement age of 60 and compulsory retirement age of 65 are far too advanced for fossil-fuel workers in danger of being terminated soon, which would require the setting of lower ages and/or setting of different conditions than that prescribed by the Labor Code.

Again, the similar question is posed. *Does the DOLE have the authority to impose a different retirement age and conditions for retirement of such workers by way of quasi-legislative rules and regulations?* It is argued that the DOLE would violate the bounds of its statutory authority should it impose a different retirement age and conditions for retirement for the affected industries. In this respect, the DOLE has a limited degree of *relative substantive* LAC.

There is potential, however, when the Department Orders on employment and working conditions of various occupations or types of work issued by the DOLE through its rulemaking power over the years are considered. Some of these include workers in audio-visual production,[233] health personnel in the private healthcare industry,[234] collectors in the debt collection

---

232   Art. 302.

233   DOLE-Film Development Council of the Philippines (FDCP) Joint Memo. Circ. No. 001-20 (2020). Guidelines Governing the Working Conditions and Occupational Safety and Health of Workers in the Audio-Visual Production

234   DOLE Dep't Order No. 182-17 (2017). Guidelines Governing the Employment and Working Conditions of Health Personnel in the Private Healthcare Industry.

industry,[235] security guards and other private security personnel in the private security industry,[236] and drivers and conductors in the public utility bus transport industry.[237] Labour advisories have been issued as well for workers in the movie and television industry[238] and delivery riders in food delivery and courier activities.[239] The appreciation of these issuances is admittedly tricky, because it must be asked whether the DOLE expands and further affirms the statutory protections, or it merely echoes what has already been said in the Labor Code—but only reorganized for the quick reference of the referred industry and agency officials.

Nonetheless, the workers in carbon-intensive industries will definitely benefit from such an issuance, although limited, because it is in a way a guide to the various rights and remedies available to the workers as well as the employers in those industries. There is a relatively high degree of *relative substantive* LAC herein.

5.7.2   Employees' Compensation Commission

The current employees' compensation programme includes work-connected injury or sickness, resulting in either disability or death as compensable contingencies.[240] Compensation comes in the form of loss of income benefit, medical benefit, rehabilitation service, carer's allowance, or death benefit.[241] By instituting the programme, the State recognizes not only the risks that workers may be subjected to in the course of their employment, but also the responsibility of the State as well as the employers to create a system of compensation for any untoward incident that may happen.

Further, it is not farfetched to think that the compensation programme is also a transition measure, similar to the provisions on termination and retirement

---

235   DOLE Dep't Order No. 155-16 (2016). Rules and Regulations Governing the Employment and Working Conditions of Collectors in the Debt Collection Industry.

236   DOLE Dep't Order No. 150-16 (2016). Revised Guidelines Governing the Employment and Working Conditions of Security Guards and Other Private Security Personnel in the Private Security Industry.

237   DOLE Dep't Order No. 118-12 (2012). Rules and Regulations Governing the Employment and Working Conditions of Drivers and Conductors in the Public Utility Bus Transport Industry.

238   DOLE Labor Advisory No. 04-16 (2016). Working Conditions in the Movie and Television Industry.

239   DOLE Labor Advisory No. 014-21 (2021). Working Conditions of Delivery Riders in Food Delivery and Courier Activities.

240   Lab. Code, art. 172; ECC, Amended Rules on Employees' Compensation (1987), Rule III, §§ 1–3.

241   ECC, Amended Rules on Employees' Compensation (1987), Rule VII, § 1.

discussed above. In this case, the employee's transition arises neither from his willful action, from the employer's exercise of management prerogative, nor from operation of law. Instead, it arises from injury or sickness—legally construed—that results in the inability to perform any gainful occupation for a period of time or for a permanent state.

For purposes of this analysis, sickness as defined by the Labor Code as well as the ECC's List of Occupational and Work-Related Diseases will be explored.[242] As mentioned, the ECC was granted the power to determine the compensable sickness and the conditions for its compensability.[243] There are currently thirty-three (33) occupational and work-related diseases included in ECC's list, the newest of which is COVID-19.[244] Some of the others are cancer of the lungs, liver and brain among vinyl chloride workers or plastic workers poisoning by cadmium among workers in battery factories, who are exposed to cadmium fumes; and peptic ulcer for any occupation involving prolonged emotional, or physical stress, as among professional people, transport workers and the like.[245]

To clarify, the exclusion of a particular sickness in the List of Occupational Diseases does not automatically preclude any claim for it. The Labor Code provides a catch-all *proviso* where it must be proven by substantial evidence that the risk of contracting the disease is increased by the working conditions, which is also known as the increased-risk theory.[246] However, it is obvious

---

242   ECC, Amended Rules on Employees' Compensation (1987), Annex A. List of Occupational and Compensable Diseases. "For an occupational disease and the resulting disability or death to be compensable, all of the following conditions must be satisfied:

   1.   The employee's work must involve the risks described herein;

   2.   The disease was contracted as a result of the employee's exposure to the described risks;

   3.   The disease was contracted within a period of exposure and under such other factors necessary to contract it;

   4.   There was no notorious negligence on the part of the employee."

243   Lab. Code, art. 173 (l); ECC, Amended Rules on Employees' Compensation (1987), Rule III, § 3. "The Commission is hereby authorized to determine and approve additional occupational diseases and work-related illnesses with specific criteria based on peculiar hazards of employment."

244   ECC, Board Resolution No. 21-04-14 (2021). Conditions for the Compensability of COVID-19 under the ECC List of Occupational and Work-related Disease or Annex A of the Amended Rules on Employees' Compensation (EC).

245   ECC, Amended Rules on Employees' Compensation (1987), Annex A. List of Occupational and Work-related Diseases.

246   ECC, Amended Rules on Employees' Compensation (1987), Rule III, § 1(b); ECC, Board Resolution 93-08-0068 (1993), § 3. "There is increased risk if the illness is caused or precipitated by factors inherent in the employees' nature of work and working conditions.

that proving one's claim to that extent, especially for a worker himself or an orphaned heir, is costly and inefficient.[247]

In the shift to a low-carbon economy, while the primary driver is cutting emissions and reversing the trend of climate change, the necessary consequence of the shift is also to ensure that workers in carbon-intensive industries are removed from the harmful risks and hazards presented by those industries. As advocated by some just transition scholars, if these flaws and inequities are not solved or at least minimized in the shift, then low-carbon development is done at the expense of workers—truly contrary to just transition.[248] Thus, there is a two-way response to this: one that provides compensation to the workers for diseases resulting from the hazards of carbon-intensive industries; and one that ensures that the new industries are required to prioritize a humane and healthful working environment.

Studies have identified factors in carbon-intensive industries particularly the fossil fuel energy sources that greatly contribute to the health risks of workers therein.[249] Long term exposure to hazardous air pollutants (HAPS) prevalent in power plants, such as carbon monoxide and heavy metals present in coal ash, leads to pulmonary diseases. For example, exposure to inorganic gases (i.e. carbon monoxide, sulfur oxides, nitrogen oxides) may cause central nervous system damage; lung and heart disease cancers of the lung, larynx, bladder, esophagus, stomach, pancreas. On the other hand, hydrocarbons (i.e. benzene, styrene, polycyclic aromatic hydrocarbons) may lead to cataracts; kidney and liver damage; stomach, respiratory, blood cancers.[250] Workers such

It does not include aggravation of a preexisting illness; and [t]o establish compensability of the claim under the increased risk theory, the claimant must show proof of work-connection. The degree of proof required is merely substantial evidence as a reasonable mind may accept as adequate to support a conclusion;". See also *Dabatian vs. Gov't. Service Insurance System*, G.R. No. L-47294, 149 SCRA 123, 126–127 (1987).

247 See, e.g. *Lorenzo v. Gov't. Service Insurance System*, G.R. No. 188385, 706 SCRA 602 (2013); *Gov't. Service Insurance System v. Ct. of Appeals*, G.R. No. 124208, 542 SCRA 367 (2008); *Latagan v. Employees' Compensation Comm'n*, G.R. No. 55741, 213 SCRA 715 (1992), although the cases involved employees in government service.

248 See Cha, *supra* note 50.

249 See, generally K Bridbord, et al., 'Occupational Safety and Health Implications of Increased Coal Utilization' (1979) 33 *Environmental Health Perspectives* 285. See also E Burt, P Orris and S Buchanan, *Scientific Evidence of Health Effects from Coal Use in Energy Generation* (University of Illinois 2013); Health and Environment Alliance, *The Unpaid Health Bill: How Coal Power Plants Make Us Sick* (HEAL 2013).

250 D Bezrutczyk, 'Occupational Diseases in the Power Plant and Utility Industry' *Lung Cancer Center*, https://www.lungcancercenter.com/who-lung-cancer-affects/power-plant-utility/ (accessed 5 January 2022). See also *supra* note 249.

as ash handlers, maintenance engineers, and general plant personnel, among others, are most prone to exposure.[251]

Proceeding to the analysis herein, it is clearly within the power of the ECC to include occupational diseases that are most common to workers in carbon-intensive industries or the class of workers in such industries in the covered conditions of compensability. However, such exercise of power still heavily depends on the consultations among stakeholders pursuant to the principle of tripartism and must hurdle opposition thereto. Also, the input of the medical and scientific community on technical matters must not be discounted. Notwithstanding this obstacle, in this respect, the ECC has a high degree of *relative substantive* LAC.

Briefly on injury in the context of employees' compensation, the Labor Code does not give a similar leeway for the ECC, in a quasi-legislative sense, to determine what injuries are compensable. Instead, the standard "arising out of and in the course of employment" is provided, which has been repeatedly interpreted by the ECC as a quasi-judicial body and by the courts.[252] To illustrate, the ECC has recently issued a Board Resolution where disability or death due to injuries sustained by the employee while working from home in their residences or dwellings is made compensable.[253] Definitely, such issuance was caused by the work-from-home arrangements during the COVID-19 pandemic. Although the ECC can expand the bounds of a compensable injury through an issuance, the final determination of compensability is still subject to the courts. In this respect, the ECC has a medium degree of *relative substantive* LAC.

It must be noted that, similar to the discussion on separation pay arising from authorized cause for termination, this paper does not make a normative statement on the *correct* amount of compensation for injury and sickness contemplated by law.

---

251   *Ibid.*

252   See, e.g. *Valeriano v. Employees' Compensation Comm'n*, G.R. No. 136200, 333 SCRA 441(2000), for 24-hour-duty doctrine; *Iloilo Dock & Engineering Co. v. Workmen's Compensation Comm'n*, G.R. No. L-26341, 26 SCRA 102 (1978), for ingress-egress proximity rule; *Alano vs. Employees' Compensation Comm'n*, G.R. No. L-48594, 158 SCRA 669 (1988) for "going to or coming from work" rule. See also Azucena, *supra* note 54, 479, for a more exhaustive list.

253   ECC, Board Resolution No. 21-03-09 (2021). Policy on the Compensability of Disability or Death under P.D. No. 626, as amended, due to Injuries Sustained by Employees in the Public and Private Sectors while in the Performance of their Duties or Assigned Tasks in their Residences or Dwelling Places. *See also* ECC, Board Resolution No. 3914-A on July 5, 1988.

5.7.3   Social Security Commission

Without repeating some of the measures already discussed above, this section will focus on the recently introduced measure called unemployment insurance or involuntary separation benefits under the Social Security Act of 2018. The law provides that an SSS member, subject to the conditions and contributions required therein, "shall be paid benefits in the form of monthly cash payments equivalent to fifty percent (50%) of the average monthly salary credit for a maximum of two (2) months."[254] This benefit may only be availed of once every three years.[255] It must be noted, however, that this is different from the separation pay granted by the Labor Code for terminated employees.

Relating this to the shift to a low-carbon economy, workers who are terminated, presumably after being granted the statutory separation pay, may claim unemployment insurance from the SSS under this measure. Again, the propriety of the amount of unemployment insurance benefit is beyond consideration herein. The question therefore is whether the SSC, supposing it deems the benefit insufficient for one reason or another, with its existing powers has the authority to increase the unemployment insurance due to such then-workers and now-unemployed individuals. Based on the statutory grant to the SSC, it has no authority to change such amounts through administrative rule-making. In this respect, the SSC has a limited degree of *relative substantive* LAC.

To add, however, the power granted by Section 4(a)(10) of the law to the SSC to "develop and administer a special social security program for workers, with unique economic, social, and geographic situations"[256] has a potential for crafting a special social security programme for workers in carbon-intensive industries. Through this effort, the SSC can create a social security measure that caters especially to such class of workers, which can then incentivize the management of such enterprises to shift to low-carbon industries. The SSC has a high degree of *relative substantive* LAC as to this matter.

6   Lessons on LAC

The previous section showed a possible application of the multi-step process in adopting the LAC analysis to other jurisdictions, fields of law, and disruptions.[257] Through the use of the newly introduced planes of the LAC analysis,

---

254   Rep. Act No. 11199 (2019), § 14-B.
255   § 14-B.
256   § 4(a)(10).
257   See *supra* Part 3 3.3 for the discussion of multi-step process.

the *absolute* and *relative* LAC, the analysis found that the DOLE, the ECC, and the SSC have high degrees of *absolute substantive* LAC, which are supported by the broad substantive goals of their respective authority-granting statutes, constitutional mandate on protection of labour, and the judicial restraint on the exercise of police power for such purposes. Considering the structure of these agencies, this means that they generally have the capacity to adjust measures and actions within the lawful bounds of authority in responding to disruptions or new phenomena.

This finding must, however, be tempered by the analysis of these agencies' *relative substantive* LAC, which shifts focus from the agency structure to the particular disruption and measures analyzed. In the limited just transition measures considered herein, the DOLE has a limited degree of *relative substantive* LAC as to modification of the amount of separation pay arising from closure or cessation of operation as an authorized cause for termination, while there is a medium degree as to issuance of the requisites for an authorized cause to be a valid ground for termination to cater specifically to circumstances unique to carbon-intensive industries. Further, there is a limited degree as to modification of retirement pay and conditions thereof, while there is evidence of high degree as to issuance of guidelines on rights and remedies in carbon-intensive industries. For the ECC, it has a high degree of *relative substantive* LAC as to determination of compensable sickness in the List of Occupational and Work-Related Diseases that may include common illnesses experienced by workers in carbon-intensive industries, while there is a medium degree as to the interpretation of injury arising out of and in the course of employment. Lastly, for the SSC, it has a limited degree of *relative substantive* LAC as to modification of the amount of unemployment insurance, but there is a high degree as to creation of special social security programme intended for workers in carbon-intensive industries. These show that while an administrative agency, as a whole, may exhibit a high degree of LAC, such LAC does vary if particular measures are examined.

There is definitely much to unpack from this research, not only on the use of LAC as a framework of analysis, but also on the substantive matters of the shift to a low-carbon economy, just transition, and Philippine labour law and related social legislation. The implications of this research to the discourse on scholarship, policy, and law as well as possible points for future research are discussed herein.

As to scholarship, this research presents just transition as an emerging field of legal scholarship in the Philippines, particularly in relation to labour law. It is expected to lay the scholarly foundation that would steer future research on this topic. Furthermore, it signals to both legal and non-legal scholars from other countries that the just transition discourse has started in this part of the world.

Moreover, this paper laid the groundwork for the further use of the LAC analysis in other jurisdictions by presenting a conceptual framework that identifies the key elements of the analysis as well as a multi-step process aimed to allow researchers to use the LAC analysis beyond the US jurisdiction, climate change, and environmental and natural resources law. It shows that the LAC analysis originally developed by Camacho and Glicksman, and herein refined, has a potential of explaining the dynamics between other types of law as well as other disruptions, which greatly enlarges the significance of LAC.[258] Future research is expected to adopt and to improve the theoretical framework and methodology used in this present paper for a more nuanced analysis of legal mechanisms—for researchers need to *adapt* to new phenomena as well.

As to policy, this paper, similar to the other studies on LAC, seeks to inform policy decisions, especially on how agencies are structured, how state policy and substantive goals are pronounced, and how adaptive agencies must be to new phenomena. The LAC of the Philippine labour law and related social legislation and the respective agencies namely the DOLE, the ECC, and the SSC reflects the current state of their preparedness in facing disruptions, such as the shift to a low-carbon economy. At the very least, the study shows that there is some degree of LAC within the legal mechanisms currently in place—which is a decent starting point although must be improved policy-wise. Moreover, it does not only speak of the legislative prerogative in establishing agencies, but most importantly of the administrative capacity to adopt and implement measures as it sees fit, provided that they are within the agencies' lawful authority. Future research may include the Technical Education and Skills Development Authority (TESDA) as a legal institution, because skills training and capacity building are also essential components of just transition.[259]

Moreover, this research, in general, presents another perspective in calibrating the extent of goals and powers granted to administrative agencies. Instead of the wholesale importation of administrative agencies from other legal jurisdictions, the LAC analysis may provide a way for legislators, aided by legal scholars, to independently assess the regulatory needs of particular social behavior or relations. From such assessment, agencies that are truly fit to local

---

258   As demonstrated in this paper, the field of law and its nature within a legal system (e.g. whether there is State interest in pursuing a field of law, such as the Philippine constitutional imperative to protection of labour) greatly affect the use of LAC as a framework of analysis.

259   See Krawchenko et al., *supra* note 175; Pai et al., *supra* note 176.

needs are hoped to be established. For instance, should the Philippines heed the initiative of other jurisdictions such as Spain and Scotland, among others, in establishing a Just Transition Commission, the principles of LAC may be applied in establishing the lawful bounds of such an agency.[260]

As to law, there is indeed a potential for future research in conceptualizing the LAC analysis as a legal standard that may be used by courts in adjudicating rights and obligations. Such research may very well benefit the field of administrative law in its continuous development of legal tests and standards in settling legal issues. In this paper, it suffices for now that the Philippine legal system, particularly its administrative legal framework, was examined from the perspective of LAC, which led to the determination of *how and where they meet*.

Moreover, it cannot be overemphasized that this research introduces the legal practice of just transition in relation to the shift to a low-carbon economy within the Philippine legal jurisdiction. In particular, labour law and related social legislation are initially considered to be low-hanging fruits in what may be seen as a *just transitions law* or *law on just transitions* in the near future.[261] Just transition is mostly concerned about workers' welfare after all. Again, this method is resorted in this research due to the lack of existing constitutional or statutory mandate on just transition, aside from the general provisions on labour. Nonetheless, legislation, litigation, development of legal principles, and other means of placing just transition in the legal mainstream will definitely contribute to the legitimization—a step away from the mere *margins* of law—not only of this practice area, but also the implied recognition of rights underlying just transition, which calls for the equitable distribution of costs of the shift to a low-carbon economy.

Note on the Contributor

Jayvy R. Gamboa
Policy and Legal Research Associate, Manila Observatory; Lecturer, Department of Economics, Ateneo de Manila University; Juris Doctor, *Dean's Medal*

---

260   See The Scottish Government, *Just Transition Commission: A National Mission for a Fairer, Greener Scotland* (Scottish Government 2021); Just Transition and Equitable Climate Action Resources Center, *Spain's National Strategy to Transition Coal-Dependent Communities*, World Resources Institute Website https://www.wri.org/just-transitions /spain (accessed 5 January 2022).

261   See Doorey, *supra* note 49.

for Academic Excellence, University of the Philippines College of Law; Member, Student Editorial Board, Philippine Law Journal Vol. 92. This paper was written under the supervision of Dean Salvador T. Carlota and was awarded with the *Dean's Special Citation for Legal Writing*. The author expresses his sincerest gratitude to his adviser, Dean Carlota, for the opportunity to write an exploratory research using unconventional legal research method. The author also acknowledges Dean Antonio G.M. La Viña and Professor Arnold F. de Vera, among other teachers and colleagues, for cultivating whatever modest interest he may have had in this topic, labour policy, into a deeper level of appreciation and an interdisciplinary understanding that this paper itself embodies.

CHAPTER 8

Coal Mining Operations and Environmental Rights Violations in the East Kalimantan Province, Indonesia

Mohamad Nasir

Abstract

This article examines two issues: the environmental rights violations by coal mining operations in the East Kalimantan province, Indonesia. The second is the contribution of legislation and permits in the coal mining sector to environmental rights violations. The finding demonstrates that the operations of coal mining companies cause land conflicts and environmental degradation. Air and river pollution, clean water sources disruption, flooding, and destruction of agricultural land and settlements lead to breaches of the right to a good and healthy environment. In addition, this paper shows that the legislation and licensing system of coal mining in Indonesia itself contributed to environmental rights violations. Legislation in coal mining allows the government to issue a coal mining permit on land with land rights or in an area with other land-based activities, such as agriculture and settlements. As a result, it may lead to land conflicts and environmental degradation. Moreover, it is contrary to the role of legislation and permits in natural resources management, namely to ensure equitable access to natural resources and environmental sustainability.

Keywords

coal mining operations – human rights violation – land conflicts – environmental degradation – Indonesia

1   Introduction

Coal is a fossil fuel that dominates the world's electricity supply. It contributes 37 percent, followed by gas which provides 24 percent.[1] Since the first half of the 20th century, coal has played a significant role in the world's primary energy demand, which is predicted to continue.[2] Unlike oil and gas, coal reserves are distributed geographically and more accessible than other fossil fuels. Moreover, its abundance provides energy security to many countries because its supply will last significantly longer than oil and gas.[3] In terms of the distribution of world coal reserves, Indonesia holds 39.9 billion tonnes of coal.[4] Despite only having about 3.7 percent of global coal reserves, Indonesia has been the largest coal exporter worldwide over the last three years (2019 to 2021).[5] Most of the coal produced in Indonesia was exported, mainly to China and India.[6] However, the development of alternative energy sources and the adverse effects of coal on the environment are will likely restrain the growth of Indonesian coal export in the next five years.[7] The mining sector has been one of the key sectors contributing to Indonesia's economic growth over many decades. This industry significantly contributes to the Indonesian Gross Domestic Product. During 2017–2021, for instance, the coal mining industry contributed approximately 2.5 percent of Indonesia's gross domestic product.[8]

Besides these economic considerations, the mining sector has a negative side too: it degrades the environment. Since most of the coal deposits are close to the surface, exploiting them can apply the surface mining method (also known as open pit mining or open pit mining) – the world's most commonly used mining method. Excavating coal uses underground mining techniques

---

1   R Max, 'Why Did Renewables Become so Cheap so Fast?' https://ourworldindata.org /cheap-renewables-growth (accessed 17 August 2022).

2   BP, *Energy Outlook 2022* (British Petroleum, 2022) 33.

3   WCA, *Coal-Energy for Sustainable Development* (World Coal Association, 2012) 11.

4   BP, *Statistical Review of World Energy 2020* (British Petroleum, 2020) 44.

5   IEA, *Coal 2021* (International Energy Agency, 2021) 107.

6   MoEMR, *Handbook of Energy & Economy Statistics of Indonesia* (MoEMR 2021) 64. See also 'Export Volume of Coal from Indonesia from 2012 to 2021' *Statista* https://www.statista.com /statistics/991465/indonesia-export-volume-of-coal (accessed 21 November 2022).

7   'Indonesia Coal Market – Growth, Trends, COVID-19 Impact, and Forecasts (2022–2027)' *Mordor Intelligence* https://www.mordorintelligence.com/industry-reports/indonesia-coal -market (accessed 24 November 2022); Z Abidin 'Ekspor Batu bara Diprediksi Turun Dalam Lima Tahun Kedepan' *Indonesia Business News,* 13 September 2021, https://businessnews. co.id/2021/09/13/ekspor-batu-bara-diprediksi-turun-dalam-lima-tahun-kedepan (accessed 24 November 2022).

8   BPS, *Statistik Indonesia 2022* (Badan Pusat Statistik/BPS 2022) 683.

in case the deposit is deep in the ground.[9] Undeniably, both methods disrupt the environment. However, surface mining operation makes the impact on the environment especially acute. Squillace, for instance, highlighted that surface mining could severely erode the soil, pollute the air, and water or damage water reserves, change the landscape, destroy roads, homes, and other structures, and harm wildlife.[10] Coal mining operations often cause other environmental problems such as soil erosion, land and water degradation, and biodiversity loss.[11] Furthermore, coal mining is also considered to contribute to climate change significantly.[12] Therefore, these mining's environmental impacts could violate the right to a good and healthy environment.[13]

This article discusses the effects of coal mining operations in Indonesia, which have damaged the environment in general and robbed the livelihood and environmental rights of communities around mining areas in particular. That is to say, since coal mining requires extensive land, it triggers land rights and land use claims between coal mining companies and communities.[14] These problems are then manifested in two types of conflicts: first, disputes over land access between companies and local populations; second, the environmental conflict due to coal mining activities which have degraded the environment. This article uses the province of East Kalimantan (Kalimantan Timur on the island of Borneo) as a case study to demonstrate how coal mining operations are violating those environmental rights for three reasons.

---

9   A Gogolewska, *Surface and Underground Mining Technology* (Wrocław University of Technology, 2010) 18, 19.

10   M Squillace, *The Strip-Mining Handbook* (Environmental Policy Institute, 1990) 14.

11   IE Setiawan et al., 'Evaluation of Environmental and Economic Benefits of Land Reclamation in the Indonesian Coal Mining Industry' (2021) 10 *Resources* 60; K Izza and I Afkarina, 'Coal Mining Sector Contribution To Environmental Conditions And Human Development Index In East Kalimantan Province' (2019) 2 *Journal of Environmental Science and Sustainable Development* 192, 207; A Atteridge, MT Aung and A Nugroho, *Contemporary Coal Dynamics in Indonesia* (Stockholm Environment Institute, 2018).

12   See L Rüttinger and V Sharma, *Climate Change and Mining A Foreign Policy Perspective Legal Notice* (Adelphi 2016); B Cox et al., 'The Mining Industry as a Net Beneficiary of a Global Tax on Carbon Emissions' (2022) 3 *Communications Earth & Environment* 1, 8.

13   See Art. 28H para (1) of the 1945 Constitution; Art. 9 para (3) of the 1999 Human Rights Law; and Art. 65 para (1) of the 2009 Environmental Law.

14   See, for instance Subarudi et al., 'Kebijakan Resolusi Konflik Tambang Batu Bara Di Kawasan Hutan Di Kalimantan Timur' (2016) 13 *Jurnal Analisis Kebijakan* 53, 71; FH Tondo and R Siburian, 'Techniques of Mining and Land Grabbing: Destruction of Agricultural Activities in Kerta Buana Village, East Kalimantan – Indonesia' (2019) 35 *Asian Journal of Agricultural Extension, Economics & Sociology* 1, 14.

Firstly, this province holds 9.5 million tonnes or 38 percent of Indonesia's national coal reserves[15] and allocated about 5.2 million hectares for coal mining in its 2016–2036 spatial planning document.[16] Secondly, in terms of the number of awarded coal mining permits, this province has 1404 coal mining permits up to April 2016, or around 11 percent of the national total.[17] However, the Ministry of Energy and Mineral Resources (MoEMR) found that many of them have expired, failed to comply with administrative, technical, environmental, or financial requirements, or because a permit's area overlaps with other licenses (such as other coal mines, plantations, or protected areas). As a result, in July 2021, the MoEMR stated that of these 1404 permits, only 386 remain valid.[18] Thirdly, this province dominates the charts of coal production and exports at the national level. In 2021, for example, East Kalimantan provided a 47.35 percent share of national coal production, reaching 288 million tonnes. Meanwhile, East Kalimantan's coal exports contributed 74.37 percent of the national coal exports, or 236 million tonnes.[19] At the same time, it also confirms that coal mining sector is the central pillar of East Kalimantan's economy. Between 2017 and 2021, the coal mining sector contributed 34.5 percent to the province's gross regional domestic product.[20]

---

15   Badan Geologi ESDM, *Neraca Sumber Daya Dan Cadangan Mineral, Batubara, Dan Panas Bumi Indonesia: Status 2019* (Badan Geologi Kementerian ESDM, 2020) 61.

16   M Fadli, 'Upaya Kalimantan Timur Dalam Memenuhi Nationally Determined Contribution (NDC)' http://ditjenppi.menlhk.go.id/reddplus/images/resources/festival_iklim_2018 /kontribusi_NPS_kaltim/Pemprov_Kaltim_INDC__170118.pdf (accessed 21 August 2022).

17   Massive mining activities in East Kalimantan have left many abandoned mining pits. Based on the results of identification with high-resolution aerial photography, it is known that there are 2,385 mining holes with details of 1,953 inside the concession and 432 outside the concession areas. See Kementerian PPN/Bappenas, *Penyusunan KLHS Untuk Masterplan Ibu Kota Negara tahun Anggaran 2020* (Kementerian PPN/Bappenas, 2020) 173. Most holes were left open without fences or warning boards, even though the rules ordered them. The second is that the mining pits are close to the settlement area. Therefore, it raises the allegation that the permit issuance was carried out without an adequate feasibility study. See Komisi Nasional Hak Asasi Manusia, *Pelanggaran Atas Hak Dasar Dalam Kasus Eks Lubang Tambang Di Kalimantan Timur* (Komnas HAM 2016).

18   Dirjen Minerba ESDM, 'Status Perizinan Mineral Dan Batubara Per Juli 2021' https://www .minerba.esdm.go.id/pdf/197-Status%20IUP%20Nasional (accessed 21 August 2022).

19   Bank Indonesia, *Laporan Perekonomian Provinsi Kalimantan Timur Mei 2022* (Kantor Perwakilan Bank Indonesia Provinsi Kalimantan Timur, 2022) 47.

20   BPS Kalimantan Timur, *Kalimantan Timur dalam Angka 2022* (BPS Kalimantan Timur, 2022) 681. The enormous coal reserves are regularly described as a resource curse for the province because of the province's economic dependency on coal, corruption, collusion, and nepotism that regularly come to the fore in the province's mining industry. See JATAM, Greenpeace, ICW and Auriga, *Coalruption: Shedding Light on Political Corruption in Indonesia's Coal Mining Sector* (JATAM, Greenpeace, ICW and Auriga, 2019);

These three factors encourage massive coal mining operations in the province, which cause various problems for the environment and local communities. As an extractive industry, coal mining requires huge land areas for its operations. Therefore, rapid coal mining expansion will significantly affect Indonesia's land use and land cover (LULC) change.[21] The LULC change raises two general issues. On the one hand, land conflicts between coal mining companies and local communities on other land-based activities.[22] On the other hand, environmental degradation including disputes over pollution, degraded forests, and which pose a risk to the health of the local population[23] as well as well-being of the miners working in the pits.[24]

Bersihkan Indonesia, *Untaouchable – The Vulnerability of Reclamation and Post-Mining Guarantees to Corruption* (Auriga, 2020); H Hamzah, *Korupsi Dan Fenomena Dinasti Politik Di Kalimantan Timur* (Auriga, 2020).

21   See, for instance SA Abood et al., 'Relative Contributions of the Logging, Fiber, Oil Palm, and Mining Industries to Forest Loss in Indonesia' (2015) 8 *Conservation Letters* 58, 67; C van der Laan et al., 'Analyses of Land Cover Change Trajectories Leading to Tropical Forest Loss: Illustrated for the West Kutai and Mahakam Ulu Districts, East Kalimantan, Indonesia' (2018) 7 *Land* 108; MoEF, *The State of the Indonesia's Forests 2018* (Ministry of Environment and Forestry/MoEF, 2018).

22   BP Resosudarmo et al., 'Socioeconomic Conflicts in Indonesia's Mining Industry' in R Cronin and A Pandya (eds.), *Exploiting Natural Resources: Growth, Instability, and Conflict in the Middle East and Asia* (Stimson Center, 2009) 33, 46; A Fünfgeld, 'The State of Coal Mining in East Kalimantan: Towards a Political Ecology of Local Stateness' (2016) 9 *Austrian Journal of South-East Asian Studies* 147, 162.

23   I Anggraeni et al., 'Environmental Quality on Surrounding Community of Coal Mining Area in Samarinda, East Kalimantan, Indonesia' (2019) 5 *Public Health of Indonesia* 91, 98; R Kristanti et al., 'Institutional Performance of Mining Reclamation in Forest Areas of East Kalimantan' (2019) 25 *Jurnal Manajemen Hutan* 69, 81.

24   In the last decade (2011–2021), 40 people have died from drowning in abandoned mining pits. Of the 40 victims, almost all were teenagers and children, and only seven were recorded as adults. See CNN Indonesia, 'Lubang Bekas Tambang Kaltim: 40 Tewas sejak 2011, DidominasiAnak' https://www.cnnindonesia.com/nasional/20220204192046-12-755269/lubang-bekas-tambang-kaltim-40-tewas-sejak-2011-didominasi-anak (accessed 18 August 2022). In dealing with the deaths in these abandoned mining pits, in 2016, the National Commission on Human Rights of the Republic of Indonesia (Komnas HAM) conducted an investigation. It concluded, among others, that there had been human rights violations against the right to life, the right to health and a healthy environment, the right to justice, the right to safety and security, and child rights. In addition, Komnas HAM also considered that there had been allegations of protracted omission by state apparatus, both the central and regional governments, as regulated in Article 28I paragraph (4) of the 1945 Constitution of the Republic of Indonesia and Article 71 of Law 39 of 1999 concerning Human Rights. Komisi Nasional Hak Asasi Manusia (Komnas HAM), *Pelanggaran Atas Hak Dasar Dalam Kasus Eks Lubang Tambang Di Kalimantan Timur* (Komnas HAM, 2016) 4, 49.

This paper takes forward the investigations of the National Commission on Human Rights of the Republic of Indonesia (Komnas HAM) carried out in 2016 in respect of the breaches of human rights and the responsibilities of central and regional governmental authorities in order to identify environmental rights violations caused by coal mining operations in East Kalimantan, on the one hand; and to examine whether the legislation and permits themselves contribute to violations of environmental rights, on the other hand. Accordingly, the paper is structured in three major sections. The first section outlines the legal framework of environmental rights protection in Indonesia. The second section analyses how the operations of coal mining corporations violate environmental rights in East Kalimantan Province, Indonesia. This section examines two main issues. First is how coal mining activities give rise to land conflict and environmental degradation. The second is to what extent such conflicts and environmental degradation violate environmental rights. Subsequently, this section discusses several cases to demonstrate how coal exploitation can have disastrous consequences for environmental rights violations. The third section examines how the regulations and licensing system of coal mining in Indonesia have provided opportunities to trigger environmental rights violations.

2   Legal Framework of Environmental Rights Protection in Indonesia

The meaning and scope of environmental rights have a diverse range of conceptions.[25] It can be interpreted as the reformulation and expansion of existing human rights in the frame of environmental protection.[26] The right not only guarantees citizens a qualitative environment[27] but also their access to and the sustainable use of natural resources, such as water and food supplies.[28] In terms of scope, environmental rights cover substantive and procedural rights related to the environment. The substantive environmental rights are typically associated with the right to a healthy environment, the

---

25   See, for instance B Lewis, 'Environmental Rights or a Right to the Environment? Exploring the Nexus Between Human Rights and Environmental Protection' (2012) 8 *Macquarie Journal of International and Comparative Environmental Law* 36, 47.

26   D Shelton, 'Human Rights, Environmental Rights, and the Right to Environment' in S Vanderheiden (ed.) *Environmental Rights* (Routledge, 2017).

27   C Jeffords and JC Gellers, 'Constitutionalising Environmental Rights: A Practical Guide' (2017) 9 *Journal of Human Rights Practice* 136.

28   P Cullet, 'Definition of an Environmental Right in a Human Rights Context' (1995) 13 *Netherlands Quarterly of Human Rights* 25–40.

right to life, and the right to water.[29] Meanwhile, procedural environmental rights promote transparency, participation, and accountability. Procedural environmental rights also allow individuals to participate in policy-making regarding environmental issues.[30] These rights relate to the environment in two circumstances. First, they require specific environmental conditions or inputs for enjoyment of rights, such as the right to life. Second, many rights, especially procedural rights, are indispensable to the environmental rule of law, even if the rights apply generally and are not limited to the environmental context. Furthermore, environmental rights are recognized and protected by international human rights and environmental instruments, national constitutions and laws, and regional regulations.[31]

Within national jurisdictions, Steiger and others state that there are two levels of environmental rights regulation. First is the constitutional level. Environmental rights – as fundamental rights – are significant for the constitutional and legal order. They prevail over other legal norms, are invested with unique legal guarantees, and are only subordinate to such interests and needs, guaranteeing equal or even more robust protection. The second is the level of the so-called ordinary legislation. Environmental rights below the constitutional level enjoy less legal protection than environmental constitutional rights. The legislative body can derogate from or even abolish such rights.[32] Steiger and other continue that subjective rights are the broadest form of protection for a person. This right gives the holder a legal claim to ask that his interest in a good and healthy environment be respected. The claim has two different functions. On the one hand, the defence function implies is the inward right to defend against interference with his or her environment, which is to his or her disadvantage. On the other hand, the performance function is the right to externally demand the performance of an act to preserve, restore or improve his environment on behalf of the state to recognize one's subjective environmental rights.[33]

These defence and performance functions are present in Indonesia's constitution and ordinary legislation protecting environmental rights to a good and health environment and imposing corresponding state obligations. The 1945 Constitution recognized this right in Article 28H (1) as follows: Every person

---

29   SJ Turner, *A Global Environmental Right* (Routledge, 2014) 25–28.

30   *Ibid.*, 18, 22.

31   UNEP, *Environmental Rule of Law* (United Nations Environment Programme, 2019) 16.

32   H Steiger et al., 'The Fundamental Right to a Decent Environment' in M Bothe (ed.) *Trends In Environmental Policy and Law* (IUCN, 1980) 1, 27.

33   *Ibid.*, 32.

is entitled to live prosperous physically and spiritually, have a place to reside, acquire a good and healthy environment, and be entitled to obtain health care. Next, under Law Nr. 39 of 1999 on Human Rights (the 1999 Human Rights Law), the right to a good and healthy environment is grouped into the right to life, such as the right to life, to sustain life, and to improve the standard of living. Further, this right is also recognized and protected in Law Nr. 32 of 2009 concerning Environmental Management and Protection (the 2009 Environmental Law). This law provides the right to a healthy environment,[34] robust recognition of procedural environmental rights,[35] and guarantees that anyone who fights for such a right cannot be prosecuted.[36] The law also imposes more explicit obligations on the government[37] and provides access to in-court and out-of-court environmental dispute settlement, civil class action mechanisms, and legal standing for NGOs.[38] Moreover, regulations at the provincial, district and municipal level must also protect this right, as stipulated in the Minister of Law and Human Rights Regulation Nr. 24 of 2017 concerning Guidelines for Human Rights Content in the Formation of Legislations (The 2017 Human Rights Guidelines).

With regard to corporations, Komnas HAM[39] has issued Regulation Nr. 1 of 2017 concerning the National Action Plan for Business and Human Rights as a guideline for preventing, handling, resolving and redressing human rights violations involving business entities. This Action Plan refers to the 2011 United Nations Guiding Principles on Business and Human Rights.[40] First is protection, where the government must protect individuals from violations. Second, respect for human rights by third parties, including businesses. In this case, corporate responsibility applies to all internationally recognized human rights by avoiding, reducing, or preventing the negative impact of the company's operations. Third, remedy, namely expanding access for victims to get effective remedies through judicial and non-judicial mechanisms. When companies violate human rights, governments must provide a robust and appropriate remedy to those affected.

---

34   See Art. 65 para (1).
35   See Art. 65 para (2), (3), (4) & (5).
36   See Art. 66.
37   See Art. 62.
38   See Art. 91.
39   Komnas HAM has the function to carry out assessments, research, counselling, monitoring, and mediation about human rights. See Art. 76 para (1) and Art. 89 of the 1999 Human Rights Law.
40   Komnas HAM, *Rencana Aksi Nasional Bisnis dan Hak Asasi Manusia* (Komnas HAM, 2017) 6, 7.

3   **Environmental Rights Violations by Coal Mining Operations in East Kalimantan Province, Indonesia**

3.1   *Land Conflicts and Human Rights Violations*

According to the Mining Advocacy Network (*Jaringan Advokasi Tambang/* JATAM),[41] almost 10 percent of the total land area of Indonesia has been allocated for coal mining, 80 percent of which is under exploration. According to the same report, 19 percent of the existing land is under paddy, and 24 percent of the land with the potential for paddy cultivation is under coal mining.[42] As of 2010, 1.1 million hectares of rainforest were under coal, 85 percent of which are from the island of Borneo, in the province of Kalimantan.[43] These overlapping land use claims triggered conflict among land users.[44]

From a human rights point of view, this land conflict tends to violate the community's access to agricultural land.[45] In East Kalimantan, the presence of mining companies has annexed land and displaced communities. For example, since Kaltim Prima Coal (KPC), a coal mining company, expanded its mining areas in November 2011, an indigenous community called the Basap Dayak, who lived in Segading village, Kutai Timur district, was forced to resettle against their will. The community members decided to move from their ancestral land to take advantage of the benefits the mining company promised, such as houses, groceries, and money.[46]

The Dayak Basap tribe depends on the forest, but the company destroys it. They used to be hunters in the forest, but they could not do it anymore because there were fewer animals since the company devastated the forested

---

41   JATAM is established in 1995. It is a network of non-governmental organizations (NGO) and community-based organizations (CBO) working on issues concerning human rights, gender, the environment, indigenous people and social justice in the mining, oil, and gas industries.

42   WaterKeeper' Alliance and JATAM, *Hungry Coal: Coal Mining and Food Security in Indonesia* (WaterKeeper' Alliance and JATAM, 2017) 10.

43   M Kapoor, M Menon and V Viswanathan, *'Midcourse Manoeuvres: Community Strategies and Remedies for Natural Resource Conflicts in Indonesia'* (Center for Policy Research (CPR) – Namati Environmental Justice Program, 2018) 17, 18.

44   See M Nasir, L Bakker and T van Meijl, 'Coal Mining Governance in Indonesia: Legal Uncertainty and Contestation' (2022) 22 *The Australian Journal of Asian Law* 53, 67; A Atteridge, MT Aung and A Nugroho, *Contemporary Coal Dynamics in Indonesia* (Stockholm Environment Institute, 2018) 10.

45   See Article 40 of the 1999 Human Rights Law. For more details see sub-part 3.2.3.

46   S Maulana 'Desa Adat Dayak Basap dalam Kepungan Tambang' https://kaltimkece .id/warta/lingkungan/desa-adat-dayak-basap-dalam-kepungan-tambang (accessed 26 September 2022).

areas. They could not work for the company either as they do not have adequate education for the jobs. Furthermore, while families of those directly employed by the mine have benefitted from jobs, the communities have had to deal with significant water pollution, loss of land, and other problems.[47]

The occupation of customary lands by mining companies also occurs in the Paser district. For instance, in 2009, PT Kideco Jaya Agung (PT KJA), a coal mining company, conducted land clearing in Songka Village, a settlement of indigenous Paserese. A total of 598 hectares of the disputed land was claimed by Mrs. Noorhayati, a local villager who based her claim on a segel[48] issued in 1957. As no solution was forthcoming, they staged a six-day Belian ritual on the disputed land in June 2014. The Belian was intended to spiritually repair the consequences of PT KJA's operation on the land. However, PT KJA felt that the Belian hampered its activities, particularly the transportation of coal. Therefore, the company asked the district police to arrest Mrs. Noorhayati as the initiator of the ritual blocking the mining activities.[49] Besides, JATAM has reported that PT KJA mining activities have evicted the Dayak Paser from their homes as 27000 hectares of land were cleared for the PT KJA mining areas.[50]

Regarding the land acquisition, companies often use a different method, as happened in the village of Mulawarman, Kutai Kartanegara district. For example, a villager who refused to sell his land to the coal mining company felt intimidated because the company carried out activities just behind the fence around his house. Moreover, the company also demolished the surrounding houses that the company had bought. This situation also occurred in the rice fields in the village. Mining companies carry out activities on the rice fields they have acquired, which damages irrigation, causes pollution, and decreases rice production. Production costs are sometimes higher than yields, so farmers have no choice but to sell their land to mining companies. In this case, the coal mining companies did not force the residents to sell their land to the companies. Still, they created a situation that made the villagers uncomfortable living or farming on their land, and they eventually sold their land to the company.[51]

---

47   A Scrivener, *Banking while Borneo Burns* (World Development Movement, 2013) 27, 28.
48   A *segel* is a letter containing a statement regarding land control by a person, issued by the village head and approved by the head of the sub-district.
49   For more information about this case, see Nasir, Bakker and van Meijl, *supra* note 44, 61.
50   A Naim et al., *Deadly Coal: Coal Extraction & Borneo Dark Generation* (JATAM, 2010) 26.
51   M Muhdar, M Nasir and J Nurdiana, 'Risk Distribution in Coal Mining: Fighting for Environmental Justice in East Kalimantan, Indonesia' in *Proceedings of the 2nd International Conference of Law, Government and Social Justice* (ICOLGAS 2020) (Atlantis Press, 2020)

In terms of land claims, from January 2017 – June 2022, this study found 23 court decisions from four district courts (Berau, Kutai Timur, Samarinda, and Kutai Kartanegara) in East Kalimantan relating to allegations of obstructing or interfering with mining operations. Most of those cases are based on two causes. First, the compensation process has not been completed, and the coal mining companies have cleared the land for mining and hauling roads. Second, tensions between landowners and coal mining companies arise because the companies bought the land or provided compensation to intermediaries, not to the landowners directly.

Furthermore, such situations were also exacerbated by the people claiming the land who do not have legal documents regarding land ownership, such as certificates. The claims are mostly based on the fact that they have cultivated it for years, and some are even hereditary. On the other hand, mining companies have the law on their side since they have mining permits. As a result, courts rejected community claims which were not supported by juridical evidence of land ownership.

In those cases, mining companies also react by bringing criminal charges against people who resort to blockades and protests to assert their right to land by accusing it of obstructing or interfering with mining operations, as stated in Article 162 of the 2009 Mining Law (as amended by Law Nr. 3 of 2020). The companies' choice may end the blockades or protest, but it does not resolve the conflict; even such action violates the community's right to defend their land.

3.2   *Environmental Degradation and Human Rights Violations*
3.2.1   River Pollution and Disruption of Access to Clean Water Sources

River pollution by coal mining activities can be seen in the case of PT Indominco Mining Mandiri's (PT IMM) mining operations in the Santan Ulu, Santan Tengah, and Santan Ilir villages as well as the Marangkayu sub-district and the Kutai Kartanegara district.[52] PT IMM has 15 settling ponds to accommodate its coal mine waste. Three settling ponds are spread over the west block. Of these three, one flows into the Kare River, and two settling ponds flow into the Mayang River, which then empties into the Santan River. In addition, 12 settling ponds are in the east block where six settling ponds drain their wastewater into the Palakan River, which also empties into the Santan River.

The river crosses the three villages and is used by residents for daily needs such as bathing, washing, catching fish, and even for a drink, considering the

---

52   PT. IMM has a mining permit valid from 1998 - 2028 with a concession area of 24,121 hectares covering Kutai Kartanegara district, Bontang City, and East Kutai district, East Kalimantan Province.

water of the Santan River has good water quality. After PT IMM operates in the upstream area of the Palakan River, the quality of the river water decreased and is no longer suitable for domestic use. The test results of the Health Laboratory of the East Kalimantan Provincial Government on July 20, 2020, showed that the level of acidity (pH) reached 2.57, which means very acidic, and the iron (Fe) level reached four and a half times that of the normal health quality standard threshold. Likewise, the level of Manganese (Mn) reaches four and a half times from those health norms.[53]

Meanwhile, the impact of mining activities on people's access to clean water can be demonstrated by, for example, mining operation of two coal mining companies: PT Kitadin[54] and PT Mahakam Sumber Jaya[55] in the Kerta Bhuana village, the Tenggarong Seberang sub-district and the Kutai Kartanegara district. Since the village was turned into a coal mining area, the villagers have experienced more difficulty getting water. The groundwater which villagers consume for daily household needs may run into the deeper ex-pit mine. It can happen considering that groundwater must be pumped from the mine pit to operate an open pit. As a result, it spends groundwater content around the mine pit. The groundwater "depression" can be up to kilometres deep, depending on the depth of the mine. Some villagers had to dig as deep as 10–20 meters for water and use pumps in several places. In the 1980s, when the villagers first came to Kerta Buana, they dug down only 3–5 meters to reach groundwater. It is also exacerbated by the fact that the ex-pit mine has become one of the drinking water sources for the local community, whose land has been encircled by coal mining activities.[56]

Coal mining companies' activities causing contamination of water sources and loss of community access to clean water violate the people's right to access water resources and uses water to fulfil daily basic needs as regulated by Law Nr. 17 of 2019 concerning Water Resources.

---

53   A Rahman et al., *Membunuh Sungai* (Jaringan Advokasi Tambang (JATAM) Kalimantan Timur, 2020) 16, 20.

54   PT Kitadin began its mining operations in 1984 and renewed the permit in March 2013, valid until February 2022. The concession area reaches 2,973 hectares in the Tenggarong Seberang sub-district, Kutai Kartanegara district.

55   PT Mahakam Sumber Jaya has a mining permit valid from 2012 to 2034 with a concession area of 20,380 hectares covering Kutai Kartanegara district and Samarinda City, East Kalimantan Province.

56   Greenpeace, *Dirty Work of Banpu* (Greenpeace South East Asia, 2016) 8, 10.

3.2.2   Flooding and Abandoned Mining Pits

One of the impacts of coal mining operations is flooding, as happened in the city of Samarinda, the capital of the province of East Kalimantan. Mining concessions in this city reach 50742.76 hectares, or about 71 percent of the area of the city. Under the Samarinda Municipal Government Work Plan for 2023, all sub-districts are flood-prone areas of a high category. The Plan also documents that one of the causes of flooding is land clearing for coal mining activities.[57]

The Statistics Bureau of Samarinda Municipality states that the intensity of flooding in Samarinda is increasing. In 2018, for example, there were three floods; in 2019, 18 times; in 2020, there were 20 floods; and in 2021, there were 30 floods. [58] In addition to paralyzing the city's economy, the flood submerged thousands of residents' houses and several public facilities such as health centres, village offices, and schools. As a result, the Samarinda Municipal Government has made a master plan scenario for flood disaster management from 2016 to 2035, estimated to cost up to 5.26 trillion in 20 years.[59]

Flooding also occurred in the Kerta Bhuana village. PT Kitadin constructed a canal that channels the water discharge from the mining settling pond to the nearby river. Unfortunately, the canal passes through the middle of the village. Consequently, during heavy rain, the discharge water overflows houses and paddy fields sometimes looking turbid and oily.[60] The coal mining operations that caused flooding have violated the right to a good and healthy environment as stipulated in the 1999 Human Rights Law and the 2009 Environmental Law.

Besides being one of the triggers for flooding, mining activities also left 1,735 mine pits unreclaimed in the East Kalimantan Province.[61] According to the Ministry of Environment and Forestry, the area of the mining pits are around 154 thousand hectares.[62] Many of these abandoned and unreclaimed mining sites with enormous mine holes are located only a few hundreds of meters

---

57 Bappeda Litbang Kota Samarinda, *Rencana Kerja Pemerintah Daerah (RKPD) Kota Samarinda Tahun 2023* (Bappeda Litbang Kota Samarind,a 2022) 11-15.

58 BPS Kota Samarinda, *Kota Samarinda dalam Angka 2022* (BPS Kota Samarinda, 2022) 160.

59 Bappeda Litbang Kota Samarinda, 11-17.

60 *Ibid.*, 45.

61 'Data Jatam: Lubang Tambang Kaltim Renggut 40 Nyawa dalam Satu Dekade' *CNN Indonesia*, 9 November 2021, https://www.cnnindonesia.com/nasional/20211108155341-20-718184/data-jatam-lubang-tambang-kaltim-renggut-40-nyawa-dalam-satu-dekade (accessed 17 November 2022).

62 'Menteri LHK Ungkap Data Lubang Tambang di IKN, Total Luasnya Setara Separuh Jakarta' *Republica*, 28 March 2022, https://www.republika.co.id/berita/r9gjoy409/menteri-lhk-ungkap-data-lubang-tambang-di-ikn-total-luasnya-setara-separuh-jakarta (accessed 17 November 2022).

from residential areas.[63] From 2011 to date (November 2022), 41 children have drowned in these exposed voids.[64]

In terms of abandoned and unreclaimed mining pits, Komnas HAM conducted an investigation in June 2016. Such inquiry concluded, among others, that the coal mining companies have breached the right to life, the right to a good and healthy environment, the right to justice, the right to feel safe, and the rights of children as regulated in the 1999 Human Rights Law. In order to follow up on the conclusion, Komnas HAM asked the governor to firmly sanction the mining corporation that has proven to violate the process of exploration, exploitation, reclamation, and post-mining. Also, to evaluate companies responsible for the death of people who drowned in former mining pits. Meanwhile, Komnas HAM recommended that the coal mining companies recover the victims' rights as the realization of the corporate respect for human rights by implementing its operational activity following the third pillar of the UN Guiding Principles on Business and Human Rights as adopted by the Government of Indonesia in its 2011 Action Plan.[65]

3.2.3   The Destruction of Agricultural Land

The PT Kitadin's and PT Mahakam Sumber Jaya's mining activities have threatened the existence of agricultural land in the Kerta Buana village, the Tenggarong Seberang sub-district and the Kutai Kartanegara district. Until 2010, of the 475 hectares of rice fields, only 398 hectares of fertile rice fields are now left. It was further exacerbated by the fact that of the 390 hectares of rice fields, only 80 hectares belonged to the residents, while two mining companies controlled the rest.[66] Furthermore, in a report, Greenpeace stated that

63   T Toumbourou et al. 'Political Ecologies of the Post-Mining Landscape: Activism, Resistance, and Legal Struggles over Kalimantan's Coal Mines' (2020) 65 *Energy Research & Social Science* 14.

64   'Sudah 41 Anak Tewas di Lubang Bekas Galian Tambang, Terbaru Terjadi di Berau' *Korankaltim.com*, 9 October 2022, https://korankaltim.com/read/samarinda/57005 /sudah-41-anak-tewas-di-lubang-bekas-galian-tambang-terbaru-terjadi-di-berau (accessed 17 November 2022).

65   Komnas HAM, *The Violation of Basic Rights In The Case of Former Mining Pit In East Kalimantan* (Komnas HAM, 2016) 117, 120.

66   See J Purba, D Listiana and S Murlianti, *Integrasi Sosial Transmigran Bali di Desa Kerta Buana, Kabupaten Kutai Kartanegara, Provinsi Kalimantan Timur* (Diva Press, 2018) 180, 184; Prokaltim, 'Sawah dikepung tambang, PT Kitadin Bantah jadi penyebab' 18 June 2019, https://samarinda.prokal.co/read/news/17099-sawah-dikepung-tambang-pt-kitadin -bantah-jadi-penyebab (accessed 14 May 2020).

about half of the agricultural land area in the Kerta Buana village (about 700 hectares) had been lost to mining concessions.[67]

The destruction of agricultural land also emerged in the Mulawarman village, the Tenggarong Seberang sub-district and the Kutai Kartanegara district. Farming is the main livelihood of the people in Mulawarman village, and in 1997, the district government declared the village a rice barn for the district.[68] In 2003, the central and district governments issued several coal mining concessions in the village. The Regional Research Council of the Kutai Kartanegara Regency reported that in 2013 the entire Mulawarman village had been allocated to several coal mining companies, such as PT Kayan Putra Utama Coal, PT Azara Baraindo Energitama, PT Kemilau Rindang Abadi, PT Fisi Fernando Sejahtera, PT Insani Bara Perkasa, PT Mahakam Sumber Jaya and PT Santan Batubara.[69]

The presence of mining companies in the village is slowly reducing rice production because the rice fields are converted into coal mining areas. The head of Mulawarman village, Mulyono, emphasized that from the area of agricultural land of around 526 hectares in 1981, only 20 hectares remain. In addition, coal mining companies have damaged the irrigation system, making it difficult for farmers to grow rice. As a result, the land becomes unproductive, and it makes many villagers have no choice but to sell their fields to coal companies. Meanwhile, the liveable areas in the village have also been reduced to 65.75 hectares.[70]

Coal mining activities, as described above, have damaged and decreased the agricultural areas and threatened the people's access to adequate food. It is contrary to the community's right to a decent life regulated in Article 40 of the 1999 Human Rights Law. Although the article does not explicitly mention the right to food, according to Article 11 of the International Covenant on Economic, Social and Cultural Rights (ICESCR), this right includes the right to adequate food. Indonesia has ratified the ICESCR through Law Nr. 11 of 2005,

---

67   *Ibid.*, 7.

68   Antara Kaltim, 'Desa Lumbung Padi Terancam Emas Hitam!' 20 April 2017, https://kaltim .antaranews.com/berita/37934/desa-lumbung-padi-terancam-emas-hitam (accessed 27 May 2019).

69   DRD Kutai Kartanegara, *Kondisi Lingkungan Hidup Di Desa Mulawarman Kecamatan Tenggarong Seberang Kabupaten Kutai Kartanegara* (Dewan Riset Daerah/DRD Kutai Kartanagera, 2013) 8.

70   GM Sunan, 'Desa Mulawarman, Daerah Transmigrasi yang Terancam Punah, Relokasi Harga Mati' 19 April 2017, https://bontangpost.id/11065-desa-mulawarman-daerah-transmigrasi -yang-terancam-punah-relokasi-harga-mati/ (accessed 4 March 2020).

which requires Indonesia to be bound by the covenant, including ensuring the delivery on the right to food.

3.2.4 Air Pollution

Large-scale open pit mining can contribute significantly to air pollution, especially at the operating stage. Open pit mining activities can release N_2O, CO, SO_2, and coal dust particles into the air, where these gases can cause Acute Respiratory Infection (ARI).[71] In addition, if the surrounding community inhales the gas particles, it will interfere with their respiratory tract. ARI is one of the health problems caused by the effects of coal mining dust present with high prevalence. This situation, for instance, occurred in the Mulawarman village. The villagers have inflicted respiratory diseases caused by coal mine dust from coal mining companies operating behind their backyards.[72]

Air pollution caused by coal mining has violated the right to a good and healthy environment as stipulated in the 2009 Mining Law and Law Nr. 36 of 2009 concerning Health[73]. The phrase "good and healthy" in the right to a good and healthy environment is related to the minimum quality requirements of the environment so that humans can live well and healthy especially in terms of air quality.[74] Furthermore, Boyd states that poor air quality not only has implications for the right to a good and healthy environment but also impacts a wide range of human rights, including the rights to life, health, water, food, housing, and children's rights. In addition, poor air quality falls disproportionately on the shoulders of marginalized and vulnerable people.[75]

3.2.5 Settlements Damage

Open-pit mining activities are done by clearing land and extracting material from the target coal seam. Removing material to a particular layer above the coal sometimes contains complex rock types that must be blasted first.[76]

---

71   Z Muslim and H Helmy 'Analisis Dampak Industri Stockpile Batu Bara Tehadap Lingkungan dan Tingkat Kesehatan Masyarakat' (2020) 9 *Jurnal Visionist* 52, 59.

72   *Ibid.,* 49.

73   Art. 6.

74   F Fadhillah, *Hak Atas Lingkungan Hidup Yang Baik Dan Sehat Dalam Konteks Mutu Udara Jakarta* (Greenpeace, WALHI and ICEL, 2018) 4.

75   See DR Boyd, *Amicus Curiae Brief of the United Nations Special Rapporteur on Human Rights and the Environment* in the Citizen Lawsuit re: Jakarta Air Pollution Case Number 374/PDT.G/LH/2019/PN.JKT.PST in Central Jakarta District Court.

76   M Busyairi and A Oktaviani, 'Dampak Peledakan (Blasting) Terhadap Kesehatan Keselamatan Kerja Dan Pemukiman Penduduk Di Sekitar Lokasi PT. Safhira Gifha Kota Bangun-Kutai Kartanegara' (2018) 10 *Matrik: Jurnal Manajemen dan Teknik Industri Produksi* 92, 108.

The practice of blasting can damage people's houses if carried out in the surrounding settlements. In the environmental context, the minimum distance between the location of mining activities and residential is 500 meters.[77] When carried out, blasting often causes noise, landslides, and cracks in the houses, as happened in the Mulawarman,[78] the Kerta Buana[79] and the Buana Jaya[80] villages as well as the Tenggarong Seberang sub-district and the Kutai Kartanegara district.

In the context of human rights, mining activities that damage residential areas have violated Article 40 of the 1999 Human Rights Law, which states that everyone has the right to a decent life. In addition, it violates Article 129 (a) of Law Nr. 1 of 2011 concerning the Implementation of Settlement and Housing Areas, which states that everyone has the right to occupy, enjoy, or obtain proper housing in a healthy, safe, harmonious and orderly environment.

Several cases above demonstrated that the coal mining operations violated the rights to a good and healthy environment and breached several related rights such as rights to life, water, clean air, adequate food, housing, and children's rights. With regard to these environmental degradations, communities around mining sites rarely file civil lawsuits to demand compensation from mining companies. In this regard, most cases are settled by negotiation between both parties or mediation by the regional governments (province or district) to resolve pollution and stop further damage. This settlement should be criticized given that under the 2009 Environmental Law, compensation payments or reparation of damaged housing and other facilities cannot exclude criminal sanctions imposition. Moreover, adopting a non-litigation approach to settling environmental pollution and destruction contradicts with Article 85 of the 2009 Environmental Law, which states that a non-litigation approach cannot be applied to criminal acts.

---

77   Minister of Environment Regulation Nr. 4 of 2012 on Indicators of a Friendly Environment for Business or Activity Open Coal Mining.

78   Kaltim Post 'Terancam Longsor, Warga Desa Mulawarman Mengungsi' 20 February 2020, https://kaltim.prokal.co/read/news/367336-terancam-longsor-warga-desa-mulawarman -mengungsi.html (accessed 20 February 2020).

79   F Muliawan, 'Teka-Teki Penyebab Amblesnya Pura Prajapati di Tenggarong Seberang' https://kaltimkece.id/warta/terkini/teka-teki-penyebab-amblesnya-pura-prajapati -di-tenggarong-seberang (accessed 28 September 2022).

80   N Priambodo, 'Ketika Tambang Menguasai Desa Buana Jaya, Menggali Dekat Permukiman, Jalan pun Dipindahkan' https://kaltimkece.id/warta/lingkungan/ketika -tambang-menguasai-desa-buana-jaya-menggali-dekat-permukiman-jalan-pun -dipindahkan (accessed 28 September 2022).

Nonetheless, some cases have challenged the government's responsibility, such as the notorious citizen lawsuit of "Gerakan Samarinda Menggugat" (Samarinda Movement Sues): Komari et al. (Samarinda residents) vs. the Mayor of Samarinda, the Minister of Energy and Mineral Resources, the Governor of East Kalimantan, the Minister of the Environment, and the House of Representatives of Samarinda. The case related to the government's negligence in reducing greenhouse gas emissions and the lack of supervising mining activities. The lawsuit was filed in the Samarinda district court in June 2013. After a series of trials, in July 2014, the Samarinda District Court ordered the defendants to reformulate some climate change and mining policies.[81]

Another option for litigation is to report suspected pollution or environmental damage to the police. However, in practice, the communities as whistleblowers are asked to provide evidence of such pollution or damage (such as laboratory results), which the communities sometimes cannot fulfill. In addition, using criminal environmental instruments takes time and requires financial support in the evidentiary process.[82]

4   Regulations and Permits: Instruments for Protecting the People and the Environment or Tools for Exploiting Natural Resources?

Coal mining governance in Indonesia has gone through a number of changes in the last decade. With regard to the authority to grant coal mining permits, according to Law Nr. 4 of 2009 concerning Mineral and Coal Mining (the 2009 Mining Law), three levels of governments are bestowed with such authority, namely the district/city government (if the mining location is in a district/city), the provincial government (if across districts/cities), and the central government (if cross-provincial).[83] This division of authority was later amended by Law Nr. 23 of 2014 concerning the Regional Government. The reasons for the revocation of authority are that the district or municipal governments often issue permits without considering the ecological impacts that arise. Another argument is the lack of capacity of human resources to handle the mining sector permits. Then the withdrawal of authority also aims to facilitate supervision

---

81   See MB Daud et al., *Samarinda Menggugat: Ketika Kegelisahan Menjadi Kemarahan* (Jatam, 2017).

82   M Nasir and M Muhdar, 'Coal Mining Conflict Settlement: Between Legal Certainty and Protection of the Environment and Society' Paper presented at *the 12th conference of the European Association for Southeast Asian Studies (EuroSEAS)*, Paris-Aubervilliers, 1 July 2022.

83   See Art. 6, 7 & 8 of the 2009 Mining Law.

from the central government over natural resources management.[84] Under the latter law, only two levels of government can issue permits: the provincial government if the mining area is located within the province and the central government if the mining location is cross-provincial.[85]

In 2020, through Law Nr. 3 of 2020 concerning Amendments to Law Nr. 4 of 2009 concerning Mineral and Coal Mining (the 2020 Mining Law), the government decided to centralize the mining authority into the hands of the central government.[86] The central government argued that the revocation of the mining authority was required to synchronize the role of the central and provincial governments in the mineral and coal mining sector. Also, many cases of overlapping mining permits are the basis for why this authority is then centralized.[87]

Most revisions are related to mining permits, such as the jurisdiction to issue permits and the permit holder's rights and obligations. Furthermore, through Presidential Regulation Nr. 55 of 2022 concerning the Delegation of Authority in Mineral and Coal Mining Management, the central government delegates the authority of granting people's mining permits (*Izin Pertambangan Rakyat/* IPR) and mining services business permits (*Izin Usaha Jasa Pertambangan/* IUJP) to the provincial government.[88] Moreover, coal mining governance is dispersed over multiple sectoral laws and the Mining Law, such as those touching upon the environment,[89] land,[90] forestry,[91] regional government,[92] and spatial planning.[93] When central government, however, issued Law Nr. 11 of 2020 concerning Job Creation, it amended those laws regarding the environment, land, forestry, regional government, and spatial planning.

Licensing, in addition to statutory regulations, is an essential factor in natural resource governance in Indonesia, particularly in coal mining. The permit has two leading roles. First, a permit is the main instrument for supervising

---

84   DA Rusiana, 'RUU Pemda Wewenang Yang Dilimpahkan Ke Pemprov' *Sindonews.com*, 29 April 2014, https://nasional.sindonews.com/berita/858585/13/ruu-pemda-wewenang -yang-dilimpahkan-ke-pemprov (accessed 12 December 2022).

85   See Appendix CC concerning Distribution of Energy and Mineral Resources Government Affairs.

86   See Art. 6 of the 2020 Mining Law.

87   Dewan Perwakilan Rakyat Republik Indonesia, *Naskah Akademik Rancangan Undang-Undang tentang Perubahan Atas Undang-Undang Nomor 4 Tahun 2009 tentang Pertambangan Mineral dan Batu Bara* (DPR RI 2018) 1.

88   See Art. 2 of Presidential Regulation Nr. 55 of 2022

89   Law No. 32 of 2014 concerning Environmental Protection and Management

90   Law No. 41 of 1999 concerning Forestry

91   Law No. 5 of 1960 concerning Basic Agrarian Law

92   Law No. 23 of 2014 concerning Regional Government

93   Law No. 26 of 2007 concerning Spatial Planning

and controlling coal mining activities. Second, a permit is a means of distributing land for coal mining. Therefore, improperly granting a permit will impact the implementation of monitoring and supervision and the land distribution for the parties (communities and mining companies).[94] Accordingly, legislation and permits in coal mining provide opportunities to trigger land conflicts and environmental degradation. Furthermore, the existing condition indicates that the coal mining regulations and the licensing system lacks sufficient mechanisms to predict environmental and societal risks.[95] In other words, the regulations and permits have contributed to the violation of environmental rights.

Such ever-changing legislation on coal mining and related sectors led to various problems in coal mining governance. That is to say, according to Butt and Linsey,[96] unclear formulations of laws and lack of elucidation undermined the implementation of new legislation and created additional problems of authority arising from the application of legal instruments that are not part of the official hierarchy of laws.[97] Against this light, Nasir and others stated that coal mining governance is plagued by legal uncertainty that poses a significant obstacle to a functional and practical coal mining regime.[98] Furthermore, The Fraser Institute, in its annual survey of mining companies over the past three years (2019–2021), consistently shows a high degree of uncertainty in the interpretation and enforcement of existing regulations by the Indonesian government.

Such legal uncertainty is particular present under the Mining Law. In this regard, pursuant to the 2009 Mining Law (as amended in 2020) and its implementing regulations, the government can issue a coal mining permit on land with land rights or on an area with other land-based activities, such as plantations, agriculture, and settlements.[99] However, the permit holder must settle the land rights claim with the land rights holders or other land-based activity holders before they perform their activities. These provisions raise a number of interpretative problems on potentially conflicting rights.

Firstly, an overlap between permits and land rights emerges if a mining permit is granted on land on which land rights apply. Conceptually, land consists of two main aspects, namely control and ownership determining the legal

---

94   PM Hadjon, *Pengantar Hukum Administrasi Negara Indonesia* (Yuridika, 2002) 4, 5.

95   *Ibid.*, 49.

96   S Butt and T Lindsey, *Indonesian Law* (Oxford University Press, 2018).

97   D Sadiawati et al., *Strategi Nasional Reformasi Regulasi: Mewujudkan Regulasi yang Sederhana dan Tertib* (Bappenas, 2015).

98   Nasir, Bakker and van Meijl, *supra* note 44, 53, 67.

99   Art. 134 of the 2009 Mining Law (as amended by the 2020 Mining Law).

TABLE 8.1   Indicators and Scores on Mining Law and Policy in Indonesia by the
            Fraser Institute[100]

No	Indicators	Scores		
		2019 (76 jurisdictions)	2020 (77 jurisdictions)	2021 (84 jurisdictions)
1	Uncertainty Concerning the Administration, Interpretation, and Enforcement of Existing Regulations	65	64	61
2	Uncertainty Concerning Environmental Regulations	63	56	61
3	Regulatory Duplication and Inconsistencies	73	64	67
4	Uncertainty Concerning Disputed Land Claims	72	56	80

relationship between people and land, on the one hand; and the use and utilization governing how land is used and managed, on the other hand.[101] Under the Basic Agrarian Law of 1960 (BAL), the legal relationship with the land is called land rights (surface of the earth). In contrast, the legal relationship in using mining materials in the crust of the earth is called a permit (mining permit). Under this concept, a coal mining permit is an instrument that regulates the relationship between the permit holder and natural resources that are found below the earth's surface. Furthermore, Government Regulation Nr. 18 of

---

100   A Stedman, J Yunis and E Aliakbari, Fraser Institute Annual Survey of Mining Companies 2019 (Fraser Institute, 2020); J Yunis and E Aliakbari, Fraser Institute Annual Survey of Mining Companies 2020 (Fraser Institute, 2021); J Yunis and E Aliakbari, Fraser Institute Annual Survey of Mining Companies 2021 (Fraser Institute, 2022).

101   NFN Syahyuti, 'Nilai-Nilai Kearifan Pada Konsep Penguasaan Tanah Menurut Hukum Adat Di Indonesia' (2016) 24 Forum penelitian Agro Ekonomi 14, 27.

2021 concerning Management Rights, Land Rights, Flats Units, and Land Registration (GR Nr. 18 of 2021) explains that the space below the surface is divided into two categories.[102] First, the underground surface with a maximum depth of 30 meters from ground level. Second, the deep underground space, whose depth is more than 30 meters from ground level. This deep underground space is structurally or functionally separate from the rights to the surface land, so it is not automatically owned by the holder of the land rights above it. In the case of the profound underground having potential for oil, gas, minerals, and coal resources, the right cannot be granted to the owner of the land right. Exploring such resources requires permits. The separation of these two types of control leads to overlapping land uses. Theoretically, the legal relationship with the land (land rights) is more robust than permits. However, the development of land law in Indonesia seems different from such an understanding. In contrast, when land rights are "in conflict" with the mining business license, then the rights over the land must be "defeated".[103]

Secondly, overlap between mining licenses and other permits related to land-based activities, such as agriculture and settlement, emerges. It may occur because the licensor (central and regional government) tends to issue the permits without going through a transparent, accountable, and participatory process. In the Mulawarman village, for example, the whole area of the village has been licensed to nine coal mining companies and then triggered tenurial conflicts and environmental damages. In this regard, legally, the permit that comes later should not harm the previously granted license because it is contrary to the principles of good governance,[104] particularly the principles of accuracy and legal certainty. Earlier research in reviewing administrative court decisions regarding plantation and mining permits in the Kutai Kartanegara district (2002–2008) shows that the district government is on the losing side in court cases since it fails to comply with those principles of good governance.[105]

Legal uncertainty also prevails when land uses overlap. Under those circumstances, government policies, such as the Presidential Instruction Nr. 1 of 1976 concerning the Synchronization of Agrarian Affairs, Forestry, Mining, Transmigration, and Public Sector Works, tend to privilege mining use. Pursuant to this Presidential Instruction Nr. 1 of 1976, when overlap between mining operations

---

102   See Art. 74 of GR Nr. 18 of 2021.

103   O Sitorus, 'Penataan Hubungan Hukum Dalam Penguasaan, Pemilikan, Penggunaan, Dan Pemanfaatan Sumber Daya Agraria (Studi Awal Terhadap Konsep Hak Atas Tanah Dan Ijin Usaha Pertambangan)' (2016) 2 *BHUMI: Jurnal Agraria dan Pertanahan* 1, 11.

104   Art. 10 of Law Nr. 30 of 2014 concerning Government Administration.

105   M Nasir, *Implementasi 9 (Sembilan) Urusan Pertanahan Di Kabupaten Kutai Kartanegara* (Bagian Pertanahan Sekretariat Daerah Kabupaten Kutai Kartanegara, 2010).

and other land uses cannot be avoided, the government prioritized issuing mining permits.[106] This presidential instruction is based on a development paradigm that prioritizes economic growth over natural resource management. As a result, a society's economic potential to gain more capital ignores the variety of access and interests at stake.[107]

Undoubtedly, this tendency to prioritize coal mining often creates conflicts between mining permit holders with landowners or other land use permit holders. Nonetheless, the mining legislation does provide conflict settlement rules, which presuppose the agreement of all the parties. It then raises a question: for example, if the landowner refuses, how can the continuation of permit holder activities be? Conversely, the regulation should protect the landowners when they refuse to release their land for mining activities. In many cases, the permit holders stand behind the Presidential Instruction Nr. 1 of 1976, or when dealing with the protesting communities, the coal mining companies often accuse them of obstructing or interfering with mining operations, as stated in The 2009 Plantation Law (as amended by The 2020 Plantation Law).[108] Instead of resolving disputes, using these two regulations increases the escalation of conflict in the mining sector. *Mutatis mutandis* with Article 162 of the 2009 Mining Law (as amended by the 2020 Mining Law) whose application coal mining companies often solicit to criminalize the people who protested to assert their right to the land by accusing them of obstructing or interfering with their mining operations.

Within the East Kalimantan mining context, regional regulations on the distribution of various land use (for the cultivation of 10,451,331 hectares) indirectly contribute to environmental rights violation. The Provincial Spatial Plan (2015–2035) in table 8.2 below lists that approximately 40 percent of the province's territory has been reserved by the provincial government for coal mining. Yet, the designated areas for coal mining overlap with other land-based activities in the cultivation area. In addition, when the land allocation of each sector is added up, the total area exceeds the provided portion of the cultivation area itself. Therefore, the uncertainty of the allocation of this area has triggered environmental degradation and conflict over the land in East Kalimantan.

---

106   See point 11(ii) of Appendix of Presidential Instruction Nr. 1 of 1976.

107   I Nyoman Nurjaya, Prinsip-Prinsip Global Pengelolaan Sumber Daya Alam: Implikasinya Bagi Politik Pembangunan Hukum Nasional, *Simposium Internasional Jurnal Antropologi Indonesia ke-2*, 18–21 July 2001 at Universitas Andalas, Padang, 4.

108   Art. 162 states that every person that blocks or interferes with the mining activities of a holder of a coal mining permit can be sentenced to detention [deprivation of liberty] for a maximum period of one year or a maximum fine of one hundred million Rupiah.

TABLE 8.2   The land use allocation in cultivation area according to spatial
             planning of East Kalimantan Province (2015–2035)

Land Use	Allocation
Production forest	6,055,793 Ha
Agriculture and plantation	3,681,657 Ha
Fishery	187,304 Ha
Industry	57,176 Ha
Settlement	97,442 Ha
Tourism	396,266 Ha
Coal Mining	5,227,136 Ha
Total	**15,702,774 Ha**

SOURCE: *SPATIAL PLANNING OF EAST KALIMANTAN PROVINCE (2015–2035)*

Despite the spread of mining conflicts due to overlapping land use, the government provided a solution by virtue of GR Nr. 43 of 2021 concerning the Settlement of Incompatibilities Relating to Spatial Planning, Forest Areas, Licenses, or Land Rights (GR Nr. 43 of 2021) to prevent those conflicts. In respect of coal mining permits issued in an area where other permits or land titles have been previously allocated, the overlapped part should be excluded from that mining concession area.[109] Furthermore, the government also promulgated GR Nr. 96 of 2021 concerning the Implementation of Mineral and Coal Mining Business Activities. This GR stipulates that the central government undertakes to resolve the dispute through mediation if the parties do not reach a consensus. This mediation is coordinated by the MoEMR, the Minister of Agrarian and Spatial Planning/National Land Agency, and the regional government. Under this mediation framework, the central government can provide recommendations for resolving land rights issues.[110]

The lack of supervision on coal mining permits is another contributing factor to environmental rights violations. In East Kalimantan, since only eight mining inspectors were operating in 2017,[111] the number increased to 35 by 2020.[112]

---

109   See Art. 12 para (2) of GR Nr. 43 of 2021.

110   See Art. 175 of GR Nr. 96 of 2021.

111   T Apriando, 'Antara Ribuan Izin Dan Ratusan Lubang Tambang Batubara, Kaltim Minim Pengawas' https://www.mongabay.co.id/2017/05/31/antara-ribuan-izin-dan-ratusan-lubang -tambang-batubara-kaltim-minim-pengawas (accessed 15 September 2021).

112   See Ditjen Minerba ESDM, 'Laporan Kinerja Tahun 2020' https://www.minerba.esdm .go.id/pdf/198Lakin2020 (accessed 12 December 2022)..

However, this number is considered inadequate compared to the number of permits and concessions to be monitored, including mining areas located in remote areas. The Director of Environmental Engineering of the Directorate General of Mineral and Coal of the MoEMR stated that at least one mining inspector should be appointed to two or three coal mining concessions.[113] The other challenge is that inspections should be performed every three months. Given the lack financial and human resources, this is not the case. With the transfer of mining inspectors from the provincial to the central government level in 2016, no budget was reserved for this transfer of staff. The provincial governments refused to contribute to the supervision budget as they argued that with the adoption of the 2020 Mining Law they no longer have the authority in the coal mining sector. As a result, the provincial government refused to stop illegal mining and supervision of coal mining concessions de facto came to an end.[114] Nevertheless, the provincial government retained the authority to act against violations by using other legal instruments, such as environmental and spatial planning laws, instead of the mining regulations.[115]

Finally, corruption and conflicts between public and private interests are notably present amongst permit holders. Tempo magazine found that coal mining companies often mentioned several names of "big chiefs"– army or police generals – when supervisors handled the cases. A study conducted by an NGO coalition demonstrated that some of the owners or investors of coal mining companies in East Kalimantan belonged to the inner circle of local politicians and provide funding for their election campaigns. Against the background of those election campaigns, the issuance of coal mining permits increased significantly around the elections regional leaders.[116] Fearing repercussions, mining inspectors are reluctant to process company violations with such parties behind them.[117] This modus operandi continues when law

113   RD Suastha and RD Kandi, 'Pemangkasan Anggaran Sri Mulyani Repotkan Penga-wasan Tambang' https://www.cnnindonesia.com/nasional/20160907093436-75-156607/pemangkasan-anggaran-sri-mulyani-repotkan-pengawasan-tambang/ (accessed 20 August 2019).

114   MS Ardan, 'Jubir Gubernur Sebut Pemprov Bisa Digugat Jika Hentikan Tambang Ilegal, Jatam Tantang Debat Terbuka' https://kaltimkece.id/warta/lingkungan/jubir-gubernur-sebut-pemprov-bisa-digugat-jika-hentikan-tambang-ilegal-jatam-tantang-debat-terbuka (accessed 24 May 2022).

115   See Constitutional Court Decision No. 64/PUU-XVIII/2020.

116   Bersihkan Indonesia, Coalruption: Shedding Light on Political Corruption in Indonesia's Coal Mining Sector (Bersihkan Indonesia, 2019) 8, 9.

117   Tempo, 'Kerlip Bintang Di Tanah Tambang' https://majalah.tempo.co/read/laporan-khusus/140178/kerlip-bintang-di-tanah-tambang? (accessed 20 April 2022).

enforcers confront the violators.[118] This close relationship between the owners or shareholders of coal mining companies and local authorities often causes local government officials to be unwilling to enforce the law.

5   Conclusion

Indonesia recognizes and protects environmental rights in the 1945 Constitution and legislation regarding human rights and the environment as the right to a good and healthy environment. At the regional level, the Minister of Law and Human Rights Regulation Nr. 24 of 2017 concerning Guidelines for Human Rights Content in the Formation of Legislations orders the regional government to protect this right. Furthermore, in dealing with corporations, Komnas HAM has promulgated Regulation Nr. 1 of 2017 concerning the National Action Plan for Business and Human Rights, which provides a guideline for preventing, handling, resolving, and redressing human rights violations involving business entities.

Although laws and policies to protect environmental rights are available, violations of the rights still occur across coal mining operations in the province of East Kalimantan. Coal mining activities cause two problems. First is the land conflicts between coal mining and other land-based activities. This land conflict violates the community's access and rights to natural resources, especially land. In this regard, coal mining companies grabbed land and displaced local communities. The second is environmental degradation. This study identifies that the exploitation of coal resources causes the communities to lose their rights to a good and healthy environment, such as air and river pollution, disruption of clean water sources, flooding, and destroyed agricultural land and settlements. More specifically, the coal mining operations have also breached several related rights to a good and healthy environment, such as the right to life, water, clean air, adequate food, housing in general and children's rights in particular.

This paper also shows that coal mining regulations provide loophole to violate the right to a good and healthy environment. It is, for instance, demonstrated by the 2009 Mining Law (as amended in 2020) and its implementing

---

118   Kompas, 'Ada Tambang Ilegal Di Mengaku Dibekingi Pangdam Dan Kapolda' https://regional.kompas.com/read/2022/03/26/060649278/ada-tambang-ilegal-di-wilayah-kutai-kartanegara-mengaku-dibekingi-pangdam (accessed 8 June 2022); Monitor Indonesia, 'Nama Kapolri Dicatut Pemain Batubara Di Kaltim Untuk Menakuti Warga' https://monitorindonesia.com/2021/06/pemain-batubara-di-kaltim (accessed 8 June 2022).

regulations, which allow the government to issue a coal mining permit on land with land rights or on an area with other land-based activities, such as agriculture and settlements. As a result, it may lead to land conflicts and environmental degradation. It is contrary to the purpose of legislation and permit, which aims to ensure equitable access to natural resources and environmental sustainability. However, the practices on the grounds have failed to meet the expectations. As a result, coal mining activity cannot prevent the marginalization of the nearby community and environmental degradation. In addition, this study also finds that changes in the authority of coal mining supervision have influenced the supervisory budgeting policy, which impacts the lack of supervisory activities on coal mining activities. Finally, this study also underlines that supervision cannot be carried out effectively if the owners or shareholders of coal mining companies have a close relationship with those in the centre of political power in the region.

Note on the Contributor

Mohamad Nasir
Lecturer, Faculty of Law, Universitas Balikpapan, Balikpapan, Indonesia. Correspondence: mohamad.nasir@uniba-bpn.ac.id

PART 3

Human Rights Protection of Vulnerable Persons

∴

CHAPTER 9

Marital Rape in South Asia: Colonial Origins and Postcolonial Challenges

Saumya Uma

Abstract

This article traces the colonial origins of the marital rape exemption in criminal law, and critically examines the socio-legal efforts taken in Bangladesh, India, Nepal, Pakistan and Sri Lanka, in grappling with this exemption. It argues that the exemption of marital rape from the criminal offence of rape in the penal codes of some countries, and differential treatment in sentencing policy between marital and non-marital rape in other countries, violate international human rights standards as well as a constitutional promise of equality. Despite varied postcolonial developments, the article highlights and discusses similar challenges faced by the five countries. It draws upon feminist theory and praxis and concludes that a removal of the exemption and sameness in treatment of marital and non-marital rape are not panacea for all violence and discrimination that married women are subjected to, in the absence of radical social reforms. It advocates for accepting and respecting young women's exercise of choice and agency in marriage, as a necessary pre-condition for negotiating sexual intercourse within marriage. It also advocates for strengthening a transnational feminist exchange of socio-legal strategies and solidarities to end impunity for marital rape in South Asia.

Keywords

marital rape – South Asia – exemption – immunity – discrimination – equality

1 Introduction

Rape is rape, and rapist is a rapist, so should all forms of rape—within and outside marital and intimate relationships—not be treated the same? Can the offence of rape, which is otherwise treated as a serious offence under most penal codes, cease to exist as a criminal offence only because the perpetrator is not "any person" but a husband? These questions may seem rhetorical, yet their answer is neither straightforward nor unidimensional in the South Asian context.

"South Asia" as a region did not exist in colonial times. For the British, their empire in India defined the entire region.[1] The British Raj—the period of direct British colonial rule over the Indian sub-continent—commenced in 1858, through the Government of India Act 1858. British India was partitioned into India and Pakistan (which comprised East and West Pakistan) in 1947, and East Pakistan subsequently became the independent nation of Bangladesh in 1971. Nepal was not colonised but was a British protectorate from 1815 to 1923. Sri Lanka was under British colonial rule from 1796 to 1948. This common colonial legacy led to common legal origins in the five countries under examination in the present article.

A 2021 report on sexual violence in South Asia notes that the rate of lifetime intimate partner/ spousal sexual violence is 27.3% in Bangladesh, 6.6% in India, 7.7% in Nepal and 6.8% in Sri Lanka.[2] These figures are indicative only, as the patriarchal attitudes of parties to marriage, women's acceptance of a perceived subordinate position within the same, social stigma and the exemption of marital rape in criminal law in most South Asian countries exacerbate the low rate of reporting/recording of marital rape incidents.

In this first part, this article outlines the contours of the issue, particularly from a South Asian perspective. In the second part, it examines the colonial origins of the marital rape exemption. It argues that the combined effect of the biblical notion of "one flesh" and the doctrine of coverture stripped married women of any right to independent identity; given this context, legal recognition of marital rape was an impossibility. In the third part, it traces the criminal law provision on marital rape in the South Asian countries of Bangladesh, India, Nepal, Pakistan, and Sri Lanka, and critically evaluates legislative and judicial reforms pertaining to the same. In the fourth part, the article draws linkages between common challenges faced in all five countries. In the fifth part, the article discusses feminist theory and advocacy initiatives at the ground level, that have contributed to an enabling environment for socio-legal discourse on

---

1   S Joshi, 'Colonial Notions of South Asia' (2003) 1 *South Asian Journal* 6.
2   Equality Now & Dignity Alliance International, 'Sexual Violence in South Asia: Legal and Other Barriers to Justice for Survivors' (2021) 14https://d3n8a8pro7vhmx.cloudfront.net /equalitynow/pages/3578/attachments/original/1618920590/Sexual_Violence_in_South _Asia_Legal_and_other_Barriers_to_Justice_for_Survivors_-_Equality_Now_-_2021 _%281%29.pdf?1618920590 (accessed 1 February 2022).

marital rape. This is followed by possible ways forward in the concluding part of the article.

2 The British Colonial Origins of the Marital Rape Exemption in Criminal Law

Colonial rule in India consisted of a "civilising mission" when the British rulers sought to initiate reforms in India, by projecting themselves to be the harbingers of progress and modernity.[3] According to Chitnis and Wright, the tussle between the British colonial authorities and the native male elite in this regard was fought on the backs of Indian women because it was the alleged degraded position of Indian women and the 'barbaric' actions of Indian men that justified the colonial mission in the first place. Despite the extremely poor legal and social status of women in England, the colonial rule in India was justified, ironically, on the ground of improving Indian women's status.[4]

In England, in the 1700s, married couples were governed by the biblical notion of "one flesh"—that is, the woman's flesh merged with that of her husband's flesh after marriage. The ramifications of marriage for women in England were grave—they lost their independent existence, identity and basic rights. The doctrine of "one flesh" formed the basis for the doctrine of coverture by which married women lost (or were presumed to have surrendered) their rights, identity and independent legal status in exchange for the husband's protection and authority over them. In the oft-quoted words of Blackstone:

> By marriage, the husband and wife are one person in law: that is, the very being or legal existence of the woman is suspended during the marriage, or at least is incorporated and consolidated into that of the husband; under whose wing, protection, and cover, she performs everything; and is therefore called in our law-French e feme-covert.foemina viro co-operta; is said to be covert baron, or under the protection and influence of her husband, her baron, or lord; and her condition during her marriage is called her coverture.[5]

---

3   V Chitnis and CD Wright, 'The Legacy of Colonialism: Law and Women's Rights in India' (2007) 64 *Washington and Lee Law Review* 1315, 1317.

4   S Uma, 'Wedlock or Wed-Lockup? A Case for Abolishing Restitution of Conjugal Rights in India' (2021) 35 *International Journal of Law, Policy and the Family* 1, 5.

5   W Blackstone, *Commentaries on the Laws of England*, Vol. 1 (Clarendon Press 1765) 430.

Blackstone stated, "our law considers marriage in no other light than as a civil contract."[6] Yet Pateman tells us that this is not to be interpreted literally, as an agreement on equal terms between two equal parties. In her words:

> The original contract is a sexual-social pact; but the story of the sexual contract has been repressed. Standard accounts of social contract theory do not discuss the whole story and contemporary contract theorists give no indication that half the agreement is missing. The story of the sexual contract is also about the genesis of political right, and explains why exercise of the right is legitimate - but this story is about political right as patriarchal right or sex-right, the power that men exercise over women. The missing half of the story tells how a specifically modern form of patriarchy is established. The new civil society created through the original contract is a patriarchal social order.[7]

Thus, the civil contract was premised on the husband's domination and superiority and the wife's subordination and inferiority. As Ryan observes, the meaning behind the husband's superiority appears circular when viewed from a contemporary perspective—the husband had a superior status because his status was superior.[8] The underlying presumption was that the wife would submit to the authority of her husband and provide him "consortium" which included sexual intercourse, in exchange for the husband protecting her and providing for the family's financial and other needs.[9]

A combination of the doctrines of one flesh and coverture led to a legal position where a husband was legally the owner of his wife's person as well as her property, and her legal identity was absorbed by and subsumed in her husband's identity. The practice of sale of wives in England, as originally recorded by Lawrence Stone, referred to and documented by Barnett, is a further indication of how married women were treated as chattels of their husbands.[10] Barnett states that where the marriage had broken down and a divorce was not possible to obtain or the expenses for obtaining the same were prohibiting, husbands would auction their wives; as a public affirmation of his ownership

---

6   *Ibid.*, 432.

7   C Pateman, *The Disorder of Women: Democracy, Feminism and Political Theory* (Stanford University Press, 1989), 1.

8   RM Ryan, 'The Sex Right: A Legal History of the Marital Rape Exemption' (1995) 20 *Law & Social Inquiry* 941, 944.

9   S Uma, 'Fidelity, Male Privilege and the Sanctity of Marriage: Examining the Decriminalization of Adultery in India' (2021) *Women & Criminal Justice* 1, 4.

10   H Barnett, *Introduction to Feminist Jurisprudence* (Cavendish Publishing Ltd., 1998) 35.

rights, a leather collar would be placed around the wife's neck and the husband would bring her to the auction with a chain attached to the collar, he noted. Bacon affirmed the power of the husband to "discipline" his wife and gain her obedience through the following words: *a husband 'hath by law power and dominion over his wife, and he may keep her by force within the bounds of duty, and may beat her, but not in a violent or cruel manner'.*[11] Within this legal scheme, where married women had no right to an independent identity or rights within marriage, legal recognition of marital rape was a misnomer.

Sir Matthew Hale—the Chief Justice of the King's Bench from 1671 to 1676—codified the marital rape exemption through the following words: "The husband cannot be guilty of a rape committed by himself upon his lawful wife, for by their mutual consent and contract the wife hath given up herself in this kind unto her husband, which she cannot retract."[12] This exemption defined the sexual meaning of the marriage contract and is also one origin of its legal privilege.[13] While Geis called Hale a "pious misogynist",[14] Han wished to be fair to Hale and noted that Hale was "writing at a time when marriage was regarded as a lifelong institution".[15] While explanations may vary, it is true that in contemporary discourse on marital rape, Sir Hale's quote is often cited as the legal authority for and justification of criminal law exemption for the act.

In the UK, the Married Women's Property Act 1870 recognized, for the first time, married women's right to own property, including their earnings from work, separate from their husbands. The Married Women's Property Act 1882 gave legal recognition to married women as independent entities, responsible for their own debts. This diluted husbands' exercise of ownership over their wives. More than a century later, the Court of Appeal and the House of Lords in United Kingdom upheld the conviction of a husband for marital rape, stating that a marital rape exemption did not exist in English law, and that it was possible for a husband to be held guilty of marital rape.[16] This landmark judgement provided a finality to the illegality of marital rape exemption in English criminal law.

---

11   M Bacon, *A New Abridgment of the Law, Alphabetically Digested Under Proper Titles in Five Volumes*, 4th edition (printed by ER Nutt and R Gosling (assigns of E. Sayer) for H Lintot, 1736), quoted and discussed in the Australian judgment of *La Rovere v La Rovere* [1962] 4 FLR 1, 7.

12   M Hale, *The History of the Pleas of the Crown*, Vol. 1 (Payne, 1736) 628–629.

13   RM Ryan, *supra* note 8, 947.

14   G Geis, 'Lord Hale, Witches, And Rape' (1978) 5 *British Journal of Law and Society* 26.

15   TC Han, 'Marital Rape – Removing the Husband's Legal Immunity' (1989) 31 *Malaya Law Review* 112, 121.

16   *R v R* [1991] UKHL 12 (23 October 1991).

The criminal offence of rape is a gender-specific crime against women in South Asian countries, based on the British criminal law during colonial rule. It has remained a gender-specific crime against women in all the five countries in the post-colonial context due to the historical experiences of women in the region. Constitutional guarantees of right to life, liberty, dignity, privacy, equality and non-discrimination co-exist uncomfortably with laws that either exclude marital rape from the purview of the criminal offence of rape (as in the case of India and Sri Lanka), or treat rape within and outside marriage differently, as two different categories of crimes in law and/or warranting two different sets of punishments (as in the cases of Bangladesh and Nepal). Patriarchal interpretation of religious texts in relation to women's marital obligations and a lack of sexual autonomy for women have often led to an internalised acceptance of marital rape among women, even where the law formally criminalises marital rape (as in the case of Pakistan).

3   The Law and Jurisprudence on Marital Rape in South Asia

In all the five South Asian countries, marital rape exists to differing degrees, and has been addressed through legislative and/or judicial initiatives, with varying degrees of success. This section of the article examines such initiatives.

3.1   *Bangladesh*
The issue of marital rape gained high visibility in October 2020 due to the death of Nurnahar, a fourteen-year-old schoolgirl, 34 days after her marriage. The death was caused by forced sexual intercourse by her 34-year-old husband, leading to excessive genital bleeding. The incident from Tangail, a city in Bangladesh, was widely reported in national dailies.[17] The incident indicates the shocking complicity of the husband, who continued to rape his minor wife even as she painfully bled for over thirty days, and his parents who took her for medical treatment to the local village doctor only when it was too late to save her life.[18]

Nurnahar's was not an isolated incident of marital rape in Bangladesh, although it helped galvanise public discourse against it. A National Survey of

---

17   See for instance, A Al Numan, 'How a Child Bride Died 34 Days After Marriage' *Dhaka Tribune*, 27 October 2020; T Huda, 'Marital Rape Killed a Child in Our Country. Why is it Still Legal?' *Daily Star*, 29 October 2020.

18   *Ibid.*

Violence Against Women conducted by the Bangladesh Bureau of Statistics—
an official body—found that 27.3% of ever-married women or 5390 out of
19,987 ever-married women interviewed by the Bureau said that they were
forced to have sexual relations with their husbands.[19] It further found that
where the woman had experienced sexual violence from her husband in the
last twelve months, she was subjected to such violence multiple times.[20]

3.1.1 The Penal Code

The legal situation on marital rape in Bangladesh is best understood through
the co-relation of three laws: Bangladesh Penal Code 1860; *Nari o Shishu Nirjaton
Domon Ain* (Women and Children Repression Prevention Act) 2000 and Child
Marriage Restraint Act. S 375 of the Bangladesh Penal Code 1860, which defines
the criminal offence of rape, provides for an exception, worded as follows:
"Exception. Sexual intercourse by a man with his own wife, the wife not being
under thirteen years of age, is not rape." Thus, the rape of Nurnahar by her
husband is legally not considered rape under the criminal law of Bangladesh.
S 376 of the Penal Code further states as follows:

> Whoever commits rape shall be punished with imprisonment for life or
> with imprisonment of either description for a term which may extend
> to ten years, and shall also be liable to fine, *unless the woman raped is his
> own wife and is not under twelve years of age*, in which case he shall be
> punished with imprisonment of either description for a term which may
> extend to two years, or with fine, or with both (emphasis added).

S 376 provides differential treatment for the criminal offence of rape based
on the victim's marital status: when it is for non-marital rape, the punishment
prescribed in life imprisonment or ten years' imprisonment with fine, but for
marital rape of wife under twelve years of age, the punishment prescribed is up
to two years with/or fine. This glaring disparity in the punishment illustrates
the legislative failure to treat marital rape, particularly of minor girls, as a
serious criminal offence.

---

19   Bangladesh Bureau of Statistics, *Report on Violence Against Women (VAW) Survey 2015*
      (2016), https://evaw-global-database.unwomen.org/-/media/files/un%20women/vaw/vaw
      %20survey/bangladesh%20vaw%20survey%202015.pdf?vs=2125, 19 (accessed 1 February
      2022).
20   *Ibid.*, 21.

3.1.2   Special Law for Women and Children

S 9(1) of the *Nari o Shishu Nirjaton Domon Ain* (Women and Children Repression Prevention Act) 2000—a law dealing with violence against women and children—states that if a person rapes a woman or a child, he is liable to be punished with death or with rigorous imprisonment for life and fine. But Explanation to s 9(1) provides an exception to the offence of rape, in the case of married women and girls, unless they are aged under sixteen. Under Bangladeshi law, individuals under the age of sixteen are considered children. Through a combined reading of s 375 BPC and Explanation to s 9(1) to the 2000 Act, one can conclude that forced sex within marriage is legally permissible so long as the girl is above thirteen years of age.

3.1.3   The Child Marriage Restraint Act

The Child Marriage Restraint Act 2017 allows the marriage of girls below sixteen years of age if it is "under special circumstances," "in the best interests of the minor," "with the consent of parent/guardian" and with the permission of the court. One cannot imagine the circumstances under which a child marriage, with its grave ramifications for the minor's physical, psychological and sexual well-being, could be termed to serve the best interests of the minor, unless it is through a patriarchal discourse on protecting honour of the self and family. The "special circumstances" are not defined in law, and allow wide discretion to courts. A concern has been expressed that minor girls who are sexually assaulted or become pregnant through such sexual assaults may be forced to marry the rapist and such marriages may be legalised through such a provision.[21] It is also notable that the girl's consent or wishes do not feature anywhere in these provisions. Thus, presumably, the girl is not old enough to express consent or exercise her autonomy, but is old enough for marriage and (forced) sexual relations!

3.1.4   The Constitutional Challenge

In November 2020, a public interest litigation (class action suit) was filed in the High Court Division of the Supreme Court of Bangladesh by four civil society organizations—Bangladesh Legal Aid and Services Trust (BLAST), Bangladesh Rural Advancement Committee, Naripokkho and Manusher Jonno

---

21   Girls Not Brides Bangladesh, 'Reconsider Child Marriage Restraint Act 2016 – Girls Not Brides Bangladesh to Prime Minister' https://www.girlsnotbrides.org/articles/do-not -allow-child-marriage-under-special-circumstances-girlsnotbrides-bangladesh/ (accessed 1 February 2022).

Foundation.[22] The petition challenged the constitutionality of the exception under ss 375 and 376 of the Bangladesh Penal Code and s 9 of the 2020 Act (discussed above), on grounds that they violate the fundamental right to equality, equal protection of the law and non-discrimination on the ground of sex, including marital status (Articles 27, 28 and 31 respectively). They argued that the Exception to s 375 BPC and the provision in s 376 BPC excluding marital rape were inserted in the law in 1860 during the British colonial era, and no steps have been taken to amend the same even almost fifty years after adoption of the Constitution and fundamental rights guaranteeing equality and prohibiting discrimination on the ground of gender in Articles 27 and 28 thereof (para 10 of the petition). The British colonial origin of the marital rape exception in rape law has been discussed in the preceding part of this paper.

The petition drew the attention of the court to the judgement of the House of Lords in *R v R* (discussed above), to the legal provision in Nepal that criminalises marital rape, and to a judgement of the Indian Supreme Court—*Independent Thought v Union of India*—that criminalised marital rape of girls between the ages of 15 and 18. It contended that since law regards consent as the basis for marriage, and a marriage cannot be solemnized without consent of either party, it is implied that there must be consent in acts of sexual intercourse within marriage.[23] It further contended that it would be contrary to the recognized principles of justice and wholly arbitrary, capricious, and whimsical, as they exempt a person's culpability for rape, merely because of his relationship to the woman as her husband.[24] The petition also states that the sections under examination violate provisions of international human rights conventions ratified by Bangladesh, including the International Covenant on Civil and Political Rights (ICCPR) and CEDAW.[25]

The same month, the Supreme Court called upon the respondents to show cause why these legal provisions should not be declared void, for being discriminatory and unconstitutional.[26] The petition remains pending at this

---

22   *Bangladesh Legal Aid and Services Trust and Others vs. Secretary – Ministry of Law, Justice and Parliamentary Affairs and Others* Writ Petition No. 7758 of 2020, filed on 1 November 2020. Summary available at http://www.bdpil.org.bd/search/full_view/346 (accessed 20 November 2022).

23   *Ibid.*, para 15.

24   *Ibid.*, paras 16 and 19.

25   *Ibid.*, para 18.

26   *Ibid.*, Order dated 3 November 2020, passed by Justices Md. Mozibur Rahman Miah and Mohi Uddin Shamim http://www.bdpil.org.bd/assets/uploads/pdf/2ffa9-rule-order-wp -7758-of-2020.pdf (accessed 19 November 2022).

point in time, but it has the potential to become a landmark judgement that outlaws marital rape in the criminal law of Bangladesh.

3.2   *India*

As in the case of Bangladesh, India has a marital rape exemption in the provision of rape in the Indian Penal Code 1860. The constitutional validity of the exception was challenged through several writ petitions, which were clubbed and heard by a Division Bench of the Delhi High Court. In May 2022, the court gave a split verdict, with one of the two judges ruling that the marital rape exemption was unconstitutional.[27] In particular, one of the two judges – Justice Rajiv Shakdher - found that the marital rape exception violates the following provisions of the Indian Constitution: Article 14 (guarantee of equality before the law and equal protection by the law), Article 15 (prohibition of discrimination on grounds including of sex), Article 19(1)(a) (fundamental right to freedom of speech and expression), and Article 21 (fundamental right to life with dignity). The appeals, along with several other petitions with similar issues, are presently pending before the Supreme Court of India.

The origins of the public discourse on marital rape in India can be traced to the death of eleven-year-old Phulmonee, who died of vaginal rupture and haemorrhage in 1890 after she was raped by her 29-year-old husband, Hari Mohan Maiti.[28] Since British law penalized marital rape only if the girl was under 10 years of age, Hari Maiti could not be legally charged with rape and murder; instead, he was prosecuted for the lesser offence of committing rash and negligent acts.[29] The incident and the public debates that followed spurred the move to increase the age of consent for sexual intercourse from 10 years to 12 years, undertaken through the Age of Consent Act of 1891. This was subsequently increased to 15 years in s 375 of the Indian Penal Code.

The prevalence of marital rape in India has been confirmed by recent official statistics. The government-backed National Family Health Survey (NFHS 5) (2019–21) found that among married women aged 18–49 years, who have ever experienced sexual violence, 82% respondents said that the husband was the perpetrator, and 13.7% said that the former husband was the perpetrator.[30] Further, out of the 82% women respondents, a large majority (84%) of the

---

27   *RIT Foundation v Union of India* 2022 SCC OnLine Del 1404 (Delhi High Court) Judgment of Justices C. Hari Shankar and Rajiv Shakdher of the Delhi High Court, dated 11 May 2022.

28   For details, see T Sarkar, 'A Prehistory of Rights: The Age of Consent Debate in Colonial Bengal' (2000) 26 *Feminist Studies* 601.

29   *Queens Empress v Huree Mohan Mythee* [1891] XVIII ILR (Cal) 49.

30   P Benu, 'Marital rape: Most Married Women Are Sexually Abused by Their Husbands, Says NFHS Data' *The Hindu Businessline*, 16 May 2022.

women reported that they were "physically forced to have sexual intercourse" with the husband – in other words, they experienced marital rape.[31]

3.2.1   Intersecting Legislation

As in the case of Bangladesh, in India too there is a plethora of intersecting legislation that impinge upon marital rape. Section 375 of the Indian Penal Code (IPC) defines the offence of rape. Exception 2 to s 375 IPC, states as follows: "sexual intercourse by a man with his own wife, the wife not being under fifteen years of age, is not rape." Through a judgement of 2017, "fifteen years of age" was substituted with "eighteen years of age."[32] Pursuant to the Law Commission of India's 42nd report in 1971,[33] s 376B was inserted, which provides for sexual intercourse by a man with his wife without her consent, when she is living separately under a decree of judicial separation or otherwise, as a punishable crime. In other words, under the present criminal law in India, marital rape is punishable *only* if the wife is under 18 years of age or is living separately from her husband judicially or informally. The sentence prescribed for non-marital rape is ten years' to life imprisonment with fine, while the sentence prescribed for marital rape during separation is two to seven years' imprisonment. This disparity in the punishment prescribed is also indicative of the legislature's treatment of marital rape in situations of separation as a less grievous crime than non-marital rape.

Although married women cannot file a criminal complaint for rape, a criminal law remedy is available under s 377 IPC for "carnal intercourse against the order of nature"—commonly referred to as "unnatural sex" (including anal sex). Another criminal law remedy available to aggrieved wives is s 498A IPC, a provision that criminalises "cruelty to wives." Marital rape may be pleaded as amounting to physical and mental cruelty under the provision, and this is an argument made by feminist scholars such as Flavia Agnes in countering the demand for removing the marital rape exemption.[34] However, the efficacy of the provision has been marred by a prevailing myth of misuse by women propagated by men's rights activists, which has been given an official stamp

---

31   *Ibid.*

32   *Independent Thought vs. Union of India* (2017) 10 SCC 800.

33   Law Commission of India, *Forty-Second Report on the Indian Penal Code* (Ministry of Law 1971) https://lawcommissionofindia.nic.in/1-50/report42.pdf (accessed 29 November 2022).

34   F Agnes, 'Section 498A, Marital Rape and Adverse Propaganda,' (2015) 50 *Economic & Political Weekly* 12, 13.

by judgements of the Supreme Court.[35] In this context, women facing marital rape are unlikely to find an effective remedy from the judiciary through s 498A IPC.

The Prohibition of Child Marriage Act (PCMA) 2006 prohibits the solemnisation of child marriages, and prescribes the lawful age of marriage for girls as 18 and boys as 21. There is a current move to increase the lawful age of marriage for girls to 21, although feminist scholars are critical of the move and opine that the same will strengthen patriarchal control over a woman's choice in marriage even further.[36] It a punishable offence for those who abet, promote or solemnise child marriages, including the husband if he is above 18 years of age.

The Protection of Children from Sexual Offences (POCSO) Act, enacted in 2012, makes sexual intercourse with a person under 18 years of age a punishable offence. The law is gender neutral and makes no exemptions for consent or for marital relationships. Hence, in cases of a child bride, the husband runs the risk of being prosecuted for sexual offences (including rape) under POCSO and rape under s 375 IPC, in addition to a child marriage under PCMA 2006.

3.2.2   Official Responses for Law Reform

The Law Commission of India, in its 172nd report in 2000, engaged cursorily with the issue of deleting the marital rape exemption. It observed that it was "not satisfied that this Exception should be recommended to be deleted since that may amount to excessive interference with the marital relationship".[37]

The Report of the Committee on Amendments to Criminal Law (2013), established by the Indian government in the wake of the homicidal gang rape of Jyoti Pandey on a moving bus in Delhi in 2012, took a contrary view.[38] The committee headed by Justice J. S. Verma, stated explicitly that the exemption for marital rape "stems from a long out-dated notion of marriage which regarded wives as no more than the property of their husbands".[39] After a survey of relevant legal provisions in other countries, as well as international

---

35   For details, see BN Doddahatti, 'The Dangerous, False Myth That Women Routinely Misuse Domestic Cruelty Laws' *The Wire*, 11 August 2017; see also *Rajesh Sharma v State of U.P.*, 2017 SCC OnLine SC 821.

36   F Agnes, 'Increasing Marriage Age for Girls May only Strengthen Patriarchy' *The Times of India*, 19 December 2021.

37   Law Commission of India, *One Hundred and Seventy Second Report on Review of Rape Laws* (Ministry of Law 2000) https://cdnbbsr.s3waas.gov.in/s3caodaec69b5adc88ofb 464895726dbdf/uploads/2022/08/2022082487.pdf, 23 (accessed 28 November 2022).

38   *Report of the Committee on Amendments to Criminal Law* (Government of India 2013) https://spuwac.in/pdf/jsvermacommitteereport.pdf (accessed 28 November 2022).

39   *Ibid.*, 113.

human rights conventions[40] that the Indian government has ratified, it recommended not only the removal of marital rape exception, but also the exclusion of marital or other relationship between the perpetrator and victim as a valid defence against rape, as a relevant aspect for inquiry into consent or as a mitigating factor justifying lower sentences for rape.[41]

However, the law reform that followed the 2013 Report did not accept this recommendation on the ground that "it would place the entire family system under great stress".[42] This is discussed further in the section below on 'Post-Colonial Challenges'.

3.2.3   Recent Judgements Fortifying Removal of the Exemption Clause
The past few years have seen a spate of judgements that have fortified the move towards removing the marital rape exemption. In *Independent Thought v Union of India*, the Supreme court countered the argument of the state that reading down the marital rape exemption would have the effect of "destroying the institution of marriage".[43] Justice Lokur noted that marriage is not institutional but personal and therefore, while an *individual* marriage may be destroyed, reading down the exception does not have any implications for the *institution* of marriage. If this is an effective rebuttal to the state's argument about preserving sanctity of marriage, a Gujarat High Court judgement countered the argument even more.[44] The court observed as follows:

> The exemption given to marital rape, as Justice Verma noted, "stems from a long out-dated notion of marriage which regarded wives as no more than the property of their husbands". Marital rape ought to be a crime

---

40   The international human rights treaties and principles referred to and relied upon include the following: the Universal Declaration of Human Rights 1948, the International Covenant on Civil and Political Rights 1966, the International Covenant on Economic, Social and Cultural Rights 1966, the Beijing Principles of the Independence of the Judiciary (drawn up and agreed to in 1995 by the Chief Justices of countries in the Asia-Pacific region), the Convention on the Political Rights of Women 1954, the Convention on the Political Rights of Women 1953, The Declaration on Elimination of Violence against Women 1993 and the Convention on Elimination of all forms of Discrimination against Women 1979.

41   Supra note 38, 117.

42   Parliamentary Standing Committee on Home Affairs, *One Hundred and Sixty Seventh Report: The Criminal Law (Amendment) Bill, 2012* (Government of India, 2012) http://164.100.47.5/newcommittee/reports/EnglishCommittees/Committee%20on%20Home%20Affairs/167.pdf, 26–27 (accessed 1 February 2022).

43   *Independent Thought vs. Union of India* (2017) 10 SCC 800.

44   *Nimeshbhai Bharatbhai Desai vs. State of Gujarat* 2018 SCC OnLine (Guj) 732, para 166.

and not a concept. *Of course, there will be objections such as a perceived threat to the integrity of the marital union and the possibility of misuse of the penal provisions. It is not really true that the private or domestic domain has always been outside the purview of law. The law against domestic violence already covers both physical and sexual abuse as grounds for the legal system to intervene. It is difficult to argue that a complaint of marital rape will ruin a marriage, while a complaint of domestic violence against a spouse will not.* It has long been time to jettison the notion of 'implied consent' in marriage. The law must uphold the bodily autonomy of all women, irrespective of their marital status. (emphasis added)

In the *Anuj Garg* and *Navtej Singh Johar* judgements, the Supreme Court held that any discrimination founded on a gender stereotype would amount to a violation of a constitutional guarantee against sex-based discrimination.[45] In 2018, in *Joseph Shine v Union of India*, a five-judge bench of the Supreme Court of India held that the "delineation of private or public spheres become irrelevant as far as the enforcement of constitutional rights is concerned. Therefore, even the intimate personal sphere of marital relations is not exempt from constitutional scrutiny."[46] In *Puttaswamy*, a nine-judge bench of the Supreme Court affirmed that the right to privacy was part of the fundamental right to life guaranteed by the Indian constitution, and that bodily integrity was integral to the right of privacy.[47] However, Tarafder and Ghosh highlight the possible pitfalls of a privacy argument in the context of marital rape, which must be kept in mind.[48] Drawing upon feminist scholarship, they argue that the 'privacy' argument a) does not translate into the *de facto* realisation of liberty in most cases; and b) reinforces public-private dichotomy and establishes the sanctity of the home (especially the marital bedroom), thereby protecting certain spaces rather than individuals within them. The judgements discussed above provide a sound legal foundation for the removal of the marital rape exemption.

3.3   *Nepal*
Nepal has attempted law reform, spurred by judicial initiatives, though a chasm exists between the law and the ground realities. No. 1 of the Chapter on

---

45   *Anuj Garg and Others vs. Hotel Association of India and Others* AIR 2008 SC 663; *Navtej Singh Johar vs. Union of India* AIR 2018 SC 4321

46   2018 SCC OnLine SC 1676; para 66 of Justice Chandrachud's judgement.

47   *K.S. Puttaswamy v. Union of India*, (2017) 10 SCC 1 : 2017 SCC OnLine SC 996.

48   A Tarafder & A Ghosh, 'The Unconstitutionality of the Marital Rape Exemption in India' (2020) 3 *University of Oxford Human Rights Hub Journal* 202, 214–7.

Rape in the Country Code 1963 (referred to as *Muluki Ain*) defined rape as the act of having sexual intercourse with a girl, widow or other's wife not attaining the age of sixteen years with or without her consent in whatsoever manner or attaining the age of sixteen years without her consent in whatsoever manner either exerting threat, pressure or coercion or with undue influence. This definition excluded the act of rape of a woman by her husband.

3.3.1   The First Constitutional Challenge

In 2001, Advocate Meera Dhungana, on behalf of Forum for Women, Law and Development—a women's organization—challenged the exclusion of marital rape in Nepal's *Muluki Ain* (Country Code).[49] She contended that the exclusion violated provisions of the Constitution of the Kingdom of Nepal, namely guarantees of fundamental rights of equality and non-discrimination on the ground of sex, other constitutional guarantees as well as state obligations under international human rights conventions ratified by Nepal.[50] The writ petition also relied upon Section 9(1) of the Nepal Treaty Act 1991, which stated that if a domestic statute is in contravention of an international treaty that Nepal has ratified, the treaty law will prevail over the domestic statute to the extent of inconsistency. For these reasons, she argued that the relevant legal provisions must be declared invalid.

The Deputy Attorney General argued that equality was possible only among equals, but married and unmarried women cannot be treated alike, due to differing social position and family responsibilities.[51] He pointed to an alternative remedy—of divorce and the criminal offence of battery.[52] Interestingly, he also argued that there was no requirement for consent from one's own wife as "marriage is a permanent consent expressed for having sexual relations".[53] These arguments illustrate clearly that more than a century after the doctrine

---

49   *The Forum for Women, Law and Development v His Majesty's Government, Ministry of Law, Justice and Parliamentary Affairs* Writ No 55 of the year 2058 BS (2001–2002) (Supreme Court of Nepal).

50   Arguments summarized in the judgement, ibid., paras 1–5. The relevant international human rights treaties referred to in the judgment include the following: the Universal Declaration of Human Rights 1948; the International Covenant on Civil and Political Rights 1966; the International Covenant on Economic, Social and Cultural Rights 1966 and the UN Convention on the Elimination of All Forms of Discrimination against Women 1979.

51   *Ibid.*, para 12.

52   *Ibid.*

53   *Ibid.*

of coverture was eliminated from English law, it has entrenched and embedded itself in the Nepali socio-legal milieu.

In 2002, the Supreme Court of Nepal delivered its judgement. It observed
that the exclusion of marital rape contravened the provisions of CEDAW and
the letter and spirit of provisions of Nepal's Constitution.[54] It reasoned that if
an act is an offence by its very nature, it is unreasonable to say that it is not the
offence merely because of difference in person committing the act, and that
there was no justification in differentiating between the women who are wives
and other women.[55] It observed as follows:

> ... a marriage does not mean women to turn in to slaves. Thus, women
> do not lose human rights because of marriage. So long as a person lives
> as a human being he/she is entitled to exercise those in-born and nat-
> ural human rights. To say that the husband can rape his wife after the
> marriage is to deny independent existence, right to live with self-respect
> and right to self-determination. Any act which results in non-existence
> of women, adversely affects on self-respect of women, infringes upon
> right of women to independent decision making or which makes women
> slaves or an object or property is not compatible in the context of mod-
> ern world, rather it is a stone-age thought; ... to forcibly compel women
> to use an organ of her body against her will is serious violation of her
> right to live with dignity, right to self-determination and it is an abuse
> of her human rights. The Constitution has guaranteed the right to pri-
> vacy. Therefore, in the light of those international instruments on human
> rights, it cannot be said that marital rape is permissible.[56]

It directed Parliament to introduce a Bill for bringing the necessary amendments and to include marital rape in the *Muluki Ain* (Country Code). However,
it was not before 2006 that this was undertaken by the Parliament through
an inclusion of marital rape in S.3(6) in the Chapter on Rape in the *Muluki
Ain* (Country Code). The women's movement's struggle for equality and non-
discrimination did not end there. The punishment prescribed for marital rape
was 3 to 6 months' imprisonment while the punishment prescribed for non-
marital rape was between five and 15 years' imprisonment (varying durations
based on age of the victim). The vast disparity in the punishments stemmed
from a patriarchal perspective that rape of a woman by her husband was a

---

54   *Ibid.*, para 30.
55   *Ibid.*
56   *Ibid.*, paras 24–5.

lesser crime than rape by other men, due to the husband's right to his wife's person. This stemmed from the British doctrines of "one flesh" and coverture, the underlying notion of which was that the husband "owned" his wife, her person and property, and that her identity was subsumed and merged with his after marriage. These doctrines have been explained in greater detail in Part 2 of this article.

3.3.2   The Second Constitutional Challenge

The provision dealing with unequal punishments to marital and non-marital rape was challenged again in the Supreme Court of Nepal in 2007, by a married woman who was repeatedly subjected to marital rape: Jit Kumari Pangeni.[57] Jit Kumari's husband had been convicted of marital rape under the Country Code but was punished with the lesser punishment. The Nepali law allowed anyone sentenced to less than three years' imprisonment to be eligible for release on bail upon paying an amount. Jit Kumari was anxious that her husband would be released on bail by paying Nepali Rupees 4500, return to her matrimonial home and subject her to marital rape once again.[58]

Together with the Forum for Women, Law and Development, she filed a writ petition challenging the constitutionality of s 3(6) of the Chapter on Rape in the *Muluki Ain* (Country Code), terming it to be an inadequate remedy and a discriminatory provision under Nepal's constitution as well as under international human rights treaties ratified by Nepal. They sought a direction from the Supreme Court of Nepal to the Parliament, directing the latter to make amendments in law such that marital and non-marital rape are prescribed an equal sentence.

In response, the Secretariat of the Parliament defended the differential punishment by contending that there was a difference between marital and non-marital rape; in the case of marital rape, its effect is limited to the family of the victim and is associated with the future life of the person in question (that is, the husband), while in cases of non-marital rape, its effect is on society. It also asserted that prescribing the quantum of punishment was the prerogative of the legislature and that arguments about equality cannot be raised in a court of law.[59] The Government of Nepal, Prime Minister and the Council

---

57   *Jit Kumari Pangeni (Neupane) and Others v Prime Ministers and Council of Ministers and Others* Writ No 064-0035 of the Year 2063 (Supreme Court of Nepal) 53.

58   Summarised in the judgement, *ibid.*, para 1.

59   *Ibid.*, para 8.

of Ministers, as well as Ministry of Law, Justice and Parliamentary Affairs advanced similar arguments before the Supreme Court.[60]

A three-judge bench of the Supreme Court of Nepal adjudicated over the case. The majority judgment (by two judges) rejected their contentions and held that differential punishments to marital rape and non-marital rape was not consistent with the principle of equality under Nepal's Constitution and the international human rights conventions it had ratified. It observed as follows:

> Where, rape has been recognized as a grave criminal offence under the Chapter of Rape and where the result of such offence is the same, there is no rationality in differentiating between marital and non-marital rape. Offence is committed in lieu of any criminal act and provided, rebate on punishment is to be provided pursuant to the status of the actor, it would deem to be inconsistent with the right to equality as envisaged in the Constitution.... Where a spouse is considered as means of recreation and exploitation and contrary to the desires of the spouse, her health and needs, is raped by the closest person, then such a person committing such an offensive act, cannot be entitled to rebate in punishment merely because of his relationship with his spouse and there is no jurisprudential basis with regards to such rebate in punishment.[61]

It directed the Ministry of Law, Justice and Parliamentary Affairs to amend the discriminatory sentencing policies between marital and non-marital rape.

The dissenting judge disagreed with the majority judgement, opining that marital rape presented particular evidentiary challenges, except in situations where the spouses had a judicial separation and were living separately. He observed that forensic science may not be able to differentiate between rape and consensual intercourse, and that in situations where the couple lived together and the wife alleged rape, the life and liberty of the husband would be at risk because he would not be able to prove that the act amounted to consensual sexual intercourse.[62] For this reason, he directed the legislature to include a condition of judicial separation and living apart in the provision defining marital rape.[63] In other words, he wished that criminal law ought to recognize

---

60   *Ibid.*, paras 9–10.
61   *Ibid.*, para 19.
62   *Ibid.*, para 12 of the dissenting judgement.
63   *Ibid.*

marital rape as a criminal offence only where the couple was living apart after judicial separation.

The majority judgement focussed on normative values, international human rights standards and constitutional principles related to differential sentencing policy, while the dissenting judgement focused on evidentiary challenges in proving consent in sexual intercourse that takes place within marriage and the difficulty that may arise for the husband in proving his innocence. While one cannot disagree with the dissenting judge's concerns about difficulty in gathering evidence, it is also pertinent to ponder over whether pragmatic and evidentiary considerations ought to override the normative value of the law, and if so, to what extent.

3.3.3   The Aftermath

Pursuant to the *Jit Kumari* judgement delivered by the Supreme Court, in 2016, the Parliament revised the penal provision on marital rape, and the sentence prescribed was amended to three to five years' imprisonment. In contrast with the non-marital rape of an adult woman, punishable with imprisonment of seven to ten years, the punishment for marital rape continues to remain lower, indicating that raping one's wife is a "less serious offence" carrying a lighter sentence.

3.4   *Pakistan*

Pakistan's Penal Code 1860 contains no exception for marital rape in its statutory definition of rape. Though Pakistan and India's penal codes are drawn from the 1860 IPC, former president Zia-ul-Haq's regime passed five ordinances, called the *Hudood* Ordinances, in 1979 that treated certain offences separately. One of them was rape.[64]

3.4.1   The Zina Ordinance

The *Zina* Ordinance of 1979 is one of the five *Hudood* Ordinances, which were part of Zia-ul-Haq's "Islamisation" process. In essence, the Ordinances created new offences and also brought existing offences in conjunction with his interpretation of Shari'a law. One of the implications of the *Zina* (which itself means extramarital sex) Ordinance was that it incorporated a marital exemption into the *definition* of rape, making it definitionally impossible for a man to rape his wife. Thus, where the original Penal Code—like India's—had a marital exemption clause after the offence's ingredients, the new one resembled

---

64   M Lau, 'Twenty-Five Years of Hudood Ordinances—A Review' (2007) 64 *Washington & Lee University* 1291, 1295.

Lord Hale's airtight wording: a person could only rape a "woman or man, as the case may be, to whom he or she is not validly married".[65]

This was part of a larger trend of making it harder to file charges against and prosecute men for rape—and simultaneously making it riskier for women to do so. The *Zina* Ordinance created two levels of offences: *hadd* and *tazir*.[66] The former, in cases of rape or adultery, could lead to stoning to death as a fixed punishment; the latter—as fallback offences—had discretionary punishments.[67] Rape was made difficult to prosecute: for *hadd*, conviction could only be secured if the offender confessed or if four adult, pious Muslim men (if they were Muslim) or four adult men (if they were non-Muslim) witnessed it. While *tazir* was still possible, courts were biased against women at this level too.[68] Moreover, if a conviction attempt failed, the accusing woman could then be charged with extramarital sex, which carried a public whipping of up to a hundred lashes.

Importantly, even unmarried women sometimes bore the brunt of the exemption.[69] The effect of consent now becoming a "non-issue" for women and residing with the men in the family is that even if a man *believed* he was married to a woman, he would be acquitted.[70] Apart from removing the possibility of married women filing cases against their husbands, then, its symbolism radiated beyond marital rape to include a few cases of non-marital rape, that too, based entirely on the (male) perpetrator's word.

3.4.2   Amendments in 2006

Pakistan amended its laws in 2006 through the Protection of Women (Criminal Laws Amendment) Act, which restored rape to the Penal Code's domain.[71] S 375 of the Penal Code— which was reinstated—now largely mirrors s 375 of the IPC, albeit with the marital exemption quietly dropped. The 2006 amendment largely hollowed out the *Zina* ordinance. In 2016 Pakistan further strengthened

---

65   ZUH Muhammad, *Introduction of Islamic Laws: Address to the Nation* (Printing Corporation of Pakistan, 1979) 36.

66   MZ Abbasi, 'Sexualization of Sharīʿa: Application of Islamic Criminal (Ḥudūd) Laws in Pakistan' (2021) *Islamic Law and Society* 1, 2.

67   For details, see MH Cheema, 'Cases and Controversies: Pregnancy as Proof of Guilt under Pakistan's *Hudood* Laws' (2006) 32 *Brooklyn Journal of International Law* 121, 135.

68   Abbasi, *supra* note 66.

69   Human Rights Watch, *Crime or Custom: Violence Against Women in Pakistan* (1999) https://www.hrw.org/reports/pakistan1999.pdf, 41 (accessed 1 September 2022).

70   A Jafar 'Women, Islam, and the State in Pakistan' (2005) 22 *Gender Issues* 35, 45.

71   For a more extensive discussion on the Act, see M Lau, *supra* note 64; for a critique of the Act, see Human Rights Watch, *Proposed Reforms to Hudood Laws Fall Short* (2006) https://www.hrw.org/news/2006/09/06/pakistan-proposed-reforms-hudood-laws-fall-short (accessed 21 February 2022).

its rape laws.[72] However, this has not benefited married women's lived experiences on the ground. Indeed, while legally there is no impediment to lodging a criminal complaint for marital rape, the "rampant abuse of women" within the criminal justice system that Zia's Islamisation facilitated has not been rectified to restore trust of women in the legal system.[73]

It is important to view Pakistani women's predicament in the contemporary context against this historical telling because Zia's Islamisation continues to influence cultural norms surrounding rape. As Jafar writes, these laws established a sense of "womanhood" that has persisted long after Zia's regime.[74] This construction of "womanhood" consisted of three aspects, as highlighted by Jafar – women's sexuality as passive yet destructive, women as repositories of family honour and women as the property of men in the family.[75]

3.5   *Sri Lanka*
As in most other South Asian countries, Sri Lanka's legal framework on marital rape is replete with loopholes and contradictions.

3.5.1   Penal Code and the Exception to Marital Rape
Sri Lanka's Penal Code 02 of 1883—the primary criminal law in the country—explicitly excludes marital rape from the purview of the criminal offence of rape. Marital rape in the country is only criminalised when husband and wife are judicially separated or where the wife is under 16 years of age. Section 363(a) of the Penal Code states that a man commits rape when he has sex with a woman "without her consent, even where such woman is his wife, and she is judicially separated from the man". This amendment was made in 1995. The Report of the Leader of the Opposition's Commission on the Prevention of Violence against Women and the Girl Child in 2014 stated that in 1995, "marital rape was included without the caveat of judicial separation, but strong opposition from the Muslim and Christian lobby within Parliament resulted in the dilution of this provision".[76] The legislative reluctance to recognise marital

---

72   Criminal Law (Amendment) (Offense of Rape) Act 2016.
73   A Jafar, *supra* note 70, 43.
74   *Ibid.*, 36.
75   *Ibid.*
76   Report of the Leader of the Opposition's Commission on the Prevention of Violence Against Women and the Girl Child (Colombo 2014) 32–33.
      http://gbvforum.lk/r-library/document/Report%20of%20the%20Leader.pdf   (accessed 28 November 2022).

rape in criminal law in Sri Lanka, discussed further by Udani, echoes the situation in India.[77]

As Jezima Ismail, President of the Muslim Women's Congress in Sri Lanka, says: "There is no tradition of legal separation in Sri Lankan society ... women live separately from abusive husbands, and they go to (the) law only when they want a divorce."[78] Thus, the Sri Lankan Penal Code paid lip service to women by way of recognizing marital rape in a context that predominantly does not exist in reality! In other words, it is as good as not recognising marital rape in criminal law at all.

3.5.2   Impact of the Domestic Violence Act

If one thought that similar to the Indian context, married women had an avenue for alternative remedy through the Prevention of Domestic Violence Act of Sri Lanka No. 34 of 2005, that is not the case. The Domestic Violence Act recognises physical and psychological violence. S 23 of the 2005 Act defines "domestic violence" as an act that constitutes an offence under Schedule 1 of the Act. Schedule 1 refers to all offences contained in Chapter XVI of the Penal Code. Chapter XVI contains s 363(a) that excludes marital rape as an offence except in contexts of judicial separation. The sum and substance of the legal position is that the Domestic Violence Act of Sri Lanka does not include marital rape.

3.5.3   Under-Aged Marriages

Sri Lanka's common law does not allow marriages where parties are below the age of 18. However, the Muslim Marriage and Divorce Act 1951, which governs the law related to marriages within the Muslim community, has set no minimum age of marriage. In fact, s 23 of the 1951 Act states that a girl less than 12 years of age may be married with the permission of a *Qazi* (religious) judge. So technically, the age of marriage for girls under the 1951 Act is zero! One of the most contentious aspects of the 1951 Act has been the campaign to increase the minimum age of marriage to 18, which has met with resistance from conservative elements within the Muslim community. In recent months, efforts are ongoing to amend the same and bring a universal age of marriage in the

---

77   GIDI Udani 'Contesting the Consent: An Analysis of the Law Relating to Marital Rape Exception in Sri Lanka' (2017) 14 *International Journal of Business, Economics and Law* 43, 46.

78   V Fernando, 'Sri Lanka: Rape, Marital Rape, Incest, Law Issues, Shame' (2008) http://www .wunrn.org/news/2008/09_08/09_15_08/091508_sri.htm (accessed 20 November 2022).

country.[79] Even if this were successful, the social reality of under-aged girls being forced into marriages and raped within marriage, cannot be changed unless there is social reform accompanying the legal reform.

3.5.4 The Constitutional Perspective

Sri Lanka's rape laws are highly punitive (with a maximum of twenty years and compensation to the victim) and—where they include marital rape (rape in contexts of judicial separation)—uniform. Unlike Bangladesh, the Penal Code does not carry far lower minimum prescriptions for rape in contexts of judicial separation. However, the law is unconstitutional on the face of it. The Constitution of Sri Lanka, which was enacted in 1978, expressly entitles everyone to equality before and equal protection of the law.[80] It also prohibits sex-based discrimination.[81] Further, the Constitution provides a guarantee that no person will be subjected to harassment or inhuman and cruel treatment.[82] The exclusion of marital rape from the criminal offence of rape and from the Domestic Violence Act (except rape in contexts of judicial separation) are in direct violation of these constitutional guarantees.

In reality, women in abusive marriages find it nearly impossible to escape them due to the economic dependence on the husband. One woman who confessed to being raped by her husband in Sri Lanka reported the limitations of legal options: she could divorce him, but that would leave her without shelter or work. Her economic contingencies, linked to her husband, thus prevent her from taking one of the few ways out of her marriage.[83] Additionally, rape laws were last amended over 25 years ago. In the past few years, there have been no cases highlighting the clear unconstitutionality of the Code's marital rape exemption. Sri Lanka's poor conviction rates for non-marital rape show no sign of improving, either. In sum, even if, in the future, the marital rape exemption is abolished, Sri Lankan society's inability to offer meaningful redress to survivors portends little hope. However, it is possible that civil society in Sri Lanka may take a leaf from its neighbours' experiences, and file a petition challenging the constitutional validity of the marital rape exemption in the years to come.

---

79   See for instance, H Sethi, 'Reforms Regarding Child Marriage in Sri Lanka' (2021) https:// borgenproject.org/child-marriage-in-sri-lanka/ (accessed 2 February 2022).

80   Art. 12(1) of the Constitution of Sri Lanka.

81   Art. 12(2) of the Constitution of Sri Lanka.

82   Art. 11 of the Constitution of Sri Lanka.

83   D Colombage, 'Rapes Surge in Sri Lanka Amid Weak Laws' *Al Jazeera*, 17 August 2014 https://www.aljazeera.com/features/2014/8/17/rapes-surge-in-sri-lanka-amid-weak-laws (accessed 1 June 2022).

4   Postcolonial Challenges

Despite varied legal approaches and socio-political roadmaps in the post-colonial era, the five South Asian countries examined in this article share common challenges. Various surveys—national and international—have indicated that the incidence of marital rape in the five countries under study is high. Yet, law and policy makers have demonstrated a clear reluctance to remove the marital rape exemption from criminal law of rape, and from treating marital rape on par with non-marital rape in aspects of sentencing.

Given that rape itself has a low conviction rate, the conviction rate for marital rape is likely to be lower. Besides, as the examples of Pakistan and Nepal indicate, removing the marital rape exemption does not automatically imply that there will be a floodgate of complaints in police stations, given the stigma and victim blaming that are often associated with rape. Beyond discriminatory and inadequate legislative provisions on marital rape, South Asia's sociocultural milieu poses major obstacles in women's pursuit of justice, some of which are elaborated below.

4.1   *Social Stigma*

Sex is taboo in most South Asian countries and speaking about rape is considered dishonourable. In Bangladesh, women who face violence within the marriage face social pressure not to report the abuse or seek legal redress.[84]

Similarly, Women's Wellbeing Survey 2019—conducted by the Sri Lankan government—indicated that 20.4 per cent of the ever married women faced physical and/or sexual violence from an intimate partner in their lifetime in Sri Lanka.[85] Yet, as noted by Savithri Fernando, cultural norms inhibit women from reporting their crimes.[86] As explained by Ruhani Perera:

> Within the Sri Lankan context, the reality is that sex in itself is a taboo subject and rape within a marriage is regarded as a domestic or private matter in the legal system. The victimised woman takes her cue from the legal and social climate and opts to suffer in silence. A variety of reasons prevent such women from addressing this issue—social stigma, fear,

---

84   Human Rights Watch, *I Sleep in My Own Deathbed'—Violence Against Women and Girls in Bangladesh: Barriers to Legal Recourse and Support* (2020) https://www.justice.gov/eoir/page/file/1333811/download, 27 (accessed 1 August 2022).

85   Women's Wellbeing Survey 2019, Department of Census and Statistics, Government of Sri Lanka (2020) http://www.statistics.gov.lk/Resource/refference/WWS_2019_Final_Report (accessed 1 October 2022).

86   D Colombage, *supra* note 83.

shame, community and family disapproval, fear of losing children, negative attitudes and possible harassment at the hands of the police.[87]

Several years after the rape law in Nepal was amended to include marital rape,
many women have reportedly never heard of the term "marital rape" as it was
a taboo to talk about sex.[88] The taboo, compounded by a lack of awareness
about the law and the social stigma attached to reporting rape, along with
social, emotional, and economic factors, have resulted in women's failure to
lodge a complaint to the police about marital rape.

A 2003 survey in Pakistan indicated that 47% of women disclosed that they
were raped by their husbands.[89] The survey was conducted in three public-
sector hospitals in Rawalpindi and Islamabad, with 216 women interviewed
in total. Only a third of the women surveyed told anyone about the violence
they endured, reflecting the deep-rooted sense of shame that permeates these
offences.[90]

Political and historical impact of legislation, such as the *Zina Ordinance* in
Pakistan, also go hand in hand with cross-national associations of rape with
shame and dishonour. In South Asian communities, dishonour is closely linked
with family pride.[91] Therefore, statistics for marital rape cases are abysmal
in those countries that have criminalized the same (Nepal and Pakistan). In
India, according to the National Family Health Survey 5 (2019–21), among
married women aged 18–49, 82% of them reported sexual abuse by their
husband, of whom a large majority (84%) said that their husbands "physically
forced her to have sexual intercourse with him even when she did not want to –
in other words, marital rape".[92] Yet, the survey found that only 14% have sought
help for the violence and that 77% did not seek help or tell anyone about the
physical and sexual violence they experienced.[93] This is indicative of social

---

87 V Fernando, *supra* note 78.

88 T Bhattarai, *Lack of Awareness, Stigma Fuels Marital Rape in Nepal* (2012) https://
    globalpressjournal.com/asia/nepal/lack-of-awareness-stigma-fuels-marital-rape-in-nepal/
    (accessed 1 February 2022).

89 MA Shaikh, 'Is Domestic Violence Endemic in Pakistan: Perspective from Pakistani Wives'
    (2003) 19 *Pakistan Journal of Medical Sciences* 23.

90 *Ibid.*, 26.

91 For a detailed discussion see M Gupte, 'The Role of 'Honor' in Violence against South
    Asian Women in the United States' Manavi Occasional Paper No. 11 (2015) https://www
    .masum-india.org.in/images/honor.pdf (accessed 20 February 2022).

92 P Benu, 'Marital Rape: Most Married Women are Sexually Abused by Their Husbands,
    Says NFHS Data' *The Hindu Businessline*, 16 May 2022.

93 *Ibid.*

stigma and the perceived shame and loss of honour to the woman's family if she complained of marital rape.

4.2   *Internalised Patriarchy*

Another obstacle to women's access to justice for marital rape is internalised patriarchy. In October 2020, the Dhaka Tribune conducted a survey on sexual violence against women, and 63.8% of the respondents said rape within marriage was acceptable in Bangladesh.[94] In another survey conducted by the Bangladesh Rural Advancement Committee's Advocacy for Social Change department in February 2019, it was found that only 4% of the 4,800 respondents considered spousal rape to be a form of violence.[95] The findings of the surveys cumulatively indicate that although marital rape is widely prevalent, a large number of Bangladeshis (including women) are ready to accept the same—a clear manifestation of internalised patriarchy among women.

If one thought that law reform may catalyse social reform, this is not always the case, as the situation in Pakistan and Nepal indicate. In Pakistan, informal reports also suggest that most Pakistani women internalize the notion that women ought to acquiesce to sexual demands by their husband.[96] In Nepal, despite the law criminalising marital rape, women are ingrained with patriarchal attitudes about consent to sexual intercourse within marriage, due to the socialization process. However, due to low reporting, hardly any statistics are available, as observed by Bhattarai.[97] These show the limitations of a legal approach, that is not accompanied by efforts at unlearning patriarchal beliefs and building a consciousness about asserting one's own bodily integrity and sexual autonomy.

4.3   *Religious and Cultural Norms*

Pakistan has made progress in the legal front in criminalising marital rape. However, this did not result in married women taking legal recourse against the husband, highlighting the deep chasm that exists between law in the books and law in action, even as more and more women were filing (non-spousal) rape cases against men.[98] Openly confronting the legacy of Zia's Islamisation

---

94   KK Tithila, 'Marital Rape, Hardly Considered a Crime' *Dhaka Tribune*, 25 November 2020.

95   N Jahan & Z Islam, 'Marital Rape, Child Marriage: Issues That Are Now Even More Pressing' *The Daily Star*, 11 October 2020.

96   S Rauf, 'Silence on Spousal Sexual Assault Jarring: Doctors' *Tribune*, 8 March 2011.

97   Bhattarai, *supra* note 88.

98   Asian Human Rights Commission, State of Human Rights in Pakistan, 2010 (2010) https://reliefweb.int/sites/reliefweb.int/files/resources/5CA24C75397E12A6C12577 F4002DC589-Full_Report.pdf, 61 (accessed 1 April 2022).

and the cultural norms that cloak rape in shame for the woman is necessary to bring meaningful change into Pakistani married women's lives.

The play of religious norms in Nepal and cultural norms in India to justify retention of the marital rape exemption, or discriminatory treatment of marital and non-marital rape, pose formidable challenges to married women who attempt to assert their sexual autonomy and bodily integrity within marriage through criminal law mechanisms. Religious and cultural arguments have an emotional appeal and give a false sense of pride in a region that is fast moving towards religious majoritarianism, extremism, and nationalism.

For instance, in the first constitutional challenge before Nepal's Supreme Court, the Ministry of Law, Justice and Parliamentary Affairs took refuge to Hindu religion, tradition and values to justify the marital rape exemption. The cabinet secretariat too gave a similar reply, drawing upon the argument about Hindu religion, tradition and values. However, the court rejected the justifications and emphatically stated that no religion may ever treat marital rape as lawful because the aim of a good religion is not to hate or cause loss to anyone.[99]

In India, an observation made in the Parliamentary Standing Committee's 167th Report on Home Affairs (2013) reveals why the Indian government rejected recommendations of the Justice Verma Committee to remove the marital rape exemption. It stated as follows:

> Some Members also suggested that somewhere there should be some room for wife to take up the issue of marital rape. It was also felt that no woman takes marriage so simple that she will just go and complain blindly. Consent in marriage cannot be treated as consent forever. Several Members of the Committee, however, felt that the marital rape has the potential of destroying the institution of marriage. The committee felt that if a woman is aggrieved by the acts of her husband, there are other means of approaching the court. In India, for ages, the family system has evolved and it is moving forward. Family is able to resolve the problems and there is also a provision under the law for cruelty against women. *It was, therefore, felt that if the marital rape is brought under the law, the entire family system will be under great stress and the committee may perhaps be doing more injustice.*[100] (emphasis added)

---

99   *The Forum for Women, Law and Development v His Majesty's Government, Ministry of Law, Justice and Parliamentary Affairs*, Writ No 55 of the year 2058 BS (2001–2002) (Supreme Court of Nepal) para 32.

100 Parliamentary Standing Committee on Home Affairs, *One Hundred and Sixty Seventh Report on The Criminal Law (Amendment) Bill*, 2012 (presented to the Rajya Sabha on 1st

The above quote indicates the attempt to evoke Indian cultural norms, and to insulate the institutions of marriage and family from legal interventions. The shallowness of the argument lies in the claim that Indian cultural norms allow for marital rape—a claim which, if true, is hardly one to be proud of!

In Sri Lanka, the prevalence of intimate partner violence (IPV) is high, yet several stakeholders including the police and medical professionals believe that IPV is a personal matter, in which outsiders should not intervene.[101] It is this cultural norm and social mindset that closes the doors to effective redress from IPV, including marital rape, for women in Sri Lanka. Furthermore, perceptions of being a "good" wife, that the man should be the "boss" and the belief that the wife is obliged to have sex with her husband even if she does not want to are gendered norms seen in patriarchal societies that promote women's subordinate status.[102] Further, researchers state that women are taught that virginity, virtue, and conformity to tradition are essential for women since divorce is stigmatised and chance of remarriage is low.[103]

4.4   *Institutionalised Misogyny and Perceived "Misuse of the Law" by Women*

The low conviction rates for non-marital rape are bound to deter women from lodging a complaint to the police about marital rape, either in situations of judicial separation or otherwise. The institutionalized misogyny in law intensifies the challenge of access to justice for women. For instance, in the case of Sri Lanka, extremely low conviction rates for non-marital rape have been reported. A 2013 UN survey found that 15% of men admitted to raping women; only 5% said they had been punished and imprisoned for their crimes.[104]

March, 2013, laid on the Table of Lok Sabha on 4th March, 2013) (Government of India, 2013), http://164.100.47.5/newcommittee/reports/EnglishCommittees/Committee%20on%20Home%20Affairs/167.pdf, 26–7 (accessed 29 November 2022).

101   AC Jayatilleke et al., 'Intimate Partner Violence in Sri Lanka' (2010) 4 *Bioscience Trends* 90, 94.

102   V Jayasuriya et al. 'Intimate Partner Violence Against Women in the Capital Province of Sri Lanka: Prevalence, Risk Factors, and Help Seeking' (2011) 17 *Violence Against Women* 1086, 1098.

103   For details see IL Jayakoddy, *Gender Identity and Domestic Violence in Sri Lanka: Reading Experiences of Violence through Gender Disclosure* (Gothenburg University 2002).

104   UN Women, 'Half of Men Report Using Violence and a Quarter Perpetrate Rape According to UN Survey of 10,000 Men in Asia-Pacific' (2013) https://www.unwomen.org/en/news/stories/2013/9/half-of-men-report-using-violence-and-a-quarter-perpetrate-rape-according-to-un-survey (accessed 17 August 2022).

In Nepal, a member of Forum for Women, Law and Development—the organisation that was instrumental for filing the two constitutional challenges before the Supreme Court—was quoted as follows:

> ...even with the law amended to include marital rape, it's difficult and time-consuming for women to pursue cases...cases concerning adults take longer than cases involving minors, and many times guilty husbands receive bail and the couples have to live under the same roof during the judicial process. This might lead to more violence.[105]

A national study of Nepal's law and policy on sexual and gender-based violence by the International Federation of Red Cross and Red Crescent Societies cites the following gaps and challenges: low awareness, poor access to justice, complexity of legal proceedings and long delays in court proceedings.[106]

Similarly in Pakistan, although marital rape is included in the criminal law since 2006, there has been *no* case of marital rape per police reports.[107] Recently, one woman filed a case against her husband under s 377 (unnatural sex) and he was arrested.[108] The outcome is unknown yet. The experience of Nepal and Pakistan, and the contemporary challenges that women face in relation to marital rape, are valuable lessons for other South Asian countries where there are ongoing efforts to remove the marital rape exemption in the criminal offence of rape. They help belie the fear among law and policy makers in other South Asian countries that removing the marital rape exemption would lead to a floodgate of litigation where hapless husbands would be dragged to court by vindictive wives!

Failure of the police to discharge their mandated duties in registering criminal complaints and investigating offences against women, public prosecutors' lack of due diligence during trial, judicial biases against women and the harrowing experiences of rape victims and survivors during the legal process

---

105   Bhattarai, *supra* note 88.
106   International Federation of Red Cross and Red Crescent Societies, 'Nepal Country Case Study: Effective Law and Policy on Gender Equality and Protection from Sexual and Gender-Based Violence in Disasters. 2017' https://disasterlaw.ifrc.org/sites/default/files/media/disaster_law/2021-07/Gender-SGBV-Report_-Nepal_0.pdf, 2–17 (accessed 21 February 2022).
107   S Zaman & M Zia, 'Women's Access to Justice in Pakistan' https://www.ohchr.org/documents/HRBodies/CEDAW/AccesstoJustice/AuratFoundationAndWarAgainstRape_Pakistan.pdf (accessed 1 March 2022).
108   A Kayani, 'Man in Jhelum Arrested for "Marital Rape and Sodomy" on Wife's Complaint' *Dawn*, 18 January 2018.

in general and cross examinations, in particular, have also been documented in India.[109] In Sri Lanka, the police's first response in most cases of domestic violence (including sexual violence within marriage) is to "reconcile" the family.[110] Additionally, discriminatory evidence requirements, narrowly defined rape laws, long delays and lack of victim support leading to low conviction rates remain a few of the many barriers to justice for victims of sexual violence.[111] These are indications of institutionalised misogyny in South Asian countries in cases of non-marital rape, both among the police and the judiciary. Given that the legal institutions have entrenched gender, caste, class, religious and other biases, women are likely to face formidable challenges in approaching them for recourse for marital rape, even after the marital rape exemption is removed.

A primary concern among men in general as well as men in power, is that innocent husbands would be dragged to the police station and the court by unscrupulous and vengeful wives making false allegations of marital rape. Though this is evident in Indian public discourse, this was also alluded to in the Nepal's second constitutional challenge, by the dissenting judge. This concern arises partly through the propaganda that women misuse laws meant for their protection, and partly through a confusion about evidentiary standards and burden of proof for marital rape. The myth of misuse of laws by women has been addressed elsewhere.[112] As observed by Singh, the judicial perception of rampant misuse has persisted in part because it stems from and reinforces the patriarchal values and norms deeply embedded in the Indian social structure; over time, it has served various patriarchal ends by playing a significant role in turning the clock back on the legal protections available to women.[113] This observation is also true in the South Asian context.

---

109 See Commonwealth Human Rights Initiative & Association for Advocacy and Legal Initiatives, 'Barriers in Accessing Justice' https://cjp.org.in/wp-content/uploads/2020/10/CHRI-and-AALI-Barriers-in-accessing-justice-English.pdf (accessed 1 September 2022); Equality Now & Dignity Alliance International, 'Sexual Violence in South Asia: Legal and Other Barriers to Justice for Survivors' (2021) https://www.equalitynow.org/resource/sexualviolencesouthasia/ (accessed 28 November 2022).

110 T Weerasinghe, 'Sexual Violence: System is Stacked against Victims and It Can Begin at Police Stations' *Sunday Times* (Sri Lanka), 8 August 2021.

111 *Ibid.*

112 A Agarwal, 'Why Should the Marital Rape Exception be Removed?' (2021) 56 *Economic & Political Weekly* 33, 35; Doddahatti, *supra* note 35; F Agnes, 'Supreme Court's Judgement Ignores Lived Reality of Married Women' (2017) 52 *Economic & Political Weekly* 16–9; F Agnes, 'Protective Legislations: The Myth of Misuse' (1996) 30 *Economic & Political Weekly* 865.

113 S Singh, 'The Indian Judiciary, Domestic Violence and the Delusion of Rampant Misuse' (2012) 8 *NLUJ Law Review* 185, 212.

4.5   "Saving" the Institution of Marriage

The reluctance to delete the marital rape exemption from the offence of rape and the reluctance to prescribe punishment for marital rape on par with non-marital rape arises from a patriarchal belief that the sanctity of institutions of marriage and family ought to be protected from legislative interference. This is incongruent, given that all the five South Asian countries have legislated on domestic violence, which reiterated the necessity for state intervention when violence exists in the sites of marriage and family. In essence, various domestic violence legislations have busted the public–private dichotomy. If domestic violence laws have not undermined or weakened the institutions of marriage and family, there is no reason why removing the marital rape exemption or punishing marital rape on par with non-marital rape would. Additionally, how the sanctity of marriage would be protected by brushing marital rape under the carpet and cloaking it in the name of religion and culture, is anyone's guess. The application of the privacy argument (privacy of marriage and family) to the detriment of women's right to sex equality is precisely why Nussbaum opines that "the human liberties at stake in this debate are too important to leave them in trust to privacy, that most untrustworthy and compromised of concepts."[114] Similarly, MacKinnon's critique that the right to privacy "looks like an injury got up as a gift" and that it is difficult to convince that anything done in private "to be perceived as coercive" is relevant when we speak of privacy of marriage and family from arbitrary state interference.[115]

Deleting the marital rape exception from the criminal offence of rape is often seen to place at risk the institution of marriage itself. As Justice Hari Shankar's opinion in the Delhi High Court judgment illustrates (discussed in 3.2 above), there exists an immense reluctance in naming the husband as the wife's "rapist", even if there was forced / non-consensual sexual intercourse within marriage. The judge observed as follows:

> Introducing, into the marital relationship, the possibility of the husband being regarded as the wife's rapist, if he has, on one or more occasion, sex with her without her consent would, in my view, be completely antithetical to the very institution of marriage, as understood in this country, both in fact and in law.[116]

---

114   MC Nussbaum, 'Is Privacy Bad for Women? What the Indian Constitutional Tradition can Teach About Sex Equality' (2000 April) *Boston Review* 1.

115   C MacKinnon, *Feminism Unmodified: Discourses on Life and Law* (Harvard University Press, 1987) 100.

116   *RIT Foundation v Union of India, supra* note 27.

Saving the institution of marriage is also considered a legitimate concern of the state, thereby embedding this value in law and legal institutions. The assertion of women's right to bodily autonomy and her exercise of agency within the marital relationship is subsumed by gendered norms and roles that wives are expected to perform, in order to sustain and preserve the institution of marriage. Additionally, there has been an increasing political clout asserted by men's rights groups that aim at countering the advocacy initiatives of women's rights groups. For instance, in India, groups such as the Save Indian Family Foundation were at the forefront of protests against removal of marital rape exemption, while Men's Welfare Trust impleaded itself as an intervenor in the case before the Delhi High Court.[117] Such groups consisting of men's rights activists opposed the removal of the marital rape exemption from the Indian Penal Code and called for a "marriage strike"—a protest against marrying women for the fear of being falsely accused of marital rape.[118] Hundreds of young men in their twenties protested in social media that they will not marry if the marital rape exemption is removed. In other words, they asserted a right to rape in marriage! Such groups also lay emphasis on saving the institutions of marriage and family, on the premise that women's ability to file criminal complaints for marital rape would weaken the institutions.

In Sri Lanka, a senior police officer admitted that he was well aware of the "unprofessional approach most officers take towards these complaints," (of physical and sexual violence within marriage) and about how they "prioritise keeping the 'family' together over the physical and emotional well-being of the woman who has been attacked."[119] In Bangladesh, while there was no criminal law provision on marital rape, the law on domestic violence applied only to married women, excluding those in intimate relationships outside of marriage; reportedly, this deterred those in abusive marital relationships from seeking divorce as that would negate the applicability of protectionsunder the domestic violence law.[120]

In Pakistan, the *Aurat March* (women's march across Pakistan on International Women's Day) where women demanded an end to violence against

117   J Wallan and S Lateef, 'Men's Rights Activists Protest Introduction of Marital Rape Law in India' *The Telegraph,* 2 February 2022.

118   For more details, see DNA Web Team, 'As #MarriageStrike Trends on Social Media, Marital Rape Debate Turns into Battle of the Sexes' https://www.dnaindia.com/india/report-as -marriagestrike-trends-on-social-media-marital-rape-debate-turns-into-battle-of-the -sexes-2929799 (accessed 10 February 2022).

119   T Weerasinghe, 'Sexual Violence: System is Stacked against Victims and It Can Begin at Police Stations' *Sunday Times* (Sri Lanka), 8 August 2021.

120   Human Rights Watch, "*I Sleep in My Own Deathbed" Violence against Women and Girls in Bangladesh: Barriers to Legal Recourse and Support* (Human Rights Watch, 2020) 20.

women and gender minorities, faced an extremist backlash in the form of street protests and a Taliban condemnation of the women for "actively spreading obscenity and vulgarity", and an organized social media disinformation campaign against the organisers and supporters of *Aurat March*.[121] The persons who orchestrated the backlash include ultra-nationalists, "men's rights" activists and extremist religious groups.[122]

4.6   Prevalence of Forced Marriages

Consent is a pivotal issue that distinguishes sexual intercourse and rape. Yet, the concept of consent is often ignored with regard to women and girls. A case in point is the Child Marriage Restraint Act 2017 of Bangladesh, which allows the marriage of under aged girls with the consent of the parent / guardian, without taking into consideration the minor girl's viewpoint.

In South Asian marriages, decision-making power is often vested in the patriarch within the family and the (often male) community leaders, ignoring an exercise of agency by young women. Inter-caste, inter-class, and inter-religious marriages are actively discouraged and vehemently opposed. The high incidence of (dis)honour killings in South Asia bear evidence to the fact that women's agency and sexual/marital choices are neither recognised nor respected.[123]

Arranged marriages, which have been the prevailing form of marriage across South Asia, are alliances fixed by two families, which may or may not be consented to by the marrying couple. Families often exert considerable power over their children, keeping in mind considerations such as caste purity, class parity, protection of family property and lineage. Given the patriarchal power that governs women's sexuality, sexual choices and agency vis-à-vis marriage are often trampled upon. In this context, accepting and respecting young women's exercise of choice and agency in marriage, and their economic independence within it would need to be necessary pre-conditions that provide women with an enabling environment with negotiating power on sexual intercourse within marriage. Devoid of consent to marriage, consent to sexual intercourse within marriage may remain a lofty yet hollow ideal.

---

121   R Khurshid, 'Media: The March of Disinformation' *Dawn*, 21 March 2021.
122   *Ibid.*
123   For details on honour killings in South Asia, see T D'Lima, JL Solotaroff and RP Pande, 'For the Sake of Family and Tradition: Honour Killings in India and Pakistan' (2020) 5 ANTYAJAA: *Indian Journal of Women and Social Change* 22; L Welchman & S Hossain (eds.), *"Honour": Crimes, Paradigms, and Violence Against Women* (Zed Books 2005).

5   Feminist Theory and Praxis

The disparate treatment of marital rape, as compared to non-marital rape, may be attributed to the gendered dichotomy between "public" and "private" spheres entrenched in the psyche of the society at large, critiqued extensively by feminist scholars, yet not dislodged till today. For instance, Ortner observed that the association of women with the domestic/private sphere was a universal phenomenon across all societies and cultures,[124] while Pateman critiqued the conception of the liberal state and its use of the public–private dichotomy.[125] Liberal feminists have argued that the domain of private sphere must be reserved for individual choices and personal autonomy. In contrast, radical feminists have critiqued legal structures that reinforce and embed male dominance in intimate relationships. They have argued that the absence or lack of regulation in the private sphere (which women predominantly inhabit) leads to unequal power equations, subjugation of and violence against women within the family and in intimate relationships. MacKinnon termed the private sphere as "a means of subordinating women's collective needs to the imperatives of male supremacy".[126] Notwithstanding the difference in feminist approaches, there is consensus on the fact that "by classifying the family as private, the public–private distinction has frequently worked to shield abuse and domination within familial relations, placing them beyond political scrutiny or legal intervention".[127]

A significant feminist contribution has been to demonstrate that the family is a site of violence and discrimination against women due to unequal power equations between its members. Without the privilege of imagining violence against women as an expression of patriarchy alone, feminists of colour from both the global North and South have long argued that feminists must approach violence against women through an engagement with structural violence.[128] Kimberlé Crenshaw urges the readers to understand violence against women in the home through violent structural inequalities based on race and class.[129]

---

124   SB Ortner, 'Is Female to Male as Nature is to Culture' in L Lamphere and M Rosaldo (eds.), *Women, Culture, and Society* (Stanford University Press, 1974) 67.
125   C Pateman, *The Disorder of Women: Democracy, Feminism and Political Theory* (Stanford University Press, 1989).
126   C MacKinnon, *Toward a Feminist Theory of the State* (Harvard University Press, 1989) 188.
127   J Weintraub 'The Theory and Politics of the Public/Private Distinction' in J Weintraub and K Kumar (eds.), *Public and Private in Thought and Practice: Perspectives on a Grand Dichotomy* (University of Chicago, Press 1997) 1, 29.
128   RJ Hall, 'Feminist Strategies to End Violence Against Women' in R Baksh and W Harcourt (eds.), *The Oxford Handbook of Transnational Feminist Movements* (Oxford University Press, 2015) 394, 397–398.
129   K Crenshaw, 'Mapping the Margins: Intersectionality, Identity Politics and Violence Against Women of Color' (1991) 43 *Stanford Law Review* 1241, 1245–6.

In the South Asian context, feminists have highlighted that gender-based violence intersects with caste, religion, and other structural hierarchies.[130] For instance, Menon has highlighted a key patriarchal assumption that underlies the institution of family and marriage - the control over women's sexuality. [131] Kapur has critiqued the patriarchal construct of "good woman"—a chaste and loyal wife who maintains the integrity of her family, culture and the nation, as opposed to the "bad woman" who transgresses these norms and who, as a consequence, is neither protected by the law nor saved from punishment.[132] Feminist historians have observed the inter-linkages between caste, marriage and the family, highlighting the subordination of Dalit women's lives through the double burden of patriarchy by the dominant caste and multiple patriarchies within their own caste, in India and Nepal.[133] De Alwis has highlighted the nature and scope of patriarchy and the ways in which it operates within the institution of marriage in Sri Lanka, pushing women to become "nurturers", "reproducers" and "carriers" irrespective of their ethnicity.[134] The impact of patriarchy and religion on the status of women within the institutions of family and marriage has been examined in Pakistan and Bangladesh.[135]

The public–private dichotomy that continues to exist in the South Asian region, embedded and reinforced through judicial discourse, is best described by a quote from an Indian judgement of the 1980s:

> The Introduction of constitutional law in the home is most inappropriate. It is like introducing a bull in a china shop. It will prove to be a ruthless destroyer of the marriage institution and all that it stands for. In the privacy of the home and the married life, neither Article 21 nor Article 14 have any place. In a sensitive sphere which is at once most intimate

---

130   K Kananbiran and R Menon, *From Mathura to Manorama: Resisting Violence against Women in India* (Women Unlimited, 2007).

131   N Menon, *Seeing Like a Feminist* (Penguin Books India Pvt Ltd., 2012).

132   R Kapur, *Erotic Justice: Law and the New Politics of Postcolonialism* (Permanent Black, 2005).

133   U Chakravarti, *Gendering Caste: Through a Feminist Lens* (Sage Publications, 2003); for an analysis of the gender and caste dynamics in Nepal, see U Bhandary, 'Gender Identities and Women's Subordination: An Understanding from Deconstructionist's Lens' (2008) 1 *Socio-Economic Development Panorama* 7–20.

134   M De Alwis, *Interrogating the 'Political': Feminist Peace Activism in Sri Lanka* (Palgrave Macmillan, 2009).

135   See for instance N Kabeer, 'Subordination and Struggle: Women in Bangladesh' (1988) 168 (March-April) *New Left Review* 95–121; F M Critelli, 'Between Law and Custom: Women, Family Law and Marriage in Pakistan' (2012) 43 *Journal of Comparative Family Studies* 673–9.

and delicate, the introduction of the cold principles of constitutional law will have the effect of weakening the marriage bond.[136]

Susan Brownmiller observed as follows:

> Man's discovery that his genitalia could serve as a weapon to generate fear must rank as one of the most important discoveries of prehistoric times along with the use of fire and the first crude stone axe. From prehistoric times to the present, I believe that rape has played a critical function. It is nothing more or less than a conscious process of intimidation by which all men keep all women in a state of fear.[137]

While rape as a weapon of violence and oppression against women has been subjected to intense feminist discourse, and, in response, all countries have criminalised the same, the treatment given to marital rape is less than favourable to women. Marital rape, as a critical issue, has received less attention by the state.[138] However, it has been a subject of feminist discourse, which informs and influences feminist praxis in South Asia as well.

Although this article has largely discussed law reform processes and their social ramifications in the five South Asian countries under examination, the enabling environment for such advocacy campaigns has been created by feminist political action. In recent times, South Asia has witnessed the launch of new feminist politics and a shift in the discourse on rape, which may be termed as the process of decolonising the married woman's body and reclaiming sexual autonomy.

In India, the homicidal gang rape of a young woman on a moving bus in Delhi in 2012 led to national and global outrage and galvanised many people to occupy public spaces and protest the rape culture in India. The rights-based anti-rape movement gave an occasion, therefore, to people from a diversity of interest groups to express their rage against the neo-colonial repressive state.[139]

---

136   *Harvinder Kaur v Harmander Singh* AIR 1984 Del 356, para 34. Article 21 refers to fundamental right to life while Article 14 refers to fundamental right to equality before the law and equal protection of the law, guaranteed by the Indian Constitution.

137   S Brownmiller, *Against Our Will: Men, Women and Rape* (The Balantine Publishing Group, 1975) 14–15.

138   S Nigam, 'The Social and Legal Paradoxes Relating to Marital Rape in India: Addressing Structural Inequalities' (2015) http://www.countercurrents.org/nigam030615.htm (accessed 10 February 2022).

139   A Kurian, 'Decolonizing the Body: Theoretical Imaginings on the Fourth Wave Feminism in India' in S Jha and A Kurian (eds.), *New Feminisms in South Asia: Disrupting the Discourse through Social Media, Film and Literature* (Routledge, 2017) 15, 16.

The report of the government-appointed Justice Verma committee that examined reforms in the criminal law on rape in 2013, infused a stronger rights-based discourse into rape law. In 2020, the gang rape of a woman in the presence of her children in Lahore, and victim-blaming of the assaulted woman by the Pakistani police sparked public outrage.[140] In Pakistan, women's rights marches (referred to as *Aurat* march) are held each year, where feminist slogans such as *Mera Jism Meri Marzi* (My Body, My Choice) are used to assert women's bodily autonomy against issues such as marital rape.[141] In Bangladesh, anti-rape protests against the backdrop of a gang rape and torture of a young woman in Dhaka in 2020, led to calls for state accountability for the climate of impunity that prevailed, leading to high incidence of rape and gang rape.[142] Feminist peace activism in Sri Lanka has highlighted the interlinkages between gender, masculinity, power, and violence. In Nepal, young women's rights activists are attempting to reshape the movement against sexual violence, through campaigns such as *Ajhai Kati Sahane* (How Much Shall We Tolerate?).[143] Each year, South Asian countries participate actively in One Billion Rising and 16 days of activism against gender-based violence, providing a platform for awareness raising on women's bodily autonomy and agency in the context of violence against women.

Such flashpoints and campaigns have catalysed a shift in the discourse on rape from dishonour, shame, and stigma (to the woman/girl and her family/community) to a violation of sexual autonomy, bodily integrity, consent and privacy of every woman. The shifting of the discourse has been complemented by a call for support services, access to justice, a re-examination of rape law and a critique of institutionalised patriarchy and anti-women bias among the enforcement agencies and the judiciary within the criminal legal system. However, it would be wrong to think that feminists have spoken in one voice in favour of removing the marital rape exemption. As highlighted by Mandal, feminist engagement with the issue nuances and complicates our understanding of the varied forms of violence within marriage as manifestations of the varied power dynamics within it.[144] Further, South Asian feminist interventions also engage considerably with colonial and postcolonial history, law and literature.[145]

---

140   H Ellis-Petersen, 'Backlash in Pakistan as Police Appear to Blame Woman for Gang Rape' *The Guardian*, 11 September 2020.

141   N Pandita, 'Mera Jism, Meri Marzi' Say the Women of Pakistan' *Asian Age*, 16 April 2020.

142   See Human Rights Watch, *supra* note 80.

143   A Khadgi, 'How Young Activists are Trying to Reshape the Movement against Sexual Violence in Nepal' *Kathmandu Post*, 3 November 2020.

144   S Mandal, 'The Impossibility of Marital Rape' (2014) 29 *Australian Feminist Studies* 255.

145   See for instance A Loomba and R Lukose (eds.), *South Asian Feminisms* (Duke University Press, 2012); G Karmakar, 'On Violence and Resistance: Narratives of Women in South Asia' (2022) 24 *Journal of International Women's Studies* 1.

6   Possible Ways Forward

The first part of this article provided the socio-legal context of the issue, particularly from a South Asian perspective. The second part discussed the British colonial origins of the marital rape exemption, through the doctrine of coverture, Blackstone's writings, and Sir Matthew Hale's famous quote that the wife had given her irrevocable consent to sexual intercourse with her husband upon marriage. It foregrounded the fact that decades after the UK shirked off the regressive law, South Asian countries remain saddled with the remnants of the doctrine of coverture, embedded firmly within the legal framework and social psyche. They grapple with its ramifications, including the exemption for marital rape in criminal law, through legislative and judicial interventions, propelled by feminist advocacy campaigns. The third part of this article discussed the socio-legal status of marital rape in Bangladesh, India, Nepal, Pakistan, and Sri Lanka, tracing legal provisions and landmark judgments. The fourth part culled out common challenges faced by all five South Asian countries in ensuring justice to women victims of marital rape in the post-colonial context. In particular, obstacles posed through social stigma, internalised patriarchy, religious and cultural discourses, institutionalised misogyny, propaganda about women's potential "misuse" of the law, state's claim of preserving the institution of marriage as a legitimate concern, as well as the phenomenon of forced marriages were discussed. The fifth part foregrounded feminist theory relevant to marital rape, and feminist praxis that has resulted in advocacy initiatives in South Asia.

Marital rape violates every notion of women's human rights and cannot be justified any longer under the garb of protecting the institutions of marriage or family. Given the contemporary public discourse around sexual autonomy, agency, bodily integrity and privacy of every woman, it is not tenable any longer—legally or socially—to argue that marriage provides a blanket irrevocable consent to sexual intercourse covering its entire duration. Such an argument denies and deprives women of their personhood which is integral to their identity. While there can be no two questions about removing the marital rape exemption or bringing the sentencing policy between marital and non-marital rape on par, that is not to say that criminal law is the only or desirable solution to all ills within a marital or an intimate relationship. Traditionally, criminal law has focussed on prosecution, conviction, and punishment to the accused, with little room for reparative justice for the raped woman.

Removing the marital rape exemption or treating marital rape on par with non-marital rape in law, is only the beginning of the road to justice. These are not a quick-fix solution for all forms of violence faced by women within marital or intimate relationships. Re-orienting women to value their bodily integrity and sexual autonomy in marital and intimate relationships, re-educating men to respect consent in all acts of sexual intercourse and particularly within marriage, public awareness raising on marital rape as a criminal offence, and countering the bias and reluctance among the various stakeholders of criminal law through systems of accountability are essential measures that must accompany law reform processes. South Asian governments have an important role to play in implementing these measures, as part of their obligations to respect, protect and fulfil women's human rights.

Law has an important role in establishing a much-needed normative standard of behaviour. The marital rape exemption and disparate prescriptions of punishments to marital and non-marital rape provide immunity to the errant husband, which ought to be eliminated. However, law has its limitations in fostering a larger enabling environment in which sexual intimacy is premised on free, open and non-judgmental conversations, mutual respect, and consent between the partners. Thus, law reforms and effective implementation of the law must be accompanied by a rise in social consciousness and political activism. Additionally, transnational feminist strategy-sharing and solidarity-building are the need of the hour to counter the existing impunity for marital rape in South Asia.

Note on the Contributor

Saumya Uma
Professor and Director – Centre for Women's Rights, Jindal Global Law School, O.P. Jindal Global University, India. Prof. (Dr.) Saumya Uma teaches, researches and writes at the intersections of gender, law and human rights. The opinions expressed in this article are her own. She thanks Barristers Sara Hossain and Sharmin Akhter from Bangladesh and Attorney at Law Nimalka Fernando from Sri Lanka for providing their valuable inputs on the contents of this article. She also thanks Kieran Correia – student of Jindal Global Law School and Aditi Bhardwaj – student of Institute of Law, Nirma University for their research and editorial assistance. The author can be contacted at saumyauma@gmail.com.

CHAPTER 10

Illegitimate Children Plight and Protection under the Malaysian Dual Legal System

Nadhratul Wardah Salman, Saroja Dhanapal and Shad Saleem Faruqi

Abstract

An illegitimate child refers to a child who is born outside wedlock regardless of whether the illegitimate birth is caused by adultery or rape as well as through a 'syubhah' consummation. The high illegitimate birth rate in Malaysia has given rise to moral indignation. This article analyses the principles and application of Common Law and Syariah Law pertaining to illegitimacy in Malaysia, a country practicing a dual legal system. The study adopted a qualitative doctrinal research method based on content analysis of the Malaysian laws applicable in the civil and Syariah courts. The findings clearly indicate that there is a wide disparity in the application of these laws. The study ends with recommendation for policy changes that can bridge the discrepancies between the two systems while ensuring the principle of lineage in the Islamic law is upheld, as Islam is the official religion in the country.

Keywords

illegitimate child – society – civil law – Syariah law – rights of the child

1 Introduction

Concern about children and children's rights has been ongoing since time immemorial. This concern has increased in intensity with the increasing number of illegitimate children being born all over the world as well as in Malaysia.[1]

---

1 WAFW Ismail, AS Baharuddin, LA Mutalib, Z Mamat, and SA Shukor, 'A Comparative Study of the Illegitimate Child Term from Shariah and Malaysia Legal Perspective' (2020) 8 *Humanities & Social Sciences Reviews* 101–109.

According to Azizah and others,[2] the rise of illegitimate birth in Malaysia has significantly proved that the community in Malaysia is facing a very serious issue of moral demolition. Due to the serious concern over the issue of illegitimacy and children's rights, protecting children from any maltreatment has been a crucial focus in all nations. This is especially so for illegitimate children whose wellbeing is at a disadvantage due to the laws that differentiate them from legitimate children. The situation is worsened by society stigmatizing by calling them 'bastards'[3] as they are considered children of sinners. This is because the term 'illegitimate children', in layman's terms refers to children born out-of-wedlock. Under common law, a child born outside of a marriage is called '*filius nullius*' which means a child of nobody.[4] A child that is born in an invalid marriage is also considered as an illegitimate child.[5] Although, in the past, the harsh and derogatory term 'bastard' was commonly used to refer to these children, it is important to note that today, society's perceptions on the issue of illegitimacy are changing. Thus, it can be said that legitimacy played an important function and had greater consequences in the old days compared to now.[6] This is supported by Mahmood[7] who claims that the negative connotation in regard to 'illegitimate child' is gradually losing significance in family jurisprudence in many parts of the West but he went on to add that it is still important in India because of religious and cultural practices. This view can be applicable to countries where Islam is the official religion like Malaysia.

Malaysia, a country that practices a dual legal system adds to the growing concern on the issue of illegitimacy. This is due to the stringent Islamic perceptions of illegitimacy and in addition to the lack of clarity as to the role of federal and state law under Schedule 9 List 11.[8] As a result, there is a need for

---

2   AM Rashid, NAM Awal, AAM Shariff, NA Abd Hamid and TNAT Zainudin, 'Menangani Masalah Kelahiran Anak Tak Sah Taraf Di Malaysia: Peranan Perundangan Jenayah Syariah Dalam Masyarakat (Solving the Problem of Illegitimate Birth In Malaysia: The Role of Syariah Criminal Law in the Society)' (2019) 89 *Akademika* 5–16.

3   Illegitimate Child Definition in *Duhaime's Law Dictionary*, http://www.duhaime.org/LegalDictionary/I/IllegitimateChild.aspx (accessed 2 January 2023).

4   HH Kay, 'The Family and Kinship System of Illegitimate Children in California Law' (1965) 67 *American Anthropologist* 57–81.

5   JW Ester, 'Illegitimate Children and Conflict of Laws' (1961) 36 *Indiana Law Journal*, https://www.repository.law.indiana.edu/ilj/vol36/iss2/2. (accessed 2 January 2022).

6   JD Bock, 'Doing the Right Thing? Single Mothers by Choice and the Struggle for Legitimacy' (2000) 14 *Gender & Society* 62–86.

7   T Mahmood, 'Presumption of Legitimacy under the Evidence Act: A Century of Action and Reaction' (1972) *Journal of the Indian Law Institute* 78–89.

8   For further details, refer to the Schedule 9 List 11 of the Malaysian Federal Constitution 1957 which indicate the exemption provided to those professing the religion of Islam.

in-depth research to be carried out to identify the loopholes in the current laws in place in Malaysia related to the issue of illegitimacy. This is to ensure that Malaysia is in line with the practices of other nations as well as with its international obligation which advocates for a movement towards protecting the rights of marginalised groups. In the present case, this would be to protect the well-being of the illegitimate children. Since issues related to the identity of an illegitimate child continue to be a challenge as a result of the dual legal system adopted in Malaysia, this marginalised group's rights remain questionable. It must be noted that birth registration and the right to a name and nationality are critical for it is through this that 'all other rights of a child will naturally flow in'.[9] It must be noted that the laws and policies relating to children's rights have significantly improved with the ratification of the United Nations Convention on the Rights of the Child (UNCRC) and the enactment of Child Act 2001. Yet, Malaysia had reservation to Article 2 (discrimination) and Article 7 (birth registration, the right to a name and nationality) of the UN Convention. Thus, the current tension that has emerged as the result of the dual legal system continues to be of concern in Malaysia.

In view of this, the current research is focused on analysing the status of illegitimate children under the Malaysian laws such as Adoption Act 1952, Legitimacy Act 1961, and Child Act 2001 with reference to UNCRC that Malaysia has ratified. In addition, the research also examines the position of illegitimate children under the Syariah laws in Malaysia and concludes with recommendations and possible solutions to lessen the disparity between civil and syariah laws and to fill the lacuna in the law with an aim to protect illegitimate children's rights.

For ease of reading, this article starts with an overview of the concepts of legitimacy and illegitimacy, followed by a discussion on how illegitimacy is defined in the United Nations Convention on the Rights of the Child. Next, the article gives a detailed analysis on the issue of illegitimacy in all the key Acts of the Malaysian Civil Law as well as the Malaysian Syariah Law. The article ends with a conclusion providing recommendations for bridging the inconsistencies between the two laws where possible while upholding the key principle 'nasab' under the Syariah law as Malaysia is an Islamic country with Islam being the main religion.

---

9   *Ibid.*

2   Legitimacy and Illegitimacy

According to Cretney,[10] legitimacy is a legal concept whereby a couple's child can fully enjoy the rights as a child and be fully recognised as a member of the family. In *Re Lowe Stewart v Lowe*[11] Romer J. said that legitimacy is the question of status where it can be acquired by being legitimately born into a family or being legitimated by law. He went on saying that as the plaintiff had attained the status, it was irrelevant consideration whether she attained it in one way or the other. This is to say that without this legal status given to these children, their lives are surrounded by numerous challenges which can arise from society as well as the family. Stigmatization and the denial of inheritance rights are but a few. In Malaysia, the definition of the term illegitimacy can be found in S.112 of the Evidence Act 1950 where it is stated that the fact that any person was born during the continuance of a valid marriage between his mother and any man, or within two hundred and eighty days after the dissolution of the marriage, the mother remaining unmarried, shall be conclusive proof that he is the legitimate son of that man, unless it can be shown that the parties to the marriage had no access to each other at any time when he could have been begotten.[12] According to Mahmood,[13] this definition which is also pari materia with the Indian Evidence Act 1972 lays down some presumptions with regards to the legitimacy of children. It is immaterial to the debate whether it supersedes the contradicting principles of Hindu and Islamic laws. It is traditionally accepted that it constitutes the general law.

In addition to the landmark decision in Bin Abdullah's case,[14] the increasing statistics of illegitimate children of all races and religions in Malaysia has caused an array of concern in this issue. It was reported that between 2005

---

10   SM Cretney, *Principle of Family Law*, 4th ed. (Sweet and Maxwell, 1984).

11   In *Re Lowe Stewart v. Lowe*. [1929] 2 Ch. 210. A woman had two illegitimate children, a son and a daughter. The son died in 1919 leaving a child. The woman died in 1928 intestate. It was held that the daughter having thus been rendered legitimate as from the commencement of the Legitimacy Act 1926 to take an interest in the estate of her intestate mother as if she had been born legitimate but the child of her brother (who died before the Act came into force) was not entitled to take a share.

12   Evidence Act 1950, s. 112.

13   *Ibid.*, 10.

14   *Jabatan Pendaftaran Negara & Ors v. A Child & Ors* (Majlis Agama Islam Negeri Johor, Intervener) [2020] 4 CLJ. The issue is whether the Director General of National Registration possesses the authority under the Births and Deaths Registration Act 1957 to ascribe "bin Abdullah" instead of the name of the biological father to the name of an illegitimate Muslim child when registering the birth of that child.

and 2015, more than half a million children registered with the National Registration Department were children born out of wedlock.[15] A more recent report[16] has indicated that a total 543,363 illegitimate children was recorded by the National Registration Department which includes children born before the marriage been registered according to the regulations, children born before the fulfillment of the six months' requirement (for Muslim couples only), failure to register marriages conducted overseas and abandoned babies without knowing the identity of their parents. According to Wan-Ibrahim and others,[17] the National Registry Department has released data based on the number of illegitimate children from the year 2000 to 2009 where it reported that there is an average of 2500 cases of illegitimate children recorded each month or 83 cases per day and 1 illegitimate child for every 7 minutes. This data is shocking and is very true for in 2016, the number had exceeded 50,000.[18] In terms of illegitimate children according to racial distribution, it has been reported that the Malays as well as Bumiputera of Sabah and Sarawak recorded 20,949 babies, Indians 19,581 and Chinese 18,111.[19] Based on religion, the statistics showed 30,978 Muslims, 18,085 Hindus, 17,236 Buddhist and 3,395 Christians are born illegitimate. These statistics clearly denotes that the issue of illegitimacy is prevalent among all races in Malaysia. However, the larger number reported among Malays and Bumiputera can be reasoned by the syariah laws applicable to Muslims which is very stringent on the issue of illegitimacy. Nor Aziah Mohd Awal[20] asserts that illegitimate birth is still a taboo in Malaysia since the multi-racial society in Malaysia being very traditional and religious is ruled by laws which still differentiate between legitimate and illegitimate birth. In Malaysia, unlike other countries, the issue of illegitimacy is harsher as a result

15   T Ruxyn, 'More than 530,000 Innocent Children are Labelled "Illegitimate" in Malaysia' 11 November 2016, https://says.com/my/news/more-than-530-000-illegitimate-children -registered-with-jpn (accessed 3 January 2023).

16   *Ibid.*, 5.

17   WA Wan-Ibrahim, WARKW Abdullah, ZA Bakar and HAR Asyraf, 'Illegitimate Child in Malaysia' (2013) 7 *Advances in Natural and Applied Sciences* 369–373.

18   S Thambapillay, 'A Critical Analysis of The Statutory Framework on Maintenance of Non-Muslim Children and Young Persons in Malaysia' PhD Diss., Faculty of Medicine University of Malaya Kuala Lumpur, Malaysia (2017) http://studentsrepo.um.edu .my/7780/1/Hard_Copy_Thesis.pdf (accessed 3 January 2023).

19   MZ Norhasmah, 'Outcomes of Pregnancy Among Unmarried Mothers in Malaysia' PhD Diss., Faculty of Medicine University of Malaya Kuala Lumpur, Malaysia (2016) http:// studentsrepo.um.edu.my/6911/1/OUTCOMES_OF_PREGNANCY_AMONG_UNMARRIED _MOTHERS.pdf (accessed 3 January 2023).

20   NAM Awal, 'Legal Status and Rights of Illegitimate Children in Malaysia: The Conflicting Rights' (2009) *International Survey of Family Law* 275.

of the dual legal system adopted in the country. The civil law and syariah law impose different rules on the issue of illegitimacy.

3   Illegitimacy under the UN Convention on the Rights of the Child

Since the issue relating to illegitimate children has been in existence and has caused major debates, the Malaysian government ratified the UNCRC as early as 19 March 1995. It was one of the 196 countries which signed the Convention. Under the Convention, the countries that ratified it are bound to uphold laws that comply with the international law regarding the rights of the children.[21] The Convention consists of 45 articles which focus on the protection and welfare of children's rights and this focus is clearly indicated in the Preamble of the Convention.[22] It is clearly stipulated that the rights of an illegitimate child is given due protection like any other child. This is seen in the Preamble which states that the States Parties to UNCRC "[r]ecognizing that the United Nations has in the Universal Declaration of Human Rights and in the International Covenants on Human Rights, proclaimed and agreed that everyone is entitled to all the rights and freedoms set forth therein, without distinction of any kind, such as race, colour, sex, language, religion, political or other opinion, national or social origin, property, birth or other status", has agreed in Article 2 as follows:

> States Parties shall respect and ensure the rights set forth in the present Convention to each child within their jurisdiction without discrimination of any kind, irrespective of the child's or his or her parent's or legal guardian's race, colour, sex, language, religion, political or other opinion, national, ethnic or social origin, property, disability, birth or other status.

A key outcome of Malaysia's ratification is the Child Act 2001 (Act 611) which forms part of the protective legal environment for children in the country. Although UNCRC clearly protects the rights of illegitimate children under Article 2, it is important to take note at this point that Malaysia did not agree to all the articles in the said Convention specifically those that do not conform to the Federal Constitution and other national laws as well as policies inclusive

---

21   United Nations Convention on the Rights of the Child, https://www.ohchr.org/en /professionalinterest/pages/crc.aspx (accessed 3 January 2023).

22   See Preamble of the United Nations Convention on the Rights of the Child (UNCRC) to get a comprehensive insight as to the focus on the rights of a child.

of Article 2. However, beside ratifying the UNCRC and subsequently enacting Child Act 2001, Malaysia is indeed very protective and sensitive to the issues regarding the rights of children where the wellbeing and the needs of children continues to be one of the concerns in this country. This is evident in the status report[23] on children's rights in Malaysia where it was indicated that in 2009, the Government had introduced and modelled the National Child Policy/National Policy for Children and its Plan of Action based on the general principles of UNCRC. Further, in the same year, the National Child Protection Policy and the National Plan of Action for Child Protection were introduced. The report went on to conclude that despite these commendable actions, there is still a lot of inconsistencies especially in relation to the definition of child under civil and syariah courts. The report also indicated that there is inadequate protection for illegitimate children as they are still being marginalised and this lacuna calls for Malaysian laws to be made more specific with special provisions to handle and govern illegitimate children. This is also highlighted in the 2018 report[24] where it is stated that despite Malaysia having several laws in place for child protection and is arduously working to prevent any harm to children, there are still gaps in the substance and implementation of the law, including issues related to child marriage. Although the report does not specify illegitimate child's rights, it can be presumed that this is included in the statement on the status of child protection in Malaysia.

4   Illegitimacy under Malaysian Civil Law

It must be noted in the offset that the protection of children's rights took a leap after Malaysia ratified the UNCRC in 1995. However, the fact that Article 2 (regarding non-discrimination), Article 7 (regarding birth registration, the right to a name and nationality), Article 14 (freedom of thought, conscience and religion), Article 28(a)(1)(regarding compulsory and free primary education for all) and Article 37 (regarding torture and other cruel in human or degrading treatment or punishment and unlawful or arbitrary deprivation of

---

23   Malaysian Child Resource Institute, *Status Report on Children's Rights in Malaysia. Child Rights' Coalition* (2012), https://www.unicef.org/malaysia/Child_Rights_Coalition _Report_on_Childrens_Rights_FINAL.pdf (accessed 3 January 2023).

24   Child Rights Coalition Malaysia, *Executive Summary: Status Report on Child Rights in Malaysia 2018 Child Rights Coalition Malaysia*, https://wao.org.my/wp-content /uploads/2020/08/CRC-Report-Presentation.pdf (accessed 3 January 2023).

liberty) were reserved shows that there is still room for discrimination of children. The justification given for these 'reservations' is that these Articles do not conform to the Federal Constitution and other national laws and policies. This is similar to the justification given by the Malaysian Government when they reserved several Articles in the Convention on the Elimination of All Forms of Discrimination against Women 1979 (CEDAW), based on the ground that they are in conflict with Islamic law and the Federal Constitution.[25] According to Meerah Deiwi,[26] the reservation of the above Articles can be seen to have some negative impact on children's rights where issues related to education, healthcare, birth registration and child protection services still remain as challenges to them.[27] Despite these reservations, it must be conceded that over the years, the level of protection awarded to children has improved to a great extent with Malaysia's ratification of UNCRC. This is concurred by Md Salleh's where she asserted that Malaysia is moving forwards in protecting the welfare of the child for many efforts have been taken to reduce the gap through amendment of inefficient and impracticable old provisions and practices relating to child protection and introducing new and better laws.[28] For example, the Sexual Offences against Children Act 2017 (Act 792) and the Court for Sexual Crimes against Children among others. Before the enactment of Child Act 2001, there are a number of other legislations in place which deal specifically or indirectly with children's rights. Among these are Adoption Act 1952, Child Care Centre Act 1984, Domestic Violence Act 1994 and the Education Act 1996. There are also legislations under Syariah Law that cater to the protection of Muslim children; the Islamic Family Law (Federal Territories) Act 1984 and the Syariah Criminal Offences Act (Federal Territory) 1997.

The following discussion is based on the analysis of the various Acts with reference to UNCRC 1989 to show to what extent the rights upheld in UNCRC is already covered in Malaysian legislations and policies with view to identify if Malaysia needs to enact other laws to meet the UN Convention's requirements.

---

25 AG Hamid and KM Sein, 'Reservations to CEDAW and the Implementation of Islamic Family Law: Issues and Challenges' (2009) 3 *Malaysian Journal on Human Rights* 69–94.

26 MD Raja Gopal, 'Does Illegitimacy Status of Children Matter? A Review on Malaysian Perspectives' (2014) 5 *International Journal of Applied Psychology* 109–114.

27 Malaysian Child Resource Institute, 'Child Right Coalition Malaysia. Status report On Children's Right in Malaysia' http://www.malaysiancare.org/wp-content/uploads /2013/12/2013-CRC-Report-EN_FINAL.pdf (accessed 3 January 2023).

28 AS Md Salleh, 'Paradigm Shift in the Child's Welfare Protection in Malaysia' (2018) *The European Proceedings of Social & Behavioural Sciences* 553–562.

4.1   Definition of a Child

The following analysis of the definition of a child will cover both Acts in place in Malaysia before and after Malaysia's independence. Malaysia obtained its independence in 1957 and the Acts in Table 10.1 which were enacted prior to 1957 are those which came into effect during the colonial period and those after 1957 are the ones enacted post-independence. The analysis will indicate that with the increase in awareness on the importance of a child's rights which emerged via international instruments, the definition of a child has been given critical examination to ensure the protection vital to children is covered under specific and detailed definitions. Table 10.1 gives the definitions for the word 'child' as indicated in UNCRC as well as the laws in Malaysia.

Table 10.1 shows that under Article 1 of the UNCRC, 'a child' is defined as a person aged below 18 years unless under the law applicable to the child, majority is attained earlier. It must be noted that the UNCRC does not mention much about the rights of illegitimate children. Article 2 of the Convention specifically states that all 'children shall not experience any form or type of discrimination irrespective of the child's or his or her parent's or legal guardian's race, ethnicity, hair colour, language spoken, disability, birth or other status and that the state authority shall take precautions and preventions to ensure that the children will not be discriminated in whatsoever ways or form of discrimination mentioned earlier.' This can be taken to include the illegitimate children as the phrase 'irrespective of the child … birth' captures this group of children. Further, Article 37 of the Convention states that 'No child is entitled to any form of inhuman or degrading treatment and that all children should be treated humanely with respect like any other human being serve to be.' Paragraph (c) particularly mentions that 'Every child shall not be separated from its own parents unless it is considered as the child's best interest.' This can be taken to incorporate a situation where an illegitimate child is involved as the phrase 'No child', 'All children' and 'Every child' does not show any discrimination between legitimate and illegitimate children. Thus, the UNCRC ensures that children are protected against any form of discrimination in reference to their legal human rights by the responsible authority of a nation that rectifies the convention.[29]

In comparison, Section 112 of the Malaysian Evidence Act 1950 does not define child using direct term but rather defines who is a legitimate child. It is important to take note of two key terms used in the said section. Firstly, it

---

29   UA Ahmed, MA Aktar, and M M Alam, 'Ensuring Child Rights for a Just Society' in WL Filho, AM Azul, L Brandli, AL Salvia, PG Özuyar and T Wall (eds.) *Peace, Justice and Strong Institutions* (Springer International Publishing, 2021) 1–12.

TABLE 10.1   Analysis of Malaysian laws on children's rights in reference to UNCRC 1995 (Definition)

UNCRC 1995	Malaysian laws
Article 1 For the purposes of the present Convention, a child means every human being below the age of eighteen years unless under the law applicable to the child, majority is attained earlier.	**The Evidence Act 1950** S.112: The fact that any person was born during the continuance of a valid marriage between his mother and any man, or within two hundred and eighty days after its dissolution, the mother remaining unmarried, shall be conclusive proof that he is the legitimate son of that man, unless it can be shown that the parties to the marriage had no access to each other at any time when he could have been begotten. **Adoption Act 1952** S.2: "child" means an unmarried person under the age of twenty-one and includes a female under that age who has been divorced. **Legitimacy Act 1961** S.2(1) In this Act, unless the context otherwise requires-- "date of legitimation" means the date of the marriage leading to the legitimation or, where the marriage occurred before the prescribed date, the prescribed date. **Law Reform (Marriage and Divorce) Act 1976** S.2: "child of the marriage" means a child of both parties to the marriage in question or a child of one party to the marriage accepted as one of the family by the other party; and "child" in this context includes an illegitimate child of, and a child adopted by, either of the parties to the marriage in pursuance of an adoption order made under any written law relating to adoption. S.87: In this Part, wherever the context so requires, "child" has the meaning of "child of the marriage" as defined in section 2 who is under the age of eighteen years. **Child Act 2001** S.2 "child"— (a) means a person under the age of eighteen years; and (b) in relation to criminal proceedings, means a person who has attained the age of criminal responsibility as prescribed in section 8of the penal Code [Act 574].

discusses legitimacy of the child using the fixed time of birth as a determinant point for legitimacy, "If the child is born during the continuance of a valid marriage or if a child is born within 248 days after its dissolution with the mother remaining unmarried, the child is considered to be legitimate". The analysis of the definition of child and specifically illegitimate child shows proof that there is specific mention on the issue illegitimacy of a child in the Act as indicated in S.112. According to Paul,[30] the presumption of the legitimacy in Malaysia has its origin from the common law and is codified in this Act. As indicated, the Section gives clear indication that a child who is born during a marriage is 'conclusive proof' of legitimacy, unless it can be proven that the parties to the marriage had no access to each other at any time the child could have been conceived. In the case of Vhima v. Dhulappa,[31] it was held that this presumption is based on the principle that when a marriage is proven to exist, then its continuance must prima facie be presumed.[32] Secondly, the use of the phrase 'legitimate son' in Section 112 of the Malaysian Evidence Act 1950 denotes a patriarchal approach and this in itself calls for an amendment of the section.

The Adoption Act 1952 and the Registration of Adoption Act 1952[33] are two other legislations in Malaysia that also discuss issues related to protecting children's rights. Under the Adoption Act 1952, 'adopted child' is defined as a child who has been authorized by the court who has been adopted or re-adopted while 'child' is defined as 'unmarried person' under the age of 21 and includes a female under that age who has been divorced. Section 9 illustrates in a comprehensive manner the implication of the adoption order to include rights to inheritance similar to a child born in a lawful wedlock. With regards to illegitimate children, the term illegitimate is found under section 2, Interpretation section where it defines 'father' in relation to an illegitimate child as the natural father. It is crucial to note here that section 31 of the Act clearly indicates that the Act shall not apply to Muslims. The Registration of Adoption Act 1952, on the other hand, applies to both Muslims and non-Muslims. Section 6(1) is of crucial importance as it deals with the registration of de facto adoptions. Although the Act does not define the term 'child', S.10 (2) clearly

---

30   A Paul, *Evidence: Practice and Procedure*, 4th ed. (Lexis Nexis, 2010).
31   *Bhima v. Dhulappa* [1904] 7 Bom LR 95.
32   MA Lomte and SR Katari, 'A Critical Analysis of Legal Presumption of Legitimacy of Child under Section 112 of Indian Evidence Act, 1872' (2017) 3 *International Journal of Law* 50–52.
33   A key difference between the Adoption Act and the Registration of Adoption Act is seen in its application. The former is applicable to non-Muslims only while the latter caters for adoption by Muslims (although its application is not restricted to Muslims alone).

sets the conditions of adoption that can be registered.[34] The term 'illegitimate' is also incorporated in Section 2(b) but only in relation to the person who can adopt such a child.

The difference between the Adoption Act 1952 and the Registration of Adoption Act 1952 was encapsulated in the Federal Court's decision in *Sean O'Casey Petterson v. Chan Hoong Poh & Anor.*[35] For the purpose of this research, the differences between the Acts as indicated in the case are crucial for the first Act extinguishes all rights, duties, obligations and liabilities of the parents and guardians in relation to future custody, maintenance and education of the child but this is not so in the second Act. Furthermore, a child adopted under the Registration of the Adoption Act does not have rights to inherit any property of the adoptive parents should they die intestate. Thus, this means the legal rights of the biological parents remain as conferred by law concluding that this Act only gives custodial rights. This is an important point for the rights of the child are perceived differently under the two Acts. More importantly, the Registration of the Adoption Act retains the syariah law practices that there is no lineage between the illegitimate child and the biological father.

Unlike the Evidence Act 1950, it is generally held that the definition of a child under Adoption Act 1952 is clearer for Section 87 defines 'child of marriage' under Section 2 as referring to a child under the age of 18 years. This is similar to the definition of child under UNCRC which denotes that a child is one who is below the age of 18. The Adoption Act 1952 was amended in 2001 via Act A1098. The amendments include a new section identified as Section 25A. There are key changes under this section, specifically section 25(2)(b) which stipulates that the Registrar-General should not state the word 'adopted', 'adopter' or 'adoptive' or any word to like effect in the birth certificate. It went on to stipulate that the natural or adoptive parent/parents should surrender to the Registrar-General the original certificate of birth and be issued a new

---

34   See S.10(2) of the Registration of The Adoption Act 1952 to have a better understanding about the types of adoption that can be registered.

35   In *Sean O'Casey Petterson v. Chan Hoong Poh & Anor* [2011] 3 CLJ 722. The appellant (an American citizen) and the first respondent lived together in Las Vegas and as a result she had given birth to a child. They separated but the appellant later discovered that the child's original birth certificate contained someone else's name as the father and the child was adopted by a Muslim couple under the Registration of Adoption Act 1952. A DNA profiling test confirmed that the appellant was the biological father. James Foong FCJ dismissing the appeal, said that it is necessary to appreciate the difference. The Court asserted that the Adoption Act is referred to as a Court Adoption where the order is made through a Court process and considered adoptions de jure (as matter of law) whilst the Registration of The Adoption Act 1952 caters for de facto adoptions as matter of fact.

birth certificate.[36] According to Raymond Ma and Chloe Lim Yen Hwa,[37] this amendment which calls for a new birth certificate to be issued creates the notion that the child is a child born to the applicant in a lawful wedlock. This is a positive change for it removes the stigma attached to an illegitimate child.

Similarly, the Legitimacy Act 1961 also does not define 'child' but rather provides information on 'the date of the child's legitimacy'. This Act defines a legitimated person as one being legitimated by this statute and the other statutes such as the Legitimacy Enactment of the Federated Malay States, the Legitimacy Enactment of the State of Johor, and the Legitimacy Ordinance of the Straits Settlements.[38] Under this Act, there are two ways by which a child can be legitimated that is if the biological parents marry subsequently or through an application of legitimacy.

The Law Reform (Mariage and Divorce) Act 1976 must be commended because it gives more details with regards to who is 'a child of marriage'. Section 2 asserts that "child of the marriage means a child of both parties to the marriage in question or a child of one party to the marriage accepted as one of the family by the other party; and 'child' in this context includes an illegitimate child of, and a child adopted by, either of the parties to the marriage in pursuance of an adoption order made under any written law relating to adoption". It can be concluded that with the increase in issues related to children, it is crucial for an amendment to the laws in place to ensure a clear definition of 'child' is provided.

The Child Act 2001 is the first and foremost Act that was enacted after Malaysia ratified the UNCRC specifically addressing matters related to children in Malaysia. Under Section 2, a child is defined as a person below the age of 18 years old. This is in line with the Age of Majority Act 1971. However, it must be noted a different definition is denoted if a case is heard under a criminal proceeding. This is highlighted by Noor Aziah Mohd Awal[39] who asserted that the definition of child under the Child Act 2001 in relation to criminal proceedings means a person who has attained the age of criminal responsibility as prescribed in Section 82 of the Penal Code.

---

36   S.25(2) Adoption Act (Amendment) 2001.
37   R Mah and CLY Hwa, *Citizenship for Adopted Children – A Malaysian Perspective*, paper presented at the 24th LAWASIA Conference held in Seoul, South Korea, on 9–12 October 2011, http://www.mahwengkwai.com/citizenship-for-adopted-children-a-malaysian-perspective/ (accessed 3 January 2023).
38   S. 2(1) Legitimacy Act 1961.
39   *Ibid.*, 22.

4.2   *Protective Measures towards Children*

The foregoing section discussed the definition of the term 'child' in UNCRC as well as in the Malaysian laws applicable to children. This section analyses the provisions in the Malaysian laws in reference to children's rights with close comparison with those in UNCRC. Table 10.2 indicates the key sections that provide protective measure towards children.

TABLE 10.2   Analysis of Malaysian laws on children's rights in reference to the UNCRC 1995 (Protection)

UNCRC 1995	Malaysian laws
Article 2 1. States Parties shall respect and ensure the rights set forth in the present Convention to each child within their jurisdiction without discrimination of any kind, irrespective of the child's or his or her parent's or legal guardian's race, colour, sex, language, religion, political or other opinion, national, ethnic or social origin, property, disability, birth or other status. 2. States Parties shall take all appropriate measures to ensure that the child is protected against all forms of discrimination or punishment on the basis of the status, activities, expressed opinions, or beliefs of the child's parents, legal guardians, or family members **Article 3** 1. In all actions concerning children, whether undertaken by public or private social welfare institutions, courts of law, administrative authorities or legislative bodies, the best interests of the child shall be a primary consideration. 2. States Parties undertake to ensure the child such protection and care as is necessary for his or her well-being, taking into account	**Married Women and Children Maintenance Act (MWCMA) 1950** S.3(2) If any person neglects or refuses to maintain an illegitimate child of his which is unable to maintain itself, a court, upon due proof thereof, may order such person to make such monthly allowance, as to the court seems reasonable **Adoption Act 1952** S. 9(1) Upon an adoption order being made, all rights, duties, obligations and liabilities of the parent, guardian of the adopted child, in relation to the future custody, maintenance and education of the adopted child, including all rights to appoint a guardian or to consent or give notice of dissent to marriage shall be extinguished, and all such rights, duties, obligations and liabilities shall vest in and be exercisable by and enforceable against the adopter as though the adopted child was a child born to the adopter in lawful wedlock:

(cont.)

TABLE 10.2   Analysis of Malaysian Laws on Children's Rights in Reference to the UNCRC 1995
             (Protection) (*cont.*)

UNCRC 1995	Malaysian laws
the rights and duties of his or her parents, legal guardians, or other individuals legally responsible for him or her, and, to this end, shall take all appropriate legislative and administrative measures.	Provided that, in any case where two spouses are the adopters, such spouses shall in respect of the matters provided in this subsection and for the purpose of the jurisdiction of any Court to make orders as to the custody and maintenance of and right of access to children stand to each other and to the adopted child in the same relation as they would have stood if they had been the lawful father and mother of the adopted child, and the adopted child shall stand to them respectively to a lawful father and mother, respectively.
Article 5 States Parties shall respect the responsibilities, rights and duties of parents or, where applicable, the members of the extended family or community as provided for by local custom, legal guardians or other persons legally responsible for the child, to provide, in a manner consistent with the evolving capacities of the child, appropriate direction and guidance in the exercise by the child of the rights recognized in the present Convention.	
Article 7	S.9(2) Where, at any time after the making of an adoption order, the adopter or the adopted child or any other person dies intestate in respect of any movable or immovable property, that property shall devolve in all respects as if the adopted child were the child of the adopter born in lawful wedlock and were not the child of any other person.
1. The child shall be registered immediately after birth and shall have the right from birth to a name, the right to acquire a nationality and. as far as possible, the right to know and be cared for by his or her parents.	
2. States Parties shall ensure the implementation of these rights in accordance with their national law and their obligations under the relevant international instruments in this field, in particular where the child would otherwise be stateless.	S.9(3) In any disposition of movable or immovable property made, whether by instrument *inter vivos* or by will (including codicil), after the date of an adoption order—
	(*a*) any reference (whether express or implied) to the child or children of the adopter shall, unless the contrary intention appears, be construed as, or as including, a reference to the adopted child;

(*cont.*)

TABLE 10.2 Analysis of Malaysian Laws on Children's Rights in Reference to the UNCRC 1995 (Protection) (*cont.*)

UNCRC 1995	Malaysian laws
Article 8 1. States Parties undertake to respect the right of the child to preserve his or her identity, including nationality, name and family relations as recognized by law without unlawful interference. 2. Where a child is illegally deprived of some or all of the elements of his or her identity, States Parties shall provide appropriate assistance and protection, with a view to re-establishing speedily his or her identity. **Article 16** 1. No child shall be subjected to arbitrary or unlawful interference with his or her privacy, family, home or correspondence, nor to unlawful attacks on his or her honour and reputation. 2. The child has the right to the protection of the law against such interference or attacks.	(*b*) any reference (whether express or implied) to the child or children of the adopted child's natural parents or either of them shall, unless the contrary intention appears, be construed as not being, or as not including, a reference to the adopted child; and (*c*) any reference (whether express or implied) to a person related to the adopted child in any degree shall, unless the contrary intention appears, be construed as a reference to the person who would be related to him in that degree if he were the child of the adopter born in lawful wedlock and were not the child of any other person. S.9 (4) Where an adopted child or the spouse or issue of an adopted child takes any interest in any movable or immovable property under any disposition, whether by instrument *inter vivos* or by will (including codicil), or under any intestacy, or where an adopter takes any interest in any movable or immovable property under any disposition as provided in this section by an adopted child or by the spouse or issue of an adopted child, or under the intestacy of an adopted child or of the spouse or issue of an adopted child, any estate or other duty which becomes leviable in respect of it shall be payable at the same rate as if the adopted child had been a child of the adopter born in lawful wedlock.

(*cont.*)

TABLE 10.2   Analysis of Malaysian Laws on Children's Rights in Reference to the UNCRC 1995
               (Protection) (*cont.*)

UNCRC 1995	Malaysian laws
	S.9(5) Notwithstanding anything in this section, trustees or personal representatives may convey or distribute any movable or immovable property to or among the persons entitled to it without having ascertained that no adoption order has been made under which any person is or may be entitled to any interest in it, and shall not be liable to any such person of whose claim they have not had notice at the time of the conveyance or distribution; but nothing in this subsection shall prejudice the right of any such person to follow the property, or any property representing it, into the hands of any person, other than a purchaser, who may have received it.
	S.9(6) Where an adoption order is made in respect of a person who has been previously adopted, the previous adoption shall be disregarded for the purposes of this section in relation to the devolution of any property on the death of a person dying intestate after the date of the subsequent adoption order and in relation to any disposition of property made after that date.
	Registration of Adoption Act 1952
	S. 6(1) Where at the date when application for registration is made any child under the age of eighteen years who has never been married is in the custody of, and is being brought up, maintained and educated by any person, or by two spouses jointly, as his, her or their own child under any *de facto* adoption, and has for a period

(*cont.*)

TABLE 10.2 Analysis of Malaysian Laws on Children's Rights in Reference to the UNCRC 1995 (Protection) (*cont.*)

UNCRC 1995	Malaysian laws
	of not less than two years continuously and immediately before the date of such application been in such custody and has been so brought up, maintained and educated, the Registrar may, upon the application, in the form in the First Schedule, of such person or spouses, register the adoption if—

(*a*) such person or spouses and the child shall appear before the Registrar and shall produce to the Registrar such evidence either oral or documentary as may satisfy the Registrar that such adoption took place;

(*b*) the parents or one of the parents, or, if both the parents are dead or if neither of the parents is within Peninsular Malaysia, any guardian of the child shall appear before the Registrar and express consent to the adoption:
Provided that if the Registrar is satisfied that in all the circumstances of the case it is just and equitable and for the welfare of the child he may dispense with the consent of any parent or custodian of the child or with the appearance of any parent or custodian who shall have signified his consent by statutory declaration; and

(*c*) the prescribed fees are paid.
S. 10(2) The Registrar shall not register any adoption unless the person applying for registration, or in the case of an application by two spouses, one of the spouses —

(*cont.*)

TABLE 10.2   Analysis of Malaysian Laws on Children's Rights in Reference to the UNCRC 1995
               (Protection) (cont.)

UNCRC 1995	Malaysian laws
	(a) has attained the age of twenty-five years and is at least eighteen years older than the child in respect of whom the application is made;
	(b) has attained the age of twenty-one years and is a brother, sister, uncle or aunt, whether by consanguinity or affinity, of the child, or, if the child is illegitimate, a person who would be so related if the child were legitimate; or
	(c) is the mother or father of the child.
	Guardianship of Infant Act (GIA) 1961 S.3 The guardian of the person of an infant shall have the custody of the infant, and shall be responsible for his support, health and education.
	S.4 Subject to the rights and powers of any trustee or personal representative in whom an infant's property is vested, a guardian of the property of an infant shall have the control and management of the infant's property, and shall deal therewith as carefully as a man of ordinary prudence would deal with his own property, and may, subject to this Act, do all acts which are reasonable and proper for the realization or protection of the infant's property.
	S.5 (1) In relation to the custody or upbringing of an infant or the administration of any property belonging to or held in trust for an infant or the application of the income of any such

(cont.)

TABLE 10.2   Analysis of Malaysian Laws on Children's Rights in Reference to the UNCRC 1995
             (Protection) *(cont.)*

UNCRC 1995	Malaysian laws
	property, a mother shall have the same rights and authority as the law allows to a father, and the rights and authority of mother and father shall be equal. (2) The mother of an infant shall have the like powers of applying to the Court in respect of any matter affecting the infant as are possessed by the father. S.6 On the death of a parent of an infant, the surviving parent, if any, shall, subject to this Act, be guardian to the infant either alone or jointly with any guardian appointed by the deceased parent, and— (a) if no guardian has been appointed by the deceased parent; or (b) in the event of the death or refusal to act of the guardian or guardians appointed by the deceased parent, the Court may, if it thinks fit, appoint a guardian to act jointly with the surviving parent. S.7 (1) A parent of an infant may by deed or will appoint any person to be guardian of the infant after that parent's death. (2) Any guardian appointed under subsection (1) shall act jointly with the surviving parent, if any, but if— (a) the surviving parent objects to the guardian so acting; or (b) the guardian considers that the surviving parent is unfit to have the custody of the infant,

(cont.)

TABLE 10.2   Analysis of Malaysian Laws on Children's Rights in Reference to the UNCRC 1995
                (Protection) (*cont.*)

UNCRC 1995	Malaysian laws
	the guardian may apply to the Court and the Court may—
	(aa) refuse to make any order (in which case the surviving parent shall remain the sole guardian of the infant);
	(bb) make an order that the guardian shall act jointly with the surviving parent; or
	(cc) make an order that the guardian shall be the sole guardian of the infant.
	(3) If the Court makes an order under paragraph (2)(cc), the Court may make—
	(a) such order regarding the custody of the infant and the right of access of the surviving parent to the infant as, having regard to the welfare of the infant, the Court thinks fit; and
	(b) an order requiring the surviving parent to pay to the guardian such periodical sums towards the maintenance or education of the infant as the Court may consider reasonable having regard to the means of that surviving parent.
	(4) If guardians are appointed by deed or will by both parents of an infant, the guardians so appointed shall, after the death of the surviving parent, act jointly.

(*cont.*)

TABLE 10.2   Analysis of Malaysian Laws on Children's Rights in Reference to the UNCRC 1995
(Protection) (*cont.*)

UNCRC 1995	Malaysian laws
	(5) A guardian appointed by the Court under section 6 to act jointly with the surviving parent shall continue to act as guardian after the death of the surviving parent, but if the surviving parent has appointed a guardian, the guardian appointed by the Court shall act jointly with the guardian appointed by the surviving parent.
	S.9 The Court or a Judge may, in appointing any guardian of an infant's property, by order define, restrict, or extend the power and authority of the guardian in relation thereto, to such extent as is necessary for the welfare of the infant.
	S.11 The Court or a Judge, in exercising the powers conferred by this Act, shall have regard primarily to the welfare of the infant and shall, where the infant has a parent or parents, consider the wishes of such parent or both of them, as the case may be.
	Legitimacy Act 1961 (Revised 1971) S.3 Nothing in this Act shall operate to legitimate a person unless the marriage leading to the legitimation was solemnized and registered in accordance with-- (a) the Civil Marriage Ordinance 1952 [Ord. No. 44 of 1952]*, or the Christian Marriage Ordinance 1956 [Ord. No. 33 of 1956]*;

(*cont.*)

TABLE 10.2   Analysis of Malaysian Laws on Children's Rights in Reference to the UNCRC 1995
             (Protection) (*Cont.*)

UNCRC 1995	Malaysian laws
	(b) the Christian Marriage Ordinance [Cap. 24]* or the Marriage Ordinance 1959 [Ord. No. 14 of 1959] *, of Sabah; or (c) the Church and Civil Marriage Ordinance [Cap. 92]* of Sarawak, or any Enactment or Ordinance repealed by any of the said Ordinances. S.4 Subject to section 3, where the parents of an illegitimate person marry or have married one another, whether before or after the prescribed date, the marriage shall, if the father of the illegitimate person was or is at the date of the marriage domiciled in Malaysia, render that person, if living, legitimate from the prescribed date or from the date of the marriage, whichever is the later. S.5 (1) A person claiming that he or his parent or any remoter ancestor became or has become a legitimated person may, whether domiciled in Malaysia or elsewhere, apply by petition to the High Court praying the Court for a decree declaring that the petitioner is the legitimate child of his parents, or that his parent or remoter ancestor was legitimate; and the High Court shall have jurisdiction to hear and determine the application and to make a decree declaratory of the legitimacy or illegitimacy of that person as to the Court may seem just; and that decree shall be binding to all intents and purposes on all persons whomsoever.

(*cont.*)

TABLE 10.2   Analysis of Malaysian Laws on Children's Rights in Reference to the UNCRC 1995 (Protection) (*Cont.*)

UNCRC 1995	Malaysian laws
	S.6 (1) Subject to this Act, a legitimated person and his spouse, children or more remote issue shall be entitled to take any interest-- (a) in the estate of an intestate dying after the date of legitimation; (b) under any disposition coming into operation after the date of legitimation, in like manner as if the legitimated person had been born legitimate. S.7 Where a legitimated person or a child or remoter issue of a legitimated person dies intestate in respect of any of his property the same persons shall be entitled to take the same interests therein as they would have been entitled to take if the legitimated person had been born legitimate. S.9 A legitimated person shall have the same rights and be under the same obligations in respect of the maintenance and support of himself or of any other person as if he had been born legitimate, and subject to this Act the provisions of any written law relating to claims for damages, compensation, allowance, benefit or otherwise by or in respect of a legitimate child shall apply in like manner in the case of a legitimated person.

(*cont.*)

TABLE 10.2   Analysis of Malaysian Laws on Children's Rights in Reference to the UNCRC 1995
(Protection) (*Cont.*)

UNCRC 1995	Malaysian laws
	S.11 (1) Where, on or after the prescribed date, the mother of an illegitimate child, the child not being a legitimated person, dies intestate as respects all or any of her property, and does not leave any legitimate issue surviving her, the illegitimate child, or if he is dead his issue, shall be entitled to take any interest therein to which he or his issue would have been entitled if he had been born legitimate.
	(2) Where, on or after the prescribed date, an illegitimate child, not being a legitimated person, dies intestate as respects all or any of his property, his mother, if surviving, shall be entitled to take any interest therein to which she would have been entitled if the child had been born legitimate and she had been the only surviving parent.
	Child Act 2001 3. (1) there shall be established a Council which shall be known as the "Co-ordinating Council for the protection of Children"
	6. (1) the Council may establish such committees as it deems necessary or expedient to assist it in the performance of its functions under this act.
	7. (1) the Council shall establish throughout Malaysia groups of persons, each group to be known as a "Child protection team", for the purpose of coordinating locally based

(cont.)

TABLE 10.2   Analysis of Malaysian Laws on Children's Rights in Reference to the UNCRC 1995
             (Protection) (Cont.)

UNCRC 1995	Malaysian laws
	services to families and children if children are or are suspected of being in need of protection.
	15. (1) notwithstanding any written law to the contrary, any mass media report regarding— (a) any step taken against a child concerned or purportedly concerned in any criminal act or omission, be it at the pre-trial, trial or post-trial stage; (b) any child in respect of whom custody is taken under part v; (c) any child in respect of whom any of the offences specified in the first schedule has been or is suspected to have been committed; or (d) any proceedings under part vi, shall not reveal the name, address or educational institution, or include any particulars calculated to lead to the identification of any child so concerned either as being the person against or in respect of whom action is taken or as being a witness to the action.
	17. (1) a child is in need of care and protection under the situation listed in (a) until (k).

4.2.1   UN Convention on the Rights of the Child

Table 10.2 discusses the findings from the analysis carried out on the Malaysian laws on children's rights in reference to UNCRC 1995 in terms of the protection provided. Under Article 2 UNCRC, there is a requirement for state parties to respect and ensure that they adhere to the rights set forth in the convention for every child without discrimination in the form of race, colour, sex, language, religion, political or other opinion, national, ethnic, or social origin, property, disability, birth or other status by taking appropriate measures. Article 3 stipulates that any action taken concerning children must ensure that primary consideration is given to uphold the best interest of the children. Article 5 enforces states parties to give due respect to the responsibilities, rights and duties of parents and other stakeholders by giving appropriate direction and guidance according to the rights upheld in the convention. Article 7 provides the rights to a name, nationality and the rights to know and be cared for by his or her parents from the time of birth. These rights are implemented in accordance to their national laws as well as their obligations under the relevant international instrument. Article 8 prohibits parties from depriving the rights of the child in terms of identity, nationality, name and family relation which are recognised by law and if these deprivations are done illegally, state parties should provide assistance to re-establish these rights. Article 16 of the UNCRC protects child's right of privacy, honour and reputation.

4.2.2   Child Protection under Malaysian Federal Law

After ratifying the UNCRC, Malaysia enacted a special national law, the Child Act 2001, to reflect the protection provided under the UNCRC. However, it is crucial to note that Malaysia on its own initiative even before the existence of UNCRC had enacted laws to protect children's rights which are reflected in UNCRC. One such Act is the MWCMA 1950. Under section 3(2) of the Act, the court is given the power to order a person who neglects to maintain an illegitimate child to fulfil his obligations. This provision is commendable for it is an indication that the Act does not only protect legitimate children [section 3(1)] but also illegitimate children. According to Mazlina Mahali and others,[40] the word 'proof' under the provision[41] certainly allows the court to accept all relevant and reliable evidence such as DNA and blood tests to be admitted by the court to determine the father of a child born out of wedlock. However, this provision contravenes with the married man's ability to rebut the presumption of illegitimacy under the Evidence Act 1950. This too has created an inconsistency in the law. The term 'conclusive proof' in S.112 of the Evidence Act 1950 bars the admissibility of the DNA test. However, there are cases where it has been admitted, such as *Alesiah Junil & Chua Kin Han v. Julas Joenol*[42] and

---

40   M Mahali, R Rajamanickam and AC Ngah, 'Who's Your Daddy? The Legal Issues on Presumption of Legitimacy in Malaysia' (2016) 11 *The Social Sciences* 7300–7304.
41   S.3(2) If any person neglects or refuses to maintain an illegitimate child of his which is unable to maintain itself, a court, upon due proof thereof, may order such person to make such monthly allowance, as to the court seems reasonable.
42   *Alesiah Junil & Chua Kin Han v. Julas Joenol* [2013] I LNS 1213.

Chua Kim Suan v. Ang Mek Chong.[43] Here Mazlina and others[44] claims that the judges had misinterpreted S.112. They quoted Aitkin J in *Ainan bin Mahmud v Syed Abu Bakar bin Habib Yusoff & Ors*[45] stating that the only rebuttable fact that can be admitted is evidence of non-intercourse. The cases cited show that there is inconsistency in the law.

Another Act that provides extensive protection of children's rights is the Adoption Act 1952. The most significant section of the Act is section 9. Section 9(1), (2), (3), (4), (5) and (6) have been drafted using specific phrases that indicate protection of children's rights from discrimination especially 'birth' which is similar to article 2(1) of the UNCRC. Since the Adoption Act caters specifically for the adopted child, section 9(1) to (6) uses the phrase 'as though the adopted child was a child born to the adopter in lawful wedlock' to indicate that the child has all the rights that 'a child of lawful wedlock has'. This clearly strengthen protection against discrimination of 'birth'. The Registration of Adoption Act 1952 extends the protection provided under the Adoption Act 1952 by listing the obligations and responsibilities of the Registrar in ensuring the process of adoption is carried out properly for it to be just and equitable.

The Guardianship of Infant Act 1961 also provides protection for children's rights, but this Act is specifically enacted to cater to the special needs of an infant. In doing all these, the Act clearly imposes a strict condition that the court or the judge must have regard 'primarily to the welfare of the infant' in exercising the powers conferred under the Act (section 11). Besides the Legitimacy Act 1961, the Guardianship of Infant Act (GIA) 1961 also gives some form of protection for illegitimate children. According to Mimi Kamariah,[46] there is a distinction shown between the term 'guardianship' and 'custody'. A parent who is appointed as a guardian has powers over a child's upbringing, care, discipline and religion while 'custody' refers to the state of having certain rights over the child, such as care and control.[47] One parent might get the right to the custody while the other one might not and just be granted the right to care and control.[48] This has caused a lot of controversies where courts had to intervene to establish the rights being contested as seen in the case of *Dipper v. Dipper.*[49]

Section 3 of the Act stipulates that the guardian of the infant has custody and is responsible for his/her support, health and education. According to

43   *Chua Kim Suan v. Ang Mek Chong* [1988] 3 MLJ 231.

44   *Ibid.*, 37.

45   *Ainan bin Mahmud v Syed Abu Bakar bin Habib Yusoff & Ors* [1939] MLJ 209.

46   MK Majid, *Family Law in Malaysia* (Malayan Law Journal Sdn Bhd, 1999).

47   *Ibid.*

48   S.3 and S.5 of the Guardianship and Infant Act 1961.

49   *Dipper v. Dipper* [1980] 2 ALL ER 22.

Mimi Kamariah,[50] this indicates that the guardian is also the custodian of the infant and she interprets section 5 which allows the court to give the custody to another person as only occurring in exceptional situation. Section 4 states the duty of a guardian of the property of the infant while section 6 discusses the situation where the mother of the infant becomes the guardian of the infant and his property if the infant has no living father.

With regards to the issue on whether the GIA 1961 applies to illegitimate children, Jeffrey Tan J stated in his judgment in the case of *Sinnakaruppi a/p Periakaruppan v Bathumalai a/l Krishnan*[51] that the GIA does not apply to illegitimate children. In this case, the plaintiff, who was the natural mother of an illegitimate infant, applied to the court for a declaration that she was the lawful guardian and was therefore entitled to the custody and care of her child. However, the court decided she should seek custody by way of wardship proceeding. On the same issue, Raja Azlan Shah J observed that 'the Guardian-ship of Infant Act 1961 does not seem to provide for illegitimate children'.[52] He justified his observation by highlighting on the absence of any reference to illegitimate children except for in Section 1(2)(a). His decision followed the approach taken by Viscount Simonds in the English case *Galloway v Galloway*.[53] This decision was confirmed in T v O[54] where the court agreed to the case of *Re Balasingam v Paravathy* to the extent that the natural mother of an illegitimate child is the person in whom the parental rights and duties will be vested exclusively in the absence of any court order. Furthermore, in the case of *Tam Ley Chian v Seah Heng Lye*,[55] the court did not heed to the decision in *Re Balasingam v Paravathy* and concurred that Section 24 of the Courts Judicature Act 1964 confers the High Court with jurisdiction to appoint and control guardians of infants including illegitimate infants.

Due to the issue in the GIA 1961, the Guardianship of Infant (Amendment) Act 1999 was passed. The amendment shows some key distinguishing elements. One such change is noted in Section 5 which gives equal rights and authority to both the mother and the father in reference to the custody or upbringing of an infant or the administration of any property belonging to or held in trust for an infant or the application of the income of any such property.[56] This change is welcomed. However, the term 'right to the custody or upbringing' can create issues when it comes to the religion as seen in cases of inter-faith marriages.

---

50   *Ibid.*, 50.
51   *Sinnakaruppi a/p Periakaruppan v Bathumalai a/l Krishnan* [2001] 6 MLJ 29.
52   *Re Balasingam v Paravathy* [1970] 2 MLJ 74.
53   *Galloway v Galloway* [1955] 3 ALL ELR 429.
54   *T v O* [1993] 1 MLJ 168.
55   *Tam Ley Chian v Seah Heng Lye* [1993] 3 MLJ 696.
56   S.5(1) and S.5(2) Guardianship of Infant (Amendment) Act 1999.

This conflict was discussed in the case of Dr M Jeyaganesh (alias Muhammad Ridzwan Mogarajah)[57] where the High Court has given joint legal custody of the two boys to Muslim convert Dr M Jeyaganesh (alias Muhammad Ridzwan Mogarajah) and his Hindu wife, S. Shamala in accordance with Section 5 of the Guardianship and Infant Act 1961. According to the report in Malaysiakini, the complex issue here is not just about the adjustment of rights between a man and a woman in an estranged matrimonial relationship but also involves the rights of the children as individuals caught in an unhappy situation of adults' infidelity and custody fights.[58]

The Legitimacy Act 1961 (revised 1971) also shows Malaysia's efforts towards protecting children's rights through its extensive and clear provisions. However, it has its limitation and shortcoming. Firstly, the Act only applies to non-Muslims and secondly, it only provides protection for a child born in a valid marriage (section 3). The Act also regulates situations where an illegitimate child can become legitimate through subsequent marriage of the parents but emphasises the requirement for certain conditions to prevail. This certainly is in contradiction with the UNCRC which provides protection to all children irrespective of legitimacy. The Legitimacy Act 1961 also provides for protection of the children's interests in relation to property [section 6(1)(a)(b) and section 7] as well as rights of maintenance and support (section 9). In addition to this, the Act also has provisions in regard to what happens to the property when a mother of an illegitimate child dies as well as when an illegitimate child dies (section 11).

An analysis of the Law Reform (Marriage and Divorce) Act (LRA) 1976 clearly shows that this Act does include illegitimate child. Further according to Section 75(7) of the LRA, if the marriage is not solemnized in accordance with the provisions in Section 6, 10, 11, 22(4) and 72, the marriage will be declared as void. The consequences of this are that the children conceived during the period of this invalid marriage will be considered as illegitimate children. In the case of *Tam Lye Chian v Seah Heng Lye*,[59] the marriage was held not to have been solemnized in accordance with the LRA. Both parties bought an action to resolve the dispute as to the rights and custody of their children. The court in this case followed the common law position laid down in the case of *Re K*,[60] where the parental responsibility for an illegitimate child conceived during an

---

57   L Goh, 'Shamala Conversion Case: To the Federal Court' *The Star Online*, 28 April 2009, https://www.thestar.com.my/news/nation/2009/04/28/shamala-conversion-case-to-the -federal-court/ (accessed 3 January 2003).

58   Jeffrey, 'Custody Case: Either Syariah or Civil, Not Both' *Malaysiakini*, 22 July 2004, https:// www.malaysiakini.com/letters/28618 (accessed 3 January 2023).

59   *Ibid.*, 59.

60   *Re K* [1977] 1 WLR 533.

invalid marriage goes to the mother, in accordance to the position on the custody of an illegitimate child.

It is interesting to note that Malaysia, has adequately provided protection for children of various status (infant, legitimate, illegitimate and adopted) long before the UNCRC came into existence.

Despite there being protection provided for under the various Acts discussed, Malaysia, after ratifying the UNCRC (with certain reservations due to non-compatibility with the Constitution, national laws and national policies of the Government of Malaysia, including the Syariah law) had enacted the Child Act 2001 to fulfill its obligation to the UNCRC. Thus, the enactment of Child Act 2001 after Malaysia's ratification of UNCRC is commendable as it has clarified ambiguities and limitations in the previous Act with in-depth details that are clearly in line with the provision of UNCRC where the 'welfare of the child' is given utmost important. As discussed, under this Act, a legitimated person is defined as a person that is being legitimated by this statute and the other statutes such as the Legitimacy Enactment of the Federated Malay States, the Legitimacy Enactment of the State of Johor and the Legitimacy Ordinance of the Straits Settlements.[61] For the legitimation application to be valid by the marriage of biological parents of an illegitimate person, Section 4 of this Act provides that the subsequent marriage shall operate in a condition that the father must be a Malaysian domiciliary at the time of the marriage and that the marriage must be solemnized and registered according to Section 3. Besides that, Section 6 of this statute states that a legitimated person, his spouse and the children shall be entitled to take any interest in the estate and property.

Section 9 of the Act states that a legitimated person shall have the same rights and obligations "as if he had been born legitimate, and subject to this Act the provisions of any written law relating to claims for damages, compensation, allowance, benefit or otherwise by or in respect of a legitimate child shall apply in like manner in the case of a legitimated person". The right of an illegitimate child and his or her mother to succeed in the intestacy of the other is also stated in Section 11. This Section provides that in a situation where the mother of an illegitimate child dies intestate and does not leave any legitimate issues surviving her, the illegitimate child shall be entitled to take any interest in which he or his issue would have been entitled if he had been born legitimate.[62] Hence, it is advisable for the mother of an illegitimate child to make a will for her illegitimate child to ensure that her child is entitled to her property if she does not have any legitimate issues surviving her. Under Legitimacy Act, there are two ways in which legitimacy can be granted:

---

61   S. 2(1) Legitimacy Act 1961.
62   *Ibid.*, 42.

i.   Subsequent marriage of the biological parents[63]
ii.   Application for a declaration of legitimacy[64]

Section 2(1) of this Act provides definitions for key terms used in the Act which include 'legitimated person' and 'intestate'. 'Intestate' is said to include a person who leaves a will but die intestate as to some beneficial interest of his estate. While 'legitimated person' is defined as a person legitimated by this Act or by any of the written laws repealed by this Act.[65] It must be clearly noted that although this Act allows the legitimation of a child through the marriage of the parents, there is a condition imposed as seen in Section 3 where it states that such a legitimation does not enable the person or his spouse, children or remoter issue to take any interest in property except as expressed in the Act. According to Section 5 of the Act, legitimation can also be done by way of declaration of legitimacy where a person claiming that he or his parent or any remoter ancestor became or has become a legitimated person may, whether domiciled in Malaysia or elsewhere, apply by petition to the High Court praying the Court for a decree declaring that the petitioner is the legitimate child of his parents, or that his parent or remoter ancestor was legitimate. The case of *Lau Zhan Chen v Makoto Togase & 2 Ors*[66] clearly distinguishes Section 4 and Section 5(1). In this case, the parents of the illegitimate child did marry after the child was born but they could not legitimise the child due to the father not being domiciled in Malaysia as required under Section 4. Thus, the petitioner applied under Section 5(1) and the high court granted the declaration of legitimacy based on the blood test which showed 99.7% probability of paternity. In terms of rights of a legitimated person in reference to property, Section 6(1) clearly prescribes the conditions where legitimated person has interest in a property:

> Subject to this Act, a legitimated person and his spouse, children or more remoter issue shall be entitled to take any interest:
> a.   in the estate of an intestate dying after the date of legitimation;
> b.   under any disposition coming into operation after the date of legitimation, in like manner as if the legitimated person had been born legitimate.

---

63   S.4 Legitimacy Act 1961 (revised 1971).
64   S.5 Legitimacy Act 1961 (revised 1971).
65   The laws repealed include the Legitimacy Enactment of the Federated Malay States [Cap. 69], the Legitimacy Enactment of the State of Johore [En. 19 of 1936] and the Legitimacy Ordinance of the Straits Settlements [Cap. 85].
66   *Lau Zhan Chen v Makoto Togase & 2 Ors* [1995] 1 CLJ 841.

With regards to priority of interest, Section 6 (2) provides the criteria to be observed.[67] This Act also provides further adequate protection by way of Section 9 where it is stated that a legitimated person has the same rights as if he was born legitimate.

The Child Act was recently amended in 2016 to include provisions on child registry, community service order (cso), a family-based care and heavier penalty but these amendments will not be discussed as the changes do not affect the focus of the research discussion which is on the protection of illegitimate children. Further, all the reservations to the uncrc will not be discussed except for reservation to article 2 and article 7. Under the Child Act 2001, it is clearly shown that the Act does not recognise discrimination related to 'birth' as upheld in article 2 and article 7 of the uncrc. It must be noted that when the Child Act 2001 was enacted, it repealed three other statutes (the Juvenile Courts Act 1947, the Women and Girls Protection Act 1973 and the Child Protection Act 1991) and consolidated the laws relating to the care, protection and rehabilitation of children. The Child Act does not expressly provide for guardianship or custodial rights or loss of such rights, but this can be inferred from certain sections in Part V of the Act.[68] Section 18 provides for the taking of a child in need of care and protection into temporary custody by any Protector or police officer. Section 19 provides that a child who is taken into temporary custody shall be produced before the Court for Children within 24 hours. If there is a condition where the child cannot be brought to the Court within the time specified, a Magistrate may direct the child to be placed in a place of safety or in the care of a fit and proper person until the child can be brought to the court.

Under Section 19, the person in charge of the child shall have control over the child and be responsible for the maintenance of the child. If there is a conflict where the child is claimed by his parent or guardian, the child shall continue to be in the care of the person given responsibility under the section. This means that under this section, there is a temporary loss of guardianship or custodial rights of a parent or guardian over a child who is in need of care and protection. This is because the law takes into consideration the welfare of the child and considers it as a paramount consideration.

---

67   Please read S.6(2) of the Legitimacy Act 1961 (Revised 1971) as to the ranking of rights of the children.

68   S Thambapillay, *Recent Developments in Malaysian Family Law*, Selected Issues in the Development of Malaysian Law, Proceedings of the Inaugural University of Malaya Law Conference, Faculty of Law, University of Malaya, 2008.

The court can make an order to place the child in the custody of a fit and proper person under Section 30(1)(b) for a certain period of time. Section 30(4) provides that the parent or the guardian of the child may still claim the child, thereby suggesting that they have not lost their guardianship or custodial rights over their children under the provision previously mentioned. In the event that no such claim is made, the court may make an order placing the child for adoption by the foster parent or any person who wishes to adopt the child and dispense with the consent of the parent or guardian for the adoption. The Child Act 2001 specifically states that the protection and the rights of children are indeed important to be safeguarded. Although there is no specific provision in the Act that mentions the term 'illegitimate child', it can be understood that the term 'child' as defined in Section 2 comprises both legitimate and illegitimate children. If the lawmakers had wanted to limit this Act to only legitimate children, the term 'legitimate' would have been defined and this is not the case. Thus, the Child Act 2001 can be said to be a movement in the right direction towards creating an umbrella Act under which protection is provided to children immaterial of their birth status. This interpretation can be validated if the phrases "has no parent or guardian" or "the parent or guardian cannot be found" in Section 17(1)(d) and Section 17(1)(e) are analysed. It provides indication that this extensive and comprehensive Act does provide protection for illegitimate children that are marginalised by society.

Further evidence of the comprehensive scope of protection measures inthe Child Act 2001 can be inferred from the establishment of a co-ordinating council for the protection of children [section 3(1)], the establishment of committees necessary or expedient for the functions of the Act [section 6(1)], the establishment of child protection teams [section 7(1)], the restriction on media reporting and publication [section 15(1)] and the clear definition of child in need of care and protection [section 17(1)]. The Act also gives clear indication of the duties, powers and obligations of the various key stakeholders; parent, guardian, other person, probation officer, the courts and the minister.

5   Illegitimacy under Malaysian Syariah Law

Syariah law refers to the Islamic religious law that is in place in Malaysia dealing with matters related to personal law, marriage and divorce as well as other religious matters. The sources of Islamic law come from two main sources, that is, the Al-Quran and the Hadith. The Al-Quran is the words of Allah that has been compiled in a book. Hadith is the compilation of Sunnah which refers to all that is narrated by Prophet Muhammad (PBUH), including his actions and sayings. Syariah law has jurisdiction over all Muslims in Malaysia. In reference to issues of legitimacy, the law says that if a child is born out of wedlock, he/she cannot bear the father's name in the birth certificate. This is because illegitimate children are considered to have no relationship at all with the father and this includes the connection in the family lineage. In Islam, the lineage or 'nasab' is important as one of the five elements listed in the framework of *Maqasid al-Shari`ah* which denotes the goals and objectives of Islamic law.[69] Islam upholds the position of protecting the lineage by making the family unit as the basis of a good and protected society which can only be maintained by upholding the sanctity of marriage. Since the syariah law judges treat illegitimate children in a stringent manner where the illegitimate Muslim children in Malaysia face a harsh reality and negative social stigma from the community, the civil law under specific Acts such as the Adoption Act 1952 and Legitimacy Act 1961 provide procedures for legalising illegitimate children. This causes disparity in the law between the two systems.

Beside this inconsistency in the laws in the dual system, the issue surrounding illegitimate children has triggered further debate at diverse levels of society by the earlier decision of Bin Abdullah's case[70] where the decision shocked the Muslims in Malaysia for it ruled to allow an illegitimate child to have the right to use the biological father's name which undermined the lineage (nasab) which is an important necessity for Muslims. However, the Federal Court[71] held that Section 13A of the Birth and Death Registration Act 1957, which allows a child's surname to be stated in his birth certificate, does not apply to the registration of births of Malay Muslim children. This is because Malays, in reality and by culture and tradition, do not carry a surname. The outcomes of this case are that the words "bin Abdullah (meaning son of a servant of Allah)" must be removed from the child's birth certificate and that the biological father's name must not be inserted as part of the child's name due to the reason stated above. This decision is in line with Article 3(1) of the UN Convention on the Rights of the Child that 'best interests of the child shall be a primary consideration' in all actions taken by courts and administrative authorities concerning children in Malaysia.

In Arabic, the term for illegitimate children is *walad ghayr shar'I* or *walad al-zina* (the child born of wedlock) which is generally used to refer to children who are born out of lawful wedlock. Islam sets out the lineage (*nasab*) as one of

---

69   Z Abd al-Karim, *Al-Wajiz Fi Ushul al-Fiqh* (Maktabahal-Batsair, 1994).
70   *A Child & Ors v Jabatan Pendaftaran Negara & Ors* [2017] 4 MLJ 440 (Court of Appeal).
71   *Jabatan Pendaftaran Negara & Ors v. A Child & Ors (Majlis Agama Islam Negeri Johor, Intervener)* [2020] 4 CLJ.

the important necessities for Muslim to protect.[72] According to Abdul-Rahman al-Sheha,[73] destroying the means for reproduction by any means or tampering with it in any way for no legitimate reason is an unlawful practice according to Islam. His argument is based on the fact that the family unit is the basic structure of the society and thus by protecting the lineage, we are protecting society and maintaining the value and sacred ties of family by the means of marriage. The position of law and rules of Islamic law regarding illegitimate children is portrayed through very clear-cut provisions. This is proven in the case of *Maryam Nurisha bt Othman v Huzairin bin Basir.*[74] In this case, the marriage was solemnized on 22 August 2008 and their daughter was born on 25 September 2008. The plaintiff, who was the mother of the girl, admitted in her statement that the child was conceived before her marriage and that the information was acknowledged by the biological father and hence, it made the girl illegitimate. The court held that the girl was not to be ascribed to the biological father and cannot bear the name of the biological father, who is also her mother's current husband at that time. This case clearly illustrates that Syariah law does not accept children conceived before the marriage as legitimate children of the marriage. Furthermore, during the National Fatwa Committee's meeting,[75] it was collectively decided that an illegitimate child is a child born as a result of an adultery or rape and was not from a doubtful (*syubhah*) intercourse.[76] Illegitimate children also include those children who were born less than 6 months from the date of the parents' sexual intercourse after the proclamation of marriage.

The two legislations in place in Malaysia to deal with issues related to legitimate and illegitimate children under the Syariah are the Islamic Family

---

72   *Ibid.,* 65.

73   AR Al-Sheha (n.d.), *Human Rights in Islam and Common Misconceptions,* Revised Edition, http://hrlibrary.umn.edu/research/Egypt/HumanRightsinI-slam.pdf (accessed 3 January 2023).

74   *Maryam Nurisha bt Othman v Huzairin bin Basir* [2011] 33 JH (2) 227.

75   The administration of Islamic laws in each state empowers them to establish a fatwa committee to assist the Mufti Department in issuing fatwas. All members of the committee, including muftis and deputy muftis, are appointed by the respective sultans and Yang di-Pertuan Agong. Subject to section 51 of the Administration of the Religion of Islam (State of Selangor) Enactment 2003, the Fatwa Committee shall, on the direction of His Royal Highness the Sultan, and may on its own initiative or on the request of any person by letter addressed to the Mufti, prepare fatwa on any unsettled or controversial question of or relating to Hukum Syarak.

76   Muzakarah 64, dated on 27 July 2004.

Law (Federal Territories) Act 1984[77] and the Syariah Criminal Offences Act (Federal Territory) 1997.[78] However, it must be noted that under Syariah law, the State Legislative Assembly is empowered to enact specific laws applicable to their respective state. This is also one of the concerns that surround the issue of legitimacy as there is lack of uniformity on how the law applies to the issue of illegitimacy among Muslims in the different states of Malaysia. The Islamic Family Law (Federal Territories) Act 1984 deals inter alia, with Muslim illegitimate children and also the acknowledgment of paternity with regard to the Muslim children in Malaysia. Some states such as Kelantan, Selangor, Perak, Malacca and Johor have their own Islamic Family Law Enactments and their provisions have already been harmonised with this Act while other states adhere to the provisions in the Islamic Family Law (Federal Territories) Act itself. Section 2 of the Islamic Family Law (Federal Territories) Act 1984 states that 'illegitimate in relation to a child means born out of wedlock but not as a result of syubhah intercourse'. Thus, *nasab* (lineage) is seen as a descendant with a lawful blood relationship. Section 110 provides that when 'a child is born to a woman who is married to a man more than six qamariah months from the date of the marriage or within four qamariah years after dissolution of the marriage either by the death of the man or by divorce, the woman not having remarried, the nasab or paternity of the child is established in the man, but the man, by way of li'an or imprecation can disavow or disclaim the child before the Court'. This is shown in the case of *Norzaini Bt Alias v Mohamad Sharif bin Mohamad Taib*,[79] where the plaintiff - the mother – applied for maintenance for her 13 year old child but the father denied and stated that the child is not his. However, the court held that the child was indeed legitimate, and the father was ordered to pay the child maintenance on the ground that the child was born after ten and a half months from the date of the marriage between the plaintiff and the defendant which clearly indicated that the intercourse had taken place during their marriage.

Further, Section 111 provides that 'where the child is born more than four 'qamariah' years after the dissolution of the marriage either by the death of the man or by divorce, the paternity of the child shall not be established in the man unless he or any of his heirs asserts that the child is his issue'. This

---

77   Islamic Family Law (Federal Territories) Act 1984. Save as is otherwise expressly provided, this Act shall apply to all Muslims living in the Federal Territory and to all Muslims resident in the Federal Territory who are living outside the Federal Territory.

78   Syariah Criminal Offences Act (Federal Territory) 1997. This Act shall apply only to (a) the Federal Territories of Kuala Lumpur, Putrajaya and Labuan; and (b) to persons professing the religion of Islam.

79   *Norzaini Bt Alias v Mohamad Sharif bin Mohamad Taib* [2003] 16 JH (2) 101.

principle is illustrated in the case of *Fatimah bt Abdullah and Anor v Mat Zin bin Kassim*[80] where the court held that a child who was born within one year of the divorce of their parents was legitimate. There was proof to show that the plaintiff and the defendant had sexual intercourse during their marriage period. The child was born more than six months from the date of the intercourse in accordance with the rules. In a case of *Ismail v Kalam*,[81] the court held that a child born four years after the parent's divorce was illegitimate as it exceeded the maximum period of pregnancy provided by the Syariah law and the Islamic provisions in Malaysia.

The Syariah Criminal Offences Act (Federal Territory) 1997,[82] the other legislation related to the issue of illegitimacy deals with criminal offences which occur under the Syariah law. Islamic law does not tolerate adultery and fornication, while pregnancy out of wedlock is an offence under the law.[83] There is indeed a criminal provision which addresses the issue of an adult who gets involved in extramarital relations.[84] Section 23 of this Act provides that it is an offence for any person either man or woman to have sexual intercourse with another person who is not his/her lawful spouse. Thus, a woman who delivers a child as a result of such intercourse faces a risk of prosecution if she tries to prove paternity as she would be indirectly confessing to her illegal act.[85] It is clear under the Syariah law that a child born out of wedlock will not be able to inherit from the father's side.[86] Islamic law is fixed and inflexible as it is derived from a divine source. Thus, it is impossible to say that the rights of illegitimate children in Islam in relation to their father have been denied since such rights do not exist in Islam in the first place.[87] The punishment for this offence is a fine not exceeding five thousand ringgit and/or an imprisonment for a term not exceeding three years or whipping not exceeding six strokes or any combination of the abovementioned punishment.

---

80   *Fatimah bt Abdullah and Anor v Mat Zin bin Kassim* [2001] 14 JH (2) 225.
81   *Ismail v Kalam* [1995] 10 JH 41.
82   Syariah Criminal Offences (Federal Territories) Act 1997 (Act 559).
83   AS Sidahmed, 'Problems in Contemporary Applications of Islamic Criminal Sanctions: The Penalty for Adultery in Relation to Women' (2001) 28 *British Journal of Middle Eastern Studies* 187–204.
84   VS Chowbe *Adultery–A Conceptual and Legal Analysis*. Retrieved from SSRN 1856991 (2011) https://papers.ssrn.com/sol3/papers.cfm?abstract_id=1856991.
85   S.23, Syariah Criminal Offences (Federal Territories) Act 1997.
86   Y Yunanto, 'Recognition of Illegitimate Children in Various Laws in Indonesia' 2 *Diponegoro Law Review* 85–100.
87   K Hashemi, 'Religious Legal Traditions, Muslim States and the Convention on the Rights of the Child: An Essay on the Relevant UN Documentation' in M Baderin (ed.), *International Law and Islamic Law* (Routledge, 2017) 535–568.

For Muslim babies who are born illegitimate, the National Registration Department (NRD) will indicate the status of the information of an illegitimate child as *'tiada maklumat'* (no information) in the column for the name of father. This is if the baby was born from an unwed mother including a baby who was born less than 6 months of the parents' marriage without medical evidence from the hospital to prove that the baby is born premature.[88] As an alternative, the Muslim illegitimate child can be given 'Abdullah' as their father's name.[89] The indication of 'illegitimacy' in the registration document is also practiced in other Islamic countries such as Oman. However, in other Islamic countries such as Egypt, Indonesia, Syria and Iran, there are specific provisions for the recognition of children born out of wedlock that allows paternity search through DNA tests. If this can be proven, the child can take the father's name and the responsibility is to be shared by the father.[90]

Unlike the common law system and civil law, Islam does not permit adoption as a license to legitimise an illegitimate child. This means adoption can be done but the biological or the adoptive father's name cannot be given to the child in the birth certificate. However, the name can be included in the adoption document. This is consistent with the Syariah law that does not recognise an adopted child's rights of inheritance. Although adoption can still be made, the child is denied the name of his biological and his adoptive father as his surname. In addition to that, Islam does not recognise any change to a child's inheritance rights despite the adoption. They cannot inherit and have no rights whatsoever to the property that belongs to their biological father and adoptive parents. These rules of Islamic Inheritance law (*Faraïd*) only apply to Muslims. It must be noted here that the Registration of Adoptions Act 1952 is also silent on the rights of inheritance. Despite this, Muslim adoptive parents can use their discretion to make provisions from their estate as a gift (*hibah*) for their adopted child. This discretion can be viewed as a positive option in regard to illegitimate child's right of inheritance from their biological father and adoptive parents.

In addition to the right of inheritance, there is also a concern on issues related to the marriage of Muslim illegitimate children, especially the girls. The non-biological father cannot be the *wali* (guardian) for their marriage as the

---

88   Sisters in Islam, *Muslim Family Law*, SIS Forum (Malaysia), 2014, https://sistersinislam .org/wp-content/uploads/2019/01/Dear-Editor-layout-30May2014-Final.pdf, 12 (accessed 3 January 2023).

89   Muslim puts 'binti' or 'bin' which means 'the son of' or 'the daughter of' after their children's name and put the child father's name after it.

90   *Ibid.*, 81.

illegitimate child is considered to have no '*asbah* (male relatives on the father's side). When a Muslim bride is solemnized by a *wali hakim* (the appointed guardian to solemnize the wedding as there is no lawful guardian on behalf of the girl), it is considered to be disgraceful. This can cause a stir and disruption when the girl does not even realise that she is an illegitimate child. The possible solution when this incident happens is that the mother should open up and speak to her daughter regarding her status and to inform and leave the decision to her future son-in law whether he is willing to accept the girl despite her illegitimate status. The abovementioned issues regarding the illegitimate status of a child would not be an issue if society understands that these children do not have a choice of being born like this. They are the victims of their parents' conduct and hence, they are innocent and are not supposed to be blamed and suffer the negative consequences.

As a conclusion, it can be said that the analysis of the syariah laws in place in Malaysia clearly shows that Islam does not tolerate adultery, fornication, and pregnancy out of wedlock which are considered offences under the law. As discussed, there are federal criminal provisions specified for adults who get involved in extramarital relationships as seen in the Syariah Criminal Offences Act (Federal Territory) 1997 and the Islamic Family Law (Federal Territories) Act 1984. This indicates that Islam takes lineage as one of the fundamental necessities (*dharuriyat*) that a Muslim should protect. Islam upholds the position of protecting the lineage by making the family unit as the basis of a good and protected society which can only be maintained by upholding the union of marriage. A marriage shall uphold the status of a child as the legitimate status with promise for a better protection and future for the child. Nevertheless, to a certain extent, an illegitimate child's right is still protected under Islamic law as seen in section 80 of Islamic Family Law (Federal Territories) Act 1984 which states that 'if a woman neglects or refuses to maintain her illegitimate child who is unable to maintain himself or herself, other than a child born as a result of rape, the Court, upon due proof thereof, may order the woman to make such monthly allowance as the Court thinks reasonable'.

Many representatives from other religions have critised on how Islam interprets illegitimacy and the way the laws 'appear' to be punishing the mother and the child while the man is not affected in anyway. Beyond the individual criminal responsibility for sexual intercourse outside of wedlock, there is a misconception that the Syariah law is punishing the mother and the child. Instead, it would make the mother the sole provider for the child. From this perspective the law is upholding a concept of recognising women's right by allowing the mother to have all the rights over the child. In view of this persisting controversy, Indonesia through a judgement made by the Constitutional

Court in 2010[91] attempted to prioritise the welfare of the child over the Islamic inflexible grasp of the lineage (nasab) concept. In Islamic Law, maintaining the lineage (nasab) is one of the five objectives of Syariah (Maqashid al Shariaah).[92] Habibi states that following the judgement, Indonesia Ulema Council (the country's religious authority) has introduced what was known as the legal harmonization approach by way of issuing fatwa number 11 of 2012 concerning the position of illegitimate children in Indonesia.[93] He went on to assert that the fatwa provides advice to the authority to sentence a man who commits adultery to pay a living of his illegitimate child and after he dies, provide the child with inheritance.

6   Conclusion

The biggest issue regarding the future of illegitimate children in Malaysia pertains to their social stigma and discrimination. Despite numerous efforts undertaken by the Malaysian Government seen through the enactment of laws with the purpose to protect these children's rights, there is a lacuna in the law as indicated through the analysis of the respective Acts both under civil and syariah legal systems. The gaps in the laws are indicated by the inconsistency in the definitions of the term 'child' and 'legitimate' as well as the discrepancies in the type and level of protection provided for children under these Acts within the dual system. The findings from the document analysis and past literature clearly point to the need for more clarity and transparency in the laws under both systems taking into consideration new technological developments such as DNA test and blood test without limitation (specifically in civil law). This is to ensure that issues of illegitimacy are resolved in a more consistent manner through new laws or amendments in the existing ones to give due recognition to the Islamic perceptions on the sanctity of marriage (nasab) and also take into consideration 'the best interest of the child'.

This research being conducted by way of a doctrinal approach has its limitations. The analysis and the interpretation of the various documents can

---

91   Constitutional Court Number 46/PUU-VIII/2010.

92   Maqashid al-Shariah is the main goal of the revelation of sharia. Scholars agree that Islamic sharia was revealed to safeguard five things, namely: protecting religion, soul, mind, lineage, and honor, and protecting property. Al-Syâthibî, al-Muwafaqat, (tp: Dar ibn Affan, 1997), II, 20.

93   AR Habibi 'The Dynamics of Illegitimate Child Status in Sharia and National Law of Indonesia: Is There a Harmonization?' (2021) 3 *Al Manhaj: Journal of Indonesian Islamic Family Law* 70–80.

be further enhanced in terms of validity and reliability if future research-ers conduct interviews with the main stakeholders inclusive of lawmakers, judges, lawyers and most importantly religious scholars. The need to consult religious scholars will ensure that any change in the laws would not under-mine the basic principles of Islam. Further, the religious scholars' views are crucial because Islam is the official religion in Malaysia. The researchers are not showing disrespect for other religions or insisting that Islam is superior but are only advocating that the division between civil law and syariah law that is very prominent in regards to the rights of an illegitimate child be rec-onciled to ensure that the status of these children are given utmost priority. If this can be done alongside with maintaining the Islamic principle of lineage, the researchers believe that the best interest of these children will be upheld. One way to do this would be by bringing into force the age-old principle under Islam that the Khalifah is to provide shelter for the wellbeing of such a child. Since the Khalifah system is not in place in Malaysia, the alternative solution would be to allow the process of legitimising illegitimate children through the Births and Deaths Registration Act 1957. In order for this to happen in view of this group's plight and to ensure that their rights are protected, there is a need for an overall transformation of society's perception towards the status of illegitimate children. Furthermore, with regards to the social stigma and the discrimination that the illegitimate children face, it is advocated that the Gov-ernment, through the implementation of law, plays an active role to protect these children's rights.

This research concludes that illegitimate children are vulnerable and they fall under the category of marginalised group of society. They are sinless and innocent and do not deserve to be discriminated and treated badly just because of their status. In traditional societies, bearing a child out of marriage is considered a great sin against the moral values of the community and results in the isolation of the mother and her child. The state is held responsible for providing affirmative measures supporting this vulnerable unmarried mother and her child. However, today, with there being so much of improvement in terms of knowledge and understanding of the laws as well as religious princi-ples, it is easier for nations throughout the world to enact laws that cater to this marginalised children without discarding any religious practice.

Note on the Contributors

Nadhratul Wardah Salman
Senior Lecturer, Faculty of Law, University of Malaya, Malaysia.

Saroja Dhanapal
Former Associate Professor, UCSI University, Malaysia.

Shad Saleem Faruqi
Tunku Abdul Rahman's Chair Holder, Faculty of Law, University of Malaya, Malaysia.

This research was carried out under the University of Malaya Faculty Research Grant (GPF005M-2018). The authors would also like to thank Norfatin Zalizan for the research done towards completion of this article.

CHAPTER 11

Exploring Older Persons' Financial Abuse in Malaysia: Protecting through Empowerment, Prevention and Enforcement

Mohammad Abu Taher, Olivia Tan Swee Leng, and Siti Zaharah Jamaluddin

Abstract

Malaysia will be an aged nation in 2030 when more than 15% of its population age 60 years and above. Being an aged nation, the issues on older person's abuse, especially financial abuse need to be addressed. Older persons are targeted for financial abuse and exploitation due to their vulnerability as there is a perception that they are rich in assets and wealth, accumulated from years of working. The impact of older persons' financial abuse and exploitation can accelerate death among older persons due to financial loss, humiliation, and depression. Although there are several legislations enacted by Malaysian lawmakers to address older persons' financial abuse, these statutes are inadequate to protect the older persons from financial exploitation. This article attempts to discuss the legal framework for financial abuse in Malaysia. In this context the authors opted to use the doctrinal approach of research, whereby materials were compiled from the Malaysian legislations, case laws, journal articles, and databases. The authors believe that aside from proposing additional legal and supporting measures on protection and prevention of older persons' financial abuse and exploitation, empowering the older persons is also crucial.

Keywords

aged nation – older persons – financial abuse – empowerment – prevention

1   Introduction

In Malaysia, retirement is associated with age. At present, the age of retirement in Malaysia is 60 years for both the public and private sectors as governed by the Minimum Retirement Age Act 2012 (Act 753) and the Pensions Act 1980

(Act 227) respectively. In 2022, there were 1.6 million workers in the public sector[1] while 15.831 million worked in the private sector.[2] Those who are working in the informal sector will not have any specific age of retirement. Unfortunately, there is no record as to the number of workers in the informal sector since they are not required to register with any of the government agencies. Nevertheless, those who reached the age of retirement still have the option of continuing working or retiring for good.

After spending so many years working, older persons look forward to retirement, hoping to do what they were not able to do previously. Thus, planning for retirement is also important to ensure that older persons enjoy active lifestyle which is a key to active ageing.[3] When Malaysia increased the age of retirement from 55 years to 60 years with the introduction of the Minimum Retirement Age Act 2012, the gap of 5 years should be utilised for retirement planning including the transition to retirement. The 5-year gap allows a potential retiree to plan how he wants to spend his money and his time with specific activities including his leisure. Unfortunately, it is not uncommon for older persons to face physical mobility and health challenges which led them to seeking assistance from others, such as family members, friends or carers in carrying out their daily tasks including handling financial matters. If they are suffering from any disability or frailty, they are socially isolated and extremely dependent on others, increasing the risk and vulnerability for them to be financially abused.[4] Aside from this, the present older persons find information technology and communication (ICT) an additional challenge, more so with the increase in usage throughout their daily routine including in financial matters, resulting in more assistance needed in order to conduct their financial transactions. It has been observed that older persons' faced more difficulties during Covid-19 pandemic where digital technology was used in a large

---

1   'Civil Servants Will Not Be Forgotten in Budget 2022, Says PM Ismail Sabri' *The Malay Mail*, 27 October 2021, https://www.malaymail.com/news/malaysia/2021/10/27/civil-servants-will -not-be-forgotten-in-budget-2022-says-pm-ismail-sabri/2016461 (accessed 10 January 2023).
2   Employment and Labour Statistic, Siri 34 Bil 4/2022, December, *Ministry of Human Resources Malaysia*, https://www.mohr.gov.my/ebook/Statistikbil4/mobile/index.html (accessed 6 January 2022).
3   G Henning, A Stenling, AA Bielak, P Bjälkebring, AJ Gow, M Kivi and M Lindwall, 'Towards an Active and Happy Retirement? Changes in Leisure Activity and Depressive Symptoms during the Retirement Transition' (2021) 25 *Aging & Mental Health* 621, 631.
4   NB Che Amani, RB Kahar, RB Ibrahim and MB Hasbullah, 'Elder Financial Abuse Experience: A Qualitative Study from the Perspective of Older Persons in Malaysia' (2021) 11 *International Journal of Academic Research in Business and Social Sciences* 479, 498.

scale for the various reasons, such as the implementation of the Movement Control Order (MCO) and the used of cashless transactions.

No one is immune to cybercrime, and everyone in the population, particularly older persons, must be aware of the cyber environment's dual nature: convenience comes with the risk of cyber threats. According to Cyber Security Malaysia's Spam statistics (January to March 2020), there was a 93 percent rise in spam compared to the previous year. Furthermore, when compared to January to March 2019, the total number of cybercrime occurrences reported increased by 34%. This rising trend indicates that cyber events continue to be a problem in Malaysia. The vulnerable population, such as the older persons, would need to be more vigilant in order to avoid being victims of cyber-attacks.[5]

2   Elder Abuse and Neglect (EAN)

The World Health Organisation (WHO) has recognised elder abuse and neglect (EAN) as one of the major public health issues. EAN is categorised into five types: physical abuse, emotional abuse, sexual abuse, financial abuse, and neglect. Much has been written on the other four types of abuses, nevertheless the same cannot be said for financial abuse.[6] WHO defines financial abuse as the illegal or improper exploitation or use of funds or other resources of older persons.[7] Financial abuse is connected to monetary abuse, property abuse or legal abuse which resulted in financial loss to older persons. This definition can also cover financial exploitation, which is defined as the illegal or improper use of an older person's funds, property or assets.[8]

---

5   LS Tan, RG Vergara, N Khan and S Khan, 'Cyber Security and Privacy Impact on Older Persons amid Covid-19: A Socio-Legal Study in Malaysia' (2020) 2 *Asian Journal of Research in Education and Social Sciences* 72, 76.

6   MM Gilhooly, G Dalley, KJ Gilhooly, MP Sullivan, P Harries, M Levi and MS Davies, 'Financial Elder Abuse through the Lens of the Bystander Intervention Model' (2016) 26 *Public Policy & Aging Report* 5, 11.

7   The World Health Organisation, 'Missing voices: Views of Older Persons on Elder Abuse' (2002), http:// whqlibdoc.who.int/hq/2002/WHO_NMH_ VIP_02.1.pdf?ua=1 (accessed 16 June 2020).

8   S Wood, & PA Lichtenberg, 'Financial Capacity and Financial Exploitation of Older Adults: Research Findings, Policy Recommendations and Clinical Implications' (2017) 40 *Clinical Gerontologist* 3, 13.

3   Types of Elder Financial Abuse

There are many ways for older persons to be financially abused and exploited by family members, carers or third party. If the family members or carers are involved, the nature of such a closed personal relationship between the parties allows them access to the older persons' funds, which leads to theft, unauthorized access to accounts (cashing an elderly person's cheques without authorization or use of ATM card without permission); forging an older person's signature; misusing an older person's money or possessions; coercing or deceiving an older person into signing any document with regards to the property.[9] These transactions are within the traditional financial abuse since the perpetrators are family members or trusted person.[10] For example, a 68-year-old retired clerk with arthritis has found it difficult to go to the bank, her son persuaded her to give him the authority to handle her finances amounting to the transfer of her property to him.[11]

Financial abuse by a third party normally involves scams, through phone by using telemarketing, internet (love scam, *Macau* scam) or investment scams.[12] All these transactions require deception which influence the older persons to depart with their money or property.[13] These transactions are non-traditional financial abuse since the perpetrators are strangers and do not have a personal relationship with the victims.[14] These transactions are more complicated since the perpetrators' methods are difficult to be traced. For examples, in early 2021, a 74-year-old retired teacher fell victim to the infamous '*Macau* Scam',[15] losing

---

9   *Ibid.*
10   D Setterlund, C Tilse, J Wilson, AL McCawley and L Rosenman, 'Understanding Financial Elder Abuse in Families: the Potential of Routine Activities Theory' (2007) 27 *Ageing & Society* 599, 614.
11   S Indramalar, 'Ageing and Abused by Their Own' *The Star*, 3 November 2016.
12   S Indramalar, 'Time to Act: More Seniors Fall Prey to Scams' *The Star*, 1 October 2021.
13   D Burnes, CR Henderson Jr, C Sheppard, R Zhao, K Pillemer and MS Lachs, 'Prevalence of Financial Fraud and Scams among Older Adults in the United States: A Systematic Review and Meta-Analysis' (2017) 107 *American Journal of Public Health* e13, e21.
14   TP Ying and NH Bahaudin, 'Warning: Macau Scam Operators Have New Target and They Could Be Your Parents' *The New Straits Times*, 4 November 2018; NZ Othman, '#TECH: Many Lonely Hearts are Still Falling for Online Fake Lovers' *New Straits Times*, 14 February 2020, https://www.nst.com.my/lifestyle/bots/2020/02/565459/tech-many-lonely-hearts -arestill- falling-online-fake-lovers (accessed 20 January 2022).
15   The term "Macau scam" was coined as it is believed it originated from Macau or that the first victims came from there. The scam often starts with a phone call from someone pretending to be an officer from a bank, government or law enforcement agency or debt collector. The scammer will tell the potential victim that they owe money or has an unpaid fine, often with a very short window to settle the payment or face "dire consequences".

RM1 million to a scammer, according to a news report.[16] A few months later, another senior citizen lost RM18,000 in an online love scam and a 68-year-old housewife and a couple in their 80s in Negeri Sembilan lost close to RM300,000.00 in two separate phone scams in October 2021.[17]

The cases of older persons' abuse and neglect in Malaysia is underreported, even more so for financial abuse.[18] Due to under-reporting, there is no official estimation as to the amount of loss suffered by older persons. Nevertheless, the news had reported repeatedly about older persons who lost their savings to scams.[19] The harm and distress resulted in older persons who suffered financial abuse to die earlier as compared to those who suffered from other abuses.[20] The victims of financial abuse do not just lose money, they experience humiliation and depression, since they do not have the luxury of time to recover from the said loss. Kaspiew and others[21] highlight how financial abuse of older persons suffered depletion in their wealth, experienced psychological trauma, and exhibited a decline in quality of life. Due to the humiliation, they may not want to report such incident, thereby allowing the perpetrator to go unpunished. With the elderly population projected to increase to 15% in 2030, Malaysian lawmakers need to seriously consider financial abuse of older persons in order to accord the necessary protections to them as envisaged by the Articles 5[22] and 8[23] of the Federal Constitution.

---

16   Bernama, '74-Year-Old PJ Woman Loses RM1 Million to Macau Scam Syndicate' *The Star*, 5 February 2021.

17   *Ibid.*

18   CC Madu, GC Chuan and MA Taher, 'Profiling Financial Abuse of the Elderly in Malaysia and Nigeria: The Need for Special Legal Response' in SZ Jamaluddin et al., (eds.) *Protecting The Elderly Against Abuse and Neglect: Legal and Social Strategies* (Kuala Lumpur, University of Malaya Press, 2017) 81, 95.

19   F Zolkepli, 'Senior Citizen, 66, Cheated of 1.8 Million by Scammers' *The Star*, 19 December 2020.

20   R Sooryanarayana, CW Yuen, NN Mohd Hairi, F Hairi, SA Aziz, R Ramli, R Mohamad, K Chinna and ABA Mahmud, 'Elder Abuse in a Rural Community in Malaysia: The Who and The How' in SZ Jamaluddin et al., (eds.) *Protecting The Elderly Against Abuse and Neglect: Legal and Social Strategies* (University of Malaya Press, 2017) 65, 79.

21   R Kaspiew, R Carson and H Rhoades, 'Elder Abuse: Understanding Issues, Frameworks and Responses' (Research report no. 35, 2016), *Australian Institute of Family Studies*, https://aifs.gov.au/ sites/default/files/publication-documents/rr35- elder-abusenov18.pdf (accessed 14 February 2021).

22   Article 5: Liberty of the person.

23   Article 8: Equality.

4   The Current Legislations on Elder Financial Abuse in Malaysia

4.1   *Domestic Violence Act 1994 (Act 512)*
In Malaysia, older persons' financial abuse falls within the meaning of domestic violence in the Domestic Violence Act 1994 ("Act 512"). "Financial abuse" is
defined in the following subsections of Act 512:

i.   section 2(ea) defines as "dishonestly misappropriating the victim's prop-
        erty which causes the victim to suffer distress due to the financial loss";
ii.   section 2(e) defines as "causing mischief or destruction to or damage to
        the property which causes distress to the older person"; and
iii.   section 2(eb) defines as "threatening the older person with intent to
        cause him to fear for the safety of his property".

Act 512 provides for several remedies for the victim of abuse, such as an emergency protection order pursuant to the section 3A which can be issued within
two hours after an application is made while an interim protection order pursuant to section 4 is an order prohibiting the person against whom the order
is made from using domestic violence against the victim. The victim may
also apply for a protection order pursuant to section 5 which has the effect of
restraining the person against whom the order is made from using domestic
violence against him. Besides that, section 5 of Act 512 also provides for the
payment of compensation for the injury, loss or damage suffered by the victim which the court deems just and reasonable. Pursuant to section 11 of Act
512, the court may also order the parties to attend reconciliatory counselling
and also psychotherapy or rehabilitation counselling, if necessary. However,
the protection measures under Act 512 are available only if the victim lodged
a police report. Without the police report, the victims will not be able to enjoy
the protection given by Act 512. Recognising the importance of information
on incident of abuse, section 18 of Act 512 protects the informants, who alert
the police about such incidents, from any liability for defamation if such information was given in good faith. Unfortunately, this protection given to the
informants is general in nature and does not impose any mandatory reporting
pertaining to domestic violence incidents. The victim needs to take the first
step of reporting to benefit from Act 512.

4.2   *Penal Code (Act 574)*
Since Act 512 must be read together with the provisions of the Penal Code
("Act 574"), the definitions in Act 512 have mirrored the offences in Act 574.
The offences in Act 574 are limited to traditional financial abuse, such as, the
offence of criminal misappropriation of property (section 403 of Act 574),

criminal breach of trust (section 406 of Act 574), while cheating (section 415 of Act 574) can be applied to both traditional and non-traditional financial abuse. Although the offences in Act 574 do not distinguish between the types of perpetrators – thus covering financial abuse committed by both family members and strangers, nevertheless the usage of financial technology will impose further obstacles in enforcement. However, for internet scams, the victims may find redress under the Communication and Multimedia Act 1998 ("Act 588"). If there is evidence that there has been a spread of false content by the alleged perpetrator, it is also possible for an action to be taken under the purview of sections 211 and 233 of Act 574.

In spite of those legal guarantees, an older person faces an uphill battle to prove the elements of the offences due to age or illness.[24] Since it is a criminal offence, the victim through the Public Prosecutor will have to prove the elements of *mens rea, actus reus*, causation and harm. The offences against property require the *mens rea* of "'dishonestly'" or "'fraudulently'" to be proven. A person is said to do an act dishonestly if it causes wrongful loss or wrongful gain (Sections 23 and 24, Penal Code) while fraudulently requires the act to be done with the intention to defraud the victim (sections 25, Penal Code). As the victim, the older person will have to give evidence during the trial as to what had happened to him. Being an elderly and if he is impaired by an illness such as dementia or Alzheimer, he will find it difficult to recall what had happened or to be consistent with his evidence, more so during cross-examination (section 118, Evidence Act 1950). The fact that he is testifying against his loved one, will make the situation even more difficult. The facts can easily be confused, his testimony may vary and be inconsistent. At the end of the trial, he may not be accepted as a credible witness and his evidence may not be admissible, hampering the effort to prosecute the perpetrator. If the older person had entrusted the perpetrator with his debit card, including the pin number due to his immobility, the transactions may still be valid since there was consent.[25] The financial institution from where the money was misappropriated considered such transaction as valid since the information pertaining to the debit card, the pin number and the account were correct. Thus, there was no reason for the institution to block the transaction. Facing these hurdles, it is not a surprise that the older person prefers to suffer in silence.

The loophole in the current legal framework be it the definition, the hurdles to obtain redress or the refusal of older persons to report, have led the older

---

24 SZ Jamaluddin, JZ Mohd Yusoff, Z Tahir, S Thambapillay and MA Taher, 'Presumption of *mens rea* in Elderly Abuse and Neglect Offences in Malaysian Penal Code: An Alternative Approach?' (2019) 3 *The Law Review* 313, 328.

25 TE Lyn, 'Asia's Old Suffer Fraud, Abuse with Rising Dementia' *Reuters*, 24 November 2011.

persons to take the responsibility to protect themselves through other legal means, such as the powers of attorney under the Powers of Attorney Act 1949 ("Act 424")[26] and fiduciary duty by a trustee under the Trustee Act 1949 ("Act 208").[27] If they do not do so, being victims of financial abuse will be a very high price to pay, sometimes with their lives. To do this, the older persons will need to engage lawyers for advice and to execute the documents to formalise the instruments for powers of attorney and formation of trust. This will involve not only effort by the older persons but also expenses, provided they are aware of such mechanisms. Considering that both the powers of attorney and fiduciary duty are preventive mechanisms, these approaches should be extended and practised in the banking and financial sectors in mitigating the risks of older persons' financial abuses by specifying who can legally assist them, especially when it involves the use of financial technology as the mode of abuse.

5   Cyber Fraud and Cyber Security Protection for Older Persons during the COVID-19 Pandemic

The older persons face abuse and neglect even in the period of the COVID-19 Pandemic including cyber fraud.[28] Malaysians are also not immune to cyber-crime during the pandemic outbreak. According to the Straits Times (2020), a businessman tried to buy facemasks online but ended up losing RM266, 153 (USD61,042). The matter is being investigated for cheating under section 420 of the Act 574 (Lim, 2020). On a global level, a malware spy system disguised as a version of the legitimate 'corona live' application, which provides data from the Johns Hopkins coronavirus tracker of infection rates and deaths, was actually facilitating invasions of privacy, by gaining access to the device's images, videos, location, and camera, as well as recording video and audio without the owner's knowledge.[29] However, online scammers have a history of preying on the weak and vulnerable, particularly during the COVID-19 pandemic. The

---

26   NA Raof and NC Abdullah, 'Financial Exploitation of Elderly: Analysis of Power of Attor-ney' in SZ Jamuddin et al., (eds.) *Protecting The Elderly Against Abuse and Neglect: Legal and Social Strategies* (University Malaya Press, 2017) 165, 184.

27   U Balasingam, 'Protection from Financial Abuse: Fiduciary Duty and Protective Measures' in *ibid.* 185, 200.

28   SM Benbow, S Bhattacharyya, P Kingston and C Peisah, 'Invisible and At-Risk: Older Adults during the COVID-19 Pandemic' (2022) 34 *Journal of Elder Abuse & Neglect* 70, 76.

29   A Ng, 'Fake Coronavirus Apps Are Really Malware that Stalks You' (2020) Retrieved from https://www.cnet.com/news/fake-coronavirus-tracking-apps-are-really-malware-that stalks -its-users/ (accessed 10 March 2021).

victims were duped into purchasing low-cost gaming accounts or game assets that turned out to be fraudulent.[30] Despite the fact that Malaysia has been actively providing cyber security awareness to its citizens through cyber security Malaysia and websites like Sebenarnya (https://sebenarnya.my) to check the validity of news to determine whether news passed on social media or the like is fake or not, cyber fraud continues to be a growing problem. During the COVID-19 pandemic outbreak, cybercriminals took use of the chance to engineer their illicit activities for financial benefit.[31]

Cyber attackers perceive older persons internet users, particularly those considered wealthy, as easy targets.[32] However, little is being done to safeguard and educate the older persons, who are among the most frequently targeted by internet scams.[33] Although there are more conversations about protecting the online workforce, as the internet-using population ages, an increasing percentage of senior netizens utilise the internet without being aware of scam posting.

Despite the fact that the present statistics reflect cyber-attacks on Malaysia's broad population, there have been allegations of older people being targeted in love scams.[34] Cyber Security Malaysia has received 61 reports of love scams since 2015.[35] "Scammers initiate a friendship or relationship with the victim online", according to Cyber Security Malaysia. They have thousands of people at their hands thanks to today's dating applications, and they know some will fall for their con. Furthermore, "scammers frequently target the elderly,

---

30   C Chen, 'Covid-19: Online Game Players Were Top Target for Scammers during China's Coronavirus Lockdown' *The Star*, 25 March 2020, https://www.thestar.com.my/tech/tech-news/2020/03/25/covid-19-online-game-players-were-top-target-for-scammers-during-chinas-coronavirus-lockdown (accessed 5 April 2022).

31   J Beirne, J Villafuerte and B Zhang, 'Fintech and COVID-19: Impacts, Challenges, and Policy Priorities for Asia' (2022) *Asian Development Bank Institute*, https://www.adb.org/sites/default/files/publication/813211/fintech-and-covid-19-web.pdf (accessed 10 January 2023).

32   D Palmer, 'Cybersecurity: Why More Needs to be Done to Help Older People Stay Safe Online' *ZDNET*, 12 November 2019, https://www.zdnet.com/article/cybersecurity-why-more-needs-to-be-done-to-help-older-people-stay-safe-online/ (accessed 20 April 2022).

33   The Straits Times, 'With Online Scam on the Rise, Digital Ambassadors Prevent Vulnerable Seniors from Falling Victim' 10 June 2021, https://www.straitstimes.com/singapore/courts-crime/online-scams-digital-ambassadors-prevent-vulnerable-seniors-from-falling-victim (accessed 15 July 2022).

34   B Mat, SDM Pero, R Wahid and MS Shuib, 'Cyber Security Threats to Malaysia: A Small State Security Discourse' (2020) 5 *Sustaining Global Strategic Partnership in the Age of Uncertainties* 31.

35   NZ Othman, '#TECH: Many Lonely Hearts are Still Falling for Online Fake Lovers' *New Straits Times*, 14 February 2020, https://www.nst.com.my/lifestyle/bots/2020/02/565459/tech-many-lonely-hearts-arestill- falling-online-fake-lovers (accessed 20 January 2022).

who may be less knowledgeable, as well as lonely ladies." They persuade these victims to wire money or tempt them with a pricey mail delivery.[36]

The *Macau* scam is one of the most common forms of scams that Malaysians are subjected to. Despite frequent police warnings, many Malaysians fall for these schemes and lose enormous sums of money to the scammers— sometimes up to a six-digit number.[37] The losses from the *Macau* scam in Selangor for the first six months of 2018 were RM16 million. *Macau* scams begin with a phone call from a fraudster posing himself as a bank employee, police officer, government representative, or debt collector. The scammer will persuade his victims that they owe money or that they are under investigation for money laundering. To avoid getting banned or having their bank accounts closed, victims wind up depositing enormous quantities of money into the scammer's account.[38] This is an old-school con that targets both the older persons and the young. However, the older persons may lack the ability to undertake the necessary searches to evaluate whether a bargain is genuine or not. It usually entails a scheme to sell something that the conman (or woman) does not have the legal authority to sell. It's also possible that the product or goods don't exist, and that the titles are entirely fictitious.

6   Loopholes in the Existing Legislations on Elder Financial Abuse in Malaysia

The loopholes in the existing legal framework comprise of four important issues, namely; the limited definition on financial abuse; the issue in proving the offence; the lack of support from the other stakeholders in minimising older persons financial abuse and the lack in empowerment of the older persons.

6.1   *The Limitation in the Definition of Older Person Financial Abuse*
The main issue in addressing older person financial abuse is the lack of consensus as to the operational definition of older person's financial abuse.[39] Terminologies such as elder maltreatment,[40] elder financial abuse or financial elder abuse (United Kingdom), financial exploitation (United States of

---

36   *Ibid.*
37   D Nair, 'Scams Targeting the Elderly and How to Protect Our Parents from Them' (2018) https://ringgitplus.com/en/blog/personal-finance-news/scams-targeting-the-elderly -and-how-to-protect-our-parents-from-them.html (accessed 10 March 2021).
38   *Ibid.*
39   Madu et al., *supra* note 18.
40   World Health Organisation, 'Elder Maltreatment' Fact Sheet (June 2022), https://www .who.int/news-room/fact-sheets/detail/abuse-of-older-people (accessed 13 August 2022).

America) is used interchangeably to refer to older person financial abuse.[41] The underpinning of all these terminologies is the right and trust, which caused harm and distress to older persons. The right and trust can come based on the existing relationship between the older persons and the perpetrators (family members, trusted friends) or the trust created through misrepresentations or fraud (third party or strangers). The existing definitions are limited with regards to the manners in which the offences are committed vide misappropriation, damaging the property or threatening the property. The definitions did not take into account the undue influence, duress or culture expectations which arise out of the family relationship, leading to the financial abuse. For example, older parents would take on the child's debt, gave in to the demand of the child or allow the child to borrow their money without paying it back, due to the child-parent relationship and culture expectation.[42] These conducts indicated that they are caring parents who put their family first, even at their own perils. As such the definition of older person's financial abuse must reflect these situations. The element of dishonest or misappropriation or damaging or threatening is missing in these transactions, nevertheless the result remains the same, the older persons suffered losses, which impacted their well-being.

6.2   *The Issue in Proving the Offence*

As Act 574 is a criminal statute, the criminal liability principles and the relevant procedural requirements must be fulfilled in order to sustain a conviction. The principle of criminal liability requires the *mens rea* or the state of mind of the accused in committing the *actus reus* or the criminal act to be proven before the accused could be convicted. The trial, examination, and cross-examination maybe too much for the elderly to handle. As such perhaps as an alternative, the Penal Code can be amended to include the rebuttable presumption of *mens rea* on the accused i.e. transferring the burden to prove the *mens rea* from the prosecution to the accused. A rebuttable presumption is a conclusion as to the existence or non-existence of a fact that a judge or jury must draw when certain evidence has been introduced and admitted as true in a lawsuit but that can be contradicted by the evidence to the contrary. A presumption is an inference that a showing of Fact A implies Fact B or a sufficient likelihood of Fact B to satisfy the burden of production.[43] This approach can be seen in the existing provision in section 409B of the Penal Code. This presumption can be invoked by the court

---

41   Madu et al., *supra* note 18.

42   Amani et al., *supra* note 4.

43   SC Salop, 'An Enquiry Meet for the Case: Decision Theory, Presumptions, and Evidentiary Burdens in Formulating Antitrust Legal Standards' *Presumptions, and Evidentiary Burdens in Formulating Antitrust Legal Standards,* 6 November 2017.

once the prosecution had proved that there was a misappropriation of money by the perpetrator, which is the *actus reus*. Once this is proven, the presumption of acting dishonestly, which is the *mens rea* element will automatically arise.[44] With this presumption, the older person needs to show that the perpetrator had utilised the older person's property as his own without the consent of the older person, without having to prove that the utilisation was done dishonestly. For example, if the older person's money in his saving account was withdrawn by the perpetrator for the perpetrator's benefit, the *actus reus* is fulfilled and the perpetrator is presumed to have done it dishonestly. The burden of proving that the misappropriation is not done dishonestly will pass to the perpetrator. This will lessen the burden on the part of the older person.

6.3   *The Issue of Lacking Support from Other Stakeholders*

The existing legislations did not impose any obligations on the part of other stakeholders in preventing older person financial abuse. Section 18 of the Domestic Violence Act 1994 provides for protection to those who informed the police of abuse incidents. This provision is general in nature, not specific to anyone, but to the public at large. In the society where interfering with others' domestic lives is frowned upon, this provision does not encourage the public to report such incident. As such, the victim of abuse needs to initiate the first step in order to get the protection under the Act. For the older persons suffering from financial abuse, this may not be easy.

Therefore, it is important that the other stakeholders to lend support to the older persons in preventing them from financial abuse. Within the traditional financial abuse, an appointed agency may offer services to advise and execute the relevant documents such as powers of attorney or creating a trust, with a clear instruction as to how the older persons' properties can be administered and by whom. This agency may also undertake the responsibility to create awareness to the older persons, the carer and the younger generations, for them to be better prepared for their future. Knowledge is indeed empowering, and is the best way to assist older persons in protecting themselves.

Aside from the older persons having to be responsible for their own financial planning, they can also be assisted by financial institutions, where their money is deposited. The older persons need to be assisted by those who can detect the exploitation and fraud.[45] In this context, the financial institution is

---

44   *Chong Chiew Nam @ Chong Chee Wah v PP* [1997] 1LNS 34.

45   M DeLiema and KJ Conrad, 'Financial Exploitation of Older Adults' in X Dong (ed) *Elder Abuse* (Springer International Publishing, 2017) 141, 157; R Eisenberg, 'Elder Financial Abuse: Why Banks and Advisers Are Stepping Up' *Forbes*, 12 February 2019.

armed with the necessary facilities and skills since they can detect any unusual or extraordinary transactions within the older person's account. The staff at the financial institutions must be trained on how to detect and prevent this abuse.[46] For example, when a flustered man walked into UOB Bank's main branch trying to bank in a cheque of more than S$150,000 (RM483,735) to an offshore account, the bank's service associate Jenny Hong got suspicious. The first tell-tale sign was the name of the account holder and the account number did not match. When Hong, 46, probed the man, in his 70s, further and asked why he needed to send money to the overseas account, he grew more rattled, kept saying that it was urgent and his answers grew more incoherent. It took a while for him to understand that he was scammed.[47]

The ability to detect will enable preventive measures to be incorporated and protect older persons from such abuse. Various discussions on how this can be done is proposed including by the bystander intervention model,[48] or the routine activity theory.[49] In the bystander intervention model, 5 steps are involved: (1) noticing relevant cues to financial abuse, (2) construing the situation as financial abuse, (3) deciding the situation is a personal responsibility, (4) knowing how to deal with the situation, and (5) deciding to intervene. In the same way that a number of stages must be negotiated in cases of bystander intervention in emergencies, in non-emergencies such as elder financial abuse, the same stages must also be negotiated.[50] This approach is suitable to be adopted by the financial institutions which have the resources including financial information of the older persons who are their clients. The details as to what should be done and who should be responsible can be included in the guidelines. Those who are responsible, however, must receive sufficient trainings on elder financial abuse.

Routine activity theory discussed how day to day routine increases the opportunities for the older persons to become victim of financial abuse. According to the said theory, the criminal acts require the convergence of

---

46   L De Donder, N De Witte, D Brosens, E Dierckx and D Verte, 'Learning to Detect and Prevent Elder Abuse: the Need for a Valid Risk Assessment Instrument' (2015) 191 *Procedia-Social and Behavioral Sciences* 1483, 1488.

47   N Chua, 'SG Bankers Stop Elderly Man from Losing S$150,000 to 'Girlfriend from Netherlands' in Internet Love Scam' *The Star*, 18 September 2022, https://www.thestar.com .my/tech/tech-news/2022/09/18/sg-bankers-stop-elderly-man-from-losing-s150000-to -girlfriend-from-netherlands-in-internet-love-scam (accessed 5 October 2022).

48   Gilhooly et al., *supra* note 6.

49   M DeLiema, 'Elder Fraud and Financial Exploitation: Application of Routine Activity Theory' (2018) 58 *The Gerontologist* 706, 718.

50   Gilhooly et al., *supra* note 6.

three factors: (a) a motivated offender, (b) a suitable target, and (c) the absence of capable guardians.[51] Since the older persons do not have control over (a), it is thus important for the older persons to take additional measures to ensure that they are not the suitable target. Understanding what they need to do to protect their properties will reduce the opportunity to be defrauded. Aside from that, the family members or carers need to be aware of the older persons' mental capacity to ensure that they are able to make a sound decision. This theory requires both the older persons and the family or carers to be proactive in preventing financial abuse.

6.4   The Issue of Lacking of Older Persons' Empowerment

The current legislations did not factor in the empowerment of the older persons. Empowerment the older persons with regards to their financial matters will go a long way in protecting them against abuse. This empowerment will also change the perception of the community with regards to older persons. Most of the time, the older persons are equated with physical and intellectual decline, thus requiring only care.[52] In reality the older persons have the same range of problems, weaknesses and strength just like anyone else. This is more relevant now since, the cohort who will be older persons in Malaysia in 2030 will be those who were born in 1970, with different needs and wants from the current cohort. They had the opportunity to education, working and better environment and infrastructure, including access to information and communication technology.

Empowerment in its general sense, refers to the ability of the people to gain understanding and control over personal, social, economic and political forces in order to take action to improve their life.[53] Empowerment entails the construction of responsible communities, ones in which the individuals that comprise them take on greater control of their lives and contribute in an egalitarian way to daily life, taking into account the various collective arrangements in place and their context.[54] In order to empower the older persons with

---

51   MD Reisig and K Holtfreter, 'Shopping Fraud Victimization among the Elderly' (2013) 20 *Journal of Financial Crime* 324–337.

52   N Thompson and S Thompson, 'Empowering Older People: Beyond the Care Model' (2001) 1 *Journal of Social Work* 61–76.

53   BA Israel, B Checkoway, A Schulz and M Zimmerman, 'Health Education and Community Empowerment: Conceptualizing and Measuring Perceptions of Individual, Organizational, and Community Control' (1994) 21 *Health Education Quarterly* 149, 170.

54   IC Cavalieri and HN Almeida, 'Power, Empowerment and Social Participation-the Building of a Conceptual Model' (2018) 5 *European Journal of Social Science Education and Research* 174, 185.

regards to handling financial abuse, it is important to understand the factors that prevent them from taking actions with regards to it. The main factor is lack of awareness and information regarding abuse and neglect including financial abuse. Unlike child or spousal abuse, older persons and the community are not sure as to what, how, why, where and to whom they can go for assistance.[55]

The empowerment of the older person maybe approached from the autonomy perspective, where the right of the older persons to decide must be respected. In order for them to make an informed decision on any matters pertaining to their lives, it is important for them to have sufficient information on those matters. As such the information on what is elder financial abuse, the procedure for reporting, the choices as to the available redress and other incidental matters must be explained to them. This explanation can be done formally through the relevant agencies dealing with the would-be retirees such the Employees' Provident Fund (EPF) or Pensions, or informally through outreach programs organised by the various non-governmental organisations (NGOs), the Ministry of Women, Family and Community Development and the financial institutions.

7   Recommendations and Implications

Even though the present Malaysian legal framework has provided for older persons' financial abuse, the current provisions need to be improvised further. The following recommendations on the discussed loopholes are proposed to address the weaknesses of the present legal provisions.

7.1   *Amending the Definitions of Financial Abuse in Act 512 and Act 574*
Amending the definitions of financial abuse in both statutes to include the exploitation through undue influences, duress and culture expectations will also capture the act of scamming. Financial exploitation can be defined as "'unjust, improper, and/or illegal use of another's resources, property, and/or assets.'[56] The definition focuses on the conduct which caused unjust, improper, illegal or unauthorized use of the older persons' properties. While the Centres for Disease Control (CDC) define financial exploitation as, "'the illegal, unauthorized, or improper use of an older individual's resources' by a caregiver or

---

55   SZ Jamaluddin, JZ Mohd Yusoff, S Thambapillay, Z Tahir, MA Taher and NF Abdul Rahman, 'Empowering the Elderly and the Community in Dealing with Elder Issues: The Way Forward for Malaysia' (2017) 4 *The Law Review* 546, 560.

56   DeLiema and Conrad, *supra* note 45.

other person in a trusting relationship, for the benefit of someone other than the older individual.'"⁵⁷ The concept of a trusting relationship is not limited to just the traditional relationship but includes the non-traditional concept, including online friends and, scammers.

Act 512 needs to include a new provision on the definition of financial abuse by inserting a new section 2(ec) on financial exploitation. In the interpretation section of Act 512, the author proposes that a new definition of financial exploitation '"as unjust, improper, and/or illegal use of another's resources, property, and/or assets,'" to be included. While for Act 574, a new offence of financial exploitation should be introduced to cater for this new definition of elder financial abuse.

7.2   *Adding a New Provision on Rebuttable Presumption in the Penal Code for Property Offences*

In order to protect the older person who may have issues to give evidence due to old age or mental incapacity, a new rebuttable presumption should be introduced in the Penal Code which is limited to an elderly victim. If the rebuttable presumption is applicable, then if the victim suffered loss at the hands of the accused, the act is presumed to be done dishonestly or fraudulently. The evidence as to the loss can be proven through the bank statement, as the direct evidence. Once this is done, the presumption will be applied and it is for the accused to prove otherwise. The shifting of the burden of proving *mens rea* would assist the prosecutor in prosecuting the cases involving older persons victims. This approach is not new to the Penal Code.

Section 409B(1) of the Penal Code provides where it shall be presumed that the accused had acted dishonestly until the contrary is proved for property offences under sections 403, 404, 405, 406, 407, 408 and 409. Sections 403 and 404 dealt with dishonest misappropriation of property, while the rest of the sections touched on criminal breach of trust offences. The presumption under section 409B (1) can be invoked by the court once the prosecution had proved that there was a misappropriation of money by the accused which involves the element of *actus reus* of the section. In the case of *Public Prosecutor v Haji Maamor bin Hj Abdul Manap*,⁵⁸ the court observed that in the absence of any direct evidence to establish a dishonest intention, the prosecutor was entitled to rely on section 409B to raise the presumption of dishonest misappropriation, after proving that the accused had misappropriated the money involved.

57   J Hall, D Karch and A Crosby, 'Elder Abuse Surveillance: Uniform Definitions and Recommended Core Elements' (2016) *Centers for Disease Control and Prevention* (CDC).

58   [2002] 6 MLJ 668.

7.3   *Providing Support by the Other Stakeholders*

A specific agency should be appointed to assist the older persons who want to protect themselves against financial abuse through power of attorney or fiduciary duty. Discussion and counselling as to what methods are available will help them in making the correct decision in their financial planning. This agency can work with the relevant ministries overseeing the affairs of older persons and the NGOs advocating for older persons' issues. Advocacy and outreach programme can be introduced to older persons and adults in their late fifties for better understanding and knowledge as well as forming part of the preparation for retirement and ageing. The planning must always come earlier.

Aside from this appointed agency, the financial institutions can also play a role by incorporating two measures for their older persons clients, namely; firstly, by introducing the monitoring system for their clients who are older persons. The clients are informed of this monitoring to detect any abnormal or unusual activities of their account. If such activities were detected, the institutions should inform the clients for confirmation purposes. This monitoring will not attract too much effort since presently, the financial institutions already have to monitor the activities of their clients for money laundering. Aside from that, the financial institutions, could also introduce the appointment of a trusted person when the older persons utilised their services. This trusted person will not have access to the older person's financial information but to act as the contact person to confirm certain information. For example, if the financial institution received a request to withdraw a substantial sum from the bank account, it can contact the trusted person to find out whether the older person is need of the said sum soon. As the person nominated by the older person to be his trusted person, it is safe to assume that that person will be aware of any changes in the older person's life. These two measures hopefully will allow the financial institutions to prevent financial abuse including scamming. Monitoring via the system and confirmation with the trusted person will provide additional layers of protections for the older person. These new measures can be introduced through in house policy or regulations, without the need to amend any law.

7.4   *Inclusion of Provisions on Empowerment of the Older Persons*

The provisions on empowerment of the older persons can be approached from two perspectives. Firstly, by providing provisions that recognise the right of the older persons to autonomy. Secondly, by creating legal duties on the community or agencies to assist in empowering the older persons. The exercise of his autonomy depends very much on the sufficient information and understanding of the older persons have over financial abuse. As such the provisions of Act 512 must include an obligation on the part of the authority to ensure that advocacy and awareness are part of the strategies in preventing older persons' financial abuse. This can be undertaken by the Activity Centre for Older Persons (*PAWE*), under the supervision of the Ministry of Women, Family and Community Development. *PAWE* provides social reaching out and development program for its members including spiritual and religious classes, health and wellness, information technology and activities on economic income.[59] *PAWE* can be utilised to share the information on financial abuse, remedies and procedures with the older persons. These activities are platforms for older persons to be empowered in order to maintain their wellbeing.[60]

8   Conclusion

The older persons are clearly a distinct and unique group of people with peculiar needs and traits which require special protection. They are particularly vulnerable and subject to various forms of abuse, with financial abuse as the most devastating against which, they are helpless and under protected in the present state of the law. There is a need for special protection through a thematic legislation taking into consideration the weakness and limitations of the older persons. Malaysian laws on older persons are still evolving, in her preparation to be an aged nation in 2030. Even though the focus of the law has always been on abuse and neglect in general, nevertheless, not much has been discussed about older persons' financial abuse. Perhaps the time is right for Malaysia to review the existing legislations on financial abuse in order to encompass the financial exploitation which cover the traditional and non-traditional financial abuse. Aside from the legislations, other supports from the other stakeholders and empowering the older persons will further strengthen the protection and prevention of older persons financial abuse in Malaysia.

---

59   S Johani, K Alavi and MS Mohamad, 'Comparison of Quality of Life Level among Elderly at Elderly Activity Center in Urban and Rural Areas' (2018) 32 *Jurnal Psikologi Malaysia* 82.

60   CF Chung, KH Pazim and K Mansur, 'Ageing Population: Policies and Programmes for Older People in Malaysia' (2020) 2 *Asian Journal of Research in Education and Social Sciences* 92, 96.

Note on the Contributors

Mohammad Abu Taher
Assistant Professor, Deptartment of Law, American International University-Bangladesh (AIUB).

Olivia Tan Swee Leng
Senior Lecturer, Faculty of Management, Multimedia University, Malaysia.

Siti Zaharah Jamaluddin
Former Associate Professor, Faculty of Law, University of Malaya, Malaysia.

CHAPTER 12

The Un-peopling of Peoples: A Critical Study on the Justifiability of the Non-recognition of the Indigenous Peoples of the Chittagong Hill Tracts

Adity Rahman Shah

Abstract

Despite being a religiously pluralist and parliamentary democratic country, Bangladesh does not recognise the indigenous groups of the Chittagong Hill Tracts (CHT) area as indigenous peoples, the residence of the majority of ethnic communities on its territory. Historically, various ethnic groups in CHT have always enjoyed local autonomy and special status. However, after Bangladesh was liberated in 1971, it did not recognise any special/separate status of the CHT ethnic communities in its attempt to enforce nationalism. Consequently, the indigenous peoples of CHT lost their right to autonomy, land rights and even cultural identity. Promisingly in 2014, in *Wagachara Tea Estate Ltd. Case*, the Appellate Division of Bangladesh has expressly admitted the existence of "indigenous peoples" in the CHT region. But, in the 2016 Universal Periodic Review, the Government of Bangladesh outwardly denied the existence of indigenous peoples in the territory. Further, in 2019, a new government order came to remove the word "indigenous" from the title of every registered organisation in Bangladesh. Against such a background, this paper attempts to explore the legal and factual basis of the CHT indigenous community's claim to be recognised as "indigenous peoples" and examines the justification of Bangladesh's current approach of non-recognition of the CHT indigenous peoples under relevant IHRL. The paper also sheds light on the possible domestic legal strategy to address the situation.

Keywords

indigenous rights – Chittagong Hill Tracts – self-determination – domestic recognition – human rights – Bangladesh

1   Introduction

It has been a long urged claim of the indigenous communities of the Chittagong Hill Tracts[1] (hereinafter CHT) of Bangladesh, the residence of the majority indigenous populations in the territory, to be recognised as "indigenous peoples" (hereinafter IPs).[2] Approximately 73 ethnic groups spread in CHT and the other parts of Bangladesh.[3] However, the ethnic groups in CHT, who are the focus of this paper, unlike other indigenous communities of Bangladesh, have historically always enjoyed special status and local autonomy similar to IPs. But since the 1971 liberation, Bangladesh, being a religiously pluralist, parliamentary democratic country, has always denied the existence of any IPs in its national territorial boundary to this date. The lack of legal recognition, specifically of the CHT ethnic communities as IPs, has been one of the primary concerns of human rights bodies[4] expressed regarding Bangladesh's human rights situation.

Domestic recognition as IPs is crucial for the indigenous communities worldwide that are subject to persistent human rights violations.[5] The IHR instruments ensure that all "peoples" have the right to self-determination (hereinafter RSD)[6] and may "freely determine their political status and freely pursue their economic, social and cultural development" in a society.[7] The RSD is a jus-cogens norm,[8] and several human rights bodies have produced jurisprudences on its significance, particularly for indigenous communities.[9] Thus, RSD is the key element to avail the indigenous rights to their culture,

---

1   Situated at the south-eastern corner of Bangladesh.

2   Working Group on Indigenous Populations (WGIP), UN Doc E/CN.4/Sub.2/2002/24, para 42.

3   M Rafi, *Small Ethnic Groups of Bangladesh: A Mapping Exercise* (Panjeree Publications, 2006) 33.

4   Human Rights Committee (HRC), Concluding Observations (CO) Bangladesh, UN Doc CCPR/C/BGD/CO/1 (2017), para 11; The Committee on Economic, Social and Cultural (CESCR), Concluding Observations (CO) Bangladesh, UN Doc (E/C.12/BGD/1) (2018), para 15.

5   P Thornberry, *Indigenous peoples and Human Rights* (Manchester University Press, 2002) 18.

6   Article 1 of International Covenant on Civil and Political Rights (ICCPR) (adopted 16 December 1966, entered into force 23 March 1976) 999 UNTS 171; Article 1 of International Covenant on Economic, Social and Cultural Rights (ICESCR) (adopted 16 December 1966, entered into force 3 Jan 1976) 993 UNTS 3; Article 1 of Charter of the United Nations (24 October 1945) 1 UNTS XVI.

7   See ICCPR and ICESCR.

8   International Law Commission, UN Doc A/56/10, chap. IV, Commentary on the draft article 26 of the "Draft Articles on the Responsibility of States for Internationally Wrongful Acts".

9   CERD, 'GR No 21: The Right to Self-determination' (2003), UN Doc HRI\GEN\1\Rev.6 209; HRC, CO, Australia UN Doc A/55/40 (24 July 2000); HRC, CO, Canada, UN Doc CCPR/C/79 /Add.105 (7 April 1999).

land, and, in other words, their right to life. But, states are reluctant to provide the "peoples" status, particularly to indigenous communities, because RSD has historically been specified as a part of the decolonisation process, and any unregulated exercise of RSD is presumed to affect the territorial integrity, political stability and sovereignty of the concerned state.[10] However, the CHT indigenous communities have always asked for internal RSD through local autonomy or self-government rather than the permanent secession leading to external RSD,[11] which may negatively impact Bangladesh's territorial integrity, stability and sovereignty.

Against this backdrop, this article focuses on Bangladesh's current approach of not recognising CHT ethnic communities as IPs, which has a negative impact on their human rights. It aims to prove through legal analysis that the CHT communities are IPs under relevant standards and that such non-recognition violates Bangladesh's pertinent international human rights law obligations.

Apart from the present introduction and the conclusion, the article unfolds over three main sections. As a background of the study, the first section starts with a brief historical overview of the development of the administrative and legal status of the CHT indigenous communities in Bangladesh so far. It also sheds light on the current position of the CHT indigenous communities and their rights in the domestic legal framework. The second section outlines the identifying criteria of IPs as per the international standards and concludes with the proper factual basis that CHT indigenous communities fulfil these criteria as IPs. Finally, the third and last section explores whether the current approach of Bangladesh towards the CHT indigenous communities is justified as per the relevant IHRL and recommends possible legal strategies to improve the current situation for CHT indigenous communities.

This paper employs exploratory and analytical approaches to analyse and explore the relevant normative standards, jurisprudential and doctrinal basis of recognizing the Indigenous peoples in international human rights laws and the obligation of Bangladesh thereof. The paper adopts qualitative method in collecting and analysing data from primary and secondary sources. It uses international treaties, customary principles, legal doctrines, domestic legislation, national and international case laws, General Comments of various UN

---

10   Vienna Declaration and Programme of Action (adopted 12 July 1993), UN Doc A/CONF.157/23, para 2; Declaration on Principles of International Law Concerning Friendly Relations and Co-operation Among States in Accordance with the Charter of the United Nations (adopted 24 October 1970), UNGA Res 2625 (XXV).

11   For internal and external RSD classification see, P Thornberry, 'Self-Determination, Minorities, Human Rights: A Review of International Instruments' (1989) 38 *ICLQ* 867, 869.

Bodies (treaty/charter based), indigenous accords as primary sources, depending on the background resources popularly known as secondary sources. The secondary sources include journal articles, textbooks, UN Committee report, online materials and other resources providing explanations and commentaries on the area of the research.

2 An Overview of the Legal Position of Bangladesh Regarding the CHT Ethnic Communities

2.1 *Historical Overview*

This section portrays the present domestic position of the legal system of Bangladesh in incorporating the CHT indigenous community's right to be recognised as IPs. To start with the discourse, a brief historical overview of the development of the administrative and legal status of the CHT region of Bangladesh is essential.

The CHT Region, being the exclusive hilly area, is situated in the southeastern corner of Bangladesh. The ethnohistorical evidence reveals that the indigenous populations in CHT had an independent feudal kingdom[12] from ancient times until the Mughal period.[13] The CHT communities were always basically self-governing bodies.[14] After the defeat of Palasi (battle of Plussey) in 1757, the Mughal period came to an end, and the British colonial regime started to make its footsteps in the region.[15] In 1860, for the first time, the area in the discussion was named the "Chittagong Hill Tracts" and was placed under the British colonial administration.[16] From the very beginning, the colonial steps faced resistance from the tribal kings.[17] Notably, in 1891, the colonial rulers took

---

12   MK Chakma, JW Khokshi et al. (eds), *Bangladesher Adivasi: Ethnographio Gobeshona, Prothom Khondo* [*Adivasis of Bangladesh: Ethnographic Research, 1st Part*] (Utsho Prokashon, 2015) 28.

13   RCK Roy, *Land Rights of the Indigenous Peoples of the Chittagong Hill Tracts, Bangladesh* (IWGIA Document No. 99, 2000) 38, 39.

14   W Mey, 'The Road to Repression: Aspects of Bengali Encroachment on the Chittagong Hill Tracts 1860–1983' in Wolfgang Mey (ed), *Genocide in the Chittagong Hill Tracts, Bangladesh* (Bangladesh Groep Nederland, IWGIA Document 51, 1983).

15   WV Schendel, *A History of Bangladesh* (Cambridge University Press, 2009) 49.

16   Act XXII of 1860 (repealed by the Scheduled Districts Act 1874). The CHT, however, was first annexed by the East-India Company as their tributary in 1787 and the Company recognized CHT's quasi-independent status.

17   Capt. TH Lewin, *The Hill Tracts of Chittagong and the Dwellers Therein; with Comparative Vocabularies of the Hill Dialects* (Bengal Printing Company Ltd., Calcutta 1869) 212.

control of CHT.[18] The British rulers appraisingly acknowledged the cultural diversity, traditional customary laws and the land rights of the ethnic communities in Chittagong Hill Tracts Regulation, 1900 (Regulation of 1900).[19] This Regulation of 1900 ensured them self-government and autonomy[20] and set up a separate legal (mainly civil matters) and administrative system for the area. Even the Government of India Act of 1935[21] assigned the CHT as an "excluded area". After the 1947 decolonisation,[22] the CHT region was in the East Pakistan zone. The 1956 Constitution (the first Constitution in the Pakistan era) retained the special status of all the tribal areas in the territory, including the CHT region, being the exclusive homeland of the indigenous communities.[23] Given this trajectory, it is observed that the indigenous communities of CHT retained their autonomy this far. Unfortunately, by the 1964 Constitutional Amendment, CHT was removed from the list of tribal areas. However, the previous Regulation of 1900 was not repealed and continued to exist. After the 1971 liberation war, Bangladesh emerged as an independent state. It became a party to the ILO Convention No. 107 (hereinafter ILO C107),[24] the only international binding norm concerning indigenous communities ratified by Bangladesh so far. However, no domestic legislation in Bangladesh has accorded the CHT populations any special status to this date.

2.2   *Current Legal Position of Bangladesh*
For a clear and comprehensive concept regarding the current legal position of CHT indigenous communities in Bangladesh, the discussion has been fragmented into three parts. Firstly, how the different legal/institutional documents name the CHT ethnic communities, secondly, how their right to land and culture are incorporated in the legal system, and finally, the impact of the 1997 CHT Peace Accord.

---

18   Mey, *supra* note 14.

19   Regulation I of 1900 (entered into force 17 January 1900).

20   The local government of the CHT was entrusted with extensive rule-making power regarding every aspect of regulating the area and they may revise the existing provisions of the Regulation of 1900, *Ibid.* s 4 (2), 17 (3),18, Rule 58.

21   [26 GEO. 5. CH. 2.], https://www.legislation.gov.uk/ukpga/1935/2/pdfs/ukpga_19350002_en.pdf (accessed 13 December 2022), repealed (26 January 1950, India) (23 March 1956, Pakistan and Bangladesh).

22   The Indian sub-continent was decolonized from colonial British rule by the Indian Independence Act, 1947 and formed two separate states, India and Pakistan, the Pakistan had two parts- West Pakistan (now Pakistan) and East Pakistan (now Bangladesh).

23   Roy, *supra* note 13, 46.

24   Indigenous and Tribal Populations Convention 1957 (No. 107) (adopted 26 June 1957, entered into force 2 June 1959).

2.2.1   The Inconsistencies in the Legal Status

The indigenous communities in Bangladesh are not designated as IPs in any domestic legislative pieces. Initially, the 1972 Constitution[25] did not mention the indigenous communities residing in Bangladesh, and indigenous rights were considered to have been addressed in the section which secures the rights of the "backward section of citizens".[26] Notably, Bangladesh Constitution urges that "the people of Bangladesh shall be known as Bangalees as a nation and the citizens of Bangladesh shall be known as Bangladeshies".[27] Bangalee or Bengali is an ethnic group predominantly residing in Bengal and other parts of South Asia, having a distinct language and cultural practices and belonging to the Indo-Aryan group.[28] This constitutional provision clearly denies the existence of any other ethnic group in the state and unjustifiably forces the "Bangalee" ethnic identity over everyone residing in Bangladesh.

However, interestingly in 2011, Article 23A was inserted by the Constitution (Fifteenth Amendment) Act, which uses "tribes", "minor races" and "ethnic sects and communities" to indicate indigenous communities. Some Bangladeshi legislation refers to the CHT indigenous communities as "indigenous hillmen/ tribesmen"[29] or "aboriginal".[30] Section 2(2) of the Small Ethnic Groups Cultural Institution Act of 2010 speaks about people belonging to "small ethnic communities" or "adivasi"[31] communities. Unfortunately, no other domestic human rights legislation in Bangladesh mentions the indigenous community/rights. Also, the Preamble of the CHT Peace Accord[32] envisages "all the people in the CHT region" to refer to the CHT indigenous communities.

Thus, it is observed that Bangladesh does not directly endow the CHT ethnic communities with the legislative status of IPs. However, promisingly in 2014,

---

25   The Constitution of the People's Republic of Bangladesh, Presidential Order (PO) No 76 of 1972.

26   *Ibid.*, Article 29(3)(a).

27   *Ibid.*, Article 6(2).

28   https://www.britannica.com/topic/Bengali (accessed 23 January 2023).

29   See, ibid., *supra* note 19, Rule 4, 6, 34,45 & 50; Act No. 12 of 1995 Bangladesh; Paripatra of the Board of Revenue of 12 July 1995 Bangladesh; Administrative Regulations of 17 September 1992, 10 March 1982, 4 September 1980 and 6 April 1967; Government of the People's Republic of Bangladesh, National Board of Revenue, Application of the Income Tax Act 1922 Indigenous Hillmen residing in the Chittagong Hill Tracts, clarification regarding Memo C. No. 4 (6) Kac-5/77/589 (4 September 1980).

30   East Bengal State Acquisition and Tenancy Act 1950, s 97.

31   Means "indigenous" in Bengali language.

32   The CHT Peace Accord of 1997., https://www.ilo.org/dyn/natlex/docs/ELECTRONIC /87975/100450/F1549787842/BGD87975.pdf (accessed 15 December 2022).

in the *Wagachara Tea Estate Ltd. Case*,[33] for the first time in Bangladesh, the Appellate Division has specifically used the terminology of "indigenous peoples" and assured their existence in the CHT region. According to Article 111 of the Constitution of Bangladesh, a decision of the Appellate Division is legally binding on all. However, despite the fact, the Government of Bangladesh (GoB) outwardly denied the existence of IPs in Bangladesh in the 2016 Universal Periodic Review UPR stating that "there is no community or group of people designated or recognised as 'indigenous' in Bangladesh".[34] Further, in 2019, a government order came to remove the word "indigenous" from the title of every registered organisation in Bangladesh.[35] It proves the degree of the reluctance of Bangladesh to recognise the CHT ethnic communities as IPs. Interestingly, being a party to ILO C107, Bangladesh is obligated to uphold the rights of "indigenous populations."[36] But Bangladesh's domestic legal framework does not explicitly recognise the CHT ethnic communities even as "indigenous populations."

2.2.2   Traditional Rights to Land, Resource and Culture

The right to land and resource of the indigenous communities is largely neglected in the legal framework of Bangladesh. The domestic legal system does not have any specific provision which acknowledges the rights of the CHT ethnic communities to their ancestral lands so far. The Regulation of 1900 has attempted to incorporate the land rights, but this Regulation has been ignored by the administration and judiciary so far.[37] Approximately 20,000 acres of ancestral lands owned by the CHT IPs have been acquisitioned by the Government for various purposes.[38] According to the CHT Regional Council Act 1998,[39] the Council formed under the Act[40] shall have the right to acquire and transfer

33   *Wagachara Tea Estate Ltd vs Muhammad Abu Taher and others*, Civil Appeal No. 147 of 2007 AD (2 December 2014) 11.
34   HRC, Replies of Bangladesh to the list of issues, UN Doc CCPR/C/BGD/Q/1/Add.1 (14 February 2017), para 24.
35   Directive [Ref. No. 03.07.2666.660.66.49219.888] issued by the NGO Affairs Bureau.
36   Indigenous and Tribal Populations Convention, Article 1 (b).
37   For example, *Collector vs Azizuddin*, 23 DLR (SC)73; the High Court Division judgment in 2003 in *Ministry of Finance vs Rangamati Food Products Ltd. And others*, Writ Petition No.1774 of 2001; *Government of Bangladesh vs Rangamati Food Products Ltd. & others*, 2017 (1) LNJ (AD) 110, para 4.
38   Executive Summary of the Human Rights Report on Indigenous Peoples in Bangladesh 2017, https://www.kapaeengnet.org/executive-summary-of-the-human-rights-report-on-indigenous-peoples-in-bangladesh-2017–2728 (accessed 14 December 2022).
39   Act of 1998, s 3.
40   Members of the council shall be selected from tribal community, *ibid.* s 4.

any land in the CHT region, and the Government cannot make any law relating to land or the Council's power without notifying the Council and people living in the region. Similarly, the Rangamati, Khagrachhari and Bandarban District Council Acts of 1998[41] provide that without the prior consent of the District Council, formed with the representatives of the ethnic communities under the Act, no land transfer or settlement would take place. Unfortunately, these Councils have never been made a part of the CHT land administration.

The CHT Land Dispute Settlement Commission Act 2001[42] allows the Commission to settle the CHT land disputes with existing laws and customs.[43] However, thousands of complaints are pending without any single effective decision to this date.[44] There are allegations that the approach of the Commission is hostile to the customary laws.[45] Besides, no civil suit is permissible against the Commission's decision,[46] making the process more arbitrary. Furthermore, the Forest Act of 1927 and other supplementary legislation relevant to CHT land administration, such as the CHT Forest Transit Rules of 1973 and the CHT Land Acquisition Tenancy Regulation 1958, never included effective participation of the concerned ethnic representatives in the decision-making process. It is evident from the aforesaid discussions that the domestic legal system of Bangladesh does not protect and preserve the customary practices of collective land ownership by the CHT indigenous communities. Consequently, land grabbing takes place in the name of development projects, through forced eviction[47] and migration of Bengali settlers – apparently with Government backing.

---

41   Act no IX of 1998, s 64 (b).

42   Act 53 of 2001, s 3.

43   *Ibid.*, s 6(1)(a).

44   HRC, Summary record of the 3340th meeting, 119th Session, UN Doc CCPR/C/SR.3340 (7 March 2017), para 21.

45   Specific case references are unavailable due to Covid-19, CESCR expressed concerns on the lack of information regarding decisions of the Land Commission, CESCR, *supra* note 4, para 17.

46   Act 53 of 2001, s 16.

47   "Attacks, Land Grabs Leave Bangladesh's Indigenous Groups on Edge," 30 July 2021, https://www.aljazeera.com/news/2021/7/30/bangladesh-indigenous-groups-chakma -khasi-santal-land-grab (accessed 13 December 2022), C R Abrar, 19th November 2020, Land Grab and Resistance in the Chimbuk Hills https://www.thedailystar.net/opinion /news/land-grab-and-resistance-the-chimbuk-hills-1997245 (accessed 13 December 2022); "Commercial Rubber Plantation Evicted 21 Indigenous Families in Bandarban," https://alrd.org/news-events/11/25 (accessed 13 December 2022), "Chittagong Hill Tracts: Development Project Destroying Graveyards and Ancestral Agricultural Lands in the Bandarban District," 24 March 2020, https://unpo.org/article/21784 (accessed 13 December 2022).

The CHT indigenous communities of Bangladesh do not have any judicially enforceable rights to their culture. In 2011, Article 23A was inserted in the Constitution,[48] which says, "the State shall take steps to protect and develop the unique local culture and tradition of the tribes, minor races, ethnic sects and communities". However, Article 23A is incorporated as one of the Fundamental Principles of State Polices (hereinafter FPSP).[49] Unfortunately, the FPSPs of the Bangladesh Constitution are not judicially enforceable.[50] So the constitutional inclusion of indigenous communities' cultural rights does not emerge as an effective tool due to the legal character of Article 23A. In 2010, the GoB enacted the Small Ethnic Groups Cultural Institution Act[51] to respect, protect and preserve the distinct cultural identity of the ethnic groups in Bangladesh. Unfortunately, the law does not seem to impact the situation as it does not impose any government accountability for non-compliance. For instance, a survey reveals that almost 100% of the ethnic participants opine that their mother language is either vulnerable or endangered or extinct.[52] Also, the country's Education Policy does not incorporate the formalisation of the indigenous languages or culture in the national curriculum.[53] Thus the cultural rights of the CHT indigenous communities are highly neglected in the domestic sphere.

If the CHT community had been granted at least the internal RSD, it would have facilitated the preservation of economic, social and cultural rights relating to their land and resources from encroachment and confiscation and aided the protection of cultural rights as language and tradition. Thus, the impact of non-recognition as IPs has a harsh effect on the indigenous communities of the CHT.

2.2.3   The CHT Peace Accord

The absence of legal recognition of indigenous identity and land and cultural rights led to land grabbing, forced eviction, militarisation and countless other oppressive situations in the CHT region. Consequently, the CHT ethnic communities entered into a civil war against the state authority in demand

---

48   The Constitution (Fifteenth Amendment) Act, 2011 (Act XIV of 2011) s 14.
49   The Constitution of the People's Republic of Bangladesh, Presidential Order (PO) No 76 of 1972, Part II.
50   *Ibid.*, Article 8(2).
51   Act no. 23 of 2010.
52   Conducted by Kapaeeng Foundation, https://www.thedailystar.net/opinion/news/state -our-indigenous-languages-1783657 (accessed 20 December 2022).
53   KS Murmu, 'State of our indigenous languages' *The Daily Star* (Dhaka, 9 August 2019).

of regional autonomy.[54] To cease the longstanding hostilities, the GoB signed a peace accord with the representative of the CHT ethnic communities in 1997.[55] The Accord brings many promising clauses to assure land rights, political representation and cultural identification of the IPs. However, though the Government has enacted legislation and established organisations to implement the Accord, those remain largely ineffective. The Accord successfully ended the bloody conflicts between the rebellious CHT ethnic groups and the state. But the failure to implement the Accord has rendered the CHT ethnic communities more marginalised and oppressed.

Moreover, in 2000, the Accord was declared unconstitutional. The judiciary contended that it was a "mere" political agreement signed to facilitate the public interest and ensure a peaceful and secured environment for the CHT residents.[56] These statements downgraded the status of the Accord and thereby invalidated any chance of judicial enforceability.

As the background of the article, the current section depicts the contradictions between the current legislative framework and administrative approach regarding the status of CHT indigenous groups as IPs, which negatively impacts their rights. It also makes us realise how important it is for CHT indigenous groups to be recognised as IPs in order to exercise their rights under the state system. Moreover, as per international law, any formal recognition of "peoples" is "irrevocable."[57] Thus, the history of repeated acts of recognition and denial of the status of CHT IPs by the state authority is also not justified.

The extent of the denial of the right over land and natural resources of the indigenous community of CHT and the right over their ethnic identity makes us question the reason behind the hostile attitude of the Government of Bangladesh toward them. The concept of "nation" has been used mainly in the international legal platform to overlook national diversity.[58] The nationalists propose a single uniform community across the territory to deny any separate identity claims by the ethnocultural minority groups[59] and establish nationhood as a pre-condition of RSD. Thus, denying distinct ethnic identity curtails the opportunity of RSD by group by the society. The Liberation War

---

54   I Jamil and PK Panday, 'The Elusive Peace Accord in the Chittagong Hill Tracts of Bangladesh and the Plight of the Indigenous People' (2008) 46 *CCP* 464, 465.
55   The 1997 Accord, *supra* note 32.
56   *Mohammad Badiuzzaman vs Bangladesh* Writ Petition No. 2669 of 2000 (HCD) 7 LG (HCD) (2010).
57   W Churchill, 'A Travesty of a Mockery of a Sham: Colonialism as 'Self-Determination' in the UN Declaration on the Rights of Indigenous Peoples' (2011) 20 *GLR* 526, 542.
58   G Pentassuglia, 'Self-Determination, Human Rights and the Nation-State' (2017) *ICLR* 448.
59   *Ibid.*, 449.

of Bangladesh in 1971, generated by the RSD on the ground of Bengali ethnic origin against Pakistani nationalism, may define the reason behind forcing Bengali nationalism during the post-war period.[60] However, the unjustified state-sponsored aggression leading to confiscation and encroachment of the land and natural resources of the CHT peoples proves that economic exploitation also plays a significant role in the non-recognition of the CHT indigenous communities.

In light of this, before analysing the legitimacy of Bangladesh's approach and mapping out the state's obligations under IHRL, the next step would be to determine whether the CHT ethnic groups fall within the scope of IPs under international standards.

3   A Brief Analysis of the Concept of "Indigenous Peoples" under International Standards: An Endeavor to Determine the Status of the CHT Ethnic Communities

3.1   Defining/Identifying "Indigenous Peoples"

To identify which communities are eligible to be designated as IPs, the concept of "peoples" must be explored first. Though the existing legal instruments say that "all peoples" have the RSD,[61] they do not clarify who are "peoples". For RSD, the term "peoples" applies to "a portion of the population of an existing state",[62] i.e. a collectivity of individuals constituted by the self-identification,[63] living in a geographically separate territory, distinct ethnically and culturally from the majority population of the country.[64] Sometimes it is opined that for RSD, "peoples" includes a victimised/oppressed portion of the population.[65] However, this has not always been the case.[66] So, a minority or ethnic community does not constitute "peoples" on its own.

---

60   MA Ali, 'Place and Contested Identity: Portraying the Role of the Place in Shaping Common sociopolitical Identity in the Chittagong Hill Tracts, Bangladesh' (2012) 1 *Diversipede* 31, 33; A Ghoshal, 'Histories and Memories of the Liberation War: *Saranarthis* in Tripura' (2021) 45 *Strategic Analysis* 598.

61   *Ibid.*, 6.

62   *Reference Re Secession of Quebec*, [1998] 2 S.C.R. 217.

63   U Abulof, 'We the Peoples? The Strange Demise of Self-determination' (2016) 22 *EJIR* 536, 554.

64   UNGA Res 1541 (XV) GAOR, 15th Session, Supplement No 16 UN Doc A/4684 (15 December 1960).

65   Pentassuglia, *supra* note 58, 443, 465.

66   For example, Badinter Arbitration Commission termed Bosnian and Croatian Serbs as population, minority, and ethnic group but not as "people" while deciding their RSD, see

Now, the concern is whether indigenous communities can constitute "peoples" or not?

Duruigbo, who comprehensively enlisted four eligible classes of groups as "peoples", included "indigenous people"[67] as one of them. UNDRIP states that "Indigenous peoples have the right to self-determination".[68] Common article 1 of ICCPR or ICESCR specifies that "qll peoples have the right of self-determination".[69] So it indicates that in the context of RSD, the term "all peoples" enshrined in the international legal instruments includes IPs. So, indigenous communities are entitled to be recognised as "peoples". However, the concept of "peoples" and IPs is not the same, while the latter requires specific added requirements, i.e. deeply rooted relationship with their ancestral lands.[70]

So, who can be called IPs? While searching for the answer, it is necessary to understand that defining IPs is difficult for their cultural and characteristic diversity. The IPs are recognised by many different community names in various jurisdictions,[71] for example, "tribes, first peoples/nations, aboriginals, ethnic groups, adivasi, janajati, occupational and geographical terms like hunter-gatherers, nomads, peasants, hill people, etc.".[72] Also, the IPs have denounced themselves to have a universal definition.[73] Instead, they suggested having identifying characteristics for IPs.[74]

Though several attempts have been made, the working definition provided by the UN Special Rapporteur J. Martinez-Cobo in 1972 is one of the first consolidated approaches in this regard. The definition indicates[75] a group of people who inhabited their present residing territory before the

---

Opinion No 2, The EC Arbitration Commission of the Conference on Yugoslavia, International Legal Materials 31 (11 January 1992) 1497.

67   E Duruigbo, 'Permanent Sovereignty and Peoples' Ownership of Natural Resources in International Law' (2006) 38 *GWILR* 33, 35.

68   United Nations Declaration on the Rights of Indigenous Peoples (UNDRIP) (adopted 2 October 2007), UNGA Res A/RES/61/295, Article 3.

69   *Ibid.*, 6.

70   S J Anaya, *Indigenous Peoples in International Law* (OUP 2004) 3.

71   Thornberry, *supra* note 5, 13.

72   United Nations Permanent Forum on Indigenous Issues (UNPFII), Factsheet, https://www.un.org/esa/socdev/unpfii/documents/5session_factsheet1.pdf (accessed 14 January 2023).

73   WGIP, 14th Session UN Doc E/CN.4/Sub.2/1996/21 (16 August 1996).

74   Thornberry, *supra* note 5.

75   JM Cobo (Special Rapporteur of the UN Sub-Commission on Prevention of Discrimination and Protection of Minorities), Study on the Problem of Discrimination against Indigenous Populations, UN Doc E/CN.4/Sub.2/1986/7/Add.4 (1987), para 379.

colonisation/settlement took place by a dominant majority group of persons belonging to a different culture/ ethnic identity, and the first inhabitants still retain their distinct social and cultural identity as a non-dominant section of the society in the present state-structure. Besides, the first normative standard which locates the definition of IPs (also tribal peoples) is ILO C169,[76] which says:

> peoples in independent countries who are regarded as indigenous on account of their descent from the populations which inhabited the country, or a geographical region to which the country belongs, at the time of conquest or colonisation or the establishment of present state boundaries and who, irrespective of their legal status, retain some or all of their own social, economic, cultural and political institution.

If we follow the World Bank definition of IPs,[77] it indicates:

> a distinct, vulnerable, social and cultural group possessing the following characteristics in varying degrees: (a) self-identification as members of a distinct indigenous cultural group and recognition of this identity by others; (b) collective attachment to geographically distinct habitats or ancestral territories in the project area and to the natural resources in these habitats and territories7 (c) customary cultural, economic, social, or political institutions that are separate from those of the dominant society and culture; and (d) an indigenous language, often different from the official language of the country or region.

Thus, the standards set in the ILO C169 and the working definition by Cobo and the World Bank provide three common identifying characteristics. Firstly, it indicates a population or community which lives in a particular part of the territory to denote a special relation to that specific territory since the pre-colonial or pre-settlers time, i.e., they are the habitual residents since antiquity. Secondly, it provides that the population or community must have its own culture, language and social, economic and political system distinct from the majority population. Thirdly, they have been rendered non-dominant sections of the society by the majority segment by conquest or colonisation.

---

76   Indigenous and Tribal Peoples Convention No. 169 (adopted June 29 1989, entered into force September 5 1991), 1650 UNTS 543 Art 1 (b).

77   World Bank Operational Manual OP 4.10 – Indigenous Peoples, para 4.

Moreover, both the ILO C169[78] and the World Bank definition incorporate "self-identification" as a fundamental criterion in the indigenous status determination procedure. Considering its growing importance in IPs' status determination, the International Law Association (ILA) has assigned "self-identification" as the first criterion in the process.[79]

Thus, self-identification and the above-mentioned three common characteristics constitute four essential identifying criteria for the status determination of IPs. So, in reality, the IPs' status determination is a "two-step test",[80] i.e., first, the community fulfils the above-mentioned three indigenous definitional criteria, and next, that community identifies itself as IPs. Thus, a community becomes IPs upon the fulfilment of all these four elements, which indicates that the status of IPs does not depend on state recognition.

3.2 *Status Determination of Ethnic Communities of the CHT Region*

With the identifying criteria set, the next attempt is to examine whether the claim of the CHT ethnic communities of Bangladesh to be identified as IPs is justified or not.

3.2.1 Self-Identification

Self-identification denotes that an ethnic community must identify themselves as IPs. The IPs must certify the indigenous identity of a group or an individual as one of their own, or it may be a combination of both "personal and communal" self-recognition as IPs.[81] The CHT indigenous communities have declared their self-identification as IPs on various platforms, from the national parliament[82] to UN Forums.[83] Their self-identification as IPs has been affirmed by the Martinez Cobo Study too.[84] Moreover, in 2018, CESCR

---

78   Indigenous and Tribal Peoples Convention, Article 1 (2).

79   ILA Report of the Sofia Conference on the Rights of Indigenous Peoples (2012) para 2, https://ila.vettoreweb.com/Storage/Download.aspx?DbStorageId=1243&StorageFileGuid =401ee841-8ad2-4e35-8aaf-beebd9b3aa4e (accessed 27 April 2022).

80   M Weller, 'Self-Determination of Indigenous Peoples' in J Hohmann and M Weller (eds), *The UN Declaration on the Rights of Indigenous Peoples: A Commentary* (Oxford University Press, 2018) 125.

81   Cobo, *supra* note 74; UN Doc E/CN.4/Sub.2/1982/2/Add.6 (20 June 1982), para 210.

82   Government of Bangladesh, *Bangladesh Jatiyo Sangsad Bitorko: Sarkari Biboroni (Bangladesh Parliamentary Debates)* volume 2 (Dacca, 1972) 452.

83   UNPFII, UN Doc E/C.19/2013/18, para 32,; UNPFII, UN Doc HR/GENEVA/SEM/EXPERT /2012/BP.

84   Cobo, *supra* note, para 15.

confirmed the CHT indigenous communities' self-identification as IPs.[85] Thus, the CHT ethnic communities fulfil the first fundamental criterion.

3.2.2   The Links with the Land

The second identifying element of the IPs is the community's historical bonding with the particular geographical territory since the pre-colonial or pre-settlers period. The word "indigenous" also bears "a sense of original or first inhabitants".[86] So, it is necessary to demonstrate the historical priority of the particular community in their inhabited area.

The CHT consists of three different districts: Rangamati, Khagrachori and Bandarban. There are eleven dominant indigenous communities in these districts: Chakma, Marma, Tripura, Tangchangya, Mru, Bawm, Lushai, Pang-khua, Khumi, Khyang, and Chaks, which can be traced back to antiquity to have settled in the CHT region.[87]

In the ancient period, the Arakan State and the CHT were single State.[88] So, the aforesaid CHT ethnic communities can be located in the Arakan history to have resided in the region. The Chakma, the largest ethnic community of the CHT region, was the first-ever community to settle in the CHT region and has a historical presence of almost 1400 years.[89] The Tangchangya people were the first inhabitants of the Matamuhuri Riverbank of Bandarban since around 1418 AD.[90] The existence of the Pangkhua community as original settlers in the

---

85   CESCR, para 15.

86   Thornberry, *supra* note 5, 39.

87   Chakma, *supra* note 12, 58; Philip Gain (ed), *Survival on the Fringe, Adivasis of Bangladesh* (SEHD, 2011) 1; B Chakma, 'The Post-colonial State and Minorities: Ethnocide in the Chittagong Hill Tracts , Bangladesh' (2010) 48 *Commonwealth and Comparative Politics* 281; S Drong, *Bangladesher Biponno Adivasi* (Naoroj Kitabistan, 2010) 13, MH Sumon, *Ethnicity and Adivasi Identity in Bangladesh* (Routledge, 2022) 12; Ali, *supra* note 60; Ali, *supra* note 33; Background of Chittagong Hill Tracts, https://www.angelfire.com/ab/jumma /bground.html (accessed 23 January 2023).

88   Chakma, *supra* note 12, 415.

89   Mangal, *supra* note 12, 207; Gain, *supra* note 87; M O'Brien, 'Legal Pluralism and Stigma: A Case-study of Customary Resurgence in the Chakma Communities of Bangladesh and India' (2021) 1 *International Journal of Law in Context* 356; M O'Brien, 'Law, Culture, and Community at the Borders of the State' PhD diss., School of Oriental and African Studies, University of London, 2019, 13; "Chakma Minority: Their History, Customs And Lifestyle, Bangladesh-Ethnic Groups and Minorities," https://factsanddetails.com/south-asia /Bangladesh/Ethnic_Groups_and_Minorities_Bangladesh/entry-8181.html#chapter-2 (accessed 23 January 2023).

90   Chakma, *supra* note 12, 265; LM Surhone, MT Tennoe and SF Henssonow, *Tanchangya People* (Betascript Publishing, 2011).

Rangamati District is evident in the history of 200 years ago.[91] The Bawm community settled in the CHT around the 17th Century.[92] In 1666 AD, the Marma community was established as permanent inhabitants at the CHT port area by paying taxes to the Mughal Dynasty.[93] The Mru community established an independent state in Arakan in 2666 BC for the first time and ruled for almost 2000 years.[94] Later on, they migrated and settled down to the west side of the river Sangu and along the Matamuhuri River in the CHT.[95] The traces of the Tripura community can be found in the pre-colonial period of undivided India, where they ruled for almost 2000 years.[96] In 1513 AD, the Tripura king occupied CHT.[97] Since that time, the Tripura community had migrated and started to reside there. The Chaks used to live in Arakan for 3000 years before the birth of Buddha and later on settled permanently in the CHT at the end of the 15th ccentury.[98] The Khiyang,[99] Khumi[100] and Lusai[101] communities are believed to have migrated into the CHT region between 1700 and 1800. The Khiyang community is the first settlers of Jimran, Kukkachahari, Dhanucchari and Arachari *Mouzas*[102] of the Rangamati District.[103]

91   Chakma, *supra* note 12, 351.

92   *Ibid.*, 391; M D Miah and MM Hossain, 'Forest Dependence of the Bawm Community and the Circumstances relating to their Involvement with REDD+ Program in Bandarban' (2013) 36 *The Chittagong University Journal of Science* 69, 72; Gain, *supra* note 87, 161.

93   Chakma, *supra* note 12, 417, 418; Gain, *supra* note 87, 97; AC Marma, *The Livelihood of Marma Community in Bangladesh*, http://echo-lab.ddo.jp/Libraries (accessed 23 January 2023) 19.

94   Chakma, *supra* note 12, 469.

95   Chakma, *supra* note 12 470; Gain, *supra* note 87, 132.

96   Chakma, *supra* note 12, 304; A Ghoshal, 'From Hosts to Hostiles: Land, Migrants and the Contest for Habitat in Tripura' (2018) 33 *Journal of History* 159.

97   Chakma, *supra* note 12; Ghoshal, *ibid.*

98   Chakma, *supra* note 12, 168, 169; Gain, *supra* note 87, 30; BP Barua, *Ethnicity and National Integration in Bangladesh: A Study of the Chittagong Hill Tracts* (Harnand Publication, 2001).

99   Chakma, *supra* note 12, 97; Gain, *supra* note 87, 66.

100   Chakma, *supra* note 12, 123; N Uddin, 'Living on the Margin: The Positioning of the 'Khumi' within the Sociopolitical and Ethnic History of the Chittagong Hill Tracts' (2008) 9 *Asian Ethnicity* 33; Some think Khumi peoples migrated in Bandarban almost 1000 years ago, see Gain, *supra* note 87, 45.

101   Chakma, *supra* note 12, 522.

102   Mouza means a type of small administrative area with villages.

103   Gain, *supra* note 87, 66.

Conversely, the Bengali Community, the majority in Bangladesh, was settled in the Gangetic Delta,[104] presumably in 2000 BC.[105] The Bengali community is mainly spread in present Bangladesh and West Bengal of India, particularly in the non-hilly areas in Bangladesh.[106] In 1861 the British rulers conducted the first-ever population consensus in CHT and observed the unanimous majority of the indigenous communities compared to the Bengali community, which is respectively 97:2.[107] Thus, the historical evidence proves that from the pre-historic and pre-colonial period, the CHT indigenous communities are the original inhabitants of the CHT.

It is worth mentioning at this point that it is not sufficient to prove that the communities are the original inhabitants. They also must have strong links to their ancestral land,[108] not only in economic livelihood but also in spiritual, cultural and social identity.[109] Looking through the lens of these statements, the dependence of the CHT indigenous community on their ancestral land is undeniable. There are instances of domestic legislation which identify them through their relationship with the land they live in, for example, hill-men or forest people.[110] They are also recognised as *Jumma* people because of their dependency on the land for their traditional agricultural system, i.e., *Jum cultivation*.[111] They also maintain the common forests[112] to collect food, for hunting, for building materials[113] or handcrafts.[114] Their religious beliefs, cultural rituals, and literary activities are strongly connected to their ances-tral land and the crops they harvest.[115] In light of the preceding discussion, it can be concluded that the historical, cultural and economic relationships

---

104   Between the banks of River Ganges to River Brahmaputra.
105   PR Blood, 'Early History, 1000 B.C.-A.D. 1202' in J Heitzman and RL Worden (eds), *Bangladesh: A Country Study* (Federal Research Division, Library of Congress, 1989) 4.
106   A Bhattacharyya, 'Historical Geography of Ancient and Early Medieval Bengal' Dphil diss., University of Calcutta (1974) ch 1.
107   Chakma, *supra* note 12, 58.
108   Preamble of UNDRIP; See also, A Xanthaki, *Indigenous Rights and United Nations Standards* (Cambridge University Press, 2007) 238, 239.
109   Xanthaki, *ibid.*, 291.
110   For example, CHT Regulation of 1900 (n19); Forest Act 1927 etc.
111   Gain, *supra* note 87, 38, 77, 68, 87, 101, 122.
112   As part of their collective rights over land, Executive Summary of the Human Rights Report on Indigenous Peoples in Bangladesh 2017, 107.
113   Wood, bamboo, cane etc.
114   Gain, *supra* note 87, 107.
115   Gain, *supra* note 87, 46, 60, 61, 74, 100, 43, 121, 139, 170; see also, WV Schendel, WMey and AK Dewan, *The Chittagong Hill Tracts Living in a Borderland* (UPL, 2001).

between the CHT indigenous communities and their ancestral land are deeply intertwined.

3.2.3   A Distinct Cultural and Social Framework

Regarding the context of the third identifying requirement, the CHT ethnic community carries a distinct culture and a separate social, economic, and political system that is strikingly different from the dominant majority Bengali Community. The CHT indigenous communities have their mother tongue, aside from the state language Bangla. There are almost 37 different indigenous languages in Bangladesh. A large number of ethnic communities speak Tibeto-Burmese Language, for example, Chaks, Bawm, Pangkhua, Khuli and Chakma, Mru.[116] Apart from that, some communities have their own language. For instance, the Khiyang-kuki speaks Chinese, the Marma community has the Marma language, the Tripura community speaks in Kokborok language, and the Tanchanya language.[117] Extensive literary works are also existent in their mother tongue, depicting their rituals, beliefs and lifestyles denoting their cultural uniqueness and identity.[118]

Bangladesh is a Muslim majority country with almost 90% Muslim population and the other 10% consists of Hinduism, Buddism and Christianity. On the other hand, the ethnic communities in the CHT region are mainly animistic. For example, Chaks worship houses, trees and canals.[119] Khumis worship *Titho* as the god of crops and *Tameuh* as the universal spirit, and their most significant religious festival is *Reng* (Cow killing festival).[120] Before and after the paddy emerges, the Pangkhuas and Lushai community celebrate *Thalaiterkot* and *Kut* to celebrate Jum cultivation.[121] The traditional belief of Pangkhuas is to "maintain harmony amongst the spirit, human, animal, plant and the mineral resources" in their surroundings. Similarly, Khyang celebrates *Dabai* for the preparation of Jum, and they also worship the gods of crops.[122] The Chakmas are Buddhist by religion, but they belong to a special chakma buddisht class called Ruri or Luri, with distinct religious rituals.[123] They also

---

116   For details, see Justice Habibur Rahman, *Bangladesher Nanan Vasha [Different Languages of Bangladesh]* (Prothoma Prokashon, 2014).
117   Gain, *supra* note 87, 110.
118   Cobo, *supra* note 80, para 86; see also, Rahman, *supra* note 116.
119   Gain, *supra* note 87 32.
120   Gain, *supra* note 8, 46, 47; Drong, *supra* note 87, 212; Salek Khokon, *Adivasi Myth and Others* (New SR Press, 2011).
121   Gain, *supra* note 87, 60, 151 ,152; Drong, *supra* note 87, 135.
122   Gain, *supra* note 87, 74.
123   Gain, *supra* note 87, 85.

have a tradition of using cotton from their Jum cultivation to donate in the worshipping activities to Malokkima (the goddess of rice and wealth) and Ganga (the goddess of river and water).[124] Even being a Buddhist majority, the Marma community considers the banyan trees in their villages as sacred and a place of worship.

Similarly, Tanchangya, a Buddhist majority, worships 14 deities, and Chumulang is their most significant religious ritual.[125] The Tripura community follows Sanatana (Hindu religion). However, they perform many different rituals than traditional Hindu practices, for instance, Goria, Ker, Kharchi, Jumlai, Sakchori, Katharok, etc.[126] The Mru's religious belief revolves around Jum cultivation.[127] They worship Thurai as the Supreme deity that controls evil forces and disease on the earth. The Bawm comunity who lives in CHT had become Christian at the time of British rule.[128] However, besides their Christian faith, they worship forests, trees and rocks, rivers and waters, thinking that the spirits control these elements of nature.[129]

The religious practices of the CHT ethnic communities are clearly distinct from those of the non-indigenous population, as evidenced by the preceding discussion. Harvesting festivals, customs connected to marriage and birth rites,[130] distinct religious ceremonies, culinary preferences, clothes, and lifestyle all represent their traditional cultural expression, which is markedly different from the Bengali majority.

Moreover, the CHT indigenous communities have a distinctive social structure. Most of these ethnic communities are clan-based[131] and believe in collective ownership, unlike the Bengali community. The CHT region has had its own unique traditional administrative and judicial system for the ethnic inhabitants since the pre-British colonial periods, which are entirely different from the other parts of the country.[132] There are three hereditary circles[133] in the CHT region: the Chakma Circle, the Bohmong Circle and the Mong Circle.

---

124   Gain, *supra* note 87, 86.
125   Gain, *supra* note 87, 109, 110.
126   Gain, *supra* note 87, 123, 124.
127   Drong, *supra* note 87, 184.
128   Gain, *supra* note 87, 170.
129   Drong, *supra* note 87,196.
130   Gain, *supra* note 87, 49, 85, 124, 150, 152, 165.
131   Gain, *supra* note 87, 32, 47; Sirajul Islam, *Indigenous Communities* (Asiatic Society of Bangladesh, Academic Publishers, 2007). JP Mills, annotated by W Mey, JP Mills and the Chittagong Hill Tracts, "Tour Diary," Reports, Photographs 1926/27 (2009).
132   Chakma, *supra* note 12, 72.
133   Means community.

Each circle consists of one Circle Chief (Raja/king), one Headman per mouza[134] and a Karbari per village (Village-head). Together with the designated state officials, these community leaders manage the administrative and legal system in the CHT region. The rural local Government of other parts of the state is primarily divided into Zila (District) with the Deputy Commissioner as its head. Each such district is divided into several Upazilla Parishad[135] and Union Parishad with a chairman as their head. The urban areas are divided into City Corporations and municipalities with the Mayors as their heads.[136] The customary laws and the legal system are administered by both the tribal leaders (Circle Chief, Headman, Karbari) and the state officials in CHT. In contrast, the other parts of the states comply with the state legislation. So, it is pretty clear that the CHT indigenous communities indeed hold a very different social, political and cultural character than the other segment of Bangladesh.

3.2.4 Colonial Dominance and Marginalisation

The discourse is stepping into the fourth and last element of the identifying criteria, i.e., through conquest or colonisation, the community has become a non-dominant minority for the majority dominant section of the country. This element is crucial as it acts as an impetus for the three other identifying characteristics because it is the non-dominance and the subjugation by the colonial/majority power which necessitates the legal recognition as IPs to assert the indigenous community's RSD.

The historical sufferings and oppression of the CHT indigenous communities of Bangladesh are well-documented and evident. The ethnic communities of CHT do not have any proper constitutional recognition. This absence from the supreme law of the land has had negative impacts on them and rendered them more marginalised. Also, because of an inadequate database and undercounting, the communities remain invisible and deprived of the facilities of different governmental policies.[137] The state-sponsored authoritarian mechanisms, politically motivated in-migration of the Bengali community in the hill area, military abuses, forced eviction, ill-treatment, torture, sexual and physical violence have severely impacted the right to life, right to property and economic

---

134 Chakma, *supra* note 12, 102.
135 Administrative area with a number of villages.
136 Local government is presently operated by various laws in Bangladesh. These include Zila Parishad Act 2000; Local Government (Municipality) Act 2009; Local Government (Union Parishad) Act 2009; Local Government (Upazila Parishad) Act 1998 (amended in 2009), Local Government (City Corporation) Act 2009.
137 Gain, *supra* note 87, 17.

opportunities of these ethnic communities altogether.[138] UN Experts have expressed their concerns several times on gross human rights violations of the CHT ethnic communities.[139] Thus, the lack of security and legal protection sidelines the community in the society. Moreover, the institutional and political underrepresentation generates unequal access to healthcare, employment opportunities and education, making them vulnerable and non-dominant in their own territory.

The present section finds that the CHT indigenous communities of Bangladesh fulfil all the criteria and thereby are IPs as per international standards, irrespective of whether Bangladesh legally recognises them so or not. So, on such background, the next section would examine the justifiability of the non-recognition of CHT Peoples by Bangladesh as per the relevant IHRL.

4   An Outline of the Obligations of Bangladesh towards the CHT Peoples under IHRL and Possible Legal Strategies

4.1   Obligations of Bangladesh under IHRL towards the CHT Peoples

The present section attempts to trace the obligations of Bangladesh to recognise the CHT Peoples and examine the justifiability of non-recognition under IHRL. In this attempt, it is observed that IHR standards do not impose any direct obligation on the states to recognise the ethnic communities as IPs. Instead, they outline the rights of the IPs to be upheld by the states. It has already been observed that the CHT ethnic communities are IPs as per the theoretical framework, and technically speaking, state recognition is not even required. However, the non-recognition of IPs by the state is unjustified because a state is the primary human rights duty bearer and non-recognition

---

138   WGIP 18th Session UN Doc E/CN.4/Sub.2/2000/24 (17 August 2000) para 148; WGIP, 17th Session UN Doc E/CN.4/Sub.2/1999/19 (12 August 1999) para 112; L Karim, 'Pushed to the Margins: Adivasi Peoples in Bangladesh and the Case of Kalpana Chakma' (1998) 7 *Contemporary South Asia* 301; S Halim, S Chakma and R Chakma, *Gender and Human Rights Violation in Chittagong Hill Tracts: The Post Accord Situation* (Freedom Foundation, 2005); 'ICCPR Alternative Report Submission: Violations of Indigenous Peoples' Rights in Bangladesh,' prepared for 119th Session, Geneva (6 March - 29 March 2017) submitted by Cultural Survival, https://tbinternet.ohchr.org/Treaties/CCPR/Shared%20Documents /BGD/INT_CCPR_CSS_BGD_26640_E.docx (accessed 23 January 2023); R.A. Gray, 'Genocide in the Chittagong Hill tracts of Bangladesh'(1994) 22 *RSR* 59; There were heavy arson attack in CHT region in 2003, 2008, 2010 and 2014 resulting forced eviction, see here https://minorityrights.org/minorities/adivasis/ (accessed 23 January 2023).

139   WGIP, 18th Session, UN Doc E/CN.4/Sub.2/2000/24 (17 August 2000); recent UNHR Comm. HR/5062, OTH 84/2020, UNPFII UN Doc HR/GENEVA/SEM/EXPERT/2012/BP.1.

by the state deprives the IPs of all the significant human rights. So, this section intends to highlight the CHT Peoples' rights under relevant IHRL, which they are being deprived of because of the non-recognition of Bangladesh.

The rights of IPs are, by nature, interrelated and interdependent. The discussion will focus on the IHRL standards, both binding and soft in nature, to which Bangladesh is a party (ratified/ signed/adopted). Binding IHR standards include the International Covenant on Civil and Political Rights (ICCPR), International Covenant on Economic, Social and Cultural Rights (ICESCR), the International Convention on the Elimination of All Forms of Racial Discrimination (ICERD),[140] Convention on the Rights of the Child (CRC)[141] and the ILO Convention No. 107. The strict non-binding IHR norms in the discussion consist of UDHR,[142] Minority Declarations 1992,[143] General Recommendation (GR), General Comment (GC) and Concluding Observation (CO) on state reports provided by the UN Treaty monitoring bodies. Though Bangladesh has not adopted UNDRIP, references have been made as it is considered customary international law.[144] Some of these standards do not deal with IPs directly but with "minority"/"tribal" communities. Nevertheless, because they share inherent common factors, the rights of the "minority"/tribal community may refer to the rights of IPs.[145]

4.1.1   Right to Equality and Non-discrimination
The previous discussions demonstrate that the CHT Peoples face gross discrimination in every aspect of the private and public sphere. Though the UDHR[146] does not explicitly refer to indigenous rights, it provides for the absolute equality of every individual in dignity, rights and before the law without

---

140   Adopted at 21 December 1965, entered into force, 4 January 1969, 660 UNTS 195.

141   Adopted at 20 November 1989, entered into force 2 Sept 1990, 1577 UNTS 3.

142   Universal Declaration of Human Rights (adopted 10 December 1948, UNGA Res 217 A(III)).

143   Declaration on the Rights of Persons Belonging to National or Ethnic, Religious and Linguistic Minorities (adopted 18 December 1992 UNGA Res 47/135).

144   RB Lillich, H Hannum, SJ Anaya and D Shelton, *International Human Rights: Documentary Supplement* (Wolters Kluwer, 2009) 129–139.

145   F Viljoen, 'Reflections on the Legal Protection of Indigenous Peoples' Rights in Africa' in S Dersso (ed), *Perspectives on the Rights of Minorities and Indigenous Peoples in Africa* (Pretoria University Law Press, 2010) 75, 85.

146   Article 1, 2 and 7, the UDHR is not a legally binding treaty, but presumed to be a part of customary international law; see H Hannum, 'The Status of the Universal Declaration of Human Rights in National and International law' (1996) 25 *GJIC* 287, 289.

any discrimination. Similarly, the ICCPR,[147] ICESCR[148] and CRC[149] incorporate extensive "non-discrimination" clauses in ensuring the rights contained in the conventions in a general sense. Notably, Article 29 (d) of the CRC specifically includes equal and friendly treatment of "all peoples, ethnic, national and religious groups and persons of indigenous origin". Also, Article 1 of ICERD prohibits any "distinction, exclusion, restriction or preference" based on ethnic origin and ensures the equal enjoyment or exercise of human rights and fundamental freedoms.

Moreover, CERD, in GR No. 23, requires the state parties to ensure that IPS receive equal treatment.[150] Both Article 2(2) of the ILO Convention No. 107 and Article 4 of the Minority Declaration place the indigenous populations on equal footing in enjoying rights with other citizens. Thus, Bangladesh has obligations under several IHR norms to maintain an equal and non-discriminatory position toward the CHT Peoples.

4.1.2   Right to Culture

The cultural life of IPs denotes their religion, language, literature, livelihoods etc. As a leading standard in the context, ICESCR affirms equal economic, social and cultural rights in universalist terms.[151] Article 27 of the UDHR and Article 15(1) of the ICCPR acknowledge everyone's right to participate in cultural life freely. Notably, the UN Committee on Economic Cultural and Social Rights pointed out in General Comment No. 21 that the right to take part in cultural life is intrinsically connected with other rights, for example, the rights to life, education, self-determination and standard living.[152] Similarly, Article 2(2)(b) of ILO Convention No. 107 requires a state party to promote the social, economic and cultural development of the indigenous/tribal populations to improve their living standards. Thus, as discussed in the previous sections, as a ratifying party of ICESCR, the current approach of Bangladesh towards the right to culture of CHT Peoples is not in conformity with these IHR standards, which may consequently negate their other vital human rights.

Further, Article 27 of ICCPR and Articles 1 and 2(1) of the Minority Declaration specifically protect the right to culture, language and religion of the ethnic, religious or linguistic minorities residing within the territory. Promisingly,

---

147   Article 2(1).
148   Article 2(2).
149   Article 2.
150   CERD, 'GR No 23: Indigenous peoples' (1997), UN Doc A/52/18, annex V, para 4(b).
151   Article 2(2).
152   CESCR, 'GC No 21: Right of everyone to take part in cultural life (art. 15, para. 1a of the CESCR)' (2009), UN Doc E/C.12/21, para 2.

Human Rights Committee (hereinafter HRC) confirms in General Comment No. 23 that Article 27 applies to the IPs and imposes positive obligations on the state in that regard.[153] The Minority Declaration also uses mandatory language while incorporating state obligations.[154] So, these provisions obligate Bangladesh to take appropriate measures to protect and respect the cultural and religious rights of the CHT Peoples. In addition, ICERD promises to uphold the cultural and religious rights of the ethnic communities and requires a state to have a proper remedial procedure through courts or tribunals for violation of such obligations,[155] an obligation against which Bangladesh has no such judicial mechanism in its legal framework.

Similarly, Articles (17), 29 (c) and (30) of the CRC impel Bangladesh to adopt appropriate measures to protect the cultural, linguistic and religious identity of the children belonging to indigenous communities in different contexts. In addition, the ILO Convention No. 107 requires the state party to ensure that children of the tribal population receive education in their mother tongue.[156] The right to language, however, with limits, has also been recognised in Article 4(3) of the Minority Declaration. Unfortunately, the Children Act 2013 or any other laws of Bangladesh does not provide any such legislative pledges.

Thus, it can be inferred from the above discussion that Bangladesh does have numerous IHRL obligations to protect the cultural identity of CHT Peoples, with which the domestic legal and institutional frameworks are inconsistent.

4.1.3   Right to Land and Natural Resources
Collective land rights of IPs are a part of their RSD,[157] and they have the right to "permanent sovereignty over their natural resources".[158] Both Article 17 of the UDHR and Article 5 (d) (v) of ICERD confirm that "everyone has the right to own property alone as well as in association with others" and prohibit discrimination and arbitrary deprivation of such rights. Also, Article 3 (1) and 11 of ILO Convention No. 107 protect the property of the tribal/indigenous populations in the territory and assure individual as well as collective ownership of the land. The ILO Convention No. 107 also prohibits forced eviction,

---

153   HRC, 'GC No. 23: Article 27 (Rights of Minorities)' (1994), UN Doc CCPR/C/21/Rev.1/Add.5, para 3.2, 6.2.
154   Xanthaki, *supra* note 108, 203.
155   Article 6.
156   Article 23.
157   J Castellino, 'Conceptual Difficulties and the Right to Indigenous Self-Determination' in N Ghanea and A Xanthaki (eds), *Minorities, Peoples and Self-Determination: Essays in Honour of Patrick Thornberry* (Martinus Nijhoff, 2005) 55.
158   WGIP, 19th Session UN Doc E/CN.4/ Sub.2/2001/17 (9 August 2001), para 38.

though with some reservations on the ground of national security, economic development or health issues.[159] So, the right to communal ownership of the ancestral land of CHT Peoples is clearly acknowledged in these IHRL norms. Besides, CESCR, in General Comment No. 20 asks the state party to take special measures to ensure the land rights of the indigenous community.[160] Moreover, both in Article 28 (1) of UNDRIP and in 2009, the HRC in *Ángela Poma Poma v. Peru*[161] affirmed the requirement of the indigenous community's free, prior and informed consent on any issue relating to their ancestral land and resources. Furthermore, according to Article 12 of ILO Convention No. 107, Bangladesh may be liable for forceful evictions of the CHT Peoples without their prior consent.

Violation of the land rights of indigenous communities can make Bangladesh liable for breaching other human rights obligations as land rights are closely connected with many other essential human rights. For instance, the lack of recognition of indigenous land rights affects the right to culture and indigenous identity.[162] Also, rights to land and natural resources can be interpreted as a right to food and water, as the right to food includes rights of access to food[163] and water[164] and also the lack of such access can consequently impact the right to health.[165] Moreover, forced evictions often violate the right to life and security of persons.[166] Thus, the non-recognition of CHT Peoples' land rights in Bangladesh is legally unjustified under its existing IHRL obligation.

4.1.4   Right to Self-Determination

As a ratifying party, Bangladesh is obligated under Article 1 of the ICCPR and ICESCR and Article 1(2) and 55 of the UN Charter to ensure the RSD to the CHT Peoples. Also, HRC has repeatedly linked the right to ethnic, religious or

---

159   Article 12.

160   CESCR, 'GC No 20: Non-discrimination in economic, social and cultural rights (art. 2, para. 2, of ICESCR)' (2009), UN Doc E/C.12/GC/20.

161   HRC Communication No 1457/2006, UN Doc CCPR/C/95/D/1457/2006, para 7.6.

162   HRC, CO, Australia, UN Doc CCPR/C/AUS/CO/5 (2009).

163   CESCR, 'GC No 12: The Right to Adequate Food (Art. 11 of the Covenant)' (1999), UN Doc E/C.12/1999/5, para 13.

164   CESCR, 'GC No 15: The Right to Water (Arts. 11 and 12 of the ICESCR)' (2003), UN Doc E/C.12/2002/11, para 7,16.

165   CESCR, 'GC No 14: The Right to the Highest Attainable Standard of Health' (2000), UN Doc E/C.12/2000/4, para 4, 11, 27.

166   CESCR, 'GC No 20: Non-discrimination in economic, social and cultural rights (art. 2, para. 2, of ICESCR)' (2009) UN Doc E/C.12/GC/20, para 25, 34; CESCR, 'GC No 7: The Right to Adequate Housing: Forced Evictions (Art.11.1)' (1997), UN Doc E/1998/22, para 4.

linguistic minorities[167] with Article 1 of ICCPR, i.e. RSD.[168] But most importantly, RSD is now recognised as jus cogens[169] giving rise to "erga omnes" obligations.[170] So Bangladesh has non-derogable human rights obligation[171] to acknowledge the RSD of the CHT Peoples.

As a human right, RSD comprehensively signifies the IPs' rights. Interestingly, UNDRIP refers to the local autonomy/self-government while promising the RSD to IPs.[172] Thus, for IPs, RSD indicates the right to self-government on issues relating to political identity, the right to culture and land simultaneously.[173] The right to self-government can only be achieved through the power of self-control,[174] i.e. to have control over decisions that affects one's life and livelihood. Also, both CERD[175] and HRC[176] have emphasised the state's duty to ensure the right to the effective engagement/participation of the IPs in issues that are particularly relevant to their interest. In other words, Bangladesh needs to ensure effective political participation/representation of the CHT Peoples in the administrative framework to implement the RSD. The issue of effective participation has also been incorporated in the Minority Declaration of 1992.[177] However, in Bangladesh, no legal provision exists that affirms reserved seats or special political arrangements for the CHT Peoples to ensure political representation in either the national or the local sphere.

The purpose of this part of the present section has been to portray the nature of the extensive IHRL obligations of Bangladesh to recognise and ensure the CHT Peoples' rights and to signify the unjustified non-compliance of Bangladesh. The discourse eventually supports the article's main argument, i.e. the non-recognition of the CHT Peoples by Bangladesh is inconsistent with its IHRL obligations. In the next part, the section would attempt to outline possible scopes to improve the current situation of the CHT Peoples.

---

167   Article 27 of ICCPR.

168   HRC, *Lovelace vs Canada*, Comm. No 24/ 1977, UN Doc A/36/40 (1981); *Kitok vs Sweden*, Comm. No 197/1985, UN Doc A/43/40 (1988); *Ominayak vs Canada*, Comm. No 167/1984, UN Doc. A/45/40 (1990); *Lansman v. Finland*, Comm. No 511/ 1992, UN Doc CCPR/C/52/o/511/1992 (1993); HRC, UN Doc CCPR/C/70/D/541/199, 3 para 9.2.

169   ILC, *supra* note 8.

170   International Court of Justice, *Legal Consequences of the Construction of a Wall in the Occupied Palestinian Territory (Advisory Opinion)*, Reports 172 (9 July 2004), para 88.

171   The obligations which cannot be suspended under any circumstances.

172   Article 4.

173   UNDRIP, Article 3,4.

174   Xanthaki, *supra* note 108, 132.

175   CERD, 'GR No 21: The Right to Self-determination' (2003), UN Doc HRI\GEN\1\Rev.6 209.

176   HRC, Annual Report to UNGA, UN Doc A/49/40 (1994), para 182.

177   Article 2(3).

4.2   *Recommendation on Domestic Legal Strategies for the CHT Peoples*

Bangladesh has not accepted the individual complaint procedure of any of the legally binding IHRL treaties mentioned in the first part of this section.[178] Also, Bangladesh is an Asian country, and unlike other regions of the world, i.e. Europe, America, and Africa etc., Asia does not have any regional human rights mechanism. So, Bangladesh is not even under any regional human rights system. It means that the CHT Peoples are devoid of any universal or regional complaint mechanisms. Moreover, the legal system of Bangladesh lacks any substantial judicial mechanism to ensure indigenous rights. Therefore, for practical legal remedies, it is necessary to explore the scope of the existing domestic legal framework in light of national and international law to support the CHT Peoples' rights in domestic courts.

4.2.1   Realising Indigenous Rights through Constitutional Rights

The High Court Division (HCD) of Bangladesh holds that the domestic courts can take recourse to the international law in adjudication where there are gaps/ ambiguities in the existing provisions.[179] This precedent can be an excellent opportunity to interpret and integrate the ambiguous or absent indigenous rights into the Bangladeshi legal system.

The Bangladesh Constitution envisages the rights to culture, religion and language of the ethnic communities as FPSP.[180] Also, Article 25 of the FPSP chapter incorporates the RSD of every people through free choice to "build up its own social, economic and political system".[181] Even though these rights in FPSP are not judicially enforceable,[182] they "shall be applied by the State in the making of laws, shall be a guide to the interpretation of the Constitution and of the other laws of Bangladesh".[183] But there are judicial precedents in Bangladesh where the violations of FPSP rights have been judicially enforced because they were proved to have violated fundamental rights[184] of the Constitution. For example, despite being a part of the non-justiciable FPSP, Bangladesh

---

178   See here https://tbinternet.ohchr.org/_layouts/15/TreatyBodyExternal/Treaty.aspx?Country ID=14&Lang=EN (accessed 23 January 2023).
179   *BNWLA vs Government of Bangladesh*, Writ Petition No 8769 of 2010, para 20.
180   Bangladesh Constitution, Article 23A.
181   *Ibid.*, Article 25 (b).
182   *Ibid.*
183   *Ibid.*
184   Judicially enforceable.

courts judicially enforced the right to shelter,[185] the right to medical care[186] and public health[187] because the court held that violation of these rights amounts to violations of the right to life. The right to life is not only a non-derogatory human rights norm, but it has also been enshrined in the Constitution of Bangladesh as a fundamental right that is judicially enforceable.[188] Thus, through the right to life of the CHT Peoples may enforce their socio-economic rights, like the right to housing, health care, etc. Given that IPs are generally "at the bottom of the social and economic ladder in virtually all societies they live in",[189] ensuring the socio-economic rights of the CHT Peoples is a crucial part of their RSD.

Moreover, it has already been observed that IHRL norms connected the right to life with other rights such as the right to culture and the RSD of IPs.[190] Ensuring the right to culture through the right to life can help the CHT Peoples to get control over their right to language and education, eventually leading to the right to employment and the right to adequate housing[191] and food. Furthermore, IPs' right to culture and cultural practices are inextricably linked to and reliant on their right to land.[192] Thus, constitutional and judicial scopes need to be explored in Bangladesh to legally address the right to culture and the RSD of the CHT Peoples under the right to life.

IPs consider that land rights are the "solution to all their problems".[193] The only direct domestic legal instruments available in Bangladesh for CHT Peoples are some land rights laws that are primarily inoperative.[194] The litigators file the CHT land rights petitions under these laws and the fundamental constitutional rights to property.[195] Previous discourse in the article successfully established the relationship of land rights with the right to culture, religious

---

185 *BLAST and another vs Bangladesh and others*, Writ Petition No 2760 of 2008.

186 *National Board of Revenue (NBR) vs Advocate Zulhas Uddin Ahmed and others* 2010 39 CLC (AD).

187 *Dr Mohiuddin Farooque vs Bangladesh & Ors*, 48 DLR (1996) (HCD) 438 (1996) 2 CHRLD 107.

188 Article 32.

189 S Wiessner, 'The Cultural Rights of Indigenous Peoples: Achievements and Continuing Challenges' (2011) 22 *European Journal of International Law* 121.

190 CESCR, 'GC No 14: The Right to the Highest Attainable Standard of Health' (2000), UN Doc E/C.12/2000/4.

191 *Ibid.*

192 *Ibid.*

193 WGIP, 1st Session, UN Doc E/CN.4/Sub.2/1982/33 (25 August 1982), para 70, 72.

194 See discussion on Chapter I (B.ii).

195 Bangladesh Constitution, Article 42.

and indigenous identity, RSD[196] and most notably with the right to life.[197] So while resolving CHT land disputes, they should assimilate the land rights with the right to life of the CHT Peoples as per international practice.

In the *Saramaka Case*,[198] the *Ogoni Case*[199] and the *Endorois case*,[200] it was concluded that the lack of participation of the IPs in the decision-making process relating to their ancestral lands violated their right to property. Thus, the courts upheld the right to effective participation of the indigenous communities through their right to property. So, in Bangladesh, the litigators should interpret the right to property under Article 42 of the Constitution to include the right to effective participation of the CHT Peoples in the decision-making process as a gradual progression of implementing their right to self-government.

4.2.2 The Role of Collective Claims

Another crucial fault of the Bangladeshi indigenous rights litigations is that they lack the nature of a collective claim, i.e. only include the name of the legal aid institutions or individual claimants as litigators. Surprisingly, the cases were never filed in the name/on behalf of the community or peoples in Bangladesh.[201] The reasons are unknown. From the perspective of indigenous rights, the claims of the IPs are characteristically collective in nature.[202] Indigenous land claims stand much more valuable as collective rights than individual ones.[203] Missing this point in the litigation can surely cost any indigenous rights litigation judgment.[204] While filing cases on behalf of the CHT Peoples, litigators should keep in mind that failing to file a collective claim reduces the

---

196 See also the expansive approach in *Centre for Minority Rights Development (Kenya) and Minority Rights Group International on behalf of Endorois Welfare Council v. Kenya*, African Commission on Human and Peoples' Rights (ACHPR) Comm. No. 276/2003 (4 February 2010).

197 See also *Yakye Axa Indigenous Community v Paraguay*, IACHR Series C No. 125 (17 June 2005).

198 *Saramaka People v Suriname* (Preliminary objections, merits, reparations and costs), IACHR Series C No. 172 (28 November 2007).

199 *The Social and Economic Rights Action Center and the Center for Economic and Social Rights v. Nigeria*, ACHPR Comm. No. 155/96 (2001).

200 *Endorois, supra* note 200.

201 See here https://www.blast.org.bd/issues/adivasi (accessed 23 January 2023).

202 Viljoen, *supra* note 148, 79.

203 A Xanthaki, 'The UN Declaration on the Rights of Indigenous Peoples and Collective Rights: What's the Future for Indigenous Women?' in S Allen and A Xanthaki (eds), *Reflections on the UNDRIP* (Hart Publishing, 2011) 413, 432.

204 For example, see *Sawhoyamaxa Community v Paraguay*, IACHR Series C No 146 IHRL 1530 (IACHR 2006).

relevance of the case and undermines CHT Peoples' status as IPs and, eventually, their rights. The Bangladesh Constitution says that if "no other equally efficacious remedy is provided by law" and the issue is "being otherwise harmful to the public interest",[205] it can be filed directly to the High Court Division. As there is no effective/adequate remedy for IPs right in the legal system and a collective claim involves a significant portion of the public of the CHT region, the matter may be filed as public interest litigation opening a new legal doorway for the CHT Peoples' rights.

4.2.3   The Implementation of the 1997 CHT Peace Accord

The CHT Peace Accord has provided a special administrative arrangement for the CHT region and the opportunity for political participation of the CHT Peoples[206] to ensure the right to culture,[207] land[208] and customary laws.[209] Effective implementation of the Accord would ensure the RSD of the CHT Peoples. In 2000, the 1997 Accord was declared unconstitutional because it affirms RSD, creating a "state within a state",[210] which is inconsistent with the constitutional pledge of unitary, sovereign Government in Bangladesh.[211] Considering the significance of the RSD for an indigenous community and the nature of sovereign-friendly internal self-determination incorporated in the 1997 Accord, this decision seems highly discriminatory. Promisingly, the HCD acknowledged in 2017 that the CHT indigenous communities indeed enjoy "extra-constitutional privilege" under the present Constitution.[212] As discussed earlier, the Constitution itself provides for the RSD in FPSP with a scope of enforcement through the right to life.

Furthermore, the 1997 Peace Accord is considered to have the legal nature of an agreement because of the nature of the language used in the mutual commitment and detailed bargain provisions between the CHT Peoples and the Government.[213] On such a background, it is time to file a new petition to challenge the legal justification of the present decision on the unconstitutionality

---

205   Artcile 102 (4)(b).
206   1997 Accord, Section B, C.
207   *Ibid.*, Section D, art. 11.
208   *Ibid.*, Article 2, 3, 4, 8.
209   *Ibid.*, Article 6(b).
210   *Badiuzzaman, supra* note 56, para 17.
211   Bangladesh Constitution, Article 1.
212   *Rangamati Food Products* (AD), *supra* note 37, para 75.
213   C Bell, 'Peace Agreements: Their Nature and Legal Status' (2006) 100 *American Journal of International Law* 373, 381, 382.

of the 1997 Accord. Enforceability and the implementation of the 1997 Accord would be a milestone for the rights of the CHT Peoples in Bangladesh.

4.2.4   Legislative Measures and Policies

In 2017, the HRC recommended an immediate formal adoption of the anti-discrimination bill 2015 (it was then pending in Bangladesh), prohibiting discrimination on the grounds of ethnic origin and ensuring land rights and effective participation of the CHT peoples.[214] The 2015 bill was never adopted. A new Anti-Discrimination Bill 2022 has been placed in the parliament with similar protection.[215] The adoption of this 2022 Bill may bring new hope to the field. However, it needs to be realised that it is not always the equality that is required to protect the IPs' rights and recognition. The nature of rights which IPs have over their land, natural resources, culture, livelihoods, etc. differs from the non-indigenous groups of a state, and their "quest for cultural, political and other forms of autonomy, constitutes a demand to be treated differentially ab initio".[216] Ensuring these rights requires special provisions focused on IPs. For example, Bangladesh has a proposed Land Act, 2020 under consideration, which says that the indigenous community-owned lands should not be acquired unless necessary to develop or protect them or the environment.[217] Now the proposed Act mainly refers to the land legally owned by them, for example, their residential home or agricultural land. But the life, livelihood and spirituality of IPs are closely connected with their surrounding environment and ancestral land comprised of rivers, hills, mountains, forests or pastoral lands. But 2020 Land Act does not guarantee the protection of ancestral lands. Such protection comes only with the status of IPs, and this is why formal domestic recognition is so necessary; mere inclusion or equality is not enough.

CESCR has also suggested effective domestic legislation in line with the relevant international human rights standards to prevent violations of IPs' rights

214   HRC, Concluding Observations (CO) Bangladesh, UN Doc CCPR/C/BGD/CO/1 (2017), para 11, 12.

215   Ensuring equal rights: Anti-Discrimination Bill 2022 placed in parliament, 5 April 2022, https://www.thedailystar.net/news/bangladesh/rights/news/ensuring-equal-rights -anti-discrimination-bill-2022-placed-parliament-2998501 (accessed 23 January 2023).

216   S Wiessner, 'Faces of Vulnerability: Protecting Individuals in Organic and Non-organic Groups' in G Alfredsson and P Macalister-Smith (eds), *The Living Law of Nations* (NP Engel, 1996) 222.

217   Proposed Bangladesh Land Act and land rights of the indigenous people, MB Rafiq, 27 October 2020, https://www.thedailystar.net/law-our-rights/news/proposed-bangladesh -land-act-and-land-rights-the-indigenous-people-1984617 (accessed 23 January 2023).

in Bangladesh.[218] Thus, the committee indicated that Bangladesh should ratify ILO Conve169, adopt UNDRIP and incorporate it into the national legal framework. Bringing the changes into the domestic legislation as per the suggestions of the HRC and CESCR would be a good starting point for the appropriate legislative approach.

5   Conclusion

This article points to the unjustified non-recognition of CHT IPs in contravention of IHR standards in Bangladesh, generating systematic discrimination and structural inequalities against them in the domestic legal framework.

The identity of IPs is an inherent characteristic, and the other entities must recognise such identity rather than deny it.[219] The right to be recognised as IPs is of central importance to indigenous rights, and states cannot play a neutral or passive role in ensuring indigenous rights.[220] Thus, Bangladesh has positive obligations to recognise the CHT IPs to respect, protect, and fulfil the state's human rights obligations towards them. However, the fact of inadequate responses of Bangladesh to the national apex court decision and the relevant IHR obligations to recognise the CHT Peoples so far is unfortunate.

The success of indigenous claims depends particularly on "appropriate legal argument, judicial activism and social mobilisation".[221] Therefore, following the aforesaid recommendations may be helpful in paving the way for proper recognition of the CHT Peoples in compliance with the IHRL norms. Apart from that, Bangladesh needs to change the existing colonial authoritative power structure and establish a legal and administrative framework that incorporates effective participation of the CHT Peoples, government accountability, proper monitoring and reporting system and an impartial judiciary. Thus, adopting a holistic approach is the only option to address the unjustified non-recognition of the IPs of the CHT Peoples in Bangladesh.

---

218   CESCR, Concluding Observations (CO) Bangladesh, UN Doc (E/C.12/BGD/1) (2018), para 16.

219   *Mgwanga V Cameroon*, ACHPR Comm. No 266/2003 (27 MAY 2009), para 179.

220   P Thornberry, 'Confronting Racial Discrimination: A CERD Perspective' (2005) 5 *Human Rights Law Review* 239, 260.

221   Viljoen, *supra* note 147, 93.

Note on the Contributor

Adity Rahman Shah

Senior Lecturer, Department of Law, East West University, Bangladesh. MSt International Human Rights Law, University of Oxford. Email: adityrahman-shah@gmail.com.

PART 4

Human Rights and Democratic Values under Threat

∴

CHAPTER 13

Towards the Criminalization of Torture in Taiwan: Prospects and Challenges

Pavel Doubek

Abstract

Defining torture under international law is all but easy. The Convention against Torture establishes torture as a 'State-act' leaving behind cruelties committed by non-State actors for purely private ends. A narrow concept of torture requiring a State-nexus has been criticized as outdated and lagging behind the current international trend. To put some flesh on this conundrum, the article looks behind the scenes of the UN treaty system. It examines a path toward the criminalization of torture in the Republic of China (Taiwan) which has recently decided to 'ratify' the Convention and eradicate a 'torturous environment' sowed deeply by the previous authoritarian regime.

Keywords

Convention against Torture – torture – criminalization – public official – state-nexus

1 Introduction

Torture was endemic, widespread and systemic during the martial law period[1] in the Republic of China (Taiwan). There were no safeguards against torture in the then criminal law. On the contrary, the criminal law was misused to facilitate torture, in particular to use forced confession as a key evidence against defendants in criminal trials. In 1987, martial law was lifted and Taiwan set itself for an arduous journey toward democracy. The symbolic milestone in this process was reached on 20 December 2020 when the Taiwanese government (the Executive Yuan) adopted an implementation act of the United Nations Convention against Torture (Convention, UNCAT) and its optional protocol

---

1   Period between 20 May 1949 and 14 July 1987.

© KONINKLIJKE BRILL NV, LEIDEN, 2023 | DOI:10.1163/9789004538627_014

(OPCAT).[2] On the basis of this act, Taiwan has devoted itself to de-facto ratifying the said anti-torture documents and implementing the essential safeguards against torture and cruel, inhuman and degrading treatment or punishment (other ill-treatment).[3]

Despite the lofty aim of the Taiwan government, the implementation act has not yet been passed by the parliament (Legislative Yuan) nor has torture been defined as an absolutely prohibited act, let alone its criminalization as a separate criminal offence. This lacuna is particularly regrettable as Taiwan has been urged for years by the group of independent experts (referring to themselves as the International Review Committee, the IRC)[4] and domestic actors to implement the Convention, criminalize torture as a separate crime and establish jurisdiction of judicial bodies over alleged perpetrators of torture.[5]

Noteworthy, criminalization of torture as a separate crime (distinct from common assault or other crimes) is a matter of priority[6] and the key

---

2 Executive Yuan, 'Bill of the UNCAT and OPCAT Implementation Act' (10 December 2020) https://www.ey.gov.tw/Page/9277F759E41CCD91/56e601fa-8a7f-46af-803f-b870830b845d (accessed 1 November 2022).

3 Since Taiwan is not a Member State of the United Nations it has developed its own system of 'ratification' of the UN treaties. Treaties' obligations are implemented through an implementation act that grants international commitments a domestic legal force. Read more at https://en.covenantswatch.org.tw/treaty-reviews/ (accessed 1 November 2022). Read more about the implementation act in P Doubek, 'Implementation of the Convention against Torture in Taiwan: Filling the Gap in the International Struggle against Torture?' (2022) *Asian Journal of International Law* 1–24.

4 The IRC is not an official treaty body under the United Nations. It is a group of independent experts such as former UN officials or legal scholars. The aim of the IRC is to review Taiwan's State reports on the implementation of human rights commitments emerging from the United Nations treaties that the Taiwan government voluntarily implemented. Read more about the IRC at https://en.covenantswatch.org.tw/treaty-reviews/ (accessed 1 November 2022) or in YJ Chen, 'Human Rights Treaty Monitoring 2.0: Taiwan's Local Innovation and Implications for Global Practice' (2020) *Taiwan and International Human Rights*.

5 IRC, 'Concluding Observations and Recommendations on the Initial State Report on the Implementation of the International Human Rights Covenants' (1 March 2013) https://www.humanrights.moj.gov.tw/media/14391/5415171652675.pdf?mediaDL=true (accessed 1 November 2022), para 58; International Review Committee, 'Concluding Observations and Recommendations on the Second State Report on the Implementation of the ICCPR' (20 January 2017) https://en.covenantswatch.org.tw/wp-content/uploads/2018/12/2017-ICCPR-ICESCR-CORs_EN.pdf (accessed 1 November 2022), para 53; Q Jianrong, 'Qian Jianrong's Column: Taiwan Has Also a Crime of Torture (In Chinese: 錢建榮專欄：台灣也有酷刑罪)' 31 July 2019, https://www.upmedia.mg/news_info.php?SerialNo=68214 (accessed 1 November 2022).

6 See CAT Concluding Observations on Belgium (CAT/C/BEL/CO/3, para 8) and Sweden (CAT/C/SWE/CO/6-7, para 6). See also UN Human Rights Council, 'Report of the Special Rapporteur on Torture' (21 February 2012) Un Doc A/HRC/19/61/Add.2., p. 18, UNHRC (2008), para 73 and UN Human Rights Council, 'Report of the Special Rapporteur on Torture' (15 January 2007), UN Doc A/HRC/4/33, para 75.

commitment under the Convention.[7] It has been recognized as such on several occasions by the Committee against Torture (CAT)[8], the UN Special Rapporteurs on Torture[9] and in several country-specific studies.[10] Moreover, other UN treaty bodies and even the European Committee for the Prevention of Torture (CPT)[11] and scholars[12] are calling for the establishment of a specific offence named 'torture' in accordance, at a minimum, with the elements of torture as defined in Article 1 of the Convention.[13] Since it is broadly conceived that criminalization of torture is a pivotal norm in the fight against impunity[14] and the very first step in eradication of torture[15], it is not clear why Taiwan has

---

7   UNCAT, Article 4 in conjunction with Article 1.

8   UN Committee against Torture, 'General Comment No. 2: Implementation of Article 2 by States Parties' (24 January 2008), UN Doc CAT/C/GC/2, para 8. See also, for example, CAT criticism of the Criminal Procedure Law and the Criminal Law of the People's Republic of China (CAT/C/CHN/CO/5) or Criminal Act of the Republic of Korea (CAT/C/KOR /CO/3-5).

9   See reports of Sir Nigel Rodley (E/CN.4/2002/76, Annex I (a), T Van Boven (E/CN.4/2003/68, para 26 (a)), M Nowak (A/HRC/13/39/ADD.2, para 105 (k), JE Méndez (A/HRC/16/52, para 45), N Melzer (A/76/168, para 64).

10   L Fernandez and L Muntingh, 'The Criminalization of Torture in South Africa' (2016) 60 *Journal of African Law* 83; H Chitimira and P Mokone, 'A General Legislative Analysis of 'Torture' as a Human Rights Violation in Zimbabwe' (2017) 20 *Potchefstroom Electronic Law Journal/Potchefstroomse Elektroniese Regsblad* 20; D Carolei, 'Cestaro v. Italy: The European Court of Human Rights on the Duty to Criminalise Torture and Italy's Structural Problem' (2017) 17 *International Criminal Law Review* 567; A Marchesi, 'Implementing the UN Convention Definition of Torture in National Criminal Law (with reference to the special case of Italy)' (2008) 6 *Journal of International Criminal Justice* 195.

11   Human Rights Committee (for example, CCPR/C/UZB/CO/5, para 23), Committee on the Rights of Persons with Disabilities (for example, CRPD/C/IND/CO/1, para 33 (d); Committee on the Rights of the Child (CRC/C/UZB/CO/3-4, para 38); CPT (Visit to Greece (CPT/ Inf (2020) 15), para 91).

12   E Delaplace and M Pollard 'Torture Prevention in Practice' (2006) 16 *Association for the Prevention of Torture* 220, 227. See scholars Burgers and Danelius who have argued the opposite in HJ Burgers and H Danelius, *The United Nations Convention Against Torture: A Handbook on the Convention Against Torture and Other Cruel, Inhuman or Degrading Treatment or Punishment* (Martinus Nijhoff Publishers, 1988) 129.

13   See the full definition of torture in Article 1, para 1.

14   M Nowak et al, *The United Nations Convention Against Torture and its Optional Protocol: A Commentary* (Oxford University Press, 2019) 176. UN Human Rights Council, 'Report of the Special Rapporteur on Torture' (5 February 2010), Un Doc A/HRC/13/39/Add.5, para 255; UN Committee against Torture, 'General Comment No. 2: Implementation of Article 2 by States Parties' (24 January 2008), UN Doc CAT/C/GC/2, para 11.

15   See a comparative study of MS Berlin, which demonstrates that countries that have adopted a definition of torture in line with the standards of the UNCAT show a statistically significant reduction of torture (police torture).

not yet met this objective, in contrast to its declared will to ratify the UNCAT and take various steps in the struggle against torture.[16]

The aim of this manuscript is to shed a light on this ambivalent position of the Taiwan government and explore the reasons which might prevent it from creating a torture offense. A possible explanation would be that torture is already a 'relict of the past' in today's democratic Taiwan or its criminal law provides an adequate legal basis for investigation of torture allegations and punishment of torturers. This would mean that no specific crime of torture is, in fact, needed. A second reason could lie in a problematic definition of torture. If constituent elements of torture are ambiguous, it could be challenging for Taiwan's legislator to draw a clear *nomen juris* of a crime in its criminal code. Intriguingly, both arguments have been invoked by Taiwan's government officials.[17]

Since the definition of torture and its constituent elements is a complex issue,[18] the paper will narrow a discussion to a question of whether torture shall be criminalized as 'public torture' as required by the UNCAT or the 'public requirement' should rather be omitted. Given that torture has occurred in different timeframes and contexts in Taiwan (military suppression, totalitarian era, modern-day torture and ill-treatment), this question will be answered against the background of these contextual situations.

Besides the benefit for the Taiwanese audience, the article contributes to highlight the current debate on the criminalization of torture and contributes to scholarly understanding of a State-nexus requirement in a broader context.

The article is organized as follows. First, it explores torture in Taiwan historically. Second, it examines the attitude of the Taiwan government toward the

---

16   It, at the same time, declares a will to implement the OPCAT and to establish the National Preventive Mechanism.

17   ROC, 'Response to the Concluding Observations and Recommendations adopted by the International Group of Independent Experts on March 1, 2013' (April 2016) https://www .humanrights.moj.gov.tw/media/12225/03820041318522677e.pdf?mediaDL=true (accessed 1 November 2022), paras 191–3; ROC, 'Response to the Concluding Observations and Recommendations adopted by the International Review Committee on January 20, 2017' (June 2020) https://www.humanrights.moj.gov.tw/media/14807/04%E8%8B%B1%E6% 96%87%E7%89%88-response-to-the-concluding-observaions-and-recommendations -adopted-by-the-international-review-committee-on-january-202017.pdf?mediaDL=true (accessed 1 November 2022), paras 163–4; ROC, 'May 10, 2022. ROC Third ICCPR Report Review Meeting Day 2' (May 2022) https://www.youtube.com/watch?v=qs-O9R7TDfl&t =2953s (accessed 1 November 2022), time 8:12:12.

18   See, for example, J Harper, 'Defining Torture: Bridging the Gap between Rhetoric and Reality' (2009) 49 *Santa Clara Law Review* 893; S Dewulf, *The Signature of Evil: (Re)Defining Torture in International Law* (Intersentia, 2011).

creation of torture as a distinct crime in line with article 1 of the Convention. Third, it elaborates on the distinction between 'public' and 'private' torture against the background of different contexts in which it has occurred. In conclusion, the manuscript summarizes the reasons behind the ongoing lacuna in criminal law and provides some recommendations on how a crime of torture could be formulated in Taiwan.

2   Historical Impunity

The dark times of torture in post-war Taiwan are closely linked to the quasi-military dictatorship of the political party Kuomintang (KMT).[19] When the Republic of China (ROC) military arrived from mainland China in Taiwan in 1947, it suppressed the uprising of the Taiwan people against the ROC rule.[20] In the carnage known as the '228 Incident', thousands of Taiwan people were assaulted and killed[21] across the island.[22] Unlike the subsequent period of political terror after the retreat of the ROC government to Taiwan from the mainland (known as 'the White Terror' era) targeted mostly at political opponents, the massacre of Taiwanese people in March 1947 had a systematic and widespread character. As it went beyond a mere suppression of the revolt but threatened the existence of Taiwanese identity as such, some call the massacre an act of genocide ('Formosa genocide').[23] There were plenty of incidents when soldiers were shooting indiscriminately at people in the streets including women and children.[24] There is a great deal of information that soldiers

---

19   MS Kuo & HW Chen, 'Killing in Your Name: Pathology of Judicial Paternalism and the Mutation of the 'Most Serious Crimes' Requirement in Taiwan' in J Cohen et al. (eds), *Taiwan and International Human Rights* (Springer, 2019) 334.

20   TJ Shattuck, *Transitional Justice in Taiwan - A Belated Reckoning with the White Terror* (Foreign Policy Research Institute 2019) 8. For a historical overview see also TH Lai et al, *A Tragic Beginning: The Taiwan Uprising of February 28, 1947* (Stanford University Press, 1991) 141–167.

21   BR Roth, 'Human Rights and Transitional Justice: Taiwan's Adoption of the ICCPR and the Redress of 228 and Martial-Law-Era Injustices' in J Cohen et al, *Taiwan and International Human Rights* (Springer, 2019) 54. Learn more in Lai et al (n 20), 158–160.

22   The largest casualties were in Taipei, Chia-i, Keelung and Kaohsiung. See Lai et al., *supra* note 20, 156.

23   Tekkhiam Chia, 'Taiwan's massacre was genocide' Taipei Times (8 March 2019) https://www.taipeitimes.com/News/editorials/archives/2019/03/08/2003711057 (accessed 1 November 2022).

24   Lai et al., *supra* note 20, 155–7, 161.

shot at random at civilians passing by,[25] looting houses and shops, raping women,[26] arresting and torturing people in various official and unofficial places of detention.[27]

Once the ROC government successfully suppressed the uprising, it consolidated its power on the island by introducing martial law[28] which nullified a wide range of civil and political rights. Thirty-eight years long martial law[29] was known for systematic torture, extrajudicial executions, enforced disappearances and other grave human rights violations.[30]

The use of torture was a key instrument in criminal proceedings for obtaining a confession,[31] often leading to capital punishment or long years in prison under cruel and inhumane conditions.[32] Despite the horrific record of human rights abuses in the authoritarian-led era, no exact account of victims of torture and other forms of ill-treatment have been documented.[33] Take an example of a military trial with political opponents in the so-called 'Kaohsiung

---

25   *Ibid.*, 155–7, 161.

26   *Ibid.*, 155.

27   Memorial Foundation of 228, 'Scars on the Land: The Historic Sites Related to the February 28 Incident in Northern Taiwan Second part: In the Wake of Gunshots' (18 July 2021) https://www.228.org.tw/en_exhibition-view.php?ID=16 (accessed 1 November 2022).

28   See Temporary Provisions against Communist Rebellion which effectively nullified the constitution and established martial law in Taiwan.

29   The Martial Law was declared on 19 May 1949 by the Declaration of Martial Law in Taiwan Province (臺灣省戒嚴令) by the then chairman of the Taiwan Provincial Government and commander of Taiwan Garrison Command, Chen Cheng. Under martial law, political liberties were restricted, such as freedom of the press and freedom of assembly. The power was concentrated in the hands of the ruling Kuomintang party and no other political parties were allowed. Read more about martial law in Taiwan, for example, in I Neary, *Human Rights in Japan, South Korea and Taiwan* (Routledge, 2002).

30   Neary, *ibid.*

31   C Hoyle 'Unsafe Convictions in Capital Cases in Taiwan – A Report Based on the Research and Findings of Chang Chuan-Fen' (2019) https://www.deathpenaltyproject.org/wp-content/uploads/2019/03/Taiwan-Unsafe-Convictions-Report-FINAL_Printed.pdf (accessed 1 November 2022), 15.

32   See a prison at Green Island which was notorious for inhuman conditions and cruel treatment of prisoners during the Martial Law era.

33   The cases of historical injustice are under intensive research. See the final report (in Chinese) of the Transitional Justice Commission, an independent Taiwanese governmental agency that investigated injustices committed between 15 August 1945 and 6 November 1992. In: Transitional Justice Commission (2022) https://gazette2.nat.gov.tw/EG_FileManager/eguploadpub/ego28098/ch01/type7/gov01/num2/Eg.htm?fbclid=IwAR0ak_hpOX0Pjg-OwuE7r1muedjYcmD_vm8OSOSb1VqdM7KCmQ2VAkEKfho (accessed 1 November 2022). See also the Taiwan Innocence Project, a Taiwanese non-governmental organization which addresses the issue of wrongful conviction in Taiwan: https://twinnocenceproject.org/ (accessed 1 November 2022).

incident'.[34] Jacobs has pointed out that it is unclear whether the defendants were 'physically tortured', however almost all defendants were 'kept awake and questioned by police in relays until, under what was called 'fatigue bombing', they were willing to say and agree to anything that the police wanted.'[35] Jacobs has further emphasised that neither less visible forms of physical torture such as prolonged standing, nor mental torture, including threats, sleep deprivation, imposition of fear,[36] or 'fatigue questioning' up to a hundred hours[37] have been acknowledged as torture by the authorities at that time.[38] Accordingly, if the above-mentioned acts were not considered torture, there are no official reports on victims of torture,[39] let alone the prosecution of torturers.

The key legislative changes that first laid down guarantees of a fair trial and safeguards against torture were fuelled by public anger at flagrant cases of miscarriage of justice, in particular, wrongful convictions that resulted in unjust execution. A breaking point was a highly publicized case of torture and suicide of Wang Ying-Xian (王迎先) in 1982 that for the first time, constituted a defendant's right to retain a defence counsel before trial.[40] As Yu-Jie Chen explains, this was the very first momentum that propelled the then-authoritarian KMT government to adopt unprecedented reform resulting in the amendment of the code of criminal procedure.[41]

However, the struggle for democracy did not go smoothly[42] and despite the repeal of martial law in 1987, torture remained endemic to the criminal justice system for at least a decade. Forced confessions obtained by torture continued to be regarded as the king of evidence[43] in criminal proceedings and resulted in a number of wrongful convictions including capital punishment.[44] These

---

34 BJ Jacobs *The Kaohsiung Incident in Taiwan and Memoirs of a Foreign Big Beard* (Koninklijke Brill, 2016) 23–28.

35 *Ibid.*, 44.

36 *Ibid.*, 49–50, 69, 89.

37 *Ibid.*, 67.

38 *Ibid.*,125.

39 No compensation law was adopted to redress victims of torture.

40 YJ Chen 'One Problem, Two Paths: A Taiwanese Perspective on the Exclusionary Rule in China' (2010) 43 *N.Y.U. Journal of International Law and Politics* 713, 717. Read more about the development of the right to counsel in Taiwan in YJ Chen 'Lawyers' Activism and the Expansion of the Right to Counsel in Taiwan' in M McConville and E Pils (eds.) *Comparative Perspectives on Criminal Justice in China* (Edward Elgar Publishin,g 2013).

41 Chen (2010), *supra* note 40, 716. Code of Criminal Procedure (Xíngshì sùsòng fǎ), Article 27.

42 YH Chang, *Lee Teng-Hui and the democratization of Taiwan* (Taiwan Advocates, 2006).

43 Chen (2010), *supra* note 40, 716.

44 See, for example, cases of Cheng Hsing-tse (鄭性澤); Hsu Tzu-chiang (徐自強); Su Ping-kun (蘇炳坤).

appalling cases of injustice could be demonstrated in the notorious case of torture and execution of Chiang Kuo-Ching in 1997 or the torture and long-term imprisonment of the Hsichih trio (acquitted in 2012).[45] The legacy of the torturous past remains to date, as witnessed by the oldest criminal case of Chiou Ho-shun (邱和順) who still remains in prison based on a confession that was extracted by torture more than 30 years ago.[46]

In spite of the initial reform of criminal procedure, changes in practice were rather symbolic. Chen refers to a survey conducted among legal professionals and police in 1995 which shows that torture was still a common practice during police interrogation throughout the 1980s and '90s.[47] Meaningful reform of the criminal justice from inquisitorial to adversarial model was achieved at the beginning of the century, which for the first time laid down the fundamental procedural guarantees for a fair trial[48] including the incorporation of the exclusionary rule (non-admissibility of evidence and confession extracted by violence, threat, inducement, fraud, exhausting interrogation, unlawful detention or other improper means).[49] Another significant achievement became the requirement for mandatory recording of all stages of interrogation during the criminal proceedings.[50]

Despite several procedural safeguards, law enforcement continued to show a deaf ear to allegations of torture and carried out neither an effective investigation of torture allegations nor adequate prosecution and punishment of torturers. Based on the information provided by the Taiwan Innocence Project, when torture allegations were raised, police commonly required the victims to summons the amount of evidence by themselves, rather than to initiate ex officio investigation. Since the only source of such evidence was commonly in

---

45   See, for example, the case of Cheng Hsing-tse (鄭性澤); Hsu Tzu-chiang (徐自強); Su Ping-kun (蘇炳坤) and Hsichih Trio - Su Chien-ho (蘇建和), Chuang Lin-hsun (莊林勳) and Liu Bin-lang (劉秉郎).

46   See an investigation report in Control Yuan, 'Investigation Report of Qiu He-shun' (10 June 2020) https://www.cy.gov.tw/CyBsBoxContent.aspx?n=133&s=17154.

47   Chen (2010), *supra* note 40, 718.

48   Ibid at 720.

49   See the evolution and conceptualization of exclusionary rule in Taiwan in Chang (n 42). See Code of Criminal Procedure (Xíngshì sùsòng fǎ), Articles 98, 156 and 158-2, para 3. The Criminal Code provides no legal definition of the 'other improper means', hence it is questionable whether various techniques of psychological torture would be, in practice, regarded as 'improper means'.

50   See the amendment of the Code of Criminal Procedure in 2003 that adhered to the requirement of cross-examination in criminal procedure (new articles 287, para 1 and 287, para 2).

the possession of the police officers, it was unlikely that victims were able to bear the burden of proof.[51]

Several alleged victims of torture have also underscored excessive delays in the investigation which often led to the end that traces of slight injuries such as bruises disappeared in a course of time – depriving the victim of the only tangible evidence. Even in a situation when the victim described in detail torture which he was subjected to[52] and exposed a visible injury,[53] these facts also did not lead to the investigation and prosecution of perpetrators. To make things even more outrageous, even when State authorities recognized that torture was truly inflicted,[54] it again did not result in any response of criminal law prosecution of the perpetrators. This could be well illustrated in the torture case of Chiang Kuo-ching, who admitted his guilt on the basis of a confession extracted by torture. Although Mr Chiang was later exonerated in a posthumous trial and the use of torture was officially declared,[55] no perpetrators have been ever brought to justice.[56]

Plausibly, of the numerous allegations of torture and ill-treatment, only few of them resulted in criminal convictions. One case concerns the abuse and death of a soldier Zhong-qiu Hong (洪仲丘) in military detention.[57] Another incident relates to torture of Chiou Ho-shun (邱和順). Despite perpetrators

---

51 For example, in the torture case of Hsieh Chih-Hung (謝志宏) in 2000, police claimed to lose the disc with a recording of the interrogation during which Mr Hsieh confessed to committing a crime (Taiwan Innocence Project). See also study in C Hoyle, 'Unsafe Convictions in Capital Cases in Taiwan – A Report based on the Research and Findings of Chang Chuan-Fen' (2019) https://www.deathpenaltyproject.org/wp-content/uploads/2019/03/Taiwan-Unsafe-Convictions-Report-FINAL_Printed.pdf (accessed 1 November 2022), 16. Study reveals that in almost all cases where the defendants maintained they had been tortured, the police claimed to have lost the audio or videotapes of interrogations.

52 For example, Su Ping-kun (蘇炳坤) was allegedly subjected to waterboarding, an airstrike siren against his ear and kicking in his waist. He drew several pictures detailing how he was being tortured, however, no perpetrator was indicted (Taiwan Innocence Project).

53 See, for example, a case of Cheng Hsing-tse (鄭性澤) who suffered a bruise on his left eye, however, the medical record did not mention any injury (Taiwan Innocence Project).

54 In Su Ping-kun case, the court has explicitly acknowledged that Mr. Su was subjected to physical and mental torture. See in Su Ping-Kun case (Judgment) Taiwan High Court 臺灣高等法院107年度再字第3號 (8 August 2018).

55 Control Yuan has investigated the case and has confirmed that torture was used to extract a confession. See in Control Yuan, 'Investigation into Chiang Kuo-Ching Case: Posthumous Exoneration' (24 March 2020) https://www.cy.gov.tw/EN/News_Content.aspx?n=252&s=16384 (accessed 1 November 2022).

56 The only result of this case was a formal apology from the Ministry of National Defence and monetary compensation to Chiang's family.

57 Mr. Hong was subjected to strenuous exercise drills and suffered a heatstroke for which fell into a coma and died.

being punished in criminal trials, the convictions brought very lenient prison sentences which counted for only several months.[58]

A historic milestone in human rights development in Taiwan occurred in 2009 when the Legislative Yuan passed the ratification act of the International Covenant on Civil and Political Rights (ICCPR) and International Covenant on Economic, Social and Cultural Rights (ICESCR)[59] and set forth to abide by the obligation of prohibition of torture under Article 7 of the ICCPR.[60]

In 2013, the International Review Committee carried out a periodic review of the initial State report on the implementation of the ICCPR and recommended that Taiwan ratify the Convention against Torture and insert a crime of torture, as defined in Article 1 of the Convention, as a separate crime with adequate penalties in its criminal code.[61] The IRC also underscored the need to investigate promptly and thoroughly all allegations or suspicions of torture by an independent and impartial body with full criminal investigation powers.[62]

Four years later, in 2017, the IRC noted that this recommendation has not been implemented, thus reiterated to incorporate a separate and specific crime of torture with adequate penalties into the criminal code.[63] The IRC also noted with dissatisfaction that no progress has been achieved in implementing the previous recommendation regarding an effective investigation of torture allegations.[64]

The demand for a specific crime of torture was raised again by the IRC in 2022 during the periodic review of the third ICCPR State report. The IRC has underscored the urgency in the implementation of such obligation and reiterates 'in the strongest terms' the need for incorporation of a separate and specific crime of torture with adequate penalties into the Criminal Code

---

58   Torturers in the Chiou Ho-shun case were sentenced to imprisonment between 5 and 6 months, and the alleged torture of Zhong-qiu Hong was punished by sentences between 12 and 14 months. Interview with Taiwan Innocence Project, 27 March 2021; See for more details Zhong-qiu Hong case (Judgment) Taiwan High Court 臺灣高等法院有關105年度軍上重更(一)字第1號 (28 June 2017).

59   Act to Implement the International Covenant on Civil and Political Rights and the International Covenant on Economic, Social and Cultural Rights (Gōngmín yǔ zhèngzhì quánlì guójì gōngyuē jí jīngjì shèhuì wénhuà quánlì guójì gōngyuē shīxíng fǎ).

60   See Human Rights Committee (1992) 'General comment No. 20: Article 7 (Prohibition of torture, or other cruel, inhuman or degrading treatment or punishment)' UN Doc A/44/40, 10 March 1992, para 8.

61   IRC (2013), *supra* note 5, para 58.

62   *Ibid.*

63   IRC (2017), *supra* note 5, para 53.

64   *Ibid.*, para 54.

'without further delay'.[65] The IRC's criticism is fuelled by the fact that of 1945 complaints received by correctional institutions between the years 2015 and 2019, only 2 cases were further processed to a court (disciplinary court).[66] This gap has been underscored by a committee member, Manfred Nowak: 'Since there is no crime of torture, there is no consequence. Since there is no consequence, there is no deterrence. And that is why torture is continuing to take place in the country.'[67] Nowak further pointed to the absence of effective investigation of torture allegations and independent authority to investigate and prosecute torture.[68]

3   The Crime of Torture and the Defensive Position of the Taiwan Government

Notwithstanding the widespread impunity of torture perpetrators and constant recommendations of the IRC to establish a distinct crime of torture, the Taiwan government has insisted that existing legislation already provides a sufficient legal basis for addressing torture. Hence, it implies that there is no need for creating a brand-new type of criminal offense that differs from the existing crimes.[69]

In the initial State report on the implementation of the ICCPR (Article 7), the government did not refer to the notion of 'torture' within the meaning of Article 7, but used the term 'brutal penalty', in which torture is referred to as an example of brutal penalty ('physical brutal penalty') rather than a crime *per se*. Moreover, the report did not consider other forms of physical and

---

65   IRC, 'Concluding Observations and Recommendations on the Third State Report on the Implementation of the International Human Rights Covenants' (13 May 2022) https://covenantswatch.org.tw/wp-content/uploads/2015/12/concluding-observations-and-recommendations_taiwan-international-review-2022-0516修正.pdf (accessed 1 November 2022), para 74.
66   ROC (2022), *supra* note 17, time 7:50:10.
67   *Ibid.*, time 8:00:11.
68   *Ibid.*, time 7:53:20.
69   In particular, Article 125 of the Criminal Code (abuse and other offenses committed by public official charged with the duty of investigation or bringing offenders to justice), Article 126 of the Criminal Code (acts of violence and cruelty committed by public official charged with the custody, or conveyance of prisoners) and Article 44 of the Criminal Code of the Armed Forces (abuse of subordinate by the commander). See similar arguments raised by the government of Switzerland (CAT/C/SVK/CO/3, para 7), Denmark (CAT/C/DNK/CO/6-7, para 10) or Japan (CAT/C/JPN/2, paras 1–3). See also an assessment of these approaches in Marchesi, *supra* note 10, 197–198.

psychological pain and suffering (for example, prolonged standing, water-boarding, long-term solitary confinement, sleep deprivation, etc.) as a form of torture as these acts are noted separately from the notion of torture.[70] The government has further specified that these forms of 'brutal penalty' are criminalized under various provisions of the criminal code, in particular Article 125 and Article 126.[71]

In 2016, the government has argued that '[t]he country already has laws that prohibit crimes similar to what is described as torture in Article 7 of ICCPR and Article 1 of the UNCAT'[72] and referred again to various provisions of the criminal code and other statutes.[73] In 2020, the government has again defended its position arguing that existing regulations[74] are those that 'expressly prohibit and impose penalties on torture and cruel treatment.'[75] The same arguments were invoked again in 2022, which were clearly rejected by Nowak stating simply that 'this is not what is required by the Convention'[76] and lamenting that 'the government does not feel the necessity of enacting the crime of torture.'[77]

While it is commendable that criminal law contains offenses that could punish improper behavior of public officials and thus have some preventive effect[78], none of the said provisions is neither called 'torture', nor define torture in line with articles 1 and 4 of the Convention as an intentional and purposeful act of severe pain or suffering committed by a public official or private person on his behalf. Alarmingly, even the Taiwan Supreme Court does not consider Article 125 of the criminal code as a provision that directly protects the victim, but rather a rule that protects the general principle of fairness of justice.

---

70   ROC, 'Implementation of the International Covenant on Civil and Political Rights–Initial report submitted under article 40 of the Covenant' (September 2012) https://www.humanrights.moj.gov.tw/media/14393/541517201510.pdf?mediaDL=true (accessed 1 November 2022), paras 99–106.

71   *Ibid.*, paras 100–6.

72   ROC, 'Implementation of the International Covenant on Civil and Political Rights – Second report submitted under article 40 of the Covenant' (April 2016) https://www.humanrights.moj.gov.tw/media/12227/26920041318521f5b5.pdf?mediaDL=true (accessed 1 November 2022), para 83.

73   In particular articles 125 and 126 of the Criminal Code and article 44 of the Criminal Code of the Armed Forces. See ROC, *ibid.*, paras 81–3 and ROC (2016), *supra* note 17, paras 191–3.

74   Article 125 and Article 126 of the Criminal Code and Article 44 of the Criminal Code of the Armed Forces.

75   ROC (2020), *supra* note 17, paras 163–4.

76   ROC (2022), *supra* note 17, time 7:39:54.

77   *Ibid.*, time 7:49:15.

78   See crime of 'abusing authority' (Criminal Code, Article 125, para 1). The term 'abuse' is defined as 'any act of abuse or maltreatment of another person in a violent, coercive or inhumane way' (Criminal Code, Article 10, para 7).

Therefore, victims are not entitled to raise the case under this provision by themselves, but the proceeding must be initiated by the public prosecutor.[79]

On top of that, the above provisions of criminal code fall short to regard torture as an absolutely prohibited act as the said offenses are subjected to a statute of limitations[80] and amnesties, pardons[81] and immunities.[82] Moreover, the minimum penalty for the said crimes is considerable lenient[83] considering the severity of torture and comparable crimes in Taiwan's criminal code.[84] Nevertheless, it seems that these provisions are actually not used in practice as the utmost penalty resulting from torture allegations is often a reprimand (a disciplinary action) imposed by a disciplinary court.[85]

Despite the reassurance given by the Taiwan government that 'judiciary, prosecution, police, investigation authority ... follow the related legal procedures to eliminate torture...'[86], it is rather perplexing how they could do so if torture has not yet been defined as a crime.[87] On the contrary, it is credible to believe that rare investigations of allegations of torture and scant conviction of torture perpetrators show a systematic pattern instead that is, to a large extent, rooted in this obvious legal vacuum. In a similar vein (besides the repetitive IRC's criticism examined above), Taiwanese civil society group, the Covenants Watch, has questioned the existing provisions of the criminal code as having

---

79   See Interpretation of Article 125 of the Criminal Code (Judgment) Taiwan Supreme Court, 最高法院 91 年度台上字第 2467 號 刑事判決 (2 May 2002).

80   Crimes under Articles 125 and 126 of the Criminal Code and Article 44 of the Criminal Code of the Armed Forces are subject to 20 years of statute of limitations.

81   See Constitution of the Republic of China (Taiwan), Article 40 and Amnesty Act (Shèmiǎn fǎ, 赦免法).

82   UN Committee against Torture 2008, *supra* note 8, para 8; L Oette 'Implementing the Prohibition of Torture: the Contribution and Limits of National Legislation and Jurisprudence' (2012) 16 *International Journal of Human Rights* 717, 724; Cestaro v. Italy, Application No 6884/11, Judgment of 7 April 2015, para 208; Abdülsamet Yaman v. Turkey, Application No 32446/96, Judgment of 2 November 2004, para. 55.

83   Principle punishment for crimes under Articles 125 and 126 of the Criminal Code is imprisonment between 1 and 7 years and for a crime under Article 44 of the Criminal Code of the Armed Forces, imprisonment between 3 and 10 years.

84   For example, a crime of serious physical injury is sanctioned by imprisonment between 5 and 12 years (Criminal Code, Article 278 para 1).

85   ROC (2022), *supra* note 17, time 7:51:30.

86   ROC, 'Replies from Republic of China (Taiwan) to the List of Issues to be Taken up in Connection with the Consideration of its Third Report (ICCPR)' (October 2021) https://covenantswatch.org.tw/wp-content/uploads/2015/12/2021_ICCPR_Replies_to_LOIs_Bilingual.pdf (accessed 1 November 2022), 33.

87   See similar questions raised by Pollard: M Pollard 'Panel 1: Are Adequate Legal Frameworks in Place at the Domestic Level? Torture as a Specific Criminal Offense in Domestic Laws' (2009) 16 *Human Rights Brief* 1, 1.

any substantial effect or being merely 'decorative statutes ... with no genuine binding force.'[88] Similarly, Su Yiu-Chen has emphasised that making torture a crime in Taiwan would help to deter torture, reduce the occurrence of injustice and safeguard human rights.[89]

There is no doubt that Taiwan's criminal law fails to provide sufficient legal norms to criminalize torture and to investigate and prosecute torture perpetrators. Given this lacuna and the number of torture allegations, it is also likely, as noted by Nowak, that torture is happening in today's Taiwan. This regrettable observation heightens the ambivalent character of the current implementation process of the UNCAT since the criminalization of torture seems to be a *condition sine qua non* for a successful implementation.

Notwithstanding this reluctance, it was invoked by Taiwan government officials that a discussion is still needed on what elements constitute torture.[90] Although the government has not yet identified any specific challenges concerning a definition of torture and its constituent elements, it is likely that given different contexts in which torture has occurred in Taiwan, finding an adequate definition for the crime of torture could be rather a challenging task.[91] Therefore, a question is raised whether all the elements of torture provided for in Article 1 of the UNCAT should be incorporated as systematically recommended by the CAT or whether the Taiwan government should challenge the definition of the Convention and build a different construction.

4   Elements of Torture: A Need for a State-Nexus?

Notwithstanding a clear definition of torture in Article 1 of the Convention, various definitions can be seen in domestic criminal codes of the UNCAT States Parties. In order to avoid any interpretation and implementation problems,

---

88   Covenants Watch, 'Initial Parallel Report on the Implementation of the International Covenant on Civil and Political Rights' (30 November 2012) https://en.covenantswatch .org.tw/treaty-reviews/ (accessed 1 November 2022), 43.

89   YC Su, 'Stop Torture by Making It a Crime' *Taipei Times*, 16 December 2017, http://www .taipeitimes.com/News/editorials/archives/2017/12/16/2003684043 (accessed 1 November 2022).

90   ROC (2022), *supra* note 17, time 8:12:12.

91   Gaeta explains that notion of torture always depends upon the particular context in which it is used. She compares the torture phenomenon to a chameleon which changes its skin colour depending on where it finds itself. See P Gaeta, 'When is the Involvement of State Officials a Requirement for the Crime of Torture?' (2008) 6 *Journal of International Criminal Justice* 183, 192–193.

Nowak has suggested a verbatim incorporation of Article 1 in domestic criminal law.[92] He noted that States will be on 'the safe side' and simply 'do better' to follow the UNCAT's definition since such definition covers all aspects of torture.[93]

It appears, however, that 'public official' requirement, one of the constitutive compotents of torture under Article 1 of the Convention[94], is rather a controversial element today, since it complicates addressing torture which might not be clearly attributed to public officials. Therefore, there is no surprise that a State-nexus requirement is a subject to frequent criticism.[95] Nowak himself has admitted that the 'very narrow definition of torture of the UNCAT is outdated', hence clarifying that States should do both, follow the definition of torture in article 1 and also recognize the crime of torture beyond the official State-nexus.[96]

There is no doubt that torture inflicted by law enforcement during interrogation is the archetypal form of torture that falls fully within its definition under Article 1 of the Convention. There is no difference in that classification whether the torture was committed during the martial law era or within the democratization process after 1987 as the definition is not limited to any context and depends solely on its constituent elements. Therefore, if Taiwan ensures verbatim incorporation of Article 1 in offense of torture it surely provides an adequate norm to address police torture committed during interrogation. It would be more challenging, however, to extend Article 1 definition to torture committed in the context of the 228 incident and modern-day incidents of torture committed by a number of quasi-public officials or entirely private subjects.

4.1   Torture in the Context of the 228 Incident

It is plausible to believe that military suppression of Taiwan's uprising of the 228 Incident could be classified as a 'systematic and widespread attack directed

---

92   UN Human Rights Council, *supra* note 14, para 143. See, on the contrary, Harper suggests that states enjoy a considerable degree of discretion when defining the term. In Harper, *supra* note 18, 895.

93   M Nowak, 'Can Private Actors Torture?' (2021) 19 *Journal of International Criminal Justice* 415, 418.

94   Pain or suffering must be inflicted by or at the instigation of or with the consent or acquiescence of a public official or other person acting in an official capacity. UNCAT, Article 1, para 1.

95   Harper, *supra* note 18; Dewulf, *supra* note 18.

96   Nowak, *supra* note 93, 419.

against civilian population' under international criminal law.[97] As torturing civilians by the ROC troops between 28 February and 16 May 1947 were a part of the said attack, these acts of torture could be regarded as crimes against humanity in the meaning of the Rome Statute of the International Criminal Court (ICC).[98]

Unlike the UNCAT, the ICC Rome Statute does not regard torture as a purposeful State crime committed by public official, but defines it as 'an intentional infliction of severe pain or suffering, whether physical or mental, upon a person in the custody or under the control of the accused.'[99] Gaeta explains that the requirement of a State official is not needed anymore in the context of war crimes or crimes against humanity as this context (systematic disregard to the mental and physical integrity of human beings) is so serious that it turns the infliction of severe pain or suffering into a crime of international concern.[100]

The distinction between wartime and peacetime context is relevant for redressing the events of historical torture that was committed as part of a war crime or a crime against humanity. It should be noted in this regard that the CAT has repeatedly urged several countries to redress the torture that occurred far in history. Take Japan as an example. The Committee has pressured the Japanese government to investigate cases of military sexual slavery committed by its soldiers during World War II and to prosecute the perpetrators.[101] However, as noted above, one would remain puzzled how the Japanese authorities should apply the Convention definition to prosecute torturers who committed these crimes in the context of the war.[102] Should Japan adhere to a State-nexus definition of torture under the UNCAT or rather apply a definition under international criminal law? The same goes for Taiwan in redressing the historical torture of the 228 Incident.

---

97   Read more in ICTY, 'Prosecutor vs. Kunarac Dragoljub and others' Appeals Chamber Judgment of 12 June 2002, No IT-96-23 & IT-96-23/1-A, para 94.

98   Rome Statute of the International Criminal Court, Art. 7 para 1 (f).

99   ICC Rome Statute.

100   Gaeta, *supra* note 91, 183; P Gaeta and A Clapham 'Torture by Private Actors and 'Gold-Plating' the Offence in National Law: An Exchange of Emails in Honour of William Schabas' in MM de Guzman and DM Amann (eds) *Arcs of Global Justice: Essays in Honour of William Schabas* (Oxford University Press, 2018) 287–295.

101   See CAT Concluding Observations on Japan (CAT/C/JPN/CO/1, para 13). See similar CAT recommendations addressed to Chile, Uruguay or South Africa.

102   It is worth noting that since the definition of torture under Article 1 of the Convention does not represent customary international law outside the framework of the Convention (see ICTY (n 97) 148.), it will be erroneous to transfer it to the realm of international criminal law. See Gaeta, *supra* note 91; ICTY, *supra* note 97; 495.

It is certainly methodologically correct to distinguish between torture as 'crime *per se*' under the international human rights law on the one hand and torture as 'crime against humanity' under the international criminal law on the other hand. It is therefore credible, as underscored by Gaeta, that given the different purposes of these crimes, the two definitions are not identical and shall not be assimilated.[103] However, what does this theoretical distinction mean for practical investigation and prosecution of torture, more so, if torture occurred in relation to both normative contexts?

Let's presume that a private torturer (for example, an off-duty policeman[104]) tortured his victims during the active hostilities of the 228 Incident and continued doing so even months after the ceasefire had been declared.[105] While he will be held responsible for torture during the 228 Incident, because the definition of torture according to the ICC Rome Statute does not require a State-nexus, he will not be held liable for consequent torture, because this will be outside the context of the crimes against humanity and the UNCAT requires a State-nexus element.[106]

The question then arises as whether the time elapsed between 'wartime' and 'peacetime' should really make a difference for criminal law to see the same things through a different lens?[107] Evidently, a similar puzzle could appear today with regard to torture committed by various paramilitary groups, kidnappers involved in human trafficking or terrorist organizations where there might be neither a State-nexus nor visible wartime context.[108] Against this background, Clapham has underscored that in the 21st century, we do not really know whether there is peacetime or wartime, hence the torture rule shall not be limited to these contexts but applies at all times.[109]

Against this background, a series of questions emerge. Should Taiwan's criminal code omit the public official requirement and extend its application to the context of the 228 Incident? Should it rather keep all elements of

---

103   Gaeta, *supra* note 91, 189.
104   See more on the accountability of off-duty policemen in Fernandez and Muntingh, *supra* note 10, 96.
105   The persecutions were officially closed on May 23, 1950 in Lai et al, *supra* note 20, 183.
106   This is, of course, an illustrative case. UNCAT was not applied anyway since it entered into force four decades later, but answering this question could be relevant for present-day conflicts.
107   See similar question raised by Clapham in Gaeta and Clapham, *supra* note 100, 295.
108   Nowak has acknowledged that this contradiction is today present in various States' legislations. See Nowak, *supra* note 93, 419–20.
109   A Clapham, 'Thinking beyond the Offence of Torture' (2021) 19 *Journal of International Criminal Justice* 439, 444.

Article 1 definition to respond only to archetypal torture under police custody? Or should it be best to establish more crimes of torture, each for a particular context?

4.2   *Torture Committed by Various State and Non-State Actors*

It has been explained above that on the basis of the definition of torture under the Convention, the act of severe pain and suffering will not be considered torture unless there is a link established between the perpetrator and the State. The link might be relatively strong, as for cases where public officials are directly involved (e.g., police torture) or rather weak as torture is attributed to the State on the basis of its failure to protect victims against both public and private offenders (failure to due diligence, acquiescence).[110]

It is rather uncontroversial that a wide range of public actors such as law-enforcement officers, military and civil servants such as school teachers, medical personnel, social workers and other personnel working in public and private detention centres would all be considered as torturers under the Convention.[111] On the contrary, if a perpetrator performs some abuse for a completely private end, he or she will not be likely considered as torturer under the Convention. Hence, human trafficking, domestic violence or rape may not be considered torture, despite severe pain or suffering that the victim must endure.[112]

As seen in Taiwan criminal code, the notion of 'public official' is conceptualized very narrowly and linked to the merit of a particular crime.[113] For example, Article 125 of the criminal code defines public officials as one who is 'charged with the duty of investigation or bringing offenders to justice'[114] and one who is 'charged with the custody or conveyance of prisoners'.[115] Article 44 of the Criminal Code requires a public official to be a military commander.[116] Apparently, this narrow conception of public officials leaves behind many situations

---

110   UNCAT, Article 1 para 1. See further State responsibility for human trafficking committed by non-State actors in L McGregor 'Applying the Definition of Torture to the Acts of Non-State Actors: The Case of Trafficking in Human Beings' (2014) 36 *Human Rights Quarterly* 210.

111   Dewulf, *supra* note 18, 365.

112   McGregor, *supra* note 110; K Fortin 'Rape as Torture – An Evaluation of the Committee against Torture's Attitude to Sexual Violence' (2008) 4 *Utrecht Law Review* 145.

113   See similar deficiency, for example, in Criminal Code of the Republic of Korea, Art. 125.

114   Article 125 of the Criminal Code of the Republic of China (Taiwan).

115   *Ibid.*

116   Article 44 of the Criminal Code of the Armed Forces of the Republic of China (Taiwan). See definition of 'commander' in Article 8.

where torture could occur, such as torture of patients in health-care and social-care settings, children in children homes, etc. Alarmingly, legal understanding of a public official was further restricted by the Taiwan Supreme Court which held that public officials embodied in article 125 of the criminal code are tantamount to prosecutors and judges only.[117] Hence, besides prosecutors and judges, no other public officials not alone 'other persons acting in official capacity' are plausibly regarded as torture perpetrators in Taiwan.[118]

Noteworthy, civil society groups have repeatedly illuminated cases of torture and ill-treatment with vulnerable people and detainees, such as excessive use of restraints in prisons[119], coercive training in military[120], disproportionate use of police power against demonstrators[121] or compulsory hospitalization of people with disabilities.[122]

Besides that, it has been well-documented that Taiwan constantly fails to protect vulnerable people from crimes and abuses committed by private persons. Take an example of persistent exploitation of migrant workers on Taiwan fishing vessels[123] which has reached, on several occasions, the severity of forced labour and trafficking in person. An illustrative case could be a verdict of Cambodian court over six Taiwanese citizens in 2014 for the crime of human trafficking of more than 1000 Cambodian fishermen. Remarkably, at least four convicts remain at large in Taiwan and the law enforcement remains indifferent to their whereabouts and bringing them to justice.[124]

It is true that Taiwan's indifference to crimes committed by private persons may establish a link based on acquiescence between these 'private offenders' and the State, hence making Taiwan authorities responsible under the UNCAT.[125]

---

117 Qian (n 5), Interpretation of Public Official (Judgment) Taiwan Supreme Court, 30 年上字第 511 號 (4 January 2019).

118 Qian, *supra* note 5.

119 Covenants Watch, *supra* note 88, 51–2.

120 See Hung Chung-Chiu case analysed in Covenants Watch, 'Shadow Report 2016 on the Implementation of the International Covenant on Civil and Political Rights' (4 September 2016) https://en.covenantswatch.org.tw/wp-content/uploads/2018/12/2017-ICCPR-State-Report-Parallel-Report_EN.pdf (accessed 1 November 2022), 49–50. See also a collection of stories of various forms of abuses and deaths in military settings in B Chen and R Li, *21 phone calls: Bingge's late-night call for help* (21通電話：阿兵哥的深夜求救) (Yushan Society 2018).

121 Covenants Watch, *supra* note 120, 51–4.

122 *Ibid.*, 57–9.

123 Covenants Watch, *supra* note 88, 64–73, Covenants Watch, *supra* note 120, 54–5.

124 Greenpeace, 'Misery on Sea: Human Suffering in Taiwan's Distant Water Fishing Fleets' (24 May 2018) https://drive.google.com/file/d/1t34YxiodIXAFsdu-41Vk6PcbiyGVpHbA/view (accessed 1 November 2022), 20–5.

125 UN Committee against Torture, *supra* note 8, para18.

One may therefore believe that verbatim incorporation of article 1 of the Convention including all forms of public involvement (infliction, incitement, consent and acquiescence) will provide an adequate legal basis for addressing such deficiencies. Realistically, it would be challenging if not impossible for law enforcement to embrace such a broad interpretation of public officials based on unclear terms, in particular the elements of consent and acquiescence.[126] If today even the police and prison officers are not considered *de lege lata* public officials, it will be surprising if, all of sudden, the Taiwan prosecutors will be able to extend the State-nexus to situations where private persons are acting based on State's consent or acquiescence.

Similar to problematic accountability of torturers for torture in the context of the 228 Incident, it is likely that adherance to a State-nexus requirement may compromise the investigation of today's cases of torture committed by various public officials, quazi-public officials and solely private persons.

5   Conclusion

Torture is a crime of opportunity.[127] By reducing the opportunity, as aptly noted by Carver and Handley, the incidence of torture falls; and if torturers are effectively investigated and prosecuted, it falls further.[128] It is therefore a pivotal aim of the criminal law to send 'an unequivocal message that such conduct will not be tolerated'[129] by putting in place a clear definition of torture as a specific crime. The criminalization of torture as a separate offence is therefore nothing controversial and a matter of course for those who are serious about the struggle against torture. The lacuna in the criminalization of torture in Taiwan on the one side and the widespread impunity for torture on the other demonstrates the above inferences. What is alarming, is the ambiguity between declared will of Taiwan government to ratify the Convention and actual political reluctance to implement the very first step in eradication of torture.

---

126   See similar struggles in criminal law of Latvia (CAT/C/LVA/CO/6, paras 6–7), Kazakhstan (CAT/C/KAZ/CO/3, para 24) or Japan (CAT/C/JPN/CO/1, para 10).

127   NS Rodley 'Reflections on Working for the Prevention of Torture' (2009) 6 *Essex Human Rights Review* 21.

128   R Carver and L Handley, *Does Torture Prevention Work?* (Liverpool University Press, 2017), 627.

129   European Committee for the Prevention of Torture and Inhuman or Degrading Treatment or Punishment (CPT), UN Committee against Torture, 'Combating Impunity – Extract from the 14th General Report of the CPT' (2004) CPT/Inf (2004) 28-part, 25.

During the IRC meeting in March 2022, Nowak stated uncompromisingly that 'the way how Taiwan's government deals with the death penalty is the litmus test of whether or not it is willing to really take the international human rights obligations seriously or not.'[130] I believe that the same goes for the criminalization of torture under the current UNCAT implementation process.

Not only is the criminalization of torture a litmus test of the UNCAT implementation. It also indicates whether or not the Taiwan model of de-facto ratification of the human rights treaties outside the framework of the United Nations is viable, i.e. resulting in tangible advances in human rights. There is no doubt that changes in Taiwan's criminal law carried out as a direct consequence of the present de-facto 'ratification' would foster the legitimacy of this ratification model and could be also a welcome impetus for ratification of UN treaties elsewhere.

In the effort to explain ongoing Taiwan's reluctance to criminalize torture, one should bear in mind a special stigma attached to torture. Harper has correctly emphasised that the power of the term often prevents States to label illegal acts as 'torture' because of the stigma associated with this term.[131] It is plausible that the Taiwan government is likewise reluctant to label torture as torture since the official recognition that torture occurs in today's Taiwan might be viewed as undermining its international perception as a freedom-loving democratic State.[132] Consequently, wrapping torture in terms such as 'abuse of authority'[133] may shadow a torturous environment to outside scrutiny, distort the data on incidents of torture and shield law enforcement from domestic and international condemnation.

Against this background, the present implementation act might be viewed as an opportunity to 'call a spade a spade' and show the genuine intention in the fight against torture. There is no doubt that speedy implementation of the Convention against Torture and establishing a specific offence of torture will be a significant leap forward in the fight against impunity in Taiwan. And of course, a clear message will be sent to torturers at home and around the globe that Taiwan is no longer a safe haven for them.

A puzzle remains, whether or not all elements of torture stipulated in Article 1 of the Convention shall be incorporated into a crime of torture in Taiwan.

---

130   ROC (202), *supra* note 17, time 6:22:54.
131   Harper, *supra* note 18, 915.
132   See, for example, Taiwan's condemnation for forced labour which was taken very apprehensively by local stakeholders in Control Yuan, 'Investigation Report' (6 May 2021) https://www.cy.gov.tw/News_Content.aspx?n=125&s=20285 (accessed 1 November 2022).
133   Criminal Code of the Republic of China (Taiwan), Article 125.

Although Article 1 is broadly considered as a model definition worldwide[134] it appears that international law is moving toward the omission of the State-nexus.[135] Arguably, nothing in the international law prevents States to expand the definition of torture beyond what is set forth in paragraph 1[136] and criminalize torture as a general offence including private torture. Although the CAT has, on some occasions, criticized States for doing so and recommended maintaining the State-nexus, it is credible to believe that such an approach would take a regrettable step backwards.[137]

As Taiwan is not a formal member of the United Nations, it does not need to be bound by that restrictive interpretation of the CAT and could advance the torture definition by utilizing the best international practices and recommendations by leading scholars.[138] It has been shown that adhering to the public official requirement may be problematic to redress the historical torture of the 228 Incident as well as addressing current challenges where torture is committed by private entities or where the distinction between 'the public' and 'the private' is not clear.

Besides better accountability of incidents of torture, omitting the State-nexus requirement could send a clear deterrent message to anyone that no act of torture whatsoever will be tolerated. And this seems to best respond to the objective of the Convention. It might also foster the general understanding of the prohibition of torture as such and enhance the prevention of torture and ill-treatment in the broadest possible way.

To sum up, in order to avoid the peril of a narrow definition of torture which may increase the risk of impunity, Taiwan shall be invited to criminalize torture as a specific crime without the State-nexus requirement. It might further increase the deterrent effect if the State-nexus is perceived as an

---

134   See further discussion on global acceptance of this definition in MD Evans, 'Getting to Grips with Torture' (2002) 51 *International and Comparative Law Quarterly* 365, 376 and footnote 48. Harper uses the term 'most widely accepted definition' in Harper, *supra* note 18, 897. Gaeta refers to 'baseline definition' in P Gaeta 'Another Step in What It Means to Be Human – Prohibition v. Criminalization of Torture as a Private Act: An Interview with Paola Gaeta' (2021) 19 *Journal of International Criminal Justice* 425, 426.

135   Harper, *supra* note 18, 925–6; Nowak, *supra* note 93, 419; Dewulf, *supra* note 18, 477; Clapham, *supra* note 109.

136   On the basis of UNCAT, Article ,1 para 2: '*This article is without prejudice to any international instrument or national legislation which does or may contain provisions of wider application.*'

137   UN Committee against Torture, 'Fourth Periodic Report Submitted by Belgium under Article 19 of the Convention Pursuant to the Optional Reporting Procedure, due in 2017' (7 January 2019) UN Doc CAT/C/BEL/4, 4–9.

138   Clapham, *supra* note 109, 443; Harper, *supra* note 18, 925; Dewulf, *supra* note 18, 477.

aggravating circumstance for the basic *nomen juris* of a crime of torture.[139] On the contrary, it does not seem adequate to establish more crimes of torture for various contexts as this might be rather confusing and could also trivialize the severity of torture.[140]

Note on the Contributor

Pavel Doubek

Dr. Pavel Doubek (PhD, Judicial Assistant at the Supreme Administrative Court, Czech Republic), Member of the Czech Centre for Human Rights and Democracy; former post-doctoral research fellow at the Taiwan Foundation for Democracy and the Academia Sinica in Taiwan. I wish to thank my friend Amity Hsieh from Academia Sinica for her kind help with translations, research consultations and overall assistance throughout my research period in Taiwan. Big thanks also belong to all Taiwanese scholars, legal practitioners and human rights activists who provided me with valuable insight into the local human rights situation. Last but not least, I wish to appreciate helpful comments from Kristina Kironska on the earlier draft of this manuscript.

---

139   This must be distinguished from a situation where the definition of torture as such is used as a mere aggravating circumstance for other crimes, which surely does not constitute torture as a separate offence and has been rightly criticized by the CAT. See, for example, the Italian Penal Code (Art. 613-bis) and its criticism in Carolei, *supra* note 10, 579–580. See also Penal Code of Denmark (CAT/C/DNK/CO/6-7, paras 3–10).

140   See a peril of having two crimes of torture in CAT Concluding Observations on Macao (CAT/C/CHN-MAC/CO/5, paras 14–5).

CHAPTER 14

From the Socialist Past towards Democratization and Back to the Authoritarian Regime: A Look through the Constitutional "Development" of Russia

Sergey Marochkin

Abstract

The article focuses on the return from the brief period of democratization in Russia back to the authoritarian organization of the society and the state governance of its socialist past. The key thesis of the paper is that a short period of democratization ended with a U-turn to the authoritarian autocracy characterized by super-centralization of power, the erosion of federalism and local government, the absence of independent judiciary and real market economy and the instrumental role of law. The 2020 constitutional amendments testify to this normative development and are the subject of analysis here. A general assessment of the amendments' legitimacy rather than an in-depth examination is the objective of this study. They not only reveal a quick fix to the status quo but also set out a particular vision for the future constitutional path of the country.

Keywords

1993 Constitution – democratization – rule of law – 2020 constitutional amendments – legitimized authoritarian autocracy – personalization of the state power

1 Introduction

The Russian Federation (hereafter RF, Russia) has been living through a return from a short period of democratization back to authoritarianism. This article argues that liberation from the past socialist authoritarian regime does not necessarily and inevitably lead to democracy but can also revert to a new type of authoritarianism for the interests of higher state authorities. After the fall of the USSR (Union of the Soviet Socialist Republics), Russia once declared its intentions to become a democratic rule-of-law state[1] which is yet to become a reality. On the contrary, a small ruling group instrumentalises the law and uses vehicles of power and state machinery for their own interests.

The article explores the controversial pathways on those critical turning points away from authoritarian rule – i.e. the first period after socialism towards a democratic future – and back to it through the prism of the development of the Russian constitution whose final changes culminated in its 2020 amendments.

Those amendments are analysed here in their entirety rather than in detail nor in comparison with the text of the previous Constitution. The article criticises those academic accounts which see the amendments as codifying and institutionalizing the *status quo*[2] as if they finalize and fix some results of the created scheme of governing the country. This is true but needs clarification. The article attempts to assess the 'action' taken place from a different angle, namely to show the most obvious destruction of the foundations of the constitutional order and to evaluate the crucial role of the amendments in strengthening the authoritarian regime.

2   The First Period after Socialism: Towards a Democratic Future?

The advent of globalization and the fall of the socialist systems in the USSR and Eastern European countries initiated various processes in their domestic and international policymaking which included liberation from the authoritarian past. The dissolution of the USSR in December 1991, in particular raised great anticipation for a full departure from the former socialist political and economic system. There was real hope for a straightforward path towards a democratic state proclaimed earlier. With the adoption by the First Council of RSFSR People's Deputies (Russian Soviet Federative Socialist Republic) of the Declaration on the State Sovereignty on 12 June 1990,[3] a new society based

---

1   See, Konstitutsiia (Osnovnoi Zakon) Rossiiskoi Federatsii – Rossii [Constitution (Basic Law) of the Russian Federation – Russia] of 12 April 1978 (as amended on 21 April 1992), http://con stitution.garant.ru/history/ussr-rsfsr/1978/red_1978/5478730/ (accessed 15 December 2022).

2   W Pomeranz and R Smyth, 'Russia's 2020 Constitutional Reform: The Politics of Institutionalizing the Status-Quo' (2021) 6 *Russian Politics* 1, 1.

3   Declaration of the State Sovereignty of the Russian Soviet Federative Socialist Republic of 12 June 1990, Site of the Constitution of the Russian Federation, http://constitution.garant .ru/act/base/10200087/chapter/b869049cc45bcef2cfb16f0d1a285119/ (accessed 15 December 2022).

on the market economy, human rights, and freedoms would see the light. As a prominent researcher, Professor Alekseev, the first and the last Chairman of the USSR Constitutional Review Committee (1990–1991), wrote that "there was a brief surge of the recognition and rise of law"[4] in those years in Russia. Nevertheless, this path has been nonlinear and has included complex stages riddled with controversies. The denial by and acquisition of freedom under a former state or a social-political regime do not necessarily and inevitably lead to a democratic state.

In 1992, after the communist regime, a short-term liberalization period started and inspired many democratic changes. The 1978 Soviet Constitution of Russia was last amended on 10 December 1992[5] after the USSR's breakdown and before the adoption of the current Constitution on 12 December 1993. The 1993 Constitution of the Russian Federation[6] enshrined key democratic principles, such as human rights as the supreme value, separation of powers, federalism, multiparty system, private property, freedoms of speech and information, of mass media and peaceful assembly, the hierarchy of generally recognized international norms on human rights over domestic laws. Russia would from now onwards be a rule-of-law and social state, privileging free elections, competition and freedom of economic activity, and political and ideological diversity. Article 15.4 in particular stated a new approach to international law: "Generally recognized principles and norms of international law and international treaties of the Russian Federation shall be an integral part of its legal system. If an international treaty of the Russian Federation establishes other rules than those provided for by a law, the rules of the international treaty shall apply." They constitute the fundamental principles of the Russian constitutional order and no other provisions of the Constitution may contravene them (Article 15.1). A considerable number of new codes and federal laws were adopted to develop these fundamental principles.[7]

This clearly marked a radical move of openness towards the international community and its institutions. Although the Russian state was not democratic yet at that time, it encouraged the development of democratic

---

4   SS Alekseev, 'Krushenie prava. Polemicheskie zametki' ['Crash of Law: Polemic Notes'] in SS Alekseev, *Sobranie sochinenii. v 10 tomakh. Tom 7: Filosofiia prava I tepriia prava* [*Collected Works. In 10 Volumes. Vol. 7: Philosophy of Law and Theory of Law* (Statut, 2010) 504.

5   Database of legal information: http://www.consultant.ru (accessed 15 December 2022).

6   Official portal of the legal information: http://www.pravo.gov.ru (accessed 15 December 2022).

7   E.g. Civil Code, Criminal Code, Labor Code, Civil Procedure Code, Arbitration Procedure Code, Federal Law on RF International Treaties, etc.

and liberal trends. Consequently, the roots of a new economic, political, and civil life sprouted. Nevertheless, in the meantime, the Constitution did give the president immense power making him a central figure in the state machinery. It also granted the constituent entities of the country too much freedom, which threatened its disintegration. The initial version of the 1993 Constitution is assessed as 'a flawed but forward-looking document with much of its liberal potential'.[8]

3   The Turn and the Path Back

The mentioned first period after socialism lasted less than ten years. Some scholars called the state organization in certain Eastern European countries different forms of 'illiberal democracy' or, 'managed democracy'[9] in Russia. However, regarding Russia, it would be fair not to refer to some kind of democracy ('managed' or some other) but rather about a U-turn or backlash and rollback from its short experience of liberalization and democratization starting in the beginning of 1992 up to the end of 1999 and gradually ending after 2000. It does not make any difference whether one calls the current Russian regime 'illiberal' or 'managed'; it fundamentally lacks the traits of a democracy. Even under such a 'democratic umbrella' as regular 'so-called' elections, the current regime cannot hide its non-democratic and authoritarian features.

In Russia, this second period of authoritarianism started at the beginning of the new millennium and century and has still been ongoing. Many of the democratic trends, freedoms, and diversity witnessed during the first stage – in particular, free fair elections, freedom of speech, independence and diversity of mass media, and political pluralism – were tightened and limited over the first decade of the new millennium. The last more than ten year-period is marked by further rollback of the democratic liberalization agenda and increase of authoritarian governance and illiberal anti-democratic practices. It in fact is a return to Russia's traditional and habitual authoritarian regime of the socialist period of 1917–1985. This can be called 're-traditionalization' describing this

---

8   WE Pomeranz, 'Putin's 2020 Constitutional Amendments: What Changed? What Remained the Same?' (2021) 6 *Russian Politics* 6, 6.

9   See e.g. JW Mueller, 'Eastern Europe Goes South. Disappearing Democracy in the EU's Newest Members' (2014) 93 *Foreign Affairs* 14; I Krastev, 'The Strange Death of the Liberal Consensus: Is Central Europe Backsliding?' (2007) 18(4) *Journal of Democracy* 56–63; A Buzogány, 'Illiberal Democracy in Hungary: Authoritarian Diffusion or Domestic Causation?' (2017) 24 *Democratization* 1307–1325.

process of return to previous over-centralized one-person governance. In addition to the socialist features, some new ones characterize this regime:

- interventionist state capitalism, including state monopoly on several sectors;[10]
- diminishing a real market economy and competition; oligarchic state governance, *i.e.* governance oriented to oligarchy groups' interests;
- the political monopoly of one ruling political party that has captured the state and has been in power for more than twenty years;
- an evident lack of political pluralism and oppression of any opponent views and activities;
- the complete absence of institutional 'checks and balances' (or counterbalancing influences to ensure entire political power is not invested in only one individual or group);
- the consolidation of political power in the hands of one state's higher official and the lack of power turnovers;[11]
- the irremovability and non-transparency of power; and
- reliance of authority on tough violent measures of the security, police, and military forces.

The rule of law state was also rolled back in this second period. Since any state politics and governing regime need to be legally framed, the law was considered as a mere vehicle through which a chosen policy is implemented to achieve development.[12] The laws are used as a tool for re-traditionalization to promote national patriotism, mystical so-called 'traditional national values' (with no explanation what they are), and the defence of state sovereignty. The *Russia File* blog of the Kennan Institute mentions that a characteristic aspect of the Central and Eastern European countries, especially with authoritarian regimes, is to make use of the law to promote right-wing populism. This appears to be just the case for Russia. One key populist goal is to defend the nation and state sovereignty. For instance, the Federation Council (the Upper Chamber of the Russian parliament) established a special commission to protect state sovereignty and prevent interference in the Russian Federation's internal affairs. The trend is equally characteristic for both the domestic and foreign policies

---

10   *See* MA Arefiev, AG Davydenkova, ID Osipov, 'Vnutrennii konservatizm i neokonsrvatizm: obshee i osobenno' [Domestic Conservatism and Neoconservatism: General and Special] (2015) 7 *Philosophy and Humanities in the Information Society*, http://fikio.ru/?p=1519 (accessed 1 May 2020).

11   *See* AN Mochkin, *Paradoksi neokonservatizma (Rossiia I Germaniia v kontse XIX – nachale XX vekov)* [*Paradoxes of Neoconservatism (Russia and Germany in the late XIX - early XX centuries*] (Moscow, 1994) 194.

12   See YS Lee, *Law and Development. Theory and Practice* (Routledge, 2019) 3.

of the country, as well as for its legislation and institutional structure including the judiciary.

In this regard, the judiciary serves as a mechanism for the interests of executives on their road to authoritarian governance. In the cases involving disputes between the state authorities and an individual, the courts are inclined to take the authorities' side, running counter to one of the most significant principles of the Russian constitutional order (Article 2), namely: "Human, his rights and freedoms are the highest value. Recognition of, compliance with, and protection of the rights and freedoms of man and citizen shall be the duty of the State." The most 'vivid' examples of such cases are the judgments of the RF Constitutional Court (hereafter RCC, Court). Due to the specifics of its competence, the RCC most often hears cases involving conflicts of public (the state) and private (an individual or a group) interest favouring the former over the latter. The dissenting opinion of Judge A.L. Kononov in a 2007 case on challenging the constitutionality of some provisions of the RF Civil Code emphasized this paradoxical feature: "...between private and public interests the Court always leads somehow to the preference of public motivations."[13]

Examining the rule of law issue in Russia, Kahn has called this a 'dual state', namely courts and law work "but only in cases considered 'normal' or uncontroversial. When sufficiently strong forces are to be found on one side of a case, the case can move to the prerogative side of the docket in which power, not law, rules."[14] Such an 'inclination' of courts is to be strengthened by the latest constitutional amendments (see section below) some of which concern reform of the judiciary amongst other issues. These amendments can have an impact on the supposed 'independence' of the judiciary since the President can now recommend the Federation Council to consider dismissing the members of the senior judiciary (Article 83 of the Constitution).

4   Culmination: Juggling with the Constitution

The trends towards authoritarian rule turned out to be a prelude to the unexpected culmination of the President's annual Address to the Federal Assembly (parliament) on 15 January 2020 where he proposed a 'few' amendments to the Constitution. From a legal perspective, the necessity of most of them was

---

13   See Postanovlenie Konstitutsionnogo Suda [Ruling of the RF Constitutional Court] of 23 January 2007 No. 1-P (dissenting opinion of Judge AL Kononov), http://www.ksrf.ru (accessed 15 December 2022).

14   J Kahn, 'The Rule of Law under Pressure: Russia and the European Human Rights System' (2019) 44 *Review of Central and East European Law* 293.

very doubtful, as some provisions existed already in legislation, and others did not have a value of constitutional norms. Within only one and a half months a quickly established working group consisting of actors, musicians, sportspeople, doctors, public figures, celebrities, and just a few lawyers and members of the parliament introduced a draft of the RF Law entitled '*On the Amendment to the Constitution of the Russian Federation*' on 2 March 2020. Depending on how one counts, the number of amendments varies from 112 to 392 but the law is called 'On the Amendment …' as if it is just a single amendment. This was done to ensure that the 'all-Russian vote' would occur as a 'single package' for the amendments and not for every amendment separately. The reason is that numerous provisions on culture, respect for fatherland history, defence of the state territory, sovereignty, social guaranties, and insurance are to cover and hide a key provision on the 'nullification' of the previous presidential terms for office.

The draft passed a complicated procedure of three readings in the State Duma (Lower Chamber of the parliament), approval by the Federation Council (Upper Chamber) and by the legislative bodies of all 85 constituent entities of the Federation within only three or four days. Furthermore, it was signed by the president, published on the legal information official portal, and given legal force on 4 July 2020; except Articles 1 and 2 (hereafter "the 2020 Law").[15] The lengthy text reveals that the initiator's (i.e., the President) main goal is not to widen the social guarantees of citizens and ensure a balance of powers, as he announced in the annual Address. In fact, it is to strengthen his presidential authority and vertical structure of power, as well as to secure the permanent and exceptional governance of the only person, which actually means the 'personalization' of the state power.

4.1 The Experts' Attitude to the Purpose and Expediency of the Amendments

Scholars have not been unanimous in assessing these constitutional amendments. Some do not go beyond the literal interpretation of the text. Taking such a purely positivist (textual) approach, they consider the amendments rather useful and believe that the updated text of the Constitution in itself can give new impetus to real life and state policy especially in the social realm.

For example, the authors of one article claim: "In particular, social amendments to the Basic Law of the country seriously strengthen the foundations of

---

15   Zakon Rossiiskoi Federatsii [Law of the Russian Federation] of 14 March 2020, No 1-FKZ, http://www.pravo.gov.ru (accessed 15 December 2022).

state policy in the field of overcoming poverty and increasing citizens' income, state policy for the development of health care, education and culture, state family policy, policy towards children, adolescents and youth. The state policy of the Russian Federation in the field of labour and employment received its more systematic and qualitative design. Environmental issues logically become one of the most important priorities of the state policy of the Russian Federation."[16] They also add: "Thus, these amendments turn the declarative provisions on the social state of the 1993 RF Constitution into socio-political realities. Moreover, it seems to us that the state social policy through these amendments forms for itself the trend of the country's movement towards a 'welfare state'. [...] The adoption of these value-symbolic and social amendments will be a significant step forward in the socio-political development of the country."[17] Others write in similar bright colours: "The adoption of 'social' constitutional amendments can be viewed as a significant step for the transition of the Russian Federation from a declarative to a real model of a social state, providing a much more effective level of implementation of social policy in relation to citizens. [...] Now, in a short period of time, a qualitative breakthrough has been made towards a social state".[18] Another group of researchers, after the adoption of the amendments, immediately began to write papers of a commentary nature with explanations of the innovations, interpretation of their meaning, and proposals for supplementing the legislation.[19]

Contrary to such welcoming positivist readings of the constitutional amendments, most scholars take the opposite view: "Opposition legal experts criticized the idea of formal constitutional amendments, insisting that most of them are superfluous. Those amendments which reflect the developments in legislation, could remain at the legislation level. Values, declarations and

---

16   See D Nechaev and O Leonova, 'Change of State Policies as a Result of Adoption of Amendments to the Constitution of Russia: Directions and Features' (2020) 15 *Central Russian Journal of Social Sciences* 116, 117.

17   *Ibid.*, 125. See also S Belov, '2020 Constitutional Amendments in Russia: A Constitutional Update?' *IACL-AIDC Blog* (30 March 2021) https://blog-iacl-aidc.org/ (accessed 15 December 2022).

18   M Bochanov and A Balashov, 'Forming a Real Model of the Social State 2.0: Political Analysis' (2020) 15 *Central Russian Journal of Social Sciences* 128, 129, 139.

19   See e. g. L Chikhladze and O Friesen, 'Implementation of Constitutional Provisions Concerning Uniformed Public Authority in the Russian Federation' (2022) 26 *RUDN Journal of Law* 7–24; S Maslennikova, 'Ideology of Constitutional Amendments of 2020 in the Sphere of Social and Economic Development' (2021) 5 *Law Journal of the Higher School of Economics* 24–47 (in Russian); E Kirichek, E Kononov and G Kodirzoda, 'The Constitution of the Russian Federation and Constitutional Identity in the Context of Global Changes' *IX Baltic Legal Forum 2020*, SHS Web of Conferences 108, 01003 (2021).

policies should not appear in legal documents, especially in the Constitution. In their view, all necessary regulation could be extracted from the Constitution through interpretation."[20] In addition, the amendments do not have an absolute substantive novelty, since they are to a certain extent based on the accumulated constitutional experience, which found expression in the current federal legislation, in the legal positions of the RCC and in the previously proposed bills on amendments.[21] From this point of view, the artificially inspired expediency of the amendments is clearly revealed. The bulk of them on social, labour, historical, patriotic, ideological and other issues cover the main goal that is strengthening the vertical of authority, ensuring the personification of power in the hands of one person, and establishing a 'zeroing' rule (not taking into account the terms of the previous presidency so that the incumbent president can again participate in the upcoming elections).

4.2   Some Legal Dimensions of the 2020 Law

The legal 'value' of the 2020 Law deserves an extensive and detailed analysis highlighting the most odious provisions that flagrantly violate the Constitution and law regarding the form, the procedure of adoption, the content, and the legal logic. Furthermore, the participation and the role of the Russian Constitutional Court due to its special status in the constitutional process will also be examined.

4.2.1   The Form

The Federal Law of 1998 "On the Procedure for Adopting and Entering into Force of Amendments to the Constitution of the Russian Federation"[22] (hereafter 1998 FZ) covers changes to the constitutional text. The "Amendment" (allegedly just one, as the title of the 2020 Law states) seems to suggest that

---

20   S Belov, *supra* note 17; see also E Anichkin, 'Konstitutsionnaya Modernizatsiya Rossii 2020 Goda: Tochechnie Popravki ili Reviziya Osnovnogo Zakona?' [Constitutional modernization of Russia in 2020: point amendments or revision of the Basic law?] (2020) 2(46) *Қазақ инновациялық гуманитарлық-заң университетінің хабаршысы* [*Herald of the Kazakh Innovation Humanitarian Juridical University*] 23, 26; P Baranov, E Kazachanskaya and A Plotnikov, 'Improvement of Modern Regulatory Policy in Russia in Conservative Legal Dimension' (2021) 27 *Journal of Law and Political Sciences* 10–33; V Krasilnikov and I Pozdeev, 'On the Issue of Amendments to the Constitution of Russia' (2021) 12 *European Researcher Series A* 109, 109.

21   Anichkin, *ibid.*, 25.

22   Federal'nyi zakon 1998 "O protsedure priniatiia i vstupleniia v silu popravok k Konstitutsii Rossiiskoi Federatsii" [Federal Law of 1998 On the Procedure for Adopting and Entering into Force of Amendments to the Constitution of the Russian Federation] (as amended on 08.03.2015), http://www.consultant.ru (accessed 15 December 2022).

the Law should contain just one amendment and deal with issues of public authority organization. In fact, it represents a large 'mosaic' of many fragments (changes), dissimilar in level, significance, and direction, embracing a wide range of provisions from social guarantees for citizens, the role of the Russian language and Russian people, mentioning of God, the defence of historical truth, the fulfilment of international obligations,[23] the organization of a higher authority, to the judicial system and court proceedings, local government, etc.

4.2.2   The Procedure

The draft of the 2020 Law was developed very quickly; the process of working on it was closed within the framework of the working group headed by the president. Different experts, researchers, civil society, and politicians could not contribute to expressing their opinions on the draft. This peculiarity of the 'closed' work on the preparation of the law on amendments was mentioned in various publications.[24] Furthermore, the 2020 Law establishes a procedure for amending the Constitution itself, which violates the procedure provided for in the 1998 FZ in an evident and visible manner. Most importantly, it violates the procedure established by Article 136 in Chapter 9 of the RF Constitution. Article 135 reads: "The provisions of Chapters 1, 2 and 9 of the Constitution may not be revised by the Federal Assembly." This undoubtedly means that the 2020 Law may not change the procedure enshrined in Article 136 of the Constitution as well as in the 1998 FZ. Moreover, as noticed, their approval through a plebiscite (popular vote) is contrary to the current legislation, which lacks such a norm of expression of the people's will in the first place.[25]

However, due to the president's designation of procedures other than those in the 1998 FZ, the working group formulated it in the draft law, and the legislator followed it without any objection. The 1998 FZ normally entitles Russia's constituent entities and legislative bodies to consider and make their decisions on the amendments within a year's time. However, all 85 entities (subjects of the Russian Federation) had done this just in one day. Consequently, the 2020 Law went through all the stages of ratification and was adopted – despite of an

---

23   See in particular L Malksoo, 'International Law and the 2020 Amendments to the Russian Constitution' (2021) 115 *American Journal of International Law* 78–93.

24   M Verlaine, A Shashkova and E Kudryashova, 'Amendments of Russian Constitution Concerning International Law and the BRICS' (2020) 7 *Journal of Constitutional Research* 337–338; Krasilnikov and Pozdeev, *supra* note 20, 109.

25   AV Glukhova and DV Shcheglova, 'Conceptual and Methodological Foundations of the Political and Legal Analysis of the Constitutional Reform in the Russian Federation 2020 (Experience of Expert Assessments)' (2020) 15 *Srednerusskii Vestnik Obshchestvennikh Nauk* [*Central Russian Journal of Social Sciences*] 88, 90.

illegal and unconstitutional procedure, – signed by the president, and officially published.

To guarantee the achievement of its main goal, the 2020 Law also provides for a 'divided' procedure to come into effect: Article 3 came in force on the day of the Law's official publication, and Articles 1 and 2 (the amendments themselves and the procedure for holding the all-Russian vote[26]) came into force after this vote.

Article 3 lists the procedural issues: implementation of the Law, its submission to the Constitutional Court for opinion, and the terms under which Articles 1 and 2 take effect. The crucial provision of Article 3 however, is the removal of presidential term restrictions stipulated by Article 81 of the Constitution on the impossibility for the person who has held the office of president for more than two terms to participate again in elections. Due to this impetuous entry into force of Article 3 after the publication, the current president has already secured the right to be elected for fifth and sixth terms, regardless of the results of popular voting on Articles 1 and 2 of this Law.[27]

An essential procedural point that guarantees to achieve the same goal of the 2020 Law is the absence of a minimum required number of participants in the all-Russian vote. It is simple arithmetic, for Articles 1 and 2 to come in force even three people with two votes in favour are enough.[28]

One more procedural trick in the Law 2020 is the lack of citizens' right to express their attitude to each amendment, for example, to support social guarantees and reject some or all the changes on authorities. Voting is possible only on the principle of an 'all in one' packaged deal.

4.2.3   The Content

In general, the amendments focus on the further centralization of power, the building of its rigid vertical, the concentration of all authority in one individual' the hands, the work of the entire state machine and all branches of power and state structures just for the President's desires and opinions, the country's complete dependence on his individual opinions, ambitions and worldview.

---

26   All-Russian means for the whole Federation.

27   E Mukhametshina and A Kornya, 'Pocthi polovina rossiian uvereny chto Konstitutsiia izmeniaetsia dlia sokhreneniia Putina u vlasti' [Almost Half of Russians Are Sure that the Constitution Is Changing in order to Keep Putin in Power] *Vedomosti*, 30 January 2020, http://www.vedomosti.ru (accessed 1 May 2020).

28   See M Domańska, 'Everlasting Putin' and the Reform of the Russian Constitution' *Centre for Eastern Studies* https://www.osw.waw.pl/sites/default/files/Commentary_322.pdf (accessed 1 May 2020).

The hasty adoption of the 2020 Law, the closeness, and the refusal of expert discussion inevitably led to inconsistency between the amendments, and as a result created an internal inconsistency in the amended text of the Constitution. The researchers drew attention to that: "these amendments have also introduced a series of contradictions into Russia's highest law that transforms an imperfect but aspirational document into a defensive one". They added that "this ambiguity – the blurring of existing formal institutional differences – is a broader feature of the 'Putin constitution'".[29] These amendments 'legitimize' wide and free discretion to make decisions based on preferability rather than not on the common interests underlying the rule of law in general and the strict framework of the constitutional system's foundations in particular.

An all-Russian expert survey carried out by two Russian scholars amid 70 experts from 25 cities of Russia who participated and answered several questions on the content of the amendments to the RF Constitution revealed various risks to the stability of the political system. According to the experts,[30] the most discomforting ones undermining the rule of law were – in descending order: the 'zeroing' of presidential terms, the popular vote and the procedure to amend the Constitution of the Russian Federation. Practically all scholars analysing the essence of the amendments noted, first of all, the tightening of the vertical of power and the strengthening of the status and powers of the president: "[i]t is first the complete restructuring of power into a rigid vertical structure with all branches subordinate to the head of the state [increasing the powers of the centre over regional and local governments]. In essence, this comes to the elimination of judicial independence and its subordination to the President's will".[31]

---

29   WE Pomeranz, 'Putin's 2020 Constitutional Amendments: What Changed? What Remained the Same?' (2021) 6 *Russian Politics* 6, 7; B Noble and N Petrov, 'From Constitution to Law: Implementing the 2020 Russian Constitutional Changes' (2021) 6 *Russian Politics* 130, 146.

30   The scientific degree of the respondents (doctors/candidates of science), as well as the field of professional activity (lawyers/non-lawyers) practically do not differ in assessing the legal nature of the amendments to the Constitution. See Glukhova and Shcheglova, *supra* note 25, 88.

31   See A Kirillov, 'Gennadiy Burbulis: pospeshnoe izmenenie osnovnogo zakona ne dobavliaet doveriia k konstitutsionnim printsipam upravleniia' [Gennady Burbulis: Hasty Change of the Basic Law Does Not Add Confidence to the Constitutional Principles of Governance], *Interactive News*, https://eanews.ru/news/gennadiy-burbulis-pospeshnoye -izmeneniye-osnovnogo-zakona-ne-dobavlyayet-doveriya-k-konstitutsionnym -printsipam-upravleniya_31-01-2020 (accessed 1 May 2020); E Teague, 'Russia's Constitutional Reforms of 2020' (2020) 5 *Russian Politics* 301, 301; see also Anichkin, *supra* note 20, 24; J Henderson, *The Constitution of the Russian Federation. A Contextual Analysis*

The centralization of power has been consistently and steadily growing for more than 20 years as the core policy of the current President. At the same time, it has not formally affected the lower level – local self-government. A distinctive feature of the 2020 amendments is that they actually put an end to the concept and policy of local self-government, 'embedding' it into a single system of power (new point 3 of Article 132 of the Constitution). The amendments introduced a new governing concept, i.e. the 'unified system of public power' from the federal centre to the lower administrative local structures. While at the surface, it kept one of the foundations of the country's constitutional order 'local self-government' which "is not included in the system of state authorities" (Article 12 Chapter 1) untouched, the amendment de facto undermined it at its root, creating a striking gap between the principle and the reality. As noted, the new constitutional notion the 'unified system of public power' formalizes the chasm between the language of the constitution and politics in practice; the new principle of unity of public government should appear in the Constitution unifying the local self-government and the state instead of the division of power between both levels.[32]

From such angle of strengthening the centralization of power, another amendment resuscitated unexpectedly the State Council. Under the former socialist rule, this body can be seen reflected in the *Politburo* (i.e. Political Bureau of the Central Committee of the Soviet Union's Communist Party – the collective consultative and decisive organ at the Secretary General of the CC CPSU). Before the reintroduction of the State Council in 2020, it was a rather insignificant and invisible structure. Some researchers consider the strengthening of the State Council to be another measure for the President to centralise his powers and control the bureaucracy. Other researchers conclude that, given the new constitutional status of the State Council, another problem of duplication of powers with the existing bodies of state power emerges. Therefore, the most important question remains unanswered about specifying its place in the existing system of separation of powers, the order and principles of its formation.[33]

(Hart Publishing, 2022); The tendency on building of vertical of power was noticed much earlier: HE Hale, *Patronal Politics. Eurasian Regime Dynamics in Comparative Perspective* (Cambridge University Press, 2014).

32   Noble and Petrov, *supra* note 29, 146; Belov, *supra* note 17; see also Teague, *ibid.*, 314–315.

33   EN Savinova and LA Zubova, 'Institutionalization of the State Council in Russia in the Context of the 2020 Constitutional Reform' (2020) 15 *Central Russian Journal of Social Sciences* 172, 173; see also Teague, *supra* note 31.

4.2.4   The Legal Logic

One of the universally accepted legal principles holds that when a law changes the status, functions, or competence of an official or elected body, the law shall come into force after the expiration of the official's or elected body's terms of office. This provision legally guards against the temptation to revise the law 'for oneself/themselves'. One of the working group members made such a proposal to the 2020 Law, but the President immediately and firmly rejected it. Because the Law has already come into force, the current President and members of parliament have successfully amended the Constitution for their own purposes.

In light of this logic, it is not hard to explain why the 2020 Law was initially drafted in violation of the 1998 FZ, and then adopted and took effect as a law of a higher level. This is necessary if the 2020 Law is to enjoy priority and include rules that diverge from the 1998 FZ. (Un)surprisingly, the Constitutional Court in its Conclusion on the 2020 Law circumvented this point and argued in the 'hither and thither' manner to which it often resorts in complicated and politicized cases. The Court claimed to not assess this Law's particular compliance with the 1998 FZ but rather note that its provisions which had entered into force "take precedence over the aforementioned Federal Law as being contained in a special and newer legal act, moreover, having greater legal force" (point 2.1).[34]

Point 6 Article 3 of the 2020 Law on the 'nullification' of the previous terms of the presidency is also incompatible with legal logic. Notably, as mentioned above, this rule appears twice in the Law; differently formulated, but keeping the same essence. This is explicitly done to guarantee that the rule comes into force regardless of the outcome of the popular vote. Moreover, this rule lacks any legal justification and argumentation. It is just stated as a fact of desire of the President.

Additionally, the rule on the 'nullification' of previous presidential terms, which allows the current president to run for election again and which appears twice (point 15 Article 1 and point 6 Article 3 of the 2020 Law) is not a legal norm, since it is a one-time 'technical' rule designed for a single application to one person. Moreover, due to this one-time technical nature, it is not to be a constitutional provision.

The abovementioned RCC Conclusion confirmed this in point 6.2 and did not even mention that a non-normative, especially unconstitutional provision is included in the Law and in the Constitution. At the same time and

---

34   Zakliuchenie Konstitutsionnogo Suda RF [Conclusion of the RF Constitutional Court] of 16 March 2020 No 1-Z, http://www.ksrf.ru (accessed 15 December 2022).

contradicting the general principle of law, this one-time rule enjoys a mandatory and even retroactive force, *i.e.*, it is applied to situations and cases that existed before its adoption.[35]

4.2.5   Participation and the Role of the Constitutional Court

The RCC had seven days for a thorough legal analysis and assessment of the 2020 Law. But the Court followed the 'speedy example' of the federal and regional legislators in passing the Law and delivered its 'verdict' – the Conclusion on the Law – in barely one or two days. It is hardly possible to evaluate such a long document and provide a detailed conclusion based on a thorough legal examination such a short period; unless a predetermined opinion and purpose was made.

Moreover, according to the Constitution and laws, the Court did not have legal grounds for such a conclusion as both the Constitution and the 1998 FZ do not assign it a role in the adoption of a new Constitution or amendments to it. The 1994 Federal Constitutional Law "On the Constitutional Court of the Russian Federation" (last amended on 01.07.2021)[36] detailing the Court's competence (Article 3) does not provide it with the right to verify the constitutionality of provisions of laws that have not entered into force (in our case, Articles 1 and 2 of the 2020 Law), as well as amendments to the Constitution. Lastly, the 1994 Law (Article 71) does not provide for such a type of the Constitutional Court's opinion as a 'Conclusion' on constitutional amendments.

The Court's entire conclusion boils down to Point 2.1 mentioned above. It is invoked to give a highly professional legal character to an analysis that otherwise fails to show any logical rigor or coherency regarding the ornate and confusing phrasing of almost every article of the 2020 Law. In this regard, the Court went well beyond its competence and evaluated both the legal and political issues, substantiating the norms of the Law under review and its Conclusion with political reasoning instead.

The Court's wording of the central provision on 'resetting to zero' the terms of presidency in the 2020 Law serves as one of many examples. In 1998, in the determination of the case on the interpretation of Article 81.3 of the RF Constitution regarding the maximum number of terms for the presidency, the Court stated its strict view on the time limit.[37] This determination was and still remains to be of a legal and precedential value. It made it clear that 'two is two'

---

35   Domańska, "'Everlasting Putin' and the Reform of the Russian Constitution.'

36   http://www.consultant.ru (accessed 15 December 2022).

37   Opredelenie Konstitutsionnogo Suda RF [Determination of the RF Constitutional Court] of 5 November 1998 No 134-O, http://www.consultant.ru (accessed 15 December 2022).

even though the 1993 Constitution was adopted after the first election of then-President Boris Yeltsin, and thus did not provide him with the right to be elected for the second time under the new Constitution. Conversely, in its Conclusion of 16 March 2020, the Court easily circumvented its earlier legal position by arguing that its 1998 determination emphasized that the Constitution did not contain a clause that the previous term of the presidency was not to be included in the terms provided for in Article 81. The Court tried to assure that its determination "confirms the possibility of regulation provided by the Law for this aspect" (point 6.2) (*i.e.* the possibility of such a clause and 'resetting to zero' the terms of presidency in the 2020 Law). With alchemic proficiency or the *visa versa* logic, the Court overturned a 'no' into a 'yes'. This Conclusion of the Court is just one more to add to the many unjust and politicized Court decisions, but it is especially blatant in its cynicism and shameless of juggling of words, law provisions, the Constitution, and its own legal positions.

From its conception then to fast drafting and the content, straight through to its adoption procedure, the 2020 Law and its attendant RCC Conclusion is a constitutional coup. This is also, how many lawyers, political scientists, and observers in numerous articles, posts, and blogs have characterized this 'action'. Moreover, more than 420 lawyers, scientists, journalists, and writers sent an open letter to the President protesting the anti-constitutional coup.[38] About 200,000 people signed the "Open appeal of Russian citizens to the Council of Europe on the legal examination of the amendments to the Constitution of Russia and the procedure for their adoption".[39] The Venice Commission adopted an Opinion on the Draft Amendments to the RF Constitution on 18 June 2020 related in particular to the execution of decisions of the European Court of Human Rights in Russia.[40] At the same time, there were no further discussions in the country since the webpage with the Open appeal was deleted by the authorities.

4.3 An Impact of the Amendments on the Fundamentals of the Constitutional Order: Undermining without Disturbing

The crucial thing is that although the amendments do not formally alter Chapters 1, 2 and 9, which may not be 'touched' and revised by the parliament, they 'inject' provisions into Chapters 3 through 8. In fact, they contradict many

---

38   https://echo.msk.ru/blog/echomsk/2606224-echo/,   https://echo.msk.ru/news/2606412
-echo.html (accessed 30 March 2020).
39   https://www.change.org/ (accessed 30 March 2020) (the page was removed afterwards from this site).
40   Opinion No. 981/2020, CDL-AD(2020)009.

key foundations of the country's constitutional order and human rights protections contained in Chapters 1 and 2, such as a democratic rule-of-law state; the people as the sole source of power; the prohibition to usurp power, federalism, or separation of powers; local self-government; the secular quality of the state; and equality of all before the law.

Almost all researchers covering this topic in their publications noted that the amendments do in fact relate to the foundations of the constitutional system and even contradict them: "the amendments were scattered across the remaining sections of the constitution even though many of the provisions touched upon the fundamental principles articulated in the first two chapters". They continued that "the authorities initiated the introduction of the amendments to the RF Constitution, many of which in their content contradict the 'inviolable' chapters of the Basic Law of the country (1,2 and 9), although purely formally appear in other chapters, namely from 3 to 8".[41]

Above all, the amendments on strengthening centralization and amplification the vertical of power were covered up under the veil of social reforms. This inevitably undermined one of the central foundations of the constitutional order, i.e. the principle of separation and balance of powers (Article 10 Chapter 1 of the Constitution). A striking discrepancy between the words of the Presidential Address on initiating amendments and the result in the text of the renewed Constitution is clearly noted in this issue: "In his January 2020 address, [he] argued that a 'greater balance between the branches of power' was needed; however, despite some new competences for the parliament, the general tendency of the amendments is to make the President even more powerful than at present".[42]

As a result, the insertion into the Constitution of a new concept and scheme of governing the country under 'the unified system of public power' has nullified the principle of local self-government (Article 12 Chapter 1 of the Constitution). According to Noble and Petrov, "the 'unified system of public power' also undermines the formal autonomy of local self-government, even though Article 12 remains unchanged in stating that this layer of governance remains separate from the state".[43] As E. Teague develops, although "Putin spoke of the need 'to expand and strengthen the powers and real capabilities

---

41 Pomeranz, *supra* note 8, 18; Glukhova and Shcheglova, *supra* note 25, 90; see also Anichkin, *supra* note 20, 26.

42 M Russell, 'Constitutional Change in Russia: More Putin, or Preparing for Post-Putin?' *European Parliamentary Research Service,* http://epthinktank.eu (accessed 15 December 2022).

43 Noble and Petrov, *supra* note 29, 146.

of local self-government' [in his *Poslanie,* i.e. address], many of the amend-ments as finally approved in March appeared intended not to expand, but to reduce the powers of local government bodies by bringing them under closer federal control. This appears directly to contradict Article 12 of Chapter 1 of the constitution."[44]

According to Part 2 of Article 13 Chapter 1 of the RF Constitution, the exist-ence of a state and mandatory ideology is prohibited. To the contrary, some researchers pointed out as a result of the constitutional amendments new ideological provisions have appeared in the Constitution. Noteworthy, these ideological provisions are placed in Chapter 3 'Federal structure' of the Con-stitution, while they mainly affect the constitutional order's foundations. They are as follows: the prohibition of actions aimed at alienation of the part of the Russian territory (Part 2.1 Article 67), preserving the memory of the ances-tors who conveyed to us the ideals and belief in God (Part 2 Article 67.1), honouring the memory of defenders of the Fatherland, ensuring protection of historical truth, the prohibition of diminution of the heroic deed of the people defending the Fatherland (Part 3 Article 67.1), contributing to comprehensive spiritual, moral, intellectual and physical development of children, upbring-ing of their patriotism, civic consciousness and respect towards elders (Part 4 Article 67.1). Concerning parliamentary activity, the 'ideological' norms of the Constitution play a special role. Deputies of the parliament are forced to take one political position amid several alternatives, which are also legitimate and permissible. Therefore, relating to deputies' activities, these amendments can be interpreted as a very significant deviation from the freedom of expression.[45]

These ideological 'inclusions' also contradict with human rights and free-doms enshrined in Chapter 2 of the Constitution: "Russia's 1993 Constitution, with its declarations of universal human rights, reads very much like that of any other European country. By contrast, the amendments reflect growing nationalism, and rejection of Western liberal values. Among other things, they emphasize Russia's thousand-year history, its traditional ideals and beliefs".[46]

The amendments to Articles 79 and 125 (in Chapters 3 and 8) affecting international law and international obligations at first glance cover 'pinpoint' (specific) issues such as the causes for non-compliance with decisions of inter-national bodies and courts. In fact, they have entrenched a radical change of

---

44   Teague, *supra* note 31, 314.
45   A Gutorova, A Grokhotov, V Korovin, E Masufranova and V Yatsenko, 'Constitutional Law Restrictions on the Activities of a Deputy due to Changes in the Constitution of the Russian Federation' *SHS Web of Conferences* 108, 01002 (2021) *IX Baltic Legal Forum 2020.*
46   Russell, *supra* note 42.

Russia's perception of its legal obligations in the international community and an approach to international law in general contained in Article 15.4 (in Chapter 1) of the Constitution. Scholars highlight that asserting Russia's right to refuse to obey the decisions of international institutions if these were found not to comply with its constitution, the amendments appeared to call into question Article 15, which gave international law priority over national legislation. It is more radical: the amendment to Article 79 contradicts Article 15.[47] The country, as in former Soviet times, once again closes itself off from the rest of the world and international obligations with a 'sovereignty fence'.

5 Conclusion: Overall Results of the Current Constitutional 'Development'

The constitutional changes initiated in the Presidential Address to the parliament on 15 January 2020 and quickly embodied in the 2020 Law clearly have turned over basic principles of the rule-of-law state enshrined in the initial text of the 1993 Constitution. In the Address, he stated about dotty ('few') amendments, which actually resulted in a lengthy law with more than 200 amendments. The essence of this 'action' is accurately noted – it is not simple amendments, but the actual revision of the entire Constitution: "the 2020 amendments are not a point correction of the constitutional text, but a revision, an actual reform of the Basic law". As a result, the new revised Constitution "contains serious contradictions, fraught with domestic and foreign political risks that threaten the stable existence and development of the Russian Federation".[48]

Russia's return from the path towards democratization after the fall of socialism ending the oppression of democratic and liberal reforms to the traditional one-person authoritarian governance has been definitive with such constitutional development. Russia has turned its back to the political and legal entitlement of a new democratic society after more than seventy years of authoritarianism. In this respect, the current governance is characterized by super-centralization, the erosion of federalism and local government, the lack of the division of power, the absence of independent judiciary and a real

---

47 Teague, *supra* note 31, 309–310; see also about that Verlaine, Shashkova and Kudryashova, *supra* note 20, 338; P Kalinichenko and DV Kochenov, 'Introductory Note to Amendments to the 1993 Constitution of the Russian Federation Concerning International Law (2020)' (2021) 60 *International Legal Materials* 340–346.
48 Anichkin, *supra* note 20, 23, 27; Glukhova and Shcheglova, *supra* note 25, 91.

market economy, and the subservient role of law, which is used as a manual tool for legitimizing the purposes and interests of the ruling strata.

The 2020 Law clearly and purposefully aims to preserve and strengthen the one individual's leadership in the country for long future to come and to 'personalize' the state power in the President's hand. Such a governance scheme has come through experience and does function in some authoritarian countries. Currently, Russia is falling into line behind them. Consequently, the current Russian system can be called a 'legitimized authoritarian autocracy'. It is not an institutional governance but a personal one. This is a backward development. Regrettably, Russia has neither crawled out of its past nor radically departed it.

The amendments seem to demonstrate a movement forward in line with current trends in life, but this is a movement with the head turned back, a movement to the past. Or as Pomeranz described this constitutional development in Russia: "In the process a flawed but forward-looking document has been stripped of much of its liberal potential and instead been converted into a more traditional top-down system of governance".[49]

It is accompanied with the fact that law, which is supposed to be a means for the systemic organization of society and an equal measure of behaviour for the state and citizens, is being replaced by statutes that are subject to frequent and minor changes in the interests of the policy-makers and power structures. However, more than that, the laws/statutes are often replaced by one-time decisions of a higher official. To put it differently, the so-called 'manual governance' – the discretion and command of one state servant – replaces normative (legal) regulation. In such a situation, law ceases to be law and 'dissolves' into one-time particular decisions. This is a final constitutionalizing of the governance system over the country that the actual President established much earlier on and can be exactly called, "a pyramid of patron-client relations or a system of patronal politics".[50]

As seen from the publications discussed, foreign colleagues conducted deep and detailed analysis of the amendments. They argued "that the constitution largely codified the status-quo as it had evolved over the past decade".[51] Actually, it is clear that the amendments not only fix the *status quo*, but also create the basis for forming and strengthening the authoritarian (prospectively totalitarian) regime and for further perspectives of the country's existence. The hope that "resistance to the new distribution of powers might be expected from

---

49   Pomeranz, *supra* note 8, 6.
50   Hale, *supra* note 31.
51   Pomeranz and Smyth, *supra* note 2.

the Russian republics and regions, whose powers stood to be considerably reduced"[52] seems far too optimistic. However, it might be quite understandable since E. Teague cannot feel a real situation in the country. The strict and robust vertical of power has been created, so no voice of resistance is expected and could even or ever be given.

Democracy is not a straight and inevitable logical consequence of liberation and freedom from an authoritarian past due to the lack of democratic traditions and political culture in most countries of the former USSR. Russia has never been a democratic country. The path to the rule of law is long and hard; it requires drastic changes in the mentality of the state. The latter has demonstrated unwillingness and even rough resistance to the transformation to become a rule of law country.

Note on the Contributor

Sergey Marochkin
Professor (SJD) and Head of the Centre for International and Comparative Legal Studies, University of Tyumen (Russia). Contact: s.y.marochkin@utmn.ru

---

52   Teague, *supra* note 31, 327.

CHAPTER 15

Balancing Expectations of Privacy with Press Freedom: The UK Supreme Court's Decision in Bloomberg v ZXC and the Balancing of Privacy and Free Speech by the European Court of Human Rights

Steve Foster

Abstract

The UK government has recently announced plans to reform the Human Rights Act 1998, with one of its objects to enhance free speech and freedom of the press. A particular issue is the increasing growth of privacy rights witnessed in both the domestic courts and the European Court of Human Rights, raising concern that the over protection of privacy rights might have a chilling effect on press freedom and of reporting of matters of public interest or debate.

This article will examine two recent judicial decisions – one from the UK Supreme Court and the other from the European Court of Human Rights – which have favoured individual privacy over and above press freedom and free speech, and which might indicate a wider trend in favour of individual privacy when it is in conflict with freedom of expression. In both cases, the courts were critical of the tactics employed by the press, stressing that the press cannot, without judicial oversight, rely on its own editorial judgment to excuse what would otherwise be a breach of privacy. This issue of responsible journalism was a critical factor in the European Court's decision to favour individual privacy over press freedom, and was also relevant in the first case in establishing the rationale for the starting point of privacy expectation in investigation cases. The article will highlight these issues to identify whether these rulings are damaging to notions and values of free speech, press freedom and editorial judgement.

Keywords

press freedom – respect for private life – responsible journalism – public interest defence – investigation into criminal activity – European Court jurisprudence

1   **Introduction**

The UK Supreme Court has recently confirmed that, generally, a person under criminal investigation has, prior to being charged, a reasonable expectation of privacy in respect of information relating to that investigation.[1] Consequently, as a starting point at least, the revelation of those details will amount to a breach of an individual's expectation of privacy, unless justified by any public interest defence, or other circumstances which refute or outweigh that initial expectation of privacy. The Supreme Court stressed that this was only a general rule, or legitimate starting point, rather than a legal presumption, the finding of expectation being fact dependent. However, many fear that it will have a chilling effect on press freedom, and that it will skew the balance between privacy and free speech in this area.[2]

The decision begs the question whether such a rule is compatible with principles of free speech and press freedom, and in particular the case law of the European Court of Human Rights in this area. It also comes at a time when there is much debate about the judicial development of the law of privacy at the expense of free speech,[3] but equally, post-Leveson, when there is still much distrust of the press with respect to its investigative and reporting tactics.[4] This article argues that the decision in *Bloomberg* might set a dangerous (and potentially Convention-incompatible) precedent that might distort the balance between free speech and privacy in misuse of private information cases, and more generally might have a chilling effect on free speech.

---

1   *Bloomberg LP v ZXC* [2022] UKSC 5.
2   J Waterson, 'Bloomberg Loses Landmark UK Supreme Court Case on Privacy: Media Will Find It Harder to Publish Information about People in Criminal Investigations' *The Guardian*, 16 February 2022. See also J Rozenberg, 'Suspects and the Right to Privacy' (2022) 119 *Law Society Gazette* 11.
3   See J Kanter 'Media Groups Raise Concerns in Response to Human Rights Act Consultation' *The Times*, 22 March 2022. More specifically, the government has expressed concern over the use by wealthy business people of SLAPPs (Strategic Lawsuits Against Public Participation). At the time of writing, a Ministry of Justice publication, *Strategic Lawsuits Against Public Participation (SLAPPs); Government Response to the Call for Evidence*, provides the Government's response to its call for evidence on the use of SLAPPs, proposing the establishment of a statutory definition of SLAPPs to help identify relevant cases and form the basis for their being subject to a separate case and costs management regime.
4   *Leveson Inquiry - Report into the Culture, Practices and Ethics of the Press*, 29 November 2012. G Horton, 'Celebrity Privacy and Celebrity Journalism: Has Anything Changed since the Leveson Inquiry?' (2020) 25 *Communications Law* 10.

In addition, in *ML v Slovakia*,[5] the European Court delivered what many see as setting a trend in favour of protecting individual privacy over press freedom. In that case, the Court upheld a claim under Article 8 of the Convention (guaranteeing the right to respect for private and family life) of the mother of a deceased priest, where after his death the press had published stories of his previous convictions for sexual abuse and a possible link between it and his supposed suicide. The case will be used as an example of the European Court's alleged over reliance on privacy and due process rights when balanced with press freedom and free speech, a trend that some also feel has crept into UK domestic case law in this area.[6]

This article will examine those decisions to examine whether they might indicate a wider trend in favour of individual privacy when it is in conflict with freedom of expression. In both cases the courts were critical of the tactics employed by the press, thus stressing that the press cannot, without judicial oversight, rely on its own editorial judgment to excuse what would otherwise be a breach of privacy, or otherwise trump any other countervailing legal claim. This issue - of responsible journalism - was the critical, though not sole, factor in the European Court's decision to favour individual privacy over press freedom, and was also relevant in the first case in establishing the rationale for starting point of privacy expectation in investigation cases. The article will therefore highlight these issues in trying to identify whether these rulings are damaging to notions and values of free speech and press freedom.

2   The Facts and Decision of the Supreme Court in *Bloomberg*

In 2013, the appellants, an international news and media organisation, had reported that a UK law enforcement body (UKLEB) was investigating allegations of fraud, bribery and corruption in relation to a company. In 2016, the appellants published an article about ZXC, the chief executive of the company, in connection with that investigation, and in late 2016 published a second article in which it referred to a formal letter of request from UKLEB to a foreign government, seeking banking and business records in relation to the company and nine named executives, including ZXC. Pointing out that letters of request

---

5   Application No. 34159/17. Decision of the European Court of Human Rights.
6   S Foster 'Balancing Expectations of Privacy in Police Investigations with Press Freedom: the Supreme Court's Decision in *Bloomberg v ZXC*' (2022) 27 *Coventry Law Journal* 95. E Weinert, 'Don't Bother with Libel: Sue for Privacy Instead Following Bloomberg v ZXC' [2022] 32 *Entertainment Law Review* 149.

in general and this letter of request were labelled confidential,[7] the Supreme Court noted that the judge had found that the article contained information drawn almost exclusively from the Letter of Request, a copy of which had been obtained by the Bloomberg journalist. The Court further found that it had been given to the journalist in what must have been (and should have been recognised as) a serious breach of confidence by the person who originally supplied it.[8] Despite UKLEB's investigation into the company being in the public domain, no charges were brought against ZXC.

ZXC claimed damages for misuse of private information by Bloomberg LP and applied for an interim injunction to remove an article about the investigations from its website. That application failed, as in the court's view the Article 8 rights were likely to be outweighed by the defendant's Article 10 rights.[9] The High Court then found that ZXC's Article 8 rights outweighed the defendant organisation's Article 10 rights.[10] In the court's view, there was a clear public interest in maintaining the confidentiality of the investigations, and the justifications for the breach of ZXC's privacy did not outweigh his Article 8 rights.[11] The Court of Appeal upheld that decision,[12] finding that the judge had been right to conclude that those who simply came under suspicion by an organ of the state had, in general, a reasonable and objectively founded expectation of privacy in relation to that fact.[13]

The appellants appealed to the Supreme Court on the issue of whether the fact that information published by them about a criminal investigation originated from a confidential law enforcement document rendered that information private and/or undermined Bloomberg's ability to rely on the public interest in its disclosure. The Supreme Court also considered whether the Court of Appeal was wrong to uphold the findings of Nicklin J in the High

---

7   *Bloomberg LP v ZXC* [2022] UKSC 5, at [17]. In *National Crime Agency v Abacha* [2016] EWCA Civ 760, the Court of Appeal noted the confidential nature of such letters, accepting that it was right to start from the position that letters of request are confidential (Goss LJ, at [48]).

8   *Bloomberg LP v ZXC* [2022] UKSC 5, at [17], citing Nicklin J in *Bloomberg LP v ZXC* [2019] EWCH 970 (Ch), at [125].

9   Decision of Garnham J, 2 February 2017. In the High Court, Nicklin J was very critical of the defendant's candour in those earlier proceedings: *Bloomberg LP v ZXC* [2019] EWCH 970 (Ch), at [73–75].

10   *Bloomberg LP v ZXC* [2019] EWCH 970 (Ch).

11   *Ibid.*, at [125], at [126] and [132–133].

12   *ZXC v Bloomberg LP* [2020] EWCA Civ 611. See N Moreham 'Privacy and Police Investigations: ZXC v Bloomberg [2021] 80(1) CLJ 5.

13   *ZXC v Bloomberg LP* [2020] EWCA Civ 611, at [81–88].

Court that the claimant had a reasonable expectation of privacy and that the balancing exercise came down in favour of the claimant.[14]

In dismissing the appeal, the Supreme Court found that the general rule or legitimate starting point described by the lower courts was not a legal presumption, and whether there was a reasonable expectation of privacy was a fact-specific enquiry.[15] This would not, invariably, lead to a finding that there was a reasonable expectation of privacy in the information,[16] but that the rationale for the starting point was that publication of such information ordinarily caused damage to the person's reputation and the person's physical and social identity protected by article 8.[17]

Despite its insistence that this did not obviate the need of the claimant to prove an expectation of privacy, the Court accepted that in applying the presumption in these cases, it was likely that the expectation of privacy would be proved. The Court also recognised that it was being asked whether the general rule in relation to this category of information was similar to the general rule in relation to certain other categories of information, most strikingly information concerning the state of an individual's health, which was widely considered to give rise to a reasonable expectation of privacy.[18] It then conceded that a consideration of all the circumstances of the case, including, but not limited, to the so-called *Murray* factors,[19] will, generally, in relation to certain categories

---

14   *Bloomberg LP v ZXC* [2022] UKSC 5, at [63].

15   *Ibid.*, at [67]. It was accepted, at [77], that if someone is charged with a criminal offence there can be no reasonable expectation of privacy, that being the rational boundary, as the open justice principle in a free country is fundamental to securing public confidence in the administration of justice, citing *Scott v Scott* [1913] AC 417.

16   *Bloomberg LP v ZXC* [2022] UKSC 5, at [68].

17   *Ibid.*, at [71], citing *Niemietz v Germany* (1992) 16 EHRR 97, at [29]. Again, in the Court's view, the public's understanding of the effect on a person of publication of information that they were suspected of having committed a criminal offence was a question of fact rather than of law. The question was how others would react to the publication of information that the person was under investigation: *Bloomberg LP v ZXC* [2022] UKSC 5, at [107–108].

18   *Bloomberg LP v ZXC* [2022] UKSC 5, at [72], referring to Eady J in *McKennitt v Ash* [2005] EWHC 3003 (QB), at [142].

19   *Murray v Express Newspapers Ltd* [2008] EWCA 446. The following factors were regarded as relevant: the attributes of the claimant; the nature of the activity in which the claimant was engaged; the place at which it was happening; the nature and purpose of the intrusion; the absence of consent and whether it was known or could be inferred; the effect on the claimant; and the circumstances in which and the purposes for which the information came into the hands of the publisher.

of information, lead to the conclusion that the claimant objectively has a reasonable expectation of privacy in information within that category.[20]

In justifying the starting point, the Supreme Court noted that for some time judges have voiced concerns as to the negative effect on an innocent person's reputation of the publication of the fact that they were being investigated by the police or an organ of the state.[21] It then referred to a number of cases that had, in its view, led to a general rule or legitimate starting point that such information is generally characterised as private at stage one.[22] In particular, the Supreme Court referred to the judgment of Mann J in *Richard v BBC*,[23] where the judge had stated that as a matter of general principle, a suspect has a reasonable expectation of privacy in relation to a police investigation.[24]

With respect to the presumption of innocence, the appellants had relied on the dicta of Lord Roger in *Re Guardian News and Media Ltd*,[25] where he noted that the law proceeds on the basis that most members of the public understand that even when charged with an offence one is innocent unless and until proved guilty in a court of law. Further, that understanding applied if you are someone whom the prosecuting authorities are not even in a position to charge with an offence and bring to court.[26] However, the Supreme Court then referred to its later decision in *Khuja v Times Newspapers Ltd*,[27] where the majority of the Supreme Court held that whether the public would have equated suspicion with guilt was a question of fact; whether the public understand the difference between allegation and proof would differ from case to case.[28] The Supreme Court then justified the starting point by stating that the presumption of innocence is a legal presumption applicable to criminal trials, and that all the evidence from case law and practice in this area now

---

20   *Bloomberg LP v ZXC* [2022] UKSC 5, at [72], citing Buxton LJ in *McKennitt v Ash* [2007]
       EWCA Civ 1714, at [23].
21   *Ibid.,* at [80].
22   *Ibid.,* at [81].
23   [2018] EWHC 1837 (Ch).
24   *Richard v British Broadcasting Corporation* [2018] EWHC 1837 (Ch), at [248]. The judge
       held that if the public were universally capable of adopting a completely open and broad-
       minded view of the fact of an investigation so that there was no risk of taint either during
       the investigation or afterwards then the position might be different.
25   [2010] UKSC 1.
26   *Re Guardian News and Media Ltd* [2010] UKSC 1, Lord Rodger, at [66].
27   [2017] UKSC 49, a case where public understanding of the presumption of innocence was
       considered in the context of press reporting and open justice. See R. Craig, 'The end of
       innocence: open justice, free speech and privacy in the modern constitution – Khuja v
       Times Newspapers Ltd' (2019) 82(1) MLR 129.
28   *Khuja v Times Newspapers Ltd* [2017] UKSC 49, Lord Sumption at [9].

accepts that the person's reputation will ordinarily be adversely affected, causing prejudice to personal enjoyment of the right to respect for private life.[29]

The Court also stressed that this case turned not on identifying the nature
of the activity (potential corruption), but on the private nature of the information about the investigation. Thus, the private nature of that investigation
was not affected by the specifics of the activities being investigated.[30] Further,
although ZXC's status as a businessperson involved in a large public company
meant that the limits of acceptable criticism of him were wider than in respect
of a private individual, that had to be balanced against the effect of publication
on the claimant's reputation.[31] Finally, the Court dismissed the defendant's
argument that it had been wrong to hold that even where a claim for breach
of confidence had not been pursued, the fact that the published information
originated from a confidential law enforcement document rendered the information private and undermined its ability to rely on the public interest. The
judge at first instance treated the confidentiality of the information as a relevant and important factor at both stage one and stage two, but did not treat
it as being determinative.[32] The judge was also right to place reliance on the
public interest in the observance of duties of confidence when carrying out
the balancing exercise,[33] and that that public interest both weakens the justification for interfering with or restricting the right of privacy, and strength-
ens the justification for interfering with or restricting the right to freedom of
expression.[34]

3   The Impact of *Bloomberg* and Privacy Jurisprudence on
       Investigative Journalism, Free Speech and Privacy Protection

Following the public, and personal furore over the media tactics involved
in the case of *Sir Cliff Richard v BBC*,[35] it was feared that non-disclosure of
details with respect to early police investigations was to become the norm, the
press having to wait at least until the individual is charged. This could have

---

29   *Bloomberg LP v ZXC* [2022] UKSC 5, at [108].
30   *Ibid.,* at [129].
31   *Ibid.,* at [140–141]. Therefore, the Supreme Court found that the balance had been applied
      correctly in ZXC's favour.
32   *Ibid.,* at [148].
33   *Ibid.,* at [152].
34   *Ibid.,* at [153].
35   [2018] EWHC 1837 (Ch). For a critical commentary on the case, see T Bennett and P Wragg,
      'Was Richard v BBC Correctly Decided?' (2018) 23 *Communications Law* 151.

a chilling effect on press reporting where it raises matters of public debate, which are beyond question in this case and in *Richard*.[36] The decision has, understandably, caused fear and distrust from the media. For example, Dawn Alford, Executive Director of the Society of Editors noted that the ruling will have far-reaching implications for the British media and that legitimate public interest journalism will go unreported.[37] This observation is part of a wider concern that in the Human Rights Act era, the courts have developed the law of privacy to such an extent that free speech and media freedom has been compromised, a concern shared by the present government and one reason why it feels the Act is in need of reform.[38]

Your author argues that the decision gives rise to several areas of concern. First, when these rights are in conflict neither should be given a 'trump' status, the question of which right prevails being determined by proportionality.[39] Although the Supreme Court is adamant that its ruling has not disturbed this, the starting point is bound to have an effect on the court's balancing exercise, adding weight to the claimant's expectation of privacy due to the classification of this type of information. Despite the public interest defence being available at the second stage, the Court has in effect ruled that the defendant has, by transgressing this rule, broken a fundamental aspect of the individual's expectation of privacy, one that in normal circumstances will be upheld at both stages. This places the defendant further on the back foot, making it more difficult to justify this interference via the defence of public interest at the second stage of the enquiry.

Second, the Supreme Court insists that the nature of the claimant's activities should be restricted to the *private nature* of the commercial data, not including the *possible criminal nature* of those investigations. Again, this provides very generous protection to the Article 8 rights of the claimant, and, possibly, insufficient recognition to the argument that any reasonable expectation

---

36   See S Foster, 'Media Responsibility, Public Interest Broadcasting and the Judgment in Richard v BBC' (2018) 5 *EHRLR* 490, 501.

37   Society of Editors, 'Far-Reaching Implications of Bloomberg Privacy Ruling, says SoE' 16 February 2022. See also, J Waterson, 'Privacy Laws Could be Rolled back Following SC Ruling' *The Guardian*, 19 February 2022 (online version).

38   D Martin, 'Vow to Stop un-British 'drift' to Privacy Law as Dominic Raab Eyes Overhaul of Human Rights Act to 'Correct' Freedom of Speech Imbalance in Wake of Duchess of Sussex Court Case' *The Daily Mail*, 6 December 2021.

39   *Re S (Publicity)* [2005] 1 AC 593, where Lord Steyn identified the following considerations as being of particular importance in carrying out the balancing exercise: an intense focus on the comparative importance of the specific rights being claimed in the individual case; the justifications for interfering with or restricting each right" and the proportionality of the respective interference or restriction.

of privacy in respect of police investigations needs to be reconciled with the principle that individuals should not be allowed to suppress evidence of their own (admittedly in this case suspected) wrongdoing.[40] Accordingly, the public interest reason for the potential breach of the claimant's expectation of privacy is, at this stage at least, of no relevance. Of course, the defendant will be allowed to raise this factor at the second stage, but by that stage, the legitimate expectation is already strongly established and weighted, and the public interest arguments may rarely win out, as they can in other misuse of private information cases. Thus, once the starting point has been established, the status of the claimant, and the public interest element at the second stage, is in danger of being lost or forgotten.[41] This gives rise to real concerns over the weighting of the rights, and, more generally, the precarious position of press freedom and the public interest in these cases.

On the other hand, as we are dealing with *suspected* criminal activities, the Court's approach on this issue is probably reconcilable with its previous decision in *JR38's Application for Judicial Review, Re*.[42] In that case, the publication by the police of images of a 14-year-old boy apparently committing public order offences did not violate his Article 8 rights, as the boy could not have had a reasonable expectation that photographs of him committing the offences, taken for the limited purpose of identifying him, would not be published. In *Bloomberg*, the Court disregard the claimant's (suspected) activities because there has been a breach of the Court's starting point with respect to pre-charge revelations. This approach may also be consistent with the European Court's decision in *Axel Springer v Germany*,[43] discussed later, if we accept that the starting point is justified in cases of pre-charge disclosures, and thus that different rules apply.

Third, the Court's approach to the presumption of innocence gives scant recognition to the claim that the public can recognise the clear distinction between a person's guilt on the one hand, and the suspicion of guilt on the other, the latter carrying with it a presumption of innocence. The Court's

---

40   N Moreham 'Privacy, Reputation and Alleged Wrongdoing: Why Police Investigations Should Not be Regarded as Private' (2019) 11 *Journal of Media Law* 142. Of course, in the present case, this refers to the investigation of *suspected* wrongdoing.

41   Thus, once the Supreme Court had laid down the essential principles of its starting point, it dispensed with the question of whether the facts disclosed a breach in one sentence. – 'This case clearly falls into the category of information in which the legitimate starting point applies': *Bloomberg LP v ZXC* [2022] UKSC 5, at [145].

42   [2015] UKSC 42.

43   (2012) 55 EHRR 6 (Grand Chamber).

dismissal of Lord Rodger's dicta in *Re Guardian Newspapers*,[44] is, it is argued, overly dismissive of the public's ability to see the difference, and thus damaging to public debate on such issues; the courts' presumption of harm in these cases frustrating any public discussion and decision on the investigation and its inferences. Further, in Lord Rodger's view, publication of this information would assist the clarification of the public's perception and understanding of the issues, and failure to mention the suspects would lead to a disembodied story and the matter being given a lower priority in the media.[45] Although there might indeed be evidence that the public understanding of a particular publication is likely to be that the person was in fact guilty, to turn that possibility into a general starting point, so that we are assuming that disclosure before arrest will be damaging to the individual's reputation and expectation of privacy is a considerable judicial leap.

Finally, the decision follows a number of recent decisions unfavourable to press and media freedom, and which have thus possibly tilted the balance in favour of individual privacy. In *PSJ v News Group Newspapers*,[46] the Supreme Court held that the press could be prohibited from disclosing private information despite that information reaching the public domain and being available on social media.[47] Whist it might be legitimate to distinguish private information cases from traditional confidentiality claims in this respect,[48] maintaining injunctions in such cases can have an unnecessary effect on press freedom and free speech.[49] Further, decisions such as *Richard* have been instrumental in restricting the scope of the public interest defence where the courts find that the media have been guilty of irresponsible journalism or broadcasting, or of making a good story or good television at the expense of furthering the public interest.[50] Whilst this fact should be taken into consideration when conducting the balancing exercise, or, in *Bloomberg*, in assessing the level of

---

44   [2010] UKSC 1. See M Bohlander, 'Open Justice or Open Season?' (2010) 74 *Journal of Criminal Law* 321.

45   *Re Guardian Newspapers* (2010] UKSC 1, Lord Rodger at 60.

46   [2016] UKSC 6.

47   See J Rowbotham 'Holding Back the Tide: Privacy Injunctions and the Digital Media' (2017] 133 *LQR* 177; and K Yoshida 'Privacy Injunctions in the Internet Age: PJS v News Group Newspapers Ltd' (2016) *European Human Rights Law Review* 434.

48   *Attorney General v Guardian Newspapers* [1988] 1 AC 109.

49   U Smartt, 'Are Privacy Injunctions Futile in the Digital Age? Why Scottish Papers Choose to Name the Super Injunction A-Listers - and Why They Cannot Do So Online' (2017) *European Intellectual Property Review* 413.

50   See also the case of *Channel 5 v Ali* [2019] EWCA 677, noted by S Foster, 'Interfering with Editorial Judgment, Making "Good Television" and the Loss of the Public Interest Defence' (2019) 24 *Communications Law* 102.

the expectation of privacy, cases such as *Richard*, and now *Bloomberg*, have created rules that apply more generally in this area, and compromise the public
interest defence beyond those cases where irresponsible journalism is clearly
present on the facts.[51]

4   The Decision of the Supreme Court in *Bloomberg* and the Jurisprudence of the European Court of Human Rights

It will be interesting to see whether the appellants in *Bloomberg* choose to pursue a case before the European Court of Human Rights, and if they do what the
Court's decision would be in that case. On the one hand, if the Court appears
satisfied with the general balancing exercise carried out by the domestic courts
in these cases, and it might show due respect to the Supreme Court's ruling,
and the courts below, in their balancing of Article 8 and 10 rights, as it did in
the 'Naomi Campbell' case when it was referred to the Strasbourg Court.[52]

On the other hand, the Supreme Court's decision might be regarded as
unduly restrictive of press freedom and investigative journalism, thus clashing
with many of the principles that the Court has established in the area of public
interest free speech.[53] Specifically, the Court might feel that the presumption
or starting point might have a chilling effect on press freedom and the defendant's right to successfully raise any public interest defence. In this respect, the
European Court's rejection of Max Mosely's claim, that the press should have
a legal duty to inform an individual that they intend to publish private information, is illustrative.[54] In that case, the Court stressed that in considering
such a rule the Court had to have regard, in particular, to its implications for
freedom of expression, not limited to the sensationalist reporting at issue in
this case, but to political reporting and serious investigative journalism. Thus,
the introduction of restrictions on the latter type of journalism requires care-
ful scrutiny.[55] The Court also observed that a narrowly defined public-interest

---

51   S Foster, 'Media Responsibility, Public Interest Broadcasting and the Judgment in Richard
      v BBC' (2018) 5 *European Human Rights Law Review* 490, 503.

52   *MGN v United Kingdom* (2011) 53 EHRR 5, when it accepted that the House of Lord's
      judgment in *Campbell v MGN Ltd* [2004] 2 AC 457.

53   In particular, the principles laid down in *Sunday Times v United Kingdom* (1979) 2 EHRR
      245, *Lingens v Austria* (1986) 8 EHRR 407, *Oberschlick v Austria* (1995) 19 EHRR 389,
      Observer and Guardian v United Kingdom (1991)14 EHRR 153, and *Axel Springer v Austria*
      (2012) 55 EHRR 6.

54   *Mosley v United Kingdom* (2011) 53 EHRR 30.

55   *Ibid.*, at 121.

exception would increase the chilling effect of any pre-notification duty.[56] It is argued, therefore, that the inclusion of the starting point of privacy might have a similar chilling effect on press freedom and the availability of the public interest defence in misuse of private information cases.

As we would expect, the European Court's balancing exercise is similar to the one adopted by the domestic courts in *Murray*.[57] However, as domestic law is informed by the case law of the Strasbourg Court, the starting point is the traditional jurisprudence of the European Court in this area, as modified in the area of free speech and privacy cases. In that respect, the Supreme Court's ruling could be criticised at three levels. First, it fails to take into account the fact that the claimant in this case was a large, public company, where different rules of investigation and privacy expectation apply. Secondly, that such individuals cannot claim in respect of damage to privacy which is the foreseeable consequence of one's own actions, in this case their suspected involvement in corruption. Thirdly, and more generally, that the domestic courts have failed to give due weight to the role of the media in investigating matters of public interest.

The appellants' first argument was that the lower courts had failed to give due weight to the commercial attributes of the claimant in this case, in accordance with the principle laid down in *Oberschlick v Austria (No 2)*.[58] In that case, the Court stressed that with respect to the protection of political reputation, the limits of acceptable criticism are wider with regard to a politician acting in his public capacity than in relation to a private individual.[59] Specifically, the appellants argued that businessmen actively involved in the affairs of large public companies are not, in that sector of their lives, private individuals, but rather that they knowingly lay themselves open to close scrutiny of their acts by the media; and that the courts below had failed to give adequate consideration to the attributes of the claimant.[60]

---

56   *Ibid.*, at 126.

57   Thus, in *Axel Springer v Germany* (2005) 41 EHRR 22, the Grand Chamber established that when balancing both rights the relevant criteria were: whether the article contributed to a debate of general interest; the subject of the article and how well-known the relevant person was; the prior conduct of the person; the method of obtaining the information and its veracity; the content, form and consequences of the publication; and the severity of the sanction imposed, at [62].

58   (1997) 25 EHRR 357.

59   *Oberschlick v Austria (No 2)* (1997) 25 EHRR 357, at [29].

60   *Bloomberg LP v ZXC* [2022] UKSC 5, at [136], citing *Fayed v United Kingdom* (1994) 18 EHRR 393, at [75]: "As to enforcement of the right to a good reputation under domestic law, *the limits of acceptable criticism are wider with regard to businessmen actively involved in the affairs of large public companies than with regard to private individuals.*"

The Supreme Court accepted that the status of the claimant meant that the limits of acceptable criticism of him were wider than in respect of a private individual, but stressed that that did not mean that there is no limit to reporting, nor that that circumstance is determinative. Thus, it was a relevant consideration, but only one factor, and must be balanced against the effect of publication of the information on him.[61] The Supreme Court then reinforced the importance of the starting point by stating that the ordinary conclusion in relation to the effect of publication of information that an individual is under criminal investigation is that damage occurs whatever his characteristic or status. Indeed, the Court stated it might be that the damage to a businessperson actively involved in the affairs of a large public company would be greater than to a private individual.[62] In any case, the Court considered that the status of the claimant had been taken into account by both the judge, and by Simon LJ in the Court of Appeal, who noted that the claimant 'held a senior position in X Ltd, but was not a director, and achieved no particular prominence in his role.[63]

In *Steel and Morris v United Kingdom*,[64] the Strasbourg Court conceded that Article 10 did not, in principle, deprive multi-national and public companies of the right to bring proceedings in defamation, or to obviate the requirement for the defendants to prove the truth of any statement. Nevertheless, while stressing that there was a competing interest in protecting the commercial success and viability of companies, it stressed that such companies inevitably laid themselves open to increased public scrutiny.[65] The question in our case, therefore, is whether it is sufficient that the courts simply take the commercial attributes of the claimant into account as one, unexceptional factor, when they have already established reputational harm as, if not the leading factor, the starting point of the balance. In such cases, the European Court might feel that the balancing exercise is being distorted, and that its traditional jurisprudence on public interest speech is being undermined.

The second argument was that Article 8 should not be relied on in order to complain of a loss of reputation that resulted from the claimant's actions. Having accepted that the notion of private life covered the right to reputation,[66] the Supreme Court cited the case law of the European Court that Article 8 cannot be relied on in order to complain of a loss of reputation that is the

---

61 *Bloomberg LP v ZXC* [2022] UKSC 5, at [140].
62 *Ibid.*, at [140].
63 *Ibid.*, at [141].
64 (2005) 41 EHRR 22.
65 *Steel and Morris v United Kingdom* (2005) 41 EHRR 22, at [94].
66 *Bloomberg LP v ZXC* [2022] UKSC 5, at [145], citing *Pfeifer v Austria* (2007) 48 EHRR 8, at [35].

foreseeable consequence of one's own actions, such as, for example, the commission of a criminal offence.[67] It then noted that in *Gillberg v Sweden*,[68] the Grand Chamber had stated that any such suffering could not *in itself* amount to an interference with the right to respect for private life, extending that principle to cover not only criminal offences but also other misconduct entailing a measure of legal responsibility with foreseeable negative effects on private life.[69] The Supreme Court acknowledged that this factor could be taken into account at stage one in determining whether the claimant has established a reasonable expectation of privacy in the relevant information in a case, for instance, where a person is *actually convicted* of a criminal offence or investigated and found to have committed the alleged misconduct.[70] Thus, although the reference in *Gillberg* to "other misconduct entailing a measure of legal responsibility" was one which can be taken into account at stage one, the examples provided by the Court related to misconduct established *after* authoritative findings following an official investigation.[71]

Specifically, we need to examine the ruling in light of the European Court's decision in *Axel Springer v Germany*.[72] Although that case was concerned with the public capture of the individual's arrest and subsequent conviction of a criminal offence, as opposed to the investigation of suspected criminal activities, it is natural that the press will draw comparisons and argue that similar protection to press freedom and the public interest in publication be provided in these circumstances. In that case, a national newspaper published a front-page article about an actor being arrested in a tent at the Munich beer festival for possession of cocaine, supplemented by a more detailed article on another page and illustrated by three pictures of the actor. The further article

---

67   *Pfeifer v Austria* (2007) 48 EHRR 8, at [98]. See also *Axel Springer v Germany* (2012) 55 EHRR 6.

68   (2012) 34 BHRC 247.

69   *Denisov v Ukraine*, Application No 76639/11) (unreported) 25 September 2018, at [95], citing *Gillberg v Sweden* (2012) 34 BHRC 247.

70   *ZXC v Bloomberg*, at [123], citing *Sidabras and Džiautas v Lithuania* (2004) 42 EHRR 6, where a person was proved to be a former KGB officer, and thus lost his expectation of privacy and reputation under Article 8.

71   *ZXC v Bloomberg*, at [123]. However, the Supreme Court did not consider that misconduct was confined to a finding at the end of a criminal or other authoritative process. For instance, the example of "an armed bank-robber who held hostage a number of customers and employees in a televised three-day siege" whom he considered "could hardly claim a reasonable expectation of privacy when s/he surrendered and was arrested." This would, therefore, justify the Supreme Court's decision in *JR38*, above.

72   (2012) 55 EHRR 6; Application No 39954/08, European Court of Human Rights (Grand Chamber), 7 February 2012; [2012] EMLR 12.

mentioned that the actor, who had played the role of a police superintendent in a popular TV series for six years, had been given a suspended prison sentence for possession of drugs four years previously. The newspaper than published a second article, six months after the first one, reporting on the actor's conviction and fine for illegal possession of drugs. After the first article appeared, the actor brought proceedings against the applicants and the regional court granted an injunction prohibiting any further publication of the article and the photographs. This was confirmed six months later and the court prohibited publication of almost the entire article on pain of penalty for non-compliance, and ordered the newspaper to pay an agreed penalty.

The applicants brought an application before the European Court of Human Rights, claiming a violation of their article 10 rights. It should be stressed that the Grand Chamber's decision, in favour of the newspapers, was based on the actor's clear public profile and previous self-publicity.[73] Yet, of importance to the present discussions, it found that the articles in question, about the actor's arrest and conviction, concerned judicial facts, of which the public had an interest in being informed.[74] Thus, in the Grand Chamber's view, in principle the public did have an interest in being informed—and in being able to inform themselves—about criminal proceedings, whilst strictly observing the presumption of innocence.[75] That interest, in its view, will vary in degree, as it may evolve during the course of the proceedings—*from the time of the arrest*—according to a number of different factors, such as the degree to which the person concerned is known, the circumstances of the case and any further developments arising during the proceedings.[76] At first glance, the Grand Chamber's judgment is clearly confined to reporting of public events and judicial proceedings post arrest and charge; very different from the facts in *Bloomberg*, where the individual has not yet been charged. Clearly, an individual would have a greater expectation of privacy pre-charge, or arrest. Nevertheless, it is argued that absent a clear ruling from the Strasbourg Court, a starting point of privacy expectation in all such cases is both unnecessary and damaging to investigative journalism and the public interest.

On the other hand, it must be pointed out that the European Court has imposed limitations on the press when reporting on criminal investigations, both as a means of upholding due process and individual privacy, including the

---

73   *Axel Springer v Germany* (2012) 55 EHRR 6, at [98–101].
74   *Ibid.*, at [100].
75   *Ibid.*, at [99].
76   *Ibid.*, at [99].

right to be forgotten and to facilitate the process of rehabilitation.[77] Further, the Court has approved of restrictions that uphold the administration of justice, and where the media have misused confidential information in the reporting on the case, as the appellants had of course been guilty of in *Bloomberg*. Thus, in *Bedat v Switzerland*,[78] it was held that the state was entitled to uphold a journalist's criminal conviction when it published secret documents relating to an ongoing criminal investigation.[79]

In the Court's view, the domestic courts had properly conducted the balancing exercise when considering the competing interests under Articles 8 and 10. In particular, it noted that the manner in which confidential or secret information was obtained might be relevant to the balance of interests. Although the applicant had not obtained the information by unlawful means, as a professional journalist, he could not have been unaware of the confidential nature of the information and he had not disputed that publication might fall within the scope of the Swiss Criminal Code.[80] Again, with respect to the content of the article, the Court noted that journalists when reporting on issues of general interest must act in good faith and provide reliable and precise information in accordance with the ethics of journalism. In this case, the applicant had confined his article to sensationalism and readers would have subjectively prejudged the criminal proceedings without respect for the principle of the presumption of innocence.[81]

Although the case is mostly concerned with protecting the administration of justice and the presumption of innocence, the Court also noted that the proceedings brought against the applicant complied with the state's positive obligation to protect the accused's private life. The information disclosed by the applicant was highly personal and required the highest level of protection under Article 8, noting that the accused was not a public figure who had

77   See the cases of *Egeland v Norway* (2010) 50 E.H.R.R. 2 and *Mediengruppe Österreich GmbH v Austria* (Application No. 37713/18, decision of the European Court of Human Rights 26 April 2022, considered below).

78   (2016) 63 EHRR 15.

79   The journalist had written a magazine article concerning proceedings brought against a motorist who had driven into a group of pedestrians, killing three people and injuring eight others. One of the parties claiming damages against the motorist had lost their case file and an unknown person gave the documents to the magazine. The public prosecutor brought criminal proceedings against the applicant for publishing documents relating to the ongoing investigation, and he was sentenced to one month's imprisonment, suspended for one year, later replaced by a fine.

80   *Bedat v Switzerland* (2016) 63 EHRR 15, at [56–57].

81   *Ibid.*, at [58–61].

voluntarily exposed himself to publicity.[82] That there is in these cases two competing interests in regulating free speech and media freedom will obviously affect the strength of the Article 10 claim and any public interest defence. Although the subject of the article was a matter of public interest, there was no reason to interfere with the domestic court's finding that the article's content did not provide any insight relevant to the public debate, and served purely to satisfy the unhealthy curiosity of a particular readership regarding details of the accused's private life.[83]

There is evidence, therefore, that the Court will restrain the media's right to report on matters relating to criminal proceedings, and that post *Von Hannover*, it has been prepared to give strong weight to the privacy and due process rights of the individual. Nevertheless, the question is whether the ruling in *Bloomberg* affords sufficient weight to the public interest in publication, and whether the presumption or starting point is in conflict with that factor. The Supreme Court accepted that in considering the public interest in publication, the contribution that publication will make to a debate of general interest is a factor of particular importance.[84] Thus, in *Von Hannover v Germany*,[85] the European Court stated that it should be the decisive factor in balancing the protection of private life against freedom of expression,[86] and in *Axel Springer* it was said to be an initial essential criterion.[87] The Supreme Court is adamant that any public interest in publication was offset by the public interest in upholding the confidentiality of the letter of request, and the appellant's clear breach of such confidentiality.[88]

It is argued that despite the European Court's growing privacy jurisprudence, the Supreme Court has taken the above factors, together with the predominant weight it attaches to the starting point, to exclude any meaningful consideration of the public interest. In any case, the factor of confidentiality should not dominate the balancing exercise, and in doing so may conflict with the European Court's earlier jurisprudence. For example, in *Sunday Times v United Kingdom*,[89] the European Court found that the domestic courts' interpretation of contempt laws centred entirely on the need to secure the administration of justice, to the exclusion of the very great public interest in the matter to which

---

82   *Ibid.*, at [72–78].
83   *Ibid.*, at [62–67].
84   *zxc v Bloomberg*, at [62].
85   *Von Hannover v Germany*, (Application No 59329/00) [2004] EMLR 21.
86   *Ibid.*, at [76].
87   *Axel Springer v Germany* (2012) 55 EHRR 6, at [101]
88   *zxc v Bloomberg*, [2022] UKSC 5, at [152].
89   (1979) EHRR 245

the offending articles related to.[90] Similarly, the Supreme Court's judgment could be said to have the same effect on curtailing investigative journalism on matters of public debate, at least until the parameters of the starting point's exceptions are articulated.

There is little doubt that the starting point is favoured and adopted by all relevant state agencies, and that they regard this starting point as an unbreakable rule. However for the courts to adopt this as the starting point in their judicial balancing act, risks them attaching undue weight to the fact that the defendants had broken the law, or practice, of confidentiality, and applying that rule disproportionately in the law of misuse of private information. Thus, the courts become more concerned with this bare fact, rather than whether the claimant had suffered any real harm with respect to his legitimate expectation of privacy, and whether that can be outweighed by the public interest in publication.

5   The Decision of the European Court of Human Rights in *ML v Slovakia*

As we have seen above, the European Court has provided domestic courts with a good deal of discretion in the balancing of Article 8 and 10 rights,[91] provided the domestic courts genuinely attempt to balance both interests.[92] As a result, much of the case law tells us little of how tolerant the European Court would be if national law, within the boundaries set by the European Court, gave priority to free speech norms, including editorial discretion. Thus, it is not clear to what extent domestic law can give precedence to press freedom and public interest debate over and above privacy interests. On the other hand, recent jurisprudence provides evidence that the media will not be given a free hand as to how they report stories of a public interest, including reporting on current and past criminal proceedings and activities.[93] Indeed, one recent decision of the European Court suggests that it would favour the Supreme Court's approach in

---

90   *Sunday Times v United Kingdom* (1979) 2 EHRR 245, at [65].

91   *MGN Ltd v United Kingdom* (2011) 53 EHRR 5, and *Mosley v United Kingdom* (2013) 53 EHRR 30 on the balancing exercise carried out by the UK domestic courts.

92   P Korpisaari, 'Balancing Freedom of Expression and the Right to Private Life in the European Court of Human Rights – Application and Interpretation of the Key Criteria' (2017) 22 *Communications Law* 39.

93   See the cases of *Egeland v Norway*, Application No. 34438/04, 16 April 2009, and *Mediengruppe Osterreich GmbH v Austria*, Application No.37713/18, discussed below.

defending privacy rights over free speech, particularly where the reporting is regarded as unnecessary or unprofessional.

5.1   *The Facts and Decision in ML v Slovakia*

In *ML v Slovakia*,[94] the European Court upheld a claim of the mother of a deceased priest where after his death the press had published stories of his previous convictions for sexual abuse and a possible link between that and his supposed suicide. The articles claimed that before his supposed suicide the applicant's son had confessed to his acts and his bisexual orientation; that the bishop to whom he was subordinate had been informed of the criminal charges, following which the Church had offered a guarantee of his good behaviour; and that by virtue of that kind of guarantee, the applicant's son had either been released, not put in detention, or not convicted. The articles - one of which was accompanied by pictures of the applicant's son - mentioned his full name and many details of his private and intimate life, some of which related to the distant past, described in expressive terms and presented as stemming either from the criminal files or from the statements of people who had been approached by the journalists. The mother argued that the articles contained many false and misleading allegations which did not correspond to the domestic criminal courts' findings, and contained disproportionate value judgments characterising her son as a criminal and his acts as "disgusting paedophile orgies", the aim of which was to cause a sensation and increase the newspapers' sale figures.[95]

In giving judgment in favour of the applicant, the Court noted that, while alive, the applicant's son was not a well-known public figure or a high-ranking Church dignitary; in contrast to the domestic court's finding, that, as a parish priest, he could not be treated as an ordinary person but rather as a public figure expected to be more tolerant to criticism.[96] The Court accepted that as a general rule Article 8 cannot be relied on in order to complain of a loss of reputation that is the foreseeable consequence of, *inter alia*, the commission of a criminal offence.[97] However, it then stressed that a criminal conviction does not deprive the convicted person of his or her right to be forgotten.[98] This all

---

94   Application No 34159/17, decision of the European Court of Human Rights 2021.
95   *M.L. v Slovakia*, Application No 34159/17, decision of the European Court of Human Rights 2021, at [7].
96   *Ibid.*, at [37].
97   *Ibid.*, at [38].
98   The right to be forgotten was established by the European Court of Justice in *Google LLC v Commission Nationale de l'Informatique et des Libertes* (*CNIL*) (C-507/17) EU:C:2019:772 (ECJ (Grand Chamber).

the more so if that conviction has become spent, and that after a certain period of time, persons who have been convicted have an interest in no longer being confronted with their acts, with a view to their reintegration in society.[99]

The Court noted that the material was presented in a sensational and gossip-like manner, with flashy headlines placed on the front pages, along with (in the third article) photographs of the applicant's late son. Further, the allegations made by the tabloid press were presented as statements of fact rather than value judgments, a matter on which the domestic courts did not draw a clear distinction.[100] Although accepting that the articles raised matters of public interest and debate,[101] it was possible to inform the public adequately about the matter by means that entailed less interference with the applicant's son's legitimate interests, namely by reporting only the facts accessible from the publicly available criminal files. There was, therefore, a distinction between reporting facts capable of contributing to a debate of general public interest in a democratic society, and making tawdry allegations about an individual's private life. Although the pre-eminent role of the press in a democracy and its duty to act as a "public watchdog" are important considerations, different considerations apply to press reports concentrating on sensational and, at times, lurid news, intended to titillate and entertain, aimed at satisfying the curiosity of a particular readership regarding aspects of a person's strictly private life.[102] Accordingly, the Court held that the publication of additional, particularly intrusive information concerning the intimate sphere of the applicant's son's private life and the publication of his picture could not be justified by any considerations of general interest.[103]

5.2   *The Impact of ML on Free Speech Jurisprudence*

The European Court has always stoutly defended the values of freedom of expression and its role in a democratic society, insisting on broad mindedness,

---

99   *M.L. v Slovakia*, Application No 34159/17, decision of the European Court of Human Rights 2021, at [38]. The Court thus took into account that not only were the articles in question published several years after the applicant's son's criminal convictions, but also after those convictions had become spent (at [39]).

100   *M.L. v Slovakia*, Application No 34159/17, decision of the European Court of Human Rights 2021, at [42–43].

101   *M.L. v Slovakia*, Application No 34159/17, decision of the European Court of Human Rights 2021, at [50].

102   *M.L. v Slovakia*, Application No 34159/17, decision of the European Court of Human Rights 2021, at [53], citing *Mosley v United Kingdom*, Application No. 48009/08, decision of the European Court 10 May 2011.

103   *M.L. v Slovakia*, Application No 34159/17, decision of the European Court of Human Rights 2021, at [53–54].

pluralism and tolerance, and accepting that it includes the right to shock and offend.[104] Specifically, it has given greater weight and protection to press freedom and the right to disseminate information and ideas of public interest.[105] This has included providing the press with a greater area of editorial discretion in how and in what language it disseminates that information.[106] Further, it has stressed that politicians and other public figures must be more tolerant of criticism, and that the limits of acceptable criticism were wider with respect to (a politician) acting in his personal capacity than in relation to a private individual.[107]

The potential for the public interest defence and deference to editorial judgement in privacy cases had to be re-visited after the decision in *Von Hannover v Germany*.[108] The case had been brought after the applicant had failed to prohibit the publication of photographs taken of her, and with family and friends, by the German paparazzi and published in various German newspapers and magazines. In the domestic proceedings, the German Constitutional Court regarded her as a public figure and held that she had to tolerate the publication of photographs of herself in a public place, even though they showed her in scenes from her daily life, rather than engaged in her official duties. However, the European Court held that the publication of the various photographs fell within the scope of her private life,[109] the decisive factor being the contribution that the published material made to a debate of general interest.[110] The photographs showed the applicant engaged in activities of a purely private nature, and the photographs made no contribution to a debate of public interest, as the applicant exercised no official function.[111]

The decision had an instant impact on the UK domestic courts, and in *McKennitt v Ash*,[112] in upholding a country singer's right of privacy with respect to the revelation of details of her private life by a former friend, it was held that the claimant was not a public figure in whom there was a legitimate interest to justify or require exposure of her private life. Further, even if the claimant was a public figure in the relevant sense, there were no special

---

104 *Handyside v United Kingdom* (1979) 1 EHRR 737.
105 *Sunday Times v United v Kingdom* (1979) 2 EHRR 245.
106 *Ibid.*; *Thorgerison v Iceland* (1992) 14 EHRR 843.
107 *Obershchlick v Austria (No 2)* 1998) 25 EHRR 357.
108 (2005) 40 EHRR 1.
109 *Von Hannover v Germany* (2005) 40 EHRR 1, at [53].
110 *Ibid.*, at [60].
111 *Ibid.*, at [61].
112 [2008] QB 73.

circumstances to justify or require the exposure of her private life.[113] The decision in *McKennit* was evident of the change in judicial direction with respect to the balance between freedom of expression and the protection of privacy where the claimant is a public figure (in its general sense), but not in the specific sense of being a public official or servant.[114] This change, informed by *Von Hannover*, thus modified the circumstances in which the public interest should demand the disclosure of information relating to the private lives of public figures. *Von Hannover* restricted the public interest defence to matters of genuine, and more formal, political and public concern, and in most cases excluded information relating to the private lives of celebrities and other well-known figures. The decision in *ML* thus reflects the ideology of *Van Hannover* in the sense that the priest was not a public figure *par excellence*.

5.3   *Irresponsible Broadcasting or Journalism and the Public Interest Defence*

The decision in *ML*, however, raises issues beyond the public status of the applicant. Primarily, the ruling has focused attention on the tactics employed by the media in reporting news items, albeit of a strong public interest, and the extent to which those tactics should devalue the free speech values of any broadcast or publication. These tactics are obviously relevant to whether the media have carried out its 'duties and responsibilities' referred to in the qualifying paragraph 2 of Article 10, but the question is how much relevance that should have in public interest stories. In other words, once the Court has established that the story is of public interest, what relevance should media tactics have in deciding the balance between Articles 8 and 10, and is judicial approbation of such inconsistent with editorial judgement?

In this respect, the decision of the UK High Court in *Richard v BBC*[115] is illustrative. In that case, a famous entertainer succeeded in his action against the BBC and the police for breach of his Article 8 rights when the BBC broadcast the police's investigations into possible historical sexual abuse. In deciding that the BBC had interfered with his expectation of privacy, and that that was not overridden by any public interest, the judge considered firstly that the impact of the invasion had been very materially increased by the nature of

---

113   Lord Phillips MR, in *Campbell v MGN Ltd* [2003] QB 633, at paras 40–44.
114   See also *CC v AB* [2007] EMLR 11.
115   *Cliff Richard v BBC and The Chief Constable of South Yorkshire Police* [2018] EWHC 1837 (Ch).

the BBC's coverage, which had added drama and a degree of sensationalism.[116] Thus, the BBC went in for an invasion of Sir Cliff's privacy in a big way.[117] It was also very significant that the publication started with obviously private and sensitive information, obtained from someone who, to the BBC journalist's knowledge, ought not to have revealed it, and confirmed or bolstered with a ploy in the form of a perceived threat by the journalist to the police that he would publish the story before the police search.[118]

Without question, the judgment in *Richard* relies heavily on the tactics employed by the BBC in the gathering and dissemination of the story. This begs the question to what extent such a factor is relevant in the balancing exercise, and whether a public interest story and defence should be affected by what the court regards as irresponsible broadcasting.[119]

In attempting to impose standards of responsible broadcasting on programme makers the decision in *Richard* is unobjectionable. Such standards are imposed on and by broadcasting authorities and by the courts in areas such as defamation, contempt of court and indeed in privacy actions generally.[120] Courts thus take into account that the purpose of the programme is to entertain in reducing the public interest nature of the broadcast. Further, certain programmes made by certain companies (and broadcast on certain channels) will be assumed to have been made for purely financial or prurient reasons. This might lead to decisions being made on unfair or unprincipled purposes, and the decision in *Richard* will be of concern to programme makers who seek to combine public education and entertainment. In *Richard,* the public interest argument of the BBC in respect of the broadcast is lost because of the tactics it employed in gathering and disseminating the information. This should be relevant to the decision on the overall proportionality of the media's interference with the claimant's privacy rights; but, it is suggested, should not be allowed to dominate the balancing exercise if, as was clear in *Richard*, the investigation and broadcast concerned a matter of great public interest and debate. As was made clear by the House of Lords in *Jameel*,[121] the ultimate question must be whether publication was in the public interest, and

---

116 *Cliff Richard v BBC and The Chief Constable of South Yorkshire Police* [2018] EWHC 1837 (Ch), at [300].

117 *Ibid.*, at [301].

118 *Ibid.*, at [293].

119 See also *Ali v Channel 5 Broadcast Ltd* [2018] EWHC 298 (Ch).

120 *Campbell v MGN Ltd* [2004] 2 AC 457.

121 *Jameel v Wall Street Journal Europe* [2007] 1 AC 359.

not whether the media have broken the rules of professional journalism or broadcasting.[122]

Yet it is not simply in the UK courts that editorial discretion and media freedom has been compromised by the need to protect individual privacy and the willingness to check editorial discretion.[123] A number of decisions of the European Court have upheld restrictions on the media when reporting on criminal investigations and proceedings. For example, in *Egeland v Norway*,[124] the Strasbourg Court held that Norway was justified in imposing a fine on members of the press who photographed a convicted person leaving court. In the Court's view the protection of privacy and the fair administration of justice outweighed the interest of the press in informing the public on a matter of public concern.[125] Although the press were entitled to inform the public on matters of public concern regarding ongoing criminal proceedings, that right had to be balanced against the state's positive obligation to protect the privacy of convicted persons in criminal proceedings, as well as its obligations to ensure the fair administration of justice.[126] Although the woman's conviction, sentencing and immediate arrest had been a matter of public interest, the press owed duties and responsibilities related to protecting the reputation or rights of others and maintaining the authority and impartiality of the judiciary. Further, those duties were particularly important in relation to the dissemination to the public of photographs revealing personal and intimate information about an individual.[127]

Further, although the photographs had been taken in a public place and in relation to a public event at a time when her identity was already well-known, their portrayal of her had been particularly intrusive: all three photographs portraying her in a state of strong emotion after having been notified of a judgment in which she had been given the most severe sentence under Norwegian law.[128] In the Court's view, her reduced state of self-control in that situation

---

122   *Jameel v Wall Street Journal Europe* [2007] 1 AC 359; Lord Hope at [111].
123   In fact, some of the decisions were justified on the need to uphold the fair administration of justice, and the need to facilitate rehabilitation.
124   (2009) 50 EHRR 2.
125   The case, involving a woman who had received a 21-year sentence for a triple murder, had attracted unprecedented media attention, and the press had taken and published a number of photographs taken of her leaving the courtroom after the sentence had been announced and in a clear state of distress.
126   *Egeland v Norway* (2009) 50 EHRR 2, at [53].
127   *Ibid.*, at [59], citing *Von Hannover v Germany* (2005) 40 EHRR 1.
128   *Ibid.*, at [58]. Further, the Court also noted that her co-operation with the press on previous occasions could not justify depriving her of that protection.

lay at the core of the protection that the domestic statutory provision was intended to provide,[129] and accordingly the Norwegian authorities had acted within their margin of appreciation by enforcing domestic law on the press.[130]

More recently, in *Mediengruppe Osterreich GmbH v Austria*,[131] it was held that an injunction prohibiting an Austrian newspaper from publishing an image of an individual – a candidate for the office of Federal President of Austria - with the caption "convicted neo-Nazi", 20 years after the plaintiff's expunged conviction and, following his loss of notoriety and lack of further criminal conduct, did not violate the media's right to impart information. There was a legitimate and significant interest for convicted persons no longer being confronted with their acts after their release, with a view to their re-integration in society.[132] Distinguishing this case from previous case law, it pointed out that over 20 years had passed between the individual's criminal conviction in 1995 and the publication of the article at issue, and some seventeen years since his release in 1999.[133]

Thus, in the post *Von Hannover* period, there appears to be a growing line of authority from the Strasbourg Court that editorial judgement will not be allowed to excuse unjustified interference with privacy rights, particularly where this might obstruct the administration of justice and the individual's

---

129   *Ibid.*, at [61]. See also the case of *Peck v United Kingdom* (2003) 36 EHRR 719, a case which protected the right of a distressed individual not to have his uncontrolled public activities caught on CCTV cameras broadcast in newspapers and on television.

130   *Ibid.*, at [65]. The relevant law was contained in Section 131A of the Administration of Courts Act 1915, which provided that: "During oral proceedings in a criminal case, photographing, filming and radio or television recordings are prohibited. It is also prohibited to take photographs or make recordings of the accused or the convicted on his or her way to, or from, the hearing or when he or she is staying inside the building in which the hearing takes place, without his or her consent."

131   Application No.37713/18, decision of the European Court 26 April 2022.

132   The Court distinguished the present case from its previous decision in *Österreichischer Rundfunk v. Austria* Application No.37713/18. In that case, proceedings brought by an individual against a different media company that prohibited it from showing the individual's picture in connection with any report stating that he had been convicted under domestic law once the sentence had been executed or once he had been released on parole was held to in breach of Article 10. In the present case, the Court stressed that after a certain period of time has elapsed and, in particular, as their release from prison approaches, convicted persons have an interest in no longer being confronted with their acts, with a view to their reintegration in society: *Mediengruppe Osterreich GmbH v Austria*, at [71].

133   *Mediengruppe Osterreich GmbH v Austria*, Application No.37713/18, at [69]. The Court also noted that the applicant company's allegation that the individual was still active in the right-wing scene was not supported by any evidence other than two reports referring to his participation in events in 2009 at [71].

due process rights. Notwithstanding that, these recent decisions are arguably over-protective of privacy rights when there is a clear public interest in publication of a story that is intended to inform public debate on serious issues.

6   Conclusions

There is little doubt that the starting point established by the UK Supreme Court in *Bloomberg* is favoured and adopted by all relevant state agencies, and that they regard this starting point as an unbreakable rule. However, for the courts to adopt this as the starting point in their judicial balancing act risks them attaching undue weight to the fact that the defendant's had broken the law, or practice, of confidentiality, and applying that rule disproportionately in the law of misuse of private information. Whilst that starting point might be acceptable in the statutory law of contempt,[134] in cases where the courts' essential role is to balance the respective Convention rights, it is argued that it is both unnecessary and unjust.

As with the decision of the High Court in *Richard,* the decision of the Supreme Court in *Bloomberg* was made in the context of very loose and perhaps negligent journalistic practice. In *Richard,* that led to the High Court - perhaps inadvertently - restricting the availability of the public interest defence when the media indulge in what is perceived as unprofessional journalism, and seeking to make 'good' television.[135] This can create a chilling effect on future investigations, and promote further judicial distrust of the media, which perhaps can inadvertently be reflected in the court's balancing exercise. Similarly, in *Bloomberg,* the Supreme Court was clearly unimpressed by the tactics employed by the defendants, including their blatant disregard of the confidentiality of the letter and the need to preserve the integrity in those proceedings. Such confidentiality exists to maintain the continuation of those investigations, rather than the privacy of those under investigation, and should not justify a starting point in establishing an expectation of privacy, albeit with exceptions. It is argued that the creation of this starting point risks distorting the courts' subsequent enquiries at both stages, exacerbated by the Court's refusal to consider the public interest reason for the appellant's investigation and subsequent publication. Thus, in future cases, defendants might

---

134   For example, under s.11 of the Contempt of Court Act, creating an offence of disclosing individual identity against a judge's order.

135   S Foster, 'Media Responsibility, Public Interest Broadcasting and the Judgment in Richard v BBC' (2018) 5 *European Human Rights Law Review* 490, 503.

find that they have damned themselves by their breach of confidentiality and of this newfound presumption of privacy. Further, the claimant's expectation of privacy in this case has survived despite being an officer a large corporation who are being investigated for fraud and corruption; now outweighed by the dominant element of harm to reputation and the presumption against pre-charge disclosure.

An application to the European Court of Human Rights cannot fully remedy the potential inequalities created by this decision: the European Court is not a court of appeal on domestic law, and must decide the case based on the facts presented to it by the applicant. Only if it feels that the Supreme Court's application of the starting point test disadvantaged Bloomberg could if find a violation; otherwise, we would have to wait for a further application to the Court, on more promising and worthy facts.

This of course presumes that the European Court would regard the starting point, or presumption, as an unnecessary or disproportionate impediment to free speech and the media's opportunity to defend itself from actions in misuse of private information. The European Court's traditional jurisprudence on press freedom has certainly been modified post-*Von Hannover*,[136] and there is evidence of a greater pro-privacy approach in the last two decades,[137] illustrated most starkly by the recent decision in *ML v Slovenia*.

With respect to *ML v Slovakia,* it is perhaps too early to tell whether that decision will alter the dynamics between the protection of press freedom and privacy when those rights are in conflict. There is, however, evidence, that the UK domestic courts have grown intolerant of unreasonable media tactics employed when reporting news events, even if the story has an undoubted public interest. In such cases, the media's efforts to make 'good' television or news copy has diminished their ability to rely on any public interest defence. So too, the decision with respect to the priest's public status reduced the strength of the public interest in publication, encroaching on editorial judgement and thus having a chilling effect on investigative journalism. Nevertheless, the decision seems generally in line with previous, and subsequent, decisions that have made it clear that there is no immunity for the media in terms of reporting on criminal proceedings.

The question whether such reporting breaches Article 8 (or other rights such as the right to a fair trial) is dependent on the circumstances of the case,

---

136   MA Sanderson 'Is Von Hannover v Germany a Step Backward for the Substantive Analysis of Speech and Privacy Interests?' (2004) *European Human Rights Law Review* 631.

137   See M Tugendhat, 'Privacy, Judicial Activism and Free Speech' (2018) 28 *Communications Law* 63.

with the Court re-iterating the importance of individual privacy rights and the right to be forgotten. However, what is clear is that the dominant position of press freedom and editorial judgement has been weakened post-*Von Hannover* with the greater acceptance of individual privacy and the need to insist on responsible journalism and broadcasting.

Note on the Contributor

Steve Foster
Associate Professor in Law, Coventry University.